Tests and Measurements
in Child Development:
Handbook II

Volume 1

Orval G. Johnson

Tests and Measurements in Child Development: Handbook II

Volume 1

Jossey-Bass Publishers

San Francisco · Washington · London · 1976

TESTS AND MEASUREMENTS IN CHILD DEVELOPMENT: HANDBOOK II
Volume 1
    by Orval G. Johnson

JACKET DESIGN BY WILLI BAUM

FIRST EDITION

Code 7606

The Jossey-Bass
Behavioral Science Series

Preface

Tests and Measurements in Child Development: Handbook II is the second of two collections designed to keep researchers, evaluators, and clinicians up-to-date on the most recent developments in unpublished measures of child behavior. Both the size of the task of compiling the two volumes of *Handbook II* and the length of the final collection itself greatly exceeded our expectations. *Handbook I* and *Handbook II* combined provide access to over twelve hundred unpublished measures. Of these, about nine hundred are contained in *Handbook II,* although it covers a slightly shorter time span than *Handbook I* (nine years as opposed to ten years). The difference in the number of measures included in the two handbooks is attributable to an increase in age coverage (from birth to twelve years, to birth to eighteen years) in *Handbook II,* a search of more journals (148 as opposed to 53), and the greatly expanded activity in child research during the last decade.

Although some measurement procedures, such as "intelligence" testing of children, are being criticized by laymen and professionals, the need for appropriate assessment and evaluation procedures and tools remains. Today more than ever before, focused instruments are needed to assess specific changes in behavior and to diagnose individual characteristics and traits. More broadly, measures are needed to evaluate psychological and educational behavior-change studies, to plan training and educational strategies, and to assess the effects of ameliorative and corrective programs. The research trend toward tighter specification of objectives requires a correspondingly precise definition of measurement options.

I am indebted to my professional colleagues from many disciplines who kindly provided their measures and descriptions, and whose response, interest, and willing participation make me proud to identify myself with them.

The dedicated, energetic, and conscientious staff members of the Child Measurement Project were essential to the production of this book. Burt Dwyre's organization, sense of humor, and willingness to take on any task and carry it out efficiently were extraordinary assets to the project. Nina Johnson's journalistic skills expedited the whole search and editorial process. Mary Lawton's library skills were likewise valuable. Janna Hughes typed reams, kept voluminous records, and, most importantly, organized the office impressively.

I am grateful for the cheerful help provided by the administrators and staffs of the following libraries: Norlin Library, University of Colorado (with special thanks to Marie Campbell); Penrose Library, University of Denver; and Denison Library, University of Colorado School of Medicine.

Finally, I am indebted to James Bommarito for providing numerous leads to much useful material; to Ingrid and Lisa Johnson for contributing their typing skills during the last stages of the project and for helping to tie up the inevitable loose ends; to Laura and Kurt Johnson for valuable clerical help; and to the superintendents of the Weld County (Colorado) Board of Cooperative Educational Services (BOCES) for their enlightened appreciation of the importance of the research process.

The project was made possible by Grant No. 1 R01 MH23875 from the National Institute of Mental Health.

Boulder, Colorado   Orval G. Johnson
July 1976

Contents

Volume 2

Tests and Measurements
in Child Development:
Handbook II

Volume 1

Part One

ORGANIZATION AND PROCEDURE

Chapter 1

Criteria, Coverage, Format, and Classification System

In the *Handbook* that preceded the present volume we stated our purpose as follows:

> *Heretofore, there has been no central source to which researchers could go for specialized information on unpublished measures suitable for children. The value of a central source of information about unpublished measures appears manifold. First, since these measures are so widely scattered in various sources, there is vast duplication of effort from study to study in ferreting out of the literature the data-gathering instruments or techniques that are pertinent to each investigation. Much of that duplication of effort can be eliminated by centralizing the information on unpublished measures. Second, the individual evaluator or researcher is unlikely to cover a very wide segment of the literature in his search because of time limitations so is almost sure to miss measures that would be useful to him. Third, a central source has heuristic value. It may stimulate the planning of evaluation phases of research by increasing the number of measurement options available to the researcher. He may thus find measures more specific to his research or evaluation needs [Johnson and Bommarito, 1971, pp. 3-4].*

Handbook I has, we feel, filled the need for a central resource of unpublished measures covering the literature through the year 1965. The nine years from 1966 through 1974 saw an upsurge of interest in research and action projects with children

3

and youths. This development underscored the need to update our original collection. We did not anticipate that the resulting collection of measures—*Handbook II*—would approach three times the volume of *Handbook I*.

Handbook II is essentially an extension of *Handbook I*, being supplementary rather than overlapping. *Handbook I* covered the literature from 1956 to 1965, particularly journals. The measures described in *Handbook II* were discovered in a search of the literature from 1966 through 1974. The reader may ask, then, why the present volume includes so many more measures than the first book, especially since this search has covered a nine-year span as compared with a ten-year period in the first search. The answer is threefold: (1) The upper limit of the age range has been increased from 12 to 18, thus adding children of junior and senior high school age and consequently bringing in many adolescent measures. *Handbook I* covered ages 0 to 12, thus setting the upper limit at the sixth grade level (the last year of elementary school), a logically defensible limit. While this breadth of coverage proved useful, we were persistently vexed by difficult decisions to include or exclude a measure because, even though it overlapped the twelve-year limit, it was primarily an adolescent measure. We had to exclude, strictly on an age basis, a number of measures that we felt should have been included because of their relevance and the quality of work that went into them. The overlap was rarer when the 0 to 18 age range was used, probably because many of the measures were developed and used with school children (who normally terminate school at age 18). A measure may very well be designed for the age group 10 to 14, thus overlapping into the teens; thus, completion of high school becomes a clearer dividing point than completion of elementary school. Because of the 0 to 18 range, the whole class of adolescent measures has been included. Adult measures, unless clearly applicable to high school students (and then ordinarily only if they had been used with high schoolers) have been excluded. (2) There has been a marked increase within the past ten years in child research. (3) The current search has involved more intensive coverage of more journals as well as books, theses, other compilations of measures, and research reports.

SEARCH PROCEDURE

The professional journals continue to be the basic source of leads to new unpublished measures and to established noncommercial measures that had not been picked up previously. The procedure we adopted for finding measures was very much like the one used for *Handbook I*. Indexes, tables of contents, abstracts, and similar aids are of little help in trying to track down, for example, a reference to a measure in the middle of a sentence that does not occur again in the same article. It was often such an obscure reference, however, that set us on the trail of what turned out to be a viable instrument. Consequently we felt compelled to do a page-by-page search through most of the journals in the fields of psychology, education, psychiatry, sociology, and exceptionality. Specifically this meant scanning every page carefully enough that any mention of a measure would be picked up. Frequently a measure would be referred to, but not by name. Thus the scanning procedure had to be so precise that from a reference as vague as "Jones' test of maternal behavior was used to . . ."—which included no bibliographical citation—we were able to locate the correct Jones and correspond with him to ascertain the appropriateness of his measure for our purposes.

Of the 148 journals searched, 125 were subjected to the detailed page-by-page study. The remaining 23 were searched briefly by one of two processes. In some cases the tables of contents or indexes were scanned. With other journals an early and a late volume were selected from the 1966-1974 period, and only these were subjected to the thorough search described above. (An early and a late volume were chosen because of the possibility that the contents of the journal might change enough over that period of time to affect our decision on how intensively to search it.) In some instances the latter sampling method led to a complete study of all volumes of a journal over the 1966-1974 period. A complete listing of all journals searched appears in the Appendix.

Sources other than journals were also used in the search. Some of those described in Chapter 2 produced a number of leads to measures that were eventually included in this *Handbook*. Bibliographies frequently provided leads, as did convention programs and newsletters. Authors to whom we wrote occasionally suggested we contact certain colleagues. A few descriptions of measures were sent in spontaneously.

Some measures we could not obtain, mainly because either we could not locate an author, or when located the author did not respond, or the author responded but for some reason (the author's or ours) we decided the measure should not be included. Usually we felt assured that the absence of any one measure from the *Handbook* would create no significant gap in our coverage of the various content areas, since we had included other measures in the same area.

LOCATING TEST AUTHORS

After a reference to a new unpublished test was deemed suitable to pursue, we then had to locate the author of the measure. Since most of the test authors are members of professions with a high rate of mobility, this task was not always easy. It was, however, a comparatively simple procedure when the author's full name was given in the journal or book reference, particularly if it was noted that he was on a university or college faculty. In this case we confirmed his current address in the *National Faculty Directory* (vols. for 1973, 1974, and 1975).

If the test author appeared to be a psychologist, we consulted current directories of the American Psychological Association: *Consolidated Roster for Psychology* (1973), *Biographical Directory* (1973), and *Membership Register* (1974). Two other directories sometimes useful were the 1974-1975 *Directory of Members of the American Educational Research Association* and the 1973 *Directory of Members, American Association on Mental Deficiency*. The yearly publication of the National Society for the Advancement of Education also maintains a current list of names and addresses of its members. Another source used was the quarterly digest of the Educational Testing Service, the *Test Collection Bulletin*. Occasionally we also checked the current membership roster of the American Medical Association.

For locating test authors in England, Canada, Australia, and New Zealand we consulted the two most current volumes of the *Commonwealth Universities Yearbook* (1973 and 1974). For authors in other parts of the world we sometimes used the first edition of *World Guide to Universities* (1971).

If the sources noted above did not produce the needed information for the *senior* author of a test, we checked the same sources for known *coauthors*. Occasionally we examined any other reference work that seemed at all useful, such as the *Academic Who's Who* (1973-1974) and the *Yearbook of Higher Education* (1973-1974). If a complete address was not available but we had pinpointed the city of residence, a local telephone book was sometimes helpful.

If none of these sources supplied the necessary information for an author, we then turned our attention to the author of the article or book that mentioned the test (when this writer was not the author of the measure being sought). These writers often provided us with the necessary information, forwarded our letters of inquiry to the proper person, or made other helpful suggestions, as did university librarians, personnel in college registrar's offices, test publishing companies, and journal editors.

CRITERIA FOR INCLUSION OF MEASURES

We found it advisable after about the end of the first year of the search to cease collecting several types of measures. Behavior rating scales, behavior checklists, and certain classroom observation procedures were particularly numerous in the literature, and the duplication of items became evident. There was no readily definable point at which the decision was made, and we had no specific criteria for determining when to stop collecting any one type of measure. We made the judgment probably in much the same way that one decides to stop eating at a meal although there is still food on the table. Ideally, we might have made a detailed content analysis of each new measure to determine if it made any significant contribution (perhaps a specified percentage of new items) to the pool of measures and the items already at hand. However, our resources did not permit this kind of analysis.

We have included measures dealing with various aspects of the child's environment, as well as measures of attitudes toward children. Many scales and tests designed to measure teacher characteristics exist. Some characteristics of teachers involve their feelings about children, and some measures of those feelings are described herein. There are also numerous teacher-characteristic instruments, however, that measure personality, social attitudes, opinions about school practices, and so forth. We have not included them because they focus on the teacher, not on the child. One can argue that the attitudes of teachers constitute one aspect of children's environments, but until the attitudes are manifested in some behavior, there is obviously no effect on children. We feel that the scales and observation procedures concerned with teacher-child interaction, along with the general classroom observation instruments, measure teacher effect on children better than any teacher characteristic or attitude measure. For further discussion of measures of teacher characteristics, see McLeish (1969).

We did not include subscales of existing measures, of either published or unpublished measures. The reader interested in subscales of published measures will find relevant bibliography in Buros's *Mental Measurements Yearbooks* following the descriptions of the tests.

We did not ordinarily include achievement measures because there are many carefully developed, published academic achievement tests available, and we encountered too many unpublished tests of this type to make their inclusion feasible. We did find a few highly specialized achievement tests, however, which we included because there were few, if any, other achievement measures in that area, published or unpublished.

In general, demographic data-gathering instruments and case-history forms were not included. Long, detailed questionnaires of this type, unless they were deemed especially useful or unique in some way, were not described. Adaptations of existing measures were included if a substantial number of the items were new. Our criterion for a substantial number was roughly 50 percent.

A considerable number of sentence-completion measures turned up in the search process. One criterion we set up for the inclusion of these was the availability of a systematic, relatively objective scoring procedure. Most of the sentence-completion measures that were excluded did not qualify on this basis, although they may have met other more general criteria set up for all the measures.

FORMAT FOR DESCRIPTION

The purpose of the descriptions is to give the reader and potential user of a measure sufficient information so that he can decide whether or not to pursue the measure further. The format is only slightly modified from that used in *Handbook I.* The information provided in each description is as follows: name of measure, author, age for which the measure is appropriate, variable, type of instrument, source from which the measure may be obtained, narrative description of the measure (often with sample items), evidence of reliability and validity, and bibliography. Each of these sections is described below, with some pertinent detail and some of the problems and issues involved.

Name of Measure: The name is almost invariably provided by the author or other person drafting the description. With rare exceptions, we have retained that name. Occasionally the length of the title dictated some abbreviation. Usually the name of the measure gives a clear impression of its content.

Author: Whenever there is multiple authorship, the names are given in the order provided by the person writing the description. Whenever possible the full name (first, middle initial, and last) is provided. No positions, academic titles, or degrees are included.

Age: Age ranges for which tests are appropriate are provided in most cases by the authors. These ranges should not be viewed as restrictive, but primarily as suggestive. At the same time, authors sometimes make estimates of the range, going either above or below the ages of the children with whom they have actually used the instruments. The potential user of a measure may prefer to withhold judgment of the appropriate age range until he has seen the sample items or the complete measure. This is especially true if he is dealing with a sample from an exceptional population.

Variable: The editing of this portion of a description was difficult. A clear designation of the variable being tapped is frequently difficult, mostly because the designation may involve semantic, theoretical, and philosophical preferences. It is likely that with many measures the interjudge reliability in naming the variables would be relatively low. The number of variables for a measure is sometimes large, and they are subsumed under some broader (and consequently less precise and less useful) rubric. Study of the sample items or of the complete measure will usually clarify the variable.

Type of Measure: The reader interested in the possible use of a measure will be particularly interested in the *type* of measure being described. He will be operating in a situation that typically will impose some limitations on the kind of data-collection processes that can be used. Restrictions on available time, finances, training of personnel, accessibility to and type of subjects, physical facilities, and so forth will determine the type of measure to be used within any content category or group.

There is considerable variability in the designations different authors may use for essentially the same kind of instrument. Since there is no standard nomenclature for the classification of measuring instruments in the behavioral sciences, there is little solid basis for changing the information provided by the author on the type of measure. We have edited this information primarily for clarity and reasonable brevity, but not with any well-defined classification model.

Source from Which Measure May Be Obtained: After examining the description of a measure, the reader may wish to examine the measure itself. No measures have been described that are not available. If the complete measure is included in a publication that is generally available, that reference is given in the bibliography, and the source information follows this form: "See Smith (1974)." If the measure is available from one or more of the authors, the name(s) and address(es) are provided. In cases where addresses may change and mail addressed to a test author is not forwarded, the interested professional will find useful the sources of information on addresses described in the Locating Test Authors section of this chapter.

Description of Measure: While the items up to this point help to define a measure, this section provides a narrative description that expands the brief information previously given. It includes such information as a further detailing of the variables measured, procedures in development of the measure, normatization, administration procedures, scoring and types of scores developed, length, administration time, comments about usability or other features, and special considerations such as skills necessary for administration and scoring, any equipment needed, and precautions and restrictions on the use of the measure

In the case of some measures, examples or portions of the measure were not included because it was not feasible to include an adequate sample. Observation systems, in particular, were in our opinion difficult to represent by a few items only. Rather than bias the reader with an inadequate and possibly misleading sample, we have let the description alone carry the burden.

The question of how many and what specific items to include was a persistently vexing problem. Sometimes we found it necessary to select portions of an instrument because those items could be most readily presented. While these were bona fide items, they may not have represented the makeup of the test as well as would some items awkward to reproduce. In a few cases slight changes were made, particularly in the presentation format of items, in order to present them in the book. Many descriptions could not include sample items at all because they were of *picture* tests, or because they used other kinds of pictorial stimuli not possible to reproduce in this *Handbook.*

Reliability and Validity: Typically the data in this section were collected by the author in the process of developing and using the instrument, and sometimes in later studies by the author or colleagues. There are wide variations among measures in the amount of supportive data collected and presented. If the authors are still in the process of collecting data, we state "none reported." In many cases the user may wish to compile data on reliability and validity that are directly pertinent to the population with which he is working. Frequently the Description of Measure section includes information on the technical development of the measure, which may have a bearing on its validity.

Bibliography: According to Van Riper (Sheehan, 1970, p. 351), "No scholarly task is more onerous than the compilation of a fairly extensive bibliography. It seems unending, and it is never entirely complete or completed. Errors have a fiendish capacity for inserting themselves at every stage of publication." The same can be said of editing a limited bibliography. The bibliographies in this book are primarily reference lists as defined in the *Publication Manual* of the American Psychological Association, since they refer in most cases specifically to the development or use of the test. Thus bibliographic items pertaining to the general background of a measure are excluded, unless they specifically refer to the description. Occasionally authors submitted substantial lists of general references, none of them dealing specifically with the development or use of the measure. In these cases we have indicated "none reported." Some widely used and well-known measures are not cited because professionals are already familiar with them. The measures themselves are not referenced in the bibliography, although a formalized manual is listed if it has been prepared.

Author of Description: Most of the descriptions appearing in the *Handbook* were prepared by the authors of the measures. If someone other than the author (or the senior author, in the case of multiple authors) contributed a description, his or her name is listed at the end of the description. If several persons collaborated on a description, all of their names are given.

CLASSIFICATION OF MEASURES

There is no universally accepted classification system for measures of human characteristics, although anyone working with a large number of different measures has probably felt some need for organizing and classifying them. The basis for categorization goes beyond the personal compulsion to infuse order into an amorphous mass of data. It is based on the assumption that unorganized data are less useful than organized data. One usually imposes on the data the organization that he would find most useful and that he feels others would find useful. Sometimes the organization may conform with some articulated theoretical system, but typically the dominant theme of classification is that of usefulness.

There are several possible bases for classification of measures, all of which have been employed by various authors. (1) Frequently measures are categorized according to the content or area measured. Tests, for example, are frequently classified as tests of intelligence or academic aptitude, achievement, personality, aptitude, and interest (personal or vocational). They may also be classed more broadly as verbal versus performance or language versus nonlanguage. (2) A second classificatory mode involves the manner of administration of the measure. A distinction is made between tests that can be administered to more than one individual and tests involving a one-to-one testing situation. (3) Closely related to the group-versus-individual dimension is the response mode dimension, where measures are classed as paper-and-pencil, oral-verbal response, automated-response (button-pressing), and other less often used response modes. (4) Another classification scheme that has been employed primarily for tests is based on the scoring method and is usually referred to as objective versus subjective. This system sets up a specious dichotomy, considering the subjectivity frequently involved in determining the objectively "right" answer and the objectivity that intrudes into the conscientious scoring of essay-type questions. (5) Classification is sometimes concerned with the format of the measure, which may be a test, checklist, rating scale, observation schedule, situational task, or other. This classification is closely related to (2), (3), and (4) above since differences in measures are in large part a function of differences in administration and scoring. (6) For some purposes, measures are classified according to the subject population for whom they are designed. These include infant measures, preschool and adult measures, measures of teacher attitudes, and measures of social institutions (for example, family status characteristics). (7) Sometimes the system that appears to be most helpful is a simple alphabetical system.

These are all different ways of looking at the data-gathering process, and their value as classification systems must be determined by the usefulness of perceiving measures in any one of these frames of reference. The different classifications described above are not clearly separable ways of looking at measures. The following are examples of how the different category systems for measures are related to each other: We give paper-and-pencil tests (response mode classification) to people who can read and write (subject population classification); infant and preschool child measures (subject population) are seldom group administered (administration method); intelligence (content classification) is usually measured by tests rather than rating scales or checklists (format classification). We did not find any established system to be most useful for this project. It seemed to us that a system developed empirically and based in part on the systems described above would have maximum usefulness.

The classification system that is used herein is empirical in the sense that we looked at the data we had and, with the criterion of usefulness to the researcher in mind, set up categories that appeared to us to accommodate the data in the usefulness context. Eleven categories of measures appeared to include all the data. Some of the categories are subdivided into groups, so that there are twenty-two classes in all, the last one being a miscellaneous category. As in any situation where one imposes an organization on unstructured data, there are many cases where measures may fall into either of two and occasionally three classes. Usually, these cases could be resolved in favor of one category, with close scrutiny of the measure and the category.

Handbook II generally follows the classification of measures presented in *Handbook I*. In Category 3 (*PERCEPTIONS OF ENVIRONMENT*), the title of Group 3-a has been changed from *Attitudes toward Adults* to *Perceptions of Adults,* Group 3-b has been changed from *Attitudes toward Peers* to *Perceptions of Peers,* and Group 3-c has been changed from *Other Factors* to *Other Environmental Perceptions and Characteristics.* These changes were made to relate the Group designations more closely to the category title and to clarify the *Other Factors* group. Category 5, formerly called simply *ENVIRONMENT,* and including the three groups of *Quality of Mothering, Child-Rearing Practices,* and *Attitudes, Primarily of Parents, Toward School,* has been changed to *QUALITIES OF CAREGIVING AND HOME ENVIRONMENT* without subcategories. Not only were the first two groups very closely related but Group 5-c involved very few measures and could readily be subsumed by Category 8. Category 6 in *Handbook I* was titled *MOTOR SKILLS, BRAIN INJURY, AND SENSORY PERCEPTION*, with a separate group for each of the three areas in the title. For *Handbook II*, Group 6-b (*Brain Injury*) has been eliminated because the other two groups cover the variables from which a judgment or diagnosis of brain injury is usually inferred. Category 8, formerly *MISCELLANEOUS ATTITUDES AND INTERESTS,* without subcategories, has been changed to *ATTITUDES AND INTERESTS,* with Group 8-a called *Attitudes toward School* and Group 8-b titled *Miscellaneous Attitudes and Interests.* These changes give appropriate emphasis to the important school attitude measures. The final change in the classification system is the addition of Category 10, *VOCATIONAL*, necessitated by the number of high-school-level vocationally oriented measures found in our search.

Classification of the measures must be a careful process if it is to be useful to the reader. We were convinced that a classification system based on the content (i.e., the variable measured) would be of greatest value. How the variable is measured (meaning the type of measure) may also be crucial in terms of time, personnel, and facilities available, but the first consideration for the potential user of a measure is the variable measured.

CULTURAL BIAS IN TESTING

Because of the issue of cultural bias in testing, the collection of measures described herein should be viewed briefly within that perspective. In recent years individual and group tests of academic aptitude and achievement (as well as other types of measures) have increasingly come under attack for their middle-class orientation. The criticisms have had to do primarily with the use of tests for individual diagnosis, particularly for purposes of educational placement or for personnel selection.

A large proportion of the measures described in this *Handbook* are focused on highly specific aspects of the individual and his environment. There are relatively few of the broad-based academic aptitude tests. It should also be noted that a large proportion of the measures are research instruments that are seldom used in individual diagnosis. In those cases the cultural bias issue is not relevant except in a different sense because the measure, although not utilized to affect decisions about individuals, may be used to draw conclusions about cultural groups.

There is a persistent dilemma in the test bias issue. There is a need for diagnosis of individual strengths and weaknesses, particularly in school situations, so that the available remedial and ameliorative resources can be most economically focused. At the same time there is diminished confidence in the applicability of the traditional instruments, particularly the intelligence tests, to the linguistically and economically disadvantaged. The so-called culture-free or culture-fair tests have not provided satisfactory solutions. A more promising procedure appears to be to broaden the scope of the measurement effort, to select from a wider range of instruments and techniques, so that a number of specific skills and abilities can be assessed. Emphasis can then be placed on the abilities for which a particular culture provides learning opportunities, so that the test procedure measures to a greater extent the *ability* rather than the *opportunity* or *exposure*. If the wider range of instruments includes measures of learning processes and measures that provide a training sequence, the cultural effect will be minimized, although certainly not abolished. This *Handbook* provides the basis for an extensive and wide-ranging list of measures for adding versatility to the measurement process.

A related position is taken by the National Council on Measurement in Education through their Committee on Standards for the Development and Use of Educational Measures. The following statement comes from its Final Report, Recommendation 4-b: "The educational-measurement community must not be content in its reliance upon ability-achievement-interest measures imposed upon students in the psychometric mode. Today's problems require a focus on other subjects [also] with different methodologies."

The accumulation of data on any measures makes possible the improvement of norms and adds to the evidence on reliability and validity. For this reason, whenever possible users of unpublished measures should communicate their results to the originator of the measure, who can thus keep up to date on the usage of his instrument and the relevant statistical information and be in a better position to share it with others. As one researcher put it when asked for a bibliography of his measure, "A number of professionals have used [my test] in their research, but I have never received copies of their articles."

USING THE HANDBOOK

In order to find measures suitable to their needs, readers may follow one of two procedures—starting with the table of contents or starting with the subject index. The contents lists the titles of all categories and groups in *Handbook II*; since the titles are straightforward, they should communicate the general nature of measures in each classification. The short descriptions of all categories and subcategories, found both at the end of this chapter and preceding the category classifications in the text proper, provide further information. These descriptions should help orient readers to the sections of the book that include measures of interest to them. Then, in order to check on the relevance of measures in specific categories or groups, readers may wish to thumb through the various sections and scan the measure titles. This procedure should yield a manageable number of measures that can be studied more thoroughly.

A more limited, focused search for suitable measures can result from using the subject index as one's starting point. Following this process, readers will not be surveying as wide a variety of measures, for no one of the relatively specific terms in the subject index can cover anywhere near the number of measures found in complete categories or groups. There is an advantage, however. Although many measures assess more than one variable, these measures are still classified only under one main heading. The subject index, by including all the variables measured, provides references to variables that cross category and group boundaries. For example, a measure in Category 2 of some aspect of personality may include a section on assessing the self-concept. If a reader were only to read the category and group titles and descriptions in his search for material on the self-concept, he would limit himself to Category 4. By consulting the subject index, he will note that relevant information can also be found in other categories.

CATEGORY 1. COGNITION. These are primarily measures of various cognitive abilities, broadly interpreted. Measures of cognitive style and creativity are included here.

Group 1-a. *Intelligence, Readiness, and Maturation.* These measures generally sample broad spectra of common experiences and are frequently designed to derive an overall functioning level of the child. Other areas measured by this group are concept development and verbal reasoning. Most of the Piaget-type measures are included here. There are also many preschool screening measures.

Group 1-b. *Language and Number Skills.* While these skills often constitute parts of intelligence and readiness measures, they are important enough to warrant measures devoted exclusively to them.

Group 1-c. *Specific Achievements.* These measures are designed for assessing achievement in highly specific aspects of a child's experience.

Group 1-d. *Cognitive Style and Cognitive Processes.* This subcategory includes measures of creativity and curiosity, cognitive style, and learning processes.

Group 1-e. *Miscellaneous.* These measures involve primarily cognitive functions but could not logically be classified with the other cognitive measures.

CATEGORY 2. PERSONALITY AND EMOTIONAL CHARACTERISTICS. This category includes measures of personality and specific emotional characteristics, classified into four groups.

Group 2-a. *Personality—General.* The measures in this group are designed to sample across several or many aspects of personality. This group is composed of a large proportion of rating scales, personality checklists, and projective tests. It includes specific measures of autism.

Group 2-b. *Personality Variables.* Most of these measures are concerned with one or just a few aspects of personality. Generally the name of the measure indicates the variable involved. Measures of motivation and reinforcement preference measures are also included here.

Group 2-c. *Personality Adjustment.* The effectiveness of the child's efforts to adjust to his environment, and in particular his adjustment to school, is emphasized by these measures. Some of them measure learning problems not based primarily on perceptual processes.

Group 2-d. *Anxiety.* These measures could be classified logically in Group 2-b, but we judged that they warranted a separate group because of their number and because of the important role of the anxiety construct in research.

CATEGORY 3. PERCEPTIONS OF ENVIRONMENT. The measures in this category are concerned with the ways in which children perceive different aspects of their environment. Some direct measures of the environment are also included.

Group 3-a. *Perceptions of Adults.* These are primarily measures of children's perceptions of the influential adults in their lives—parents and teachers. Some school attitude measures (Group 8-a) also include a section on perception of teachers. Sex-role measures are included here simply because of the assumption that sex identification is closely tied to perceptions of parents or parent substitutes.

Group 3-b. *Perceptions of Peers.* These are primarily sociometric-type measures.

Group 3-c. *Other Environmental Perceptions and Characteristics.* These are miscellaneous measures, including locus-of-control measures.

CATEGORY 4. SELF-CONCEPT. These instruments are designed to measure the child's feelings about himself. Some of them are concerned with the general self-concept, while others focus on specific aspects or components of the self-concept, such as body image and capacity for responsibility. Some of these measures deal with the child's self-concept in various roles, such as that of student.

CATEGORY 5. QUALITIES OF CAREGIVING AND HOME ENVIRONMENT. Most of the measures in this category concern characteristics of parents, including their attitudes toward their children and child rearing. Measures of family characteristics such as communication patterns and integration are included here, as well as socioeconomic status and home stimulation and deprivation.

CATEGORY 6. MOTOR SKILLS AND SENSORY PERCEPTION. This category includes measures of motor skills, physical fitness, speech production, and sensory perception and discrimination.

Group 6-a. *Motor Skills.* This group includes, in addition to fine and gross motor skills, measures of physical fitness, laterality, speech articulation, rhythm, handwriting, and cerebral dysfunction.

Group 6-b. *Sensory Perception.* This group includes discrimination of visual, auditory, and tactual stimuli, and such related areas as visual memory and oral stereognosis.

CATEGORY 7. PHYSICAL ATTRIBUTES. This category includes only a few measures, but they do not logically fit elsewhere. It includes measures of wake-sleep state, physical condition, motion sickness, and health problems.

CATEGORY 8. ATTITUDES AND INTERESTS. Included here are measures of attitudes toward school and various aspects of school, and other attitudes not related to school.

Group 8-a. *Attitudes Toward School.* This group includes measures of general school attitude, attitude toward school subjects, dropout proneness, cheating, teacher reinforcement, and other school-related areas.

Group 8-b. *Miscellaneous Attitudes and Interests.* This large group includes measures of racial attitudes, attitudes toward the handicapped, political attitudes, value surveys, and a variety of other attitudes.

CATEGORY 9. SOCIAL BEHAVIOR. This category includes measures of interaction, particularly between children and the adults in their environment. Measures of aggressive behavior are included here because aggression is usually defined as involving others, thus in that sense it is social behavior. Several of the measures are frames of reference for observing social behavior.

CATEGORY 10. VOCATIONAL. Included here are measures of vocational maturity and readiness, vocational aspirations and interests, and career knowledge.

CATEGORY 11. UNCLASSIFIED. These measures could not be classified into any of the previous categories or groups.

BIBLIOGRAPHY

Johnson, O. G., and Bommarito, J. W. *Tests and Measurements in Child Development.* San Francisco: Jossey-Bass, 1971.
McLeish, J. *Teachers' Attitudes: A Study of National and Other Differences.* Cambridge, Massachusetts: Cambridge Institute of Education, 1969.
Sheehan, J. G. *Stuttering: Research and Therapy.* New York: Harper & Row, 1970.

Chapter 2

Sources of Published
and Unpublished Measures

The primary purpose of this chapter is to direct the reader to various sources of information on specific tests. Books and other sources dealing with theoretical and practical *issues* are not ordinarily included unless they include a substantial section or sections describing specific measures. A brief section of the chapter is devoted to outlining a suggested basic procedure for use by the newcomer to measurement, as a means of readily finding a measure or measures appropriate to his purposes.

PROCEDURE FOR FINDING MEASURES

There is surprisingly little information in the literature to guide the researcher, evaluator, or clinician to the kind of instruments he may need for his assessment or evaluation task. For that reason, and also to place this and the first *Handbook* in perspective with other measurement resources, the following procedure is recommended.

In most situations the search should begin with one of the publications of Buros' Institute of Mental Measurements. All of Buros' publications deal with published measures. The basic reason for starting with published measures is that, *as a rule*, they are more carefully produced and have more supportive statistical data in the way of norms and evidence on reliability and validity. A reading of this *Handbook* will verify that the previous statement is a generalization to which there are numerous exceptions, however.

Usually *Tests in Print II* (Buros, 1974) will be the most appropriate starting place. *TIP II* will be the most valuable in narrowing the search to the point where it becomes manageable, since the number of instruments in existence may be overwhelming to the conscientious researcher. Once a number of possibly useful instruments have been identified from *TIP II,* the next step is to go to the volume of the *Mental Measurements Yearbook* containing (according to *TIP II*) the description of the instruments and the critical reviews provided for many of them. Use of one of the Mental Measurements Yearbooks monographs, as described in this chapter, will help to narrow the search for the appropriate published measure.

The variety of measures needed for research, evaluation, and clinical application in all the behavioral sciences is extraordinary, and the published measures cover only those aspects where the demand is sufficient to make them commercially feasible. Therefore, the interested professional may frequently need to broaden his search to include unpublished instruments. If his interest is in measuring the behavior of children in the birth-to-18-year age range, this *Handbook* and its earlier companion should be the primary source of unpublished measures. In view of the variety of measures described in the two *Handbooks,* most searchers should be successful in finding an instrument or instruments directly pertinent to their needs. The scope and thoroughness of the search procedures we used makes us confident that most of the available unpublished measures have been included in the two collections. If a particular measure has not been described, it is nevertheless very likely that one or more similar to it have been included.

The reader interested in unpublished adult measures should consult other sources described later in this chapter. In particular, the descriptions provided by the following authors will be most useful: Comrey, Backer, and Glaser; Bonjean, Hill, and McLemore; Shaw and Wright; Robinson and Shaver; and Webb, Campbell, Schwartz, and Sechrest. (See the Bibliography at the end of this chapter for complete references.)

A section on sources of test information would not be complete without mention of publishers' test catalogues. These will provide information on relatively new measures that have not yet been reviewed in Buros' *Yearbooks.* The information is obviously biased, and it cannot provide the basis for the ultimate selection of a measure. It will, however, let the searcher know that there is an additional measure or measures available that he may wish to pursue.

The potential user of a measure will usually wish to see the instrument itself before making a final decision. There are several ways in which he may obtain the instrument, depending on whether it is published or unpublished. Test publishers sometimes send examination sets of tests, although more often for a relatively low price they will send a specimen set. Frequently universities and testing centers have test libraries available to any qualified professional, where examples of tests can be examined. The measures described in *Handbooks I* and *II* all include a source where they can be obtained. In some cases measures may be found only in journals or books or in reports not available in most large libraries, or the potential user may have access only to a relatively small community library. The interlibrary loan services of most libraries, even some of the smaller ones, will be able to procure journals and books for their patrons.

OTHER SOURCES

The primary source of information about published measures are the publications of the Institute of Mental Measurements, directed by O. K. Buros. The seven *Mental Measurements Yearbooks*, of which the first appeared in 1938 and the seventh in 1973, give a description of each measure, critical reviews, references on the construction, use, and validity of the tests, and other valuable information on specific tests as well as on other aspects of measurement. The *Seventh Mental Measurements Yearbook* (Buros, 1972) provides information on 1,157 published tests and 12,539 references on the construction, use, and validity of specific tests. It also includes original reviews of tests as well as excerpted journal reviews, a large bibliography of books on testing, and a directory of publishers.

Tests in Print II (Buros, 1974) updates *Tests in Print I* (Buros, 1961). It presents a massive amount of information on 2,467 tests in print as of early 1974 and 16,574 references through 1971 on specific tests.

All of the material in the seven *Mental Measurements Yearbooks* and in *Tests in Print II* pertinent to specific areas is included in the Mental Measurements Yearbook monographs. The areas covered are: English, foreign languages, intelligence, mathematics, personality, reading, science, social studies, and vocations, for each of which there is a separate monograph.

The abbreviated descriptions of 1,100 mental health measures collected by Comrey, Backer, and Glaser (1973) complement these *Handbooks* by covering primarily adult unpublished measures. All of these measures were selected for inclusion because they were considered to have potential utility for mental health research or service. They are classified into forty-five categories.

Chun, Cobb, and French (1975) searched twenty-six measurement-related journals over the period 1960-1970, some of them complete over that period but most with either a 20-percent systematic random sampling of articles or 1970 volumes only. They did not concentrate on child-related journals. Their volume is in two sections, the first listing the original sources for each of three thousand measures of mental health and related variables. The second section cites and annotates all of the studies in which each measure was subsequently used.

Mirrors for Behavior (Simon and Boyer, 1967, 1970) and *Measures of Maturation* (Boyer, Simon, and Karafin, 1973) are the two most comprehensive works dealing with the interaction observation system. In 1967, Research for Better Schools, Inc., headquartered in Philadelphia, published the first six volumes of what was to become a fourteen-volume anthology. Those first volumes contain twenty-six classroom interaction analysis systems, and they remain the best source for finding classroom behavior instruments. The authors include both instruments measuring the emotional climate of the classroom and those primarily concerned with thought processes. Although they are selective, the volumes pretty well cover all the classroom observation instruments in use at that time.

In 1970, *Mirrors for Behavior* was completed with an additional eight volumes in which the instruments are selected from such various fields as group dynamics, psychotherapy, medicine, industry, anthropology, and education. The total collection is made up of seventy-nine complete instruments, as well as abstracts of every instrument.

Measures of Maturation is concerned mostly with instruments for describing the behavior of very young children. Some of the systems in this four-volume anthology were designed to study individual behavior; others look at the child's interaction with his peers and his environment. Some record parent behavior only, and two were designed specifically to record the behavior of primates. Most of the seventy-three systems included in this work were designed for research purposes. Each system is abstracted for the reader, and each one is tabulated on charts showing information about coding and usage as well as the category dimensions focused on in each instrument ("individual," "social contact," and "physical environment").

Measures of Maturation, published in 1973, attempts to cover the early childhood observation systems devised over the past fifty years. The authors' intent is to describe the systems that measure some aspect of the *development* of the child. Three systems in the collection contain most of the development rating scales, which are also reported separately.

Lake, Miles, and Earle (1973) have collected and described eighty-four measures of social functioning, defined as "the properties of the individual (cognitive/perceptual, motivational, and overt behavioral) as he or she takes part in social interaction, and to the properties of the immediate social system involved (dyads, small groups, organizations)" (p. xiii). Their criteria for including any instrument were, briefly, that it be in the domain of "normal social functioning," have some theoretical or conceptual base, involve a "non-trivial amount of developmental work," be "interesting, promising, potentially useful," not have been reviewed or discussed elsewhere recently, be available to responsible researchers, and "be supported by some reasonably current information on reliability and validity."

The authors considered about three hundred instruments, from which they selected the ones that met their criteria. Some of the measures are published and some are unpublished. The authors do not describe the search procedure by which they arrived at the initial pool of measures.

The format for description of the instruments includes the following subheadings: title, authors, availability, variables, description, administration and scoring, development, critique, general comment, references, and uniterms. The uniterms are combined into a detailed index. The age-appropriateness of the measures described is not indicated in the descriptions of the individual measures or in the introduction. The authors also describe and critique twenty compendia of measures. There is an author index in addition to the uniterm index.

The staff of the Instructional Objectives Exchange (IOX) have developed a number of measures to assess attainment of educational objectives where they felt that existing measures were not adequate. Their publications include four small paperback collections of measures. Each description consists of four elements: description and rationale, directions for administration, scoring, and the measure itself, including answer sheets and scoring templates. The four collections are outlined briefly below.

Measures of Self Concept K-12 (1972) includes fifteen measures divided among the primary, intermediate, and secondary levels. The measurement procedures involve direct self-report, inferential self-report, and observational indicators. *Attitude Toward School K-12* (1972) includes twenty-three measures divided also among the three levels and three types of measurement procedure. *Judgment: Deductive Logic and Assumption Recognition 7-12* (1971) includes four measures. *Attitudes Related to Tolerance 9-12* (1971) includes twelve measures divided among these categories: paper-and-pencil instruments (direct self-report), paper-and-pencil instruments (inferential), sociometric techniques, observation forms, and unobtrusive measures.

A few of the IOX measures have been included in this *Handbook* because they appeared in another context during our search. We have not included all of them because they are already described in the IOX publications, and because we came upon them late in the search period when we already had a considerable number of instruments similar to most of the IOX measures.

The *CSE Elementary School Test Evaluations* (1970) is a product of the School

Evaluation Project of the Center for the Study of Evaluation at the University of California at Los Angeles. This paperbound compendium gives the evaluations of about 1,600 published scales and subscales for the measurement of 145 goals for elementary school grades 1, 3, 5, and 6. Twenty-four specific aspects of the measures are rated on 2- to 11-point scales. There are four categories encompassing the twenty-four specific scales, as follows: measurement validity, examinee appropriateness, administrative usability, and normed technical excellence. The ratings for each of the four categories are summarized separately in a total grade of "Good," "Fair," or "Poor." A similar publication, *Preschool/Kindergarten Test Evaluations* (1971) presents evaluations of tests for younger children.

Walker (1973) provides for the most part brief descriptions of 143 published and unpublished measures of the socioemotional domain, broadly defined. The measures are usable with young children and are classified into the following categories: attitudes, general personality and emotional adjustment, interests or preferences, personality or behavior traits, self-concept, and social skills or competency.

Goldman and Saunders (1974), on the basis of a search of twenty-nine journals for the year 1970, give skeletal descriptions of 339 unpublished experimental measures.

The Register of Questionnaires and Attitude Scales (1973, 1976) is designed to give access to questionnaires that have been used in research, mostly by members of the National Foundation for Educational Research in England and Wales. In general it is not expected that individual questionnaires will be used as they are, rather that they will be of use to researchers in the construction of their own instruments. The questionnaires were designed with a project and a restricted range of objectives in mind. Hence, verbatim use of the questionnaires should only be considered in conjunction with the publications of the specific project for which they were designed. Order forms and further information about the nearly two hundred questionnaires may be obtained from the Research Officer, Guidance and Assessment Service, NFER, The Mere, Upton Park, Slough, Berkshire, England.

Hess and others (1968, 1969) have used numerous tasks, modifications of existing measures, and some original measures in their studies of the cognitive environments of urban preschool children. Among the instruments and tasks are measures of the cognitive home environment, curiosity motivation of mothers, mothers' attitudes toward child behavior leading to mastery, mothers' roles in teacher/child and child/peer school situations, mother-child interaction, curiosity, maternal language styles, educational attitudes, and locus of control.

We have encountered relatively few measures in the broad area defined by the term *fine arts.* Lehman (1968), however, provides a resource for the researcher or practitioner concerned with measurement in the field of music. In addition to the typical (though abbreviated) introductory chapters such as those found in other measurement texts, he provides critical descriptions of eleven tests of musical aptitude and thirteen tests of musical achievement. He also briefly describes some "tests of performance and appreciation" that include procedures for rating students. Most of the measures are suitable for use with children and adults.

In his second edition Farnsworth (1969) includes a twenty-four page chapter entitled "The Measurement of Musical Abilities." Section headings in this chapter are, among others, "Tests of Verbal Knowledge," "Tests Which Stress Nonverbal Musical Skills," and "Unstandardized Aptitude Tests." In this last section the author discusses some interesting measures, most of which are published by music publishers. A description of fifteen standardized musical aptitude tests follows.

A booklet representing one of the efforts of the American Association (now Alliance) for Health, Physical Education, and Recreation (AAHPER) Perceptual-Motor Task Force, which was in operation from 1967 to 1972, is the *Annotated Bibliography on Perceptual-Motor Development* (1973). It is designed to furnish information to enhance the understanding of perceptual motor development. There are three sections. Part I is a bibliography on the work of prominent researchers in perceptual-motor development. Part II is a detailed bibliography on auditory perception and movement, body image, and movement; depth and distance perception and movement; feedback and regulation of movement behavior; figure-ground perception, field dependence, and field independence; reduced and supplementary perceptual cues and movement; and visual and size perception and movement. Part III gives brief descriptions and sources for about one hundred tests, programs, and materials sources in this area of development. This includes films as well as assessment instruments, books, and periodicals.

Sheehan (1970) details numerous studies involving the application of published and unpublished measures with stutterers of various ages.

Hearing in Children (Northern and Downs, 1974) is a new reference source for educators of the deaf, audiologists, and others dealing with hearing problems of children. The authors comprehensively review the literature regarding hearing in children, and the book contains a wealth of practical knowledge on testing procedures, interpretation of data, therapy, and methods of education. Some tests are described. Throughout the volume, the authors stress the importance of early intervention.

Cratty (1969, 1974) describes a procedure for evaluating gross-motor ability of retardates and recommends developmental motor activities to improve various gross-motor skills. He also describes (1969) some drawing tests and some measures of sex-typed game choice, a self-opinion test, and a physical fitness test.

The Osertsky Tests of Motor Proficiency have undergone a number of revisions and modifications since their inception over fifty years ago. One of the latest revisions is that of Bialer, Doll, and Winsberg (1974), who provide in addition a chronological summary of the revisions to date. They give the title of the revision, basis for modification, subject sample, scale characteristics, time needed, data on reliability and validity, and norms for twelve revisions.

Clarke (1971) describes a large number of tests or tasks designed to measure the physical and motor growth of children. His book includes measures classified under the categories of maturity, physique type and physical structure, muscular strength and endurance, and motor and athletic abilities. Other publications by this author are concerned with measurement of dynamometric-type strength tests (1967), the description and illustration of thirty-eight cable-tension strength tests (Clarke and Clarke, 1963), and a test manual for cable-tension strength batteries (Clarke and Munroe, 1970).

Clarke (1971) also discusses tests in various areas of health and physical education. Barrow and McGee (1964) include many of the tests themselves in a standard format outlining the purpose, facilities and equipment necessary, procedure, instructions, scoring, and testing personnel needed for each measure. Haskins (1972) provides nearly two hundred pages of test descriptions covering strength, endurance, attitudes, and sports skills testing. Johnson and Nelson (1969) describe many measures in a wide variety of physical education-related settings, as does Mathews (1973). Baumgartner and Jackson (1975) have written one of the most recent books in the field of physical education measurement.

Brislin, Lonner, and Thorndike (1973) concisely describe thirty published and unpublished measures usable in cross-cultural research, most of them appropriate for both adults and children. Rudolf Meis' chapter in the two-volume *Developments in Educational Testing* (Ingenkamp, 1969) describes and compares some German tests of school readiness and presents results of some research with them.

Riskin and Faunce (1972) provide a detailed review on quantifiable family interaction research over the period 1960-1972. Their article includes an extensive reference list and a glossary of key terms.

In a publication edited by Beatty (1969), Dowd and West have collated measures of affective behavior. Individual measures are described in a paragraph or so, often illustrated with typical items, along with normative data and information on administration procedures. It includes a few measures each in a variety of areas: attitude, creativity, motivation, personality, school readiness, self-concept, and miscellaneous.

A work of interest to researchers in linguistics is the Entwisle book (1967). It provides word counts of the responses of 1,160 young children, age 4-11, to ninety-six stimulus words. Norms are provided for the responses of children from preschool through fifth grade.

Fogelman's (1970) seventy-two page paperback provides information on the test performances of children in different age groups and describes some Piagetian tests. The tests are described briefly under five classes or categories, as follows, each having several subcategories: logical operations (25 tests), conservation (43 tests), transitivity and seriation (12 tests), number concepts (5 tests), and spatial concepts (4 tests). The author suggests that the teacher may want to use the measures in the classroom. The instructions for most of the measures appear to need further explication before they would be usable by anyone not already familiar with the tests.

Guilford and Hoepfner (1971) list over five hundred tests, usually with a sample item included, used by the Aptitudes Research Project in its analysis of intelligence. Oller (1973) describes the use of cloze tests and reports some of the research using that type of instrument, including also a substantial bibliography. The listing of measures for pre-kindergarten children by Mardell and Goldenberg (1972) is designed for identification of high-risk children at that age level. The extensive list includes information on publisher or other source and gives addresses.

Bonjean, Hill, and McLemore (1967) surveyed four sociological journals over a twelve-year period and found 3,609 uses and citations for 2,080 published and experimental measures. These were organized into seventy-eight categories. Extensive bibliographies are provided, and some measures judged by the authors to have been used over a long period of time are described in detail.

The Cattell and Warburton (1967) volume entitled *Objective Personality and Motivation Tests* includes descriptions of 412 measures, many designed for adults. Separate child forms exist for a number of the tests. The tests are described according to a standard format and are classified into twelve categories. Sample items are provided, and six indexes simplify the use of the book.

Shaw and Wright (1967) describe and reprint 176 attitude scales grouped into the following categories: social practices, social issues and problems, international issues, abstract concepts, political and religious attitudes, ethnic and national groups, significant others, and social institutions.

The main purposes of the McReynolds series (1968, 1971, 1975) are, as noted in the preface to volume one, "first, to describe and evaluate selected new developments in assessment technology; second, to present innovative theoretical and methodological approaches to important issues in assessment; and third, to provide summaries of the current status of important areas in the field." Thus these volumes are more concerned with issues and methodology than with specific instruments; they deal with measurement rather than with measures.

Nonreactive measures useful in sociological and psychological research and evaluation are described by Webb and others (1965). *Unobtrusive Measures* calls attention to research data derived not from tests, interviews, or questionnaires but from physical traces (such as garbage analysis), running records, episodic and private records, simple observation, and contrived observation.

The Educational Testing Service maintains an extensive library of tests and other measurement devices. A special Head Start Test Collection is available for use by any qualified person, as is the other component, the Test Collection. ETS distributes the Test Collection Bulletin as a quarterly digest of information on tests. It typically includes short descriptions of tests, both published and unpublished.

The Educational Testing Service has recently made available microfiche copies of unpublished tests in education and psychology. The first set of microfiche includes 118 test titles. Purchasers will be granted royalty-free permission to reproduce copies for their own use. An *Annotated Index* containing numerical, author, title, and subject sections has been prepared. The cost of one microfiche is $2.00, or $118.00 for the entire set of microfiche.

Pharmacotherapy of Children, a special issue (1973) of the *Psychopharmacology Bulletin,* includes behavior checklists, rating scales, parent questionnaires, interview schedules, a scored neurological exam, and the Children's ECDEU (Early Clinical Drug Evaluation Units) Battery. All of these are designed, adopted, or adapted for use in pharmacotherapy studies of children.

Meier (1973) discusses numerous early screening and assessment measures under the following chapter headings: Physical Factors, Intellectual/Cognitive Factors, Language Factors, Social/Emotional Factors, and Comprehensive Developmental Screening Systems. Studies using the measures are cited. Appendix A is an annotated index for fifty-eight selected developmental screening tests and procedures, providing summary information on the name of the measure, author, age range, reliability, validity, time required, cost per child, administration of the measure, and recommended stage at which the measure should be used in the screening system.

BIBLIOGRAPHY

Annotated Bibliography on Perceptual-Motor Development. Washington, D.C.: American Association of Health, Physical Education, and Recreation, 1973.

Barrow, H. M., and McGee, R. *A Practical Approach to Measurement in Physical Education.* Philadelphia, Pennsylvania: Lea and Febiger, 1964.

Baumgartner, T. A., and Jackson, A. S. *Measurement for Evaluation in Physical Education.* Boston, Massachusetts: Houghton Mifflin, 1975.

Beatty, W. H. (Ed.) *Improving Educational Assessment and an Inventory of Measures of Affective Behavior.* Washington, D.C.: Association for Supervision and Curriculum Development, National Education Association, 1969.

Bialer, I., Doll, L., and Winsberg, B. G. "A Modified Lincoln-Osertsky Motor Development Scale: Provisional Standardization." *Perceptual and Motor Skills,* 1974, *38,* 599-614.

Bonjean, C. M., Hill, R. J., and McLemore, S. D. *Sociological Measurement: Inventory of Scales and Indices.* San Francisco: Chandler, 1967.

Boyer, E. G., Simon, A., and Karafin, G. (Eds.) *Measures of Maturation: An Anthology of Early Childhood Observation Instruments.* Philadelphia, Pennsylvania: Research for Better Schools, 1973.

Brislin, R. W., Lonner, W. J., and Thorndike, R. M. *Cross-Cultural Research Methods.* New York: Wiley, 1973.

Buros, O. K. *The Seventh Mental Measurements Yearbook.* Highland Park, New Jersey: Gryphon Press, 1972.

Buros, O. K. *Tests in Print II.* Highland Park, New Jersey: Gryphon Press, 1974.

Buros, O. K. *English Tests and Reviews.* Highland Park, New Jersey: Gryphon Press, 1975.

Buros, O. K. *Foreign Language Tests and Reviews.* Highland Park, New Jersey: Gryphon Press, 1975.

Buros, O. K. *Intelligence Tests and Reviews.* Highland Park, New Jersey: Gryphon Press, 1975.

Buros, O. K. *Mathematics Tests and Reviews.* Highland Park, New Jersey: Gryphon Press, 1975.

Buros, O. K. *Personality Tests and Reviews II.* Highland Park, New Jersey: Gryphon Press, 1975.

Buros, O. K. *Reading Tests and Reviews II.* Highland Park, New Jersey: Gryphon Press, 1975.

Buros, O. K. *Science Tests and Reviews.* Highland Park, New Jersey: Gryphon Press, 1975.

Buros, O. K. *Social Studies Tests and Reviews.* Highland Park, New Jersey: Gryphon Press, 1975.

Buros, O. K. *Vocational Tests and Reviews.* Highland Park, New Jersey: Gryphon Press, 1975.

Cattell, R. B., and Warburton, F. W. *Objective Personality and Motivation Tests.* Urbana, Illinois: University of Illinois Press, 1967.

Center for the Study of Evaluation. *Elementary School Test Evaluations.* Los Angeles: Center for the Study of Evaluation, School of Education, UCLA, 1970.

Center for the Study of Evaluation. *Preschool/Kindergarten Test Evaluations.* Los Angeles: Center for the Study of Evaluation, School of Education, UCLA, 1971.

Chun, K. T., Cobb, S., and French, J. R. P., Jr. *Measures for Psychological Assessment.* Ann Arbor, Michigan: Institute for Social Research, University of Michigan, 1975.

Clarke, H. H. *Application of Measurement to Health and Physical Education.* (4th ed.) Englewood Cliffs, New Jersey: Prentice-Hall, 1967.

Clarke, H. H., and Clarke, D. H. *Developmental and Adapted Physical Education.* Englewood Cliffs, New Jersey: Prentice-Hall, 1963.

Clarke, H. H. *Physical and Motor Tests in the Medford Boy's Growth Study.* Englewood Cliffs, New Jersey: Prentice-Hall, 1971.

Clarke, H. H., and Munroe, R. A. *Test Manual: Oregon Cable-Tension Strength Batteries for Boys and Girls from Fourth Grade through College.* Eugene, Oregon: Microform Publications in Health, Physical Education, and Recreation, University of Oregon, 1970.

Comrey, A. L., Backer, T. E., and Glaser, E. M. *A Sourcebook for Mental Health Measures.* Prepared for the National Institute of Mental Health. Los Angeles, California: Human Interaction Research Institute, 1973.

Cratty, B. J. *Motor Activity and the Education of Retardates.* Philadelphia, Pennsylvania: Lea & Febiger, 1969.

Cratty, B. J. *Motor Activity and the Education of Retardates.* (2nd ed.) Philadelphia, Pennsylvania: Lea & Febiger, 1974.

Entwisle, D. R. *Word Associations of Young Children.* Baltimore, Maryland: Johns Hopkins Press, 1966.

Farnsworth, P. R. *The Social Psychology of Music.* (2nd ed.) Ames: Iowa State University Press, 1969.

Fogelman, K. R. *Piagetian Tests for the Primary School.* Bucks, England: National Foundation for Educational Research, 1970. In U.S., Atlantic Heights, New Jersey: Humanities Press, 1970.

Goldman, B. A., and Saunders, J. L. *Directory of Unpublished Experimental Mental Measures.* Vol. I. New York: Behavioral Publications, 1974.

Guilford, J. P., and Hoepfner, R. *The Analysis of Intelligence.* New York: McGraw-Hill, 1971.

Haskins, M. J. *Evaluation in Physical Education.* Dubuque, Iowa: Brown, 1972.

Hess, R. D., Shipman, V. C., Brophy, J. E., and Bear, R. M. *The Cognitive Environments of Urban Preschool Children.* Chicago: Graduate School of Education, University of Chicago, 1968.

Hess, R. D., Shipman, V. C., Brophy, J. E., and Bear, R. M. *The Cognitive Environments of Urban Preschool Children: Follow-up Phase.* Chicago: Graduate School of Education, University of Chicago, 1969.

Ingenkamp, K. *Developments in Educational Testing.* New York: Gordon and Breach, 1969.

Instructional Objectives Exchange. *Attitudes Related to Tolerance 9-12.* Los Angeles: Instructional Objectives Exchange, 1971.

Instructional Objectives Exchange. *Judgment: Deductive Logic and Assumption Recognition 7-12.* Los Angeles: Instructional Objectives Exchange, 1971.

Instructional Objectives Exchange. *Attitude Toward School K-12.* (Rev. ed.) Los Angeles: Instructional Objectives Exchange, 1972.

Instructional Objectives Exchange. *Measures of Self Concept K-12.* (Rev. ed.) Los Angeles: Instructional Objectives Exchange, 1972.

Johnson, B. L., and Nelson, J. K. *Practical Measurements for Evaluation in Physical Education.* Minneapolis, Minnesota: Burgess, 1969.

Lake, D. G., Miles, M. B., and Earle, R. B., Jr. *Measuring Human Behavior: Tools for the Assessment of Social Functioning.* New York: Teachers' College Press, 1973.

Lehman, P. R. *Tests and Measurements in Music.* Englewood Cliffs, New Jersey: Prentice-Hall, 1968.

McReynolds, P. (Ed.) *Advances in Psychological Assessment. Volume 1.* Palo Alto, California: Science and Behavior Books, 1968.

McReynolds, P. (Ed.) *Advances in Psychological Assessment. Volume 2.* Palo Alto, California: Science and Behavior Books, 1971.

McReynolds, P. (Ed.) *Advances in Psychological Assessment. Volume 3.* San Francisco, California: Jossey-Bass, 1975.

Mardell, C. G., and Goldenberg, D. S. *Learning Disabilities/Early Childhood Research Project.* Springfield, Illinois: Office of the Superintendent of Public Instruction, 1972. Available as ERIC document no. ED 082 408.

Mathews, D. K. *Measurement in Physical Education.* (4th ed.) Philadelphia, Pennsylvania: Saunders, 1973.

Meier, J. *Screening and Assessment of Young Children at Developmental Risk.* Publication No. (OS) 73-90. Washington, D.C.: Department of Health, Education, and Welfare, 1973.

National Foundation for Educational Research in England and Wales. *Register of Questionnaires and Attitude Scales.* Slough, Berkshire, England: NFER, 1973, 1976.

Northern, J. L., and Downs, M. P. *Hearing in Children.* Baltimore, Maryland: Williams and Wilkins, 1974.

Oller, J. W., Jr. "Cloze Tests of Second Language Proficiency and What They Measure." *Language Learning,* 1973, *23,* 105-118.

Pharmacotherapy of Children. Special Issue. *Psychopharmacology Bulletin,* 1973. Also available as Department of Health, Education, and Welfare. Publication No. (HSM) 73-9002, Washington, D.C.

Riskin, J., and Faunce, E. E. "An Evaluative Review of Family Interaction Research." *Family Process,* 1972, *11,* 365-455.

Robinson, J. P., and Shaver, P. R. *Measures of Social Psychological Attitudes.* Ann Arbor: Survey Research Center, Institute for Social Research, 1973.

Shaw, M. E., and Wright, J. M. *Scales for the Measurement of Attitudes.* New York: McGraw-Hill, 1967.

Sheehan, J. G. *Stuttering Research and Therapy.* New York: Harper & Row, 1970.

Simon, A., and Boyer, E. G. (Eds.) *Mirrors for Behavior: An Anthology of Classroom Observation Instruments.* Philadelphia, Pennsylvania: Research for Better Schools, 1967.

Simon, A., and Boyer, E. G. (Eds.) *Mirrors for Behavior: An Anthology of Observation Instruments Continued.* Philadelphia, Pennsylvania: Research for Better Schools, 1970.

Walker, D. K. *Socioemotional Measures for Preschool and Kindergarten Children.* San Francisco: Jossey-Bass, 1973.

Webb, E. J., and others. *Unobtrusive Measures.* Chicago: Rand McNally, 1965.

Part Two

MEASURES OF CHILD BEHAVIOR

Category 1. Cognition

Category 2. Personality and Emotional Characteristics

Category 3. Perceptions of Environment

Category 4. Self-Concept

Category 5. Qualities of Caregiving and Home Environment

Category 6. Motor Skills and Sensory Perception

Category 7. Physical Attributes

Category 8. Attitudes and Interests

Category 9. Social Behavior

Category 10. Vocational

Category 11. Unclassified

Category 1

Cognition

These are primarily measures of various cognitive abilities, broadly interpreted. Measures of cognitive style and creativity are included here.

Group 1-a. Intelligence, Readiness, and Maturation. *These measures generally sample broad spectra of common experiences and are frequently designed to derive an overall functioning level of the child. Other areas measured by this group are concept development and verbal reasoning. Most of the Piaget-type measures are included here. There are also many preschool screening measures.*

Group 1-b. Language and Number Skills. *While these skills often constitute parts of intelligence and readiness measures, they are important enough to warrant measures devoted exclusively to them.*

Group 1-c. Specific Achievements. *These measures are designed for assessing achievement in highly specific aspects of a child's experience.*

Group 1-d. Cognitive Style and Cognitive Processes. *This subcategory includes measures of creativity and curiosity, cognitive style, and learning processes.*

Group 1-e. Miscellaneous. *These measures involve primarily cognitive functions but could not logically be classified with the other cognitive measures.*

29

Group 1-a

Intelligence, Readiness
and Maturation

A–C (PERFORMANCE) TEST 1

AUTHOR: James G. M'Comisky

AGE: 8 years to adult

VARIABLE: Thought processes (mainly conceptualizing)

TYPE OF MEASURE: Test

SOURCE FROM WHICH MEASURE MAY BE OBTAINED: James G. M'Comisky, Psychology Department, Hull University, Hull, England HU6 7RX. Cost: Approximately £30 one test-set (test-sets prepared to individual order).

DESCRIPTION OF MEASURE: A–C (Performance) Test 1 gives two separate measures of conceptualizing, using a Vigotsky-type sorting-test. The test consists of sixteen small wooden blocks (*lignum vitae*), which differ in regard to ten characteristics: shape, solidity, and so forth. Some of the characteristics are related, for example, size, height; others are not related, for example, shape, color. Each of the two main parts of the test ("divergent" and "convergent") is subdivided, making four subtests in all. A "divergent"-"convergent" score can be estimated from the subject's performance on the test.

RELIABILITY AND VALIDITY: By the very nature of the test, it would be difficult to determine its reliability. The main validity study was an investigation of the predictive power of the test with first-year architecture students at an English university. A statistically significant relationship was found with the criterion (academic performance of the students at the end of their second year). Full details of this and other validation studies are found in the references below.

BIBLIOGRAPHY:

Freeman, J., Butcher, H. J., and Christie, J. "Creativity: A Selective Review of Research." Monograph of the Society for Research into Higher Education Ltd., 2 Woburn Square, London, England, 1965.

Freeman, J., M'Comisky, J. G., and Buttle, D. "Student Selection: A Comparative Study (Architecture and Economics University Students)." *International Journal of Educational Science*, 1969, *3*.

M'Comisky, J. G., and Freeman, L. "Concept Attainment and Type of Education." *International Journal of Educational Science*, 1967, *2*.

ACADEMIC READINESS SCALE

AUTHOR: Harold F. Burks

AGE: Kindergarten or first grade

VARIABLE: Academic readiness

TYPE OF MEASURE: Rating scale

SOURCE FROM WHICH MEASURE MAY BE OBTAINED: Arden Press, 8331 Alvarado Drive, Huntington Beach, California 92646.

DESCRIPTION OF MEASURE: This measure consists of fourteen items, each of which is rated on a 5-point scale. The areas of functioning sampled by the items are as follows: Motor, Perceptual-Motor (two items), Persistence, Memory, Attention, Counting, Word Recognition, Vocabulary, Interest in Curriculum, Social, Humor, and Emotional. For the purposes of this instrument, readiness is defined as the capacity to achieve in reading at the first-grade level and the general ability to succeed in other first-grade-level tasks.

As an example, the first item from the scale is given below:

MOTOR (moderate predictive value)

[ ]	[ ]	[ ]	[ ]	[ ]
has to be helped in most motor tasks	can do simple tasks but needs some help eating, dressing, toilet, and rest tasks	is able to care for self in eating, toilet, and rest tasks	is able to tie shoes, cut with scissors, button clothes, skip, and catch balls	holds pencil properly, rides 2-wheel bike, uses tools, combs hair, helps others at motor tasks

RELIABILITY AND VALIDITY: The reliability of this instrument was assessed by having teachers rate 110 kindergarten children ten days after the first rating period. Test-retest correlations for the categories ranged from .64 to .83. A significant positive relationship was found between all academic readiness scale categories and the Stanford Achievement Test reading scores. All of the correlations between the ARS categories on the one hand and word recognition and reading comprehension on the other hand were significant, most of them at .01 level. The factor analysis of the test indicated four identifiable factors: (1) Memory-Concentration, (2) Academic Skills, (3) Social-Emotional, (4) Perceptual Motor. Nine of the fourteen items on the scale showed significant differences between two schools: one, higher socioeconomic, and the other, lower socioeconomic.

BIBLIOGRAPHY:

Burks, H. F. "The Hyperkinetic Child." *Journal of Exceptional Children,* 1960, *27,* 18-26.
Burks, H. F. *Manual for Burks' Behavior Rating Scales.* Huntington Beach, California: Arden Press, 1968.

Prepared by Orval G. Johnson

ALBERT EINSTEIN SCALES OF SENSORIMOTOR DEVELOPMENT: OBJECT PERMANENCE

AUTHORS: Harvey H. Corman and Sibylle K. Escalona

AGE: 5 to 24 months

VARIABLE: Level of sensorimotor intelligence (object permanence)

TYPE OF MEASURE: Guttman-type scale

SOURCE FROM WHICH MEASURE MAY BE OBTAINED: Sibylle K. Escalona, Rose Fitzgerald Kennedy Center for Research in Mental Retardation and Human Development, Albert Einstein College of Medicine, Yeshiva University, Eastchester Road and Morris Park Avenue, Bronx, New York 10461. The film *The Albert Einstein Scales of Sensorimotor Development, II Object Permanence* is available (for sale, $205 or rental, $19) from the New York University Film Library, Washington Square, New York, New York 10003.

DESCRIPTION OF MEASURE: The scale is designed to measure cognitive development, with respect to object permanence, as that concept and the successive stages were defined by Piaget. The scales complement tests of general intelligence but differ in that they assess the means of problem solving available to children, but not achievement levels. It is suitable for the assessment of learning readiness and for research. A series of standard tasks, requiring the child to find objects hidden from view, and explicit instructions for administration and scoring are described in a manual. A film demonstrating scale administration is also available. One examiner experienced in infant testing and one observer/scorer are needed to obtain valid results. The several items within each stage, while of ascending difficulty, do not necessarily represent developmental progression, whereas behavior corresponding to different stages does reflect developmental status.

As an example, the fifth item of the eighteen on the scale is given below:

Interrupted Prehension
Administration: An attractive object is placed on the table, within easy reach of the subject. *After the child* has begun the reaching motion, a cloth is dropped over the toy, concealing it (and often the child's hand as well) from view *before* the hand has contacted the object.
Response: Child continues the reaching motion and grasps object, at least twice.

RELIABILITY AND VALIDITY: The original scale was administered to 119 subjects to establish reliability. Agreement among three observer/scorers was 94 percent. Spot checks during validation studies showed reliability values of no less than 92 percent. A cross-sectional validation study ($N = 113$) using Guttman scalogram analysis, corrected by Green's index of consistency, yielded a Consistency Index of 1.00 and an *eta* with age of .83 (relationship with age, not linear). Longitudinal validation was performed with fifteen subjects, all of whom showed the expected sequence of progression. Mean ages are provided for entry into and completion of each stage (Corman and Escalona, 1969).

BIBLIOGRAPHY:

Corman, H. H., and Escalona, S. K. "Stages of Sensorimotor Development: A Replication Study." *Merrill-Palmer Quarterly,* 1969, *15* (4).
Piaget, J. *The Origins of Intelligence in Children.* New York: International Universities Press, 1952.

Prepared by Sibylle K. Escalona

ALBERT EINSTEIN SCALES OF SENSORIMOTOR DEVELOPMENT: PREHENSION

AUTHORS: Harvey H. Corman and Sibylle K. Escalona

AGE: 2 to 8 months

VARIABLE: Level of sensorimotor intelligence (prehension)

TYPE OF MEASURE: Guttman-type scale

SOURCE FROM WHICH MEASURE MAY BE OBTAINED: Sibylle K. Escalona, Rose Fitzgerald Kennedy Center for Research in Mental Retardation and Human Development, Albert Einstein College of Medicine, Yeshiva University, Eastchester Road and Morris Park Avenue, Bronx, New York 10461.

DESCRIPTION OF MEASURE: The Prehension Scale reflects developmental advances in sensorimotor intelligence as defined by Piaget from the simplest primary circular reactions (early Stage II), through the more varied and complex primary circular reactions, to the second circular reactions (Stage III). A series of standard tasks and scoring criteria and procedures of administration are provided in the manual. In order to elicit the highest level of performance of which the infant is capable, examiners must flexibly adapt to the infant's state and create optimal conditions for the emergence of the relevant behaviors. Prior experience in *infant* testing is required. Scores are based on the pattern of response to stimuli; actual achievement of the "task" is irrelevant to determination of stage level. For instance, on the item testing the ability to apply squeezing motion to a squeaky toy by imitation, appropriate hand motion applied to the toy insufficient to produce sound receives a Stage III score nonetheless. The scale is constructed so as to provide several different tasks capable of eliciting the same level of response. For instance, a Stage II, substage 2 score can be attained on five different tasks that are equivalent. One examiner and an observer/scorer are needed to attain reliable test results.
    As an example, the fifth item of the fifteen on the scale is given below:

Object in Hand, Not in Visual Field
Administration: Examiner places a suitable object into the infant's hand, while the hand is not in the infant's field of vision. (Cannot be given in prone position.)

Response: (1) After the infant has held the object for three seconds he brings it to the mouth. Visual regard of object and hand is not present.

Response: (2) Grasping the object is immediately followed by bringing object to mouth in a single continuous sequence. No visual regard of object.

Response: (3) Once object is grasped infant brings it into his visual field and regards it more than transiently. If visual regard alternated with mouthing the object, a score may be given, provided the toy was regarded as soon as it entered the visual field, and *before* it was brought to the mouth.

RELIABILITY AND VALIDITY: The original scale was administered to a sample of fifty-one infants ranging from 1 to 10 months in age. Guttman scalogram analysis employing Green's index of consistency yielded a Consistency Index of .66 and a *rho* of .85 with chronological age. Subsequently longitudinal validation was performed with fourteen infants, all of whom showed the expected progression from each stage to the next. Mean ages for entry into and completion of each stage are provided (Corman and Escalona, 1969). Reliability (agreement among three observer/scorers) was .96 during pilot studies and .97 among two observers when spot checked during validation studies.

BIBLIOGRAPHY:

Corman, H. H., and Escalona, S. K. "Stages of Sensorimotor Development: A Replication Study." *Merrill-Palmer Quarterly*, 1969, *15* (4).

Piaget, J. *The Origins of Intelligence in Children*. New York: International Universities Press, 1952.

Prepared by Sibylle K. Escalona

ALBERT EINSTEIN SCALES OF SENSORIMOTOR DEVELOPMENT: SPATIAL RELATIONSHIPS

AUTHORS: Harvey H. Corman and Sibylle K. Escalona

AGE: 5 to 25 months

VARIABLE: Level of sensorimotor intelligence (spatial relationships)

TYPE OF MEASURE: Guttman-type scale

SOURCE FROM WHICH MEASURE MAY BE OBTAINED: Sibylle K. Escalona, Rose Fitzgerald Kennedy Center for Research in Mental Retardation and Human Development, Albert Einstein College of Medicine, Yeshiva University, Eastchester Road and Morris Park Avenue, Bronx, New York 10461. The film *The Albert Einstein Scales of Sensorimotor Development, III Spatial Relationships* is available (for sale, $285 or rental, $24) from the New York University Film Library, Washington Square, New York, New York 10003.

DESCRIPTION OF MEASURE: The scale measures cognitive development in the realm of spatial relationships, as successive stages in the capacity to adapt to the objective properties of physical space were defined by Piaget. The scale complements tests of general mental development but differs from such tests in that it is the means of problem solving that are assessed, not achievement. It is suitable for diagnosis of a specific learning deficit, for assessment of learning readiness, and for research. A series of twenty-one tasks yield behavioral responses, each of which is scorable; that is, there are no "failures," rather performance is scorable at one or another stage level. Items within a stage represent alternate and often equivalent means to obtain the same developmental score. They do *not* represent a sequence of ascending difficulty. A manual is available, as is a film depicting administration and scoring. One examiner experienced in infant testing and one observer/scorer are needed to obtain valid results.

As an example, the first of the twenty-one items on the scale is given below:

Lateral Displacement of Object

Administration: Child is seated on floor or on couch (propped, if necessary, with pillows). Child focuses on toy held at eye level, by *E*. Once his gaze is focused, the object is moved and placed to the right of and slightly behind the child (movement must be fast enough to avoid visual following during the displacement). This procedure is to be repeated with displacement to the left.

Response: Child searches with hand and/or moves body in direction of trajectory taken by object in order to retrieve it twice on the left and right.

RELIABILITY AND VALIDITY: A pilot study using 119 subjects yielded a reliability measure of 95 percent (agreement among three observer/scorers). Spot checks during validation studies maintained agreement above 93 percent. A cross-sectional validation study involving eighty-three infants yielded a Consistency Index of .98 (Guttman scalogram analysis corrected by Green's index of consistency). Correlation with age was *eta* = .84 (not a linear relationship). A longitudinal study involving sixteen infants was then performed; all subjects progressed in the expected sequence. Mean ages are provided for entry into and completion of each stage (Corman and Escalona, 1969).

BIBLIOGRAPHY:

Corman, H. H., and Escalona, S. K. "Stages of Sensorimotor Development: A Replication Study." *Merrill-Palmer Quarterly,* 1969, *15* (4).

Piaget, J. *The Origins of Intelligence in Children.* New York: International Universities Press, 1952.

Prepared by Sibylle K. Escalona

APPLICATION OF GENERALIZATIONS TEST (AGT)

AUTHOR: Norman E. Wallen

AGE: Grade 5 and above (data on grade 6 only)

VARIABLE: Ability to apply generalizations

TYPE OF MEASURE: Fixed response test (true-false format)

SOURCE FROM WHICH MEASURE MAY BE OBTAINED: See Wallen and others (1969).

DESCRIPTION OF MEASURE: The test is designed to measure the ability to apply generalizations to new situations in order to make defensible inferences. The focus is specifically on generalizations emphasized in the Taba Social Studies Curriculum. Before using in other contexts, potential users should evaluate both content and scoring key. The format is based on an earlier test, Social Studies Inference Test (Taba, 1966). It consists of seven short paragraphs, each describing a hypothetical situation in a society. Each passage is followed by seven to thirteen statements, each of which is to be answered as "probably true" or "probably false." Passages and statements may be read aloud.

There are sixty-five items in all, of which ten from the Hunteros and Farmanos section are given below as examples. The titles of the other sections are Mercano and Growland, Mr. Jones' Grocery Store, Pambo and Tom, Mr. Smith's Land, and the People of Dicto. An abbreviated statement of the intended generalization appropriate to each item appears in the right column. The italicized words should be clarified by the examiner.

Hunteros and Farmanos

This is about two groups of people, the Hunteros and the Farmanos, who live in the same valley surrounded by mountains. The Hunteros hunt and fish to get food. They often have to move because the herds of animals move from place to place. Most of the Farmanos are farmers. However, some of them make simple tools.

Remember: *Hunteros* are hunters
Farmanos are farmers

(PT)   1. The Farmanos have more schools for their children than the Hunteros.

1. Geographic stability and increased technology lead to more formalized educational institutions, permanent buildings, etc.

(PF)   2. The Hunteros' way of life shows that their ability to learn is less than the Farmanos.

2. "Way of life" is not a good index of learning ability—it is a product of many factors.

(PT)   3. The Farmanos should be worried if the Hunteros have a poor hunting season.

3. Interdependence of groups in same geographic area. If one group suffers, it has repercussions on others.

(PT)   4. The Farmanos will develop modern conveniences before the Hunteros.

4. Technology breeds technology.

(PF)   5. The Hunteros have practically no contact with the Farmanos.

(PT)   6. The Farmanos are *suspicious* of the Hunteros.

(PT)   7. The Hunteros will be more concerned that their leaders be daring than will the Farmanos.

(PF)   8. The Hunteros *do not* have musical or artistic activities.

(PT)   9. The Farmanos will increase in numbers (population) faster than the Hunteros.

(PT) 10. If both groups had their *lodgings* destroyed, this would harm the Farmanos more than the Hunteros.

5. Groups living in same geographic area almost certainly interact.

6. Strangeness or differences usually lead to distrust or suspicion.

7. Expectations of leaders depend largely on group needs.

8. All cultures or societies have some forms of art.

9. Geographic stability and a less hazardous life lead to population growth.

10. Geographic stability leads to greater investment, economically and psychologically, in permanent structures.

RELIABILITY AND VALIDITY: The primary data were obtained from two samples of sixth graders, each in excess of 220 cases. The first sample consisted of ten classrooms teaching the Taba Curriculum. The second was a comparison set of ten classrooms equated as to judged teacher competence and academic and socioeconomic level of students. A wide range of economic levels, academic performance, and ethnic make-up was represented. Kuder-Richardson formula 20 and split-half reliabilities over an eight-month interval were .67 and .69. Item analysis data are reported (Wallen and others, 1969). Correlations with other fixed response tests especially designed to measure thinking skills, with the STEP Social Studies Test and with the Lorge-Thorndike verbal and nonverbal tests, ranged from .42 to .60. Correlations with teacher ratings of thinking skills made three times during the year ranged from .15 to .85 with 64 percent over .40. Additional validity evidence was obtained from a separate sample of thirty-one sixth graders who were interviewed as to their reasons for their answers as they responded. The taped responses were independently analyzed by two judges as to the quality of thought demonstrated. Judge agreement was .89, and correlations with the score based on response only were .83 and .88. Further, seven of the "Taba" teachers took the test and analyzed it after the end of the school year. They made few errors, indicating agreement with the scoring key, and judged the test as a valid measure of what they had been attempting to teach.

BIBLIOGRAPHY:

Taba, H. *Teaching Strategies and Cognitive Functioning in Elementary School Children.* U.S. Office of Education, Cooperative Research Project, No. 2404, 1966.

Wallen, H., and others. *The Taba Curriculum Development Project in Social Studies.* U.S. Office of Education, Cooperative Research Project, No. 5-1314, 1969. (Also available from Addison-Wesley, Menlo Park, California.)

BASIC ABILITY TESTS

AUTHORS: Cyril J. Adcock and M. Webberley

AGE: High school to adult

VARIABLE: Reduced structure of intellect schema

TYPE OF MEASURE: Test

SOURCE FROM WHICH MEASURE MAY BE OBTAINED: Cyril J. Adcock, Department of Psychology, Victoria University of Wellington, P.O. Box 196, Wellington, New Zealand. Cost: $3.00 for postage and copying.

DESCRIPTION OF MEASURE: These tests are designed for research only and have been used with standard representative tests in an endeavor to reduce the Guilford Structure of Intellect schema to simple form for practical purposes. For this reason some of the tests are open-ended. The major dimensions and relationships of the tests are as follows: (1) *Reasoning:* Matching Triads, Circles Test, Missing Words. Research suggests a common factor in figural and semantic material. (2) *Flexibility of Semantic Closure:* Word Transformations, Missing Link Test. (3) *Flexibility of Figural Closure:* Letter Matrices, Hidden Figures. (Disguised Letters was probably too easy for students and loaded on intelligence.) (4) *Speed of Figural Closure:* Figural Matrices (not available), Blots. (5) *Speed of Semantic Closure:* Word, Letter, and Figural Matrices all related to this factor suggesting a common verbal element as with reasoning. This factor seems to be a major part of general intelligence. (6) *Fluency:* Figural fluency appeared as a separate factor in speeded naming of *objects square, cube-shaped, or spherical* in form. This is part of the general factor. (7) *Perceptual Speed:* Perceptual Speed and Reading Speed came out on a common factor, but the latter with intelligence overlap. (8) *Two memory factors:* not represented among the tests.

As examples, the first three keyed items of Reasoning: Matching Triads are given below:

In each of the problems below you have to match three people with their respective jobs. The information given provides the clues.

1. *Telephonist, Supervisor and Buyer*
   Alice is a close friend of the telephonist.
   The supervisor does not like the telephonist.
   Margaret and Diane do not get on well together.
   Who is the buyer?   (Alice)
2. *Accountant, Cashier and Boss*
   Jones beat the accountant at chess.
   Davis had dinner with the boss.
   Smith loaned $5 to the accountant.
   Jones lives in the same suburb as the boss.
   Who is the boss?   (Smith)
3. *Accountant, Cashier and Boss*
   Bill and the cashier share a car.

John always arrives before the boss.
Tom beat the accountant at golf.
The boss does not play golf.
Who is the boss?   (Bill)

RELIABILITY AND VALIDITY: None reported.

BIBLIOGRAPHY:

Adcock, C. J., and Martin, W. A. "Flexibility and Creativity." *Journal of General Psychology,* 1971, *85,* 71-76.
Adcock, C. J., and Webberley, M. "Primary Mental Abilities." *Journal of General Psychology,* 1971, *84,* 229-243.

BEHAVIOR MATURITY CHECKLIST (BMCL)

AUTHOR: Donald C. Soule

AGE: All ages, mental age 6 to 54 months

VARIABLE: Behavior maturity

TYPE OF MEASURE: Checklist

SOURCE FROM WHICH MEASURE MAY BE OBTAINED: Psychology, Research and Evaluation Section, O'Berry Center, Goldsboro, North Carolina 27530.

DESCRIPTION OF MEASURE: The BMCL is a measure of behavior maturity for severely and profoundly retarded children and adults. It is also useful for younger moderately retarded children. The BMCL yields a total behavior age as well as subtest scores in the area of grooming, eating, toileting, language, social interaction, total self-care, and total interpersonal skills. Norms were established on 206 severely and profoundly retarded subjects in institution and community programs.

The test is made up of fifteen items yielding scores in seven areas. As examples, one grooming (G) item, one eating (E) item, and one social interaction (S) item are given below:

(G) *Keeping Nose Clean*
    0. Is not aware of nose running, makes no attempt to clean.
    1. Is aware of nose running, may brush with hand or snuff it up.
    2. Will come to parent and cooperate in having nose cleaned.
    3. Will wipe own nose when told to do so but cannot adequately and completely blow and clean without help.
    4. Can adequate clean nose but often needs to be reminded.
    5. Completely and independently cleans nose when necessary without reminding.

(E) *Drinking*

    0. Cannot drink from cup or glass even held by parent.

    1. Needs to have cup or glass held.

    2. Can hold glass but needs to have it handed to him and taken away.

    3. Can hold glass, pick it up, and put it down using both hands, may sometimes spill.

    4. Can use glass and cup with one hand but not pour into it.

    5. Can pour from pitcher or bottle and use glass, cup, or straw.

(S) *Errands*

    0. Has no concept or understanding which would permit sending him on errands.

    1. Cannot be sent on errands because is not dependable enough or memory is too short.

    2. Can be sent on errands *within* area of home or cottage with note.

    3. Can be sent on errands *within* area of home or cottage without note.

    4. Can be sent on an errand *outside* of the home or cottage with note.

    5. Can be sent on an errand *outside* of the home or cottage without note.

RELIABILITY AND VALIDITY: A number of reliability checks have been done, including: retest after six months $N = 20$, $r = .93$; same examiner, different informant $N = 30$, $r = .95$; different examiner, different informant $N = 30$, $r = .90$.

BIBLIOGRAPHY:

Bostic, F., and Shelton, A. "Work Activity Program for Severely and Profoundly Retarded Adults." *Research and the Retarded,* Fall 1974.

Laufer, J. "Reliability of the Behavior Maturity Checklist." *Research and the Retarded,* 1975, *2* (2), 25-28.

Snipes, S., and Soule, D. "Some Characteristics of the Behavior Maturity Checklist." *Research and the Retarded,* Spring 1973.

Snipes, S., Soule, D., and Wilson, S. "The Developmental Learning Unit." *Research and the Retarded,* Spring 1974.

Soule, D. "Teacher Bias Effects with Severely Retarded Children." *American Journal of Mental Deficiency,* 1972, 77, 208-211.

Soule, D. *Behavior Checklist Manual.* Goldsboro, North Carolina: O'Berry Center, 1974.

BINGHAM BUTTON TEST

AUTHOR: William J. Bingham

AGE: 3 to 6 years

VARIABLE: Readiness

TYPE OF MEASURE: Test

SOURCE FROM WHICH MEASURE MAY BE OBTAINED: William J. Bingham, 46211 North 125th Street East, Lancaster, California 93534.

DESCRIPTION OF MEASURE: This test is designed to measure a child's knowledge and understanding of simple terms and relationships that he will encounter in his primary school years. The materials for this measure are remarkably simple, consisting of ten buttons of varying size, shape, and color in a plastic container. The test has a total of fifty items, ten items for each of the following categories: colors, numbers, sizes and comparisons, object/object relations, and person/object relations. Examples of items from the five areas sampled by the test are: (1) Colors: "Show me the *white* button." (2) Numbers: "Put *one* button in the jar." (3) Sizes and Comparisons: "Put your finger on the *big* button." (4) Object/Object Relations: "Put the button *in* the cap." (5) Person/Object Relations: "Take the button *away* from my hand." Age and percentile norms are provided, based on highly disadvantaged children over a period of two years. Use of this test for children of higher socioeconomic backgrounds might not be suitable other than to make general estimates of ability.

RELIABILITY AND VALIDITY: A group of four children were randomly selected from fifteen different classes and were given the test at six-week intervals. Using a Kuder-Richardson split-half reliability, a coefficient of .89 was obtained. To verify the reliability of the current edition of the test, a test-retest was administered the following summer to thirty-one of the first Head Start group. A reliability coefficient of .87 was obtained using the Chi-square method.

Four psychometrists administered the Bingham Button Test, with a series of other simple tasks, to a selected group of Head Start children. These results were compared to teacher ratings of the same group after eight weeks. Using the Chi-square method of comparisons, a correlation coefficient of .76 was obtained for all five sections of the test.

BIBLIOGRAPHY:

Mardell, C. G., and Goldenberg, D. S. *Learning Disabilities/Early Childhood Research Project.* Springfield, Illinois: State Office of the Superintendent of Public Instruction, 1972.

Prepared by Orval G. Johnson

BKR DEVELOPMENT AND TRAINABILITY
ASSESSMENT SCALE (DATA)

AUTHORS: Louise M. Bradtke, William J. Kirkpatrick, Katherine P. Rosenblatt, and Alexander Bannatyne

AGE: To 5 years

VARIABLE: Psychophysical areas of development

TYPE OF MEASURE: Test

SOURCE FROM WHICH MEASURE MAY BE OBTAINED: BKR Educational Projects, Inc., 1790 SW 43rd Way, Fort Lauderdale, Florida 23317. Cost: Manual, Curriculum, Handbook, and Activity cards: $25.00; package of 25 assessment forms: $15.00.

DESCRIPTION OF MEASURE: DATA yields a detailed assessment of a wide range of tasks and skills common to the first few years of life: recognition of purpose, spatial relations, form-shape sorting, color sorting, diameter-size sorting, texture sorting, number counting, rhythm, visual, auditory (nonlanguage), basic language, fine motor, gross motor, social self, personal skills, and direction. DATA may be used to assess very young normal children or mentally retarded people who are functioning on a low developmental age level.

The DATA Scale is a basic for prescriptive teaching. The educator incorporates the items' results with his/her objective observations, and noting the child's needs and strengths develops an individualized, prescriptive, educational program for the child utilizing activity cards as a starting point. The activity cards are utilized as examples of activities that may be incorporated into an individualized prescriptive educational program for the child. The cards are indexed and cross-indexed. These indices are developmentally sequenced to further aid the educator in the programing of the child.

DATA is also a measure of trainability, indicating the most effective teaching techniques for each child, and of the spontaneity shown by the child.

The DATA Scale also assists the educator in determining the best reinforcers to use and the child's susceptibility to verbal persuasion. DATA assists the educator in investigating the child's knowledge (What does the child know?); in investigating the child's achievement (What can the child do?); in investigating the child's learning potentials (What can the child learn?); and in investigating the child's learning styles (How does the child best learn in terms of techniques and reinforcers?).

As examples, selected items from the Basic Language area of DATA are given below. Performance is rated on a scale from 6 to 0, as follows: 6 = Spontaneously or imitatively well done; 5 = Spontaneously or imitatively, but poorly done; 4 = Physical positioning required, but well done; 3 = Reinforcement required, but well done; 2 = Physical positioning required, but poorly done; 1 = Reinforcement required, but poorly done; 0 = Failure, rejection, no attempt.

+3 *Babbles spontaneously*
Administration: This item is rated from Examiner's observations of child during the assessment.

Scoring Criteria:

Good Performance—Child repeats a combination of similar speech sounds in an apparent rhythmical pattern.

Poor Performance—Child makes isolated vowel sounds and other speech sounds, but not in an apparent rhythmical pattern.

Failure—Child does not repeat a combination of similar speech sounds in an apparent rhythmical pattern.

+8 *Says three of four recognizable words*

Administration: Examiner may assess the child on this item either by presenting the child with various objects and asking him "what's this?" or by observing the child during the assessment and noting spontaneous word production.

Scoring Criteria:

Good Performance—Child says three or more recognizable words in context.

Poor Performance—Child says only one or two recognizable words and sometimes uses them out of context.

Failure—Child does not say any recognizable words in context.

+16 *Reads simple words*

Administration: Examiner prints words "go" "cat" "mom" "stop" on sheet of paper (letters one half inch high).

Scoring Criteria:

Good Performance—Child reads 3 or 4 words.

Poor Performance—Child reads 1 or 2 words.

Failure—Child does not read the words.

RELIABILITY AND VALIDITY: None reported.

BIBLIOGRAPHY:

Bradtke, L. M., Kirkpatrick, W. J., and Rosenblatt, K. P. "Intensive Play: A Technique for Building Affective Behaviors in Profoundly Mentally Retarded Young Children." *Education and Training of Mentally Retarded,* 1972, *7,* 8-13.

Bradtke, L. M., Rosenblatt, K. P., Cortazzo, A. D., and Kirkpatrick, W. J. "Innovations in an Institution for the Mentally Retarded." *Children's Magazine,* 1971 (July-August).

Prepared by William J. Kirkpatrick

BOYD DEVELOPMENTAL PROGRESS SCALE

AUTHOR: Robert D. Boyd

AGE: Birth to 8 years; most efficient at 3 to 6 years

VARIABLE: Growth and development

TYPE OF MEASURE: Test and structured interview

SOURCE FROM WHICH MEASURE MAY BE OBTAINED: Inland Counties Regional Center, Inc., P.O. Box 6127, San Bernardino, California 92408. Cost: Softbound, $9.00; hardbound, $12.00; worksheets, $3.00 per 100.

DESCRIPTION OF MEASURE: The Boyd Developmental Progress Scale is a combination of tested items and items scored on the basis of a structured interview. The scale measures general level of growth and development in Motor, Communication, and Self-Sufficiency areas. The results are pictorially shown on a record sheet, and no attempt is made to derive a precise score in any area. The areas of Motor and Communication are intended to measure actual and demonstrated abilities of the child, while the Self-Sufficiency section measures, on the basis of the parent interview, what the child typically does. This allows for comparison to determine whether the child is typically functioning at or near his level of capability or whether there are areas of deficiency that need further evaluation. The intent of the scale is to screen for possible developmental inadequacies, which in turn may lead to appropriate treatment or training. It should be useful to both professionals and paraprofessionals who work with children below school age.

As examples, three of the 150 items are given below. They come from the Self-Sufficiency skills section of the scale, with the age levels shown.

Birth to 6 Months
2. Recovers Toy From Chest
   Administration: Give the baby a rattle to play with for a short period of time. Place the baby on his back, take the rattle from him and place it on the chest. This may be repeated as desired.
   Scoring: Credit if the child succeeds in securing the rattle. Chance success is not credited.
2 to 3 Years
21. Feeds—Uses Fork to Spear
   Administration: Ask parent, "What implements or tools are used in eating?" If parent indicates a fork is used, ask, "What does he do with the fork, for example, with pieces of meat?"
   Scoring: Credit if child uses fork for *both* scooping and spearing food.
22. Blocks—Give "Just One"
   Administration: Place the blocks in front of the child. Ask, "Give me just one block." (Do not pull hand away after receiving one block until child indicates he is through.)
   Scoring: Credit if child gives *only* one block.

23. Washes, Dries Own Hands

Administration: Ask parent, "What does your child do if he is asked to wash his own hands?"

Scoring: Credit if child is able to manage washing and drying without help. He need not be expected to turn on faucets or get a towel beyond his reach.

RELIABILITY AND VALIDITY: Each item on the 150-item scale was selected on the basis of two criteria: (1) There must be good research evidence that the behavior of skill under consideration typically emerged within the general age level to which it was assigned with the general criterion of 60-70 percent passage; and (2) no scale item was selected unless the skill, directly or indirectly, had "survival value"—defined as a behavior which would, immediately or eventually, lead to more efficient living. With these criteria and the fact that no score is derived, more specific measures of reliability and validity were not feasible, although studies of cross-cultural comparisons (particularly with Self-Sufficiency items) are now in process.

BIBLIOGRAPHY:

Boyd, R. D. *Boyd Developmental Progress Scale Manual.* San Bernardino, California: Inland Counties Regional Center, 1974.

BRITISH INTELLIGENCE SCALE

AUTHORS: C. D. Elliott, L. S. Pearson, D. J. Murray, F. W. Warburton, T. F. Fitzpatrick, J. Ward, and M. Ritchie

AGE: 3 to 17 years

VARIABLE: The scale provides a profile of abilities

TYPE OF MEASURE: Individually administered tests

SOURCE FROM WHICH MEASURE MAY BE OBTAINED: As the items in the scale are still undergoing development, they are not available except for experimental work strictly under the control of the Project Director. (Colin D. Elliott, Director, British Intelligence Scale Project, University of Manchester, Manchester, England, M13 9PL.) It is anticipated that the final version will be marketed in 1977.

DESCRIPTION OF MEASURE: The British Intelligence Scale consists of a wide range of test materials designed to provide a profile of abilities. It is intended that the scale should to a large extent replace the Stanford-Binet and WISC scales, which are presently used by educational psychologists in Britain.

During the phase of test development between 1965 and 1970, a large number of items were written and tried out on over 1,200 children. There is a wide range of content areas, each of which may produce one or more subscales in the final version. The content areas in the try-out version (some of which may be deleted in the final version) were as follows:

Content Area	Description
Vocabulary	Ranges from object and colored-picture recognition to an orthodox vocabulary scale based on published lists of words from children's vocabulary. The items cover an understanding of a degree of abstraction rather than a knowledge of rare words.
Information	This aspect is covered in two ways. Orthodox items dealing with general knowledge assess the child's understanding of a variety of subject areas and his knowledge of himself and his environment. The second type of item examines the child's reasoning about everyday events. The psychologist is given an opportunity to recognize qualitative levels of reasoning, especially among bright children.
Comprehension	Items are designed to investigate the quality of a child's concepts, ranging from the understanding of simple words and instructions to items in a similarities scale.
Ideational Fluency	Items in this area will hopefully provide measures of both the number and quality of ideas produced. Typical items would ask the child to imagine unusual uses for common objects— e.g., a brick—or to imagine the consequences of unlikely occurrences—e.g., if we had no moon.
Visual Memory	Ability to recognize pictures and arrangements and to reproduce designs from memory.
Matrices	Pattern completion and operations in which addition, seriation, inversion, etc. are carried out on content varying in size, shape, and texture. The child must put in the missing parts by placing counters or drawing.
Induction	The discovery and application of rules; responses are similar to those of the Matrices test. The rules involve constancy, rotation (clockwise and counterclockwise), alternation (horizontal and vertical), and randomness.
Operational Thinking	Tasks ranging from sensorimotor operations through classification (by shape, color, and pattern) to the analysis of formalized thinking involving implication and negation. Some inference problems are included.
Number Ability	This scale enables the tester to investigate the child's understanding of number concepts. It covers conservation of number, length, and area; seriation; reversibility; proportionality; and practical calculation. There are also a number of more orthodox computational items.
Block Design	Employs similar but not identical blocks to those used in currently available tests. Items require the reproduction of patterns using identically patterned cubes.
Visual Spatial	This scale requires the subject to visualize shapes and patterns that are turned over and turned around. Later items require more complex spatial reasoning.

The task of the present phase of the project is to perform item analyses and conduct further item development work with the aim of producing a reduced and more refined version of the scale and standardizing it on approximately 3,000 children. It is hoped that the standardization will be completed and the scale will be ready for publication during 1977. No normative or other statistical information is yet available. The scale is described in much greater detail in the references listed below.

RELIABILITY AND VALIDITY: None reported.

BIBLIOGRAPHY:

Elliott, C. D. "Intelligence and the British Intelligence Scale." *Bulletin of the British Psychological Society* (in press).

Elliott, C. D. "The British Intelligence Scale Project: Phase II." *Journal of the Association of Educational Psychologists* (in press).

Fitzpatrick, T. F. "The New British Intelligence Scale." *The Mensa Journal*, 1967, *105*, 1-2.

Fitzpatrick, T. F., and Davidson, I. "A New Intelligence Test—with a Canadian Identity." *Orbit* (Ontario Institute for Studies in Education), 1971, *7*, 16-19.

Gillham, W. E. C. "The British Intelligence Scales: à la recherche du temps perdu." *Bulletin of the British Psychological Society* (in press).

Warburton, F. W. "The Construction of the New British Intelligence Scale." *Bulletin of the British Psychological Society*, 1966, *19*, 59.

Warburton, F. W. "The British Intelligence Scale." In W. B. Dockrell (Ed.), *On Intelligence.* London: Methuen, 1970.

Warburton, F. W., Fitzpatrick, T. F., Ward, J., and Ritchie, M. "Some Problems in the Construction of Individual Intelligence Tests." In P. Mittler (Ed.), *The Psychological Assessment of Mental and Physical Handicaps.* London: Methuen, 1970.

Ward, J. "The New British Intelligence Scale: A Brief Progress Report." *Journal of School Psychology*, 1972, *10*, 307-313.

Ward, J. "The Saga of Butch and Slim." *British Journal of Educational Psychology*, 1972, *42*, 267-289.

Ward, J., and Fitzpatrick, T. F. "The New British Intelligence Scale: Construction of Logic Items." *Research in Education*, 1970, *4*, 1-23.

Ward, J., and Fitzpatrick, T. F. "Characteristics of Matrices Items." *Perceptual and Motor Skills*, 1973, *36*, 987-993.

Ward, J., and Pearson, L. S. "A Comparison of Two Methods of Testing Logical Thinking." *Canadian Journal of Behavioral Science*, 1973, *5*, 385-398.

CAROLINA DEVELOPMENTAL PROFILE

AUTHORS: David L. Lillie and Gloria L. Harbin

AGE: 2 to 5 years

VARIABLE: Developmental abilities: motor, perceptual, reasoning, language

TYPE OF MEASURE: Criterion-referenced checklist

SOURCE FROM WHICH MEASURE MAY BE OBTAINED: David L. Lillie and Gloria L. Harbin, 803 Churchill, Chapel Hill, North Carolina 27514. No cost at present.

DESCRIPTION OF MEASURE: The Carolina Developmental Profile is a criterion-referenced behavior checklist designed to be used as the first stage or step in an instructional system. This particular system is presented in *Early Childhood Education* (Lillie and Harbin, 1975). In this instructional system, the goal is to increase the child's developmental abilities to the maximum level of proficiency in order to prepare him for the formal academic tasks he will face in the early elementary-school years. The profile is designed to assist the teacher in establishing long-range objectives to increase developmental abilities in six areas: fine motor, gross motor, visual perception, reasoning, receptive language, and expressive language. The items on the Carolina Developmental Profile are presented in sequence by area. A task number, a description of the task, and a developmental age are given for each item. The items on the checklist were developed after a careful review of the literature and extensive testing on young children. In other instruments, similar items are standardized and age ranges are given. This instrument also includes age designations, but care should be taken not to apply these age ranges precisely. The purpose of this checklist is not to compare or assess the child in terms of age normative data; it is not a test, nor should it be used as such. Issues of reliability and validity in a traditional sense are not relevant to its use.

As examples, the four items in the fine motor part of the measure, for developmental age 2, are given below. They are scored either "can do" or "cannot do."

1. Turns a few pages in child's storybook, one at a time with definite control and ease.
2. Builds a standing tower of six to eight 1-inch cubes. (Demonstrate, and leave tower in place as a model. Allow three trials.)
3. Strings at least two beads in no more than 2 minutes. (Demonstrate. Count any bead put on string past plastic tip, even if it comes off later.)
4. Unwraps piece of twisted-end wrapped candy without any help. (Demonstrate if necessary.)

RELIABILITY AND VALIDITY: None reported.

BIBLIOGRAPHY:

Lillie, D. L., and Harbin, G. L. *Early Childhood Education: An Individual Approach to Developmental Instruction.* Palo Alto, California: Science Research Associates, 1975.

Prepared by Gloria L. Harbin

CHILDREN'S ASSOCIATIVE RESPONDING TEST (CART)

AUTHOR: Thomas M. Achenbach

AGE: 10 to 16 years

VARIABLE: Degree of reliance on associative responding rather than on reasoning

TYPE OF MEASURE: Paper-and-pencil test

SOURCE FROM WHICH MEASURE MAY BE OBTAINED: Thomas M. Achenbach, Department of Psychology, Yale University, New Haven, Connecticut 06510. Single copies may be obtained without charge.

DESCRIPTION OF MEASURE: The CART is designed for either group or individual administration. There is no time limit, although most children finish in 15 to 30 minutes. The primary score is the difference (D score) between the number of foil errors and the number of nonfoil errors. The purpose of the D score is to categorize children as associative or nonassociative responders. The D score is not expected to correlate in a linear fashion with other variables. Children with D scores $\leqslant 1$ (including negative scores) are considered to be nonassociative responders, while children with D scores of $\geqslant 4$ are considered to be associative responders who are not using their available reasoning powers. Children obtaining D scores of 2 or 3 are not clearly classifiable. Children who make forty-six or more errors are considered to be responding randomly and are not classifiable. The total number of errors is quite highly correlated with IQ and is a better predictor of actual school performance than are group or individual IQ test scores (see articles cited below).

As examples, fifteen of the fifty test items are given below. The correct answer is italicized; the foil item is boldfaced. Items 2, 7, and 14 are excluded from this version.

1. *Pig* is to *boar* as *dog* is to: **cat**   smoke   ant   turtle   *wolf*
3. *Sun* is to *solar* as *moon* is to: *lunar*   radar   sonar   diameter   motor
4. *House* is to *build* as *carpet* is to: **rug**   melt   *weave*   grand   coat
5. *Keep* is to *retain* as *have* is to: pain   lot   power   recess   *possess*
6. *Birds* is to *peck* as *kittens* is to: punch   **cat**   box   *scratch*   ram
8. *Affection* is to *friend* as *anger* is to: **mad**   *enemy*   spoon   cart   tray
9. *Animal* is to *zoo* as *blossom* is to: sidewalk   picture   paper   **flowers**   *garden*
10. *Taller* is to *height* as *broader* is to: stiff   overcome   amount   long   *width*
11. *Slowly* is to *walk* as *quietly* is to: rang   *speak*   want   open   fall
12. *Clear* is to *glass* as *hard* is to: *steel*   left   sweet   out   **soft**
13. *Defend* is to *attack* as *for* is to: great   yet   laugh   pray   *against*
15. *Teach* is to *teacher* as *sell* is to: shade   pole   *merchant*   **buy**   mailman
16. *Food* is to *starved* as *sleep* is to: *exhausted*   create   switch   needed   feared
17. *Bear* is to *cave* as *boy* is to: top   letter   **girl**   shell   *house*
18. *Wish* is to *future* as *memory* is to: think   mind   head   *past*   hunter

RELIABILITY AND VALIDITY: See Achenbach (1969, 1970a, 1970b, 1971) and Kerner and Achenbach (1971).

BIBLIOGRAPHY:

Achenbach, T. M. "Cue-Learning, Associative Responding, and School Performance in Children." *Developmental Psychology,* 1969, *1,* 717-725.
Achenbach, T. M. "The Children's Associative Responding Test: A Possible Alternative to Group IQ Tests." *Journal of Educational Psychology,* 1970a, *61,* 340-348.
Achenbach, T. M. "Standardization of a Research Instrument for Identifying Associative Responding in Children." *Developmental Psychology,* 1970b, *2,* 283-291.
Achenbach, T. M. "The Children's Associative Responding Test: A Two-Year Follow-Up." *Developmental Psychology,* 1971, *5,* 477-483.
Achenbach, T. M. "A Longitudinal Study of Relations Between Associative Responding, IQ Changes, and School Performance from Grades 3 to 12." *Developmental Psychology* (in press).
Kerner, M., and Achenbach, T. M. "The Children's Associative Responding Test: Its Relation to Individual Tests of Recall, Comprehension, and Concept Formation." *Psychological Reports,* 1971, *29,* 119-125.
Salomon, M. K., and Achenbach, T. M. "The Effects of Four Kinds of Tutoring Experience." *American Educational Research Association Journal,* 1974, *11,* 395-405.

CONCEPT DEVELOPMENT TEST V2

AUTHOR: P. S. Freyberg

AGE: 6 to 10 years

VARIABLE: Conceptual understanding

TYPE OF MEASURE: Test

SOURCE FROM WHICH MEASURE MAY BE OBTAINED: For single copies for research purposes, write P. S. Freyberg, Department of Education, University of Waikato, Hamilton, New Zealand.

DESCRIPTION OF MEASURE: This is a research instrument designed to examine Piaget's contention that certain kinds of concepts develop contemporaneously. The test is suitable only for children who can read at a level normally attained after a year and a half of schooling. The items are arranged in groups of four, each group dealing with a separate kind of concept. The concepts, four items for each, are: numerical correspondence, conservation (continuous quantity), conservation (discontinuous quantity), numerical equivalence, numerical associativity, class concepts (visual), class concepts (nonvisual), conservation mass, additive composition (money)–v, additive composition (money)–nv, conservation (weight), positional relationships, speed concepts, transitive relationships, causal relationships, age concepts, kinship relationships, and ordination.

As examples, a few items from the seventy-two-item test are given below. The items are read to the subjects, who simultaneously have before them a test booklet that includes pictures to help clarify the instructions.

1. Here are some red flowers and some white vases. I want to put one flower in each vase. Which answer is right?
   a. There are more *vases*
   b. There are more *flowers*
   c. There is *one flower for each vase*
5. First, Bill had a glass of lemonade and Tom had a glass of raspberry. Can you see them? They both had the same amount to drink. Afterwards, Tom poured all his raspberry into two little glasses. Which is right then?
   a. Afterwards *Tom* had more to drink
   b. Afterwards *Bill* had more to drink
   c. Afterwards they both had the *same* to drink
9. First, I have one jar with 18 black beads in it and another jar with 20 red beads in it. Afterwards, I pour the black beads into a tall glass like the one in the picture. Which is right?
   a. Afterwards I had more *red* beads
   b. Afterwards I had more *black* beads
   c. Afterwards I had the *same* number of both
13. Here are some daisies and some poppies. Which is right?
   a. There are more *daisies*
   b. There are more *poppies*
   c. There are the *same* number of each
17. Mary is given some white counters and Jill some red ones. There they are. Which is right?
   a. *Mary* has more counters
   b. *Jill* has more counters
   c. They both have the *same* number
21. Here are some red and white beads. Some of the beads are round and some of them are square. Which would make the biggest necklace?
   a. The *red* beads
   b. The *square* beads
   c. The *round* beads

RELIABILITY AND VALIDITY: Test-retest reliability was .91 for a three-year age-span ($N = 99$); the median was .81 for single grades. Seventeen objective test items correlated .72 with scores on similar questions obtained in a clinical setting, but for groups of items relating to various concepts, the correlation with equivalent clinical tests is estimated at .83 (Spearman-Brown formula).

BIBLIOGRAPHY:

Freyberg, P. S. "Concept Development in Piagetian Terms in Relation to School Attainment." *Journal of Educational Psychology,* 1966, *57,* 164-168.

Freyberg, P. S. "Stages in Cognitive Development—General or Specific?" *New Zealand Journal of Educational Studies,* 1967, *1,* 64-77.

Freyberg, P. S. "Reply to Dr. McNaughton's Comments on 'Stages in Cognitive Development—General or Specific?'" *New Zealand Journal of Educational Studies,* 1968, *3,* 82-85.

CONCEPT OF LINEAR MEASUREMENT TEST

AUTHORS: Doyal Nelson and Werner W. Liedtke

AGE: 4 to 8 years

VARIABLE: Conservation of length

TYPE OF MEASURE: Structured interview

SOURCE FROM WHICH MEASURE MAY BE OBTAINED: See Liedtke (1968).

DESCRIPTION OF MEASURE: There are six short subtests. The necessary materials are listed, and administration instructions are detailed. The six subtests are designated as follows: I. Reconstructing relations of distance; II. Conservation of length; III. Conservation of length with a change of position; IV. Conservation of length with a distortion of shape; V. Measurement of length; and VI. Subdividing a straight line.

RELIABILITY AND VALIDITY: None reported.

BIBLIOGRAPHY:

Liedtke, W. W. "Linear Measurement Concepts of Bilingual and Monolingual Children." Unpublished master's thesis. University of Alberta, Edmonton, Alberta, Canada, 1968.
Liedtke, W. W., and Nelson, L. D. "Concept Formation and Bilingualism." *Alberta Journal of Educational Research,* 1968, *14,* 225-232.
Piaget, J., and others. *The Child's Conception of Geometry.* New York: Basic Books, 1960.
Towler, J. O., and Nelson, L. D. "Spatial Concepts of Elementary School Children." *Alberta Journal of Educational Research,* 1967, *13,* 43-50.

CONCEPT FAMILIARITY INDEX (CFI)

AUTHOR: Francis H. Palmer

AGE: 21 to 60 months

VARIABLE: Acquisition of knowledge about concepts

TYPE OF MEASURE: Test

SOURCE FROM WHICH MEASURE MAY BE OBTAINED: Francis H. Palmer, New Graduate Chemistry Building, Room, 431, SUNY at Stony Brook, Stony Brook, New York 11794.

DESCRIPTION OF MEASURE: There are three versions of the CFI for three age groups: CFI-I for 21 to 29 months, CFI-II for 34 to 40 months, and CFI-III for 41 to 50 months. The measure assesses the child's acquisition of concepts related to size, touch, motion, surfaces, states, position, and form. The measure assesses the child's knowledge of concepts related to size (e.g., big, littlest); touch (e.g., hard, smooth); motion (e.g., fast, backward); surfaces (e.g., top, side); position (e.g., up, next to); and form (form boards). Norms exist for Ns of 200 for CFI-I; 500 for CFI-II, and 300 for CFI-III. Separate norms are available for black, white, Puerto Rican (New York and San Juan), Mexican (southwest U.S.), urban, and rural. The CFI is available in Spanish for Mexican and Puerto Rican. It is extensively used in cross-cultural studies: Antigua, BWI; Puerto Rico; Japan. It is valid for preverbal children. The child indicates by demonstration or recognition his knowledge of some sixty concepts over the three forms.

As examples, five items from the index are given below.

1. *Into* (box and small animals)—Place box with three small animals inside and three other small animals in front of child, saying, "See the box. See the little animals. Put them into the box."
2. *Up* (doll)—Put doll in front of child with its hands outstretched—straight out. Move doll's hands to indicate that they move. Make sure the child knows which are the hands. Say, "Where are the dolly's hands?" Then say, "Put the dolly's hands up."
3. *Geometric Form* (square insert and square, triangle, and circle forms)—Place square form to your left, circle form to your right, and triangle form in the middle. Put the square insert immediately in front of the child. Say, "Put this where it belongs." *Alternate:* "Put this back in its hole." Scoring: If the child places the square in its form without trial and error, score his response with one plus (+) and the letter V. If he uses trial and error to achieve the correct response, score with one plus (+) and the letter T.
4. *Biggest* (three plastic cups)—Place the cups in a line in front of the child with the biggest to your right. Say, "Look at the cups. Give me the biggest cup." *Alternates:* (1) Drink from the cups, putting all cups in succession to your mouth or a doll's mouth. Replace in original position. Say, "Take a drink from the biggest cup—or give a dolly a drink from the biggest cup." (2) Put small animals in biggest cup. (3) Put any favored object in biggest cup.
5. *Open* (two clear containers and tops)—Place the containers on the table, the open container on your left with the cover to its right, the closed container on your right. Say, "See the boxes; open the box." *Alternate:* Open the box and put any favored object into it.

RELIABILITY AND VALIDITY: CFI-I (24 months) achieved a Kuder-Richardson reliability coefficient of .74 with a sample of 120 black males. CFI-II has achieved reliabilities in the .80s depending upon the sample for which the statistic was derived. No reliability for CFI-III is available at this time. Validity coefficients for 300 black males for all three forms are available for school performance and Manhattan Achievement Tests at age 10.

BIBLIOGRAPHY:

Nelson, K. "Some Evidence for the Cognitive Primacy of Categorization and its Functional Basis." *Merrill-Palmer Quarterly*, 1973, *19*, 21-39.
Palmer, F. H. "Socionomic Status and Intellective Performance Among Black Male Preschool Children." *Developmental Psychology*, 1970, *3*, 1-9.
Palmer, F. H. "Minimal Intervention at Ages Two and Three." In R. Parker (Ed.), *The Preschool in Action.* Boston: Allyn & Bacon, 1971.

CONCEPTUAL BEHAVIOR BATTERY:
CONSERVATION OF NUMBER

AUTHOR: Rosemary A. Swanson

AGE: Approximately 3 to 7 years

VARIABLE: Conservation of number

TYPE OF MEASURE: Criterion-referenced test

SOURCE FROM WHICH MEASURE MAY BE OBTAINED: Office of Child Research, Arizona Center for Educational Research and Development, College of Education, University of Arizona, Tucson, Arizona 85721.

DESCRIPTION OF MEASURE: The conservation assessment instrument comes in two parallel forms that are articulated to a hierarchical task analysis of behavioral objectives related to conservation performance. The parallel forms cover exactly the same objectives (there is one item per objective per form) but employ different stimulus objects. To date the test has only been employed for experimental studies designed to teach specific conceptual behaviors to Papago Indian children and is therefore specifically articulated to a television teaching sequence. The test is used by paraprofessionals in individual assessment situations and is administered in the primary language of the child. The score employed is the total of items correct in both Forms I and II, but the forms may be administered either in one testing session or in two. Currently this instrument is in the process of extensive revision and will be extended to include more complex stimulus arrangements.

As examples, the first three items of Test I are given below.

Now, we are going to play a new game with these poker chips that I have here. After we have finished the game you can have a treat, okay? Let's start.

1. Place 2 rows of chips on table in front of child.

   (A)   ◯   ◯   ◯   (red chips)

   ◯   ◯   ◯   (white chips)

Look at the two rows of chips I have here on the table. One row is red, the other is white. They are the same. There are as many red chips as white chips. Now watch what I do with these chips. Watch me very carefully. I'm moving these chips and these chips.

Look at the two rows of chips now. Here is the red row and here is the white row. Are the two rows the same or does one have more chips? If incorrect: Which row has more? Why? If correct: Why?

2. Return to standard: *They are the same. Watch me again. Look, I'm moving these chips and these chips.*

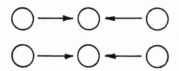

Now look at the two rows of chips. Here is the red row and here is the white row. Are the two rows the same or does one have more chips? If incorrect: Which row has more? Why? If correct: Why?

3. Return to standard: *They are the same. Now, watch what I do. I'm moving this chip over here.*

Now, I have a row of red chips and a row of white chips. Do both rows have the same number of chips, or does one have more? If incorrect: Which row has more? Why? If correct: Why?

RELIABILITY AND VALIDITY: Spearman-Brown split-half reliabilities have been calculated on the measure. Since Forms I and II cover the same objectives, they constitute the correlated half-test. Reliabilities ranged from .80 in a pretest situation with nonconserving children, to .96, and in another situation, .93 to .98. Since the measure is a criterion-referenced one, traditional validity data have not been collected.

BIBLIOGRAPHY:

Henderson, R. W., Zimmerman, B. J., Swanson, R., and Bergan, J. R. "Televised Cognitive Skill Instruction for Papago Native American Children." Mimeographed. Tucson: Arizona Center for Educational Research and Development, University of Arizona, 1974.

CONCEPTUAL BEHAVIOR BATTERY: NUMERICAL OPERATIONS

AUTHOR: Rosemary A. Swanson

AGE: Approximately 3 to 7 years

VARIABLE: Judgment of quantity relationships

TYPE OF MEASURE: Criterion-referenced test

SOURCE FROM WHICH MEASURE MAY BE OBTAINED: Office of Child Research, Arizona Center for Educational Research and Development, College of Education, University of Arizona, Tucson, Arizona 85721.

DESCRIPTION OF MEASURE: The numerical operations instrument comes in two parallel forms that are articulated to a hierarchical task analysis of behavioral objectives related to the conceptual behaviors in question. The parallel forms cover the same objectives but employ different stimuli. The measure includes items that assess (1) counting with one-to-one correspondence: (2) matching sets; and (3) making judgments of same, more, and fewer with regard to sets of different objects and object configuration. This test is designed so that the child's responses can be made through motor behavior instead of requiring verbalization. Furthermore, even children who do not possess any of the conceptual behaviors under consideration can still participate in the assessment situation.

Two examples of the sixteen items comprising Enumeration Test I are given below. The parallel form is Enumeration Test II.

6. (Use cards: one for examiner and three for child. Place cards for child in a row in front of him. Examiner has one card with two spots on it; child has three cards with two spots, three spots and one spot respectively.)
   (name), *Here are some sets for you, and here is a set of 6 for me. My set has 2 spots. Give me your set that has 2 spots. Give me the one with 2.*
7. (Replace card for child. Remove your card from sight.)
   Now (name), *give me the set with 3 spots. Give me the one with 3.*

RELIABILITY AND VALIDITY: Split-half reliabilities ranged from .85 to .90.

BIBLIOGRAPHY:

Henderson, R. W., Zimmerman, B. J., Swanson, R., and Bergan, J. R. "Televised Cognitive Skill Instruction for Papago Native American Children." Technical report on grant no. OCD-CB-479 from the Office of Child Development, Department of Health, Education and Welfare. Tucson: Arizona Center for Educational Research and Development, University of Arizona, July 1974.

Henderson, R. W., Swanson, R., and Zimmerman, B. J. "Inquiry Response Induction in Pre-School Children Through Televised Modeling." *Developmental Psychology,* 1975, *11,* 523-524.

Henderson, R. W., Swanson, R., and Zimmerman, B. J. "Training Seriation Responses in Young Children Through Televised Modeling of Hierarchically Sequenced Rule Components." *American Educational Research Journal,* 1975, *12,* 479-489.

CONCEPTUAL BEHAVIOR BATTERY: SERIATION A AND B

AUTHOR: Rosemary A. Swanson

AGE: Early childhood—approximately 3 to 7 years

VARIABLE: Piagetian concept of seriation

TYPE OF MEASURE: Criterion-referenced test

SOURCE FROM WHICH MEASURE MAY BE OBTAINED: Office of Child Research, Arizona Center for Educational Research and Development, College of Education, University of Arizona, Tucson, Arizona 85721.

DESCRIPTION OF MEASURE: Both these measures come in two parallel forms that are articulated to a hierarchical task analysis of behavioral objectives related to the concept in question. Seriation B is a refinement and extension of Seriation A. The parallel forms cover exactly the same objectives but employ different stimulus arrangements in administration. So far the tests have been used for experimental studies designed to teach specific conceptual behaviors to Papago Indian children and hence are specifically articulated to a television teaching sequence. While the tests have been used only with Papago children, the test stimuli and language are not designed to be culturally specific. The tests are designed to be administered individually by paraprofessionals in the primary language of the child being tested. The score used is the total items correct on both Forms I and II, but the forms may be administered in either one or two testing sessions.

As examples, the first seven items from Seriation Form A, Test I are reproduced below, without the line drawings.

Determination of Size Relationships:
1. Present child with 3 linear objects on one side of tray. *Look at these three sticks here* (point to side of tray). *Find the longest stick and put it over here* (point to other side of tray).
2. Present child with 4 linear objects. *Look at these four sticks here. Find the biggest stick and put it over here.*
3. Present child with 5 linear objects on one side of tray. *Look at these five sticks here. Find the longest stick and put it over here.*
4. Present child with 6 linear objects on one side of tray. *Look at these six sticks here. Find the longest stick and put it over here.*

Recognition of Order:
5. a. Present child with 3-object array. *Look at these 3 sticks* (point). *Are they in the right order from longest to shortest? How do you know?*
   b. Present child with 3-object array. *Look at these 3 sticks. Are they in the right order from longest to shortest? How do you know?*
6. a. Present child with 4-object array. *Look at these 4 sticks. Are they in the right order from longest to shortest? How do you know?*
   b. Present child with 4-object array. *Look at these 4 sticks. Are they in the right order from longest to shortest? How do you know?*

7. a. Present child with 5-object array. *Look at these 5 sticks. Are they in the right order from longest to shortest? How do you know?*

  b. Present child with incorrect 5-object array. *Look at these 5 sticks. Are they in the right order from longest to shortest? How do you know?*

RELIABILITY AND VALIDITY: Spearman-Brown split-half reliabilities have been calculated on the measures. Since Forms I and II cover the same objectives, they constitute the correlated half-tests. Reliabilities for Seriation A ranged from .89 to .96 when calculated on the Papagos preschool sample. Reliabilities for Seriation B ranged from .84 to .93 on a similar sample. Since the tests are criterion-referenced and based on precise behavioral objectives, traditional types of validity information would not be appropriate. The objectives serve as the criterion standard against which the child's performance on a test is judged. The test score can be used, then, to reveal the number of behavioral objectives the child has mastered.

BIBLIOGRAPHY:

Elkind, D. "Discrimination, Seriation, and Numeration of Size and Dimensional Differences in Young Children: Piaget Replication Study VI." *Journal of Genetic Psychology,* 1964, *104,* 275-296.

Henderson, R. W., Zimmerman, B. J., Swanson, R., and Bergan, J. R. "Televised Cognitive Skill Instruction for Papago Native American Children." Mimeographed. Tucson: Arizona Center for Educational Research and Development, University of Arizona, 1974.

CONSERVATION OF LENGTH (*See note, p. 60)

AUTHOR: Jean Piaget (adaptation and scoring by Lawrence Kohlberg and Rheta DeVries)

AGE: Normal children 4 to 8 years

VARIABLE: Development of invariance of length relationships

TYPE OF MEASURE: Structured interview

SOURCE FROM WHICH MEASURE MAY BE OBTAINED: See DeVries (1971).

DESCRIPTION OF MEASURE: Three classical tasks are selected from the variety of Genevan procedures. After aligning two sticks to make sure the child knows which is longer, he is asked to point to the longer one in each of the following arrangements, using different materials each time: (1) One is moved away from him, (2) one is moved toward him, and (3) the longer one is bent in an arc so that a straight line drawn between its end points is shorter than the length of the shorter stick. Colored cylindrical gum straws were used in this version, although it can be done with inedible materials such as pipe cleaners. While Piaget used equal lengths horizontal to the child's line of sight, this version uses the vertical plane (with sticks moved toward or away from the child instead of to his right or left). Ss are scored on an 8-point Guttman scale from 0 to 7. Norms are available for 143 bright and average children chronologically aged 5 to 7 years and retarded children mentally aged 5 to 7 years, according to Stanford-Binet IQ (DeVries, 1971).

As an example, the first section of the interview is given below.

PQA. *Say:* Here are two gum sticks (4-inch yellow stick and 4½-inch green stick, placed parallel to child's line of sight, with ends farthest from child aligned). Show me the bigger and longer one.

　　　　　　　　　　_____Correct green
　　　　　　　　　　_____Incorrect yellow

Now, when I say so, you can pick the bigger one that has more gum to chew. If you don't pick the one with more to chew, you won't get any this time. You'll get another chance to get gum later. Now, before you pick, I put them like this (place card over aligned ends and push protruding longer stick into alignment with shorter stick). Is one gum stick longer now? Show me the longer one with more gum to chew.

　　　　　　　　　　_____Correct green
　　　　　　　　　　_____Incorrect yellow
　　　　　　　　　　_____Both same

How did you know that one had more to chew? Which one had more to chew before I covered them?

RELIABILITY AND VALIDITY: Interscorer agreement on 140 items for twenty randomly selected Ss was 85 percent. Piaget's findings with this task have been replicated many times. Cross-cultural research is reviewed by Dasen (1972).

BIBLIOGRAPHY:

Dasen, P. R. "Cross-Cultural Piagetian Research: A Summary." *Journal of Cross-Cultural Psychology,* 1972, *3,* 23-40.

DeVries, R. *Evaluation of Cognitive Development with Piaget-type Tests: Study of Young Bright, Average and Retarded Children.* Final report to the Department of Program Development for Gifted Children, Illinois Office of Public Instruction, 1971. ERIC document no. ED 075 065.

DeVries, R. "Relationships Among Piagetian, IQ, and Achievement Assessments." *Child Development,* 1974, *45,* 746-756.

Piaget, J., and others. *The Child's Conception of Geometry.* New York: Basic Books, 1960.

Prepared by Rheta DeVries

*GENERAL NOTE ON TASKS (applies to this test and the four that follow):

These Piagetian or Piaget-type tasks were psychometrized (standardized and quantified) in order to examine certain issues empirically (e.g., whether invariant developmental sequentiality on Piagetian tasks can be empirically demonstrated). Piaget never intended them to be used for individual assessment. While they are useful predictors of an individual's level of reasoning, it must be remembered that, as Inhelder (1943) cautions, the psychologist "must never confine his observations to one experiment only, and he should be careful not to give too absolute a value to the results" (p. 303).

Psychometrization of these tasks involved selecting task items from a large set of possibilities so that each subject is presented the same problems. Although some of the advantages of the more flexible exploratory method used by Piaget are thus lost, these versions include standardized probes that permit the experimenter to pursue the child's responses sufficiently to determine his honest beliefs and reasoning. The attempt was thus to provide a standard situation but to retain as much as possible of the exploratory method.

Guttman scales were constructed for quantification of children's performance on these tasks aimed at qualitative aspects of thought. The scales are intended to reflect developmental sequentiality in the Piagetian sense. Thus, following Kohlberg (1963), each scale met three criteria suggested as minimal to claim developmental sequentiality of a set of "pass/fail" items (in lieu of large-scale longitudinal data from divergent cultural groups). First, Guttman scaling, using Green's (1956) stringent statistical criteria, established the order of difficulty. Second, the scale orders the items in the same hierarchy formed by the age of appearance and completion; that is, the percentage of Ss passing each item increases with age. Finally, the order of items follows from a plausible theory as to why each is a prerequisite to the next. Each of the scales mentioned here meets these criteria, with the exception that in the case of a few items one might argue that they are not strictly developmental in nature. While the scale items are scored as either "pass" or "fail," this is not intended to imply that development on each aspect of knowledge occurs in additive fashion. Rather, each "fail" occurs when the child reasons with a logic that is different from adult logic. From the Piagetian point of view, the child's "wrong" way of thinking is logical and internally consistent.

There are many pitfalls in Piagetian testing, and it is essential that a tester be trained by someone skilled in both Piagetian testing and in Piaget's exploratory method. Despite the fact that these tasks are standardized, the basic procedures are the same as the Genevan methods and cannot be administered like a Stanford-Binet. The tester must be able to recognize many subtleties that often occur in children's responses in order to use the standardized probe intelligently. If the procedures are followed in a purely mechanical fashion, children's responses will often be misinterpreted.

Green, B. F. "Method of Scalogram Analysis Using Summary Statistics." *Psychometrika*, 1956, *21*, 79-88.

Inhelder, B. *The Diagnosis of Reasoning in the Mentally Retarded.* New York: Day, 1968 (first published in French, 1943).

Kohlberg, L. *Stages in Children's Conceptions of Physical and Social Objects in the Years Four to Eight.* Unpublished monograph, 1963.

CONSERVATION OF LIQUID (*See note, p. 60)

AUTHOR: Jean Piaget (adaptation and scoring by Lawrence Kohlberg and Rheta DeVries)

AGE: Normal children 4 to 9 years

VARIABLE: Children's development of conservation of continuous quantity

TYPE OF MEASURE: Structured interview

SOURCE FROM WHICH MEASURE MAY BE OBTAINED: See DeVries (1971).

DESCRIPTION OF MEASURE: Two classical tasks are selected from the variety of Genevan procedures. After establishing that the child recognizes that one of two identical beakers contains more, the greater quantity is poured into a wider beaker. In the second task, the lesser quantity is poured into a taller, skinnier container. In each case the child is asked which container has more in it to drink. This adaptation differs from Genevan procedures in that Coca-Cola is used instead of colored water. Also, the quantities to be compared are unequal rather than equal. This version contains a variety of control items to avoid the interference of possible artifacts and consequently requires 10 to 15 minutes. However, since the research indicates these possible artifacts do not generally affect children's performances, the basic tasks could be administered in about 5 minutes. Ss are scored on a 9-point Guttman scale from 0 to 8. Norms are available for 143 bright and average children chronologically aged 5 to 7 years and retarded children mentally aged 5 to 7 years, according to Stanford-Binet IQ (DeVries, 1971).
    As an example, one section of the interview appears below.

2. (Two 10 ml. beakers and one 5 ml. graduate). *Say:* Now, let's fill these two glasses. Now I fill this glass (one of the 10s) up to the very top. I don't fill this (other 10) glass up. Now, see, I put more Coke in one glass than the other. You don't need to show me, but can you see that one glass has more Coke?
                    Yes   No
When I say so, you can pick the bigger one to drink. If you don't pick the biggest one, you won't get to drink any this time. You'll get another chance to drink some later. Now, before you pick, I take this one (10 ml. size with lesser amount) and pour the Coke all out into this one (graduate). Now look at them (pause). If you can show me the one with more to drink, I'll give it to you to drink.
          Picks correct beaker   Picks incorrect graduate
                                      (Do not let child drink yet)
Does that have more? How could you tell? Show me how you could be sure.
If child says because empty had less: But how can you tell when it's like this (pointing to graduate)?
With "+" indicating a conservation response, the sequence of questioning is as follows"
+1, +2: Does it change when it's poured in here? Why not?

RELIABILITY AND VALIDITY: Interscorer agreement on 160 items for twenty randomly selected Ss was 91 percent. Piaget's (1941) findings on this task have been replicated many times. Cross-cultural research is reviewed by Dasen (1972).

BIBLIOGRAPHY:

Dasen, P. R. "Cross-Cultural Piagetian Research: A Summary." *Journal of Cross-Cultural Psychology,* 1972, *3,* 23-40.
DeVries, R. *Evaluation of Cognitive Development with Piaget-type Tests: Study of Young Bright, Average, and Retarded Children.* Final report to the Department of Program Development for Gifted Children, Illinois Office of Public Instruction, 1971. ERIC document no. ED 075 065.
DeVries, R. "Relationships Among Piagetian, IQ, and Achievement Assessments." *Child Development,* 1974, *45,* 746-756.
Piaget, J. *The Child's Conception of Number.* London: Routledge & Kegan Paul, 1952 (first published in French, 1941).

Prepared by Rheta DeVries

CONSERVATION OF MASS (*See note, p. 60)

AUTHOR: Jean Piaget (adaptation and scoring by Rheta DeVries)

AGE: Normal children 4 to 9 years

VARIABLE: Development of children's notions about invariance of substance quantity

TYPE OF MEASURE: Structured interview

SOURCE FROM WHICH MEASURE MAY BE OBTAINED: See DeVries (1971).

DESCRIPTION OF MEASURE: Two items selected from the variety of Genevan procedures present the classic problems of rolling one of two balls into a sausage shape and then one of two balls into a pancake shape. In this version, soft fondant candy instead of clay is used, and unequal rather than equal quantities are used. Candy is not essential. The interview requires only about 5 to 8 minutes. An 8-point Guttman scale is used to quantify responses from 0 to 7. Norms for boys aged 4 to 7 years are available (Kohlberg, 1963, using clay and a slightly different procedure). Norms are also available for 143 bright and average children chronologically aged 5 to 7 years and retarded children mentally aged 5 to 7 years, according to Stanford-Binet IQ (DeVries, 1971).

As an example, one section of the interview appears below.

2. *Say:* Here are two more balls of candy. (Present two unequal balls, smaller to child's right.) Which one has more to eat? Yes, that has more. (*E* begins to press smaller ball into pancake shape about 4 inches in diameter, as he talks.) In a minute when I say so, if you can pick the one that has more to eat, you may have it. If you don't pick the one with more to eat, you won't get any candy this time, but you'll have another chance to get some later. I put this one like this. Which has more to eat?

Ball   Pancake

How do you know that's more to eat? Which is bigger? Which had more to eat before I flattened it?

                    Ball   Pancake

Did this (point to pancake) really get to be more candy to eat? If no: Why not? If yes: How does that happen?

RELIABILITY AND VALIDITY: Interscorer agreement on the 140 scale items for twenty randomly selected Ss was 97 percent. This task, especially, has been often replicated and cross-culturally validated (Dasen, 1972, for example).

BIBLIOGRAPHY:

Dasen, P. R. "Cross-Cultural Piagetian Research: A Summary." *Journal of Cross-Cultural Psychology*, 1972, *3*, 23-40.

DeVries, R. *Evaluation of Cognitive Development with Piaget-type Tests: Study of Young Bright, Average, and Retarded Children.* Final report to the Department of Program Development for Gifted Children, Illinois Office of Public Instruction, 1971. ERIC document no. ED 075 065.

DeVries, R. "Relationships Among Piagetian, IQ, and Achievement Assessments." *Child Development*, 1974, *45*, 746-756.

Kohlberg, L. *Children's Conceptions of Physical and Social Objects in the Years Four to Eight.* Unpublished manuscript, 1963.

Piaget, J., and Inhelder, B. *Le Development des Quantités Chez l'Enfant.* Neuchatel: Delachaux et Niestle, 1941.

Prepared by Rheta DeVries

CONSERVATION OF NUMBER (*See note, p. 60)

AUTHOR: Jean Piaget (adaptation and scoring by Lawrence Kohlberg and Rheta DeVries)

AGE: 3 to 8 years

VARIABLE: Conception of number

TYPE OF MEASURE: Structured interview

SOURCE FROM WHICH MEASURE MAY BE OBTAINED: See DeVries (1971).

DESCRIPTION OF MEASURE: Three items selected from the variety of Genevan procedures present the classic problem of lengthening one of two rows of objects (M&Ms in this version). For 5 to 10 minutes the child is interviewed regarding this judgment about the relative quantity of the two rows. This version of the task differs from that most commonly used by Piaget in that unequal quantities are used, five candies in one row and six in the other. (Piaget had children establish equivalence of two rows and then judge whether they were still equivalent when one row was made longer than the other.) In this adaptation, Item 1 begins with six candies in a longer row on one pizza plate and five in a shorter row on an adjacent plate. After establishing the nonequivalence, the six M&Ms are constricted into a row shorter than the row of five, and the child's judgment of quantity is probed. Item 2 is designed to ascertain the effect of counting on the child's conservation. (It should be noted that although Piaget in his later thinking concluded that small numbers—up to about eight—should be considered "perceptual numbers" because children can sometimes maintain invariance through perceptual means rather than logicomathematical reasoning, the results of this study showed almost identical age norms to those reported by Piaget. Nevertheless, it might be wise for researchers wishing to utilize this adaptation to work with eight and ten objects, rather than five and six.) Ss are scored on a 10-point Guttman scale from 0 to 9. Norms are available for bright and average children chronologically aged 5 to 7 years and for retarded children mentally aged 5 to 7 years, according to Stanford-Binet IQ (DeVries, 1971).

RELIABILITY AND VALIDITY: Interscorer agreement on 261 items for twenty randomly selected Ss was 97 percent. Many replications of this task demonstrate its validity. See Dasen (1972) for a cross-cultural report.

BIBLIOGRAPHY:

Dasen, P. R. "Cross-Cultural Piagetian Research: A Summary." *Journal of Cross-Cultural Psychology,* 1972, *3,* 23-40.

DeVries, R. *Evaluation of Cognitive Development with Piaget-type Tests: Study of Young Bright, Average, and Retarded Children.* Final report to the Department of Program Development for Gifted Children, Illinois Office of Public Instruction, 1971. ERIC document no. ED 075 065.

DeVries, R. "Relationships Among Piagetian, IQ, and Achievement Assessments." *Child Development,* 1974, *45,* 746-756.

Piaget, J. *The Child's Conception of Number.* London: Routledge & Kegan Paul, 1952 (first published in French, 1941).

Prepared by Rheta DeVries

CONSTANCY OF GENERIC IDENTITY: PHOTOGRAPH FORM (*See note, p. 60)

AUTHORS: Rheta DeVries and Lawrence Kohlberg

AGE: 3 to 8 years

VARIABLE: Children's beliefs about the invariance of generic identity

TYPE OF MEASURE: Structured interview

SOURCE FROM WHICH MEASURE MAY BE OBTAINED: A set of the five glossy 5 X 7 photographs may be obtained by sending a check for $5.50 made out to the University of Illinois at Chicago Circle, to Mr. Edward Retel, Photographic Laboratory, 112 Burnham Hall, University of Illinois at Chicago Circle, Chicago, Illinois 60680. The procedure, its rationale, and norms may be found in DeVries (1971).

DESCRIPTION OF MEASURE: The photograph form of this task is based on Kohlberg's (1963) original schematic drawing task and on DeVries' (1969) live form of the task. In the live form of the task children are introduced to a live animal (a cat or a cat wearing a ferocious dog mask) and see a "transformation" of the animal into another generic identity (cat to dog, dog to cat, or cat to rabbit). The photograph form of this task (requiring 5 to 8 minutes) utilizes the following black-and-white photographs: (1) side view of cat with whiskers accentuated, in standing position; (2) cat with whiskers accentuated in crouching position; (3) side view of cat (same as photograph 1) with whiskers missing; (4) cat in crouching position (same as photograph 2) with whiskers missing; (5) side view of cat wearing dog mask, in standing position. Using only photograph 1, the interviewer first asks whether the cat can be a dog if he "really wants to," and, if the child responds affirmatively, the interviewer probes to find whether the child believes he would be a *real* dog. Using photograph 1, then, in various combinations with other pictures, the interviewer asks the child whether various combinations of changes in appearance and/or behavior would bring about a real change in the identity of the cat in photograph 1. Ss are scored on a 9-point Guttman scale, from 0 to 8. Norms for the drawing form (on a 5-point scale) are available for sixty-four children 4 to 7 years of age (Kohlberg, 1963). Norms are available for the photograph form for 143 bright and average children chronologically aged 5 to 7 years and retarded children mentally aged 5 to 7 years, according to Stanford-Binet IQ (DeVries, 1971).

RELIABILITY AND VALIDITY: The live form of the Generic Identity task not only validated Kohlberg's findings with the schematic-drawing task but strengthened his conclusion that before age 6 to 7, children do not believe that generic identity is necessarily a constant characteristic of a live animal. A low correlation between the schematic drawing form and the live form (r = .21) cannot be interpreted because the drawing form was administered prior to the live form. Interscorer agreement on 104 items for thirteen randomly selected Ss on the photograph form was 96 percent.

BIBLIOGRAPHY:

DeVries, R. "Constancy of Generic Identity in the Years Three to Six." *Society for Research in Child Development Monographs,* 1969, *34,* Serial No. 127, 1-67. (Primarily a report on the use of the live form, but including the schematic, and a useful theoretical discussion.)

DeVries, R. *Evaluation of Cognitive Development with Piaget-type Tests: Study of Young Bright, Average, and Retarded Children.* Final report to the Department of Program Development for Gifted Children, Illinois Office of Public Instruction, 1971. ERIC document no. ED 075 065.

DeVries, R. "Relationships Among Piagetian, IQ, and Achievement Assessments." *Child Development,* 1974, *45,* 746-756.

Kohlberg, L. *Stages in Children's Conceptions of Physical and Social Objects in the Years Four to Eight.* Unpublished monograph, 1963.

CREATIVE-RESPONSE MATRICES TEST

AUTHOR: Philip E. Vernon

AGE: 8 to 12 years

VARIABLE: Nonverbal intelligence, or "g"

TYPE OF MEASURE: Test

SOURCE FROM WHICH MEASURE MAY BE OBTAINED: Philip E. Vernon, Department of Educational Psychology, University of Calgary, Calgary, Alberta, Canada T2N 1N4.

DESCRIPTION OF MEASURE: The test is given individually (though it could be adapted for group form with modified instructions and practice items). Twenty items, graded in difficulty, are based on Xs and Os, or abstract shapes, each with a gap at the end for completion of the pattern. Subjects learn how to do the test by having each of the first ten items explained (unless they give the correct response unaided). Norms for English children age 10½ are available, together with results for boys in several less developed cultures: Jamaicans, East Africans, Canadian Indians, and Eskimos. Factor analyses show it to have a high "g" saturation. The test takes 10 to 15 minutes.

RELIABILITY AND VALIDITY: Repeat reliability is not available. Internal consistency is obtained through item analysis and construct validity through factor analysis. The type of problem is similar to that in Raven's Progressive Matrices for whose reliability and validity there is a large amount of evidence. This version was produced in order to make it easier to relate to culturally deprived and test-unsophisticated children.

BIBLIOGRAPHY:

Vernon, P. E. "Ability Factors and Environmental Influences." *American Psychologist,* 1965, *20,* 723-733.
Vernon, P. E. "Environmental Handicaps and Intellectual Development." *British Journal of Educational Psychology,* 1965, *35,* 9-20, 117-126.
Vernon, P. E. "Abilities and Educational Attainments in an East African Environment." *Journal of Special Education,* 1967, *4,* 335-345.
Vernon, P. E. *Intelligence and Cultural Environment.* London: Methuen, 1969.

DRUMCONDRA VERBAL REASONING TEST

AUTHORS: William G. Gorman and Thomas Kellaghan

AGE: 10 to 12 years

VARIABLE: Verbal reasoning ability

TYPE OF MEASURE: Group test

SOURCE FROM WHICH MEASURE MAY BE OBTAINED: Educational Research Centre, St. Patrick's College, Dublin 9, Ireland.

DESCRIPTION OF MEASURE: The test consists of 110 items and was designed as a measure of the ability to use and reason with verbal symbols. It contains sections on analogies, the identification of words opposite in meaning to a given stimulus, the identification of concepts as belonging to a single category, and problems in inductive and deductive reasoning. The test has been standardized on a sample of Irish students aged 10 to 12 years with a mean of 100 and standard deviation of 15.

RELIABILITY AND VALIDITY: Internal consistency measures (Kuder-Richardson) were .98 at age 10, .96 at age 11, and .98 at age 12. Coefficient of stability over a two-week period was .94 and over a nine-week period, again .94. The standard error of a test score is approximately 3.3 points of standardized score. Several small-scale studies of the validity of the test have been carried out. Performance on the test was found to correlate .84 with performance on the WISC verbal scale, .80 with performance on the California Short-Form Test of Mental Maturity, .77 with the Standard Progressive Matrices, and .90 with Morrisby's General Ability Test (verbal section). Correlations with teachers' estimates of pupils' aptitude for scholastic achievement ranged between .72 and .81.

BIBLIOGRAPHY:

Gorman, W. G. "The Construction and Standardization of a Verbal Reasoning Test for Age Range 10 Years 0 Months to 12 Years 11 Months in an Irish Population." Unpublished doctoral dissertation. University College, Dublin, Ireland, 1968.

Kellaghan, T., and Greaney, V. "Factors Related to Choice of Post-Primary School in Ireland." *Irish Journal of Education,* 1970, *4,* 69-83.

Kellaghan, T., and MacNamara, J. "Family Correlates of Verbal Reasoning Ability." *Developmental Psychology,* 1972, *7,* 49-53.

Prepared by Thomas Kellaghan

EVALUATION OF LEARNING SKILLS

AUTHOR: Eileen M. Earhart

AGE: 3½ to 6½ years

VARIABLE: Basic learning skills

TYPE OF MEASURE: Performance tests

SOURCE FROM WHICH MEASURE MAY BE OBTAINED: Eileen M. Earhart, Family and Child Sciences Department, Human Ecology Building, East Lansing, Michigan 48823. A minimal charge will be made to cover reproduction costs.

DESCRIPTION OF MEASURE: The evaluation of Learning Skills is designed to measure the child's performance on basic learning tasks. The tasks include matching, identifying, copying, memory and listening, naming, sequencing, tactile discrimination, classifying, concept formation, and coordination. The skills are basic to success in formal learning situations such as reading and mathematics. Manipulative materials such as wooden cubes, design or parquetry shapes, cut-out numbers, and cut-out letters are used for the major portion of the assessment procedures. Pictures and abstract designs are also incorporated in several items; the child uses a pencil to complete two items. Paper-and-pencil items are purposely limited because the fine motor control required in these tasks is frequently inadequately developed in the young child. Manipulative materials that are enjoyable and appropriate for the developmental level, therefore, have been used extensively in this instrument. Piaget's theory of development places the young child in the preoperational stage in which manipulation of, or interaction with, the environment is a major factor in the child's development. Piaget's work has served as a general foundation for the development of the learning skills evaluation. The child's performance on each skill is recorded on a protocol sheet. An overall profile is useful to the teacher who plans learning activities for the children. (Learning activities to develop deficit skills have also been designed to accompany the assessment procedure.) The assessment is administered to each child individually and can easily be divided into sections to be given at different times or by different people at a series of tables. The instrument has been used at the beginning of kindergarten in some school districts to help the teacher specify the learning needs of each child. At the end of kindergarten, the performance level is again assessed. Teachers of preschool children have used the simpler items at the beginning of the evaluation procedure and omitted the more complex items requiring higher levels of skill development. The assessment procedure has also been used by teachers of learning-disabled children to ascertain levels of skill development, so that a plan of instruction can be designed to develop deficit skills.

Examples of three tasks included in the evaluation procedure are given below.

Memory: Place three wooden cubes on the table. Say: "Look carefully at these blocks because I am going to take one away." Cover the blocks with a box lid or a piece of paper while you remove one of the blocks. Be sure the child cannot see the block you remove. You could ask him to also close his eyes; however, many children have difficulty following that direction. Place the set of twelve blocks near the child.

"show me a block in the box like the one I took away." The blocks to use and the one to take away for each trial follow: (1) red, blue, yellow . . . take away red; (2) green, orange, purple, blue . . . take away purple; (3) yellow, red, orange, blue, purple . . . take away orange.

Copying a model: In this task six triangular blocks (red, purple, yellow, brown, blue, and green) are placed around a point on the table so that the tips of the triangles all meet at the point and their bases form a regular hexagon. Build the block design above the child's working space and ask him to make one like it.

RELIABILITY AND VALIDITY: None reported.

BIBLIOGRAPHY:

Earhart, E. M. *Evaluation of Learning Skills.* East Lansing: Michigan State University, n.d.

EVALUATION SCALE FOR 4- AND 5-YEAR-OLD CHILDREN

AUTHOR: Annie L. Butler

AGE: 4 to 5 years

VARIABLE: School behavior in affective, cognitive, and physical areas

TYPE OF MEASURE: Observation guide

SOURCE FROM WHICH MEASURE MAY BE OBTAINED: Publications in Education, School of Education, Indiana University, Bloomington, Indiana 47401. Cost: $1.25.

DESCRIPTION OF MEASURE: The Evaluation Scale for 4- and 5-Year-Old Children was developed for use by the classroom teacher in evaluating the maturity and growth of individual children in relation to the child's self-concept, physical development, social interactions, and cognitive processes. Items in four areas correspond with the four areas of program goals. Two columns describing different levels of behavior for each item are included to help the teacher identify a frame of reference for making an evaluation. These columns do not necessarily describe behavior typical for any age, although to insure usability with both nursery school and kindergarten children, the scale was developed through careful observation of 4- and 5-year-old children. A profile can be prepared on the basis of the teacher's observations of the child at intervals throughout the year.

As examples, two of the twenty-nine items on the scale are given below. The teacher rates the child on a 5-point scale ranging from 1, a lower level of behavior than is described in the left-hand column, to 5, behavior that reaches or exceeds that described in the right-hand column.

C. Progress toward self-sufficiency

1	2	3	4	5

Needs constant direction or support from the teacher, or shows much dependence on another child.

Needs only a minimum of direction by the teacher to become involved in productive activity. Abides by his own idea of what he wants to do in his relationships with children.

B. Sensitivity to the feelings of others

1	2	3	4	5

Shows more egocentrism than awareness of the feelings of others—is frank to the point of cruelty—"I don't like that."

Words his comments to show awareness of another child's response to a situation. Tries to soothe another child's hurt; makes comments which help the child feel better.

RELIABILITY AND VALIDITY: None reported.

BIBLIOGRAPHY:

Butler, A. L. "An Evaluation Scale for Four- and Five-year-old Children." *Bulletin of the School of Education,* Indiana University, 1965, *41* (2).

FOUR MUSIC CONSERVATION TASKS

AUTHORS: Marilyn Pflederer Zimmerman and Lee Sechrest

AGE: 5, 7, 9, and 13 years

VARIABLE: Conservation in the development of musical concepts

TYPE OF MEASURE: Music listening and structured interview

SOURCE FROM WHICH MEASURE MAY BE OBTAINED: See Zimmerman and Sechrest (1968). Also available at nominal cost for reproducing tasks from Marilyn P. Zimmerman, 11 Carriage Place, Champaign, Illinois 61820.

DESCRIPTION OF MEASURE: The four musical tasks designed by Zimmerman are patterned from Piagetian conservation tasks. The tasks consist of four phrases selected from Bartòk's piano music *For Children,* in which systematic variations are made in order to test for conservation. The variations paired with each original phrase are as follows:

x_i change of instrument x_t change of tempo
x_h change of harmony x_r change of rhythm
x_m change of mode x_c change of contour
x no change x_{in} change of interval

Each task is preceded by the following directions. The directions are not recorded.

"You will hear this short tune played several times." (Play the stimulus.) "Each time that it is played you will hear it followed by a second tune. I would like you to answer these questions about the two tunes": (a) "Is the second tune the same or is it different from the first tune?" (b) Then, according to the subject's answer: "What was different about it?" "Are they the same in any way?" "How do you know?" "Tell me more about what you heard."

RELIABILITY AND VALIDITY: The tasks were administered to 198 subjects distributed over four age levels (approximately 5, 7, 9, and 13) who had been randomly assigned to experimental and control training groups before the tasks were administered. All responses were analyzed both quantitatively and qualitatively. Product-moment correlations were computed in order to establish the ability of the two authors to apply the scoring system. The correlations indicating judge agreement ranged from .74 for change of interval to .97 for change of instrument. An analysis of variance was performed on the recognition scores with experimental condition and age of subjects represented as main effects and type of stimulus treated as a repeated measure. Age produced a highly significant effect, as did type of stimulus. A second analysis of variance performed on conservation scores conformed in all respects to the first analysis.

BIBLIOGRAPHY:

Pflederer, M., and Sechrest, L. "Conservation-type Responses of Children to Musical Stimuli." *Council for Research in Music Education,* 1968, 1319-1336.
Zimmerman, M. P., and Sechrest, L. *How Children Conceptually Organize Musical Sounds.* Evanston, Ill.: Northwestern University, 1968. ERIC document no. ED 028 200.
Zimmerman, M. P., and Sechrest, L. "Brief Focused Instruction and Musical Concepts." *Journal of Research in Music Education,* 1970, *18,* 25-36.

GRASSI BASIC COGNITIVE EVALUATION

AUTHOR: Joseph R. Grassi

AGE: 4 to 8 years

VARIABLE: Basic cognitive development

TYPE OF MEASURE: Test

SOURCE FROM WHICH MEASURE MAY BE OBTAINED: Joseph R. Grassi, 3501 Jackson Street, No. 110, Hollywood, Florida 33021. Cost: Manual, $20.00; Record Forms, package of 50, $5.00.

DESCRIPTION OF MEASURE: The Grassi Basic Cognitive Evaluation identifies basic cognitive deficits that have been shown to be related to both preacademic and academic learning. It rapidly samples twenty-six individual basic cognitive areas in 20 to 30 minutes. It has been used successfully with preschool children to identify cognitive developmental deficits and with school children experiencing learning problems. However, its greatest effectiveness is with children from age 4 to 8. On the basis of the data revealed by the testing of 84,000 children in psychological clinics and remedial reading programs, it became apparent that the usual conventional intellectual development model had serious short-comings because it was too restrictive. A new paradigm evolved recognizing three inter-related dimensions of intelligence: sensorimotor, basic cognition, and the intellect. The Basic Cognitive Evaluation was designed to fill the gap between the sensorimotor and intellect dimensions. Extensive studies were carried out to identify basic cognitive areas that could close the gap and that have direct relationship to success with early reading, spelling, number work, and writing. The following areas were identified and included in the Grassi Basic Cognitive Evaluation: (1) Visual discrimination of colors, forms, sizes, and combinations of these. (2) Basic concepts: ability to form simple dichotomies, such as same and different, or more and less. (3) Identification (naming) of colors, numbers, and letters. (4) Directional orientation: ability to see numbers, letters, and words without inverting and/or reversing the images. (5) Visualization: ability to see a whole from its part. (6) Number concepts: ability to deal with simple numerical concepts and quantities. (7) Auditory discrimination: ability to hear likenesses and differences. (8) Kinesthesia: ability to reproduce geometric forms. (9) Sequencing of forms, numbers, and letters (auditory and visual). (10) Recall of forms, numbers, and letters (visual and auditory).

RELIABILITY AND VALIDITY: Four hundred children were followed during the primary grades. Those who had basic cognitive deficits were unsuccessful, whereas those who had intact cognitive developments were successful. The validity correlation was .85. One hundred and fifty children were retested after a one-month interval. The Pearson product-moment correlation was found to be .94. Comparisons of 200 Binet IQs and Basic Learning Quotients revealed a poor correlation of .58. This suggests that the two instruments tap different dimensions. A comparison of Binet IQs with B.L.Q.s of 400 disadvantaged children revealed a correlation of .15. A five-year study of over two thousand disadvantaged children (data to be published) provided an opportunity to study the extent of their cognitive deficits. Not only do disadvantaged children have severe deficits but over 80 percent of them are affected. The study clearly demonstrated that early academic failure of disadvantaged children is caused not simply by lack of intelligence but by severe basic cognitive deficits. A special remedial program based on the Basic Cognitive Evaluation has been developed using electronic apparatus and sequential programing. These were used with the disadvantaged children with outstanding results. Data regarding the above will be furnished on request to those who have a specific interest in utilizing the program.

BIBLIOGRAPHY:

Grassi, J. R. "Prevention of Learning Disabilities by the Scoptec Method." *Academy News*, 1973, *4*, 2-5. In *Exceptional Child Education Abstracts*, 1974, *5*, 573.

GREENSPAN'S MATRIX TEST OF
REFERENTIAL COMMUNICATION

AUTHOR: Stephen Greenspan

AGE: Middle childhood and early adolescence

VARIABLE: Communicative egocentrism

TYPE OF MEASURE: Test, individually administered

SOURCE FROM WHICH MEASURE MAY BE OBTAINED: A complete description of the test materials, administration, and scoring is contained in Greenspan and Barenboim (1975). This paper may be obtained from Stephen Greenspan, Psychology Department, University of Rochester, River Station, Rochester, New York 14627.

DESCRIPTION OF MEASURE: The test uses a board divided into a three-by-three matrix. The subject is given sixteen forms that come in three common geometric shapes, three colors, and two sizes. Communicative egocentrism is assessed by asking the subject to dictate instructions that would help a hypothetical other child (unable to see the subject's board) to replicate (on another board) a design the subject is asked to make by filling in the matrix with objects of his or her choice. Since there are five bits of necessary information (size, shape, color, column, and row) for each of the nine cells, scores could range from a nonegocentric low of 0 errors to an egocentric high of 45 errors. The test was designed to assess children's cognitive and behavioral performances in an area of functioning that plays an important part in Piagetian theory. While designed primarily as a measure of cognitive-developmental level, the test may have possible usefulness as an index of socioemotional functioning as well.

RELIABILITY AND VALIDITY: Greenspan and Barenboim (1975) found the test to be highly reliable. A test-retest correlation coefficient of .86 was obtained when sixty elementary-school children (grades 1 to 6) were retested three weeks after an initial assessment. An interrater reliability correlation coefficient of .98 was obtained when the test protocols of thirty-eight subjects were independently scored by two raters.

Greenspan and Barenboim (1975) conducted two validity studies. The first looked at developmental correlates of performance on the test, and the second looked at socioemotional correlates. A highly significant age effect ($p < .001$) occurred in children's performances across grades 1 through 6. Significant age jumps in this sample (120 subjects, with twenty at each of the six grade levels) occurred between first and second grade ($p < .01$) and between fifth and sixth grade ($p < .02$).

A number of measures of socioemotional competence were also found to be significantly correlated with performance on the matrix test. Matched groups of normal and emotionally disturbed 11- and 12-year-old children were found to be significantly different ($p < .001$) in their performance on the test, with the disturbed sample much more egocentric. Within an emotionally disturbed sample there was a mixed pattern of results, with some indication that egocentric children are more likely to be perceived both by peers and teachers as significantly less adjusted. In a longitudinal follow-up there was a similar mixed pattern of results, which gave some indication that improvement in referential communication performance is predictive of positive change in behavioral adjustment.

Chandler, Greenspan, and Barenboim (1974) used the test as a means of evaluating the effectiveness of two different forms of perspective-taking training. It was found that emotionally disturbed children who were trained in referential communication skills would improve significantly more on the test than would children who received noncommunicative role-taking training or who were in a no-treatment control group ($p < .01$).

BIBLIOGRAPHY:

Chandler, M. J., Greenspan, S., and Barenboim, C. "Assessment and Training of Role-Taking and Referential Communication Skills in Institutionalized Emotionally Disturbed Children." *Developmental Psychology,* 1974, *10,* 546-553.
Greenspan, S., and Barenboim, C. "A Matrix Test of Referential Communication." Paper presented at the Fifth Annual Symposium of the Jean Piaget Society. Philadelphia, Pennsylvania, June 1975.

HANNAH/GARDNER PRESCHOOL LANGUAGE SCREENING TEST

AUTHORS: Elaine P. Hannah and Julie C. Gardner

AGE: 3 to 5½ years

VARIABLE: Perceptual and cognitive development

TYPE OF MEASURE: Series of developmental tasks categorized for visual, auditory, motor, or conceptual emphasis

SOURCE FROM WHICH MEASURE MAY BE OBTAINED: Joyce Motion Picture Company, 8613 Yolanda, P.O. Box 458, Northridge, California 91324. Cost: $69.95.

DESCRIPTION OF MEASURE: The Preschool Language Screening Test is a set of seventy developmental task items that have been categorized according to their primary emphasis as visual, auditory, motor, or conceptual. The test is designed to screen the perceptual and cognitive development of preschool children. Since this is a developmental period during which learning lags are often present but ignored, the test is a battery that will give some indication that the child is not meeting the age norms in areas of development vital to later academic performance. It is arranged on a modality base, and the specific tasks represent specific academic learning skills (memory span, figure-ground activity, sequencing, and closure). It is particularly useful to the examiner who might wish to suggest a remedial direction in either the classroom or the clinic during the period preceding formal school entrance and testing with more complex instrumentation. The test is designed to be administered by a paraprofessional as well as a teacher or clinician. The instrument also contains a small battery of eleven elementary pretest items indicating whether the child can even participate in a formal examination situation. Both middle and lower socioeconomic norms have been provided. A Spanish version with separate norms is in preparation.

As examples, twelve of the seventy items are given below.

4. Shuffle the five sets of paired cards. Spread them out on the table and say, "Find the ones that go together." Score as correct two sets of three.

7. Give the child the face with missing parts and a pencil. Say, "Some parts of this face are missing. Can you finish it for me?" Score any representation of two eyes and a mouth as correct.

13. (No Materials) Say, "Can you stand on one foot?"

16. (Box) Say, "Can you put the matches in the box for me?"

26. (No Materials) Say to the child, "Listen to me and then say the same thing I do." Say the following at one-second intervals: "Ball . . . Dog."

29. (Box) Get out the ball and cup. Ask the child to "Take the ball out of the cup, bounce it once, and give it to me."
(Picture File) Say to the child, "Show me: Two boys are the smallest."

37. (Box) Place the cup, the spoon, the ball, and a red, blue, and yellow block in front of the child. Say, "Put the yellow block on the spoon."

44. "Listen and see if you can finish this: Jack and Jill _____." Any part of the rhyme is accepted.

56. Take a block and the spoon out of the box, replace lid. Place the spoon 5 or 6 inches from the box. Say, "Put the block in back of the box."

61. Say, "Show me empty."

67. "Which is up, the floor or the sun?"

RELIABILITY AND VALIDITY: The original scales were composed of items based on skills that previous research indicates are within the capabilities of normal children at specific developmental stages and age levels. The test battery is controlled for perceptual or cognitive emphasis and within each perceptual scale for the complexity of skill activities listed above. Each task is included at the level at which 90 percent of the subjects of specific age range passed it. Subsequent studies of reliability using the Pearson product-moment correlation method indicate a test-retest correlation of .95 and an interexaminer reliability of .93. Using Friedman's two-way analysis of variance, a comparison of scores achieved by three matched groups of thirty children who had either language problems, articulation problems, or no deficit indicated a difference significant at the .01 level. A similar comparison of the scores of children with language deficits on the Preschool Language Screening Test and the ITPA indicated a correlation (Spearman rank correlation method) of .87 for total scores.

BIBLIOGRAPHY: None reported.

ILLINOIS CONDITIONAL REASONING TEST (ICRT)

AUTHORS: Barbara Moor Sanner, Robert H. Ennis, Marilyn Martin, Edward L. Smith, and Joanne Sturgeon

AGE: Grades 1 to 9

VARIABLE: Children's conditional reasoning skills

TYPE OF MEASURE: Multiple-choice/fill-in (administered individually and verbally)

SOURCE FROM WHICH MEASURE MAY BE OBTAINED: Barbara Moor Sanner, School of Education, Campion Hall, University of San Francisco, San Francisco, California 94117.

DESCRIPTION OF MEASURE: The Illinois Conditional Reasoning Test (ICRT) is a condensed and altered version of the Smith-Sturgeon Conditional Reasoning Test (SSCRT), Part I (Ennis, Finkelstein, Smith, and Wilson, 1969; see also p. 000). There are six items for each of four logic principles: contraposition, transitivity, inversion, and conversion, for a total of twenty-four items. The items may also be grouped according to valid (contraposition and transitivity) and invalid (inversion and conversion) principles. All items are in conditional form, and content is based upon principles of chemistry. No time limit is involved in administering the test. For a child to get credit for an item he must give both the correct conclusion and an adequate justification. This procedure prevents the child from getting credit for an answer because he guessed or gave the right conclusion for the wrong reason. The ICRT differs from the SSCRT in two major ways: (1) The content of the ICRT is all of one type—principles of chemistry. Some work with Part II of the SSCRT, which was based on principles of electricity, indicated that children were responding to those items based upon their experience with light switches. (2) Six items in the SSCRT contain negatives in the major premise. In order to create items with as much similarity and simplicity as possible, none of the major premises in the twenty-four ICRT items have negatives.

As an example, Item 1 of the twenty-four ICRT items is given below. The format of the other items is essentially the same. The child is introduced to the materials and procedures through a short demonstration experiment.

Item 1: Contraposition–Suppositional
   (A powder didn't bubble when we added vinegar. Is the powder soda? (No))
       1. *Does vinegar make soda bubble?* (Yes)
       2. *I'm going to ask you to pretend something. Then I want you to tell me what we're pretending. Pretend there's a white powder in here; we add vinegar and it doesn't bubble. What are we pretending?*
       3. (We're pretending that we added vinegar and the powder didn't bubble.) *Do you think the powder would be soda, wouldn't be soda, or is there no way to tell?* (a) "would be soda" (b) "wouldn't be soda" (c) "there's no way to tell"
       4. *Tell me how you decided that . . .*
               (Replace empty)

Scoring: *Item 1: Contraposition–Suppositional*
(Pretend a powder doesn't bubble when we add vinegar. Would the powder be soda?)
A. Conclusion:
      1. _____ Would be soda
      2. _____ Wouldn't be soda
      3. _____ There's no way to tell
      4. _____ No answer
B. Justification:
      4. _____ Skeptical reasoning
          "I don't know because I can't see if it is soda from the orange bottle."
      5. _____ No justification
          "I really don't know why I chose that. I just know that I am right."
      6. _____ Indeterminate
          "You haven't told me enough to judge whether or not the stuff is soda."
      7. _____ Other (write in)
      8. _____ Strong
          "If it is soda, it bubbles when vinegar is added; the white stuff didn't bubble."
      9. _____ One premise
          "When you add vinegar to soda it bubbles."
      10. _____ "The white stuff didn't bubble."
      Comments:

  C. Valid: 8, 9, 10

RELIABILITY AND VALIDITY: The test was administered to a sample of fifty urban fifth graders. The children came from diverse socioeconomic backgrounds, were racially mixed, and had a wide range of IQ scores with verbal and nonverbal means near 100. Test scores on each of the principles and on the principles grouped into valid and invalid categories were obtained. These scores were used for several statistical comparisons, including correlations to age, sex, and IQ. Raw score rankings by principle were also analyzed. Two statistical measures of test reliability were computed—the Kuder-Richardson formula 20 for internal consistency of items and test-retest correlations. The Kuder-Richardson scores for the four principles and for scores grouped according to validity and invalidity ranged from .74 to .94. Ten children were randomly selected to be retested. The individual principle scores and scores grouped according to valid and invalid principles were all significant at the .05 level and ranged from .77 to .90.

    Validity may be argued on four different grounds: (1) Item format reflects approved fundamental principles of logic; (2) there is a wide range of item difficulty (from .14 to .92); (3) items tended to discriminate positively and well, with almost all the items discriminating at .50 or above (except for contraposition items, which could not register high discrimination since most children had high contraposition scores); and (4) comparisons with external measures parallel results found in other studies or can be explained.

BIBLIOGRAPHY:

Ennis, R. H., Finkelstein, M., Smith, E. L., and Wilson, N. H. *Conditional Logic and Children.* Ithaca, New York: Critical Thinking Project, Cornell University, 1969.
Sanner, B. M. "A Study of the Ability of Fifth Graders to Handle Conditional Logic." Unpublished doctoral dissertation. University of Illinois, Urbana, 1974.

INFANT COGNITIVE DEVELOPMENT SCALE

AUTHOR: Albert Mehrabian

AGE: Birth to 2 years

VARIABLE: Representational ability

TYPE OF MEASURE: Piagetian test

SOURCE FROM WHICH MEASURE MAY BE OBTAINED: See Mehrabian and Williams (1970). A list of the materials necessary for administering the measure is available from Albert Mehrabian, University of California, Los Angeles, Department of Psychology, 405 Hilgard Avenue, Los Angeles, California 90024.

DESCRIPTION OF MEASURE: This series of twenty-eight items was devised to measure cognitive development on the basis of Piaget's concepts, because his approach seemed most appropriate for examining cognitive development in relation to subsequent linguistic functions. It is assumed that the ability to represent or communicate is not restricted to the linguistic medium, and that there are clearly other nonverbal media of gesture, movement, and intonation through which a child can communicate his desires and attitudes and can denote objects or the relationships among objects. The purpose of this measure is to identify those preverbal skills that are most directly related to representational ability. The items were selected for their relevance for representational ability, the ease with which they could be administered, and their interesting quality for children. The total set was, of necessity, restricted to a small number so that all of the items could be administered to each child. The final set of items evolved from a series of pilot experiments in which the ease of administration and the difficulty of the various items were explored. Such preliminary data were used to order the items in terms of difficulty.

As examples, the first three items from the scale are given below.

Item 1, Denotation and Representation, I

E gives S a small rubber toy. Score 5, if S hands the toy back to E or names it (if S hands it back, he is asked, *What is this called?*); 4, if S plays with the toy in a manner appropriate to that toy; 3, if he plays with it in an inappropriate manner; 2, if he examines the toy; 1, if he attempts to place, or succeeds in placing, the toy in his mouth; 0, if he continues to grasp the toy outside his field of vision.

Items 2 and 3, Denotation and Representation, II and III

A library desk bell is presented in *S*'s field of vision, at a distance close enough for him to touch but beyond his grasp. *E* must ensure that *S* cannot reach the toy. After the presentation, *S* is allowed to play with the bell to minimize frustration. Following a brief play period, the bell is removed and a grip ball presented in the same manner. *E* manipulates each object to produce the sound it makes (the ball is squeezed, the bell is rung). *S*'s responses to the desk bell and grip ball are scored separately, as two different items. Score 8, for consensual naming of the object; 7, for idiosyncratic naming; 6, if *S* points to the object without making call sounds; 5, if *S* touches the object to explore it but does not attempt to grasp it; 4, if *S* emits call sounds while pointing to the object (pointing is distinguished from grasping by the absence of finger movements and palm not being held face up); 3, if *S* emits call sound without attempting to grasp object; 2, if he attempts to grasp object while emitting call sounds; 1, if he attempts to grasp object; 0, if there is no appreciable reaction from *S*.

RELIABILITY AND VALIDITY: The interjudge reliability figures were obtained by correlating the scores of the two raters for each item, over all the children. The reliability figures indicate a high level of consistency in the two judges' scoring of the various items, the median *r* being .93. A total score was computed for each child by summing his *z*-scores for the entire set of items. The correlations of individual item scores with total scores also suggest a high degree of internal consistency in the items, in that two-thirds of these correlations exceed the .50 level. The correlations of item scores with age provide validity information for the various items in terms of their hypothesized relationship to cognitive development. To obtain test-retest reliability for the scale, a sample of forty-three subjects from the original pool returned after four months and were administered the scale for a second time. The correlation of total scale test-retest for these subjects was .72.

To explore the dimensionality of the scale, the data were analyzed using a multidimensional homogeneity scaling technique developed by Bentler (1971). This method was used in conjunction with Horst's (1965) basic structure successive factor rotation program. The first factor extracted through this method included 80 percent of the items along with age. This analysis also provided a matrix coefficient of homogeneity of .93 (Bentler, 1971). Bentler's index also assesses the extent to which the items form an ordinal scale. The obtained matrix homogeneity coefficient indicates that the items included within this test of cognitive development exhibit strong ordinal relationships.

BIBLIOGRAPHY:

Bentler, P. M. "Monotonicity Analysis: An Alternative to Linear Factor and Test Analysis." In R. Green (Ed.), *Measurement and Piaget.* New York: McGraw-Hill, 1971.

Horst, P. *Factor Analysis of Data Matrices.* New York: Holt, Rinehart and Winston, 1965.

Mehrabian, A., and Williams, M. "Piagetian Measures of Cognitive Development for Children up to Age Two." *Journal of Psycholinguistic Research,* 1971, *1,* 113-126.

Prepared by Orval G. Johnson

INFANT RATING SCALE

AUTHOR: Janet L. Hoopes

AGE: Less than 12 weeks

VARIABLE: Developmental pattern

TYPE OF MEASURE: Rating scale

SOURCE FROM WHICH MEASURE MAY BE OBTAINED: See Hoopes (1967).

DESCRIPTION OF MEASURE: The instrument was devised to yield quantitative and some qualitative data that might improve the prediction for normal intellectual growth. It was considered an experimental instrument that would scale data available in case files or from observation of the infant, and hence alert the practitioner to deviant growth patterns. The scale contains items that reflect cumulative research (in 1958) in the field of prenatal perinatal factors and information on early behavioral patterns that might have significance for later development. It proved to have practical applicability in an adoption agency and was used as a screening device. It is important to remember that no one danger signal has significance in and of itself. Results of the follow-up study showed that an accumulation of danger signals might be predictive of slower growth. Although the specifics of the rating scale can be easily taught to a paraprofessional, it is strongly recommended that a professional trained in infant observations work in conjunction with the paraprofessional. (See Hoopes, 1966, 1967.) Information from five different areas is scaled: (1) intelligence of the parents and other members of the natural family group, (2) medical information on the mother during prenatal course, (3) birth and delivery, (4) early behavior of the infant, and (5) medical condition and progress of the infant.

As examples, eight selected items of the twenty-nine item scale are given below.

Background
1. Mother's intelligence (estimate unless IQ is known)

1	2	3	4	5
Retarded	Dull	Average	Bright	Superior
IQ 80	81-94	95-109	110-124	125

Mother's Medical
8. Bleeding during pregnancy

Extreme	Moderate	None
(threatened miscarriage)	(some straining)	

Birth History
1. Type of delivery

Breech	Caesarian	Normal

2. Length of labor

Less than 3 hours	3 to 23 hours	24 hours or more

4. Birth weight

Less than 5 lbs.	5 lbs. to 5, 15 oz.	6 lbs. to 6, 15 oz.	7 lbs. to 7, 15 oz.	8 lbs. to 8, 15 oz.	9 lbs. to 9, 15 oz.	10 lbs. or more

5. Condition at birth

| Poor (Apgar 4 or less) | Fair (Apgar 5 to 7) | Good (Apgar 8 to 10) |

Placement (0 to 8 weeks)

1. Eating

Weak suck (milk dribbles out of mouth)	Moderate suck (bottle removed easily)	Strong suck (bottle removed with difficulty)
Frequent spitting up whole bottle	Moderate amount	No spitting

| Small feeding, 1 to 2 ounces | Moderate, 3 to 4 ounces | | Large quantity, 5 ounces or more |

3. Body strength

| Passive, weak, floppy | Average strength and body control | Active, strong, moves a lot— head up when on tummy—"travels" in crib | Hypertonic and tense |

RELIABILITY AND VALIDITY: Reliability was tested by interrater agreement between caseworker and psychologist based on (1) record data only, and (2) actual observation of the infant. Agreement ranged from 70 percent in the section on early behavior of the infant to 95 percent on medical information. The obtained agreement falls within acceptable levels of significance. Data on validity are obtained in the follow-up study reported in Hoopes (1967).

BIBLIOGRAPHY:

Hoopes, J. L. "Development of an Infant Rating Scale and Its Use in Adoption Practice." Mimeographed. Philadelphia, Pennsylvania: Children's Aid Society, 1966.
Hoopes, J. L. *An Infant Rating Scale: Its Validation and Usefulness.* New York: Child Welfare League of America, 1967.

INVENTORY OF READINESS SKILLS

AUTHORS: Jack Shelquist, Barbara Breeze, and Bette Jacquot

AGE: 4 to 7½ years

VARIABLE: Readiness for formal instruction

TYPE OF MEASURE: Test

SOURCE FROM WHICH MEASURE MAY BE OBTAINED: Educational Programmers, Inc., P.O. Box 332, Roseburg, Oregon, 97470. Cost: Specimen set (includes 1 test, 1 teacher's manual, 1 set visual memory cards, and 1 mask), $3.75; complete set (includes 20 tests, 1 each of manual, mask, and visual memory cards), $8.95; 100 tests (only), $32.95 or $.35 each if purchased in small lots; manual, $2.25; mask, $.25; visual memory cards, $.65.

DESCRIPTION OF MEASURE: The Inventory of Readiness Skills consists of eighty-two items divided into the following eight subtests: Auditory Memory Sequential, Word Discrimination, Body Awareness, Locational and Directional Concepts, Color Discrimination, Visual Motor Coordination, Visual Perception of Letters, and Letter Names. The child responds either verbally or tactually to the examiner's directions. No special training is required of the examiner before using the test. It is an individually administered test designed to assist the teacher in making a diagnostic assessment of the child's understanding of those eight fundamental skills considered essential to successful participation in the school's formal instructional program. It aids in pinpointing areas of strength and weakness in order to determine where reinforcement is necessary.

The test has been developed as an aid for the evaluation of children attending preschool, kindergarten, first grade, or special-education classes. It has been primarily designed for use as a criterion-referenced test; however, descriptive norm-referenced material is available. An individual profile is provided on the front of each test. If a child falls below the line graph on the individual profile, which indicates an acceptable performance level, the teacher should initiate an instructional program to raise the child's level of performance in that area.

In the Body Awareness subtest, the examiner asks the child to identify parts of his body in one of several ways, such as, "Touch your head," "Show me your hands," "Put your hand on your neck," or "Raise your hand." The first five of the eighteen items of this subtest are head, hands, knees, right hand, and back. In the Locational and Directional Concepts subtest the examiner gives the child ten directions to follow. The first three are: (1) Say, "Make a mark *on* the soap." (2) Say, "Make a mark *outside* the circle." (3) Say, "Make a mark *above* the pan."

RELIABILITY AND VALIDITY: The test was administered to 1,344 subjects, from which 448 children were chosen by random sample. The children included 277 from preschool or Project Headstart, seventy-four from kindergarten, and ninety-seven from first grade. Their ages ranged from 3 years, 7 months to 9 years, 9 months with 80 percent between 5 years and 7 years. Information concerning the mean and standard deviation for Auditory Perception Skills and Visual and Motor Skills are included in the manual. Because there is only one test form and because split-half computations are not appropriate due to the shortness of some of the subtests, the test-retest method of determining reliability (Hays formula) was used. Test-retest statistics and an item analysis table are included in the manual. Content validity was determined by the great emphasis current research has placed on the specific skills tested in each subtest area.

BIBLIOGRAPHY:

Seymour, J., Jr. "Education and Information." *CANHC-GRAM* (Newsletter of the California Association for Neurologically Handicapped Children, Los Angeles), 1971, *5* (7).

IOWA TEST OF PRESCHOOL DEVELOPMENT (ITPD)

AUTHOR: Ralph Scott

AGE: 2 to 5 years

VARIABLE: Readiness skills in four areas: language, visual motor, memory, and concepts

TYPE OF MEASURE: Preschool achievement test

SOURCE FROM WHICH MEASURE MAY BE OBTAINED: Go-Mo Products, Inc., 1906 Main, Cedar Falls, Iowa 50613. Cost: $89.95.

DESCRIPTION OF MEASURE: The Iowa Test of Preschool Development (ITPD) is an achievement-oriented preschool instrument designed specifically for children from 2 to 5 years of age. There are two levels of the ITPD: Level I is for youngsters from 2 to 3½ years old, Level II for children from 3½ to 5 years old. Both levels yield a total Preschool Achievement Index (PAI). Children's responses are grouped into four subtest areas (Language, Visual Motor, Memory, and Concepts), which in turn yield eight Skill Area Achievement Indexes (SAAIs) on Level I and eleven SAAIs on Level II.
     As examples of items from each skill area, the child:

1. Points to an object that has been orally described by the examiner (Receptive Language skill area)
2. Orally describes a picture (Expressive Language)
3. Throws a bean bag into a can (Large Motor)
4. Copies a straight line (Small Motor I)
5. Places pegs in a pegboard (Small Motor II)
6. Recalls the label of an object previously shown him/her (Visual Memory)
7. Recalls the labels of a series of objects stated verbally by the examiner (Auditory Memory)
8. Points to a "red" object, on request of examiner (Receptive Concepts)
9. Uses the color term "red" on request of examiner (Expressive Concepts) (In Level I, Receptive and Expressive Concepts scores are combined into a single Concepts score; on Level II separate scores are secured for Receptive and Expressive Concepts)
10. Finds two shapes which are alike (Similarities and Differences: Level II only)
11. Puts a block "near" a doll (Spatial Relationships: Level II only)

RELIABILITY AND VALIDITY: Norming of the ITPD was based on scores of 569 Ss, divided into fifteen age groups formed at three-month intervals. The split-half method, corrected by the Spearman-Brown formula, was employed to determine reliability of the instrument. On Level I the resulting coefficients ranged from .94 to .99, with a mean correlation of .97 (seven CA groups); on Level II the coefficients ranged from .81 to .97 with an average correlation of .94 (eight CA groups). In assessing concurrent validity, correlations were secured on total ITPD scores and Stanford-Binet IQs of sixty-four Ss (mean CA 2 years 11 months at time of initial testing) for whom long-term assessment was conducted. Intervals between administration of the two measures varied from one to ten days, and order of testing was counterbalanced. The resulting correlation was .64. Predictive validity measures were obtained by comparing total ITPD attainments of the same sixty-four Ss (evaluated longitudinally) when their mean CA was 35 months (Level I) and again at 44 months (Level II), with first grade total Primary Mental Abilities (PMA) IQs in first grade (mean CA 78 months). The resulting correlations were .58 (Level I) and .68 (Level II) respectively. Additional information concerning predictive validity was obtained by comparing total ITPD scores with later first grade *PMA* IQs (mean CA 6 years 6 months) of three separate groups of children, 37 (*N* = 12), 44 (*N* = 27), and 57 (*N* = 34) months of age at time of ITPD testing. The resulting correlations of total ITPD and total *PMA* IQs were .73, .70, and .52 respectively.

BIBLIOGRAPHY:

Scott, R. "Home Start: Family-Centered Preschool Enrichment for Black and White Children." *Psychology in the Schools,* 1973, *10,* 140-146.
Scott, R. "Research and Early Education." *Child Welfare,* 1974, *53,* 112-119.
Scott, R. "Translating Intra-Child Achievement Differences into Individualized Enrichment for Children from 2 to 5 Years of Age." *The School Psychologist,* 1975, *29,* 4.
Scott, R., and Kobes, D. A. "The Influence of Family Size on Learning Readiness Patterns of Socioeconomically Disadvantaged Preschool Blacks." *Journal of Clinical Psychology,* 1975, *31,* 85-88.
Scott, R., and Seifert, K. "Family Size and Learning Readiness Profiles of Socioeconomically Disadvantaged Preschool Whites." *Journal of Psychology,* 1975, *89,* 3-7.
Scott, R., and Smith, J. E. "Ethnic and Demographic Variables and Achievement Scores of Preschool Children." *Psychology in the Schools,* 1972, *9,* 174-182.
Scott, R., and Smith, J. E. "Ethnic and Demographic Variables and Achievement Scores of Preschool Children." *The School Psychology Digest,* 1972, Fall, 29-32.

J-K SCREENING TEST

AUTHORS: Rosalie C. Johnson and Rose K. Kenney

AGE: 5½ to 6½ years

VARIABLE: Learning difficulties of first-grade students

TYPE OF MEASURE: Screening test

SOURCE FROM WHICH MEASURE MAY BE OBTAINED: J-K Screening Service, 124 Solano Street, San Rafael, California 94901. Cost: $.50 per test, $2.50 per teacher's manual.

DESCRIPTION OF MEASURE: The Johnson-Kenney (J-K) Screening Test consists of ten subtests that sample a variety of perceptual-motor and cognitive skills considered important in the educational process. These subtests involve visual-motor coordination, visual and auditory recognition and discrimination, perceiving abstract relationships, and the perception of spatial relationships. The tasks on the test are those most children of that age group can be expected to accomplish without difficulty. The range of the test is narrow in scope so that difficulties of a child in any area can be detected immediately. One behavioral area that plagues elementary school teachers is the inability to make accurate early assessment of learning difficulties. This screening test was developed for identifying first-grade students with learning problems that significantly interfere with school performance.

The subtests and their descriptions are given below.

Subtest	Physical Description	Task Description
I. Number Concepts A. Counting Objects	Series of 10 pictures and 10 numerals arranged vertically.	Child counts the number of objects in a box and draws a line to the corresponding numeral on the opposite side of the page.
B. Writing Numerals	7 rows of objects to be counted.	Child counts the number of objects in each row and writes that number in the box at the end of the row.
II. Visual-Motor Coordination	A series of 12 pairs of squares with the first square in each pair containing a simple design. The second square in the pair is blank.	Child is asked to reproduce the design contained in the first square of each pair.
III. Discrimination of Form	Series of 6 pictures arranged horizontally on the first page; series of 6 words on the second page.	Child marks the picture or word that is different from the others.
IV. Symbol Recognition	Series of 9 alphabetical symbols placed in rows.	Child identifies similar letters by marking them with an "X."
V. Spatial Relations	8 pairs of 2 squares containing the same number of dots. The first square has a line drawn through several of the dots.	Child reproduces the first square "model" by drawing it in the second square.
VI. Position in Space	Series of 7 horizontally arranged pictures.	Child identifies the picture that is different from the others.
VII. Perceiving Relationships	5 rows of 4 pictures each.	Child marks the picture that does not belong.
VIII. Auditory Discrimination	5 rows of 3 pictures each and 5 rows of 3 words.	As the tester names the pictures or words, the child marks the 2 pictures or words that have the same beginning sound.

Subtest	Physical Description	Task Description
IX. Color Recognition	6 numbered circles in boxes.	Child colors the circles according to the directions of a tester.
X. Draw-a-Person	One 8½ X 11½ in. piece of paper (blank).	Child is asked to draw a picture of a person.

RELIABILITY AND VALIDITY: Three separate studies were done to investigate the predictive validity of the J-K Screening Test. (1) In the initial pilot project the screening test was administered at the beginning of the fall term to 171 first graders in four elementary schools in the Marin County area in California. At the end of the academic year, teachers' dichotomous subjective ratings ("satisfactory" or "unsatisfactory") for each student's academic performance were collected. In order to determine roughly the relation of the student's performance in the first grade and the score on the screening test, a Pearson product-moment correlation was computed involving each student's total test score and the teacher's ratings. The resulting correlation of .66 was significant ($p < .001$). (2) In the second study the J-K Test was given during the first month of school to 375 beginning first graders in two elementary school districts in the San Francisco area. At the end of the first grade, each student's teacher rated the pupil in terms of academic performance. A Pearson product-moment correlation was computed, comparing each student's total J-K score with the teacher's dichotomous rating (satisfactory or unsatisfactory). The Pearson correlation of .65 was significant ($p < .001$). In addition, a point biserial r was computed so that a more conservative estimate of association for discrete dichotomous data might be used, which does not assume a normally distributed population. The resulting biserial r was identical in value to the previously reported Pearson r and also was statistically significant ($r = .65; p < .001$). (3) The third validity study involved fifty-two first graders who were administered the J-K Test at the beginning of the fall term of 1973. Following completion of the first-grade year, each student was rated by his teacher on the Pupil Rating Scale (Myklebust, 1971) in terms of the student's auditory comprehension, spoken language, general orientation, motor coordination, and personal-social behavior. With the exception of the Draw-A-Person subtest, all of the J-K subtests positively correlated with the Pupil Rating Scale to a statistically significant degree when Pearson product-moment correlations were computed. Of particular importance is the remarkably high correlation between the total J-K score and the total Pupil Rating Scale ($r = .85; p < .001$).

Subtest reliabilities are as follows (values in parentheses are communalities; others are KR-20 coefficients): Counting and Recognition (.81); Writing Numerals (.35); Visual Motor Coordination (.99); Discrimination of Form (.51); Symbol Recognition (.43); Spatial Relations .95; Position in Space (.48); Perceiving Relationships .74; Auditory Discrimination (.82); Color Recognition .68; Draw-A-Person (.16).

BIBLIOGRAPHY:

Myklebust, H. R. *The Pupil Rating Scale.* New York: Grune & Stratton, 1971.

Seitz, F. C., Johnson, R. C., and Kenney, R. K. "Detection of Learning Difficulties in First Grade: Preliminary Analysis of the Johnson-Kenney Screening Readiness Test." *Psychological Reports,* 1973, *33,* 219-225.

Seitz, F. C., and Johnson, R. C. "The J-K (Johnson-Kenney) Screening Readiness Test as a Measure of First Grade Learning Difficulties: A Cross-Validation Study." *Psychological Reports* (in press).

Seitz, F. C., Willis, P. M., and Johnson, R. C. "The J-K Screening Readiness Test as a Measure of First Grade Learning Difficulties: A Cross-Validational Study." *Psychological Reports* (in press).

JOHNS HOPKINS PERCEPTUAL TEST (JHPT)

AUTHOR: Leon A. Rosenberg

AGE: 3 to 9 years

VARIABLE: General cognitive skills

TYPE OF MEASURE: Test

SOURCE FROM WHICH MEASURE MAY BE OBTAINED: Leon A. Rosenberg, Johns Hopkins Hospital, 601 North Broadway Street, Baltimore, Maryland 21205. Duplicating and mailing cost.

DESCRIPTION OF MEASURE: The Johns Hopkins Perceptual Test (JHPT) requires a child to select one of a group of forms that matches a standard form. There are thirty such forms. Item difficulty is varied by differences in number of angles in the figure and in number of alternatives (either two, three, or five). The designs are "random" and are produced following techniques developed by Attneave and Arnoult (1956) and LaBerge and Lawrence (1955). The complexity continuum is defined in terms of the amount of information inherent in each design (Attneave, 1957). The instrument is still a research tool, and extensive norms are not available. The original hope that the instrument would be culture-fair has not been realized fully. Recent research has indicated a small but significant relationship between JHPT scores and the mother's education.

RELIABILITY AND VALIDITY: JHPT $\times$ Peabody Picture Vocabulary Test: $r = .62$ ($N = 50$); JHPT $\times$ Draw-A-Person Test: $r = .70$ ($N = 37$); JHPT $\times$ Columbus Mental Maturity Scale: $r = .80$ ($N = 25$); JHPT $\times$ Peabody Picture Vocabulary Test: $r = .76$ ($N = 71$); JHPT $\times$ Columbus Mental Maturity Scale: $r = .76$ ($N = 71$); test-retest: $r = .90$ ($N = 61$); alpha coefficient = .76 ($N = 1,410$); alpha coefficient = .73 ($N = 1,317$); item r-biserials range between .27 and .72 ($N = 1,410$); factor analyses ($N = 1,410$, $N = 1,317$) show highest loading on a factor of general cognitive skills.

BIBLIOGRAPHY:

Attneave, F., and Arnoult, M. D. "The Quantitative Study of Shape and Pattern Perception." *Psychological Bulletin,* 1956, *53,* 452-471.

Attneave, F. "Physical Determinants of the Judged Complexity of Shapes." *Journal of Experimental Psychology,* 1957, *53,* 221-227.

Gilbert, L. N., and Shipman, V. C. *Johns Hopkins Perceptual Test: Technical Report Number 9.* ETS-Headstart Longitudinal Study. Princeton, New Jersey: Educational Testing Service, 1972.

LaBerge, D. L., and Lawrence, D. H. "A Method of Generating Visual Forms of Grades Similarity." *American Psychologist,* 1955, *10,* 401.

Rosenberg, L. A. "A Culture-Fair Instrument for Intellectual Assessment." In J. Hellmuth (Ed.), *Disadvantaged Child.* Vol. 2. New York: Brunner/Mazel, 1969.

KNI DEVELOPMENTAL SCALE

AUTHOR: Eldene Woellhof

AGE: Birth to 5 years

VARIABLE: Developmental maturation

TYPE OF MEASURE: Rating scale

SOURCE FROM WHICH MEASURE MAY BE OBTAINED: Psychology Department, Kansas Neurological Institute, 3107 West 21st Street, Topeka, Kansas 66604.

DESCRIPTION OF MEASURE: The eighty items of the scale relate to the four major areas of functioning: socialization (S), communication (C), physical development (P), and self-help (SH), and they are separated into age-level intervals. The first two years are divided into three-month intervals with one item from each category included; the third through fifth year into six-month intervals with two items from each category included. This provides a rough visual estimate of functioning by either total age level or category level. By obtaining detailed information from observations or from the informant, the examiner scores the item (+) if it is clear the child has demonstrated the ability of the specified item and (−) if it is clear the child has not consistently done so. By multiplying the number of items passed in each area by three months, a crude developmental age estimate may be obtained. The total score may be obtained by multiplying the total number of items passed by three-fourths months. Since the items of the scale were selected by permission from standardized instruments, one cannot validly score the selected items to arrive at standardized developmental age levels for the various areas. The wording of some of the selected items had to be slightly altered to meet the atypical environment of institutionalized retarded children.

As examples, three items each from the four areas of functioning, designated (S), (C), (P) and (SH), are given below.

(S)   1. Focuses eyes briefly and intently on *P* who bends into his field of vision
       17. Shows or offers toy to adult
       49. Likes to share, beginning realization of social demands

(C)   2. Coos and chuckles when happy
        18. Indicates wants by pointing *before* event
        51. Likes to name things
(P)   3. Hand usually open when lying on back
        19. Walks without support *few* steps
        53. *Down* steps, one per tread
(SH)   4. Grasps objects within reach
        20. Cooperates in dressing by lifting limb
        55. Washes and dries hands and face adequately with a reminder

RELIABILITY AND VALIDITY: None reported.

BIBLIOGRAPHY:

Nihira, K. "Measurement of Adaptive Behavior: A Descriptive System for Mental Retardates." *American Journal of Orthopsychiatry*, 1968, *38,* 622-634.

LEARNING POTENTIAL ASSESSMENT DEVICE: ANALOGY TESTS

AUTHORS: Reuven Feuerstein and others

AGE: 9 to 14 years in normal children; 10 years to adulthood for retarded performers

VARIABLE: General intelligence based on figural and logico-verbal modalities

TYPE OF MEASURE: Test

SOURCE FROM WHICH MEASURE MAY BE OBTAINED: Reuven Feuerstein, Hadassah Wizo Canada Research Institute, 6 Karmon Street, Beit Hakarem, Jerusalem, Israel. Experimental editions only.

DESCRIPTION OF MEASURE: The test is composed of four distinct instruments: test, retest, training materials, and shift. The whole set of materials is constructed in a way to permit the establishment of a base line, the use of the result as an indicator for the type of training procedure to be used with the specific examinee, a posttest measuring the modifiability of the individual as reflected by the difference between the base line and the results obtained after training, and, finally, a shift test which is a more elaborate measure of the transfer of the acquired principles and skills onto new, more complex situations.

About fifteen hundred adolescents were examined with this test. About one thousand of them were culturally deprived and socially disadvantaged retarded performers placed in prevocational schools and preparatory classes within the framework of Youth Aliyah. About five hundred children were examined within a regular elementary school, and norms have been obtained for grades 2 to 8. Seventh and eighth graders of a retarded school were also examined for modifiability. The test was constructed on the basis of a theoretical model and attempted to come as close as possible to the concept of proportionality by using a taxonomy of relationships. The theoretical model and the findings are to be found in Feuerstein and others (1972).

RELIABILITY AND VALIDITY: Partial validation of the test was done against intrinsic and extrinsic measures.

BIBLIOGRAPHY:

Feuerstein, R., and others. *Studies in Cognitive Modifiability.* Vol. 2. Jerusalem, Israel: Hadassah Wizo Canada Research Institute, 1972.
Narrol, H., and Bachor, D. G. *An Introduction to Feuerstein's Approach to Assessing and Developing Cognitive Potential.* Toronto, Canada: Ontario Institute for Studies in Education, 1975.

LEARNING POTENTIAL ASSESSMENT DEVICE: RAVEN'S PROGRESSIVE MATRICES VARIATIONS 1 AND 2

AUTHORS: Reuven Feuerstein and others

AGE: 8 years to adulthood in normal children; 11 years to adulthood in retarded performers

VARIABLE: Cognitive modifiability in general intelligence

TYPE OF MEASURE: Test

SOURCE FROM WHICH MEASURE MAY BE OBTAINED: The distribution of this test at this time is limited to research and experimental work and can be obtained from Reuven Feuerstein, Hadassah Wizo Canada Research Institute, 6 Karmon Street, Beit Hakarem, Jerusalem, Israel.

DESCRIPTION OF MEASURE: The test consists of two books, Feuerstein and others, Volume 1 (1972), which contains thirty variations on B8 to B12 problems of the Raven matrices, six variations per task, and Feuerstein and others, Volume 2 (1972), which consists of fifty-eight variations based on five tasks of the Ravens' matrices from series C, D, E, and Adults. The construction of the LPAD Raven variations is based on the LPAD model described in detail in Feuerstein and others (1972). The major characteristic is the use of test-teach-test model where the latter test is constructed in a way to provide the examinee with an opportunity to apply the principles, skills, and motivations acquired during the teaching session to a series of tasks becoming progressively more complex and remote from the problem taught initially. The test measures the capacity of the individual to use previous experiences for adaptation to progressively new situations. The decision to use the tasks derived from Raven's progressive matrices was made because of the extensive data offered by Raven. This data led him to conclude that below certain IQ levels there is no way to train the individual for proper functioning in certain parts of the test, especially B8 to B12 and even less so in the series C, D, and E.

Our findings show that low-functioning individuals from 50 to 70 IQ may become very successfully involved in solving the more difficult parts of these variations providing us with the proof of modifiability. The test has been used with a great variety of retarded performers ranging from 50 to 80 IQ with early adolescents and young adults and has proven helpful in pointing to the capacity of the individual to become involved in a learning process, use his cognitive functions, and become modified in his level of functioning in very significant tasks.

The major use of these instruments is in an individual clinical session. However, experiments done recently have proven their feasibility for use in group settings, with the understanding that the group setting can be considered only for screening purposes and the students thus identified must be reexamined individually. The application of LPAD both individually and by means of group sessions requires a period of training and familiarization of the examiner with the theoretical model of the dynamic assessment, the characteristics of the instruments, the teaching phase determining the nature of the interaction between the examiner and examinee, and, finally, the interpretation of results. Volumes 1 and 2 offer a theoretical orientation for these three aspects of the examination. However, personal training is highly recommended.

RELIABILITY AND VALIDITY: Reliability measures are presented in Feuerstein and others (1972), but since this was written, a great amount of data have been gathered on both the reliability and the validity of the tests. Reliability for two retest periods (after one to two months and after seventeen months): for the short period the range is .57 to .85; for long periods, .57 to .80. The more important aspect of the LPAD test is its clinical validity. A measure of this validity can be shown by the great number of adolescents previously described and treated as retardates who have, following LPAD assessment, been integrated into normal educational settings and have proved to cope successfully with normal requirements. One of the more important aspects of the LPAD measures (to be described later) is the capacity to derive a prescriptive intervention.

BIBLIOGRAPHY:

Feuerstein, R., and others. *Studies in Cognitive Modifiability*. Vols. 1 and 2. Jerusalem, Israel: Hadassah Wizo Canada Research Institute, 1972.
Haywood, C., and others. "Behavioral Assessment in Mental Retardation." In P. McReynolds (Ed.), *Advances in Psychological Assessment*. Vol. 3. San Francisco: Jossey-Bass, 1974.
Mental Tests and Cultural Adaptation—Cognitive Assessment of the Socioculturally Deprived Child and Adolescent. Jerusalem, Israel: Hadassah Wizo Canada Research Institute, n.d.
Narrol, H., and Bachor, D. G. *An Introduction to Feuerstein's Approach to Assessing and Developing Cognitive Potential*. Toronto, Canada: Ontario Institute for Studies in Education, 1975.

LEXINGTON DEVELOPMENTAL SCALE AND LEXINGTON DEVELOPMENTAL SCALE SCREENING INSTRUMENT (LDS AND LDSSI)

AUTHORS: John V. Irwin, Margaret Norris Ward, Carol C. Deen, Ann B. Greis, Valerie Cooley, Alice Auvenshine, and Flonnia C. Taylor

AGE: Birth to 6 years

VARIABLE: Motor, language, personal-social, cognitive, and emotional development

TYPE OF MEASURE: Assessment

SOURCE FROM WHICH MEASURE MAY BE OBTAINED: United Cerebral Palsy of the Bluegrass Child Development Centers, Inc., P.O. Box 8003, 465 Springhill Drive, Lexington, Kentucky 40503.

DESCRIPTION OF MEASURE: The Lexington Development Scale (long form) evaluates children on 414 documented items in four important areas in the development of the child: motor, language, personal-social, and cognitive. Each of the four areas is scored in years on the basis of developmental age. The LDS is a continuous scale divided into two overlapping sections. The Infant section covers ages zero to 2 years, and the Early Childhood section continues from 2 to 6 years. The long form of the LDS is designed for the classroom teacher to assess the behavior of children at the beginning and end of the school year. This is accomplished by incorporating assessment items into daily classroom activities, usually for the first two weeks of school. Charts facilitate assessment of individual children during group activities. Some items may be assessed on an individual basis.

The instrument is useful to teachers in making prescriptive teaching plans for each child, in interpretation to parents of a child's weaknesses or strengths through the use of the profile charts, and in administrative accountability. The computerization of the data helps an administrator know whether expenditures on programs are worthwhile and also which classes achieve the greatest results with children as individuals or in a group.

The Lexington Developmental Scale Screening Instrument has half the items of the long form. It was designed as a screening tool for teachers, nurses, social workers, and homemakers to assess children individually during a 30-minute clinic or home visit, and for day-care workers and early childhood teachers with limited time, personnel, and equipment. Item analysis comparing the long and short forms on 207 Head Start children revealed that the short form is just as sensitive as the long form in determining the developmental age and the developmental quotient. Classroom teachers prefer the more detailed information discerned from the long form, especially if the child's profile shows developmental lags.

RELIABILITY AND VALIDITY: Data from preliminary reliability studies, by both item and area, suggest high reliability. There has been no formal attempt to establish validity; however, items were taken from standardized tests, and the Stanford-Binet was administered to the reliability group. Scores from Stanford-Binet and the LDS Language and Cognitive Area were comparable. Recent comparison with ITPA, Peabody, Draw-A-Person, and Goldman-Fristoe show that the LDS is more sensitive in some cases than others and compared favorably in all areas with the above tests. Preliminary investigations of the correspondence between the short and long forms of the LDS suggest that as far as the establishment of the performance age by area is concerned, the two forms are virtually interchangeable.

BIBLIOGRAPHY:

United Cerebral Palsy of Bluegrass, Inc. *The Lexington Developmental Scale: An Instrument of Measurement—First Revision.* Lexington, Kentucky: United Cerebral Palsy of Bluegrass, 1973.

United Cerebral Palsy of Bluegrass, Inc. *The Lexington Developmental Scale, Short Form: An Instrument of Measurement for Infant and for Early Childhood.* Lexington, Kentucky: United Cerebral Palsy of Bluegrass, 1974.

Prepared by Rhea A. Taylor

LOGICAL DISCOVERY TASK

AUTHOR: Sheila Becker

AGE: 5 to 12 years

VARIABLE: Concept attainment

TYPE OF MEASURE: Card game

SOURCE FROM WHICH MEASURE MAY BE OBTAINED: See Becker (1974); also available from Sheila Becker, Montreal Oral School for the Deaf, 5000 Iona Avenue, Montreal, Quebec, Canada.

DESCRIPTION OF MEASURE: The Logical Discovery Task, adapted for young children from a concept attainment task used with college students by Brunner and Goodnow (1956), is a nonverbal technique in the form of a card game. As the basis of a study with deaf and hearing children (Becker, 1974), the Logical Discovery Task, was used to: (1) evaluate the children's levels of cognitive development as outlined by Piaget (1960), (2) compare the performances of deaf and hearing children, (3) study and compare the thinking strategies or styles of deaf and hearing children, and (4) study the influence of language development on concept attainment in deaf children.

The test materials of this task consist of twenty-seven 3 X 5 cards. Each card has one, two, or three identical figures on it; the figures are triangles, circles, or squares, and they are colored yellow, blue, or red. No two cards are alike. The child is presented with a sample card that matches one of the twenty-seven cards, and through successive choices from the twenty-seven cards he is asked to discover which of the three variables is being sought by the examiner. Eight different sample cards are used in the eight trials, five of which are designed to measure the discovery of a concept and three to measure the application of this concept. The manner in which the child reaches his answer allows the examiner to determine which type of strategy he uses, if any.

RELIABILITY AND VALIDITY: None reported.

BIBLIOGRAPHY:

Becker, S. "The Performance of Deaf and Hearing Children in a Logical Discovery Task." *The Volta Review,* 1974, *76,* 537-545.
Bruner, J. S., and Goodnow, J. J. *A Study of Thinking.* New York: Wiley, 1956.
Piaget, J. *Psychology of Intelligence.* Patterson, New Jersey: Littlefield, Adams, 1960.

MARSHALLTOWN BEHAVIORAL
DEVELOPMENT PROFILE (MBDP)

AUTHOR: Marshalltown Project

AGE: Birth to 6 years (developmental age)

VARIABLE: Communication, motor, and social skill

TYPE OF MEASURE: Developmental checklist

SOURCE FROM WHICH MEASURE MAY BE OBTAINED: The Marshalltown Project, 507 East Anson, Marshalltown, Iowa 50158. Cost: $3.00.

DESCRIPTION OF MEASURE: The MBDP contains 327 developmental skill items to evaluate preschoolers. Three subtests measure communication, motor, and social development. Items are directly keyed to a set of three prescriptive teaching manuals. Examples of items are given below.

Category	Age	Item
Communication	7 months	Looks at some common objects when their names are spoken.
Motor	30 months	Stacks rings on pegs in order.
Social	48 months	Puts on socks.

Profile manual includes sample score sheet, list of items needed for testing, and test administration and scoring directions. Score sheets may be ordered.

RELIABILITY AND VALIDITY: A missing data correlations study was done with 189 test batteries of preschool children who were being served by the Marshalltown Project because they exhibited a developmental lag. Pearson product-moment correlations of several measures with MBDP were: Stanford-Binet, .62; Slosson Intelligence Test for Children and Adults, .55; Alpern-Boll, Mean Score .61, IQ .55. The MBDP mean was 93.19 and *SD* of 15.04, compared with a Stanford-Binet Form L-M mean of 93.45 and *SD* of 13.28.

BIBLIOGRAPHY:

Alpern, G. D., and Boll, T. J. *Developmental Profile.* Indianapolis, Indiana: Psychological Development Publications, 1972.
Slosson, R. L. *Slosson Intelligence Test (S.I.T.) for Children and Adults.* East Aurora, New York: Slosson Educational Publishers, 1963.

Prepared by Mel Walden

MAUSER PICTURE SENTENCE TEST (MPST)

AUTHOR: August J. Mauser

AGE: Preschool to grade 1

VARIABLE: Listening ability

TYPE OF MEASURE: Test

SOURCE FROM WHICH MEASURE MAY BE OBTAINED: August J. Mauser, Department of Special Education, Graham Hall 223, Northern Illinois University, DeKalb, Illinois 60115.

DESCRIPTION OF MEASURE: The MPST was designed to measure the child's comprehension of oral language of sentences. The instrument is a measure to predict success in beginning reading instruction. Originally field-tested on first-grade children in 1965 and used in the author's 1968 dissertation, the test consists of sixty stimulus sentences arranged in order of increasing difficulty. The child is read each sentence and is asked to respond to the appropriate picture from a four-picture plate showing a boy, girl, adult, or animal involved in some type of action. The stimulus sentences were originally developed from words included in the Gates Vocabulary List of 1,500 most common words, the Dale List, Dolch's Storytellers Vocabulary, and also from the graded vocabulary list of several basal readers. Administration and scoring are relatively simple in that raw scores and percentile scores are derived from subtracting the errors that the child makes from the total number of items of the test, giving a raw score total.

The following are the first ten of the sixty stimulus sentences:

1. Jeff is eating an apple.
2. Susie has a doll.

3. Tom is riding a bicycle.
4. Dick is sleeping in the bed.
5. Nancy is looking at a book.
6. Father and Jeff are riding on horses.
7. Linda is holding a big ball.
8. Mary is going into the house.
9. Mother is not happy with Jane.
10. Carol has a hat on her head.

RELIABILITY AND VALIDITY: The MPST has sufficient variability and internal consistency when administered on entrance to first grade. It correlates moderately (r = .43 to .53) with the Peabody Picture Vocabulary Test (PPVT), Metropolitan, and Ginn Recall Tests, and it has low relationships to tests such as the Alphabet Test and Gates Word List Tests. The correlation of MPST scores with success in beginning reading was .36.

BIBLIOGRAPHY:

Ellson, D. G., Harris, P., and Barber, L. "A Field Test of Programmed and Directed Tutoring." *Reading Research Quarterly,* 1968, *3,* 307-367.
Mauser, A. J. "First Grade Children's Comprehension of Oral Language in Sentence and Success in Beginning Reading Instruction." Unpublished doctoral dissertation. Indiana University, Bloomington, 1968.

MICHILL GENERAL ABILITY TEST (MGAT)

AUTHOR: M. Y. Quereshi

AGE: 10 years and up

VARIABLE: General mental ability (inductive reasoning)

TYPE OF MEASURE: Test

SOURCE FROM WHICH MEASURE MAY BE OBTAINED: M. Y. Quereshi, Department of Psychology, Marquette University, 617 North 13th Street, Milwaukee, Wisconsin 53233. Cost: Estimates on request.

DESCRIPTION OF MEASURE: The Michill General Ability Test (MGAT) consists of forty-four items designed to assess general intellectual ability, especially of the inductive-reasoning type. Each item consists of English alphabets arranged according to a certain rule that the subject must discover and then provide the last missing letter in each series. The test can be used with children between the ages of 10 and 18 years, but it is not suitable for children below age 10.

As examples, the first five of the forty-four items of Form A are given below.

1. M A S M B S M C S M —
2. D X E W F V G U H T I S —
3. O P Q V W —
4. M N O M N O P Q R P Q R S —
5. F X E F X D E F X C D E F X —

RELIABILITY AND VALIDITY: The reliability and validity indices were computed from the data collected on 250 children between the ages of 10½ and 17½ years, divided into four age groups (10½ to 11½, 12½ to 13½, 14½ to 15½, and 16½ to 17½). There were 119 boys and 131 girls in all groups combined. Three types of reliability indices were computed: (1) internal consistency (odd-even corrected by the Spearman-Brown formula), (2) test-retest reliability (over a period of three months), and (3) parallel-form reliability. The internal consistency indices ranged between .69 and .85, and the parallel-form reliability ranged between .64 and .82. The validity data were based on the same samples as described above. Correlations of MGAT scores with Wechsler Intelligence Scale for Children and Wechsler Adult Intelligence Scale scores ranged between .57 and .65. In a separate study based on 137 high school boys, the correlation between MGAT Form A and grade-point average was found to be .43. Although a parallel Form B is available, the data reported here are only on Form A, since more research has been done on Form A.

BIBLIOGRAPHY:

Quereshi, M. Y. "An Application of Votaw's Test of Compound Symmetry to a Multi-form Scale of Inductive Reasoning." *Journal of General Psychology,* 1969, *80,* 99-105.
Quereshi, M. Y., and Veeser, W. R. "Mental Test Performance as a Function of Various Scoring Cutoffs." *Journal of General Psychology,* 1970, *82,* 241-250.
Veeser, W. R. "Mental Test Performance as a Function of Item Order and Scoring Cutoffs." Unpublished doctoral dissertation. Marquette University, Milwaukee, Wisconsin, 1968.

MINNESOTA CHILD DEVELOPMENT INVENTORY

AUTHORS: Harold Ireton and Edward Thwing

AGE: Mothers of children 12 months to 6 years

VARIABLE: Preschool development

TYPE OF MEASURE: Inventory

SOURCE FROM WHICH MEASURE MAY BE OBTAINED: Behavior Science Systems, 5701 Hawkes Terrace, Minneapolis, Minnesota 55436. Cost: Specimen set (includes Manual, Inventory booklet, answer sheet, and male and female profile forms), $5.00;

complete set, packed in a desk box (includes Manual, 10 Inventory booklets, 100 answer sheets, 500 male and female profile forms, and scoring templates), $32.50.

DESCRIPTION OF MEASURE: The Minnesota Child Development Inventory is a systematic means for the developmental evaluation of children and for the preliminary identification of children with developmental disorders. It can be used for the step-one evaluation of the individual child whose development is suspect and for screening of groups of children. The Inventory consists of a booklet, an answer sheet, and a profile. The booklet contains 320 statements describing the behaviors of children in the first 6½ years of life. These statements were selected on the basis of: (1) representation of developmental skills, (2) observability by mothers in real-life situations, (3) descriptive clarity, and (4) age-discriminating power. The mother is asked to indicate those statements that describe her child's behavior by marking "Yes" or "No" on the answer sheet. Scoring the answer sheet is a simple clerical task involving the use of templates. Machine scoring is also available. The score for each developmental scale is summarized on the Minnesota Child Development Inventory Profile. The profile pictures the child's development in comparison to norms for both children his age and children of other ages. The age norms of the profile are based upon a sample of 796 white suburban children aged 6 months to 6½ years (395 males, 401 females). Age norms are provided for each sex separately. The scores on the developmental scales are interpreted in terms of the age norms and below-age guidelines.

As examples, the developmental scales, followed by the first ten of the 320 items in the test booklet, are given below.

General Development:	A summary scale, providing an overall index of development and consisting of the most age-discriminating items from the other seven scales.
Gross Motor:	Locomotion and related behaviors involving strength, balance, and coordination.
Fine Motor:	Visual-motor skills, from simple eye-hand coordination to complex fine motor behavior.
Expressive Language:	Expressive communication, from simple gestural, vocal, and verbal behavior to complex language expression.
Comprehension–Conceptual:	Language understanding, from simple comprehension to concept formulation.
Situation Comprehension:	Nonverbal understanding of, and interaction with, the environment through observation, discrimination, imitation, and motor behavior.
Self-Help:	Self-help skills, including eating, toileting, and dressing.
Personal-Social:	Personal and social behavior, including initiative, independence, social interaction, and concern for others.

1. Walks without help.
2. Unbuttons one or more buttons.
3. Says two or more words clearly.
4. Rides tricycle using pedals.
5. Increases activity when shown a toy.
6. Actively refuses to obey.
7. Says "Thank you."

8. Plays games with guns, such as cowboys, cops and robbers, or spaceman.

9. Tells what an object is made of.

10. Feeds self a cracker or cookie.

RELIABILITY AND VALIDITY: Split-half reliability coefficients for the individual scales are as follows: GD (.90), GM (.77), EL (.88), SC (.68), SH (.78), and PS (.80). Validity of the scales for the norm group is demonstrated by systematic increases in mean score with increase in age and by low incidences of children scoring appreciably below their age level. A clinical study of 109 preschool-age children referred for psychological evaluations showed that subaverage MCDI results were predictive of a variety of developmental problems measured by direct psychological evaluation.

BIBLIOGRAPHY:

Ireton, H., and Thwing, E. "The Minnesota Child Development Inventory in the Psychotic-Developmental Evaluation of the Preschool-Age Child." *Child Psychiatry and Human Development,* 1972, *3,* 102-114.

Ireton, H., and Thwing, E. *Manual for the Minnesota Child Development Inventory.* Minneapolis, Minnesota: Interpretive Scoring Systems, 1974.

Ireton, H., and Thwing, E. "Pediatric Developmental Evaluation of the Preschool-Age Child Utilizing Maternal Report: The Minnesota Child Development Inventory." Mimeographed report, 1975.

Ireton, H., Thwing, E., and Currier, S. "Minnesota Child Development Inventory Identification of Children with Developmental Disorders." Mimeographed report, 1975.

MORAL JUDGMENT INTERVIEW (FORMS A AND B)

AUTHOR: Lawrence Kohlberg

AGE: Elementary school to adult

VARIABLE: Stage of moral judgment

TYPE OF MEASURE: Structured interview

SOURCE FROM WHICH MEASURE MAY BE OBTAINED: Moral Education and Research Foundation, Roy E. Larsen Hall, Appian Way, Harvard University, Cambridge, Massachusetts 02138.

DESCRIPTION OF MEASURE: Each of the two forms of the Moral Judgment Interview is comprised of three stories with accompanying questions that sample different aspects of the moral issue. Detailed scoring guides with numerous examples are provided to exemplify responses characteristic of five hypothesized stages of moral development.

As an example, one of the stories, and five of the eleven questions based on it, are given below.

Story VII.

Two young men, brothers, had gotten into serious trouble. They were secretly leaving town in a hurry and needed money. Karl, the older one, broke into a store and stole $500. Bob, the younger one, went to a retired old man who was known to help people in town. Bob told the man that he was very sick and he needed $500 to pay for the operation. Really he wasn't sick at all, and he had no intention of paying the man back. Although the man didn't know Bob very well, he loaned him the money. So Bob and Karl skipped town, each with $500.

1. Which would be worse, stealing like Karl or cheating like Bob? Why?
2. Suppose Bob had gotten the loan from a bank with no intention of paying it back. Is borrowing from the bank or the old man worse? Why?
3. What do you feel is the worst thing about cheating the old man?
6. Which would be worse in terms of society's welfare, cheating like Bob or stealing like Karl? Why?
8a. What or who tells you what is right or wrong?

RELIABILITY AND VALIDITY: None reported.

BIBLIOGRAPHY:

Kohlberg, L. "Stages and Sequence: The Cognitive-Developmental Approach to Socialization." In D. Goslin (Ed.), *Handbook of Socialization Theory.* Chicago: Rand McNally, 1969.

Kohlberg, L. *Moral Judgment Interview and Procedures for Scoring.* Manual. Cambridge, Massachusetts: Moral Education and Research Foundation, 1971.

Kohlberg, L., and Turiel, E. "Moral Development and Moral Education." In G. Lesser (Ed.), *Psychology and Educational Practice.* Glenview, Illinois: Scott Foresman, 1971.

Rest, J. R. *The Hierarchical Nature of Moral Judgment: A Study of Patterns of Comprehension and Preference of Moral Stages.* Cambridge, Massachusetts: Moral Education and Research Foundation, 1971.

Prepared by Orval G. Johnson

MOTOR-ACADEMIC-PERCEPTUAL (M-A-P) SKILL DEVELOPMENT CHECKLIST

AUTHOR: Donna Kwall Smith

AGE: 2 to 8 years

VARIABLE: Motor, academic, and perceptual skills

TYPE OF MEASURE: Checklist

SOURCE FROM WHICH MEASURE MAY BE OBTAINED: Limited number of copies available for $1.00 (to cover postage and handling) from Donna K. Smith, ARIN Intermediate Unit No. 28, 120 North Fifth Street, Indiana, Pennsylvania 15701.

DESCRIPTION OF MEASURE: This checklist is designed to provide the teacher of multiply handicapped young children with a behavior-oriented evaluation of the child's skills in the following areas: Motor Skills—gross motor skills, manipulative skills, self-care skills, exhibiting body awareness; Academic Skills—general readiness, communication skills, early skill development; Perceptual Skills—visual discrimination skills, non-visual discrimination skills. Through the frequent use of this single measure, appropriate learning objectives can be established for each child. The checklist may be completed easily (within half an hour) through teacher observation of the child as he or she is involved in classroom activities. Since the facets of each skill are arranged hierarchically, the chart can be used to establish appropriate subsequent learning objectives for the child.

As examples, four of the seven items in Category II-A, Academic Skills, general readiness, are given below.

	1	2	3	4	5
1. Participation in the group	Shows no awareness of the group	Joins the group with little involvement	Joins the group; attempts to pay attention to what is happening around him	Attends to task within the group	Participates in the group
2. Listening	Does not listen	Listens to some commands	Interrupts with extraneous comments while listening	Needs reminders while listening	Listens attentively while under group supervision
3. Following directions	Does not follow directions	Follows one-step directions with assistance	Follows one-step directions independently	Follows two-step directions independently	Follows complex directions independently
4. Handling books	Destroys books	Does not destroy books	Explores and manipulates books	Shows interest in pictures	Turns pages in anticipation

RELIABILITY AND VALIDITY: None reported.

BIBLIOGRAPHY: None reported.

NEONATAL BEHAVIORAL ASSESSMENT SCALE

AUTHOR: T. Berry Brazelton

AGE: 1 month

VARIABLE: Neonatal behavior

TYPE OF MEASURE: Rating scale

SOURCE FROM WHICH MEASURE MAY BE OBTAINED: See Brazelton (1973). Three training films are available from Education Development Center, 55 Chapel Street, Newton, Massachusetts 02158. Cost: Rental fee, $15.00; purchase price, No. 1, $115.00; No. 2, $115.00; No. 3, $130.00.

DESCRIPTION OF MEASURE: The Brazelton Behavioral Assessment Scale is intended as a means of scoring interactive behavior. It is not a formal neurological evaluation, though the neurological implications of such a scale make it necessary that a few basic neurological items be included. These are based on the descriptions of neurological assessment outlined in Prechtl and Beintema (1964). The main thrust of the evaluation is behavioral. It is an attempt to score the infant's available responses to his environment and thus, indirectly, his effect on the environment. It is essentially aimed at evaluating the normal newborn infant, and its use in comparing infants within and across cultures has been demonstrated (Brazelton, Koslowski, and Tronick, 1971; Brazelton and Robey, 1965; Brazelton, Robey, and Collier, 1969; Freedman and Freedman, 1969; Horowitz and others, 1971; Scarr and Williams, 1971). The score sheet includes twenty-seven behavioral items, each of which is scored on a 9-point scale, and twenty elicited responses, each of which is scored on a 3-point scale. The exam takes about 30 minutes to perform and 10 to 15 minutes to score using the manual. It is in use at present as a research instrument but should be considered for a clinical tool in early assessment of the neonate's contribution to his environment.

As an example, one of the twenty-seven behavioral items, with the scoring scale, is given below.

6. *Orientation Response—Inanimate Auditory*

This is a measure of his response to the rattle or a soft bell (nonsocial) as a stimulus when he is in an alert state. The auditory stimuli should be presented to one side and out of sight (at least 6 inches away and no more than 12 inches) so that one can observe the infant's eyes and head as they respond to the lateralized stimulus. This scores his best performance in one of the awake states to the stimulus. Latency altering degree of eye shift and head turning to the stimulus are scored. Brightening of face and eyes can be seen, and they are evidences of his attention to the stimulus.

1—No reaction.
2—Respiratory change or blink only.
3—General quieting as well as blink and respiratory changes.
4—Stills, brightens, no attempt to locate source.
5—Shifting of eyes to sound, as well as stills and brightens.
6—Alerting and shifting of eyes and head turns to source.
7—Alerting, head turns to stimulus, and search with eyes.

8–Alerting prolonged, head and eyes turn to stimulus repeatedly.

9–Turning and alerting to stimulus presented on both sides on every presentation of stimulus.

RELIABILITY AND VALIDITY: Reliability of .85 is obtainable in two days of training. Reliability can be maintained for 1 to 2 years. Published reports indicate reliabilities of independent testers trained at the same time as ranging from .85 to 1.00. In addition, testers can be trained to a .90 criterion of reliability, and the level of reliability remains at .90 or higher for a prolonged period. The most extensive test-retest stability data were collected. Using an earlier version of the scale, sixty infants (thirty males and thirty females) were tested on the third or fourth day of life and then again at 1 month of age. Reliabilities for each item as well as for each subject were computed. The subjects were Caucasian upper-lower-, middle-, and upper-middle-class infants. All were of normal birth-weight with Apgar scores at 5 minutes well within the normal range of 8 or higher. Infants with any known medical problems were eliminated from the study. The mean age for females at the time of the first test was 3.13 days with a range of 3 to 5 days; for males the mean age was 3.47 days with a range of 2 to 5 days. For the retest at approximately 4 weeks of age, the mean age for females was 27.87 days with a range of 24 to 33 days; for males the mean was 27.79 days with a range of 24 to 34 days.

BIBLIOGRAPHY:

Brazelton, T. B. "Psychophysiologic Reactions in the Neonate: I. The Value of Observation of the Neonate." *Journal of Pediatrics,* 1961, *58,* 508.

Brazelton, T. B. *Neonatal Behavioral Assessment Scale.* Philadelphia, Pennsylvania: Lippincott, 1973.

Brazelton, T. B., Koslowski, B., and Tronick, E. "Neonatal Behavior in a Group of Urbanizing Blacks in Zambia." Paper presented at the Society for Research in Child Development annual meeting. Minneapolis, Minnesota, April 1971.

Brazelton, T. B., and Robey, J. S. "Observations of Neonatal Behavior: The Effect of Perinatal Variables, in Particular that of Maternal Medication." *Journal of the American Academy of Child Psychiatry,* 1965, *4,* 1965.

Brazelton, T. B., Robey, J. S., and Collier, G. A. "Infant Development in the Zinncanteco Indians of Southern Mexico." *Pediatrics,* 1969, *44,* 274.

Freedman, D. G., and Freedman, J. "Behavioral Differences Between Chinese-American and European-American Newborns." *Nature,* 1969, *224,* 1227.

Horowitz, F. D., Self, P. A., Paden, L. Y., Culp, R., Laub, K., Boyd, E., and Mann, M. E. "Newborn and Four-Week Retest on a Normative Population Using the Brazelton Newborn Assessment Procedure." Paper presented at the Society for Research in Child Development annual meeting. Minneapolis, Minnesota, April 1971.

Osofsky, J. D., and Danzger, B. "Relationships Between Neonatal Characteristics and Mother-Infant Interaction." *Developmental Psychology,* 1974, *10,* 124-130.

Prechtl, H., and Beintema, D. *The Neurological Examination of the Full Term Newborn Infant.* Clinics in Developmental Medicine, No. 12. London: Spastics Society with Heinemann Medical, 1964.

Scarr, S., and Williams, M. "The Assessment of Neonatal and Later Status in Low Birth-Weight Infants." Paper presented at the Society for Research in Child Development annual meeting. Minneapolis, Minnesota, April 1971.

OBJECT AND PERSON PERMANENCE SCALE

AUTHOR: Silvia M. Bell

AGE: 6 months to 2 years

VARIABLE: Development of the concept of the object—animate and inanimate

TYPE OF MEASURE: Test

SOURCE FROM WHICH MEASURE MAY BE OBTAINED: Silvia M. Bell, Department of Psychiatry, U.S. Public Health Service Hospital, Baltimore, Maryland 21211.

DESCRIPTION OF MEASURE: This eleven-item measure was developed from Piaget's descriptions of the development of the concept of object permanence. The development of *person* permanence is an original adaptation of the object scale. The scale is administered in a fixed order, starting with items that aim to measure Piaget's stage three (secondary circular reactions) to stage six (the beginning of thought) as well as transitional positions between the major stages. More complete information is available from the author.

As examples, the first three of the eleven test items are given below.

Item and Description	*Scoring*	*Stage*
1. *Reconstruction of the whole from a visible part.* The baby's attention is attracted to the object or person, which is then completely covered by a screen. Subsequently a small part of the object or the person's forehead (but not the eyes) is exposed.	Success entails obtaining the object.	3b
2. *Interrupted prehension.* As the baby is reaching toward the object or person it is completely hidden.	Success entails obtaining the object.	3b-4
3. *Retrieval of an object which is completely hidden.* The baby's attention is attracted toward the person or object, which is then completely hidden.	To pass, the baby must find the hidden object in both places.	4

RELIABILITY AND VALIDITY: None reported.

BIBLIOGRAPHY:

Bell, S. M. "The Development of the Concept of Object as Related to Infant-Mother Attachment." *Child Development*, 1970, *41*, 291-311.
Piaget, J. *The Construction of Reality.* New York: Basic Books, 1954.

PACIFIC INFANTS PERFORMANCE SCALE (PIPS)

AUTHORS: Ian G. Ord and John Schofield

AGE: 4 to 6 years

VARIABLE: Intelligence and school readiness in developing countries

TYPE OF MEASURE: Performance scale

SOURCE FROM WHICH MEASURE MAY BE OBTAINED: Ian G. Ord, Department of Behavioral Science, Darling Downs Institute of Advanced Education, Toowoomba, Queensland, Australia. Cost: $10 (Australian).

DESCRIPTION OF MEASURE: The PIPS was developed in 1967-1968 as a test of general cognitive capacity in Papua, New Guinea, at the request of its Director of Education. It was used initially over the period 1968-1972 as an index of school readiness in the screening of pupils in more remote schools where aspirants far exceeded available places. It was used extensively by indigenous teachers. It is virtually a downward extension of three of the subtests of the New Guinea Performance Scale (Ord, 1970), a test for preliterates aged 8 to adult levels, extensively used in Papua, New Guinea, and with Australian Aboriginies. The PIPS has subsequently been used fairly extensively in New Zealand (Brooks, 1972; Klippel, 1973; St. George, 1974) but also experimentally in Fiji, the Cook Islands (St. George and St. George, 1974), Nepal, and Malaysia. Age norms at six monthly intervals from 4½ to 6½ years have been established for New Zealand and Cook Island children. The test is administered by mime. Cultural differences in performance are minimal. In New Zealand there were no significant differences between Maori and white performances.

The PIPS consists of three subtests: (1) *Block Tapping.* This is a downward extension of a Knox Cube Imitation type test. It uses two sets of instruments: three and four equidistant wooden cubes respectively on wooden bases, which are first tapped in set sequences by the tester and then imitated by the testee. There are twelve items. (2) *Bead Threading.* Not unlike Binet bead threading items, it has large spherical cylindrical and cubical beads. The tester threads bead sequences onto stiff plastic covered wire, knotted at one end. After fixed display times the beads are hidden and the testee is invited to copy the sequences, which are then compared. It contains seven items. (3) *Design Making.* This is a Koh's Block type test, but uses flat red and white tiles representing the sides of the blocks. There are two flat container trays in which the tester makes a pattern, which the testee then copies. It consists of twelve items. Both the Bead Threading and Design Making tests are preceded by sorting tasks to draw the testee's attention to essential differences in the materials.

RELIABILITY AND VALIDITY: For Papua, New Guinea, children a Kuder-Richardson formula 20 reliability figure of .82 was found for two hundred 6-year-olds at school entry level. In New Zealand for some four hundred Maori and white children, using Rulon's split-half method and correcting for length with the Spearman-Brown formula, a reliability of .87 was obtained. For Papua, New Guinea, children, validity of concealed performances at school entry was assessed against the criteria of school teachers' rankings on attainment, at the completion of the first year of schooling. For four separate classes Spearman rank order (*rho*) correlations ranged between .55 to .70. Similarly, in New Zealand rank order correlations were made for one class of new entrant children against teachers' rankings on general ability, giving a figure of .71. As a measure of concurrent validity a Pearson product-moment correlation of .73 for the same class was obtained for the PIPS with the Anton Brenner Developmental Gestalt Test of School Readiness. For the Papua, New Guinea, groups referred to above, mean item validity measured against upper and lower 27 percents of total scores was .68. Item difficulty orders were virtually identical for Papua, New Guinea, and New Zealand children, indicating something of the generalizability of the PIPS.

BIBLIOGRAPHY:

Brooks, I. R. "A Cross-Cultural Study of Cognitive Abilities in Maori and Pakeha Four-Year-Olds." *New Guinea Psychologist,* 1972, *4,* 54-64.

Klippel, M. D. "A Cross-Cultural Study of Two Approaches to the Measure of Intelligence." Unpublished master's thesis. University of Auckland, New Zealand, 1973.

Ord, I. G. *Mental Tests for Pre-literates.* London: Ginn, 1970.

Ord, I. G. "Assessing Cognitive Capacities of Nonliterate New Guinea Adults and Children." In L. J. Cronbach and P. J. D. Drenth (Eds.), *Mental Tests and Cultural Adaptation.* The Hague, Netherlands: Mouton, 1972.

Ord, I. G., and Schofield, J. "An Infant Performance Scale: A Prospective Test for Use at School Entry." *New Guinea Psychologist,* 1969, *1,* 18-20.

Ord, I. G., and Schofield, J. *Manual: Pacific Infants Performance Scale.* Brisbane, Australia: Jacaranda, 1970.

St. George, A. *The Pacific Infants Performance Scale: Some Preliminary and Comparative New Zealand Studies.* Psychology Research Papers. Hamilton, New Zealand: University of Waikato, 1974.

St. George, R., and St. George, A. *A Field Study of Testing in the Cook Islands.* Palmerston North, New Zealand: Massey University, 1974.

St. George, R., and St. George, A. "The Intellectual Assessment of Maori and European School Children." In P. Ramsey (Ed.), *The Family at School.* Sydney, Australia: Pitman, 1975.

PENNSYLVANIA PRESCHOOL INVENTORY (PPI)

AUTHOR: Russell A. Dusewicz

AGE: 3 to 6 years

VARIABLE: Cognitive development

TYPE OF MEASURE: Test

SOURCE FROM WHICH MEASURE MAY BE OBTAINED: Russell A. Dusewicz, West Chester State College, West Chester, Pennsylvania 19380.

DESCRIPTION OF MEASURE: The Pennsylvania Preschool Inventory (PPI) is designed to assess the cognitive development of preschool children from 3 to 6 years of age. It has been designed to be as straightforward and efficient as possible in order to minimize the difficulties usually faced in using standardized tests with young children. To administer the PPI one needs no technical knowledge of testing, since all the information needed is included in the manual. The form of the PPI that accompanies the manual is presently a research version consisting of sixty-one items of various types. They are divided into the following categories: passive vocabulary (fifteen items), complimentary relationships (eleven items), noncomplimentary relationships (ten items), number concepts (seven items), verbal analogies (eleven items), and awareness of self (seven items). In its present form the PPI can serve as a rapid but reliable means of evaluating the relative cognitive readiness of preschool children. The test requires about 15 minutes to administer, and the answer sheets are easily scored by hand.

Below are two sample items and two items from the test.

a. "Here is a picture of a toothbrush (point). Look at all these other pictures (point to other four pictures). Which one of these do we use with a toothbrush?"
b. "Here is a shoe and a slipper (point). They are like each other because we wear them on our feet. Show me something else like a shoe and slipper."
45. "We cry when we're sad, we laugh when we're _____."
46. "We drive in a car, we sail in a _____."

RELIABILITY AND VALIDITY: A Kuder-Richardson formula 20 reliability of .93 was obtained for a sample of eighty-five children tested from area nursery schools. A validity study on a separate sample of sixty-eight children yielded correlations with the Stanford-Binet of .90, with the Peabody Picture Vocabulary Test of .91, and with the Slosson Intelligence Test of .86.

BIBLIOGRAPHY:

Dusewicz, R. A. *The Pennsylvania Preschool Inventory Testing Manual.* Harrisburg, Pennsylvania: State Department of Education, 1973.
Dusewicz, R. A. "A Preschool Inventory of Cognitive Functioning." Report based on paper presented at American Research Association annual meeting. Washington, D.C., 1975.

PICTURE WORD GAME: A NONVERBAL TEST OF THE ABILITY TO USE LANGUAGE-RELATED SYMBOLS (PWG)

AUTHORS: Milton Budoff, Louise Corman, and Elisha Babad

AGE: Grades 1 to 4

VARIABLE: Training-based assessment of "g" intelligence

TYPE OF MEASURE: Test

SOURCE FROM WHICH MEASURE MAY BE OBTAINED: Research Institute for Educational Problems, 29 Ware Street, Cambridge, Massachusetts 02138. Cost: Sample set consisting of one test and training booklet, training instructions, and report of research, $1.00; package of ten training booklets, $2.50; package of ten test booklets, $3.50.

DESCRIPTION OF MEASURE: The Picture Word Game (PWG) is a completely revised version of the Semantic Test of Intelligence developed by Rulon and Schweiker (1953). The child learns geometric symbols representing pictorially presented meanings, including nouns, verbs, and quantities, for example, △ = woman; ◠ = dog; + = standing; and ⌒ = running. The student "reads" the sequence of geometric forms and chooses which picture best represents the meaning of the geometric forms composing the sentence. Conversely, a picture may be presented and the child must "read" the correct sequence of symbols, for example, boy pulling dog. Test items are presented in both formats after a group or individual training session in which the student learns the symbol-picture combinations. No memory is required because the child works with a key, which includes all the symbol-picture combinations. The task aims at examining the young child's capability to use the language-type format without recourse to words, a skill in which the low school-achieving poor and/or minority group child is often deficient. The untimed power test consists of thirty-seven "sentences"; one one-symbol, seven two-symbol, nine three-symbol, nine four-symbol, and eleven five-symbol sentences. Vocabulary comprises sixteen symbols: five nouns (cat, dog, woman, boy, horse); five intransitive verbs (sit, lie down, walk, stand, run); three transitive verbs (pull, chase, carry); and three numbers (two, three, and four). The training session is conducted before the administration of the test. A training booklet, which teaches ten of the nouns and verbs appearing in the test, is used in conjunction with slides. Six symbols are used in the test that are not taught to ascertain the child's understanding of the task and his ability to apply the format to novel symbols. Half of the items require translation from picture to symbol; the remainder from symbol to picture. Posttraining score indicates competence with nonverbal materials structured in sentence formats.

RELIABILITY AND VALIDITY: The original form of the PWG, composed of sixty items, was administered to 205 students distributed equally, up to the fifth grade, from a low-income urban school district. The test showed a high degree of internal consistency reflected in a Kuder-Richardson formula 20 reliability coefficient of .95. Difficulty levels and discrimination indices were obtained for each item. The revised test of thirty-seven items was composed of items that met these three criteria: (1) The difficulty level of test items for the total sample was evenly distributed throughout the test (approximately equal numbers of easy and moderate-to-hard items were retained); (2) to the extent it was possible, each item selected showed a gradual increase in difficulty from grades 1 to 5; and (3) the discrimination index of each item was not less than .25 for the total sample. The sample ($N = 90$) for the revised version of the test was drawn from the same community as the subjects included in the pilot testing. Subjects were five (grades 1 through 5) classes, twenty-five children per grade. Kuder-Richardson formula 20 reliability coefficient of .93 reflected a high degree of internal consistency. Mean item difficulties revealed were as follows: (1) Items requiring translation from symbol to picture were significantly harder than items that required translation from picture to symbol ($F = 63.64$, 1/85 df, $p < .001$); (2) the difficulty of items increased linearly as the number of symbols increased from two to five ($F = 70.27$, 3/255 df, $p < .01$); and (3) the two most difficult sets of items on the test were items employing the concept of numbers that had not been taught, and all of them had three, four, or five symbols (mean percent correct = 50 to 60 percent). Despite the effectiveness of these procedures, however, mean total scores (in terms of percent correct for each grade) revealed a probable ceiling effect for children beyond the third grade whose average score exceeded 30 percent correct. Scores on the PWG were correlated with two subtests of the Stanford achievement test to provide evidence of the PWG as a language measure. While these coefficients are low in terms of concurrent validity (.39), they are similar in magnitude to the validity coefficient obtained by Rulon and Schweiker (1953).

BIBLIOGRAPHY:

Budoff, M. "Learning Potential: A Supplementary Procedure for Assessing the Ability to Reason." *Seminars in Psychiatry,* 1969, *1,* 278-290.
Corman, L., and Budoff, M. *The Picture Word Game: A Nonverbal Test of the Ability to Use Language-Related Symbols.* RIEP print 77. Cambridge, Massachusetts: Research Institute for Educational Problems, 1974.
Rulon, P., and Schweiker, R. *Validation of a Nonverbal Test of Military Trainability.* Final report. Washington, D.C.: Department of the Army, June 1953.

PIKUNAS GRAPHOSCOPIC SCALE (PGS) I

AUTHOR: Justin Pikunas

AGE: 5 to 16 years

VARIABLE: Intelligence and certain personality variables

TYPE OF MEASURE: Psychodiagnostic drawing test

SOURCE FROM WHICH MEASURE MAY BE OBTAINED: Justin Pikunas, Department of Psychology, University of Detroit, 4001 West McNichols Road, Detroit, Michigan 48221.

DESCRIPTION OF MEASURE: The PGS I consists of a set of ten framed plates arranged on a heavy flexible bond sheet measuring 18 X 14 inches, each space except the tenth containing achromatic or chromatic perceptual cues. The first plate presents fairly structured stimuli intended to evoke drawing of several basic content categories, that is, inanimate nature, plant, animal, and human. It is also intended to evoke a pattern for drawing the subsequent plates. The partially begun form and color can be completed, colored, and labeled by the subject. Up to the age of 3 years, however, most children accept the drawing as satisfactory in form and color if only to a small extent. This fairly structured space is counterbalanced by the last plate, which is blank. Both plates measure 5 X 5½ inches. The remaining plates (2 through 9), each measuring approximately $3\frac{5}{8} \times 3\frac{1}{4}$ inches, present semistructured perceptual cues of varying form and color, offering almost unlimited opportunities for drawing any content and thus offering the opportunity for projection of Ss motivational tendencies and needs. Spaces 2 through 5 contain stimuli meant to suggest animate objects, whereas spaces 6 through 9 stimulate inanimate content. Two questions are added, to which the subject draws or writes his responses: (1) "What is the thing you most often draw? Draw it in the empty space on the right." (2) "What else would you like to draw?"

RELIABILITY AND VALIDITY: Pikunas and Carberry (1961) standardized the PGS content for Detroit area children (N = 350) between the ages of 5 and 15. The group as a whole tended most frequently to draw human individuals, manufactured objects, animals, and houses. The content changed noticeably from age to age, and the percentage differences were significant at the .01 level. The findings by Demko (1957) for ages 9 to 11 are consistent with this investigation. In Kuntz's (1962) investigation of intelligence and adjustment of mental retardates (N = 57), it was found that PGS I correlates with the Stanford-Binet .78, while its adjustment scores correlated .69 with a pupil adjustment inventory. This study concluded that the PGS is a valid measure of intellectual capacity and adjustment of lower level intelligence, excepting mongoloid children. Gardecki (1964) used PGS I to determine the relationship between academic ability and self-concepts of 141 second-grade children. The PGS revealed significantly more favorable perception of themselves than do those children who are poor readers, as expressed in such drawing variables as opposite sex identification, sketchy lines, and incompleteness. Morrisette (1967), using three groups (bright, normal, and subnormal) of preadolescent girls (N = 90), found that the PGS I served effectively as a differential assessment tool. A very broad range of content choice is a mark of intellectual superiority. The groups differed significantly on the choice of several categories of content. With increasing IQs girls produced more original responses, as well as more human responses.

BIBLIOGRAPHY:

Bushey, J. T. "The Relation Between Intelligence as Shown on the PGS and School Success of Children Between the Ages of 7 and 9." Unpublished master's thesis. University of Detroit, Michigan, 1955.

Demko, D. "The Relation Between Adjustment as Shown on the PGS and Teacher's Ratings of Children Between the Ages of 10 and 12." Unpublished master's thesis. University of Detroit, Michigan, 1957.

Gardecki, B. "The Self-Concept of Good and Poor Readers." Unpublished master's thesis. University of Detroit, Michigan, 1964.

Golen, M. "A Comparison of WISC and the PGS in Prediction of School Achievement." Unpublished master's thesis. University of Detroit, Michigan, 1965.

Kuntz, P. "The Pikunas Graphoscopic Scale as a Measure of Intelligence and Adjustment in the Testing of Mental Retardates." Unpublished master's thesis. University of Detroit, Michigan, 1962.

Morrisette, P. "The Use of Categories by Bright, Normal, and Subnormal Preadolescent Girls on the Pikunas Graphoscopic Scale and the Stephens' Categorization Tasks." Unpublished doctoral dissertation. University of Oklahoma, Norman, 1967.

Neville, H. A. "A Diagnostic Evaluation of the PGS II as Compared to the MMPI." Unpublished master's thesis. University of Detroit, Michigan, 1964.

Pikunas, J. *Manual for the Graphoscopic Scale (PGS)*. Detroit, Michigan: University of
    Detroit, 1975.
Pikunas, J., and Carberry, H. "Standardization of the Graphoscopic Scale: The Content
    of Children's Drawings." *Journal of Clinical Psychology*, 1961, *17*, 297-301.

PRE KINDERGARTEN SCALE

AUTHOR: Timothy M. Flynn

AGE: 3 to 5 years

VARIABLE: Cognitive skills, self-control, relationship with achievement model, dependency

TYPE OF MEASURE: Observer rating scale

SOURCE FROM WHICH MEASURE MAY BE OBTAINED: Timothy M. Flynn, Department of Child and Family, Southern Illinois University, Carbondale, Illinois 62901.

DESCRIPTION OF MEASURE: Since the preschool teacher has the opportunity to observe the child in a variety of situations over an extended period of time, an approach requiring only the most elementary act of judgment between the teacher's recall of these observations and recording the behavior was needed. The multiple-choice format used by the Prekindergarten Scale accomplishes this by defining the possible behaviors as unambiguously as possible. Thus the teacher does not have to use her own personal referents to describe the child being rated, as she merely selects the behavior that best describes the child's usual mode of behavior in the presented situation. The four responses for each of the twenty-five items are weighted 1 to 4.

As examples, one item from each of the five sections of the scale are given below.

Personal skills
1. When communicating with his teacher, this child:
    1. nearly always expresses a complete thought.
    2. usually expresses a complete thought.
    3. uses incomplete thoughts.
    4. uses gestures only.
    5. Have not observed.

Relationships with Teacher
7. When emotionally or physically upset, this child:
    1. turns to his teacher for comfort and reassurance.
    2. accepts and responds to unsolicited comfort and reassurances from the teacher.
    3. passively accepts unsolicited comfort and reassurance.
    4. resists teacher's attempts at comfort and reassurance.
    5. Have not observed.

Peer Relations

11. When this child is engaged in group activity such as singing, class games, etc., he can usually be observed:
    1. leading the group activity.
    2. actively following the group.
    3. following the group only after some urging.
    4. observing the group without actively participating.
    5. Have not observed.

Personal Behavior

16. When this child spills something, he:
    1. nearly always begins cleaning up without prompting.
    2. occasionally requires prompting to begin cleaning up.
    3. begins cleaning up only after prompting.
    4. does not attempt to clean up even after prompting.
    5. Have not observed.

Cognitive Skills

25. When this child is given instructions on how to perform a task, he has:
    1. little difficulty in following the instructions.
    2. some difficulty, but he does not require assistance.
    3. difficulty, in that he requires some assistance from others to finish the task.
    4. such difficulty that he cannot complete the task even with assistance.
    5. Have not observed.

RELIABILITY AND VALIDITY: Factor analysis was performed on the ratings of 144 3- and 4-year-old children to obtain the following four factors: cognitive skills, self-control, relationship with achievement model, and dependency (Flynn, 1971). Factor coefficients were obtained from the principal component (orthogonal analysis), using three separate ratings by the child's teacher and two teacher aides. The twenty-five sets of factor coefficients (one for each factor) were applied to another sample consisting of 153 migrant children who had been rated by their teachers and two teacher aides. Each child received four factor scores from each of the three raters for a total of twelve factor scores. The three sets of factor scores for each child made it possible to adapt Campbell and Fiske's (1959) convergent-discriminant validation procedure to validate the four factors. Comparing the correlations between the four factor scores of three different observers provided a method of evaluating both the divergent and convergent validity of the four traits. The matrix constructed demonstrated that the correlations between two different observers (methods) measuring the same trait were higher than the correlations between the unlike traits measured tby the same or different observers. A comparison between the twelve validity coefficients (average = .43 with the average of .11 for the thirty-six coefficients not on the validity diagonal) provides support for the overall discriminant validity of the four traits (Flynn, 1971).

BIBLIOGRAPHY:

Campbell, D., and Fiske, D. "Convergent and Discriminant Validation by the Multi-trait-Multi-method Matrix." *Psychological Bulletin,* 1959, *56,* 81-105.

Flynn, T. M. "Development of a Multiple Choice Behavioral Observation Scale." Paper presented at Annual Meeting of American Educational Research Association. Minneapolis, Minnesota, March 1970.

Flynn, T. M. "The Effect of a Part-time Special Education Program on the Adjustment of EMR Students." *Exceptional Children,* 1970, *36,* 680-681.

Flynn, T. M. *Convergent-Discriminant Validation of Behavioral Ratings.* Abstracts of AERA 1971 National Convention. Washington, D.C.: American Educational Research Association, 1971.

Flynn, T. M., and Curtis, H. A. "Traits Related to Achievement Motivation in Migrant Children." Migrant Project Report. Florida State University, Tallahassee, 1970.

PRESCHOOL RATING SCALE (PRS)

AUTHORS: William F. Barker, Louise Sandler, Agnes Bornemann, and Gail Knight

AGE: 2½ to 6½ years

VARIABLE: Personal-social development

TYPE OF MEASURE: Rating scale (Guttman)

SOURCE FROM WHICH MEASURE MAY BE OBTAINED: William F. Barker, Center for Preschool Services, Room 469, Franklin Institute Research Laboratories, Philadelphia, Pennsylvania 19103. No cost at this time.

DESCRIPTION OF MEASURE: The Preschool Rating Scale (PRS) consists of twenty four- and five-choice Guttman scaled items that purport to assess a preschool child's personal-social development. The ratings in five areas (coordination, verbal expression, auditory understanding, orientation, and social relations) are provided by the day-care worker based upon her/his perceptions derived from at least one month of continuous contact with the child. The item choices are behaviorally specific and avoid the use of technical jargon as much as possible. Based upon the experience of at least fifty child-care workers, it seems clear that (1) the scale is easy to use, (2) useful information is provided to both the researcher and the day-care worker, and (3) the day-care worker is forced to consider each child in useful ways that she/he may not have done in the past.

Norms are available for 1,040 children in six 6-month age groups from 36 to 71 months of age. The norms were developed from both urban and suburban advantaged and disadvantaged males and females. Results from extensive statistical analysis indicate that one set of norms is appropriate for all groups for each age group. Although the data are cross-sectional in nature, the norm scores indicate a developmental trend in that they increase as older age groups are examined.

The PRS was developed as an evaluation instrument to assess the personal-social development of preschool children with problems over time. Experience gained over the past two years would seem to indicate that it can be used (1) for screening, (2) for programs evaluation, (3) to act as a guide to the day-care worker in identifying specific areas of development that may need remediation, (4) to alert day-care workers to areas of development they should be aware of, and (5) to assess day-care workers' effectiveness.

As examples, three items from the twenty on the scale are given below. In the first area, *coordination*, the two items are gross motor and fine motor; in *verbal expression* the three items are vocabulary, grammar, and sharing ideas and experiences; in *auditory understanding* the six items are vocabulary, individual instructions (shown), group discussions, memory, story listening, and rhythm; in *orientation* the five items are relationships, environment, organization, occupation (shown), and adaptability; and in *social relations* the four items are individual approach to group, group approach to individual (shown), cooperation, and egocentricity. The day-care worker chooses one response for each item.

Individual Instructions

1. Cannot follow directions, confused even if gestures are used.
2. Follows simple instructions but often needs special help and sometimes gestures.
3. Usually remembers and follows 3-stage directions.
4. Exceptionally skillful in retaining and following complex directions and is one of the first in class to do so.

Occupation

1. Activities must always be initiated by others (teacher, peers).
2. Has difficulty finding something to do for himself and continuing without adult help.
3. Sometimes organizes or suggests activities for himself.
4. Usually finds acceptable activities for self and other.

Group Approach to Individual

1. Child is avoided by others.
2. Child is tolerated by others.
3. Child is sought out, primarily for reasons other than friendship (i.e., fear of his aggression).
4. Child is sought out, primarily because he is liked.

RELIABILITY AND VALIDITY: Based upon the ratings of 125 children by two groups of raters (pairs of raters rated fifteen to twenty children each independently), the average of interrater correlation coefficient estimates was .74. Further work is in progress to improve the reliability of the scale. Some item choices are being reworded, and more detailed and specific rating procedure directions are being developed. Several types of judgmental validity (construct, user, and face) have been obtained. The construct validity was obtained via comparison between the item choices and the original scale outline. The user validity was obtained via discussions with at least fifty day-care workers who used the scale. Finally, the face validity was obtained via discussions with users as well as with other kinds of day-care, mental health, and psychometric professionals.

More sophisticated statistical procedures have been used to indicate the predictive and inferential validity. The predictive validity was determined through the use of a discriminant analysis. This analysis indicates that the PTS can classify children as typical or nontypical with a high degree of accuracy. Inferential validity is indicated by noting that the mean score increases as older age groups are examined. This result is consistent with the hypothesis that the PTS is a developmental scale. Information is now being collected that will allow the determination of congruent, concurrent, and factorial validity of the scale.

BIBLIOGRAPHY:

Barker, W. F., Sandler, L., Bornemann, A., and Knight, G. "The Preschool Rating Scale." Paper presented at annual meeting of National Council for Measurement in Education. Washington, D.C., April 1975.

PRIMARY GRADE RETARDED-TRAINABLE CHILDREN'S REFERRAL AND BEHAVIOR RATING FORM

AUTHORS: Rolf A. Peterson, Sally Gorski, and Rhoda L. Kreisman

AGE: 5 to 12 years (retarded); 2 to 4 years (normal screening)

VARIABLE: Developmental level and behavior problems

TYPE OF MEASURE: Rating scale and checklist

SOURCE FROM WHICH MEASURE MAY BE OBTAINED: Rolf A. Peterson, Department of Psychology, University of Illinois at Chicago Circle, Box 4348, Chicago, Illinois 60680.

DESCRIPTION OF MEASURE: The Primary Grade Retarded-Trainable Children's Referral and Behavior Rating Form (PGRC Referral and Behavior Rating Form) consists of fifteen developmental subscales (Walking, Stairs-Up, Stairs-Down, Toilet Training—Soiling, Toilet Training—Setting, General Toilet Behavior—Independence, General Toilet Behavior—Dressing, General Toilet Behavior—Washing, Eating—Motor, Drinking, General Language Use, Language-Response Behavior, Commands, Dressing, and Socialization) and forty-seven behavior problem items. Each developmental subscale contains several items arranged in developmental order. The referrer selects the developmental level (item) that best describes the child's present functioning level. Besides direct communication of the present developmental level on each of the fifteen skills, a set of estimate norms is provided. Thus the approximate developmental age can be obtained for each of the skills. No overall developmental score is statistically derived, but informal estimates of an overall social developmental level and verbal developmental level have been successfully used. An example of the developmental scales follows:

Stairs-Up

_____ 1. Crawls upstairs.
_____ 2. Walks upstairs with assistance of an individual taking one step at a time.
_____ 3. Walks upstairs unassisted one step at a time.
_____ 4. Walks upstairs with assistance one step per tread.
_____ 5. Walks upstairs unassisted one step per tread.

The forty-seven behavior problem items were selected on the basis of educational and clinical relevance. The items were rationally grouped into the subcategories of Eating Behaviors, Communication Behaviors, Response to Commands, Group Activity Behaviors, Individual Task Behaviors, and Personal-Social Behaviors. No evidence is available that these groups function as factors, and thus far the forty-seven items have been considered as independent problem behaviors. Weighted scores, based on teacher ratings of importance of cause for referral, can be calculated. The items within the Group Activity Behaviors category provide an example:

Group Activity Behaviors

_____ Begins an independent project during group activity but does not disturb others' participation.

_____ Ignores group activities but sits quietly.

_____ Loses interest in group activities after 4-5 minutes.

_____ Wanders off during group activities.

_____ Interrupts group activity (e.g., refuses to wait his turn, disturbs other children, and so forth).

RELIABILITY AND VALIDITY: A series of mock-referral studies were run to determine if the form indicated more developmental and behavioral problems for referred than nonreferred children. In general, the scores obtained indicated specific problems and discriminated between groups, on both the developmental scales and behavior checklist. Based on clinical use, the form also appears to provide important diagnostic and planning information.

Several estimates of reliability have been obtained. When two ward personnel, both highly familiar with the child, were used as raters, agreements on exact developmental level and/or behavior problems ranged from 67 percent to 93 percent. Teacher ratings were obtained to determine interrater agreement and six-week test-retest reliability. The correlation coefficients overwhelmingly fell in the .80 and above range. Exact agreement on only those behavior problem items checked by either or both raters is low, that is, 52 percent for test-retest and 38 percent for interrater. These low percent agreement scores appear to be due to the ambiguous instructions provided to the raters.

BIBLIOGRAPHY:

Barker, R., and Peterson, R. A. "The Use of a Referral and Behavior Rating Scale in an Educational Setting." _Education and Training of the Mentally Retarded_ (in press).

Peterson, R. A. "Rater Reliabilities on the Primary Grade Retarded-Trainable Children's Referral and Behavior Rating Form: An Extended Report." Unpublished report. University of Illinois at Chicago Circle, 1975.

Peterson, R. A., Gorski, S., and Kreisman, R. "A Primary Grade Retarded-Trainable Children's Referral and Behavior Rating Form—Expectation and Referral Data: An Extended Report." Unpublished report. University of Illinois at Chicago Circle, 1973.

Peterson, R. A., Gorski, S., and Kreisman, R. "A Referral and Rating Form for Trainable Children." _Exceptional Children,_ 1973, _39,_ 36.

PROFILE TEST

AUTHOR: Alex F. Kalverboer

AGE: Approximately 4 to 10 years

VARIABLE: Spatial-constructive development

TYPE OF MEASURE: Drawing test

SOURCE FROM WHICH MEASURE MAY BE OBTAINED: A. F. Kalverboer, Experimental Clinical Psychology Unit, Department of Clinical Psychology, University Hospital, Groningen, Netherlands; or, Swetz-Zeitlinger Publishers, Keizersgracht 487, Amsterdam, Netherlands.

DESCRIPTION OF MEASURE: The test requires the completion of a face profile, the outline of which is given. Instructions and scoring system have been standardized. A score is obtained by summing up the number of correctly added details. Scores are interpreted in terms of Piaget's theory. Preliminary norms have been established for age groups from 4 to 12 years, for lower and middle/higher socioeconomic classes separately. The test seems to be a promising tool in research programs and screening procedures focusing on problems of school readiness or developmental lags in children in the age range from 4 to 8.

RELIABILITY AND VALIDITY: The test has been administered to approximately 1,100 children, aged 3 to 12 years. It discriminates between children of various ages and preschool children who are not yet ready for school and controls (Kalverboer and Sanders-Allersma, 1973). The scoring system can be reliably used (Spearman-Brown correlation is .95 between two independent scorers on four hundred profiles). The internal consistency of the sum scores ranges from .62 to .82, depending on the age group.

BIBLIOGRAPHY:

Kalverboer, A. F., LeCoultre, R., and Casaer, P. "Implications of Congenital Ophthalmoplegia for the Development of Visuo-Motor Functions (Illustrated by a Case with the Moebius Syndrome)." *Developmental Medicine and Child Neurology,* 1970, *12,* 542-654.

Kalverboer, A. F., and Sanders-Allersma, H. J. "A Profile-Test for Spatial-Construction Development." In A. P. Cassee, P. E. Boecke, and J. T. Barendregt (Eds.), *Clinical Psychology in Netherlands.* Vol. 2. Deventer, Netherlands: J. T. Van Loghum Slaterus, 1973.

PROGNOSTIC TEST FOR EARLY CHILDHOOD (PTEC)

AUTHOR: Jerry B. Ayers

AGE: 60 to 72 months

VARIABLE: School readiness

TYPE OF MEASURE: Test

SOURCE FROM WHICH MEASURE MAY BE OBTAINED: Jerry B. Ayers, College of Education, Tennessee Technological University, Cookeville, Tennessee 38501.

DESCRIPTION OF MEASURE: The materials used to administer the PTEC are a manual, reusable test booklet, and separate answer sheets. The test can be administered by a classroom teacher in less than 10 minutes. During the administration, the examinee is either asked to perform in some manner or asked a simple objective question. His score is the sum of the acceptable responses. The instrument has also been administered to children as young as 43 months with some degree of success. It has been used on a limited basis in measuring children's understandings of materials from the American Association for the Advancement of Science program *Science: A Process Approach* (Ayers, 1969).

As examples, the first seven of the thirty-five items of the PTEC are given below, with scoring criteria.

1. "Which direction is up?" Child should point up or in some other manner indicate which direction is up.
2. "Wave your right hand." Child must wave his right hand or indicate which is his right hand.
3. "What month is this?" Child must respond with the correct name of the month.
4. "Two sounds I am going to say are of the same kind and one is different from the others. Which one is different? Meow-meow, Quack-quack, Tick-tock." Child must respond with "Tick-tock" or the last sound. (Tick-tock is different from the others in two ways. The first two sounds are generally associated with animals and both are repeated sound words, while the third sound, "Tick-tock," is a sound associated with a clock; also it is composed of two different words.)
5. "Show me the triangle." Child must point to the triangle.
6. Examiner points to the ellipse. "What is this shape called?" Child must respond with the word "ellipse." No other response is considered acceptable.
7. Examiner points to the yellow rectangle. "What color is this?" Child must respond with the word "yellow."

RELIABILITY AND VALIDITY: The instrument was administered to a sample of eighty-two children as they entered the first grade and again at the end of the year (total lapsed time of nine months). The Kuder-Richardson formula 20 reliability was .80. Correlation of total score from the PTEC with scores from the Metropolitan Readiness Test was .75 (administered at the time the children entered first grade). Correlations of the PTEC with scores from the Metropolitan Achievement Test were as follows: Word Knowledge, .76; Word Discrimination, .65; Reading, .34; and Arithmetic,

.79. Correlation of the fall administration of the PTEC with the spring administration was .72, indicating significant cross-year reliability.

BIBLIOGRAPHY:

Ayers, J. B. "Evaluation of the Use of Science: A Process Approach with Preschool-Age Children." *Science Education,* 1969, *53,* 329-334.

Ayers, J. B., and Johnson, C. E. "A Prognostic Test for Early Childhood." *Educational and Psychological Measurement,* 1970, *30,* 983-987.

PURDUE CONSERVATION TEST

AUTHOR: Grayson H. Wheatley

AGE: 5 to 8 years

VARIABLE: Ability to conserve

TYPE OF MEASURE: Group film test

SOURCE FROM WHICH MEASURE MAY BE OBTAINED: Grayson H. Wheatley, Mathematical Science Building, Purdue University, West Lafayette, Indiana 47907. Cost: approximately $90.00.

DESCRIPTION OF MEASURE: This instrument is a 30-minute group-administered 16 mm. film test (in color) of the Piagetian conservations. Of the twenty-three conservation items, there are three of number, three of length, five of quantity, two of mass, four of area, one of weight, and five of volume. All directions are contained on the film, and children respond on picture answer sheets. A typical item shows liquid being poured from one container to another after initial equality has been established. The child must mark a picture symbol to indicate which container has more "juice." The test is useful to teachers in obtaining a measure of readiness for first-grade mathematics and to researchers investigating cognitive development. It has been used to assess changes in a compensatory program.

RELIABILITY AND VALIDITY: The correlation with an individually administered test using concrete objects was .86, and the test-retest correlation, .83. Tests with similar content had a predictive correlation of .85. The test has an internal consistency of .91.

BIBLIOGRAPHY:

Wheatley, G. "The Development of a Group Film Test of Certain Piagetian Conservations." Paper presented at annual meeting of American Educational Research Association. Chicago, Illinois, 1972.

Wheatley, G. "Socioeconomic Status and Mode of Presentation as Factors in Children's Concept Attainment." *Journal of Experimental Education,* 1975, *43,* 6-14.

Wheatley, G. "A Motion Picture Test of Piagetian Concepts." *Psychology in the Schools,* 1975, *12,* 21-25.

RAPID DEVELOPMENTAL SCREENING CHECKLIST

AUTHORS: Committee on Children with Handicaps, American Academy of Pediatrics, District II, Margaret J. Giannini, Chairman

AGE: 1 month to 5 years

VARIABLE: Developmental lags

TYPE OF MEASURE: Checklist

SOURCE FROM WHICH MEASURE MAY BE OBTAINED: Margaret Giannini, Mental Retardation Institute, 1249 Fifth Avenue, New York, New York 10029.

DESCRIPTION OF MEASURE: This forty-item checklist is a compilation of developmental landmarks matched against the age of the child. These are in easily scored question form and may be checked "Yes" or "No" by a physician or his aide, by direct observation. The selection of items by the designing committee was guided by the following criteria: (1) The item should be simple and the scoring clear, without additional instruction. (2) The item should be familiar to those who work with children. (3) The age at which an item appears is one that can be passed by the vast majority of the normal population, and one that if failed constitutes a probable developmental lag. This was established by consensus of the committee. (4) The items should contain an appropriate mixture of gross motor, fine motor, adaptive, verbal, and social landmarks. (5) It should not be ambiguous, complex, too technical, or too time-consuming. Scoring should not require too much equipment or special training. "No" responses at the appropriate age may constitute a signal indicating a possible developmental lag. If there is a substantial deviation from these values, the child should be evaluated more carefully, considering the wide variability of developmental landmarks. Adjustment for prematurity, prior to 2 years, is made by subtracting the time of prematurity from the age of the child. For example, a 2-month-old infant who was 1 month premature should be evaluated as a 1-month-old infant.

As examples, ten of the forty items of the checklist are given below.

1 month—Can he raise his head from the surface while in the prone position?
3 months—Does he follow a moving object?
5 months—Can he reach for and hold objects?
7 months—Can he transfer an object from one hand to another?
10 months—Can he pull himself up at the side of his crib or playpen?

12 months—Can he wave bye-bye? Can he walk with one hand held? Does he have a two-word vocabulary?

18 months—Can he build a tower of three blocks? Does he say six words?

2½ years—Can he jump lifting both feet off the ground? Can he build a tower of six blocks? Can he point to parts of his body on command?

4 years—Can he stand on one foot? Can he copy a cross?

5 years—Can he follow three commands? Can he copy a square? Can he skip?

RELIABILITY AND VALIDITY: Items were chosen by clinical consensus of the fifteen authors. It is meant as a screening instrument and it has been found effective in clinical application.

BIBLIOGRAPHY:

Giannini, M. J., and Chusid, E. "Rapid Developmental Screening Checklist: A One-Year Pilot Project." Report to the Mental Retardation Institute, New York Medical College. Valhalla, New York, 1972.

REVISED GESELL PRESCHOOL EXAMINATION

AUTHORS: Louise B. Ames, Clyde Gillespie, Jackie Michaels, and Richard N. Walker

AGE: 2½ to 6 years

VARIABLE: Developmental abilities (motor, adaptive, language, personal-social)

TYPE OF MEASURE: Age scales

SOURCE FROM WHICH MEASURE MAY BE OBTAINED: Revision is still in preparation; for earlier version see Gesell (1940).

DESCRIPTION OF MEASURE: This updating of the Gesell Preschool Examination includes revision of item content, administration methods, norms, and method of scoring. The format of an age scale will be obtained, with three to six items to be scored pass-fail in the four areas (motor, adaptive, language, personal-social) at each half-yearly age level. But total scores for the four areas and for the full battery will be derived via standard scores. In order to preserve some of the clinical richness of the examination, qualitative descriptions of developmental trends on a number of the test items will supplement the pass-fail scoring.

RELIABILITY AND VALIDITY: The Revised Examination has been administered to 640 children: forty boys and forty girls at each of eight age levels. Subjects were selected to fill a schedule stratified for socioeconomic level by father's occupation. Nearly all were tested within a month of their yearly or half-yearly birthday. The sample is entirely a New England one and is slightly underrepresented for black children (about 8 percent); it is anticipated that later editions may call for slight adjustment of norms. Reliability: Scorer agreement is a focus of concern as scoring standards are being developed; extent of agreement will be reported. Test-retest reliability over short (one-month) intervals will be determined for samples of children at several ages. Validity: As in all age scales, evidence will be presented that mean scores and percentage-passing statistics change substantially with age. More importantly, a large proportion (over half) of the normative subjects are being located and retested as they reach 8 years of age. The follow-up data will play a small role in initial item selection (though that has already been principally done on the basis of many years of experience with the items, as well as of the curves of percentage passing by age); it will mainly serve to determine the predictability of the early tests.

BIBLIOGRAPHY:

Gesell, A. L., Halverson, H. M., Thompson, H., Ilg, F. L., Castner, B. M., Ames, L. B., and Amatruda, C. S. *The First Five Years of Life: A Guide to the Study Of the Preschool Child.* New York: Harper & Row, 1940.

Prepared by Richard N. Walker

RING AND CUBE TEST

AUTHOR: Reuven Kohen-Raz

AGE: 5 to 10 months

VARIABLE: Bimanual coordination and skill in reaching

TYPE OF MEASURE: Test

SOURCE FROM WHICH MEASURE MAY BE OBTAINED: See Kohen-Raz (1966).

DESCRIPTION OF MEASURE: The principal innovations of this instrument, when compared with traditional infant tests requiring manipulation and grasping of objects, are as follows: (1) The time of performance is limited to a maximum of 240 seconds, or 4 minutes; and (2) the individual performance is objectively measured by recording manually characteristic behavior categories, using a specially designed coding system. Two scores are computed. The Latency Score measures the time elapsing between the presentation of the object and the first interaction by *S*. It is computed from the Raw Latency Score, which is the sum of five latency subscores, each represented by the ordinal number of the 15-second interval, during which the following five responses occurred: (1) first touch of object by left hand, (2) first touch of object by right hand, (3) first grasp of object by left hand, (4) first grasp of object by right hand, and (5) first simultaneous grasp by both hands. The second score, the Activity Score, is the sum of points given to types of activities according to the following system of credits and weights: (1) One point is credited for each interval during which one hand is active in grasping the object. Points are given separately for each hand. (2) In a similar way, half a point is given for each interval for the touch activities. This reduction of weight is based on the assumption that touching is a more primitive response than grasping. (3) One additional point is scored for each interval during which both hands are simultaneously active in grasping. No such score is given for simultaneous touch. (4) One point is given for each single incidence of six response categories.

RELIABILITY AND VALIDITY: The reliability of the Activity Score was tested by split-half rank correlation between part-Activity Scores computed for the two halves of the test, each containing an equal number of 15-second intervals. In order to obtain the most conservative measure of reliability, chronological age was kept constant, and Ss of the institutionalized population, who showed the lowest performance, were excluded, which assumedly ensured an additional partial control of "mental age." Reliability coefficients are satisfactory and would be still higher if computed for the total sample, combining age and environment. At age 6 months, for the Ring Test ($N = 22$) rho = .87, and for the Cube Test ($N = 15$) rho = .94; at age 8 months, for the Ring Test ($N = 13$) rho = .88, and for the Cube Test ($N = 13$) rho = .71. All coefficients are significant at the .01 level.

There is a consistent progression by age in Activity and Latency Scores on both Ring and Cube Tests and in three environmental groups: home, kibbutz, and institution. Combining the three environmental groups, age differences are significant between ages 5 and 6 months for the Ring Test, between ages 6 and 8 months for both Ring and Cube Tests, and between ages 8 and 10 months for the Latency Score of the Cube Test only. Keeping environmental groups separated, some of the age differences are still significant in spite of the shrinkage of N.

BIBLIOGRAPHY:

Kohen-Raz, R. "The Ring-Cube Test: A Brief Time Sampling Method for Assessing Primary Development of Coordinated Bilateral Grasp Responses in Infancy." *Perceptual and Motor Skills*, 1966, *23*, 675-688.

Prepared by Orval G. Johnson

RUTGERS DRAWING TEST (FORM B)

AUTHOR: Anna S. Starr

AGE: 6 to 9 years

VARIABLE: Intelligence, perception, motor skill

TYPE OF MEASURE: Drawing test

SOURCE FROM WHICH MEASURE MAY BE OBTAINED: Anna S. Starr, 126 Montgomery Street, Highland Park, New Jersey 08904. Cost: One test, $.06; 500 copies or more, $.05 each; manual, $1.00. Postage and insurance added.

DESCRIPTION OF MEASURE: Form B of the Rutgers Drawing Test is designed as an upward extension of Form A of the test (Johnson and Bommarito, 1971), the Form B designs being more complex. The test consists of sixteen designs, which the child is asked to copy once. There is no time limit. It may be used with an individual or with a small group of children. Each figure is scored on a 3-point scale ranging from 0 to 2. The manual gives examples of scoring for each of the designs drawn by regular class pupils and neurologically impaired pupils. Norms are provided based on 2,074 children aged 5-0 to 9-11. Beginning with age 6-0, 6-1, there are norms for every two-month age interval up to age 9-10, 9-11, including range, median, mode, mean, interquartile range, and drawing score.

RELIABILITY AND VALIDITY: Test-retest reliability of 100 second and third graders tested a week apart was .79. Forty-three retest scores were within a point of the original scores. The test-retest correlation, with a one-week interval, of the scores of 105 7-year-olds was .69. The Rutgers correlated .35 with the Stanford Achievement Test and .38 with the Draw-a-Person Test (N = 100 children aged 7-6 to 8-10). Yudin (1967) tested 110 children aged 4 to 7 with the WISC, Stanford-Binet, and Rutgers Drawing Test. When a drawing quotient was computed, the mean WISC or S-B IQ was greater than the Rutgers Drawing IQ, and the Rutgers and WISC performance scores were most similar. The correlation between Rutgers Drawing IQ and the three WISC scales were .56, .69, and .63. Correlation between S-B IQ and Rutgers Drawing IQ was .70.

BIBLIOGRAPHY:

Balinsky, J. L. "A Configurational Approach to the Prediction of Academic Achievement in First Grade." Unpublished doctoral dissertation. New Brunswick, New Jersey: Rutgers—The State University, 1964.
Denson, T. A., and Michael, W. B. "Rutgers Drawing Test as a Midyear Kindergartner Predictor of End-of-Kindergarten Readiness for First Grade." *Educational and Psychological Measurement,* 1974, *34,* 999-1002.
Dudek, S. Z., Goldberg, J. S., Lester, E. P., and Harris, B. R. "The Validity of Cognitive Perceptual-Motor and Personality Variables for Prediction of Achievement in Grade 1 and Grade 2." *Journal of Clinical Psychology,* 1969, *25,* 165-170.
Dudek, S. Z., Lester, L. P., and Harris, B. R. "Variability on Tests of Cognitive and Perceptual-Motor Development in Kindergarten Children." *Journal of Clinical Psychology,* 1967, *23,* 461-464.
Johnson, O. G., and Bommarito, J. W. *Tests and Measurements in Child Development: A Handbook.* San Francisco: Jossey-Bass, 1971.
Jones, R. W. "Cross-sectional and Longitudinal Views of Visual Reproduction and the Effects of Visual Distraction on Visual Reproduction by Brain-damaged Retardates, Familial Retardates and Normal Children." Unpublished doctoral dissertation. University of Miami, Florida, 1963.
Kaczmarek, H. J. "Rutgers Drawing Test as an Identifier of Learning Difficulties." Unpublished doctoral dissertation. Arizona State University, Tempe, 1975.

Leton, D. A. "A Factor Analysis of Readiness Tests." *Perceptual and Motor Skills,* 1963, *16,* 915-919.

Panther, E. E. "Prediction of First-Grade Reading Achievement." *Elementary School Journal,* 1967, *68,* 44-80.

Starr, A. S. "The Rutgers Drawing Test." *Training School Bulletin,* 1952, *49,* 45-64.

Starr, A. S. *The Rutgers Drawing Test, Form B, Manual.* Unpublished manuscript. Highland Park, New Jersey, 1973.

Yudin, L. W. "The Rutgers Drawing Test and Intelligence: A Preliminary Comparative Study." *Perceptual and Motor Skills,* 1967, *24,* 1038.

SANTA CRUZ BEHAVIORAL CHARACTERISTICS PROGRESSION (BCP)

AUTHOR: Office of the Santa Cruz County Superintendent of Schools

AGE: Preschool to high school

VARIABLE: Behavioral characteristics of school children

TYPE OF MEASURE: Observation system

SOURCE FROM WHICH MEASURE MAY BE OBTAINED: VORT Corporation, P.O. Box 11132, Palo Alto, California 94306. Cost: Complete set, $17.85.

DESCRIPTION OF MEASURE: The BCP is part of Santa Cruz County's Special Education Management Project, serving as the major assessment, instructional, and communication tool. It is a nonstandardized continuum of behaviors in chart or booklet form, consisting of 2,400 observable traits referred to as behavioral characteristics. Ages and labels have been discarded and behavioral characteristics have been grouped into categories called behavioral strands. Most of the fifty-nine strands include fifty roughly sequential characteristics, the last few of which approximate what society considers "appropriate" or "acceptable" adult behavior. The BCP has identifying behaviors describing some of the handicapping behaviors that mentally, behaviorally, and physically exceptional children might display in each of the behavioral strands. These identifying behaviors assist the teacher in focusing on the basic need areas of the pupil and in determining priorities of learner objectives. The BCP chart format displays the behavioral characteristics in a way that permits visual consideration of the relationships between and among the strands. The BCP is tied in systematically with an ordered procedure for the delivery of services to children with learning difficulties. The system also includes a progression of about seven hundred tasks or activities the staff member must accomplish if the learner is to achieve specific behavioral objectives.

RELIABILITY AND VALIDITY: None reported.

BIBLIOGRAPHY:

Office of the Santa Cruz County Superintendent of Schools. *Special Education Management System,* Booklets 1 to 4. Palo Alto, California: VORT Corporation, 1973.

Prepared by Orval G. Johnson

SAPIR DEVELOPMENTAL SCALE AND PROFILE

AUTHOR: Selma G. Sapir

AGE: 4 to 7 years

VARIABLE: Developmental level

TYPE OF MEASURE: Test

SOURCE FROM WHICH MEASURE MAY BE OBTAINED: Selma Sapir, 60 Biltmore Avenue, Yonkers, New York. Cost: Test forms, administration, directions, and form boards, $50.00.

DESCRIPTION OF MEASURE: The test taps three major areas: (1) perceptual motor, which includes visual discrimination, visual memory, auditory discrimination, auditory memory, and visual motor; (2) bodily schema, which includes visual motor spatial, body image, and directionality; and (3) language, which includes orientation and vocabulary. This is an experimental edition. Its major purpose is to be a teaching tool. After giving the test and scoring it on the developmental profile, it enables a teacher to develop a teaching plan that will promote optimal growth. It is designed to single out high-risk children.

RELIABILITY AND VALIDITY: Eighty-five percent of the children selected to be high risk with the scale were identified independently by a pediatric neurologists.

BIBLIOGRAPHY:

Sapir, S. G. "Sex Differences in Perceptual Motor Development." *Perceptual and Motor Skills,* 1966, *22,* 987-992.

Sapir, S. G. "Learning Disability and Deficit Centered Classroom Training." In J. Helmuth (Ed.), *Cognitive Studies No. 2: Deficits in Cognition.* New York: Brunner/Mazel, 1971.

Sapir, S. G., and Nitsburg, A. *Children with Learning Problems: A Developmental Interaction Approach.* New York: Brunner/Mazel, 1973.

Sapir, S. G., and Wilson, B. "A Developmental Scale to Assist in the Prevention of Learning Disability." *Educational and Psychological Measurement,* 1967, *27,* 1061-1068.

SCALE OF GESTURAL IMITATION

AUTHORS: Ellen Winkelstein and Gail H. Wolfson

AGE: 6 to 24 months

VARIABLE: Gestural imitation

TYPE OF MEASURE: Developmental scale

SOURCE FROM WHICH MEASURE MAY BE OBTAINED: Ellen Winkelstein, 504 Beacon Street, Boston, Massachusetts 02115. Cost: $.50 to cover printing and distribution.

DESCRIPTION OF MEASURE: The scale is a diagnostic tool for determining an infant's level of development in gestural imitation. It is based on the Hunt-Uzgiris Scale of Gestural Imitation (Uzgiris and Hunt, 1966) and was developed as part of an infant curriculum development project (Winkelstein, 1974). It is designed for use by people such as day-care staff without special skills in measurement. Detailed step-by-step instructions for administration and scoring are provided, as well as training in following these instructions. The scale is composed of three stages of gestural imitation with eight specific gestures to be presented to the infant to imitate at each stage. A description of the three stages, with an example from the scale of a gesture from each stage, follows: Stage One, Imitation of Familiar Gestures, during which infants imitate gestures they have already done on their own; Stage Two, Imitation of Unfamiliar Gestures, during which infants imitate gestures they have not already done on their own; and Stage Three, Imitation of Invisible Gestures, during which infants imitate gestures they cannot see themselves perform. Examples from the scale: familiar gesture from Stage One: "clap hands"; unfamiliar gesture from Stage Two: "rubs something with fist"; invisible gesture from Stage Three: "rubs top of the head with an object."

RELIABILITY AND VALIDITY: The reliability was studied by having three day-care staff members give the scale to six infants ranging in age from 6 to 24 months. Their results were compared with those of an experienced tester. There was 100-percent agreement on specifying the stage of gestural imitation for each infant. The validity of the scale is derived from two sources: (1) observations of a wide range of infant gestural imitation indicating that the specific gestures selected for each stage do represent those imitated by infants at that stage of development, and (2) recent data (Uzgiris, 1971) supporting the sequence and behavioral content of these developmental stages. Additional work on establishing the validity and reliability is under way.

BIBLIOGRAPHY:

Uzgiris, I. "Patterns of Vocal and Gestural Imitation in Infants." Paper presented at the International Society for the Study of Behavioral Development Symposium. The Netherlands, July 1971.

Uzgiris, I., and Hunt, J. M. *An Instrument for Assessing Infant Psychological Development.* Unpublished manuscript, February 1966.

Winkelstein, E. "The Development of a Systematic Method by which Day-Care Staff Can Select Gestural Imitation Curriculum Procedures for Individual Infants." *Child Study Journal,* 1974, *4,* 169-178.

SCALE FOR RATING PUPIL DEVELOPMENT–
KINDERGARTEN AND FIRST-GRADE LEVEL (SRPD)

AUTHOR: Joseph S. Renzulli

AGE: 5 to 7 years

VARIABLE: Developmental learning skills; social and emotional development

TYPE OF MEASURE: Rating scale

SOURCE FROM WHICH MEASURE MAY BE OBTAINED: Joseph S. Renzulli, School of Education, University of Connecticut, Storrs, Connecticut 06268. Send stamped, self-addressed envelope for a single copy.

DESCRIPTION OF MEASURE: The Scale for Rating Pupil Development–Kindergarten and First-Grade Level measures traits and levels of performance that are expressed in terms of observable and relatively unambiguous behaviors. The scale was designed for the twofold purpose of diagnosing specific areas of weakness and evaluating the effectiveness of various remedial approaches to learning. Part I of the SRPD consists of fifty-seven basic learning skills or tasks that children should be able to master at the kindergarten and first-grade levels. Part II deals with five areas of social development and four areas of emotional development. Items included in the scale generally fall into the areas of: observing, listening, manipulating, socializing, communicating, interacting with others, and developing favorable interests and attitudes toward school. The scale is based on research studies in child psychology that deal with the developmental tasks of primary-grade youngsters.

As examples, given below are selected items from Level I (twenty-four items) and Level II (thirty-three items) of Part I, Developmental Skill of Kindergarten and First Grade. Part II is Social Development (five items) and Emotional Development (four items).

LEVEL I
5. Can memorize words and melodies for group singing.
11. Can print first name.
15. Can recognize land and water masses on globe.
22. Knows the difference between left and right (e.g., parts of body, pages in book).
LEVEL II
4. Can count by 2s, 5s, and 10s through 100.
9. Knows how to use the ruler to measure things that are a certain number of inches in length.
12. Knows the number of days in a week = 7.
30. Can read orally with some degree of expression and make use of punctuation marks.

RELIABILITY AND VALIDITY: Content validity for the present version of the SRPD is based on feedback and recommendations from primary-grade teachers who participated in field studies with the first two experimental editions of the instrument. Factor analysis procedures were also used to help establish the construct validity of the instrument. Correlations between scores on Part I of the SRPD and the Metropolitan

Readiness Test are as follows: Word Meaning, .64; Listening, .71; Matching, .75; Alphabet, .77; Numbers, .42; Copying, .69; Total, .68. *Alpha* internal consistency reliability ranged from .77 to .82, and interrater reliability was .88.

BIBLIOGRAPHY:

Renzulli, J. S. "Evaluating Programs for the Culturally Disadvantaged." *Connecticut Teacher,* 1969, *36,* 10-13, 20.

SCHENECTADY KINDERGARTEN RATING SCALE (SKRS)

AUTHORS: W. Glenn Conrad and Jon E. Tobiessen

AGE: Kindergarten

VARIABLE: Language, controls, cognitive, motor, and social development.

TYPE OF MEASURE: Rating scale

SOURCE FROM WHICH MEASURE MAY BE OBTAINED: W. Glenn Conrad, Schenectady County Child Guidance Center, Inc., 821 Union Street, Schenectady, New York 12308.

DESCRIPTION OF MEASURE: The Schenectady Kindergarten Rating Scales (SKRS) are a battery of thirteen teacher-administered rating scales that have been developed as an economical measure for screening large numbers of children in kindergarten so that preventive or remedial programs can be provided for those who are deficient in language, motor, cognitive, or social development.

The scales are listed and briefly described here in the order in which they appear in the rater's booklet: (1) Waiting and Sharing (WS), a 7-point scale measuring the child's ability to wait for things, to share possessions, and to take turns. (2) Level of Organization of Play (LOP), a 5-point scale concerning the degree to which a child organizes the play material at his disposal. (3) Clarity of Speech (CS), a 6-point scale involving the clarity of a child's speech and how easily it can be understood. (4) Use of Materials (UM), a 5-point scale concerning the child's ability to represent reality using art materials. (5) Restraint of Motor Activity (RMA), a 7-point scale involving the length of time a child can engage in a quiet, subdued activity. (6) Cooperation with Adults (CoA), a 5-point scale involving the child's willingness to comply with requests by adults. (7) Verbal Skill (VS), a 5-point scale regarding the complexity of a child's vocabulary and sentence structure. (8) Fearfulness (Fr), a 5-point scale involving the extent to which a child seems apprehensive. (9) Frequency of Anger Toward Adults (FAA), a 7-point scale concerning the frequency of physical and verbal expressions of anger toward adults in the classroom. (10) Use of Scissors (US), a 5-point scale involving the child's ability to manipulate scissors. (11) Type of Motor Activity

(TMA), a 7-point scale regarding the degree to which a child engages in large-muscle as opposed to small-muscle activities. (12) Activity vs. Passivity of Speech (APS), a 5-point scale involving the amount of speaking done by a child. (13) Frequency of Anger Toward Children (FAC), a 7-point scale concerning the frequency of physical and verbal expressions of anger toward peers.

As an example, Item 4 of the measure, one of the shortest of the thirteen items, is given below:

Use of Materials (4 UM)

1. This child uses crayons, paints, and clay in crude, aimless fashion—scribbles with crayons, scrubs with paint brush, or bangs with clay.
2. This child engages in careful experimental manipulation of these materials but shows no interest in using them to represent anything.
3. This child engages in careful manipulation of these materials and tells what he is making, although there is a total lack of resemblance between his product and what he says he has made (in the teacher's judgment).
4. This child is able to achieve some resemblance between what he produces and what he says he is making.
5. This child is able to achieve easily discernible representations of what he says he is drawing, painting, or molding.

RELIABILITY AND VALIDITY: The scales have reasonable reliability. Interrater reliability was evaluated using prekindergarten classes because of the availability of two full-time teachers in a class. The percentage of children on whom teachers agreed within 1 point ranged from 78 to 94 percent on the 5-point scales, and from 69 to 84 percent on the 7-point scales. Disagreement by 3 or more points exceeded 6 percent on only two scales (FAA, FAC). Test-retest reliability at a six-month interval ranged from 69 percent to 94 percent agreement within one scale level. Predictive validity in identifying children with potential problems in first grade ranged from 79 percent for boys and 83 percent for girls. Our experience has been that a measure of visual perception such as the Bender Gestalt obtained in small groups improves the predictive power of the screening process by including those children with visual-perceptual or visual-memory deficits.

BIBLIOGRAPHY:

Conrad, W. G., and Tobiessen, J. "The Development of Kindergarten Behavior Rating Scales for the Prediction of Learning and Behavior Problems." *Psychology in the Schools,* 1967, *4,* 359-363.
Tobiessen, J., and Conrad, W. G. "The Schenectady Kindergarten Rating Scales Manual." Mimeographed. December 1970 (available from authors).
Tobiessen, J., Duckworth, B., and Conrad, W. G. "Relationship Between the Schenectady Kindergarten Rating Scales and First-Grade Achievement and Adjustment." *Psychology in the Schools,* 1971, *8,* 29-36.

SCIENTIFIC CONCEPT ATTAINMENT TEST

AUTHOR: W. H. King

AGE: 7 to 14 years

VARIABLE: Concept development

TYPE OF MEASURE: Test

SOURCE FROM WHICH MEASURE MAY BE OBTAINED: See King (1961, 1963).

DESCRIPTION OF MEASURE: The exploratory research for this quickly administered test of scientific sophistication is based on the work of Piaget. The original schedule of seventy items was reviewed by a panel of primary teachers and accepted as being suitable for children in English Junior Schools. Those questions were listed under five headings, later reduced to four: (1) Length, weight, time, and direction; (2) Volume and weight; (3) Miscellaneous concepts, mainly mechanical; and (4) Living things, seasons. The original test was given to more than twelve hundred children; it was not the aim of this research (King, 1961) to establish norms, although the rate of increase in score with increase in age was investigated. In the later study (1963), a shortened twenty-item version called Science Schedule was given to 801 children in a verbal form. Rate of growth of scientific knowledge was found to be similar for boys and girls; boys and girls aged 10 years showed no significant differences in knowledge of science concepts, but there was significant differentiation in secondary-school children.

As examples, seven items selected from the four sections of the test are given below.

1. Estimate time between two taps (15 seconds). (Accept 10 to 20 seconds)
2. Estimate length of blackboard (or a horizontal length about 12 to 18 feet) to the nearest foot. (Accept $1 \pm \frac{1}{6}$)

1. Water in jar (jam jar): stone added. Is level of water higher, equal, or lower?
   Water in jar: sand added. Is level of water higher, equal, or lower?

1. Which of the following substances are able to turn into water? tea, sugar, steam, hail, salt, clouds, soap, snow.

1. Is the—sun, tree, dog, flower, fire, candle—alive? (Yes, No, Don't know)
3. Are all things that move living? (Yes, No, Don't know)

RELIABILITY AND VALIDITY: Reliability of the Science Schedule in one study (King, 1963) was .60, slightly higher for boys than for girls.

BIBLIOGRAPHY:

King, W. H. "I—The Development of Scientific Concepts in Children." *British Journal of Educational Psychology*, 1961, *31*, 1-20.
King, W. H. "II—The Development of Scientific Concepts in Children." *British Journal of Educational Psychology*, 1963, *33*, 240-252.

SENSE OF SELF-IDENTITY QUESTIONNAIRE

AUTHORS: Carol J. Guardo and Janis B. Bohan

AGE: Kindergarten to Grade 3

TYPE OF MEASURE: Questionnaire

VARIABLE: Sense of self-identity

SOURCE FROM WHICH MEASURE MAY BE OBTAINED: Questionnaire, categories of response, and scoring procedures contained in NAPS document no. 01652, available from ASIS National Auxiliary Publication Service, c/o CCM Information Corp., 440 Park Avenue South, New York, New York 10016. Cost: $3.00 for each microfiche, $6.50 for each photocopy.

DESCRIPTION OF MEASURE: The measure consists of a set of fourteen single or multiple questions comprising a semistructured interview. The last five questions are used to double-check on the information received from previous questions. The questionnaire is designed to tap four dimensions of sense of self-identity: humanity, sexuality, individuality, and continuity (from the past and into the near and remote future). The double-check item that deals with the effect on self-identity if the child's name is taken away from him also provides an index of nominalism.

The interview is administered individually and tape recorded as a basis for coding and categorizing. It takes 15 to 20 minutes to administer. Three response categories (yes, no, or conditional, where some qualification of an if-then variety is cited) are used for scoring the answers to all critical questions except the one dealing with continuity from the past. In this case, responses are assigned to one of four categories: don't know, too short, too long, or always. The reasons given for answers to each of the critical questions are placed in eleven categories for scoring: (1) name, (2) physical characteristics, (3) age, (4) sex, (5) behavior, (6) mental functions, (7) possessions, (8) origins, (9) humanity, (10) personeity, and (11) miscellaneous. The dimensions of self-identity are explained in Guardo (1968) and Guardo and Bohan (1971).

As examples, five selected items from the questionnaire are given below. Item 1a. is a double-check item.

2. You said your name is X, so *you are* X, right?
3. Now then, could *you be* Y? (Individuality)
6. Could you be your dog (cat, fish, or whatever), A? (Humanity) Why? (or) Why not?
7. When you get in the higher grades in school, will you still be the same boy (girl)? (Continuity into the Near Future) Why? (or) Why not?
8. When you get to be grown up, will you still be the same boy (girl)? (Continuity into the Remote Future) Why? (or) Why not?
1a. If someone took your name away, would you still be the same? Why? (or) Why not?

RELIABILITY AND VALIDITY: Each of the authors independently coded all responses from the tapes and categorized both the basic responses and the reasons given for responses. Agreement ranged from 93 to 100 percent for all age-sex groups.

BIBLIOGRAPHY:

Guardo, C. J. "Self Revisited: The Sense of Self-Identity." *Journal of Humanistic Psychology,* 1968, *8,* 137-142.
Guardo, C. J., and Bohan, J. B. "Development of a Sense of Self-Identity in Children." *Child Development,* 1971, *42,* 1909-1921.

SERIES LEARNING POTENTIAL TEST (SLPT)

AUTHORS: Elisha Babad and Milton Budoff

AGE: Grades 1 to 4 (6 to 10 years)

VARIABLE: Training-based assessment of "g" intelligence utilizing a learning-potential model

TYPE OF MEASURE: Test

SOURCE FROM WHICH MEASURE MAY BE OBTAINED: Research Institute for Educational Problems, 29 Ware Street, Cambridge, Massachusetts 02138. Cost: Sample set consisting of a manual, two test forms, and training booklet, $2.50; package of ten test booklets, $3.50; package of ten training booklets, $2.50.

DESCRIPTION OF MEASURE: The logic of a learning-potential assessment paradigm has been reviewed by Budoff (1975). This training-based assessment is a more culture-fair testing paradigm for examining a low-income and/or minority group and/or non-English-speaking child's capacity to show his/her capacity to understand and perform on reasoning problems, estimating "g" (intelligence) utilizing a process-oriented conceptualization. Posttest scores reflect the child's ability under optimized conditions in which all subjects are familiar with the task and its demands and have had the opportunity to learn and apply task-relevant strategies. Two other nonverbal reasoning tasks have systematic training procedures and can be used in a learning-potential format: altered versions of the Kohs Block Designs and Raven Progressive Matrices. These have been particularly useful for assessing ability among low IQ, low SES children who are culturally and/or linguistically different from middle-class children, for children suspected of borderline or mild levels of mental retardation, and for those who are moderately, severely, or profoundly mentally retarded. Forms of the SLPT and data are available on English-, Spanish-, Hebrew-, and Arabic-speaking children.
    The SLPT utilizes a group procedure and provides sessions held on three separate days including pretest, problem-relevant training, and posttest. Two forms (A and B) are available for use as a pre- and posttest; each is composed of sixty-five items.

The testee's task is the completion of a series of pictures or geometric forms arranged in a pattern in which the figures change systematically. Each item presents a horizontal row of cells, each of which contains a stimulus figure. One cell is blank and may be placed in any part of the series. The testee must identify among the multiple choices which one best completes the series. Four concepts may vary in the series: semantic content (meaningful or geometric figures), size (large/small), color (black/white), or orientation (up/down or left/right). None of the seventeen items in the coaching booklet is identical to any of the 130 test items. Five strategies are taught and practiced during the class-size training session of 30 to 45 minutes: (1) The student learns to identify each concept that changes; (2) he learns to "sing the tune" for each concept, one at a time, as an organizational aid to identify the pattern of each concept; (3) to reduce the memory load in a multiconcept item, the student crosses out the wrong choices for each concept so identified; and (4) the child learns to reverse the direction in which the tune is sung when the location of the blank space calls for such reversal, for example, the blank at the beginning of a series.

RELIABILITY AND VALIDITY: Extensive information regarding reliability and validity of the SLPT is available (Babad and Budoff, 1974a; Corman and Budoff, 1973). Most completely, with American populations, the psychometric characteristics of the test forms have been determined with some seventeen hundred low and middle SES black and white students in grades 1 to 4. Test-retest reliabilities computed using 120 nontrained subjects for Form A and 93 similarly selected subjects for Form B yielded coefficients of .87 and .93 for Forms A and B, respectively. Form equivalence, determined by correlating pre- and posttest scores of 106 nontrained students, half of whom had received Form A on the pretest, Form B on the posttest, and vice versa, yielded a coefficient of .87. Kuder-Richardson formula 20 reliability coefficients, determined by using all students who received the pretest, were .95 for both forms. Students included in the training study were randomly assigned to a trained or nontrained group and to Form A or Form B.

Item analyses and factor analyses calculated on each form before and after training showed that both the difficulty level and loading of any given item were comparable. The percentage of students who passed many items rose after training. A four-way repeated analysis of variance including grade (four levels), group (trained/nontrained), and test form (A and B) as the between-subjects factors, and test session (pre- and posttraining) as the within-subjects factor indicated the following significant main effects: grade (F = 36.54, $p < .001$) and test session (F = 94.96, $p < .001$). The Group X test session interaction (F = 20.88, $p < .001$) indicated that the trained group had a greater increase in mean score from pre- to posttest than did the nontrained group.

Mean pre- to posttest differences for the trained and nontrained groups by social class revealed the greatest mean score increase for second and third graders from lower-class communities. In the middle-class group, first and second graders showed the highest mean increase. The fact that fourth graders improved little with training regardless of social class suggests a possible ceiling effect of the test; that is, training appeared not to be beneficial after the third grade. Of all lower-class students in the sample, 51.3 percent exceeded the middle-class pretest mean after training, in contrast to 34.9 percent who exceeded this mean before training. The Israeli adaptation has attempted to increase the de facto effects of this ceiling. Primarily Puerto Rican low SES Spanish-speaking students ($N = 189$), ranging in age from 6 years, 2 months to 14 years, 10 months, were administered the SLPT. Posttraining scores increased significantly (t = 3.32, df = 73, $p < .01$ for primary students; t = 2.56, df = 110, $p < .05$ for intermediate students). The lower average gain displayed by the older students suggested the tendency of children older than 9 years of age to attain a de facto ceiling.

To test the predictive power of LP and IQ measures, a stepwise multiple-regression analysis was performed on each of the six Inter-American General Abilities Series (IAGAS) achievement measures (Spanish and English scores on the verbal, nonverbal, and numeric subtests). Independent variables were Series posttraining scores, WISC performance IQ, and Spanish and English WISC vocabulary scores. The best combination of predictors of nonverbal and numeric achievement in both Spanish and English was provided by the Series posttraining LP score, age, and WISC performance IQ.

BIBLIOGRAPHY:

Babad, E., and Bashi, J. *An Educational Test of the Validity of Learning Potential Measurement.* Final report on research performed under Ford Foundation grant. RIEP print 91. Cambridge, Massachusetts: Research Institute for Educational Problems, June 1975.

Babad, E., and Budoff, M. *A Manual for the Series Learning Potential Test.* Unpublished. Cambridge, Massachusetts: Research Institute for Educational Problems, 1974a.

Babad, E., and Budoff, M. "Sensitivity and Validity of Learning Potential Measurement in Three Levels of Ability." *Journal of Educational Psychology,* 1974b, *66,* 439-447.

Budoff, M. "Measuring Learning Potential: An Alternative to the Traditional Intelligence Test." In G. R. Gredler (Ed.), *Ethical and Legal Factors in the Practice of School Psychology: Proceedings of the First Annual Conference in School Psychology.* Philadelphia, Pennsylvania: Temple University, 1975.

Budoff, M., Gimon, A., and Corman, L. "Learning Potential with Spanish-Speaking Youth as an Alternative to IQ Tests: A First Report." *Inter-American Journal of Psychology,* 1974, *8,* 233-246.

Corman, L., and Budoff, M. *The Series Test as a Measure of Learning Potential.* RIEP print 47. Cambridge, Massachusetts: Research Institute for Educational Problems, 1973.

Gimon, A., Budoff, M., and Corman, L. *Applicability of Learning Potential Measurement with Spanish-Speaking Youth as an Alternative to IQ.* Final report. Grant OEG-1-72-0020 (509). Washington, D.C.: Office of Education, 1974.

SET MATCHING INVENTORY/MATHEMATICS (SMI/M)

AUTHORS: Jack Victor and Alan Coller

AGE: Preschool

VARIABLE: Ability to match stimuli according to common attributes

TYPE OF MEASURE: Test

SOURCE FROM WHICH MEASURE MAY BE OBTAINED: Jack Victor, 82-25 218th Street, Hollis Hills, New York 11427.

DESCRIPTION OF MEASURE: The SMI/M, one of the Early Childhood Inventories (see Index of Measures), is an individually administered inventory designed to evaluate the child's receptive ability to match stimuli according to their common attributes. The child is asked to point to a box, from among four alternatives arranged in boxed quadrants at the corners of the test page, that contains only the "standard" item(s) indicated by the administrator. The standard appears unboxed in the center of the page.

The SMI/M consists of twelve items divided into two parts. The first contains the "easier" unmixed sets. At this level the child must choose the alternative whose components are all identical to the standard. For example, the four alternatives in one item are (1) four books, (2) three glasses and one book, (3) two glasses and two books, and (4) four glasses. Since the standard is a glass, the child must choose the set containing only the glasses. The second level contains the "harder" mixed or conjunctive sets. Here the child must choose the alternative that contains only the components of the standard. For example, the four alternatives in one item are (1) a dog, a fish, a rabbit, and a snake; (2) a turtle, a snake, a fish, and a rabbit; (3) a turtle, a rabbit, a dog, and another rabbit; and (4) a rabbit, a turtle, another rabbit, and another turtle. Since the standard is a turtle and a rabbit, the child must choose the fourth box. For purposes of retesting and to aid in the evaluation of guess and response set behaviors, equivalent forms of the SMI/M have been developed. The two forms differ in the stimuli used and in the position of the correct alternative.

RELIABILITY AND VALIDITY: None reported.

BIBLIOGRAPHY:

Coller, A., and Victor, J. *Early Childhood Inventories Project.* New York: New York University, Institute for Developmental Studies, 1970.

Ryan, T. J., and Moffitt, A. R. "Evaluation of Preschool Programs." *Canadian Psychologist,* 1974, *15,* 205-219.

Prepared by Alan Coller, Jack Victor, and John Dill

SEX CONSTANCY (*See note, p. 60)

AUTHORS: Lawrence Kohlberg and Rheta DeVries

AGE: Normal children 3 to 8 years

VARIABLE: Development of children's beliefs about sex constancy

TYPE OF MEASURE: Structured interview

SOURCE FROM WHICH MEASURE MAY BE OBTAINED: The set of drawings used by Kohlberg and DeVries is available from Rheta DeVries, College of Education, University of Illinois at Chicago Circle, Chicago, Illinois 60680. A different version of this measure and a manual for test administration are available from Educational Testing Service, Princeton, New Jersey 08540.

DESCRIPTION OF MEASURE: Four schematic drawings are used in this interview (requiring about 5 to 10 minutes for most children), designed to assess children's beliefs about the invariance of the attribute of femaleness. The drawings show: (1) girl in dress with long hair, (2) girl in dress with crew-cut hair, (3) girl with long hair in boy's clothes, and (4) boy with crew-cut hair in boy's clothes. Drawing 1 is presented first and, after the child sees it as a girl, she is asked whether the girl could be a boy if she really wanted to. This drawing is then used in conjunction with each of the other drawings, and the child is questioned about the possibility of a real sex change with various appearance and behavioral transformations. The examiner is to be careful on each of the six items in the task to probe when the child says the girl would become a boy. This probe takes the form, "Would the child be a *real* boy then (in a slightly questioning tone)?" Ss are scored from 0 to 9. Norms are available for 143 bright and average children chronologically aged 5 to 7 years and retarded children mentally aged 5 to 7 years, according to Stanford-Binet IQ (DeVries, 1971). Norms for boys 3 to 6 years may be found in DeVries (1969).

As examples the first three of the six items of the interview are given below.

1. If this child (point to girl picture) really wants to be a boy, can she?
   Yes   No   *If no:* Why not?
2. (Show girl picture and picture of girl with guns.) If this (point to girl) child played with guns and did boy things (point to girl with guns), what would it (point to girl) be? Would it be a boy or girl?
   Boy   Girl   *If girl:* Why would it still be a girl?
3a. (Show girl picture and picture of girl with hair cut.) If this child's (point to girl) hair were cut short (point to girl with hair cut), what would it (point to girl) be? Would it be a boy or a girl?
    Boy   Girl   *If girl:* Why would it still be a girl?

RELIABILITY AND VALIDITY: Interscorer agreement on 261 items for twenty randomly selected Ss was 96 percent. Validity of the developmental scale is indicated by the increasing success on each scale item with increasing age, and validity of the phenomenon of lack of identity is supported by research by Emmerich (1973, pp. 123-144), Emmerich and Goldman (1972), and Shipman and others (1971).

BIBLIOGRAPHY:

DeVries, R. "Constancy of Generic Identity in the Years Three to Six." *Society for Research in Child Development Monographs,* 1969, *34* (127), 1-67.

DeVries, R. *Evaluation of Cognitive Development with Piaget-type Tests: Study of Young Bright, Average, and Retarded Children.* Final report to the Department of Program Development for Gifted Children, Illinois Office of Public Instruction, 1971. ERIC document no. ED 075 065.

DeVries, R. "Relationships Among Piagetian, IQ, and Achievement Assessments." *Child Development,* 1974, *45,* 746-756.

Emmerich, W. "Socialization and Sex-Role Development." In J. R. Nesselroade and H. W. Reese (Eds.), *Life-Span Developmental Psychology.* New York: Academic Press, 1973.

Emmerich, W., and Goldman, D. *Boy-Girl Identity Task.* Technical report 1. Princeton, New Jersey: Educational Testing Service–Head Start Longitudinal Study. December 1972.

Shipman, V., Barone, J., Beaton, A., Emmerich, W., and Ward, W. "Disadvantaged Children and Their First School Experiences: Structure and Development of Cognitive Competencies and Styles Prior to School Entry." Report no. 71-19. Princeton, New Jersey: Educational Testing Service, 1971.

Prepared by Rheta DeVries

SHAW BLOCKS TEST

AUTHOR: David Lester

AGE: 9 years and up

VARIABLE: Intelligence, originality, rigidity

TYPE OF MEASURE: Block arrangement test

SOURCE FROM WHICH MEASURE MAY BE OBTAINED: See Lester (1967a). It may not be reproduced for profit, by order of the designer Harold Shaw.

DESCRIPTION OF MEASURE: The Shaw Blocks Test is a quick test to measure intellectual/cognitive performance. It was designed to measure intelligence without penalizing creativity or originality. Obviously, however, since it consists of only one type of intellectual performance, it is probably less valid as a measure of overall intellectual performance than the standardized individual intelligence tests. Unlike them, however, it does not penalize creative and original responses. The four blocks differ on a number of attributes (shape, color, weight, letters on them, and so forth), and the subject has to arrange the blocks in sequences based on as many principles as he/she can think of. The more sequences, the higher the score.

RELIABILITY AND VALIDITY: The Kuder-Richardson reliability (by the method of rational equivalence) on a sample of old persons was .87. In samples of college students, prison inmates, and eighth-grade students, scores on the Shaw Blocks Test did not correlate with IQ scores. This suggests that it measures something different from standard IQ tests which is potentially useful, but it should be regarded as a research and experimental tool for the present until further validity studies are carried out. In a sample of graduate students, scores on the Shaw Blocks Test correlated highly with the Miller Analogies Test (.82) and with the Graduate Record Examination verbal and quantitative tests (.49 and .43). Lester (1967a) has noted how it might be used to measure originality and rigidity, but no work has been done on the reliability and validity of these measures. Scores for originality of response did not correlate with the intelligence score for graduate students.

BIBLIOGRAPHY:

Bromley, D. "Some Experimental Tests of the Effect of Age on Creative Intellectual Output." *Journal of Gerontology,* 1956, *11,* 74-82.
Heim, A., and Lester, D. "Performance of Children on the Shaw Blocks Test." *Perceptual and Motor Skills,* 1964, *19,* 740.
Howson, J. "Intellectual Impairment Associated with Brain-Injured Patients Revealed in the Shaw Test of Abstract Thought." *Canadian Journal of Psychology,* 1948, *2,* 125-133.
Lester, D. "Consistency and Validity of the Shaw Blocks Test." *Perceptual and Motor Skills,* 1966, *22,* 134.
Lester, D. "The Shaw Test: A Description." *Journal of Clinical Psychology,* 1967a, *23,* 88-89.
Lester, D. "The Shaw Test: Simultaneous Measures of Intelligence, Originality, and Rigidity." *Perceptual and Motor Skills,* 1967b, *24,* 1106.
Lester, D., Bird, K., Brown, K., and Massa, J. "Validity of Shaw Blocks Test." *Perceptual and Motor Skills,* 1973, *37,* 442.

SITUATIONAL TEST OF SELF-HELP SKILL TRAINING

AUTHORS: M. R. Minge and T. S. Ball

AGE: Unlimited

VARIABLE: Self-help skills

TYPE OF MEASURE: Situation or work-sample test

SOURCE FROM WHICH MEASURE MAY BE OBTAINED: See Ball, Seric, and Payne (1971).

DESCRIPTION OF MEASURE: Eleven commands are given pertaining to three categories of behavior: Attention, Undressing, and Dressing. The subject is given 20 seconds to respond. Detailed descriptions of these commands follow:

A. *Attention*
1. *S* seated, *GL* (Patient's own group leader in ward setting) directly in front of *S* and seated. Command, "_____, look at me."
2. *S* seated. *GL* five feet away. *S* stays seated 30 seconds. Command, "_____, stay."
3. *S* seated. *GL* five feet away. *S* stands up on command, "_____, stand up."
4. *GL* standing next to chair. *S* five feet away. *S* sits on command, "_____, sit down."
5. *S* seated. *GL* five feet away. *S* comes to *GL* on command, "_____, come to me."

B. *Undressing*
1. *S* seated. *GL* seated directly opposite. *S* removes shirt on command, "_____, take your shirt off."
2. *S* standing with elastic-banded boxer shorts on. *GL* directly opposite *S*. *S* removes pants on command, "_____, take your pants off."
3. *S* seated with both socks on. *GL* opposite *S*. *S* removes one sock at a time on command, "_____, take your socks off."

C. *Dressing*
1. *S* seated, shirt off. *GL* hands T-shirt to *S* with bottom open and toward *S*. Command, "_____, put your shirt on."
2. *S* standing, pants off. *GL* hands elastic-banded boxer shorts to *S* with front forward and waist open. Command, "_____, put your pants on."
3. *S* seated. *GL* hands *S* one sock at a time with heel down and closest to *S* and top of sock open and directed upward. Command, "_____, put your socks on."

Data for each of the eleven items show outcomes of two trials per item given. The number of items given is determined by the number of correct responses emitted by the subject. Specifically, the subject has to respond correctly on both trials of any two of the first three items in Category A (Attention) in order to be given the fourth and fifth items in that category. If in either Category B (Undressing) or Category C (Dressing) the subject did not respond correctly on both trials of at least one of the first two items, the third item in the respective category is not given. According to this method, a subject can be tested on at least six and at most eleven items, yielding a total of between twelve and twenty-two trials. Scores thus range from 0 to 22.

RELIABILITY AND VALIDITY: The eleven test items correspond closely to the terminal steps for each of the tasks in a program of self-help skill training (Minge and Ball, 1967). Assessment of interjudge reliability for the Situational Test total score yielded a correlation coefficient of .96 (Ball, Seric, and Payne, 1971).

BIBLIOGRAPHY:

Ball, T. S., Seric, K., and Payne, L. E. "Long-Term Retention of Self-help Skill Training in the Profoundly Retarded." *American Journal of Mental Deficiency*, 1971, 76, 378-382.

Minge, M. R., and Ball, T. S. "Teaching of Self-Help Skills to Profoundly Retarded Patients." *American Journal of Mental Deficiency*, 1967, *71*, 864-868.

Prepared by Thomas S. Ball

SIX MUSIC CONSERVATION TASKS

AUTHOR: Marilyn Pflederer Zimmerman

AGE: 5, 7, 9, and 13 years

VARIABLE: Tonal and rhythmic conservation

TYPE OF MEASURE: Music listening and interview

SOURCE FROM WHICH MEASURE MAY BE OBTAINED: See Zimmerman and Scherest (1968). Also available at nominal cost for reproducing tasks from Marilyn P. Zimmerman, 11 Carriage Place, Champaign, Illinois 61820.

DESCRIPTION OF MEASURE: The Six Musical Tasks designed by Zimmerman are patterned after Piagetian conservation tasks. The tasks consist of the following: Task I, Conservation of Duration; Task II, Conservation of Meter; Task III, Conservation of Rhythm Pattern with Tonal Pattern Varied; Task IV, Conservation of Melody with Tempo Varied; Task V, Conservation of Tonal Pattern with Pitch Levels Varied; Task VI, Conservation of Tonal Pattern with Rhythm Pattern Varied. Each of the tasks is presented in a simulated classroom setting. The tasks and responses are recorded.

As an example of an item in the measure, the first item of Task III uses as a stimulus three quarter notes played on A of the treble clef. The four response options are: (1) three quarter notes (C, D, E); (2) a dotted quarter, an eighth, and a quarter note (G, F, E); (3) three quarter notes (E, D, C); and (4) three quarter notes (A, A, A). One exact repetition of the stimulus (4) is included in each item to separate memory from conservation. The respondent is asked to say whether each response is the "same" as or "different" from the stimulus. If he replies that it is different, he is asked to explain.

RELIABILITY AND VALIDITY: The tasks were administered to eighty subjects distributed over four age levels: ten boys and ten girls each at ages (approximate) 5, 7, 9, and 13. The analysis of variance showed a highly significant ($F = 74.89$; $df = 3,72$; $p < .001$) main effect for age and virtually no variance attributable to sex. The large F for tasks occurred because the tasks are scored on different metrics and the means differed widely. A significant ($F = 19.84$; $df = 15,360$; $p < .001$) interaction between individual tasks and age suggests that the different tasks separated the age groups to differing degrees. Split-half reliabilities (Spearman-Brown corrected) were calculated for each task at each age level and for each task across all age levels. Tasks III, V, and VI had low reliabilities of .02, .49, and .57 respectively. Task I was found to be completely unreliable.

BIBLIOGRAPHY:

Pflederer, M. "The Responses of Children to Musical Tasks Embodying Piaget's Principle of Conservation." *Journal of Research in Music Education,* 1964, *12,* 251-268.
Pflederer, M. "A Study of the Conservation of Tonal and Rhythmic Patterns in Elementary School Children." *California Journal of Educational Research,* 1966, *17,* 52-62.
Pflederer, M., and Sechrest, L. "Conservation in Musical Experience." *Psychology in the Schools,* 1968, *5,* 99-105.
Zimmerman, M. P., and Sechrest, L. *How Children Conceptually Organize Musical Sounds.* Northwestern University, Evanston, Illinois, 1968. Available as ERIC document no. ED 028 200.

SMITH-STURGEON CONDITIONAL REASONING TEST

AUTHORS: Edward L. Smith and Joanne Sturgeon

AGE: 5 to 10 years

VARIABLE: Conditional reasoning ability

TYPE OF MEASURE: Individual test

SOURCE FROM WHICH MEASURE MAY BE OBTAINED: The script, description of materials, and test information are included in *Conditional Logic and Children,* available from The Critical Thinking Project, 371 Education Building, University of Illinois, Urbana, Illinois 61801. Cost: $2.00 for postage and handling.

DESCRIPTION OF MEASURE: The test makes use of real situations with embedded "if-then" relationships. Certain of these relations are made explicit by the test administrator, who follows a standardized pattern. When given a reasoning problem the child being tested is reminded of any "if-then" relationship needed in the problem; is shown, or asked to suppose, some other fact; and is asked what, if anything, follows about some object (e.g., a light). An answer is regarded as correct only if—upon probing with the question "why?"—it is followed by an adequate justification.

The test consists of two main parts, the house part and the chemicals part, both of which are quite extensive. As examples, two brief samples of the measure are given below.

The following conditional statements represent the information from which children are asked to reason on the *house* part:
1. If the big handle is up, then the bell works.
2. If the light is on, then the big handle is up.
3. If the bell does not work, then the big handle is down.
4. If the big handle is down, then the light is not on.
At the beginning of the house part the child is shown that there are two handles, but he is not allowed to find out about the function of the small one. He is allowed to find out that the bell does not always ring. Thus, the possibility that the small handle being up also implies that the bell will work is left open, as is the possibility that it will work only when the large handle is up. The child is shown and assured only that the large handle being up is a sufficient condition for the bell to work.

The following conditional statements represent the information from which the children are asked to reason on the *chemicals* part:
5. If a white powder is soda, then it bubbles when vinegar is added.
6. If a white powder is sugar, then vinegar added to it turns white.
7. If a liquid is vinegar, then it makes soda bubble.
8. If a liquid makes soda bubble, then it turns litmus paper red.
At the beginning of the chemicals part, the children are shown several different reactions with vinegar and unidentified white powders. Thus, they have experience with white powders that bubble when vinegar is added and with white powders that turn vinegar milky. The possibility that several different white powders will bubble when added to vinegar is left open. The same is true for powders that turn vinegar milky.

RELIABILITY AND VALIDITY: The following are Kuder-Richardson reliabilities (twenty-four items): grade 1, $N = 30$, $r = .81$; grade 2, $N = 28$, $r = .85$; grade 3, $N = 29$, $r = .83$. An argument for content and construct validity is offered in Ennis, Finkelstein, Smith, and Wilson (1969).

BIBLIOGRAPHY:

Ennis, R. H. "Conditional Logic and Primary School Children: A Developmental Study." *Interchange,* 1971, *2,* 126-132.

Ennis, R. H. "An Alternative to Piaget's Conceptualization of Logical Competence." Paper presented at the meeting of the Society for Research in Child Development. Denver, Colorado, April 1975.

Ennis, R. H., Finkelstein, M., Smith, E., and Wilson, N. H. *Conditional Logic and Children.* Ithaca, New York: Critical Thinking Project, 1969.

Roberge, J. J. "Recent Research on the Development of Children's Comprehension of Deductive Reasoning Schemes." *School Science and Mathematics,* 1972, *72,* 197-200.

Sanner, B. M. "A Study of the Ability of Fifth Graders to Handle Conditional Logic." Unpublished doctoral dissertation. University of Illinois, Urbana, 1974.

Prepared by Robert H. Ennis

SOUTHEASTERN DAY-CARE PROJECT RATING FORM

AUTHOR: Compiled by staff under the direction of Nancy E. Travis

AGE: Infant to 5 years

VARIABLE: Developmental level

TYPE OF MEASURE: Rating scale

SOURCE FROM WHICH MEASURE MAY BE OBTAINED: Day Care and Child Development Council of America, Inc., 1012 14th Street NW, Washington, D.C. 20005.

DESCRIPTION OF MEASURE: The SDCP Rating Form is a compilation of items describing behavior, knowledge, and skills appropriate for various age levels and indicative of normal child development patterns. The items have all been standardized for children from infancy through 5 years of age. This instrument is particularly designed to be used by workers in day-care programs to help them assess children with whom they are working in order to individualize programs for each child. It is specifically designed *not* to result in a test score that could be misused.

There are four separate rating forms: birth to 30 months (twenty-six items), age 2 (twenty-seven items), age 3 (twenty-six items), and age 4 to age 6 (fifty-one items). All items are to be answered "yes" or "no." As examples, the first two and last two items from the infants' scale are given below.

Birth to 3 Months
  1. Lifts head when held at shoulder
  2. Smiles spontaneously
Seventeen to 30 Months
51. Recognizes and points to five pictures
52. Makes sentences of two or three words

The items on the other forms cover cognitive skill, social and emotional skills, motor skills, and hygiene and self-help.
The first "cognitive skill" item for 3-year-olds is given below.

Cognitive
1. Compares size   Extends "matching" concept to size, as "big" or "little." Comparisons may be easy, but should be verbalized.

RELIABILITY AND VALIDITY: Reliability and validity vary little, although a sampling of back-up ratings was done by outside observers and the differences were not significant for these purposes.

BIBLIOGRAPHY: None.

Prepared by James A. Harrell

TEACHERS' RATING QUESTIONNAIRE (TRQ)

AUTHOR: E. N. Wright

AGE: Kindergarten to grade 9

VARIABLE: Achievement and development of children

TYPE OF MEASURE: Rating scales

SOURCE FROM WHICH MEASURE MAY BE OBTAINED: Research Department, Board of Education for the City of Toronto, 155 College Street, Toronto, Ontario, Canada M5T 1P6.

DESCRIPTION OF MEASURE: This measure has been considerably revised and additional statistical information provided since it first appeared in *Handbook I.* In using the Teachers' Rating Questionnaire, teachers rate their students on several aspects of development on a Likert-type scale. The questionnaire is conceived as a method of getting at diverse properties of "achievement" and also ascertaining the degree and character of the teacher-child interaction. The rating scale exists in different but roughly equivalent forms for kindergarten, grade 1, grade 2, and grade 3, and in addition a "three plus" (3+) form appropriate for use in grades 3 to 9. In its original format there were five subsections dealing with English language, social interaction, and emotional, mental, and physical variables. Based on detailed analyses, all forms have now been divided into three sections, which exclude the physical items. No attempt is made to label the three sections, but it appears that the grouping includes one collection of items related to school achievement, a second collection of items related to social and emotional development, and a third collection of items related to inventiveness, creativity, self-expression, and independence. Means and standard deviations, based on large numbers of children, were obtained from senior kindergarten through grade 6 (excluding grade 5). The grade 3+ form, in a slightly modified fashion, was used in a large-scale study conducted in grades 5, 7, and 9. The means and standard deviations show nearly identical distributions of the data and nearly identical means and standard deviations for these three grade levels.

As an example, an item from the third section in the grade 2 form (with a total of twenty-three items) is given below. The other four forms contain items varying from eleven to twenty-seven.

Frequently participates in making and carrying out plans with little or no help from the teacher.
    Rate 0: —never has anything to offer in planning situations, or
               —needs much help in carrying out plans.
    Rate 2: —seldom participates in planning, or
               —needs help in carrying out plans.
    Rate 4: —frequently participates in making and carrying out plans with little or no
               help from the teacher.
    Rate 6: —usually participates in planning, and
               —can carry out plans without help from the teacher.

Rate 8: —has much to offer in planning and can carry out plans without help from
the teacher, and
—often helps others to carry out plans.

RELIABILITY AND VALIDITY: A somewhat similar form has been administered over
an interval of time by different teachers to the same children. The reliability data obtained in this fashion were, in effect, coefficients of stability and equivalence, though
strict equivalence is somewhat questionable since the three forms of the scale included
different numbers of items. Using these data, a special analysis technique was developed for estimating reliability coefficients (Wyman and Wright, 1974). The estimated
reliability coefficient for repeated administrations of the same version is .78 and .66
between two versions of the TRQ. Validity appears to rest primarily on concurrent
validation from the correlations between the various items of the language and mental
subscales of the TRQ with five subtests of the Metropolitan Achievement Test (MAT):
word knowledge, word discrimination, reading, spelling, and arithmetic. Children's
scores on the MAT in grade 1 were correlated with their scores on the kindergarten
form of the TRQ. These coefficients ranged between .37 (spelling on the MAT vs. language on the TRQ) to .68 (reading on the MAT vs. language on the TRQ). More elaborate information relating to validity appears elsewhere (Schroder and Crawford, 1970).

In spite of the fact that a principal components analysis was used to regroup
the items, the test user can expect intercorrelations among the subscales to remain
fairly high. Furthermore, individual evidence suggests that there will be less variation of
mean scores among scores on the TRQ from different schools than there would be
among the same scores on achievement-test data. Thus this test, even in its revised
form (Wright and Wyman, 1974), will provide a test user with somewhat different
kinds of information than would be expected from a typical standardized test. This
factor will be a limitation in some conditions and an asset in others.

BIBLIOGRAPHY:

Schroder, C., and Crawford, P. "School Achievement as Measured by Teacher Ratings
and Standardized Achievement Tests." Report no. 89. Research Department,
Board of Education for the City of Toronto, Ontario, Canada, 1970. ERIC
document no. ED 051 264.
Wright, E. N., and Wyman, W. C. "Trimming the TRQ (Revised Forms for Use in
Toronto)." Report no. 125. Research Department, Board of Education for the
City of Toronto, 1974. ERIC document no. ED 106 311.
Wyman, W. C. "Exploring the TRQ: Technical Supplement." Report no. 124. Research
Department, Board of Education for the City of Toronto, 1974. ERIC docu-
ment no. ED 106 310.
Wyman, W. C., and Wright, E. N. "Exploring the TRQ—An Assessment of the Effective-
ness of the Teachers' Rating Questionnaire." Report no. 123. Research Depart-
ment, Board of Education for the City of Toronto, 1974. ERIC document no.
ED 106 316.

TERRITORIAL DECENTRATION TEST

AUTHOR: Joseph P. Stoltman

AGE: 5 to 14 years

VARIABLE: Geographical/spatial stages

TYPE OF MEASURE: Structured individual interview

SOURCE FROM WHICH MEASURE MAY BE OBTAINED: See Stoltman (1972b) or write Joseph P. Stoltman, Department of Geography, Western Michigan University, Kalamazoo, Michigan 49001. Cost: $1.25.

DESCRIPTION OF MEASURE: The Territorial Decentration Test was designed to extend the spatial and geographical stages research of Piaget in Switzerland and Jahoda in Scotland to a sample of U.S. children. The instrument contains four subtests: (1) Verbal Territorial Identification, (2) Verbal Territorial Relationships, (3) Territorial Inclusion Using Written Symbols, and (4) Territorial Inclusion Using Props. Throughout the test the child is requested to respond verbally and manually with props to questions regarding the spatial relationships of geographical territories in the child's expanding environment (e.g., city/town, county, state, and nation). Verbal inquiries regarding prop placement behaviors enable the researcher to ascertain the application of territorial inclusion principles by the child. The measure is appropriate for assessing the effects of social science curricula upon the development of the child.

    As examples, given below are the instructions for the first five of nine items on Subtest C, entitled Territorial Inclusion Using Written Symbols. Subtests A, B, and D are Verbal Territorial Identification (ten items), Verbal Territorial Relationships (nine items), and Territorial Inclusion Using Props (ten items).

Item	Directions	Verbal Instructions
1. (1.3)	Show child the circle printed on page 1 of the response booklet. Record response to the *why*. Be certain child understands circle may be any size and any place on page.	Look at this circle. It shows (name local county). You draw a circle on this page which shows (name local city/town). Why did you put the circle showing (name local city/town) there?
2. (1.3)	Show child the circle on page 2. Record response to the *why*.	Look at this circle. It shows (name local state). You draw a circle which correctly shows (name local city/town). Why did you put the circle showing (name local city/town) there?
3. (2.3)	Show child the circle on page 3. Record response to the *why*.	Look at this circle. It shows (name local state). You draw a circle which correctly shows (name local county). Why did you put the circle showing (name local county) there?
4. (2.3)	Show child the circle on page 4. Record response to the *why*.	Look at this circle. It shows (name local city/town). You draw a circle which correctly shows (name local county).

Item	Directions	Verbal Instructions
5. (3.3)	Show child the circle on page 5. Record response to the *why*.	Why did you put the circle showing (name local county) there? Look at this circle. It shows (name nation). You draw a circle which correctly shows (name local state). Why did you put the circle showing (name local state) there?

RELIABILITY AND VALIDITY: The Territorial Decentration Test was administered to 204 children in the state of Georgia stratified proportionally by sex, race, and urban-rural background. Reliability of the instrument was determined using Kuder-Richardson formula 20 for the total test, as well as using the behavioral and explanation components. The coefficients were: total test (sixty items) = .98, behavioral component (thirty-eight items) = .96, and explanation component (twenty-two items) = .94. The construct validity of the instrument was established by comparing it with the tasks originally utilized in research by Piaget and Jahoda. Such a comparison showed that the verbal and prop manipulation tasks were essentially similar.

BIBLIOGRAPHY:

Stoltman, J. P. "Territorial Decentration and Geographic Learning." In W. Adams and F. Helleiner (Eds.), *International Geography 1972.* Toronto, Ontario, Canada: University of Toronto Press, 1972a.

Stoltman, J. P. *Manual: Territorial Decentration Test.* 1972b. ERIC documents nos. ED 065 512 and ED 065 513.

THREE-MINUTE REASONING TEST

AUTHOR: James Hartley

AGE: 11 years and up

VARIABLE: Logical reasoning

TYPE OF MEASURE: Sentence checklist

SOURCE FROM WHICH MEASURE MAY BE OBTAINED: James Hartley, Department of Psychology, University of Keele, Keele, Staffordshire, England ST5 5BG.

DESCRIPTION OF MEASURE: This test is a simplified version of one devised by Baddeley (1968) and is suitable for use with school children. The test is based upon the belief that there is, occasionally, a need for a quick test to measure subjects' intellectual abilities. The idea is that carrying out grammatical transformations should provide an intellectual task that is familiar enough to be performed very rapidly but that is sufficiently sensitive to measure intellectual capacity. In the test subjects are asked to read a sentence such as "A follows B" and then to decide whether or not this sentence correctly describes a subsequent letter pair, for example, AB. The test items comprise the following conditions, ordered at random: (1) positive or negative sentences, (2) active or passive sentences, (3) the use of "comes before" or "comes after" or "follows," (4) A or B mentioned first, and (5) the letter pair AB or BA. There are sixty-four items in all. Initially (see Hartley and Holt, 1971) students marked their answers in a true/false column. In a later version (see Hartley, Hogarth, and Mills, 1973) students ticked the sentence correct or incorrect.

As examples, the first ten items of the sixty-four on the test are given below. The respondent ticks the sentence correct or incorrect.

Examples	Response
1. B is not followed by A	BA
2. B does not come before A	AB
3. B does not come after A	AB
4. B is followed by A	AB
5. A is followed by B	BA
6. B follows A	AB
7. B comes after A	BA
8. B does not come before A	BA
9. A follows B	AB
10. A does not come after B	BA

RELIABILITY AND VALIDITY: Test-retest correlations for the test are low. In three experiments they have been found to be .79 (N = sixty-one university students: interval approximately 10 minutes); .66 (N = thirty-six 13-year-olds: interval 7 days); .32 (N = twenty-eight 13-year-olds: interval between 28 and 35 days). In terms of validity, correlations with the AH4 intelligence test reported are .70 (N = 164 15-year-olds) and .45 (N = forty-five 13-year-olds).

BIBLIOGRAPHY:

Baddeley, A. D. "A Three-Minute Reasoning Test Based on Grammatical Transformation." *Psychonomic Science,* 1968, *10,* 341-342.
Hartley, J., Hogarth, F. W., and Mills, R. L. "The Three-Minute Reasoning Test—A Reevaluation." *Educational Research,* 1973, *16,* 58-62.
Hartley, J., and Holt, J. "The Validity of a Simplified Version of Baddeley's Three-Minute Reasoning Test." *Educational Research,* 1971, *14,* 70-73.

TRANSITIVITY (*See note, p. 60)

AUTHOR: Jean Piaget (adaptation and scoring by Rheta DeVries)

AGE: Normal children 5 to 9 years

VARIABLE: Knowledge of transitive relations of lengths

TYPE OF MEASURE: Structured interview

SOURCE FROM WHICH MEASURE MAY BE OBTAINED: See DeVries (1971).

DESCRIPTION OF MEASURE: In a 10- to 15-minute interview the child is asked to make transitive inferences about the lengths of two gum straws without comparing them directly. A wooden dowel can be used by the child to measure each (one gum being shorter and one longer than the dowel). If the child does not spontaneously use the dowel to measure, the E does so and then asks which gum is longer. Other task items probe memory of the results of observed measuring and provide opportunity to assess whether the child can use the middle term to make a transitive inference after some help. A final task item confronts the child with the problem of perceptual contradiction of transitive inference (through surreptitious switching of dowels used for measuring). Although gum straws were used to enhance motivation in this study, non-edible materials can be used. Ss were scored on a 7-point Guttman scale, from 0 to 6. Norms are available for 143 bright and average children chronologically aged 5 to 6 years and retarded children mentally aged 5 to 7 years, according to Stanford-Binet IQ (DeVries, 1971).

As examples, the first of the seven task items of the interview is given below.

1. Place on two different tables on either side of the child two pieces of gum, one yellow short ($3^{13}/_{16}$ inches) and one green long ($3^{15}/_{16}$ inches).
                    Green long   Child   Yellow short
Present child with wooden stick, $3^{7}/_{8}$ inches long.
Say: Now, when I say so, I want you to find out which of these two pieces of gum is bigger, which has more gum to chew. If you can pick the bigger one, I'll give it to you to keep. If you don't pick the bigger one, you won't get gum this time; you'll have another chance to get gum later. You have to tell which one is bigger without moving the pieces of gum away from the tables, but you can use this wooden stick any way you want; you can move it to the tables if you want to. Go ahead, find out which is bigger. Point to the bigger one that has more gum to chew. (Hand child $3^{7}/_{8}$-inch stick.)
              _____Measures spontaneously   _____Does not measure
Ask: How do you know it's bigger?
If child does not measure: What if I thought this (child's nonchoice) is the bigger one, how could you show me it's not? Can you measure with the stick and make sure?
If child chooses green long and measures, move to Q6.
If child chooses yellow short or does not measure, move to Q2.

RELIABILITY AND VALIDITY: Interscorer agreement on 180 items for twenty randomly selected Ss was 100 percent. Regarding scale validity, it should be noted that the item related to the perceptual contradiction of logical inference should probably be omitted. It was intended to control for the possibility that on the nondeceptive items children might be able to see the length differences and thus make the test one of perception rather than transitive inference. However, the length differences were so small that it is unlikely that children could actually see the difference. The contradiction item could not be accomplished smoothly because it was mechanically difficult, which seemed to make some children suspicious. It was clear that some children capable of transitive inference simply preferred to trust their perceptual judgment in the case where they could actually see such a large difference in length.

BIBLIOGRAPHY:

DeVries, R. *Evaluation of Cognitive Development with Piaget-type Tests: Study of Young Bright, Average, and Retarded Children.* Final report to the Department of Program Development for Gifted Children, Illinois Office of Public Instruction, 1971. ERIC document no. ED 075 065.
DeVries, R. "Relationships Among Piagetian, IQ, and Achievement Assessments." *Child Development,* 1974, *45,* 746-756.

Prepared by Rheta DeVries

VALUE CHOICE STORIES

AUTHOR: Helena Harris

AGE: 7 to 12 years

VARIABLE: Moral judgment

TYPE OF MEASURE: Structured interview

SOURCE FROM WHICH MEASURE MAY BE OBTAINED: See Harris (1970).

DESCRIPTION OF MEASURE: Value Choice Stories is an instrument based on the research of Jean Piaget (1948) and consists of thirteen items that require the subject to make evaluative choices. Administered as a structured interview, the test has the subject make choices along four dimensions of moral judgment as follows: Consequences vs. Intentions, Immanent Punishment, Solutions to Transgression, and Meaning of Rules. These four dimensions are represented by five subtests on which the subject may be scored dichotomously as either "mature" or "immature."

As examples, three of the thirteen items making up the interview are given below.

6. Alice asked her mother to buy her a new toy. Her mother told her that she had enough toys already, and that she didn't want to give her money to buy a new toy.

But Alice wanted the toy, so when her mother was not looking, she took some money out of her mother's purse and bought the toy. The next day Alice became sick and had to stay in bed.

   a. If Alice had not taken the money from her mother's purse, would she have become sick? Tell me more about it.

   b. If you were Alice's mother, what would you do?

7. There was a boy named Tom. His father had gone out and Tom thought it would be fun to play with his father's fountain pen. First he played with the pen, and then he made a little blot on the table cloth. . . . A boy named Jim once noticed that his father's fountain pen was empty. One day when his father was away, he thought of filling the pen so he would find it full when he came home. While he was opening the ink bottle, he made a big blot on the table cloth.

   a. Did one boy do something worse than the other boy? Who? Why?

   b. If you were Tom's (or Jim's, or their) parent, what would you do?

9. If you wanted to explain to someone why he should not break other people's things, what would you tell him?

RELIABILITY AND VALIDITY: None reported.

BIBLIOGRAPHY:

Harris, H. "The Development of Moral Attitudes in White and Negro Boys." *Developmental Psychology*, 1970, *2*, 376-383.

Piaget, J. *The Moral Judgment of the Child.* Glencoe, Illinois: Free Press, 1948.

VISUAL ALERTNESS SCALE FOR NEWBORN INFANTS

AUTHORS: Anneliese F. Korner and Evelyn B. Thoman

AGE: Premature and full-term infants

VARIABLE: Degree of visual alertness

TYPE OF MEASURE: Rating scale

SOURCE FROM WHICH MEASURE MAY BE OBTAINED: See Korner and Thoman (1970).

DESCRIPTION OF MEASURE: The Visual Alertness Scale has been used to score the level of alertness of full-term newborns in response to various soothing interventions. The scale can also be used for evaluating spontaneous visual behavior or the infant's response to visual stimuli. There is no reason why the scale cannot also be applied to prematures or to infants up to 1 month of age. The scale is very simple. Scores are given as follows: 0—infant does not open eyes, 1—infant opens eyes momentarily or minimally several times, 2–infant opens eyes over a sustained period (anything in excess of five seconds), 3–infant scans drowsily or nonalertly, 4–infant alerts with bright and shiny eyes, 5–infant scans with bright alert eyes. In the authors' application (Korner and Thoman, 1970) the highest level of alerting achieved was scored during a 30-second observation period.

RELIABILITY AND VALIDITY: Complete agreement between two observers was reached in 92 percent of 251 ratings.

BIBLIOGRAPHY:

Korner, A. F. "Visual Alertness in Neonates: Individual Differences and Their Corre-
lates." *Perceptual and Motor Skills*, 1970, *31*, 499-509.
Korner, A. F., and Thoman, E. B. "Visual Alertness in Neonates as Evoked by Maternal
Care." *Journal of Experimental Child Psychology*, 1970, *10*, 67-78.

WALKER READINESS TEST FOR DISADVANTAGED PRESCHOOL CHILDREN (FORMS A AND B)

AUTHOR: Wanda H. Walker

AGE: 4 to 6 years; standardized on 3 to 9 years

VARIABLE: Readiness of children for first school experiences

TYPE OF MEASURE: Culture-fair, nonverbal, readiness test

SOURCE FROM WHICH MEASURE MAY BE OBTAINED: Wanda Walker, Northwest Missouri State College, Marysville, Missouri 64468. Cost: $.75 for microfiche; $7.45 for hard copy (available in microfiche and hard copy only from ERIC Document Repro-duction Service, 4936 Fairmont Blvd., Bethesda, Maryland 20014); $20.00 for xerox copy of entire final report. The tests alone with enough statistical data for valid inter-pretation of results are available from the Regional Office of Education, Bureau of Research, Kansas City, Missouri 66101; one copy each of Forms A and B free of charge.

DESCRIPTION OF MEASURE: This measure was designed to be a culture-fair, non-verbal readiness test for rural and urban disadvantaged preschool children. The test was developed in two forms—Form A to be administered early in the school year to iden-tify weaknesses and set up individual remedial programs, and Form B to be adminis-tered during the final weeks of the year to assess the efficiency of the program used and the progress of the child. The test is untimed, but each form can be administered to a child in 8 to 10 minutes. Scoring may be done by an aide or volunteer with the use of the answer sheets and a scoring stencil. The test consists of fifty items divided as follows: Part I: Likeness or Similarities (twenty-five items); Part II: Differences (fifteen items); Part III: Numerical Analogies (five items): Part IV: Missing Parts (five items). All of the items are pictorial. Norms are provided, based on a sample of several thousand children—boys and girls, urban and rural, and enrolled in year-round and summer-only programs. They include, for seven age groups from ages 4-0 down to 6-7 up, means, medians, quartiles, standard deviations, and percentiles.

RELIABILITY AND VALIDITY: None reported.

BIBLIOGRAPHY:

Walker, W. *A Readiness Test for Disadvantaged Preschool Children, PREP Kit No. 22.* ERIC document no. ED 037 253.

WIDE-RANGE INTELLIGENCE TEST

AUTHORS: Paul I. Jacobs and Mary Vandeventer

AGE: 6 to 12 years

VARIABLE: General intelligence ("g")

TYPE OF MEASURE: Test

SOURCE FROM WHICH MEASURE MAY BE OBTAINED: Paul I. Jacobs, 30 Valley Road, Princeton, New Jersey 08540. The test is in color. A xeroxed copy will be made available at the current cost for xeroxing.

DESCRIPTION OF MEASURE: This fifty-seven item test of double-classification skills uses those logical relations uncovered in a survey of 201 different aptitude and intelligence tests. It was constructed in the following manner: a 2 X 2 or 3 X 3 matrix of 2-inch square cells was printed on each of fifty-seven 8½ X 11-inch sheets of paper. On a given sheet each cell contains a painted shape except for the lower-right-hand cell, which is empty. The *S*'s task, as in Raven's Colored Progressive Matrices Test, is to determine what belongs in the empty cell. Along the bottom of each sheet are four response alternatives: the correct answer, the figure directly above the missing cell, the figure directly to the left of the missing cell, and a "relevant other." On each sheet these four alternatives are arranged in random order.

    The fifty-seven matrices are grouped into twelve sets based on the relationships involved. With exceptions, within each set color and shape are each paired with one of nine basic relations: size, shading, elements of a set, number series, addition, added element, reversal, flip-over, or movement in a plane. Two forms of the test have been developed.

RELIABILITY AND VALIDITY: None reported.

BIBLIOGRAPHY:

Jacobs, P. I. *How to Win at Intelligence.* Princeton, New Jersey: Alcourt Press (in press).

Jacobs, P. I., and Vanderventer, M. "The Learning and Transfer of Double-Classification Skills: A Replication and Extension." *Journal of Experimental Child Psychology,* 1971, *12,* 240-257.

Jacobs, P. I., and Vanderventer, M. "Evaluating the Teaching of Intelligence." *Educational and Psychological Measurement,* 1972, *32,* 235-248.

WOLFE-BLUEL SOCIALIZATION INVENTORY (WBSI)

AUTHORS: Sharon Wolfe and Kathy Bluel

AGE: Mental age of about 6 months to 5 years

VARIABLE: Social Maturity and self-care skills

TYPE OF MEASURE: Rating scale

SOURCE FROM WHICH MEASURE MAY BE OBTAINED: See Heal (1972).

DESCRIPTION OF MEASURE: The WBSI consists of sixty-two behavioral and quasi-behavioral items organized into seven subscales: (1) Self-care (seven items)—toilet training and cleanliness; (2) *Environmental orientation* (ten items)—awareness of the animate and inanimate objects in one's environment; (3) *Independence* (eight items) —disposition or ability to play or function without help; (4) *Communication* (nine items)—verbal or nonverbal communication; (5) *Emotional Maturity* (ten items)—socially approved or disapproved behaviors; (6) *Group Interaction* (eleven items)—cooperative socializing behaviors; (7) *Intellectual Growth* (seven items)—primitive cognitive skills. Each item specifies a behavior that may or may not characterize the subject being evaluated. The respondent's task is to assign a number to each item, depending upon whether the behavior characterizes his subject never (0), rarely (1), sometimes (2), or usually (3). Because the WBSI depends upon impartial but accurate judgments provided by a respondent, it should be administered by a carefully instructed observer who has frequent opportunity to observe the subject.

As examples, the first two of the seven subscales are given below.

Self-Care

1. Indicates when pants are wet or soiled.
2. Has bowel movements in toilet.
3. Urinates in toilet.

4. Remains dry entire night.

5. Shows discomfort when other clothing is wet or soiled.

6. Attempts to brush teeth after meals.

7. Shows distaste for dirty hands and/or face.

Environmental Orientation

1. Recognizes familiar people.

2. Shows awareness of danger.

3. Responds to facial expressions appropriately (returns smiles, etc.).

4. Is able to differentiate male from female.

5. Shows preference for some things (such as foods, colors, clothing, places, etc.).

6. Identifies own image in a mirror.

7. Regards other family members as "special" to him.

8. Conscious of adult approval or disapproval.

9. Anticipates with excitement upcoming special events.

10. Uses play or learning materials as they should be used (meaningfully attends to music, TV programs, pictures, books, etc.).

RELIABILITY AND VALIDITY: The field-testing of forty-nine children from three orthopedic schools and a research group ranging in age from 6 to 14 years from three orthopedic schools and a residential research project produced an interrater reliability of .506 for the total WBSI score. Reliabilities on individual items ranged from .10 for Environmental Orientation to .792 for Communication. The two-year test-retest reliability for twenty-five subjects was .694 for the total score and ranged from .425 to .781 for the seven subscales. Individual-item correlations are included with the norming data, making it possible to improve the instrument by judicious item selection.

BIBLIOGRAPHY:

Heal, L. W. *Evaluating an Integrated Approach to the Management of Cerebral Palsy.* Vol. III. Final report for Grant No. OEG-0-9-592149-450 (032), United States Office of Education, 1972.

Prepared by Laird W. Heal

ZEITLIN EARLY IDENTIFICATION SCREENING (ZEIS)

AUTHOR: Shirley Zeitlin

AGE: 4 to 6 years

VARIABLE: Screening for potential high-risk and very able students

TYPE OF MEASURE: Test

SOURCE FROM WHICH MEASURE MAY BE OBTAINED: Shirley Zeitlin, Campus Learning Center, State University College, New Paltz, New York 12561.

DESCRIPTION OF MEASURE: The ZEIS (research edition, 1975) is a short, individually administered instrument designed to identify early kindergarten and prekindergarten children who may have special learning needs. It screens out children who need further diagnosis to determine if they are potential high-risk learners or are so able that they could benefit from enriched learning experiences.

The screening consists of twelve sets of questions relating to language, cognitive development, auditory and visual memory, gross motor, visual motor development, body image, directionality, and laterality. The questions are divided into three parts: verbal, pencil-and-paper tasks, and nonverbal performance. The ZEIS is scored on the basis of 100 points. The questions cover a developmental range of 3 to 7 years with emphasis on 4- to 5-year-old development. There is a checklist for recording relevant observable behaviors, such as independence-dependence and speech. A checklist of Koppitz emotional indicators is also included, to be used by the school psychologist to evaluate the figure drawing question. Individual questions are not intended to be a measure of competence but are only part of an overall indication of the child's development. The screening may be administered by teachers, paraprofessionals, and other educational personnel after one training session. In addition to its use for individual screening, the ZEIS gives an overview of the entering kindergarten population and allows the staff the opportunity to adjust its curriculum accordingly. Included with the ZEIS are instructions for scoring and interpretation. All necessary materials are readily available in a school. The development and use of local norms are recommended. Normative data are being computed on a sample of three thousand (75 percent minority group) children from urban and rural areas of New York state.

As examples, two of the twelve sets of questions on the test are given below. The scoring for each correct answer and for the total item is shown in parentheses to the right of the questions.

1. Information
    a. "What is your name?" If first name only given, ask: "Do you
       have another name too?" First name (1), first and last (2).   (2)
    b. "How old are you?"   (2)
    c. "On what street do you live?"   (2)   (6) _____
5. Concepts
    a. Place the nine cubes of one color on the table, say: "Let me
       hear you count out loud the number of blocks I have."   (3)
    b. Group the blocks according to color in three groups (9-3-1) and
       ask: "Which group has the most blocks?"   (3)
    c. Place the 6-inch pencil and the 3-inch pencil on the table and
       ask: "Pick up the longer pencil."   (3)   (9) _____

RELIABILITY AND VALIDITY: None reported.

BIBLIOGRAPHY: None.

Group 1-b

Language and Number Skills

ALPHABET NAME INVENTORY/PRINTED UPPER CASE (ANI/PUC) AND ALPHABET NAME INVENTORY/PRINTED LOWER CASE (ANI/PLC)

AUTHORS: Alan Coller and Jack Victor

AGE: Preschool

VARIABLE: Knowledge of the upper- and lower-case alphabet

TYPE OF TEST: Nonverbal and verbal identification tests

SOURCE FROM WHICH MEASURE MAY BE OBTAINED: Jack Victor, 82-25 218th Street, Hollis Hills, New York 11427.

DESCRIPTION OF MEASURE: The ANI/PUC and the ANI/PLC, two of the Early Childhood Inventories (see Index of Measures), are individually administered inventories designed to evaluate the child's ability to identify the twenty-six upper- and lower-case letters of the alphabet. The ANI/PUC and ANI/PLC each consist of two separate tasks—a nonverbal task and a verbal task. In the *nonverbal receptive* task, the child is presented with twenty-six arrays of four letters each. The child is asked to point to specific letters present in each array as they are named by the administrator. The first thirteen letters asked for are those that occur most frequently in words typically used to teach initial reading and spelling skills. Each array contains two relatively high-frequency letters and two relatively low-frequency letters. The distractor letters are both visually and aurally highly discriminable from the critical letter. Familiar pictures are systematically placed among the nonverbal items to draw the child's attention to all positions in the arrays. In the *verbal expressive* task, the child is presented with each letter one at a time and is asked to name it. Two alphabet wheels are used to present the stimulus in this task. The nonverbal task is administered first, followed by the verbal task.

   Alternate forms of the nonverbal task have been developed to aid in the evaluation of guessing and positional response set behaviors. If accurate diagnostic information is desired for very young children, both nonverbal forms should be administered. The two forms of the ANI/PUC and the ANI/PLC differ only in the arrangement of the numerals in the same array. In Set B of each inventory, position 1 contains the numerals that were in position 3 in Set A. Positions 1, 2, 3, and 4 in Set A become, respectively, positions 3, 4, 1, and 2 in Set B.

RELIABILITY AND VALIDITY: Alternate form reliabilities were obtained for a sample of inner-city children in prekindergarten to first grade. The correlations are .84 for prekindergarten, .94 for kindergarten, and .92 for first grade.

BIBLIOGRAPHY:

Coller, A., and Victor, J. *Early Childhood Inventories Project.* New York: New York University, Institute for Developmental Studies, 1970.
Ryan, T. J., and Moffitt, A. R. "Evaluation of Preschool Programs." *Canadian Psychologist,* 1974, *15,* 205-219.

Prepared by Alan Coller, Jack Victor, and John Dill

AMBIGUITY TEST

AUTHOR: Frank S. Kessel

AGE: 4 years and up

VARIABLE: Comprehension of ambiguous sentences

TYPE OF MEASURE: Semistructured task

SOURCE FROM WHICH MEASURE MAY BE OBTAINED: See Kessel (1970).

DESCRIPTION OF MEASURE: The materials for the Ambiguity Test are comprised of a set of twelve ambiguous sentences and four line drawings for each sentence. The sentences are grouped into three ambiguity types drawn from linguistic theory—lexical, surface structure, and deep structure—and there are four sentences for each type. Two pictures represent the correct meanings of each ambiguity, and two pictures represent incorrect meanings; at least one of the latter is designed to add insight into the way the sentence is being interpreted. Each sentence is read with full intonation (repeated with alternative intonation for surface structure ambiguities) and the child chooses the picture(s) that "go with" the sentence. A period of semistructured questioning (along the lines of Piaget's "clinical method") then seeks to improve "diagnostic validity" by establishing the reasons for the child's picture choice (compare the incorrect picture). Although this cross-questioning differs from sentence to sentence, it follows a largely consistent pattern for any one sentence (Kessel, 1970). On the basis of picture choice and responses to cross-questioning, the child's comprehension of each sentence is scored "correct," "partially correct," or "incorrect."

As examples, four of the twelve ambiguous sentences that accompany the line drawings are given below.

1. She was bothered by the cold.
2. He put gas in the tank.
3. She hit the man with glasses.
4. They fed her dog biscuits.

RELIABILITY AND VALIDITY: There are no formal data on reliability and validity. Further studies (Brause, 1974; Jergens, 1971; Shultz and Pilon, 1973), while introducing variations to the task, have confirmed the basic findings: (1) Lexical ambiguities are comprehended earlier than surface-structure ones, which are in turn comprehended earlier than deep-structure ones; (2) the correct comprehension of all ambiguity types does not occur until early adolescence, and perhaps later. The variations introduced are of several kinds: (1) additional ambiguity types, (2) a paraphrase measure of comprehension, (3) sentences read with "neutral" intonation, (4) use of older subjects, and (5) relating comprehension of linguistic ambiguity to other cognitive processes and skills (e.g., appreciation of riddles). These variations and the interesting data they have yielded suggest that the Ambiguity Test should have been used less as a test and more as a flexible task in research aimed at broad issues in cognitive and language development.

BIBLIOGRAPHY:

Brause, R. S. "On Ambiguity: Development of the Ability to Understand Aspects of Semantic Ambiguity." Unpublished doctoral dissertation. New York University, New York, 1974.

Jurgens, J. M. "Perception of Lexical and Structural Ambiguity by Junior and Senior High School Students." Unpublished doctoral dissertation. George Peabody College for Teachers, Nashville, Tennessee, 1971.

Kessel, F. S. "The Role of Syntax in Children's Comprehension from Ages Six to Twelve." *Monographs of the Society for Research in Child Development,* 1970, *35* (139), 1-95.

Shultz, T. R., and Pilon, R. "Development of the Ability to Detect Linguistic Ambiguity." *Child Development,* 1973, *44,* 728-733.

ANALYTIC SCALE FOR MEASURING
THE SEMANTIC NOVELTY OF POEMS

AUTHOR: Gerald G. Duffy

AGE: 8 to 12 years

VARIABLE: The semantic (nonprosodic) elements of children's poetry-writing performances

TYPE OF MEASURE: Rating scale

SOURCE FROM WHICH MEASURE MAY BE OBTAINED: Gerald G. Duffy, 357 Erickson Hall, Michigan State University, East Lansing, Michigan 48824.

DESCRIPTION OF MEASURE: The theory of poetry writing was studied and statements of poets, critics, and language arts experts were used to identify the seven semantic, or nonprosodic, elements of poetry found in the scale. To score poems, three raters award points for each of the seven criteria, comparing the poem being scored with the descriptive statements and illustrative poems in the instrument and assigning points on the basis of this analysis. The scores of the three raters are then averaged. All raters are trained in the use of the instrument prior to the start of scoring. To insure a common interpretation of the criteria, raters revise slightly the wording of criterion items causing communication difficulties and cooperatively score poems for practice both prior to and periodically during scoring sessions. Rater bias is neutralized by removing all identifying characteristics and by typing all poems in an identical fashion prior to scoring.

As an example, a portion of Part I of the scale is reproduced below. The two other categories in Part I rate organization and "solving the problem and/or ending the poem." Part II of the scale rates Sensitivity, which includes stimulus perception, emotional depth, and language. Part III, Expressive Richness, rates "combining ideas and/or things in unusual relationships."

Part I. Content

    A. Theme. The writer says something which is either new or is communicated in a unique manner.

        0—The writer has no "message" or the idea is not conveyed clearly to the reader.

            The tree is merrily showing its bud,

            As the sun is drawing up all the mud;

            The flowers are really showing their faces,

            As the birds are flying to all different places.

        1—The writer communicates a "message" to the reader, but neither the idea nor the approach to the idea is unique.

            In the morning air

            You can hear the birds singing

            Like a flute playing.

        2—The writer's "message" is unique or is expressed in a unique manner.

            Swinging on its slender stalk,

            The unknown flower

            Enjoys itself every day,

            Playing tag with

            The others of its kind.

RELIABILITY AND VALIDITY: Statistical techniques were utilized to determine the validity and reliability of the instrument. First it was hypothesized that if the instrument were valid, the scores assigned to poems by raters would correlate highly with the writer's subjective prediction of what those scores would be, raters using it would discriminate between nonsense poems having few of the semantic elements being measured and those having received critical acclaim for such elements, and the scores assigned to poems would reflect the growth of verbal skills from grade to grade. If the instrument were reliable, a substantial relationship would exist from rater to rater in the scoring of each poem. The resultant data indicate that a valid and reliable instrument has been developed for measuring the semantic elements of poetry-writing performance.

BIBLIOGRAPHY:

Duffy, G. G. "Instruction in Prosody as It Affects the Semantic Novelty of Poems Written by Intermediate Grade Children." Unpublished doctoral dissertation. Northern Illinois University, De Kalb, 1966.

Duffy, G. G. "Insights in the Teaching of Poetry Writing." *The Elementary School Journal,* 1968, *69,* 32-37.

Duffy, G. G. "The Construction and Validation of an Instrument to Measure Poetry Writing Performance." *Educational and Psychological Measurement,* 1968, *28,* 1233-1236.

ANASTASIOW AND HANES REPETITION TASK

AUTHORS: Nicholas J. Anastasiow and Michael L. Hanes

AGE: 4 to 12 years

VARIABLE: Language development of children who speak subcultural vernacular

TYPE OF MEASURE: Test

SOURCE FROM WHICH MEASURE MAY BE OBTAINED: See Anastasiow and Hanes (1974).

DESCRIPTION OF MEASURE: The Sentence Repetition Technique is designed as a diagnostic tool to assist early-childhood education, kindergarten, and elementary-grade teachers in distinguishing among children who speak a different vernacular and are normal in language development from those children who speak a different vernacular and are developmentally delayed. The instrument contains twenty-eight well-formed English sentences with a wide variety of English language structures, for example, interrogative, simple declarative, and so on.

The sentences are designed to yield two scores. The first is the Reconstruction Score. This score is a measure of how many words that have equivalents in nonstandard dialect the child "reconstructs" or changes to his own vernacular. For example, the child might repeat: "She isn't a good singer" and "She ain't no good singer." At least one standard form having an equivalent form in nonstandard vernacular is included in each sentence. Most sentences have more than one form that can be reconstructed into nonstandard vernacular. The second score is the Function Word Omissions. The sentences are constructed to contain at least one abstract function word to determine the degree of difficulty children are having with these forms. It is suspected that children with high Function Words Omissions scores are developmentally delayed in their language acquisition (Anastasiow and Hanes, 1974).

The instrument is designed to aid the teacher in determining whether a child is repeating abstract terms (Function Words Correct), is developmentally delayed (Function Words Omissions), or is reconstructing (word is changed to an equivalent form in poverty vernacular). In addition, a fourth category is included. It was found that children will substitute words for the ones they are asked to repeat. The words substituted frequently are equivalent to the one given in the sentence; for example, for "neater" the child might substitute "cleaner." These substitutions are considered correct if they maintain the meaning of the sentence.

As examples, the first fifteen of the twenty-eight statements are given below.

1. He was tied up.
2. She isn't a good singer.
3. Where can he do what he wants?
4. Then he went to the movies by himself.
5. She said, "Whose toys are those?"
6. Did an accident happen while your mother was in the store?
7. Jim, who tried to escape, was caught and then beaten up.
8. Although I want ice cream, I bet I'm not going to get any.

9. The boy was hit by the girl who jumped rope in the street.

10. He runs home quickly after school because he has a bicycle to ride.

11. If you want to see an elephant's baby, then you will have to go to a zoo.

12. Joe is good when he feels like it.

13. His mother wouldn't let him go to school because he had no shoes to wear.

14. I think Mary is absent because her mother thought she was sick.

15. The boys were given lots of milk by the ladies in the lunch room.

RELIABILITY AND VALIDITY: The original scale was administered to 229 first through fourth graders. The sentences were modified, and a pilot sample of seventeen kindergarten and first-grade students' test-retest reliabilities yielded an r of .95 for Function Words Correct, and $r = .92$ for Reconstruction Words Correct. Validity was inferred from the significant grade effects that were obtained on Function Words Correct scores from an administration of the revised scale to 230 inner-city blacks, 140 Puerto Ricans, and 319 rural whites. All grade effect Fs from first through third grade were significant at the $p < .05$ level. In addition, validity was inferred from the statistically significant negative correlations of Number of Reconstructions and Iowa Basic Skill Test ($r = -.55$) and the Metropolitan Achievement Test ($-.47$ to $-.52$). In addition, Function Words Omissions is negatively correlated with the Iowa Basic Skills Test ($r = -.50$ to $r = 0.56$) and the Metropolitan Reading Achievement Test ($-.49$ to $-.52$).

BIBLIOGRAPHY:

Anastasiow, N. and Hanes, M. "Cognitive Development and the Acquisition of Language in Three Subcultural Groups." *Developmental Psychology*, 1974, *10*, 703-709.

ARITHMETIC CONCEPT INDIVIDUAL TEST (ACIT)

AUTHORS: Gerald Melnick, S. Freeland, and Barry Lehrer

AGE: Primary- and intermediate-level educable mentally retarded children

VARIABLE: Arithmetic readiness skills

TYPE OF MEASURE: Individual test

SOURCE FROM WHICH MEASURE MAY BE OBTAINED: Curriculum Research and Development Center in Mental Retardation, Department of Special Education, Ferkauf Graduate School of Humanities and Social Sciences, Yeshiva University, 55 Fifth Avenue, New York, New York 10003.

DESCRIPTION OF MEASURE: The test is designed to assess the process by which students attack quantitative relations and to provide a diagnosis as to why particular children do not progress in their arithmetic skills. The test is based upon Piagetian concepts and on research concerning the relations between Piagetian concepts and arithmetic achievement. Tasks related to seriation, classification, class inclusion, differentiation of length and number concepts, one-to-one correspondence, conservation of number, and spatial relations are included.

As examples, four items from the Classification and Class Inclusion portion of the measure are given below.

Materials: 12 small and 2 big blocks of wood
1. Take out the blocks. Point to a small block and say, "Here's a bunch of grapes." Point to a large block and say, "Here's some apples. Put together the ones that belong together." (Note what the child does.) "Why did you put these (point to one group) together? Why did you put these together (point to the other group)?" Continue with 2 if S does not group the fruits correctly; otherwise, go to 3.
3. "How many apples are there? How many grapes are there?" It is not necessary that S give the correct number, merely that he recognize that there are more of one kind of fruit.
4. "Are the apples fruits? Are the grapes fruits? Tell me what a fruit is."
5. "Do we have more grapes or more fruits on this table? Why?"

RELIABILITY AND VALIDITY: The ACIT was administered to thirty EMR children, mean CA 10.4, MA 6.8, and IQ 66.3. Reliability data were not collected. Pearson product-moment intercorrelations indicate performance on Piagetian tasks was quite heterogeneous. Intercorrelations between subtest scores ranged from low to moderate positive. The highest correlation (.48) was between seriation and conservation of number. Interrelations of Piagetian tasks with arithmetic skills measured on the Arithmetic Concept Screening Test (ACST) were generally moderate and significant. Seriation proved to be the best predictor of arithmetic skills performance ($r = .70$). With the exception of seriation, IQ and MA were consistently better predictors of arithmetic skills performance ($r = .50$ and .68 respectively). With MA partialed out, seriation remained highly related to arithmetic skills ability. Seriation and class inclusion were significantly related to MA and IQ ($r = .65$ and .61 for seriation, and .40 and .40 for class inclusion).

BIBLIOGRAPHY:

Melnick, G., Bernstein, J., and Lehrer, B. *Interrelationships Between Piagetian Tasks and Arithmetic Achievement in Primary-Level EMRs.* New York: Curriculum Research and Development Center in Mental Retardation, Yeshiva University, 1973.

Melnick, G., Bernstein, J., and Lehrer, B. "Piagetian Tasks and Arithmetic Achievement in Retarded Children." *Exceptional Children,* 1974, *40,* 358-361.

Melnick, G., and Freedland, S. *Arithmetic Concept Individual Test.* New York: Curriculum Research and Development Center in Mental Retardation, Yeshiva University, 1972.

ARITHMETIC CONCEPT SCREENING TEST (ACST)

AUTHORS: Gerald Melnick, George Mischio, Jerry Bernstein, and Barry Lehrer

AGE: Primary and intermediate level

VARIABLE: Arithmetic skills

TYPE OF MEASURE: Group-administered test

SOURCE FROM WHICH MEASURE MAY BE OBTAINED: Curriculum Research and Development Center in Mental Retardation, Department of Special Education, Ferkauf Graduate School of Humanities and Social Sciences, Yeshiva University, 55 Fifth Avenue, New York, New York 10003.

DESCRIPTION OF MEASURE: The ACST is designed for placement and evaluation of EMR children in respect to their arithmetic skills. The test is designed to control for extraneous factors that cause MR children to fail, that is, presence of irrelevant stimuli, abstract test stimuli and responses, and lack of intermediary reinforcement. The test consists of 123 items divided into five subtests reflecting six levels of ability. Each test is administered separately. Concepts include: Basic Concepts, One-to-One Correspondence, Form and Size Discrimination, Rational Counting, More and Less, Visual Clustering, Before and After, Identification of Symbols, Reversability of Addends, Number Sequence, Rational Counting, Rule of Likeness, Ordinal Numbers, Addition and Subtraction Facts, Multiplication and Division Readiness, Multiplication and Division, and Money Concepts.

RELIABILITY AND VALIDITY: The ACST was administered to seventy-nine EMR students, mean CA 9-9 (SD = 1.4), mean MA 6-5 (SD = 1.0), and mean IQ 66.9 (SD = 7.6). Kuder-Richardson internal consistency estimates were obtained for items within each of the four subtests. The reliabilities for each of the five subtests were .74, .82, .90, .89, and .95. Content validity was derived from several sources. Independent item analysis for the subtests yielded a relatively low standard error of measurement (range 1.56 to 1.98) and a relatively high mean discrimination index (range .37 to .67). Varimax Rotation Factor Analysis for each subtest yielded factors corresponding to the concepts at each level except for one mixed factor, and the absence of factors corresponding to two concepts tested by only single items. Content validity was also indicated by a high number of significant correlations between scores at the various levels, confirming the hierarchical nature of the abilities upon which the tests were based. The intercorrelations of the ACST scale scores with IQ and MA were generally significant and in the moderate range.

BIBLIOGRAPHY:

Melnick, G., Bernstein, J., and Lehrer, B. "Piagetian Tasks and Arithmetic Achievement in Retarded Children." *Exceptional Children,* 1974, *40,* 358-361.
Melnick, G., Mischio, G., Bernstein, J., and Lehrer, B. *An Arithmetic Screening Test for Primary Level Retarded Children.* New York: Curriculum Research and Development Center in Mental Retardation, Yeshiva University, 1974.

Melnick, G., Mischio, G., and Lehrer, B. *Arithmetic Concept Screening Test Manual.* New York: Curriculum Research and Development Center in Mental Retardation, Yeshiva University, 1971.

BASIC CONCEPTS OF NUMBER

AUTHOR: Alec T. Brace

AGE: 4 to 7 years

VARIABLE: Number concepts

TYPE OF MEASURE: Test, interview type

SOURCE FROM WHICH MEASURE MAY BE OBTAINED: Alec T. Brace, Memorial University of Newfoundland, St. Johns, Canada A1C 557, at nominal cost.

DESCRIPTION OF MEASURE: The instrument is designed to assess the discrepancies between the young child's ability to count and his underlying ideas of numbers. It consists of six subtests with appropriate manipulative materials familiar to the children in the area in which the assessment is being done. Administration is by personal interview with each child. The tasks are primarily Piagetian-type and attempt to measure such things as cardinal number in one dimension, conservation of number and quantity (continuous), group recognition with groups up to five in pattern and random arrangement, group recognition with groups above five, comparisons of two groups, and cardinal number in two dimensions.

RELIABILITY AND VALIDITY: None reported.

BIBLIOGRAPHY:

Brace, A. T. "The Preschool Child's Concept of Number." Unpublished master's thesis. University of Alberta, Edmonton, Canada, 1963.
Churchill, E. M. "The Number Concepts of the Young Child." Unpublished doctoral dissertation. University of Leeds, England, 1958.
Dodwell, P. C. "Children's Understanding of Number and Related Concepts." *Canadian Journal of Psychology,* 1960, *14,* 191-205.
Hyde, D. M. "An Investigation of Piaget's Theories of the Development of the Concept of Numbers." Unpublished doctoral dissertation. University of London, 1959.

BOWEN LANGUAGE BEHAVIOR INVENTORY

AUTHOR: Mack L. Bowen

AGE: Mental age 3 to 6 years

VARIABLE: Receptive and expressive language behaviors

TYPE OF MEASURE: Individually administered test

SOURCE FROM WHICH MEASURE MAY BE OBTAINED: Mack L. Bowen, 1502 West Hovey, Normal, Illinois 61761.

DESCRIPTION OF MEASURE: This language test was developed to address a number of problems in assessing language behaviors in young children: (1) measuring language development/behavior in developmentally disabled children, (2) evaluating language based on criterion-referenced testing procedures, (3) sampling language ability on a receptive-motoric-expressive basis, and (4) sampling a number of language behaviors based on well-formulated theoretical constructs. These issues are represented in the language inventory, in that identifiable language behaviors necessary for functional language usage and for receptive and expressive language are included. Eight subtests representative of current learning theory are provided. A learning hierarchy approach was utilized to structure the inventory around the types of learning described by Gagné in *The Conditions of Learning* (1971). Five of the eight types of learning defined in Gagné's hierarchy were used to describe the levels of language learning attained by severely retarded children, ages 3 to 6 years. A review of literature on language behavior and language assessment, elaboration of the theoretical base, administration and scoring criteria, test format, age norms, and reliability and validity measures are provided in detail.

RELIABILITY AND VALIDITY: Based on a sample of 160 subjects, aged 6½ to 10 with Stanford-Binet IQs from 35 to 55, significant differences in performance were analyzed on the variables of age, IQ, and sex. Item statistics for each subtest include mean, median, standard deviation, standard error of measurement, frequency distribution, ranking by fifths, proportion passing, Kuder-Richardson formula 20, reliability coefficients, and point biserial correlations. Results and implications drawn from the described population and instrument are also available.

BIBLIOGRAPHY:

Bowen, M. "Some Procedures for Evaluating Language Development in Young Retarded Children." Unpublished doctoral dissertation. University of Illinois, Urbana, 1971.

Bowen, M. "Application of Learning Theory to the Evaluation of Language Development in Young Retarded Children." Paper presented at 50th Annual International Convention Council for Exceptional Children. Washington, D.C., March 1972.

Bowen, M. *The Development of a Language Behavior Inventory for Use with Young Children.* Paper presented at American Educational Research Association annual meeting, New Orleans, Louisiana, 1973.

Gagné, R. M. *The Conditions of Learning.* New York: Holt, Rinehart and Winston, 1971.

CARROW ELICITED LANGUAGE INVENTORY (CELI)

AUTHOR: Elizabeth Carrow-Woolfolk

AGE: 3 to 8 years

VARIABLE: Diagnosis of elicited language

TYPE OF MEASURE: Test

SOURCE FROM WHICH MEASURE MAY BE OBTAINED: Learning Concepts, 2501 North Lamar, Austin, Texas 78705. Cost: Kit (includes manual, training guide, training tape, 25 scoring/analysis forms, 10 verb protocol sheets), $39.95; additional scoring/analysis forms, $4.25/package of 25; additional verb protocol sheets, $4.50/package of 25.

DESCRIPTION OF MEASURE: The Carrow Elicited Language Inventory (CELI) has fifty-two stimuli ranging from two-word phrases to ten-word sentences. The test is normed for children ages 3 to 8. The scoring/analysis form includes a recording section where the child's errors are marked, a scoring section that breaks each phrase or sentence into grammar structure (articles, adjectives, nouns, and so forth) and error type (substitutions, omissions, additions, transpositions, and reversals), and a summary section where percentile rankings are recorded for each area. If the child has many errors in the verb column, the therapist may use the Verb Protocol form to further analyze the verb structure. With this diagnosis a therapist can write a descriptive plan for each child.

The following sentences are examples of items given to the child, which he repeats to the examiner: "The children don't play, do they?" "The man likes painting by himself." "Why is the doll broken?" "The boy is chased by the dog."

RELIABILITY AND VALIDITY: Three methods of validity were obtained. Two of these methods involved concurrent validity and one involved congruent validity. The first method showed that as age increased, so did test scores. The second method showed that the test could differentiate between language-disordered children and normal children. The third method used the CELI and the Developmental Sentence Scoring (DSS) to test twenty children whose language severity had already been established by outside experts. The rank order correlation (*rho*) between outside experts and the CELI was .77. The correlation between the CELI and the DSS was −.79.

BIBLIOGRAPHY:

Carrow, E. *Elicited Language Inventory*. Austin, Texas: Learning Concepts, 1974.
Cornelius, S. "A Comparison of the Elicited Language Inventory with the Developmental Syntax Scoring Procedure in Assessing Language Disorders in Children." Unpublished master's thesis. University of Texas, Austin, 1974.

Prepared by Betsy Waddell

COMPREHENSIVE MATHEMATICS INVENTORY

AUTHORS: Robert E. Rea and Robert E. Reys

AGE: 3 to 5 years

VARIABLE: Math competencies and skills of young children

TYPE OF MEASURE: Inventory

SOURCE FROM WHICH MEASURE MAY BE OBTAINED: NAPS document no. 00613, ASIS National Auxiliary Publication Service, CCM Information Sciences, Inc., 440 Park Avenue South, New York, New York 10016. Cost: $3.00 for microfiche, $6.50 for photocopy.

DESCRIPTION OF MEASURE: This 200-item inventory is administered orally and individually in two parts (separated in time), requiring approximately 30 minutes' total time. A sheet of procedures is available from the authors. Test fatigue has not been a factor with the CMI, as children have regarded it as a "game." The authors have trained teams of students, teachers, and others and achieved virtually complete scorer agreement. The instrument has not been normed and is not available commercially. The test administration booklet is complete enough to allow for reconstruction of the kit of materials.

As examples, sample items from five of the subscales are given below. Number and Pattern Identification complete the seven subscales.

Geometry	Material:	Board with cutouts and six wooden geometric shapes
	Procedure:	Place board in front of child. Lay pieces beside board. Ask child: "Place these shapes in the board for me."
Measurement	Material:	Thermometer (constructed of durable tag board and strip of dyed elastic)
	Procedure:	Set at 90°. Slowly move to lower settings (40°). Ask: "Is it getting hotter or colder?"
Money	Material:	Card 2 (penny, dime, and nickel mounted on card)
	Procedure:	Say: "Show me the penny. Show me the nickel. Which one will buy most?"
Recall	Material:	Pencil for child and examiner
	Procedure:	Tap pencil on table. Ask child to repeat by tapping his pencil: (1) tap; (2) taps; (3) taps
Vocabulary	Material:	Small animal
	Procedure:	Place animal on table facing child. Ask: "Place your hand *over* the animal. Place your hand *under* the animal. Place your hand *in front* of the animal. Place your hand *behind* the animal."

RELIABILITY AND VALIDITY: The Kuder-Richardson formula 20 produced coefficients ranging from .91 to .94 for Part I and from .83 to .87 for Part II. These data came from the analysis of scores from thirty groups of kindergarteners.

BIBLIOGRAPHY:

Rea, R. E., and Reys, R. E. "The Comprehensive Mathematics Inventory: An Experimental Instrument for Assessing Youngsters Entering School." *Journal of Educational Measurements,* 1970, *7,* 45-47.

Rea, R. E., and Reys, R. E. "Mathematical Competencies of Entering Kindergarteners." *The Arithmetic Teacher,* 1970, *17,* 65-74.

Rea, R. E., and Reys, R. E. "Competencies of Entering Kindergarteners in Geometry, Number, Money, and Measurement." *School Science and Mathematics,* 1971, *71,* 389-402.

Rea, R. E., and Reys, R. E. "Mathematical Competencies of Negro and Non-Negro Children Entering School." *Journal of Negro Education,* 1971, *40,* 12-16.

Reys, R. E., and Rea, R. E. "The Comprehensive Mathematics Inventory: An Experimental Instrument for Assessing the Mathematical Competencies of Children Entering School." *Journal for Research in Mathematics Education,* 1970, *1,* 180-186.

CRAIG LIPREADING INVENTORY

AUTHOR: William N. Craig

AGE: School-age deaf children; may be used with adults

VARIABLE: Lipreading and lipreading with hearing words

TYPE OF MEASURE: Words and sentences in multiple-choice format

SOURCE FROM WHICH MEASURE MAY BE OBTAINED: William N. Craig, Western Pennsylvania School for the Deaf, 300 Swissvale Avenue, Pittsburgh, Pennsylvania 15218. Although the test may be presented by an examiner, a filmed version with soundtrack is available. The cost for each filmed word test is $55.65 and for each sentence test, $42.93.

DESCRIPTION OF MEASURE: Frequently a measure of lipreading or lipreading with the addition of sound is desired in order to gain a more complete assessment of the communication levels of deaf students or deaf adults. To be maximally effective, this tool should provide meaningful lipreading scores for individuals having either fairly extensive or rather limited vocabularies and should at the same time maintain a representative inventory of English phonemes. Both the manner in which the individual responds to the test items and the consistency of test presentation must also be carefully assessed. To accomplish these objectives, a test was devised using two forms of a thirty-three-item word test of inventory-selected phonemes and two forms of a twenty-four-item sentence test to assess lipreading for more complete language patterns. The administration of this test has been described in Craig (1964). This set of four tests was subsequently filmed in color and was first used in this type of presentation by Quigley (1969). A soundtrack permits the use of this test for lipreading alone or with the use of residual hearing. The test has been broadly used to assess the lipreading performance of deaf people, and it appears in Jeffers and Barley (1971).

As examples, the first ten items of the Sentence Recognition Form A subtest are given below.

 1. A coat is on a chair.
 2. A sock and a shoe are on the floor.
 3. A boy is flying a kite.
 4. A girl is jumping.
 5. A boy stuck his thumb in the pie.
 6. A cow and a pig are near the gate.
 7. A man is throwing a ball to the dog.
 8. A bird has white wings.
 9. A light is over a door.
10. A horse is standing by a new car.

RELIABILITY AND VALIDITY: This inventory was designed to differentiate among lipreaders at all age levels between the end of the first grade through the tenth grade. The answer booklet provides pictures, simple words, and sentences in order to minimize the level of language competency needed to respond. In the original preschool study, the means for those who attended and those who had not attended preschool are presented for each form. Correlations with sex, mental age, hearing loss, and age are available as well. A summary of the word-test results obtained more recently is as follows, with the validity indicated by improving test scores with students' ages:

Age	Number	Mean	SD	Mean Hearing Loss
3	14	6.86	3.87	91.6
4	52	11.62	4.66	93.8
5	52	14.92	5.90	92.5
6	26	18.89	5.49	92.5
11	87	24.10	4.43	94.5

Sentence-test results for the 11-year-old group indicate a mean of 15.25 with a standard deviation of 4.81 on the same sample of eighty-seven students. Since many factors such as hearing loss, schooling, mental age, and others can contribute to lipreading competency, tests of this skill are best used to compare groups rather than to meet established norms. A list of studies in which this instrument has been employed is available (Craig and Craig, 1974).

BIBLIOGRAPHY:

Craig, H. B., and Craig, W. N. *Evaluation Manual.* Vol. 2. Pittsburgh, Pennsylvania: Western Pennsylvania School for the Deaf, 1974.

Craig, W. N. "Effects of Preschool Training on the Development of Reading and Lipreading Skills of Deaf Children." *American Annals of the Deaf,* 1964, *109,* 280-295.

Craig, W. N., Craig, H. B., and DiJohnson, A. "Preschool Verbotonal Instruction for Deaf Children." *Volta Review,* 1971, *33,* 236-246.

Jeffers, J., and Barley, M. *Speechreading (Lipreading)*. Springfield, Illinois: C. C Thomas, 1971.

Quigley, S. P. *The Influence of Fingerspelling on the Development of Language, Communication, and Educational Achievement in Deaf Children*. Research Report RD 1299s. Washington, D.C.: Rehabilitation Services Administration, Department of Health, Education and Welfare, 1969.

DEEP STRUCTURE RECOVERY TEST (DSRT)

AUTHOR: Herbert D. Simons

AGE: Grades 4 to 8

VARIABLE: Ability to recover the deep structure of sentences (underlying subject-object relations)

TYPE OF MEASURE: Test

SOURCE FROM WHICH MEASURE MAY BE OBTAINED: Herbert D. Simons, School of Education, University of California, Berkeley, California 94720.

DESCRIPTION OF MEASURE: The DSRT is a measure of children's skills in recovering the deep structure, that is, the underlying subject-object relations, of sentences. It consists of twenty-five items. Each item consists of three sentences. Two sentences in each item are paraphrases of each other and have the same deep structure and the same meaning. These two sentences have different surface structures due to the application of one or more extra transformations to one of them. The third sentence has a surface structure that is the same or similar to one of the other two sentences, but it has a different deep structure and consequently a different meaning from the other two sentences. Subjects are asked to choose the sentence that has a different meaning from the other two sentences. In doing this it is assumed that they must recover the deep structure of at least two of the sentences. In taking the test subjects are asked to work as fast as they can, but no time limits are set.

As examples, the first five items of the test are given below.

1. The boy gave a book to the girl.
   The book was given the girl by the boy.
   The book was given to the boy by the girl.
2. What the boy would like is for the girl to leave.
   For the boy to leave is what the girl would like.
   What the girl would like is for the boy to leave.
3. He painted the red house.
   He painted the house red.
   He painted the house that was red.

4. The girl asked the boy when to leave.
   The girl asked the boy when she should leave.
   The girl asked the boy when he should leave.
5. The girl who the boy hit fell down.
   The boy the girl hit fell down.
   The boy who the girl hit fell down.

RELIABILITY AND VALIDITY: On a sample of 103 fifth-grade subjects the DSRT correlated .732 with a Cloze Test of Reading Comprehension and .476 with the Reading Subtest of the Metropolitan Achievement Test. Both are significant at the .01 level. On the same sample the internal validity of the items as measured by a biserial correlation between the test items and the total score showed correlations ranging from .36 to .84. The Kuder-Richardson formula 20 reliability of the total DSRT is .796.

BIBLIOGRAPHY:

Simons, H. D. "The Relationship Between Aspects of Linguistic Performance and Reading Comprehension." Unpublished doctoral dissertation. Harvard University, Graduate School of Education, Cambridge, Massachusetts, 1970.

Simons, H. D. "Linguistic Skills and Reading Comprehension." In H. Klein (Ed.), *The Quest for Competency in Teaching Reading.* Newark, Delaware: International Reading Association, 1972.

DEEP TEST OF /S/ PERCEPTION

AUTHORS: J. L. Keely and C. L. Madison

AGE: 5 to 10 years

VARIABLE: Discrimination of /s/ from /θ/

TYPE OF MEASURE: Test

SOURCE FROM WHICH MEASURE MAY BE OBTAINED: C. L. Madison, Communication Disorders Clinic, Washington State University, Pullman, Washington 99163.

DESCRIPTION OF MEASURE: The test evaluates S's ability to distinguish /s/ from /θ/ in isolation and in the initial, medial, and final positions of real and nonsense words. The listening task was originally prerecorded on audiotape in a sound-treated booth. A Sony 530 stereo tape recorder and Sony MTL F-96 low-impedance microphone were used. The recorded task was presented to subjects via Telex ST-20 headphones. Children are advised to listen for /s/, depressing a clicker every time they hear the phoneme. As a pretraining task Ss are asked to differentiate the /s/ from other consonants selected to elicit gross differentiations between sounds. The pretraining task included as many items as were needed to insure a child's understanding of the task. Test items are presented individually at 5-second intervals. Positive responses to /s/ (click) and no response for /θ/ (no click) are counted as correct.

RELIABILITY AND VALIDITY: Test-retest reliability was established at .96.

BIBLIOGRAPHY:

Keely, J. L., and Madison, C. L. "Articulation and Speech Sound Perception of Primary Age Children for the Phoneme /s/." Paper presented at the annual convention of The American Speech and Hearing Association. Detroit, Michigan, 1973.

Prepared by C. L. Madison

DEVELOPMENTAL SENTENCE ANALYSIS

AUTHORS: Laura L. Lee and Roy A. Koenigsknecht

AGE: 2 years to 6 years, 11 months

VARIABLE: Grammatical development in children's spontaneous language

TYPE OF MEASURE: Weighted scores for a developmental sequence of grammatical structures

SOURCE FROM WHICH MEASURE MAY BE OBTAINED: Northwestern University Press, 1735 Benson Avenue, Evanston, Illinois 60201. Cost: *Developmental Sentence Analysis,* $13.50; *Interactive Language Development Teaching,* $15.00.

DESCRIPTION OF MEASURE: Developmental Sentence Analysis is a procedure for assessing a child's use of grammatical and morphological rules from a tape-recorded sample of spontaneous conversation with an adult. Eight grammatical categories are evaluated: indefinite pronouns, personal pronouns, main verbs, secondary verbs, negatives, conjunctions, interrogative reversals, and questions. Weighted scores are assigned to a developmental sequence of grammatical structures in each of these categories. A mean score per sentence is called the Developmental Sentence Score (DSS). Norms were produced from the analysis of a language sample of two hundred children ages 2-0 to 6-11 from middle-income homes where standard American dialect was spoken. The use of Developmental Sentence Analysis leads to the formulation of prescriptive teaching goals for children with language-learning problems.

RELIABILITY AND VALIDITY: A detailed statistical analysis of the DSS procedure indicated that significant differences were produced between age groups by the overall scoring and by each of its component grammatical categories. The overall internal consistency as measured by Coefficient Alpha was .71. The within-subject interval consistency was assessed in a split-half procedure, which resulted in an estimate of reliability of .73. A repeated measures procedure indicated that the DSS procedure could be repeated with confidence at intervals of 4 months. There was consistency on the DSS samples elicited by different interviewers.

BIBLIOGRAPHY:

Koenigsknecht, R. A. "Statistical Information on Developmental Sentence Analysis." In L. L. Lee, *Developmental Sentence Analysis.* Evanston, Illinois: Northwestern University Press, 1974.

Lee, L. L., Koenigsknecht, R. A., and Mulhern, S. T. *Interactive Language Development Teaching: The Clinical Presentation of Grammatical Structure.* Evanston, Illinois: Northwestern University Press, 1974.

DISCRIMINATION OF SPATIALLY CONFUSABLE LETTERS

AUTHORS: Doreen Asso and Maria A. Wyke

AGE: 5½ to 7 years

VARIABLE: Ability to match, copy, name, and write to dictation confusable letters

TYPE OF MEASURE: Test individually administered

SOURCE FROM WHICH MEASURE MAY BE OBTAINED: See Asso and Wyke (1971).

DESCRIPTION OF MEASURE: A measure of the ability to discriminate spatially confusable letters (p, q, d, b, u, n, h, y, w, and m) using four basic methods of testing: (1) asking the subject to reproduce (by drawing) a letter from a standard example (copying), (2) asking the subject to match a particular letter with an identical letter selected from an array of similar letters (matching), (3) asking the subject to attach a correct verbal label to a specific letter (naming), (4) asking the subject to write down a letter in response to the appropriate verbal command (dictation). Copying followed by matching are easier tasks than naming and writing letters to dictation. Accuracy of copying and matching indicates the development of a visual spatial ability, which is not necessarily accompanied by the ability to discriminate letters as purely verbal symbols.

RELIABILITY AND VALIDITY: None reported.

BIBLIOGRAPHY:

Asso, D. and Wyke, M. "Discrimination of Spatially Confusable Letters by Young Children." *Journal of Experimental Child Psychology,* 1971, *11,* 11-20.

Prepared by Maria A. Wyke and Doreen Asso

FAIRVIEW LANGUAGE EVALUATION SCALE (FLES)

AUTHOR: Alan Boroskin

AGE: Birth to 6 years

VARIABLE: Language skills

TYPE OF MEASURE: Behavior rating scale

SOURCE FROM WHICH MEASURE MAY BE OBTAINED: Research Department, Fairview State Hospital, 2501 Harbor Boulevard, Costa Mesa, California 92626.

DESCRIPTION OF MEASURE: The FLES is designed for use with the institutionalized severely and profoundly retarded. It is quite short, easy to administer by parent or caretaker, and easy to score. The measure is capable of assessing various levels of verbal and nonverbal language so that change can be quickly detected. The observer checks any of a list of speech-related handicaps the patient exhibits. The scale is composed of ten levels. Levels I through V are comprised of eight items each and Levels VI through X of six items each. The levels are arranged in *descending* order of language age in order to circumvent the need for obtaining a basal age. It is essential that the observer be familiar with the patient and that language proficiency be rated in terms of present status and not in terms of past performance or assumed potential. The abilities are in terms of "does" and not "can."
As an example, Level IV of the scale is given below.

LEVEL IV. (3 points per item)
_____ 1. Understands three prepositions (for example, in, on, off, down, from).
_____ 2. Knows concept of "one."
_____ 3. Repeats two digits (for example, two/seven or eight/four).
_____ 4. Can eat chewy meats (for example, steak, pork chop, hamburger).
_____ 5. Says simple sentences and phrases (that is, three or more words).
_____ 6. Names five or more common objects on command.
_____ 7. Points out doll's eye, ear, nose, mouth, and hair on command.
_____ 8. Says and answers to own name.

RELIABILITY AND VALIDITY: Four ward technicians each evaluated fifteen patients on their ward and evaluated them again after two weeks. The reliability coefficient was .95. When each ward technician evaluated approximately fifteen patients whom he knew best, and three months later the same group of observers evaluated the patients whom they had evaluated before, all coefficients of correlations were greater than .84, and most of them were above .90. A simply constructed language rating scale composed of two parts—"speech" and "understanding"—was administered to 138 mentally retarded patients. Each part was composed of six statements ranging from *No* (speech/ understanding) *at all* to (speech/understanding) *is excellent for age.* A score of 0 to 5 (0 = *no speech/understanding*) was assigned to each scale. The scales were filled out by ward personnel who were familiar with the patient and who did not have previous knowledge of the patient's FLES score. The correlation of LA with "understanding" was .76 and with "speech," .80. The correlation of LA with the combination of speech and understanding scores was .84.

BIBLIOGRAPHY:

Boroskin, A. *Manual for the Fairview Language Evaluation Scale.* Costa Mesa, California: Fairview State Hospital, 1971.

Prepared by James S. Giampiccolo, Jr.

FLEXIBILITY IN FINDING MEANINGS (FFM)

AUTHOR: Walter H. MacGinitie

AGE: 9 to 14 years

VARIABLE: Ability to recognize word (homograph) meanings in misleading contexts

TYPE OF MEASURE: Test

SOURCE FROM WHICH MEASURE MAY BE OBTAINED: Walter H. MacGinitie, Department of Psychology and Education, Teachers College, Columbia University, New York, New York 10027.

DESCRIPTION OF MEASURE: The purpose of this test is to measure the ability to shift conceptual sets in order to find an appropriate meaning for a multiple-meaning word. The test is in the form of a vocabulary test in which the correct answer is embedded among other words that are associated with a different meaning. An example is given below. Two common meanings of *bear* are "animal" and "carry." It is easier to recognize "carry" as one meaning of *bear* when "carry" occurs in the context "burden, weight, load" (as in line 3) than when "carry" occurs in the context "forest, wild, paw" (as in line 2). Similar reasoning applies to the two items (line 1 and line 4) based on the other meaning of bear ("animal"). In the actual test, of course, the correct answer is not always in last position.

1. BEAR	forest	wild	paw	animal
2. BEAR	forest	wild	paw	carry
3. BEAR	burden	weight	load	carry
4. BEAR	burden	weight	load	animal

There are three forms of the test: A, B, and C. Each form contains twenty-five sets of four items or a total of 100 items. Each of the twenty-five stem words (such as *bear*) appears once on each of the four pages of the test form. The order of the stem words and the particular item of each set of four that appears on a given page is randomized. All words used in the test are common words, occurring at least fifty times per million in the Thorndike-Lorge (1944) count. Ideally, it would be desirable to measure how long it takes a subject to find the right answer in the misleading context compared to how long it takes him to find the same answer in the helpful context. As an alternative, the measure that has been used is the number of answers correct when the answers appear in misleading contexts compared to the number of answers correct when the same answers appear in helpful contexts. The test is thus scored for each individual as follows: Inflexibility score = Ch–Cm/Ch where Ch is the number of answers correct when the answer appeared in a helpful context and Cm is the number of answers correct when the answer appeared in a misleading context.

RELIABILITY AND VALIDITY: The Inflexibility Score is based on a difference between two highly correlated variables and has, therefore, a relatively low reliability. Data from 456 school children in grades 4 through 8 and from 103 deaf children have been analyzed. The analysis recognized that an item contributes to the Inflexibility Score only when it is right or wrong at the same time that a related item is right or wrong. Item data from the hearing children showed a modest internal consistency. Of the discrimination indices for the seventy-five sets of items, only six were negative, forty were .10 or higher, twenty-three were .15 or higher, and twelve were over .20. Reliability estimates based on these discrimination indices were .36, .18, and .60 for Forms A, B, and C respectively. By combining all three of the preliminary forms, a reliability of about .66 would be expected. The average hearing child got about 15 percent fewer correct answers when the answers were in a misleading context than when these same answers were in a helpful context. There was no clear trend according to grade. Item context had essentially no effect on the deaf subjects, a result consistent with the notion that deaf children do not distinguish very clearly between denotative and associative relationships.

BIBLIOGRAPHY:

MacGinitie, W. H. "Flexibility in Dealing with Alternative Meanings of Words." In J. Rosenstein and W. H. MacGinitie (Eds.), *Verbal Behavior of the Deaf Child: Studies of Word Meanings and Associations.* New York: Teachers College Press, 1969.

HORST REVERSAL TEST

AUTHOR: Maria Horst

AGE: 5 to 6 years; also any age with reading difficulties

VARIABLE: Reading readiness; reading disability due to reversal problem

TYPE OF MEASURE: Test

SOURCE FROM WHICH MEASURE MAY BE OBTAINED: Maria Horst, Ménerbes, St. Hilaire, Vaucluse, 84560 France. Cost: $7.00 for set of 25 copies and instructions.

DESCRIPTION OF MEASURE: The test consists of a booklet of six short pages, the front page serving as an example of the task. It shows a row of six chairs, of which the first one is separated from the others by a double line. The chairs differ in facing direction and the child has to mark the chairs that are faced in the same direction. The items of the test involve objects, geometric forms, and letters. If the child reaches the limit of his ability before the end of the test, the test is stopped. The child's score is the number of errors made, an error being a faulty crossing or an omission. If a child becomes aware of an error by himself, he is told that he can indicate this by putting a mark under the item. Time limits do not appear to greatly affect the test results. The reversal is only one factor in the process of learning to read—but a very important one. The test is used mostly in batteries that concern other aspects of reading ability.

RELIABILITY AND VALIDITY: The test was given in the beginning of the first grade, and at the end of the school year the Wide Range Achievement Test was given. Correlations were found as follows: Horst Test—WRAT = .69, Horst Test—Teachers Rating = .66, WRAT—Teachers Rating = .84.

BIBLIOGRAPHY:

DeHirsch, K. *Predicting Reading Failure.* New York: Harper & Row, 1966.
Horst, M., and Wiegersma, S. *Nederlands Tijdschrift voor de Psychologies, Het onder- zoek van de leesrijpheid by zesjarige kinderen.* Leiden: Nederlands Instituut voor Preventieve Geneeskunde, 1958.
Inizan, A. *Le Temps d'Apprendre a Lire.* Paris: Librarie Collin, 1963.
Simon, J. "Les Dyslexies d'Evolution et la Psycho-Pédagogie de la Lecture." *Efrance,* 1954, *9* (November-December).
Zazzo, R., Ajuriaguerra, J., Borel-Maisonny, S., Galifret-Granjon, N., Stamback, M., Simon, J., and Chassagny, C. *L'Apprentissage de la Lecture et Ses Troubles.* Paris: Presses Universitaires de France, 1952.

ILYIN ORAL INTERVIEW

AUTHOR: Donna Ilyin

AGE: Fifth grade through high school

VARIABLE: Ability to understand and speak original English sentences

TYPE OF MEASURE: Structured interview in context

SOURCE FROM WHICH MEASURE MAY BE OBTAINED: Newbury House Publishers, 68 Middle Road, Rowley, Massachusetts 01969. Cost: Illustrated test book, $12.50; manual of instructions, $2.95; answer sheets (50), $1.95.

DESCRIPTION OF MEASURE: The purpose of the Ilyin Oral Interview is to place students in levels of English-second-language instruction by testing their ability to answer and ask questions in a picture-controlled interview situation. It is also used to identify the person who can ask and answer questions with the correct information but whose language structure patterns are incorrect. There are two forms of the test entitled, respectively, Bill and Sam. The examiner uses one of the two alternate test forms with pictures. In the conversational setting, he asks controlled questions about pictures in the book and records the student's score. The examiner may use a tape recorder and score at a later time. Each item has a possible score of 4 points on information, word order, verb structure, and other structures.

A sample item might be:

Examiner: What is Bill doing in this picture? *Student:* Watching TV. *Examiner:* Good. Tell me in a complete sentence. *Student:* He is watching TV.

In the sample the student would receive the following score: Information = 1, Word Order = 1, Verb Structure = 0, Other = 1. A student is not rated lower for foreign-accented pronunciation or for intonation patterns. If he says *washing* instead of *watching,* he still gets 1 point for Other. The context would make this remark understandable to a native speaker. However, he does not get a point for the verb because he did not say *is* or put an *s* on *he.* That is a structural error, not an accent. The main concerns are: (1) Can a native speaker of English understand him? (2) Is his information correct according to the context? (3) Are the structure patterns correct?

RELIABILITY AND VALIDITY: Reliabilities, most of which were derived from Kuder-Richardson formula 20, were high, ranging from .86 to .98 and centering in the low to mid .90s. Correlations of the Ilyin Oral Interview with other measures are: Michigan Aural Achievement Test, .56; Michigan English Language Placement Test, .67; Michigan Aural Achievement and MELP combined, .68; English Placement Test (lower level), .85; English Placement Test (upper level), .40.

BIBLIOGRAPHY:

Ilyin, D. "Structure Placement Tests for Adults in English-Second-Language Programs in California." *TESOL Quarterly,* 1970, *4,* 323-330.

Ilyin, D. "Placing Adults in ESL Classes by Guess or by Test?" Paper presented at TESOL annual meeting. New Orleans, Louisiana, 1971.

Ilyin, D. *Developing a Placement Test for Adults in English-Second-Language Programs in California,* 1970, ERIC document no. 036 766.

INTERPRETATION TEST

AUTHORS: Norman F. Watt and Thomas B. Benjamin

AGE: At least fifth- or sixth-grade reading ability

VARIABLE: Semantic meaning

TYPE OF MEASURE: Test

SOURCE FROM WHICH MEASURE MAY BE OBTAINED: Norman F. Watt, Tobin Hall, University of Massachusetts, Amherst, Massachusetts 01002.

DESCRIPTION OF MEASURE: The Interpretation Test measures certain forms of semantic confusion in interpreting the meaning of ambiguous words. It consists of forty-eight multiple-choice items in which the respondent is required to choose from among three answers, the one which makes most sense to him being an interpretation of the meaning of the sentence he has just read. Each sentence contains a key word for which more than one meaning is possible. The context of the sentence makes discrimination among the answers possible.

As examples, five of the forty-eight items of the Interpretation Test are given below.

1. *Every Friday Jim paid for his board at his rooming house.* This means:
    A. He paid for a flat piece of wood.
    B. He paid for his rollerskates.
    C. He paid for his meals.
2. *The critic praised the acting but found the plot dull.* This means:
    A. He didn't like the color of the car.
    B. He didn't like the main story.
    C. He didn't like the section of land.
3. *The night watchman could not find the right key.* This means:
    A. He sang the wrong musical pitch.
    B. He received two playing cards.
    C. He lost a metal object for opening a lock.
4. *The Chinese coolie was fined for throwing his junk in the bay.* This means:
    A. He had dumped his trash in the water.
    B. He had lowered his small sailboat into the water.
    C. He had washed the supper dishes.
5. *Philip's car has too little power to make such a grade.* This means:
    A. He should take another route.
    B. He should study more.
    C. He should enter the priesthood.

RELIABILITY AND VALIDITY: None reported.

BIBLIOGRAPHY:

Benjamin, T. B., and Watt, N. F. "Psychopathology and Semantic Interpretation of Ambiguous Words." *Journal of Abnormal Psychology*, 1969, *74*, 706-714.

Watt, N. F. "Developmental Changes in the Semantic Interpretation of Ambiguous Words." *Journal of Abnormal Psychology,* 1971, *77,* 332-339.

JAMES LANGUAGE DOMINANCE TEST

AUTHOR: Peter James

AGE: Kindergarten and grade 1

VARIABLE: Language dominance (Spanish/English)

TYPE OF MEASURE: Test

SOURCE FROM WHICH MEASURE MAY BE OBTAINED: Learning Concepts, Inc., 2501 North Lamar, Austin, Texas 78705.

DESCRIPTION OF MEASURE: The James Language Dominance Test categorizes Mexican-American children into one of five categories: (1) Spanish dominant, (2) bilingual in comprehension and production with Spanish as a home language, (3) bilingual in comprehension with English and Spanish as home languages, (4) bilingual in comprehension with English as a home language, and (5) English dominant. The test consists of twenty items in the comprehension section and twenty in the production section for both English and Spanish. The test is first administered in Spanish and then in English. Scoring is recorded during test administration on a separate Scoring/Analysis Form. Scoring information is found in the manual of instructions, as well as test history, administration instructions, content and criterion-related validity, and normative data. A special feature of this test is its use with all groups of Spanish speakers. The test allows for dialectical variations by accepting an alternate response if a certain percentage of the students use the alternate word in comprehension or production.

RELIABILITY AND VALIDITY: The Validity and Normative Data section of the manual includes evidence on content and criterion-related validity (James, 1974). It also contains the discriminant powers of the test, group norms, expectancy tables, and probability of misclassification between adjacent groups.

BIBLIOGRAPHY:

James, P. *James Language Dominance Test Manual, English/Spanish.* Austin, Texas: Learning Concepts, Inc., 1974.

Prepared by Betsy Waddell

KALKULIA II

AUTHOR: Ladislav Košč

AGE: 8½ to 17½

VARIABLE: Mathematical ability

TYPE OF MEASURE: Pencil-and-paper test

SOURCE FROM WHICH MEASURE MAY BE OBTAINED: See Košč (1969, 1971, and 1974) and Košč and Čečer 1967-1968).

DESCRIPTION OF MEASURE: Kalkulia II comprises 120 items in which the subject has to determine the exact number of balls in a pattern consisting of 10 X 10 and 25 X 4 regularly arranged circles. The number and placement of the black balls in the pattern varies, ranging from forty-eight to seventy-four in a symmetrical arrangement: along both axes of symmetry, only along the vertical axis, only along the horizontal axis, or along the diagonal axis of symmetry. The arrangement of the black balls is structured in such a way as to enable manipulation when counting them, not with the balls individually but with their *group* arrangement. The total of counted balls should come out as a result of the sum or (on account of the symmetry of the arranged elements) as a multiple of groups of manipulated elements. Partial written computations can be made beside each test item, and the total sum is then recorded in a specially assigned place so that the test can be scored with the aid of a special stencil. The administration of the test takes 35 minutes. The scores of correctly solved items serve as a starting point for the quantitative analysis; in the scoring system, the corresponding mathematical age (convertible into a mathematical quotient) is given to each total score. The subject can also be assigned a grade from 1 to 5, in accordance with the score distribution within each age group. The *Manual* (Košč, 1969) describes intratest scatter procedures to obtain scores on type of symmetry of the ball arrangement. The test discriminates between mathematically gifted and mathematically untalented disabled children (Košč, 1974), especially when the spatial component in the structure of their mathematical abilities is disturbed.

As examples, three specimen items from the test are given below.

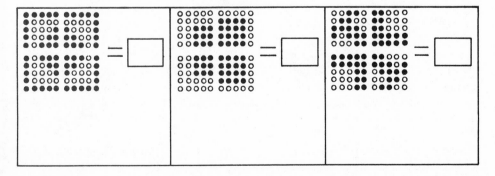

RELIABILITY AND VALIDITY: Kalkulia II is a substantially improved version of the original Kalkulia I. This new version was applied to 787 children (423 boys and 364

girls) selected randomly from Bratislava, Czechoslovakia schools for normal children aged 8½ to 16½. In addition the children were given other tests of mathematical abilities and mathematical knowledge. Kalkulia II correlated significantly with all these tests as well as with the school marks in mathematics. No substantial differences were found in the performances of boys and girls, and the score distribution for groups was approximately normal in each age group. The test clearly discriminates both within and between age groups. With regard to internal consistency, corrected split-half correlations and Kuder-Richardson formula 21 values were .8 or higher. Test-retest reliability for a special group of adult university students was .74, although this test is not suitable for the assessment of the level of mathematical abilities in adults.

BIBLIOGRAPHY:

Košč, L. *Test Kalkulia II Manual.* Bratislava, Czechoslovakia: Psychodiagnostika, 1969 (in Slovak).
Košč, L. "Psychology of Mathematical Abilities." *Studia Psychologica,* 1970, *12,* 159-162 (in English). Bratislava, Czechoslovakia: Štátne Pedagogické Nakladateľstvo, 1971 (in Slovak).
Košč, L. "Developmental Dyscalculia." *Journal of Learning Disabilities,* 1974, *3,* 164-177 (in English).
Košč, L. and Čečer, M. "A New Test for Measurement and Differentiation of Mathematical Abilities in Children." *Psychologia a Patopsychológia Diet'at'a,* 1967-1968, *2,* 325-336 (in Slovak).

KNOWN WORD TEST

AUTHOR: Elizabeth J. Levinson

AGE: 5½ to 7 years; also older retarded children

VARIABLE: Ability adequately to define words known to the child, and quality or cognitive level of definition

TYPE OF MEASURE: Test

SOURCE FROM WHICH MEASURE MAY BE OBTAINED: For original form of the test see Levinson (1963). The Scoring Key and the Scoring Guide for the revised test can be obtained from Elizabeth J. Levinson, 78 North Main Street, Orono, Maine 04473. Cost: $3.00.

DESCRIPTION OF MEASURE: This test was devised for use in an experiment testing the hypothesis that the intellectual functioning level of children can be improved by learning to define words in a cognitively more mature fashion. The measure is designed (1) to measure inability to define, as distinct from ignorance of word meanings; and (2) to permit qualitative assessment of the definitions given. It consists of thirty words chosen from the lists published by Murphy (1957) of words used in speaking by children in kindergarten and in the first three grades. These words were also checked against similar lists published by Rinsland (1945) of words used in writing by children in grades 1 to 8. The test contains ten words similar in difficulty to the first ten words of the Stanford-Binet vocabulary test falling into similar meaning categories, and two additional sets of ten words well known to children. The fact that they belong to similar meaning categories permits scoring of the definitions on the Known Word Test for correctness by the scoring directions provided for the first ten words of the Stanford-Binet. For further information regarding the test and its qualitative scoring, see Levinson (1963), and for this plus statistical results see Levinson (1971).

Given below are the first ten words of the Stanford-Binet Vocabulary Test, the thirty words of the Known Word Vocabulary Test, and four examples from the scoring key governing type or quality of the definitions given.

Known Word Vocabulary Test

S-B words	First ten words	Second ten words	Third ten words
orange	cake	apple	candy
envelope	package	bag	box
straw	cloth	grass	sand
puddle	lake	mud	hill
tap	crash	blow	clap
gown	raincoat	dress	coat
roar	whistle	sing	cry
eyelash	head	nose	hand
Mars	moon	sun	star
juggler	driver	clown	teacher

7b. Synonym or paraphrase, including constitutive material, specified further by statement of *extrinsic function*.

(cake) "Food. You cook it"
(hill) "Part of a road. You drive up and then down"
(mud) "Dirt. It's sticky, and you make mud pies"
(sand) "It's little rocks. You play in it"

6e. Synonym or paraphrase, including constitutive material, not specified further.

(cry) "A noise" (cake) "Food"
(sing) "Talk in a different way"
(sand) "Little teeny rocks"
(elbow) "The bend in your arm"

4b. Function, extrinsic, nonsynonym, specified further

(dress) "You wear it. It's soft"
(apple) "To eat. It has seeds"
(city) "Where you live in. Sometimes you go in stores and buildings"

2a. Poor or poorly expressed function, intrinsic, specified further.

(mud) "It holds you up so you won't fall through the ground. It's softer out in the road"

RELIABILITY AND VALIDITY: Levinson (1963) scored and rescored fourteen protocols with 92-percent agreement. Validity is believed to be supported by the improvement shown following training by the verbal group of experimental subjects in both MA and Known Word point score.

BIBLIOGRAPHY:

Levinson, E. J. "The Effect of Training in the Verbalization of Protoconcepts on Intelligence." Unpublished doctoral dissertation. University of Maine, Orono, 1963. Ann Arbor, Michigan: University Microfilms, No. 64-6800.

Levinson, E. J. "The Modification of Intelligence by Training in the Verbalization of Word Definitions and Simple Concepts." *Child Development*, 1971, *42*, 1361-1380.

Murphy, H., and others. "The Spontaneous Speaking Vocabulary of Children in Primary Grades." *Journal of Education*, 1957, *140*, 1-105.

Rinsland, H. D. *A Basic Vocabulary of Elementary School Children.* New York: Macmillan, 1945.

LEARNING POTENTIAL ASSESSMENT DEVICE: NUMERICAL PROGRESSIONS

AUTHORS: Reuven Feuerstein and others

AGE: 10 years to adult with normal population; 12 years to adult with retarded performers

VARIABLE: General intelligence based on numerical relationships

TYPE OF MEASURE: Paper-pencil test

SOURCE FROM WHICH MEASURE MAY BE OBTAINED: Distribution of this test at this time is limited to research and experimental work, and it can be obtained only from the author under specified conditions: Reuven Feuerstein, Hadassah Wizo Canada Research Institute, 6 Karmon Street, Beit Hakarem, Jerusalem, Israel.

DESCRIPTION OF MEASURE: The test consists of two parts: six training sheets and forty-six paper-and-pencil test items. The training is mainly oriented toward teaching the examinee the process of deducing a relationship, such as intervals in a numerical series; he must then apply the deduced rule to extend the progression. Training uses a great variety of strategies to produce flexibility and the proper methodology for the discovery of the underlying rule and its proper application. Both in the training and in the test, simple numerical tasks are used that do not require full mastery of basic arithmetic. The emphasis is on deductive processes, followed by use of rhythm and intervals.

The test provides the examinee with a great variety of opportunities to apply, in a varied way, the principles, skills, and strategies acquired during the training phase.

Supportive devices are interspersed throughout the test in order to ensure continuous interest maintained by the examinee's experience of success. The tasks are of increasing complexity, even though for the sake of encouragement, easier tasks are introduced. Thus we insure ourselves against the discontinuation of the work by the child, which is so often observed.

Because the test does not require basic arithmetic mastery, it can be used with low-functioning children who have learning disabilities and deficiencies in this area. The test may be used in clinical situations as well as for group testing. The time necessary for individual testing ranges from about 30 to 45 minutes. The group test may take longer because of the necessity of ensuring mastery of the rules by all the participants.

RELIABILITY AND VALIDITY: Reliability in group testing of 150 subjects for two retest periods (after 1 month and after 1 year) was, for the total sample: .67 over the long range from pre- to post- and .69 from mid- to post-; .72 between pre- to mid- on the short interval of a month. More than one thousand adolescents and young adults, ranging from above-average normals to the level of EMR from 50-75, were examined by individual and group tests, mainly the latter. They proved their ability to use efficiently the training session as manifested by their mastery of the test. No validity data are available at this date, but work-up of data is in progress.

BIBLIOGRAPHY:

Narrol, H., and Bachor, D. G. *An Introduction to Feuerstein's Approach to Assessing and Developing Cognitive Potential.* Toronto, Canada: Ontario Institute for Studies in Education, 1975.

LETTER DISCRIMINATION TEST

AUTHOR: Helen M. Popp

AGE: 5 to 8 years

VARIABLE: Ability to differentiate *b* from *d* in various contexts

TYPE OF MEASURE: Matching to sample test

SOURCE FROM WHICH MEASURE MAY BE OBTAINED: Xerox copy of the twenty-two pages constituting the three subtests and the instructions are available at the present time only *for research purposes*. They may be obtained by writing to Helen Popp, Harvard Graduate School of Education, 205 Larsen Hall, Appian Way, Cambridge, Massachusetts 02138. Cost: $2.00.

DESCRIPTION OF MEASURE: The Letter Discrimination Test consists of three subtests: (1) a subtest (thirty-six items) of *b* vs. *d* in isolation, in bigrams, and in trigrams in initial, medial, and final positions where possible; (2) a similar subtest (thirty-six items) for *u* and *e*; and (3) a subtest (thirty-six items) of bigram and trigram reversals (e.g., *ib* vs. *bi, bid* vs. *dib*). In subtests 1 and 2, items other than *b* vs. *d* items are included to test the ability to discriminate easier items (e.g., *dig* vs. *tig* in subtest 1, and *tid* vs. *dit* in subtest 3). An individual's performance on subtests 1 and 3 indicates specific *b-d* confusions.

RELIABILITY AND VALIDITY: The test was used in a research study as a pre- and postmeasure with intervening training on *b-d* discrimination. The cutoff point used in the study to select a "treatment" group was six or more errors on either subtest of thirty-six items (18-percent error). Data on the posttest were interpreted to indicate that a score of 10 or more errors on subtest 1 identified children who benefited from a letter/word discrimination training program ("benefited" meaning that they *succeeded* on the posttest whereas their matched controls did not). Reliability estimates from the Kuder-Richardson formula 21 for the three subtests are .89, .84, and .91.

BIBLIOGRAPHY:

Popp, H. M. "The Measurement and Training of Visual Discrimination Skills Prior to Reading Instruction." *Journal of Experimental Education,* 1967, *35,* 15-26.

LINGUISTIC CAPACITY INDEX

AUTHORS: Frederick H. Brengelman and John C. Manning

AGE: Primary-grade pupils

VARIABLE: English language readiness

TYPE OF MEASURE: Test

SOURCE FROM WHICH MEASURE MAY BE OBTAINED: Frederick H. Brengelman, Department of Linguistics, Fresno State College, Fresno, California 93710.

DESCRIPTION OF MEASURE: The Linguistic Capacity Index is based on a contrastive analysis of English and Spanish grammar and phonology. It is intended for use with primary-grade pupils whose native language is Spanish. The test may be used as a measure of English language readiness to assist the classroom teacher in grouping pupils for more effective English language instruction. The index may also be used to assess pupil achievement in learning English as a foreign language.

The Linguistic Capacity Index consists of three sections: Vocabulary Recognition, Contrastive Phonology, and Contrastive Grammar. The Vocabulary Recognition section contains twenty items measuring recognition of noun, verb, preposition, and adjective forms. In addition, all sixty items measure vocabulary development. The twenty items of the Contrastive Phonology section measure the pupil's ability to distinguish the following pairs of sounds, which are contrasted in English but not in Spanish:

(bean-bin)	(bought-boat)	(ship-chip)
(mane-men)	(pull-pool)	(lather-ladder)
(cat-cot)	(bad-bed)	(cupboard-covered)
(cot-cut)	(Sue-zoo)	(think-sink)

The Contrastive Grammar section of twenty items measures the pupil's understanding of English function words, word order, and inflectional constructions, which do not correspond to semantically similar constructions in Spanish.

can plus a simple verb	negative in verb—plus auxiliary constructions
be plus *ing* as present tense	*do*—auxiliary constructions
has plus *en* as perfect tense	*er* and *est* adjective comparison
noun as indirect object	noun as noun-modifer
likes	passive with *be* plus past participle

Total test time is about 35 minutes. A pretest is provided to familiarize the children with the mechanics of taking the test. The stimuli for the test are provided by the test booklet, which includes pictures and designs, and the accompanying stimulus-instructions, which are in the six-page manual of instructions.

RELIABILITY AND VALIDITY: None reported.

BIBLIOGRAPHY:

Jameson, G. "The Development of a Phonemic Analysis for an Oral English Proficiency Test for Spanish-Speaking School Beginners." Unpublished doctoral dissertation. University of Texas, Austin, 1967.

Prepared by Orval G. Johnson

LINGUISTIC READING TESTS I AND II

AUTHORS: Nicholas J. Anastasiow and Duncan Hansen

AGE: Grades 1 and 2

VARIABLE: Linguistic competency in decoding print

TYPE OF MEASURE: Paper-and-pencil test

SOURCE FROM WHICH MEASURE MAY BE OBTAINED: Nicholas J. Anastasiow, Institute for Child Study, 10th and Bypass 46, Bloomington, Indiana 47401.

DESCRIPTION OF MEASURE: The linguistic reading tests are designed to provide criterion measures for reading programs that emphasize the structural nature of phonological and syntactic systems rather than word frequency or story content (look-say approaches). The tests are designed to measure general linguistic competencies in decoding print. They are paper-and-pencil tests and can be administered in one period to an entire class. The specific subtests are designed to measure specific aspects of the decoding process pertinent to beginning reading. In Linguistic Test I, the first subscale requires the decoding of a key word embedded in a meaningful grammatical sentence and associating it with a pictorial representation (e.g., a picture of a deer on the left is to be matched by the sentence "See the deer run" as opposed to an incorrect alternative like "See the dare run"). The second subscale requires the child to demonstrate explicit phoneme-to-letter correspondence rules within the constraints of a graphemic environment (e.g., the word *not* is listed and the child is required to add the letter *e* in order to form the word *note*). Subscale three requires the child to form a compound word from two unbounded morphemes (e.g., the child should form the compound *bathmat* from the array *mat, bet, bath, man*). Subscale four requires the child to identify legitimate numbers of a form-class within the context of the sentence (e.g., from the sentence "Pat gave Nat a ball" the child should select the column "ball, pen, hat" as opposed to the alternative "ball, tall, fine"). Subscale five requires the child to judge the grammar of phrase structures (e.g., the child should select the phrase "a big hug" as opposed to the alternatives "hug a big" or "a hug big"). Subscale six requires the child to construct a grammatical sentence from three or four arrays of words (e.g., the child should construct a sentence "Pat ran home" from the three arrays "Pat, fat, under, like; like, ran, you, to; he, not, got, home"). Finally, subscale seven requires the child to listen to linguistic utterance units and correctly associate them with written representatives (e.g., the child would listen to "I wanna" and should pick "I want to"). All the subscales are introduced by one illustrated example.

Linguistic Reading Test II contains eight subscales constructed in the same manner as Test I, and the subscales contain content from simple letter-to-sound decoding to syntactic reading analysis of sentences. The subscale titles include: key word discrimination, phoneme-to-letter correspondence, morphemes, sentence structure, form class, compound words, suffix reading, and sentence transformation.

RELIABILITY AND VALIDITY: The revised edition of Linguistic Test I was administered to 232 first graders in ten separate classrooms. The Pearson product-moment r (odd-even) for the total test was .94. The revised edition of Linguistic Reading Test II was administered to 213 second-grade children. The split-half r was .97. Correlations of Gates Primary Reading and Linguistic Test I scores were .76 for Primary Word Reading, .52 for Paragraph Reading, .80 for Advance Word Reading, and .53 for Advance Paragraph Reading. Linguistic Reading Test II correlated with Gates Advanced Paragraph Reading, $r = .68$ and with Gates Advanced Word Reading, $r = .78$. Teacher's rating of children's success in first grade correlated with Linguistic Reading Test II for total scale, $r = .67$. Additional information can be found in Anastasiow and Hansen (1967, 1968).

BIBLIOGRAPHY:

Anastasiow, N. J., and Hansen, D. "Criteria for Linguistic Reading Programs." *Elementary English,* 1967, *44,* 231-235.
Anastasiow, N. J., and Hansen, D. "Linguistic Reading Test Number II." *Journal of Educational Measurement,* 1968, *5,* 243.

MACKEY'S PROFILES OF LANGUAGE BEHAVIOR

AUTHOR: William Francis Mackey

AGE: Self-administered, 8 years and up; parent-administered, under 8 years

VARIABLE: Distribution of languages and/or dialects in behavior

TYPE OF MEASURE: Frequency distribution checklist

SOURCE FROM WHICH MEASURE MAY BE OBTAINED: See Mackey (1972, 1974, or in press) or Beebe and Mackey (in press). Also available from the Information Officer, International Center for Research on Bilingualism, Cité Universitaire, Laval University, Quebec, Canada G1K 7P4.

DESCRIPTION OF MEASURE: This is a checklist-type of questionnaire of 100 items designed to produce a profile of individual language behavior by scale and frequency distribution. Intended for the description of bilingual, bidialectal, and other multilingual situations, the questionnaire may be simplified for more general use. Its original purpose was to distinguish and interrelate home, neighborhood, and school language behavior, but it has also been used in the development of language arts curricula for bilingual communities. Dimensions include: demography, language proficiency, language use, type of home, attitudes, school behavior, group homogeneity, and distribution of languages and dialects in total behavior of child. An expanded sociolinguistic version of 200 items also produces language profiles for the community, the teachers, and the school (in the context of its language policy). The profiles are then used to establish objectives (Beebe and Mackey, in press) in bilingual and multilingual situations.
    As examples, three of the eight sets of items from the two-hundred-item checklist for evaluating bilingual education are given below.

3.4 What sort of homes do they come from?
    3.4.1 Do the parents intend to preserve a language?
    3.4.2 What is their social and income level?
    3.4.3 How long have they been at that level?
    3.4.4 How long have they been in the area?

3.4.5 How much education do they have?

3.4.6 How much do they want their children to get?

3.4.7 How active are they in the community?

3.4.8 Do they attend school activities?

3.5 How do they feel?

3.5.1 About their home language?

3.5.2 About the second language?

3.5.3 About the school?

3.5.4 About learning in general?

3.5.5 About their ethnic group?

3.5.6 About their future?

4.4 What sort of people are they?

4.4.1 How many languages are used and by how many people?

4.4.2 How many ethnic organizations are there and of what strength?

4.4.3 Are some of the jobs in the hands of certain ethnic groups?

4.4.4 What sort of ethnic organizations are there: church, school, social, political?

4.4.5 Do some have special political or social status?

4.4.6 Are some more bilingual than others?

4.4.7 How much contact is there between the ethnic groups?

RELIABILITY AND VALIDITY: Testing and retesting was done in 1970 on a thousand bilingual children at the John F. Kennedy School in Berlin, Germany. The age range was 6 to 18. The instrument produces quantification of all relevant types of language behavior in school, in the home, and in the neighborhood, in addition to a profile of language background.

BIBLIOGRAPHY:

Beebe, V., and Mackey, W. F. *Bilingual Schools for Biethnic Communities.* Rowley, Massachusetts: Newbury House (in press).

Mackey, W. F. *Bilingual Education in a Binational School.* Rowley, Massachusetts: Newbury House, 1972.

Mackey, W. F. *L'Ecologie éducationnelle du bilinguisme.* Quebec: International Center for Research on Bilingualism, 1974 (French version).

Mackey, W. F. *Bilinguisme et contact des langues.* Paris: Klincksieck (in press) (French version).

NUMBER AND RELATED MATHEMATICAL CONCEPTS

AUTHOR: Alec T. Brace

AGE: 5 to 9 years

VARIABLE: Number concepts

TYPE OF MEASURE: Structured interview

SOURCE FROM WHICH MEASURE MAY BE OBTAINED: Alec T. Bruce, Memorial University of Newfoundland, St. John's, Newfoundland, Canada, A1C 5S7, at nominal cost.

DESCRIPTION OF MEASURE: The measure is designed to assess the thinking of young children on numbers and related concepts as revealed by the manipulations of a variety of materials in situations contrived by the researcher. Specifically it seeks to determine the extent to which cultural and environmental factors may affect children's thinking with respect to number and related concepts. The instrument consists of three subtests with appropriate familiar manipulative materials for each: conservation of numbers, conservation of continuous quantity, and relational thinking. The tasks are basically Piagetian-type.

RELIABILITY AND VALIDITY: The reliability of each subtest was established using the Kuder-Richardson formula 21. Conservation of numbers—.88 ($N = 162$), conservation of continuous quantity—.94 ($N = 162$), and relational thinking—.76 ($N = 162$).

BIBLIOGRAPHY:

Copeland, R. *How Children Learn Mathematics.* New York: Macmillan, 1970.
Lovell, K. *The Growth of Understanding in Mathematics.* Toronto, Canada: Holt, Rinehart and Winston, 1971.

NUMERAL NAME INVENTORY (NNI)

AUTHORS: Jack Victor, Alan Coller, and John Dill

AGE: Preschool

VARIABLE: Ability to identify common numbers

TYPE OF MEASURE: Nonverbal and verbal identification test

SOURCE FROM WHICH MEASURE MAY BE OBTAINED: Jack Victor, 82-25 218th Street, Hollis Hills, New York 11427.

DESCRIPTION OF MEASURE: The NNI, one of the Early Childhood Inventories (see Index of Measures), is an individually administered inventory designed to evaluate the child's ability to identify twenty common numbers, from 0 to 19. The NNI consists of two separate tasks—a nonverbal task and a verbal task. In the *nonverbal receptive* task, the child is presented with twenty arrays of four numbers (or pictures of objects) each. The child is asked to point to specific numbers present in the arrays as they are named by the administrator. Each array contains the critical numeral, two distractors (which are visually and aurally highly discriminable from the critical number—one a single digit and one a two-digit numeral), and one distractor, which is the unit or teen number containing the same number as the critical unit (e.g., 12 for the critical number 2, 16 for 6, and so forth). This arrangement of the arrays requires the child to make finer discriminations than is ordinarily the case and does not easily permit the child to make a correct choice because he knows a part of the numeral (the 6 of the 16, for example). Familiar pictures are systematically placed among the nonverbal items in order to draw the child's attention to all positions in the arrays.

In the *verbal expressive* task, the child is presented with each number one at a time on a number wheel and is asked to name it. The nonverbal task is administered first, followed by the verbal task. Alternative forms of the nonverbal task of the NNI have been developed to aid in the evaluation of guessing and positional response set behaviors. If accurate diagnostic information is desired for very young children, both nonverbal forms should be administered. The two forms differ only in the arrangement of the numerals in the same array.

RELIABILITY AND VALIDITY: Alternative form reliabilities were obtained for a sample of inner-city children in prekindergarten to first grade. The correlations are .71 for prekindergarten, .89 for kindergarten, and .85 for first grade.

BIBLIOGRAPHY:

Coller, A., and Victor, J. *Early Childhood Inventories Project.* New York: New York University, Institute for Developmental Studies, 1970.

Ryan, T. J., and Moffitt, A. R. "Evaluation of Preschool Programs." *Canadian Psychologist,* 1974, *15,* 205-219.

Prepared by Alan Coller, Jack Victor, and John Dill

ORACY RESEARCH UNIT LISTENING COMPREHENSION

AUTHORS: Andrew M. Wilkinson, Leslie Stratta, and Peter Dudley

AGE: 11+, 13+, and 17+ years

VARIABLE: Listening comprehension

TYPE OF MEASURE: Multiple-choice test

SOURCE FROM WHICH MEASURE MAY BE OBTAINED: Write Macmillan Educational, Houndmills, Basingstoke, Hants, United Kingdom RG21 2XS, for *Learning Through Listening*, three tapes with stencils for test booklets and manual. Cost not yet established.

DESCRIPTION OF MEASURE: Each test battery consists of a tape and a multiple-choice answer booklet. The batteries are typically tests of content, phonology, use of contextual constraints, register and style, and relationship. Their uses are intended to be diagnostic, for examination purposes, for second-language comprehension. They are also seen as having value as developmental materials, since the tapes focus upon particular linguistic points. All the material on the tapes is genuine or simulated spoken language and not the written language read aloud.

RELIABILITY AND VALIDITY: The tests are validated on large samples of equivalent populations.

BIBLIOGRAPHY:

Wilkinson, A. M. (with contributions by A. Davis and D. Atkinson). *Spoken English.* (2nd ed.) Birmingham, England: University of Birmingham School of Education, 1965.

Wilkinson, A. M. "The Implications of Oracy." *Educational Review,* 1968, *20* (2).

Wilkinson, A. M. "Research in Listening Comprehension." *Educational Review,* 1970, *12,* 140-144.

Wilkinson, A. M., and Stratta, L. "The Evaluation of Spoken English." *Educational Review,* 1969, *21* (3).

Wilkinson, A. M., and Stratta, L. "Listening Comprehension and 13 Plus." *Educational Review,* 1970, *22* (3).

Wilkinson, A. M., and Stratta, L. "Listening and Language." *Educational Review,* 1972, *25* (1).

Wilkinson, A. M., Stratta, L., and Dudley, P. *The Quality of Listening.* Houndmills, Basingstoke, Hants, United Kingdom: Macmillan Education, 1974.

Wilkinson, A. M., Stratta, L., and Dudley, P. *Learning Through Listening.* Teacher's manual. Houndmills, Basingstoke, Hants, United Kingdom: Macmillan Education, 1975.

ORAL LANGUAGE ASSESSMENT (OLA)

AUTHOR: John R. Munden

AGE: Unlimited

VARIABLE: Oral language ability

TYPE OF MEASURE: Structured interview

SOURCE FROM WHICH MEASURE MAY BE OBTAINED: John R. Munden, 1205 East Manhatton Drive, Tempe, Arizona 85282.

DESCRIPTION OF MEASURE: The OLA test is based on the Indiana Conference Scheme of Oral Language Analysis developed at Indiana University under Dr. Ruth Strickland and others. Some limited modification of that scheme has been made on the basis that children seldom use certain syntactical patterns, and that the in-depth analysis is not necessary for the purposes of the instrument. Pictures are used to elicit language, which is first taped, then transcribed for analysis. Data are listed in terms of syntactical patterns, movables, connectors, and total words used in the sample. It is suggested that the test be used on a pre-post basis with a random sample rather than a total population because of the time involved. It is especially useful where an accurate look at language structure is desired for any age group. A second simple test used to measure growth only is also available, although developed outside the original study. The GROWTH test simply lists total words in complete syntactical patterns, incomplete syntactical patterns, and totals for both as well as average sentence length. Detailed information on administration and interpretation is available with the tests, both of which are quickly and easily administered after a couple of practices. Both tests are currently being revised. No normative data are available for the tests. It is suggested that local norms be established for districts desiring to use the test.

RELIABILITY AND VALIDITY: Reliability and validity were established for the Indiana Conference Scheme during its development at Indiana University.

BIBLIOGRAPHY:

Hammer, E. F. "A Comparison of the Oral Language Patterns of Mature and Immature First Grade Children." Unpublished doctoral dissertation. Arizona State University, Tempe, 1969.

Loban, W. D. "The Language of Elementary School Children." Reading research report no. 1. Champaign, Illinois: National Council of Teachers of English, 1963.

Strickland, R. G. *The Language of Elementary School Children: Its Relationship to the Language of Reading Textbooks and the Quality of Reading of Selected Children.* Bloomington, Indiana: Bureau of Educational Studies and Testing, Indiana University, 1962.

Wakefield, M. W., and Whitney, F. L. *An Evaluation of Syntactical Oral Language Patterns of Migrant Farm Workers' Children in Nine Arizona Elementary Schools.* A summary report for the State Superintendent of Public Instruction. Phoenix, Arizona, 1968.

ORIGINAL WRITTEN LANGUAGE INVENTORY (OWL)

AUTHOR: Helen B. Craig

AGE: 6 to 14 years

VARIABLE: Written language development

TYPE OF MEASURE: Test

SOURCE FROM WHICH MEASURE MAY BE OBTAINED: Western Pennsylvania School for the Deaf, 300 East Swissvale Avenue, Pittsburgh, Pennsylvania 15218.

DESCRIPTION OF MEASURE: The Original Written Language Inventory (OWL) was designed to help assess the development of vocabulary, syntax, and functional linguistic categories of young deaf children, as demonstrated by their performance on a narrative composition task. Four sets of stimuli are included, two sets geared to the vocabulary most familiar to young children (6 to 8) and two sets for older children (9 to 14). The stimuli are seven-picture sequences depicting simple stories of specific interest to the two age levels (e.g., for the younger children, one sequence shows the rescue of a treed cat; for the older, the adventure centers on a youth piloting an airplane in a storm). The students, in small groups of four or five, are instructed to write a story about the pictures. The compositions are then scored following a model that includes word tokens and types, type/token ratio, phrase tokens and types, number of sentences, complexity of sentences (number of functional slots, subordinate clause transformations, and so forth). For example, a sentence such as "The little flea bit the pudgy young pup" would be counted as a three-slot sentence (NVN) containing eight word tokens, seven types, two phrases (three- and four-word), and no subordination. A sentence score is computed on the whole composition based on the number of functional units per sentence. This provides a relatively simple measure of growth in the early stages of language development. A more complex scoring model, directly based on transformational grammar, is being tested. The OWL may also be used to elicit sequential oral language, which may be taped and then scored in the same way as the written.

RELIABILITY AND VALIDITY: The OWL has been administered to 168 deaf children in the 6 to 8 age range and to 265 deaf students age 9 to 14. The validity of the test as a developmental measure is indicated by the degree of increase from one age level to the next. At age 6, for example, the number of words written was 14.91, the number of sentences 1.89, and the sentence score (indicating use of functional units) was 3.55. At the age of 7, these scores had increased to 22.95, 3.44, and 7.02 respectively. At the age of 10, with the second set of stimuli, the scores on these variables were 74.62, 7.17, and 17.68; at age 11 they were 90.77, 10.24, and 26.72. No reliability data are available.

BIBLIOGRAPHY:

Craig, H. B. "Expansion of Educational Environment for Hearing-Impaired Children." 89: 313 Report. Pittsburgh, Pennsylvania: Western Pennsylvania School for the Deaf, 1971.

Craig, H. B. "Facilitation of Creative Response by Deaf Students." 89:313 Report. Pittsburgh, Pennsylvania: Western Pennsylvania School for the Deaf, 1973 and 1974.

Craig, H. B., and Craig, W. N. *Evaluation Manual.* Vol. 2. Pittsburgh, Pennsylvania: Western Pennsylvania School for the Deaf, 1974.

OTT TEST OF ORAL LANGUAGE

AUTHORS: Elizabeth Ott (with Gloria Jameson and Southwest Educational Development Laboratory for Part I and revisions of Part I)

AGE: Approximately 5 to 12 years

VARIABLE: Fluency and proficiency in oral language usage

TYPE OF MEASURE: Test—tape-recorded questions with visual stimuli

SOURCE FROM WHICH MEASURE MAY BE OBTAINED: Elizabeth Ott, Southwest Educational Development Laboratory, 211 East 7th Street, Austin, Texas 78701.

DESCRIPTION OF MEASURE: The Ott Test of Oral Language is designed to assess level of proficiency in oral language production, including the principal elements of language: phonemic distinctions, intonation, and syntax. The test consists of two parts. Part I is a test of the more common phonemic differentiations recognized as problems for Spanish speakers learning English. It renders eleven subscores and a total score (range 0 to 132). Part II tests fluency in English, including elaboration and intonation, which are scored for each of three kinds of responses: descriptive, inferential, and imaginative. Range of the total score is 0 to 96.

    Part II—Fluency: This test is administered in a conversational setting with appealing pictures accompanied by oral, verbal stimuli. The questions are structured so as to involve the pupil personally in the pictured situation. By moving from the descriptive level into the abstract (inferential, imaginative), opportunity is established for the expression of relations having to do with causality, quantity, quality, time space, and human relationships. A total of twenty-four verbal probes is used with eight pictures. Pupil responses are original and spontaneous. The test package consists of test equipment and a test guide. The test equipment includes synchronized master tape recordings (cassettes or reels) of the test (one for each part); and a set of slides, flimstrips, or pictures (for Part II). The guide includes (1) a list of test equipment, (2) instructions for use of the test equipment, (3) instructions for administering the test, (4) script of the test, (5) scoring procedures for Part I and Part II, and (6) scoring sheets for Part I and Part II.

    In Part I (Phonemic Analysis), the respondent is asked, among other things, to say thirty-three sentences. The first five sentences are:

1. Mother is *shopping.*
2. Mary's making a *wish.*
3. The water's in the *ditch.*
4. The *rack* is by the door.
5. There's a *tag* on the rug.

In Part II (Fluency), the respondent is asked twenty-four questions about eight pictures. Two of the picture situations (with questions) are:

Slide 2. Close-up of three girls.
    4. Q: What do you see in *this* picture?   Descriptive
    5. Q: What are the girls looking at?   Inferential
    6. Q: What are they thinking?   Imaginative
Slide 3. Picture of four boys looking up.
    7. Q: Tell me what they are doing.   Descriptive
    8. Q: *Why* are they looking up?   Imaginative
    9. Q: Is the sun shining? How do you know?   Inferential

RELIABILITY AND VALIDITY: Reliability and validity data were compiled using first-, second-, and third-grade children selected by their teachers on the basis of reluctance to respond orally, excessive shyness, or dialect deviations. Internal consistency coefficients (Kuder-Richardson formula 20) for 120 primary-grade children were .78, .79, and .80 for the three subscales descriptive, inferential, and imaginative, and for the total scale, .91. Reliabilities are also provided by grade level by scale and for the total. Test-retest results for 271 predominantly first graders (total score) was $r = .67$. The measure was used in connection with evaluation of the Communication Skills Program, a Title III project implemented in five Louisiana parish school systems. Comparative data were collected from experimental and control schools. Significant differences between experimental and control groups were found on the Descriptive and Imaginative subscales and on the total test. Differences on the inferential subscale were at the .07 level.

BIBLIOGRAPHY:

Brett, S. M. "A New Measure of Language Maturity." *Elementary English,* 1965, *42,* 666-668.
Horn, T. D. *A Study of the Effects of Intensive Oral-Aural English Language Instruction, Oral-Aural Spanish Language Instruction, and Non-Oral-Aural Instruction on Reading Readiness in Grade One.* Austin: University of Texas Press, 1966.
Jameson, G. "The Development of a Phonemic Analysis for an Oral English Proficiency Test for Spanish-Speaking School Beginners." Unpublished doctoral dissertation. University of Texas, Austin, 1967.

PARAGRAPH BOUNDARY TEST

AUTHORS: Frank M. Koen, Alton Becker, and Richard Young

AGE: 17 years to adult

VARIABLE: Paragraphing ability

TYPE OF MEASURE: Test

SOURCE FROM WHICH MEASURE MAY BE OBTAINED: Order NAPS Document NAPS-00222 from ASIS National Auxiliary Publications Service, 440 Park Avenue South, New York, New York 10016. Cost: $3.00 for microfiche, $6.50 for photocopy.

DESCRIPTION OF MEASURE: A total of eleven passages of English prose served as the original set of stimuli. The number of sentences per passage ranged from fifteen to fifty-two; the number of words from 216 to 592. Each passage is printed on a single page with brackets placed between sentences and at the beginning and end of the passage. Passages one through ten were converted to nonsense by replacing all nouns, verbs, adjectives, and adverbs with nonsense paralogs of equal average syllabic length. For example, the sentence "Sloths have no right to be living on the earth today; they would be fitting inhabitants of Mars, where a year is over six-hundred-days long" becomes "Smars have no mirt to be lewling on the kust reteb; they would be tibbing nonentants of Ness, where a reet is over nus cantron tels dan." Word-endings that play a grammatical role (e.g., *-ed, -ly, -s, -ing*) are retained, as are all sentence punctuation marks, including commas, semicolons, periods, and quotation marks. All paragraph indentions are removed. In the nonsense version, a given paralog replaces one and only one English word and is repeated at every occurrence of the latter. *S*s are asked to read the passage carefully and to place paragraph markers at the places that seem right to them without regard to where the author may have put them. It is pointed out that each passage might or might not begin and end with a paragraph.

RELIABILITY AND VALIDITY: Kuder-Richardson formula 20 was used to measure interjudge agreement for each passage. The formula is used here to express the consistency among *S*s rather than among items (that is, sentence junctures). It may be interpreted as an index of the ambiguity of the "paragraphing signals" occurring in the passages. In every case but one (Passage 3) interjudge agreement, in terms of Kuder-Richardson formula 20, is greater for English than for nonsense versions of the same passage. Even in the nonsense passages, however, reliability ranges from .53 to .92 with a median of .75. These findings indicate that the paragraph is a psychologically real unit. The inference that paragraphing signals are not entirely semantic is supported by Pearson product-moment correlations between E and N versions of the same passage; they range from .42 to .95, with a median of .71. These figures represent the correspondence between the proportions of *S*s placing paragraph markers at common sentence junctures in the two versions. Developmental changes in paragraphing are shown by the correlation of the children's paragraph marking with that of adults. At ages 7 to 8, the correlations are either very low or negative, increasing at ages 10 to 12, and finally at ages 14 to 16 being .81 for nonsense paragraphs and .85 for English paragraphs.

BIBLIOGRAPHY:

Koen, F. M., Becker, A., and Young, R. "The Psychological Reality of the Paragraph."
Journal of Verbal Learning and Verbal Behavior, 1969, *8,* 49-53.

Prepared by Orval G. Johnson

PREPOSITIONS INVENTORY/LINGUISTIC CONCEPTS (PI/LC)

AUTHORS: Alan Coller and Jack Victor

AGE: Preschool

VARIABLE: Ability to recognize use of prepositions

TYPE OF MEASURE: Test

SOURCE FROM WHICH MEASURE MAY BE OBTAINED: Jack Victor, 82-25 218th
Street, Hollis Hills, New York 11427.

DESCRIPTION OF MEASURE: The PI/LC, one of the Early Childhood Inventories
(see Index of Measures), is an individually administered inventory designed to evaluate
the child's ability to recognize the use of sixteen prepositions—*against, among, around,
away from, behind, between, beside, down, in, in front of, on, over, through, toward,
up,* and *under.* The child is presented with sixteen arrays of four pictures each and is
asked to point to the picture that represents the preposition named by the administrator. For example, in one array a kitten is shown *under, in front of, behind,* and *on*
a sofa. In another array a bee is shown *among, over,* going *toward,* and going *away
from* a bunch of flowers. The sixteen arrays are designed so that each may be used to
evaluate at least two different prepositions. Thus the PI/LC has equivalent forms that
may be used for retesting and to aid in the evaluation of guessing and positional response set behaviors. If accurate diagnostic information is desired for very young children, both forms should be administered.
    As examples, the first five of the sixteen items of Sets A and B are given
below.

Put your finger on the picture where the:
Set A
1. Cat is *under* the couch.
2. Plane is *over* the hanger.
3. Bee is *among* the flowers.
4. Squirrel is *going down* the tree.
5. Boy is *behind* the chair.
Set B
1. Cat is *in front of* the couch.

2. Plane is *beside* the hanger.
3. Bee is *over* the flowers.
4. Squirrel is *going up* the tree.
5. Boy is *going toward* the chair.

RELIABILITY AND VALIDITY: None reported.

BIBLIOGRAPHY:

Coller, A., and Victor, J. *Early Childhood Inventories Project.* New York: New York University, Institute for Developmental Studies, 1970.
Ryan, T. J., and Moffitt, A. R. "Evaluation of Preschool Programs." *Canadian Psychologist,* 1974, *15,* 205-219.

Prepared by Alan Coller, Jack Victor, and John Dill

PRESCHOOL LANGUAGE SCALE

AUTHOR: Title III ESEA Early Prevention of School Failure Project Staff, Peotone, Illinois.

AGE: 2 to 9 years; emphasis on 4½ to 6 years

VARIABLE: School readiness of integrated auditory and visual perceptual modalities

TYPE OF MEASURE: Individual diagnostic test

SOURCE FROM WHICH MEASURE MAY BE OBTAINED: Curriculum Service, Title III, 114 North Second Street, Peotone, Illinois 60468.

DESCRIPTION OF MEASURE: The following is a brief description of each of the five sections of the test, which takes approximately 15 minutes to administer. I. Visual Vocal Integration—A picture is shown to the child while the examiner asks a question concerning an aspect of the picture, such as: "Peanut butter and jelly come in a (jar)." This is a chain response requiring visual-auditory-vocal association, discrimination, and memory. II. Vocabulary—At the preschool level, vocabulary responses are generalized and are difficult to score. Rather than to allow greater subjectivity, specific questions are asked leading to definitive qualities, such as: "How does ice feel? (cold/wet)." Only discrete concepts are scored. III. Auditory Response—In its simplest form Auditory Response may be considered as the ability to follow directions. The test items become progressively more difficult by chaining more than one direction, by increased prepositionality, and by phoneme similarity, such as: "Put the bat beside the doll and make all balls roll." IV. Integrative Auditory Memory—This test is similar to the grammatic closure section of the ITPA. Items are selected to assess long-term auditory memory of discrete phonemes represented by proper or related parts of speech, such as: "Ground is dry, but a river is (wet)." V. Discriminative Visual-Auditory Memory—This test is very similar to the visual sequential memory section of the ITPA. Shapes made of felt may be coded visually by shape or auditorily by name. These are placed in sequential order, then exposed for 5 seconds. The child is then told: "Put them back like I had them." Memory method is left to the child.

As examples, one selected item from each of the first four sections of the test is given below.

I. *Visual Vocal Integration*
_____(Button) What is this? What color is it?
II. *Vocabulary*
_____What do you do with television (see, look, watch, hear)?
III. *Auditory Response*
_____Find a block, car and sock. Put them here (point to the large green area).
IV. *Integrative Auditory Memory*
_____This car is in the box. Now the car is: *out.*

RELIABILITY AND VALIDITY: During the three years of development the Preschool Language Scale has been administered to over 2500 prekindergarten children. The PLS has gone through a series of six revisions leading to its final form. The correlation of pretest and posttest language scores was .77, significant at the .001 level. The Stanford-Binet Intelligence Test was administered by two examiners to fifty-seven randomly selected students in the testing population. The Pearson correlation of raw score and the Binet mental age was .78 (significant at the .001 level). The present formula for predicting mental age from the language score is: MA = 40.16 + .876 (language score). In 98.6 percent of the cases it was possible to predict the mental age to within ± 20 percent.

BIBLIOGRAPHY: None.

Prepared by Lee Simonek

PUPIL PROFILE OF READING SKILLS (PPRS)

AUTHORS: Alfred L. Lazar and Patricia E. Lazar

AGE: 5 to 14 years

VARIABLE: Progress in reading skills development

TYPE OF MEASURE: Checklist

SOURCE FROM WHICH MEASURE MAY BE OBTAINED: See Lazar and Lazar (1973/1974).

DESCRIPTION OF MEASURE: The PPRS consists of 110 items of reading behavior that may be completed by a teacher or resource specialist who is familiar with the child. The checklist measures six dimensions of reading behavior: (1) perceptual reading skills, (2) word identification and attack skills, (3) comprehension, (4) oral reading, (5) study skills for effective reading, and (6) interpretation and appreciation reading skills. The scoring uses three symbols: (1) H—implies student has demonstrated skill to an acceptable criterion, (2) D—implies a deficit and an area for remediation, and (3) NA—not applicable or not assessed this time. The measure is used for planning individualized instruction and remediation plans.

As examples, selected items from the following six dimensions of the checklist are given below.

I. *Perceptual Reading Skills*
   A. Auditory Skills:
      5. recognizing syllable length
   B. Visual Skills:
      10. discriminates between shapes and knows names
   C. Motor Skills:
      17. one-foot balance with eyes open
II. *Word Identification and Attack Skills*
   A. Sight Vocabulary
      23. can associate pictures to words
   B. Phonic Analysis Skills:
      28. recognizes consonant sounds
   C. Structural Analysis Skills:
      34. recognizes affixes
   D. Context Clue Skills:
      39. uses experiences
   E. Syllabification Skills:
      45. can recognize syllables.
III. *Comprehension*
   A. Comprehension Skills:
      50. can match definitions and word symbols

RELIABILITY AND VALIDITY: Several studies are in progress that will provide interjudge *r*s.

BIBLIOGRAPHY:

Lazar, A., and Lazar, P. "Profile Development—for Educational Remediation." *Academic Therapy,* 1973/1974, *9,* 175-181.

QUANTITY MATCHING INVENTORY/
MATHEMATICS (QMI/M)

AUTHORS: Jack Victor and Alan Coller

AGE: Preschool

VARIABLE: Ability to match quantity

TYPE OF MEASURE: Test

SOURCE FROM WHICH MEASURE MAY BE OBTAINED: Jack Victor, 82-25 218th Street, Hollis Hills, New York 11427.

DESCRIPTION OF MEASURE: The QMI/M, one of the Early Childhood Inventories (see Index of Measures), is an individually administered inventory designed to evaluate the child's receptive ability to match quantities regardless of the nature of the attributes of the stimulus items. The quantities the child is asked to match range from one through five. The child has to choose from among four alternatives (located at the corners of the page), the correct choice having the same quantity as a standard (located at the center of the page). The QMI/M is divided into four levels of complexity based on variations of irrelevant stimulus attributes. (1) In the first level, the only difference between the alternatives is the quantity itself. For example, the four alternatives in one item are two, three, four, and five identical white circles, and the standard in the center is two identical white circles. (2) In the second level, the child must select the quantity match from alternatives that are of different achromatic color (black or white) from the standard. For example, the four alternatives in one item are two, three, four, and five identical white circles, and the standard in the center is three identical black circles. (3) In the third level, the alternatives differ in shape from each other, as well as from the standard shape. For example, one item uses two circles, three rectangles, four crosses, and five hearts as alternatives, and the standard in the center is five triangles. (4) In the fourth level, the child must select the quantity match from alternatives having mixed shapes. For example, the four alternatives in one item are: (a) a cross and a circle; (b) a heart, a circle, and a cross; (c) a square, a cross, a heart, and a circle; and (d) a triangle, a circle, a heart, a cross, and another circle. The standard in the center is a circle, a triangle, and a square.

For the purpose of retesting and to aid in the evaluation of guessing and response set behavior, equivalent forms of the QMI/M have been developed. The forms differ in the stimuli used and in the position of the correct matching alternatives.

RELIABILITY AND VALIDITY: None reported.

BIBLIOGRAPHY:

Coller, A., and Victor, J. *Early Childhood Inventories Project.* New York: New York University, Institute for Developmental Studies, 1970.

Ryan, T. J., and Moffitt, A. R. "Evaluation of Preschool Programs." *Canadian Psychologist,* 1974, *15,* 205-219.

Prepared by Alan Coller, Jack Victor, and John Dill

R-B NUMBER READINESS TEST

AUTHOR: Dorothy M. Roberts

AGE: 4 to 6 years

VARIABLE: Number readiness

TYPE OF MEASURE: Test

SOURCE FROM WHICH MEASURE MAY BE OBTAINED: Dorothy M. Roberts, 1428 East 7th Street, Plainfield, New Jersey 07062.

DESCRIPTION OF MEASURE: The test consists of twenty pictorial items designed to measure the concepts of counting, cardinality, ordinality, one-to-one correspondence, vocabulary (shorter, longer, longest, more than, most, order) ordinality, writing of single numerals, recognition of shapes and patterns involving shapes, and recognition and matching of numerals. It must be administered orally to groups of not more than eight children at a time, preferably with at least one assistant to check less mature children in turning pages, following directions, and so forth. A raw score is obtained, which assists in ranking the children or identifying those in need of additional readiness activities prior to formal mathematics instruction.

As examples, four selected items of the twenty on the test are given below.

C. Put your finger on the picture of the balloons. Find out how many balloons there are. Put a mark on the *numeral* that tells *how many* balloons there are.
E. (1) Put your finger on the picture of the flowers. Put a mark on the *tallest* flower.
   (2) Point to the picture of the flags. Put a mark on the *shortest* flagpole.
   (3) Point to the pencils. Put a mark on the *longer* pencil.
   (4) Point to the paint brushes. Put a mark on the *shorter* paint brush.
G. Look at the pictures in the bottom row. There is a boy, a girl, a baseball, and a book. Put a mark on the *third* picture.

RELIABILITY AND VALIDITY: None reported.

BIBLIOGRAPHY:

Bjonerud, C. E. "Arithmetic Concepts Possessed by the Preschool Child." *Arithmetic Teacher,* 1960, *7,* 347-350.
Roberts, D. M., and Bloom, I. "Mathematics in Kindergarten—Formal or Informal?" *Elementary School Journal,* 1967, *67,* 338-341.

READING AND FOLLOWING DIRECTIONS TEST

AUTHOR: Clarence R. Calder, Jr.

AGE: 8 to 11 years

VARIABLE: Ability to read and follow instructions

TYPE OF MEASURE: Test

SOURCE FROM WHICH MEASURE MAY BE OBTAINED: Clarence R. Calder, Jr., School of Education, Department of Elementary Education U-33, University of Connecticut, Storrs, Connecticut 06268.

DESCRIPTION OF MEASURE: The Reading and Following Directions Test consists of seventeen items that allow subjects to read directions and perform simple manipulative paper-and-pencil tasks. The directions become more complex with each succeeding item. Items are scored using the following point system: items one to six, 1 point; items seven to nine, 2 points; items ten to thirteen, 3 points; and items fourteen to seventeen, 4 points. The maximum score is 40 points.

    As an example, the directions for five of the seventeen items are given below.

1. Put a one in the square and a cross in the circle.
3. Draw a line from the cat to the ball that will go up over the fish and put a cross on the fish.
7. Put a three in the largest circle and a cross in the smallest circle.
10. Cross out the number six, cross out every number that is in the twenties, and cross out the largest number.
16. Cross out the six in the circle, the three in the square, the number in the third circle, the biggest number that is in a square, and the four in the circle.

RELIABILITY AND VALIDITY: None reported.

BIBLIOGRAPHY:

Calder, C. R., Jr., and Zalatimo, S. D. "Improving Children's Ability to Follow Directions." *Reading Teacher,* 1970, *24,* 227-231, 238.

READING/EVERYDAY ACTIVITIES IN LIFE (R/EAL)

AUTHOR: Marilyn Lichtman

AGE: Junior high school and up

VARIABLE: Functional or practical literacy

TYPE OF MEASURE: Test

SOURCE FROM WHICH MEASURE MAY BE OBTAINED: CAL Press, 76 Madison Avenue, New York, New York 10016. Cost: 1 to 100 booklets, $.65 each, discounts on quantity; cassettes, $4.85 each; examiner's manual, $3.50 each.

DESCRIPTION OF MEASURE: R/EAL is a forty-five-item test that covers the following nine categories of common printed material, with specific examples in parenthesis: (1) signs and labels (road signs), (2) schedules and tables (T.V. schedule), (3) maps (road maps), (4) categorized listings and indices (want ad), (5) high-interest factual narrative (narcotics article), (6) illustrated advertisements (food store), (7) technical documents (apartment lease), (8) set of directions (recipe for pizza), and (9) fill-in-blank form (job application). Directions and questions are administered via cassette tape. The student writes his responses directly in the test booklet. items are scored according to an objective scoring key. Successful response to at least 80 percent of the items is indicative of functional literacy. Normative information based on a group of 16- to 21-year-old disadvantaged youths is provided. Individual test item construction was based on task analyses of each of the nine reading criteria.

RELIABILITY AND VALIDITY: The test was validated on a sample of 434 16- to 21-year-old disadvantaged youths in a residential program aimed at development of basic education and vocational skills. Point-biserial item-total test correlations ranged from .25 to .66 with a median value of .51. The Kuder-Richardson formula 20 reliability coefficient was .93. A validity coefficient of .74 was calculated between R/REAL and the Stanford Achievement Test. Criterion-referenced validity was developed based on task analyses for each of the criteria.

BIBLIOGRAPHY:

Lichtman, M. "Development and Validation of R/EAL, an Instrument to Assess Functional Literacy." *Journal of Reading Behavior,* 1974, *6,* 167-184.

Pacific Training and Technical Assistance Corporation. "Evaluation of the Community-Based Right-to-Read Program." Report submitted to U.S. Office of Education, Office of Planning, Budgeting, and Evaluation. Contract no. OEC-1-73-5174, SB-3-2-0-8-(a)-73 (c) 380. September 1974.

RECEPTIVE-EXPRESSIVE EMERGENT LANGUAGE (REEL) SCALE

AUTHORS: Kenneth R. Bzoch and Richard League

AGE: Birth to 3 years

VARIABLE: Receptive and expressive language skills

TYPE OF MEASURE: Ratings scale using mother as informant

SOURCE FROM WHICH MEASURE MAY BE OBTAINED: Anhinga Press, 420 Boulevard, P.O. Box 13501, Gainesville, Florida 32604. Cost: Handbook, $9.00 (Hardbound, $12.00); REEL Scale Forms, package of 25 for $6.50; REEL Kits, Softbound $14.50, Hardbound $17.50.

DESCRIPTION OF MEASURE: This systematic way of obtaining information through a knowledgeable informant (mother) allows measuring and relating *chronological* age to *receptive* language age to *expressive* language age. Discrepancies at any level between receptive and expressive language age give differential diagnostic information regarding the environmental influence on early language acquisition (as contrasted to organic or retardation abnormalities related to language). Norms are based on 100 consecutive well-baby studies over an eight-year period. The scale is presently being used to contrast infants born with cleft palate, deafness, and other organic problems. Scale items can be used as a guide in parental counseling for home speech and language stimulation training of handicapped children.

RELIABILITY AND VALIDITY: Test-retest reliability was .71. Validity studies are in progress.

BIBLIOGRAPHY:

Bannatyne, A. "Programs, Materials and Techniques." *Journal of Learning Disabilities,* 1972, *5,* 512 (a review of K. R. Bzoch and R. League, 1971).
Bzoch, K. R., and League, R. *Assessing Language Skills in Infancy: A Handbook of Multidimensional Analysis for Emergent Language.* Gainesville, Florida: Anhinga Press, 1971.

RELATIONAL CONCEPTS INVENTORY/
PRE-MATHEMATICS (RCI/PM)

AUTHORS: Jack Victor and Alan Coller

AGE: Preschool

VARIABLE: Knowledge of sets of concepts

TYPE OF MEASURE: Test

SOURCE FROM WHICH MEASURE MAY BE OBTAINED: Jack Victor, 82-25 218th Street, Hollis Hills, New York 11427.

DESCRIPTION OF MEASURE: The RCI/PM, one of the Early Childhood Inventories (see Index of Measures), is an individually administered inventory designed to assess the child's receptive understanding of sets of concepts that are prerequisite to the learning of many quantitatively related concepts and that are especially relevant to the understanding of mathematical sets. The inventory consists of twenty items. These items are used to make up ten sets of two-choice polar opposite concepts: first-last, few-many, apart-together, empty-full, equal-unequal, beginning-end, all-none, open-closed, top-bottom, and right-left. The child is asked to point to the items representing the concept asked for by the administrator. Each of the ten sets of concepts has either: (1) two pictures, each of which represents one of the two opposite concepts; for example, the concept "few-many" is depicted by a picture of a bowl full of crackers and a picture of a bowl containing only a few crackers; (2) one picture representing both concepts; for example, the concept "first-last" is depicted by a picture of horses in a race, one of which is clearly first and one of which is clearly last.

To evaluate guessing and positional response set behavior, the sets of twenty items are administered twice. The critical items asked for in the second administration are the opposite of the critical items asked for in the first administration. For example, when the child is shown the picture of the horses in the race during the second administration, he is asked to point to the horse that is last in the race rather than the one that is first. The forty items (twenty pairs, each presented twice on the RCI/PM) make it possible to obtain a reliable estimate of the child's knowledge of each *set* of polar opposite concepts (e.g., "fullness"-full-empty). Such construction also allows for the balancing of position and concept, thus controlling for influences of positional response sets.

As examples, the first eight concepts of the twenty on which the child is tested first (in this order) are given below.

Put your finger on the:
1. Child who is *first* in line to see Santa Claus.
2. *Open* window.
3. *Empty* pitcher.
4. Bars which are *unequal.*
5. Boy who has *all* the balloons.
6. Bowl with *many* crackers in it.
7. Person at the *end* of the line.
8. Babies who are playing *together.*

The first eight concepts for the second administration of the test are:

1. Child who is *last* in line to see Santa Claus.
2. *Closed* window.
3. *Full* pitcher.
4. Bars which are *equal.*
5. Boy who has *none* of the balloons.
6. Bowl with *few* crackers in it.
7. Person at the *beginning* of the line.
8. Babies who are playing *apart.*

The same pictures are used with corresponding items on both administrations of the test.

RELIABILITY AND VALIDITY: None reported.

BIBLIOGRAPHY:

Coller, A., and Victor, J. *Early Childhood Inventories Project.* New York: New York University, Institute for Developmental Studies, 1970.
Ryan, T. J., and Moffitt, A. R. "Evaluation of Preschool Programs." *Canadian Psychologist,* 1974, *15,* 205-219.

Prepared by Alan Coller, Jack Victor, and John Dill

RELATIONAL CONCEPTS INVENTORY/ PRE-SCIENCE (RCI/PS)

AUTHORS: Jack Victor and Alan Coller

AGE: Preschool

VARIABLE: Understanding of physical dimensions

TYPE OF MEASURE: Test

SOURCE FROM WHICH MEASURE MAY BE OBTAINED: Jack Victor, 82-25 218th Street, Hollis Hills, New York 11427.

DESCRIPTION OF MEASURE: The RCI/PS, one of the Early Childhood Inventories (see Index of Measures), is an individually administered inventory designed to assess the child's receptive understanding of sets of concepts related to the scaling of physical dimensions. These concepts deal with weight, temperature, height, speed, size, distance, width, humidity, and age. RCI/PS consists of ten sets of pictorial representations of two-choice polar opposite concepts: hot-cold, slow-fast, long-short, wet-dry, big-little, near-far, light-heavy, narrow-wide, fat-thin, and old-young. The child is asked to point to the picture representing the concept asked for by the administrator. For example, the child is presented a picture of a snowman and a picture of the sun and is asked to point to the one that is hot. Each of the ten sets of concepts has two corresponding sets of stimuli, for a total of twenty items. For example, the concept "hot-cold" has a picture of the sun and a snowman and a picture of a fire and ice cream.

To aid in the evaluation of guessing and positional response-set behaviors, the twenty sets should be administered twice. The critical items asked for in the second administration are the opposite of the critical items asked for in the first. For example, when the child is shown the pictures of the snowman and the sun in the second administration, he is asked to point to the one that is cold rather than the one that is hot. The forty tested items (twenty items tested twice) on the RCI/PS make it possible to obtain a reliable estimate of the child's knowledge of each *set* of polar opposite concepts. Such construction also allows for the balancing of position and concept, thus controlling for influences of positional response sets.

As examples, the first five items for the two administrations of the inventory are given below.

I. 1. Put your finger on the picture of something *cold*.
  2. Put your finger on the picture of something which moves *fast*.
  3. Put your finger on the picture of the *long* line.
  4. Put your finger on the picture of the boy who is *dry*.
  5. Put your finger on the picture of the man who is *fat*.
II. 1. Put your finger on the picture of something *hot*.
  2. Put your finger on the picture of something which moves *slowly*.
  3. Put your finger on the picture of the *short* line.
  4. Put your finger on the picture of the boy who is *wet*.
  5. Put your finger on the picture of the man who is *thin*.

RELIABILITY AND VALIDITY:None reported.

BIBLIOGRAPHY:

Coller, A., and Victor, J. *Early Childhood Inventories Project*. New York: New York University, Institute for Developmental Studies, 1970.

Ryan, T. J., and Moffitt, A. R. "Evaluation of Preschool Programs." *Canadian Psychologist*, 1974, *15*, 205-219.

Prepared by Alan Coller, Jack Victor, and John Dill

REYNELL DEVELOPMENTAL LANGUAGE SCALES

AUTHOR: Joan K. Reynell

AGE: 1 to 5 years

VARIABLE: Developmental levels of verbal comprehension and expressive language

TYPE OF MEASURE: Test

SOURCE FROM WHICH MEASURE MAY BE OBTAINED: NFER Publishing Co., Ltd., Jennings Building, Thames Avenue, Windsor, Berks SL4 1QS, England. Cost: Sterling retail price at November 1, 1975, £43.35p.

DESCRIPTION OF MEASURE: The scales are composed of (1) Verbal Comprehension Scale A, (2) Verbal Comprehension Scale B, and (3) Expressive Language Scale. Verbal Comprehension Scale A follows the development of verbal comprehension from the earliest stage of selective recognition of certain word patterns on an affective level, through gradually increasing complexity of interpretation of different parts of speech to the stage at which verbal interpretation extends to situations beyond the here and now and language becomes a true vehicle of thought. Examples of items contained in this section range from "Where is the ball?" (from a selection of four to eight toys) to the conceptionally complex "Which one barks?" (from a selection of toy animals) and finally to questions such as "This little boy has spilled his dinner. What must he do?" In these scales an attempt has been made to follow this developmental process of verbal comprehension without too much dependence on increasing the difficulty of the vocabulary used, so that it becomes a test of word knowledge and without increasing the sentence length excessively. The nine sections of this instrument progress (with some overlap) from the stage of verbal preconcepts, through several stages of increased assimilation, to the last section in which verbal comprehension is merging into higher intellectual processes. Verbal Comprehension Scale B was developed to meet the need for a test requiring only minimal response from the child, such as for cerebral palsied children or those who are very withdrawn. The questions are so constructed that they may be answered by selection (e.g., from a selection of small dolls—Bobby, Mary, Baby, and Mother—this statement is presented: "Mary and Bobby go to school. Who stays with Mother?"). This scale is intended to be parallel to Scale A in that it follows the same developmental sequence. The scales are identical for the first half, while for the second half the only real difference is that in Scale B the number of pieces of test apparatus per test item has been reduced so that an eye-pointing response is clear, and the questions are so constructed that they may be answered by selection. Simplifying the response in this way has made the scale slightly easier at the upper end, and separate norms are provided. The Expressive Language Scale can be used to give a total expressive language score, or for a comparison of the development of different aspects of language in a child. Section 1, Language Structure, is concerned with spontaneous expression and is normally scored, incidentally, during the course of the interview. Items range from vocalization other than crying through to the use of complex sentences. The second section is concerned with vocabulary, and the final part is aimed at finding out how far a child can use language creatively in describing a picture. Thus these three sections are each concerned with a different aspect of language. These sections are not entirely parallel developmentally, nor are they entirely sequential, but they are in order of development with a very considerable overlap. The earliest developmental stages (presymbolic language) are included in Section 1; naming, and the ability to describe word meanings, in Section 2; and the use of language to express consecutive ideas in Section 3. Section 2 must depend to some extent on the abilities assessed in Section 1, and Section 3 must depend to some extent on the abilities assessed in Sections 1 and 2.

A revision of the scales is in process and is tentatively scheduled for spring 1977. A supplement to the manual is provided for those who wish to use the scales with hearing-impaired children. Norms are provided in the form of age scores, standard scores, and graphs on which a child's development may be compared with normal and deviant patterns.

RELIABILITY AND VALIDITY: The nine split-half reliability coefficients (with Spearman-Brown correction) for the three scales for three age groups ranged from .77 to .92, median .84. Interscale correlations are provided in the Manual. There was a small but consistent difference in favor of girls on the scales.

BIBLIOGRAPHY:

Reynell, J. K. "Children with Physical Handicaps." In P. M. Mittler (Ed.), *Psychological Assessment of Mental and Physical Handicaps.* London: Methuen (in preparation).

Prepared by Orval G. Johnson

RYSTROM DIALECT TEST

AUTHOR: Richard Rystrom

AGE: 4 to 11 years

VARIABLE: Dialect

TYPE OF MEASURE: Test

SOURCE FROM WHICH MEASURE MAY BE OBTAINED: See Rystrom (1969). This test should be constructed and validated by each researcher using it, so that it will discriminate for the speakers in his geographic region. Using the twenty-four items of the test he should (1) make the tape recording, (2) administer this instrument, and (3) calculate reliability for his sample.

DESCRIPTION OF MEASURE: This test consists of a series of twenty-four items presented to Ss from a tape recording. Their responses are recorded on a second recorder, which does *not* record the stimulus sentences. In each item there is a grammatical sentence complementary to the stimulus sentence. The evaluator, who need not be specially trained, decides whether the *S* was repeating the A or the B sentence on the checklist, without knowing which form was presented on the stimulus tape. If the response is not clear, he marks neither choice. The test is designed to produce a bimodal distribution, one for speakers of black English (B.E.) and one for standard English (S.E.).

As examples, five of the twenty-four items on the test are given below:

  1. A. The light's burned out.
     B. The light burned out.
  5. A. They followed us.
     B. They follow us.
 11. A. His wife's parked in front of the gate.
     B. His wife parked in front of the gate.
 18. A. His feet're tired from standing all day.
     B. His feet tired from standing all day.
 24. A. The fish'll swim up the river.
     B. The fish swim up the river.

RELIABILITY AND VALIDITY: Reliability was .80 with speakers of B.E. and .85 with speakers of S.E. The test appears to have face validity.

BIBLIOGRAPHY:

Rystrom, R. "Testing Negro-Standard English Dialect Differences." *Reading Research Quarterly,* 1969, *4,* 500-511.

SAME/DIFFERENT INVENTORY-1 (S/DI-1)

AUTHORS: Jack Victor, Alan Coller, and John Dill

AGE: Preschool

VARIABLE: Understanding of concepts "same" and "different"

TYPE OF MEASURE: Test

SOURCE FROM WHICH MEASURE MAY BE OBTAINED: Jack Victor, 82-25 218th Street, Hollis Hills, New York 11427.

DESCRIPTION OF MEASURE: The S/DI-1, one of the Early Childhood Inventories (see Index of Measures), is an individually administered inventory designed to evaluate the child's receptive understanding of the concepts "same" and "different." The S/DI-1 consists of two twelve-item tasks. In the *same* task, the child is asked to point to the picture, from a set of two alternatives, that is exactly the same as the standard picture (located above and in the center of the two alternatives). In the *different* task, the child is shown the same set and asked to point to the picture that is different from the standard. (See example below.) The *same* task is administered first, followed by the *different* task. Example items precede each task.

The S/DI-1 was constructed to measure the child's conceptual understanding of same/different when there is no perceptual confusion present and without relying on highly developed discrimination skills. Following is an example from this inventory:

| Standard | | 7 | |
| Alternatives | 7 | | 3 |

As can be seen from the example above, one of the alternatives is identical to the standard, the other is perceptually quite different. Items were constructed using variations among six categories: size, shape, numerals, letters, internal design, and meaningful objects. Each of the six categories is evaluated twice, and there are four example items. The use of twelve items means that if the child makes no more than two errors the administrator can still conclude that the child has performed well enough to know the concepts. In this case the administrator may wish to regard the inventory as providing a pass/fail measure. This allowance for errors is an attempt to take into account momentary lapses of attention on the part of the young child.

RELIABILITY AND VALIDITY: None reported.

BIBLIOGRAPHY:

Coller, A., and Victor, J. *Early Childhood Inventories Project.* New York: New York University, Institute for Developmental Studies, 1970.

Ryan, T. J., and Moffitt, A. R. "Evaluation of Preschool Programs." *Canadian Psychologist,* 1974, *15,* 205-219.

Prepared by Alan Coller, Jack Victor, and John Dill

SAME/DIFFERENT INVENTORY-2 (S/DI-2)

AUTHORS: Jack Victor, Alan Coller, and John Dill

AGE: Preschool

VARIABLE: Understanding of concepts "more like" and "more different"

TYPE OF MEASURE: Test

SOURCE FROM WHICH MEASURE MAY BE OBTAINED: Jack Victor, 82-25 218th Street, Hollis Hills, New York 11427.

DESCRIPTION OF MEASURE: The S/DI-2, one of the Early Childhood Inventories (see Index of Measures), is an individually administered inventory designed to evaluate the child's receptive understanding of the concepts "more like" and more different." The S/DI-2 consists of two twelve-item tasks. In the *more like* task, the child is asked to point to the picture, from two alternatives, that is more like the standard picture (located above and in the center of the two alternatives). In the *more different* task, the child is shown the same sets and is asked to point to the picture that is more different from the standard picture. The *more like* task is administered first, followed by the *more different* task. Example items precede each task.

In the S/DI-2, in order for the child to choose correctly from the alternatives, he may attend to perceptual and/or conceptual similarities between the choices and the standard. For example, in one item the standard is a triangle and the alternatives are a disc and a small triangle (with a different orientation from the standard). The child may perceive that the standard and the "correct" comparison both have straight lines. Or, the child may identify or label the standard as a triangle and choose the "correct" alternative because it belongs conceptually to the same class of objects as the standard. As can be seen from the above example, one of the alternatives is conceptually identical and perceptually similar to the standard; the other alternative differs from the standard both conceptually and perceptually. Items were constructed using variations among six categories: size, shape, numerals, letters, internal design, and meaningful objects. Each of the six categories is evaluated twice, and there are four example items. The use of twelve items means that if the child makes no more than two errors the administrator can still conclude that the child has performed well enough to know the concepts. In this case the administrator may wish to regard the inventory as providing a pass/fail measure. The allowance for errors is an attempt to take into account momentary lapses of attention on the part of the young child.

RELIABILITY AND VALIDITY: None reported.

BIBLIOGRAPHY:

Coller, A., and Victor, J. *Early Childhood Inventories Project.* New York: New York University, Institute for Developmental Studies, 1970.

Ryan, T. J., and Moffitt, A. R. "Evaluation of Preschool Programs." *Canadian Psychologist,* 1974, *15,* 205-219.

Prepared by Alan Coller, Jack Victor, and John Dill

SAME/DIFFERENT INVENTORY-3 (S/DI-3)

AUTHORS: Jack Victor, Alan Coller, and John Dill

AGE: Preschool

VARIABLE: Understanding of concepts "exactly the same" and "different"

TYPE OF MEASURE: Test

SOURCE FROM WHICH MEASURE MAY BE OBTAINED: Jack Victor, 82-25 218th Street, Hollis Hills, New York 11427.

DESCRIPTION OF MEASURE: The S/DI-3, one of the Early Childhood Inventories (see Index of Measures), is an individually administered inventory designed to evaluate the child's receptive understanding of the concepts "exactly the same" and "different." The S/DI-3 consists of two twelve-item tasks. In the *exactly the same* task, the child is asked to point to the picture, from two alternatives, that is exactly the same as a standard picture located above and to the center of the two alternative pictures. In the *different* task, the child is shown the same sets and is asked to point to the picture that is different from the standard. The *exactly the same* task is administered first, followed by the *different* task. Example items precede each task.

The S/DI-3 was constructed to measure the child's conceptual understanding of these two concepts when some degree of perceptual confusion is present. In order for the child to choose correctly between the alternatives, he must attend closely to subtle differences. Following is a sample item:

		1	
Standard			
Alternatives	1		I

As can be seen from the example above, one of the alternatives is identical to the standard; the other differs only in the line at the top of the numeral. Items were constructed using variations among six categories: size, shape, numerals, letters, internal design, and meaningful objects. Each of the six categories is evaluated twice, and there are four example items. The use of twelve items means that if the child makes no more than two errors the administrator can conclude that the child has performed well enough to know the concepts. In this case the administrator may wish to regard the inventory as providing a pass/fail measure. This allowance for errors is an attempt to take into account momentary lapses of attention on the part of the young child.

RELIABILITY AND VALIDITY: None reported.

BIBLIOGRAPHY:

Coller, A., and Victor, J. *Early Childhood Inventories Project.* New York: New York University, Institute for Developmental Studies, 1970.

Ryan, T. J., and Moffitt, A. R. "Evaluation of Preschool Programs." *Canadian Psychologist,* 1974, *15,* 205-219.

Prepared by Alan Coller, Jack Victor, and John Dill

SCALE FOR NUMERICAL ORDERING OF
RESPONSE TENDENCIES (SNORT)

AUTHORS: Wayne Otto, Thomas C. Barrett, and Karl Koenke

AGE: Grades 1 to 6

VARIABLE: Ability to formulate the main idea in a paragraph

TYPE OF MEASURE: Rating scale

SOURCE FROM WHICH MEASURE MAY BE OBTAINED: See Otto, Barrett, and Koenke (1968).

DESCRIPTION OF MEASURE: The Scale for Numerical Ordering of Response Tendencies (SNORT) consists of a 12-point scale and three paragraphs constructed and written at a first-grade difficulty level, all three requiring synthesis of both subject and predicate. Expository rather than narrative materials are used so that responses will be more convergent than divergent. Four sentence paragraphs containing a single central thought were constructed. Nature topics were chosen as the subject matter to assure reasonable appeal across all grade levels. In addition to the operational definitions for each category, examples of acceptable statements for each paragraph are given. Ranking of main-idea responses on SNORT is based on the degree of synthesis within each response. High value is given to appropriate synthesis of both subject and predicate. A lesser value is placed on over- or undergeneralization of either element. Little or no value is given to restatements of specifics or irrelevant associations. The scale can be applied only to literal main-idea statements inferred from explicit content of the paragraphs.

As an example, one of the three paragraphs, together with three of the twelve response scoring categories of the scale, are given below.

Paragraph B:
Robins may build nests under a roof. Bluejays like nests in trees. Ducks make nests in tall grass. Woodpeckers make nests inside wood fence posts. (Main idea: Birds build nests in different places.)
Category and Examples:
1. Irrelevant or incorrect material, i.e., paraphrasing or bringing in material not directly related to the paragraph.
   a. Rabbits can be pets.
   b. Robins make nests in trees.
   c. Baby chicks need food.
2. Two elements too generally or specifically stated.
   a. Where bluejays, birds, and ducks put their nests.
   b. Robins, bluejays, and woodpeckers make their nests in high grass, under rooftops, and in fenceposts.
   c. What birds make their places in.
3. Two elements correctly stated.
   a. Birds make nests in different places.
   b. Birds build nests in many places.
   c. Different birds build nests in different places.

RELIABILITY AND VALIDITY: In Otto, Barrett, and Koenke (1968), 400 second- and fifth-grade students from four elementary schools were individually asked to read a paragraph silently while thinking about "what all the sentences say together." When the subject had completed the reading, he or she was asked to "make up just one sentence in your own words that says what all the sentences tell you." The subjects' responses were coded, scrambled, and typed on master sheets. Three judges trained in rating sample responses assigned each individual response to a SNORT category, resulting in three ratings for each response. The judges met three times throughout the scoring period to discuss and clarify the operational approaches to the task. Agreement among judges' ratings of responses was very high. The interjudge reliability coefficients for the total three paragraphs were: (1) second-grade data: .98, .97, .97; (2) fifth-grade data: .96, .96, .97. The reliability coefficients for each paragraph taken individually were higher than .91. Because of these high correlations, one might place confidence in the ratings of a single judge.

A second area of concern was whether the three paragraphs can be interchanged. The intercorrelations of the sum of the three judges' ratings for each paragraph were: (1) second grade: A-B = .56, A-C = .59, B-C = .52; (2) fifth grade: A-B = .25, A-C = .31, B-C = .53. These low interparagraph correlations show that the paragraphs are related but are not interchangeable. Again intercorrelations of individual judge's ratings of the paragraphs were almost identical to the sum of the three judges' ratings, which further supports the belief that one judge's ratings would be adequate. One conclusion that resulted from the low interparagraph correlations relates to content. A subject's contact with the concepts of a particular paragraph may enhance his ability to infer a main idea. From the findings, one might infer that instruction to help pupils derive and state a literal main idea in reading will be more efficient if they are taught this later in the elementary experience.

BIBLIOGRAPHY:

Barrett, T. C., and Otto, W. "Elementary Pupils' Ability to Conceptualize the Main Idea in Reading." Paper presented at the American Educational Research Association annual meeting. Chicago, 1968.

Otto, W., and Barrett, T. C. "Two Studies of Children's Ability to Formulate and State a Literal Main Idea in Reading." Technical report of the Wisconsin Research and Development Center for Cognitive Learning, 1968. ERIC document no. ED 024 543.

Otto, W., Barrett, T. C., and Koenke, K. "Assessment of Children's Statements of the Main Idea in Reading." *International Reading Association Conference Proceedings*, 1968, *13*, 692-697.

Prepared by Sandra White

SCREENING TEST FOR AUDITORY COMPREHENSION
OF LANGUAGE (STACL)

AUTHOR: Elizabeth Carrow-Woolfolk

AGE: 3 to 7 years

VARIABLE: Auditory comprehension of language

TYPE OF MEASURE: Screening test

SOURCE FROM WHICH MEASURE MAY BE OBTAINED: Learning Concepts, Inc., 2501 North Lamar, Austin, Texas 78705. Cost: Manual, $2.95; test booklet (one per child), $.80.

DESCRIPTION OF MEASURE: The STACL is the short form of the Test for Auditory Comprehension of Language (TACL) (see pp. 231-232). Both forms are available in Spanish and English. The STACL contains twenty-five stimuli and is designed to be group-administered to children ages 3 to 7. There are cutoff scores indicating whether children need further language diagnosis using the longer version of the measure.
Examples of items included in the test are given below.

1. "Jump"—Three pictures are available for the child to choose from: a boy sitting, a boy standing, and a boy jumping.
2. "His puppy is black and white"—Three pictures are available to choose from: a boy with his black-and-white dog, a girl kneeling with a black-and-white dog, and a girl holding a black-and-white dog.
3. "The dog is in front of the car"—Three pictures to choose from: a dog in front of a car, a dog beside a car, and a dog inside a car.

RELIABILITY AND VALIDITY: The test-retest reliability on 100 of the original 418 children was .60. There are no validity studies reported.

BIBLIOGRAPHY:

Bartel, N. R., Bryan, D., and Keehn, S. "Language Comprehension in the Moderately Retarded Child." *Exceptional Children*, 1973, *39*, 375-382.

Carrow, E. "Comprehension of English and Spanish by Pre-School Mexican-American Children." *Modern Language Journal*, 1971, *60*, 299-306.

Carrow, E. "Auditory Comprehension of English by Monolingual and Bilingual Pre-School Children." *Journal of Speech and Hearing Research*, 1972, *15*, 407-412.

Carrow, Sister M. A. "The Development of Auditory Comprehension of Language Structure in Children." *Journal of Speech and Hearing Disorders*, 1968, *33*, 99-111.

Jones, B. J. "A Study of Oral Language Comprehension of Black and White, Middle and Lower Class, Pre-School Children Using Standard English and Black Dialect in Houston, Texas, 1972." Unpublished doctoral dissertation. University of Houston, Texas, 1972.

Prepared by Betsy Woddell

SOPHISTICATION OF READING INTERESTS SCALE (SRIS)

AUTHOR: Robert S. Zais

AGE: 12 years to adult

VARIABLE: Sophistication of interest in fiction

TYPE OF MEASURE: Forced-choice rating scale

SOURCE FROM WHICH MEASURE MAY BE OBTAINED: See Zais (1968). Available from University Microfilms, Zeeb Road, Ann Arbor, Michigan 48106.

DESCRIPTION OF MEASURE: The pilot form of the SRIS consists of thirty pairs of randomly arranged story synopses with an additional five pairs of synopses included to check for faking and social desirability of responses. These include (1) ten pairs, each made up of a *least* and a *moderately* sophisticated synopsis; (2) ten pairs, each made up of a *moderately* and a *most* sophisticated synopsis; and (3) ten pairs, each made up of a *least* and a *most* sophisticated synopsis. Respondents are asked to choose from each pair the story they think they would prefer to read. The story synopses are controlled for length, subject matter, and readability. An additional five pairs are included to check for faking and social desirability of responses. By assigning values of 1, 2, and 3 to synopses that are, respectively, least, moderately, and most sophisticated, a graduated range of scores on sophistication is obtained.

As an example, the first of the thirty-five pairs of randomly arranged story synopses, with scoring values indicated, is given below.

1. a. A jammed rocket forces Captain Jon Glen to land his space craft on a strange planet. The earth men find that the strange, underground residents of the planet are peaceful; but they are in great danger from a hostile race of Beetle men. Jon and his crew use strategy and earth weapons to help defeat the Beetle men. Gratefully, the underground people give them the parts they need to fix their space ship and get back to earth.
   b. Magnetic fields shift; the earth starts to move closer to the sun. The planet is doomed and must be evacuated. Thus, a space fleet is launched to find a new planet. An ideal space paradise is found which is quite like the garden of Eden. This story describes the behavior of the first people to settle the new planet. It's a frank and brutal picture. People really do make their own heavens—and hells.

RELIABILITY AND VALIDITY: A reliability coefficient of .74 was obtained using the split-half method corrected by the Spearman-Brown formula. To determine content validity, a panel of twenty certified secondary teachers of English with a minimum of two years' teaching experience validated the story synopses for level of sophistication. Kendall coefficients of concordance ranged from .57 to 1.0 (all significant beyond the .01 level). To determine empirical validity, the scale was administered to four groups of secondary-school students (Ns = 18, 21, 24, 25), and their scores correlated with their teachers' rankings for sophistication of interests. Class coefficients ranged from .01 (NS) to .58 ($p < .01$). To determine construct validity, mean scores of the above groups were compared for age and IQ. A significant difference in means was found to exist, the older and intellectually superior subjects attaining higher SRIS scores.

BIBLIOGRAPHY:

Zais, R. S. "The Sophistication of Reading Interests as Related to Selected Personality Factors and Certain Other Characteristics of High School Students." Unpublished doctoral dissertation. University of Connecticut, Storrs, 1968.
Zais, R. S. "A Scale to Measure Sophistication of Reading Interests." *Journal of Reading,* 1969, *12,* 273-276, 326-355.

SPEECH AND LANGUAGE SCREENING TEST
FOR PRESCHOOL CHILDREN

AUTHOR: Nancy B. Fluharty

AGE: 2 to 6 years

VARIABLE: Articulation, reception, and expressive language

TYPE OF MEASURE: Screening test

SOURCE FROM WHICH MEASURE MAY BE OBTAINED: See Fluharty (1974).

DESCRIPTION OF MEASURE: This screening test for preschool children ages 2 to 6 years old is a thirty-five-item test divided into three sections: (1) identification of fifteen objects (screens articulation, vocabulary), (2) understanding of ten sentences, and (3) production of ten sentence types in imitation. Based on the transformational-generative grammar model, this test contains a variety of sentence-structure types commonly produced by preschool children. Standardization made with twelve hundred children from three socioeconomic groups found no racial or cultural bias. The test is currently being used in Cincinnati Head Start programs. It is recommended for use with all populations of preschool children, preferably by a professional familiar with transformational-generative grammar.

As examples, ten representative items from the three sections of the test are given below. Section A is scored for both identification of the object and correct articulation of the first and second phonemes. Sections B and C are scored for correct responses.

Section A:
1. *hat*
2. *bag*
3. *sock*
4. *knife*
5. *teeth*
Section B:
1. Is the leaf on the table? (Child responds "yes" or "no"((leaf, two pencils, two bags on table)

5. The ring is on the bag. (Remove rings, bags; display two combs)

9. Where is the feather? (Child must point or state)

Section C: (Place a "check" on line if repeated correctly; check missing items or record substituted response below sentence.)

1. The girl*s* ha*ve* the presents.

2. The man is a *football player.*

RELIABILITY AND VALIDITY: Mean intertester reliability involving five clinicians was .96. Test-retest procedures with twenty subjects yielded a Pearson product-moment correlation mean of .97. Preschool speech and language screening test results were compared with diagnostic evaluations of speech and language skills for sixty children, thirty who passed the screening test and thirty who failed the screening test. The Pearson product-moment correlation for validity yielded .87. Thus the screening test appears to agree favorably with the results of more thorough evaluations.

BIBLIOGRAPHY:

Fluharty, N. B. "The Design and Standardization of a Speech and Language Screening Test for Use with Preschool Children." *Journal of Speech and Hearing Disorders,* 1974, *39,* 75-88.

SPEECH RATING SCALE FOR CHILDREN WITH SEVERE SPEECH LAGS AND PSYCHOSIS

AUTHOR: Theodore Shapiro

AGE: 1½ to 8 years

VARIABLE: Speech behavior

TYPE OF MEASURE: Two-dimensional rating scale

SOURCE FROM WHICH MEASURE MAY BE OBTAINED: Theodore Shapiro, Bellevue Medical Center, New York University, 550 First Avenue, New York, New York 10016.

DESCRIPTION OF MEASURE: This scale offers a measure of communicativeness in a developmental framework. The two dimensions permit normative and deviance estimates and provide the only known quantifiable measure of communicativeness for psychotic children. Tape-recorded 10-minute interviews with psychotic children are scored in two dimensions: morphology and function. For morphology, each utterance is assigned to one of twenty-one categories that distinguish between prespeech and speech production. The speech percentage is related to intelligibility. Disjunctive syntax is also categorized. For function, twenty-five items are divided between noncommunicative and communicative speech. The noncommunicative sector includes isolated expressive speech, imitative speech, and context-disordered speech. The communicative sector includes appeal speech and signal-symbol speech.

The categories included under the heading "Context Problems" are as follows: *Vocalization out of context* refers to phrases, words, sentences having no immediate reference in the interview or its environs; typically autistic. These may be words or sentences. Examiner may know the origin (and suspect delayed echoing) or association, but it does not (fit-refer) in any common-sense (apparent) way to what is going on. *Vocalization with partial reference* refers to sentences, phrases (may be said in stereotyped manner) having oblique/tangential reference to current play or queries. *Stereotypic overelaboration* refers to answers that are overinclusive or hypermnestic; for example, asked what it is (pointing to nose), child answers, "nose, eyes, hair, teeth."

RELIABILITY AND VALIDITY: The morphological judgments are based on phonemic structure of the production and word count and were not subjected to reliability study. The transcripts of fifteen children were taken from the larger sample and scored for function by two independent raters. Each independent rater categorized each utterance into one of the five sectors of isolated speech, imitative speech, appeal speech, or signal-symbol speech. The number of utterances in each group found by each examiner was analyzed by the Pearson correlation method. The raw score interobserver correlations were: isolated speech, .97; imitative speech, .98; context disturbance, .81; appeal speech, .89; and signal-symbol speech, .98. All were significant at $p < .001$. The validity of the scale was measured by relationship to other measures, such as a symptoms severity scale (a symptom checklist) and an early classification designed by the author. The Pearson correlation between total symptom score (SSS) and communicativeness (language scale) for the first examination ($N = 30$) was $r = .68$, and ($N = 28$) $r = .81$ for a second examination ($p < .001$). Correlations using only the language subscore of the SSS and the communicativeness score were $r = .51$ ($p > .01$) for the first examination and $r = .62$ ($p < .001$) for the second examination.

BIBLIOGRAPHY:

Shapiro, T., and Fish, B. "A Method to Study Language Deviation as an Aspect of Ego Organization in Young Schizophrenic Children." *Journal of the Academy of Child Psychiatry,* 1969, *8,* 36-56.

Shapiro, T., Chiarandini, I., and Fish, B. "Thirty Severely Disturbed Children: Evaluation of Their Language Development for Classification and Prognosis." *Archives of General Psychiatry,* 1974, *30,* 819-825.

STERN'S ECHOIC RESPONSE INVENTORY
FOR CHILDREN (ERIC)

AUTHOR: Carolyn Stern

AGE: 3 to 6 years

VARIABLE: Auditory perception, range of sentence memory, and accuracy of phonemic output.

TYPE OF MEASURE: Individually administered test

SOURCE FROM WHICH MEASURE MAY BE OBTAINED: Carolyn Stern, 10323 Lorenzo Drive, Los Angeles, California 90064. Cost: $3.00 plus handling and postage.

DESCRIPTION OF MEASURE: The ERIC is part of a battery of tests (VDI, EVI, and CADI) designed to assess the prereading skills of young children. Compared to the CADI and the VDI, which require simple selection responses to indicate the ability to discriminate auditory or visual stimuli, the EVI and the ERIC are more demanding—the child must produce the appropriate verbal response. The ERIC measures the child's ability to imitate sentences with increasing morphemic and syntactic complexity.

   The test consists of a series of twenty sentences, arranged in order of linguistic difficulty as well as memory load. The vocabulary was selected from the comprehensive word lists developed for the EVI and is thus well within the repertoire of children in the 3 to 6 age range. Two parallel forms are available. The hierarchy of complexity was based on: (1) the complexity of the tree, that is, left-branching, embedding, and so forth; (2) the total number of morphemes; (3) type of transformation; (4) number of transformational rules; and (5) number of morphophonemic rules. The simplest item in Form A is: "Dogs bark." In Form B it is: "Birds fly." The most difficult items in Forms A and B are, respectively: "If the ground is wet the children won't be able to play in the park," and "If the weather is cold the children won't be able to swim at the beach." An attempt has been made to maintain a balanced affective level between the two forms. Each form takes less than 15 minutes to administer. A sentence is scored as correct even though the child makes one error. The score is not influenced by dialectical or pronunciation features.

RELIABILITY AND VALIDITY: A total of 450 children, enrolled in nursery school, children's centers, or Head Start classes in a large urban setting were tested, with 254 receiving Form A and 196 Form B. There were 216 boys and 234 girls; 149 Caucasian and 301 black; 333 from lower-class and 117 from middle-class socioeconomic groups. Three age levels were sampled: 111 3-year-old, 237 4-year-old, and 102 5-year-old children. The intratest reliability coefficient (Spearman-Brown) is .90 for Form A and .89 for Form B. Test-retest interform reliability is .91, based on a sample of forty-seven 4-year-old children from a homogeneous day-care population. Several tables including means and standard deviations for different age, sex, SES, and ethnic groupings are available, as well as norms in percentiles computed for the total sample.

BIBLIOGRAPHY:

Stern, C. "Evaluating Language Curricula for Preschool Children." *Monographs of the Society for Research in Child Development*, 1968, *33*, 49-61.

Stern, C. *Echoic Response Inventory for Children (ERIC)*. Washington, D.C.: Bureau of Research, Office of Education, Department of Health, Education and Welfare, 1969. ERIC document no. ED 039 931.

STERN'S EXPRESSIVE VOCABULARY INVENTORY (EVI)

AUTHOR: Carolyn Stern

AGE: 3 to 6 years

VARIABLE: Language facility—labeling, verbal output

TYPE OF MEASURE: Individually administered test

SOURCE FROM WHICH MEASURE MAY BE OBTAINED: Carolyn Stern, 10323 Lorenzo Drive, Los Angeles, California 90064. Cost: $3.00 plus handling and postage.

DESCRIPTION OF MEASURE: The EVI is part of a battery of tests (ERIC, VDI, and CADI) designed to assess the prereading skills of young children. It consists of a booklet of forty black-and-white line drawings to which the child is to make an appropriate response according to the verbal stimulus presented by the examiner. Extensive preliminary work was carried out in selecting the concepts included. A compilation of hundreds of words from numerous vocabulary lists and tests for this age group was prepared and tallies of frequency of occurrence made. From these tallies, 125 words were randomly selected to represent various levels of frequency, with the restriction that a pictorial stimulus could be constructed and that a variety of parts of speech would be sampled. These were presented to 104 children, and the percentage of children labeling each item was correctly determined. Items were then ranked according to difficulty, and approximately every fourth item was selected. Stimuli for noun labels present little problem; however, adjectives, adverbs, and prepositions are difficult to portray without a comparison or model instance. Thus to get the adjective "thin" there are two pictures, one of a thin lady and the other of a fat lady. The child is told: "This lady is fat; what is this lady?" The responses "skinny" and "thin" are both scored as correct. The final forty-item test includes nouns, verbs (present, present progressive, past, and future), prepositions, adjectives, adverbs, and pronouns. A fairly rigid scoring criterion is used. With few exceptions, the child's answer must include the key word or tense to be credited.

RELIABILITY AND VALIDITY: The EVI has been presented to 430 children ranging in age from 3 through 6 years. There were 204 boys and 226 girls; 145 Caucasian and 285 black children; 300 from low and 130 from high socioeconomic-status families. Test reliability (Kuder-Richardson formula 20) based on a subsample of 192 homogeneous day-care children was .88. Since the original work with this measure, the EVI has been used as a pre- and posttest with hundreds of children in various compensatory and experimental studies. However, no further statistical computations were carried out.

BIBLIOGRAPHY:

Stern, C. "Evaluating Language Curricula for Preschool Children." *Monographs of the Society for Research in Child Development,* 1968, *33,* 49-61.

Stern, C. *The Expressive Vocabulary Inventory.* Washington, D.C.: Bureau of Research, Office of Education, Department of Health, Education and Welfare, 1969. ERIC document no. ED 040 204.

SYNTACTIC STRUCTURE ELABORATION SCALE

AUTHOR: Ellis G. Olim

AGE: 8 years to adult

VARIABLE: Surface syntactic structure complexity

TYPE OF MEASURE: Reference frame for scaling

SOURCE FROM WHICH MEASURE MAY BE OBTAINED: Coding manual obtainable, without charge, from Ellis G. Olim, Department of Human Development, University of Massachusetts, Amherst, Massachusetts 01002.

DESCRIPTION OF MEASURE: The increase in elaboration and complexity of syntactic structures with language development has long been noted in developmental studies. This scale measures the frequency, elaboration, and complexity of clauses and unusual phrases in a language protocol, weighted for degree of complexity and syntactic elaboration. The ten subscales of the measure are: (1) mean sentence length, (2) adjective range, (3) adverb range, (4) verb elaboration, (5) complex verb preference, (6) abstraction scale, (7) stimulus utilization, (8) introduced content, (9) syntactic structure elaboration, and (10) mean preverb length. The coding manual gives detailed instructions for scoring each of the subscales, together with definitions and distinctions to be used by the scorer.

RELIABILITY AND VALIDITY: Three sets of language protocols were obtained from 163 subjects. These were independently scored by language coders. Reliability was checked by having two coders work independently on a 15-percent sample of the protocols. A rank-order reliability coefficient of .95 was obtained. Validity of the construct syntactic elaboration was assumed on the basis of previous research on language development. In addition, the research of the author and others supported validity of the scale in that it discriminates sharply the language complexity of persons of different educational levels and correlates highly with other linguistic measures of language developmental level.

BIBLIOGRAPHY:

Olim, E. G. "Maternal Language Styles and Children's Cognitive Behavior." *Journal of Special Education*, 1970, *4*, 53-68.

Poole, M. E. "Social Class and Code Elaboration in Written Communication." *Language and Speech*, 1972, *15*, 1-7.

Poole, M. E. "Social Class Differences in Code Elaboration: A Study of Written Communication at the Tertiary Level." *Australian and New Zealand Journal of Sociology*, 1972, *8*, 46-57.

Poole, M. E., and Field, T. W. "Social Class and Code Elaboration in Oral Communication." *Journal of Speech and Hearing Research*, 1971, *14*, 421-427.

TEST FOR AUDITORY COMPREHENSION
OF LANGUAGE (TACL)

AUTHOR: Elizabeth Carrow-Woolfolk

AGE: 3 to 7 years

VARIABLE: Auditory comprehension of language

TYPE OF MEASURE: Test

SOURCE FROM WHICH MEASURE MAY BE OBTAINED: Learning Concepts, Inc., 2501 North Lamar, Austin, Texas, 78705. Cost: Test and twenty-five scoring forms (either English or Spanish), $34.95; additional scoring forms, $3.75/package of twenty-five.

DESCRIPTION OF MEASURE: The Test for Auditory Comprehension of Language contains 101 stimuli ranging from single words to phrases and sentences. The test is currently normed on middle-income children ages 3 to 7, and additional norms are being gathered for Spanish and low-income groups. The scoring form includes ages at which 75 percent and 90 percent of the children passed each item. The scoring form also includes an analysis section clustering the items into three subareas (vocabulary, morphology, and syntax), giving the therapist a quick view of a child's deficiencies. (For short form of the test, STACL, see p. 223.)

Examples of items in the test are given below.

1. *Red.* The child points to one of the three pictures shown: a red ball, an orange ball, a yellow ball.
2. *Running.* The child points to one of the three pictures shown: a boy running, a girl sleeping, a boy watching television.
3. *The lion has eaten.* The child points to one of the three pictures shown: a lion about to eat, a lion eating, a lion with a bone in front of him.
4. *It's not black.* The child points to one of the three pictures shown: a black cat, a white dog, a black dog.

RELIABILITY AND VALIDITY: Validity evidence on the test was gathered in three ways. First, the test was constructed in a developmental sequence, meaning that with increase in age, scores will increase. Second, studies have shown that the Test for Auditory Comprehension of Language distinguishes well between children with severe handicaps and those without. The correlations between the test and IQ scores was found to be .80 among trainable retarded children. Third, it was found that as the language status improved with language-disordered children, so did the scores on the test. Reliability was obtained on both the English version and the Spanish version. Test-retest correlations were .94 on the English version and .93 on the Spanish version. Additional studies have verified the high reliabilities.

BIBLIOGRAPHY:

Bartel, N. R., Bryan, D., and Keehn, S. "Language Comprehension in the Moderately Retarded Child." *Exceptional Children,* 1973, *39,* 375-382.

Carrow, E. "Comprehension of English and Spanish by Pre-School Mexican-American Children." *Modern Language Journal,* 1971, *60,* 299-306.

Carrow, E. "Auditory Comprehension of English by Monolingual and Bilingual Pre-School Children." *Journal of Speech and Hearing Research,* 1972, *15,* 407-412.

Carrow, Sister M. A. "The Development of Auditory Comprehension of Language Structure in Children." *Journal of Speech and Hearing Disorders,* 1968, *33,* 99-111.

Jones, B. J. "A Study of Oral Language Comprehension of Black and White, Middle and Lower Class, Pre-School Children Using Standard English and Black Dialect in Houston, Texas, 1972." Unpublished doctoral dissertation. University of Houston, Texas, 1972.

Prepared by Betsy Woddell

TEST OF KNOWLEDGE OF GRAMMATICAL STRUCTURE

AUTHOR: Lois Sauer Degler

AGE: Elementary and junior grades

VARIABLE: Knowledge of grammatical structure

TYPE OF MEASURE: Test

SOURCE FROM WHICH MEASURE MAY BE OBTAINED: Test is copyrighted and may be obtained from Lois S. Degler, George Peabody College for Teachers, Nashville, Tennessee 37203.

DESCRIPTION OF MEASURE: The Test of Knowledge of Grammatical Structure consists of four forms of forty-eight items each. It includes nonsense-language sentences constructed to match four basic sentence patterns: (1) noun-verb, (2) noun-linking verb-linking verb-complement, (3) noun-verb-object, and (4) noun-verb-indirect object-direct object or noun-verb-object-complement. These patterns are varied according to three levels of structural complexity (single words, phrases, and clauses filling sentence-pattern slots). Children respond to the sentences by translating them into English sentences.

As examples, four of the items on Test Two are given below.

49. By boinging boing boings boings.
50. His boing boinged a boing boingly.
51. A boing boinged a boing another boing.
52. The boing boinged his boing what . . .

RELIABILITY AND VALIDITY: The measure was subjected to a pilot study to refine the test and testing procedures. Forty-seven fourth graders completed all four forms of the test. Coefficients of equivalence were calculated for the four forms. These were of sufficient magnitude to consider the forms equivalent. Hoyt's Analysis of Variance method was used to measure internal consistency of the total test and the four forms. Reliability coefficients for the total test and each of the four forms were .92 or higher. Data from an item analysis were used to shorten the test. Stems too hard or too easy or having low biserial correlation with the total test were eliminated. Decisions about specific sentence patterns to be included and the decision to vary sentences according to complexity of elements within pattern slots were consistent with findings and recommendations of a recent survey of the language of elementary children; thus the test is assumed to have content validity.

BIBLIOGRAPHY:

Sauer, L. E. "Fourth Grade Children's Knowledge of Grammatical Structure and Its Relation to Reading Comprehension." Unpublished doctoral dissertation. University of Wisconsin, Madison, 1968.

Sauer, L. E. "Fourth Grade Children's Knowledge of Grammatical Structure." *Elementary English,* 1970, *47,* 807-813.

TEST OF LETTER DISCRIMINATION

AUTHOR: James W. Tawney

AGE: 2 to 8 years

VARIABLE: Visual discrimination of letter forms

TYPE OF MEASURE: Test

SOURCE FROM WHICH MEASURE MAY BE OBTAINED: James W. Tawney, 730 South Limestone, University of Kentucky, Lexington, Kentucky 40506. Cost: Current cost of xeroxing.

DESCRIPTION OF MEASURE: The test consists of forty-two items requiring the respondent to select a letter to match the sample item. Matches are selected from a set of five letters most likely to be confused with the sample. The test is based upon the work of Gibson, Gibson, Pick, and Osser (1963). Test results identify specific letter confusions and may identify types of confusions, for example, orientation (M-W, b-p, A-V) confusions. These specific confusions can be directly remediated by appropriate discrimination training activities.

As examples, the first six of the forty-two items are given below.

1. C
   O C U G J
2. M
   H W M N Z
3. M
   M N H W Z

4. I
   L I T F P
5. O
   G D C Q O
6. Q
   G O Q C D

RELIABILITY AND VALIDITY: None reported.

BIBLIOGRAPHY:

Gibson, E., Gibson, J., Pick, A., and Osser, H. "A Developmental Study of the Discrimination of Letter-like Forms." In H. Levin (Ed.), *A Basic Research Program on Reading.* Ithaca, New York: Cornell University, 1963.

Tawney, J. W. "Training Letter Discrimination in Four-year-old Children." Unpublished master's thesis. University of Illinois, Urbana, 1969.

Tawney, J. W. "Training Letter Discrimination in Four-year-old Children." *Journal of Applied Behavior Analysis,* 1972, *5,* 455-475.

TEST OF LISTENING COMPREHENSION (TLC)

AUTHOR: Nancy K. Wallner

AGE: Kindergarten and beginning first grade

VARIABLE: Listening comprehension

TYPE OF MEASURE: Test

SOURCE FROM WHICH MEASURE MAY BE OBTAINED: Nancy K. Wallner Post Office Drawer CT, Mississippi State, Mississippi 39762. Test tapes and booklets will be provided at cost, determined by the size of the order.

DESCRIPTION OF MEASURE: The Test of Listening Comprehension (TLC) consists of two forms, A and B, each consisting of eighty-four items purporting to measure auditory comprehension of literal and inferential meanings. No reading skills are required. Pupils, separated from one another by screens, receive directions, story passages, questions, and response choices by listening to an audiotape through individual headsets. They are required to mark their responses in a picture answer booklet. Testing time required is 45 minutes. Test booklets must be hand-scored. The TLC is designed to assess listening comprehension ability prior to the start of formal reading instruction, so that intervention can be initiated, as needed, before deficiencies in listening are compounded into reading disabilities. Because the TLC is considered to be at the developmental level, the author reserves the right to decide its use in research studies.

RELIABILITY AND VALIDITY: Internal reliability for Forms A and B has been established at .95. Alternate form reliability has been established at .89. Each form of the TLC purports to have content validity, established by a panel of three evaluators. Predictive validity ranges from .68 with the Stanford Achievement Test to .76 with the Metropolitan Achievement Test. Concurrent validity with the Metropolitan Readiness Tests has been established at .74. Analysis of factorial validity indicates one significant factor. Statistics have remained consistent with testing of typical midwestern kindergartens, disadvantaged black first graders, affluent white first graders, and typical southern first-grade pupils.

BIBLIOGRAPHY:

Wallner, N. K. "The Development of a Test of Listening Comprehension for Kindergarten and Beginning First Grade—A Preliminary Report." *The Southern Journal*, 1972, *6*, 39-48.

Wallner, N. K. "The Development of a Listening Comprehension Test for Kindergarten and Beginning First Grade." *Educational and Psychological Measurement*, 1974, *34*, 391-396.

TEST OF PREPOSITIONS OF SPATIAL POSITION

AUTHOR: Myrtle McLeod Fisher

AGE: 3 to 5 years

VARIABLE: Understanding of spatial prepositions

TYPE OF MEASURE: Manipulative test, interview

SOURCE FROM WHICH MEASURE MAY BE OBTAINED: Myrtle McLeod Fisher, 2404 Olympia Drive, SE, Calgary, Alberta, Canada T2C 1H5.

DESCRIPTION OF MEASURE: The test measures children's understanding of twenty prepositions by having them place objects in an indicated spatial position (nonverbal part), answer "yes" or "no" to questions containing spatial prepositions (controlled verbal part), and supply missing words (prepositions) in a story told to the child where the examiner manipulates objects into positions (free verbal part). The model farm was used as a testing device because the population tested had discussed the farm environment in school prior to testing. A model would have to be constructed before the test could be used.

As examples, six of the twenty items on the nonverbal part of the test are given below.

1. Put the cow *underneath* the tree.
2. Put the tractor *beside* the barn.
3. Make the dog jump *over* the fence.
4. Put the rooster *on the right* of the henhouse (determine with child which is the front).
5. Put the rooster *on* the roof.
6. Make the cow go *through* the barn.

RELIABILITY AND VALIDITY: Interjudge reliability was consistently high.

BIBLIOGRAPHY:

McLeod, M. *Kindergarten Children's Understanding of Prepositions of Spatial Position.* Unpublished master's thesis. University of Alberta, Edmonton, Canada, 1969.

TEST OF PRESCHOOL LANGUAGE PROFICIENCY

AUTHOR: Norman C. Graham

AGE: 3 to 5 years

VARIABLE: Ability to imitate, comprehend, and produce sentences

TYPE OF MEASURE: Test

SOURCE FROM WHICH MEASURE MAY BE OBTAINED: N. C. Graham, Department of Education, University of Aston in Birmingham, Gosta Green, Birmingham, England B4 7ET. Anticipated cost: £10 (Sterling).

DESCRIPTION OF MEASURE: The test was devised to study the dual role of short-term memory and knowledge of linguistic structure in language development of normal preschool and educable subnormal school children. There are three subtests: imitation (I), comprehension (C), and production. There are two equivalent forms of I and C. The production test is difficult to administer. A word-span test for comparison purposes is also provided.

As examples, the first five of the twelve items on Form A of the imitation subtest are given below. The child is asked to repeat each item.

1. Is Johnny drawing a cat on the board?
2. The girl has not picked up the crab.
3. Boys stand up if the girls sit down.
4. The breaking of the window brought the policeman.
5. Mary has a ribbon and so has Teddy.

RELIABILITY AND VALIDITY: Scores on the test with a sample of 100 ESN children were compared with teachers' ratings on a 5-point scale of children's comprehension and expressive language ability as follows:

	Imitation	Test Comprehension	Production
Teacher rating, Comprehension	.67**	.62**	.77**
Expression	.79**	.70**	.78**

Relevant to the question of reliability, intercorrelations of item difficulty were computed for each subtest on three different groups—preschool, dull-normal, and educable subnormal:

	Imitation		Test Comprehension		Production	
	Preschool	Dull-Normal	Preschool	Dull-Normal	Preschool	Dull-Normal
Subnormal	.65*	.79**	.66*	.56*	.98**	.96**
Preschool		.73**		.60*		.95*

**$p < .01$
*$p < .05$

BIBLIOGRAPHY:

Graham, N. C. "Memory Span and Language Proficiency." *Journal of Learning Disabilities,* 1968, *1,* 644-648.

Graham, N. C. "Short-Term Memory and Syntactic Structure in Educationally Subnormal Children." *Language and Speech,* 1968, *11,* 209-219.

Graham, N. C. "The Language of Educationally Subnormal Children." Department of Education and Science research report. Birmingham University, England, 1970.

Graham, N. C. *A Test of Preschool Language Deficiency, Experimental Edition.* Birmingham, England: School of Education, University of Birmingham, 1970.

Graham, N. C. "Toward a Test of Language Production." *Educational Review,* 1971, *24,* 34-46.

Graham, N. C. "A Psycholinguistic Approach to Language Deficiency." In *The Child and the Outside World: Proceedings of the Twenty-ninth Biennial Conference of the Association for Special Education.* Coventry, England, 1973.

Graham, N. C. "A Critique of Survey of Curricula and Performance in Modern Language." *Audio-Visual Language Journal,* 1974, *12,* 108-109.

Graham, N. C. "Response Strategies in the Partial Comprehension of Sentences." *Language and Speech,* 1974, *17,* 205-221.

Graham, N. C. "The Role of Grammatical Rules in Interdisciplinary Research." Paper presented to the International Colloquium. University of Bielefeld, Germany, 1975.

Graham, N. C., and Gulliford, R. "A Psycholinguistic Approach to Language Deficiency." *Educational Review,* 1968, *20,* 136-145.

TESTS AH2 AND AH3

AUTHORS: Alice W. Heim, K. P. Watts, and V. Simmonds

AGE: 10 years to adulthood

VARIABLE: Verbal, numerical, and perceptual reasoning

TYPE OF MEASURE: Group tests

SOURCE FROM WHICH MEASURE MAY BE OBTAINED: National Foundation for Educational Research (NFER) Publishing, 2 Jennings Buildings, Thames Avenue, Windsor, Berks SL4 1QS, England.

DESCRIPTION OF MEASURE: AH2 and AH3 are parallel tests of general reasoning. They are similar in form, difficulty-gradient and number of items, mean and standard deviation, differing only in content. They share the same manual and the same preliminary examples. Both tests comprise three sets of forty questions, the first set consisting of verbal items (V), the second of numerical (N), and the third set of perceptual (P) items. "Perceptual" here denotes material that is either diagrammatic or pictorial. All items are multiple-choice, offering six responses from which to choose. The total test score (maximum 120) yields a measure of general intelligence, the V-N-P profile yielding a qualitative assessment of the individual.

Examples of the verbal and numerical items only are given below.

1. Which one of the six lower words means *either* the same as *or* the opposite of the top word?

large

over-fed	wide	rich	small	castle	light
1	2	3	4	5	6

2. Which one of the six lower words is *like* the top two but unlike the other five?

rivet   in

bolt	hand	nail	foot	elbow	leg
1	2	3	4	5	6

3. *14* is to *7* as *10* is to

5	4	17	2	14	6
A	B	C	D	E	F

4.

9   6   4

Multiply the smallest figure by the largest and divide the result by the middle figure.

5	30	6	36	3	none of these
A	B	C	D	E	F

RELIABILITY AND VALIDITY: The table below shows (1) the test-retest reliability of the tests and (2) the AH2/3 intertest correlations, that is, a measure of their degree of parallelism. The subjects were 11-year-olds; the time interval was ten months.

	Test-Retest Consistency Same tests	Intertest Correlations Parallel tests
Verbal	.81*	.77*
Numerical	.83*	.84*
Perceptual	.76*	.68*
Total Score	.91*	.88*
n	90	86

Very similar results were found with 13-year-olds, with a six-week time interval. The second table shows the split-half correlations obtained from 200 students at technical colleges.

	AH2	AH3
Verbal	.84*	.85*
Numerical	.86*	.85*
Perceptual	.70*	.83*
Total	.92*	.94*
n	100	100

*p < .001

Validity for AH2 and AH3 has been determined by comparing the tests with (1) well-established psychometric tests, group and individual, the time interval between testings ranging from a few hours to twenty-two months; (2) academic examinations in English, mathematics, and more general school subjects; (3) other criteria, such as streaming and setting in school, and rise in score with age. These comparisons yielded very satisfactory results from the viewpoint of both total score and separate V, N, and P scores.

BIBLIOGRAPHY:

Heim, A. W., Watts, K. P., and Simmonds, V. *AH2/AH3 Manual.* Windsor, England: National Foundation for Educational Research Publishing, 1974.

Heim, A. W., Watts, K. P., and Simmonds, V. "AH2 and AH3: Parallel Tests of Reasoning." *British Journal of Psychology,* 1974, *65,* 493-503.

VERBAL MATURITY SCALE

AUTHORS: Albert G. Packard, Elaine E. Lee, and M. Adele Mitzel

AGE: 3, 4, and 5 years

VARIABLE: Verbal ability

TYPE OF MEASURE: Criterion-referenced test

SOURCE FROM WHICH MEASURE MAY BE OBTAINED: Baltimore City Public Schools, 3 East Twenty-fifth Street, Baltimore, Maryland 21218.

DESCRIPTION OF MEASURE: The Verbal Maturity Scale consists of sixty questions. It was developed to be used with 3- and 4-year-old children in Head Start or Early School Admissions Programs. It is a measure of a child's ability to understand and to respond verbally to questions about himself and his environment. It provides an estimate of a child's general fund of knowledge and his ability to recall and express that knowledge without the use of visual clues. The emphasis in the test is not on total score but in determining what a child does or does not know about himself and his environment when he enters a preschool program and when he leaves.

The questions are arranged in blocks, such as "Let's Talk About You," "Let's Talk About Some of the Animals You Know," and so forth. It is individually administered by a teacher or a psychologist. The questions are scored either right or wrong, but several questions may have more than one answer. For example, the answer to "What color is the sky?" may be blue, white, or grey. "What does a bee do?" A bee may fly, buzz, hum, sting, make honey, and so forth. The test can be used as a pre- and postmeasure, and the answers to the questions and the concept represented by the questions are meant to be taught.

As examples, one item from each of the seven subtests is given below. The entire test consists of sixty items.

A. Let's Talk About You
   1. Where do you live?
B. Let's Talk About Some of the Things You Do
   9. What do you wear on your hands when it is cold?
C. Let's Talk About Some of the Things You Might Use
   15. What do we use a boat for?
D. Let's Talk About Some of the Animals You Know
   23. What animal gives milk?
E. Let's Talk About Some of the People You Know
   32. Who brings letters to your house?
F. Let's Talk About Some of the Colors You Know
   38. What color is butter?
G. Let's Talk About Some of the Other Things You Know
   44. Which is more—a nickel or a quarter?

RELIABILITY AND VALIDITY: Content validity was determined by teachers and psychologists assigned to Head Start programs. Predictive validity was estimated by correlations with teachers' grades in kindergarten and PMA scores. These correlations ranged in the high .70s and .80s.

BIBLIOGRAPHY:

Stine, O. C., Saratsiotis, J. B., and Furno, O. F. "Children in the Extremes of Physical and Psychological Measurements." *Journal of School Health,* 1969, *39,* 636-641.

Prepared by M. Adele Mitzel

VOCABULARY AND GRAMMAR TESTS

AUTHOR: Albert Mehrabian

AGE: 2½ to 5 years

VARIABLE: Grammatical skill and vocabulary

TYPE OF MEASURE: Test

SOURCE FROM WHICH MEASURE MAY BE OBTAINED: See Mehrabian (1970).

DESCRIPTION OF MEASURE: These six measures can be viewed as assessing the child's ability to use language to refer to events of increasing complexity and to distinguish correct from incorrect usage. Test 1, Picture Vocabulary, is a thirty-five-item measure. Test 2, Comprehension of Simple Commands, contains items like "Put the pencil on the book" and "Put the string, but not the book or the pencil in the box." There are fifteen such items. Test 3, Comprehension of Meaningless Commands, consists of eight items of the following type: "Drop the box on the floor; drop the floor on the box." Test 4, Inflection, consists of eleven items such as, "this is a block; here are two (blocks) (of them)." Test 5, Judgment of the Grammaticalness of Sentences and Phrases, has thirteen items of the following type: "I no want the pencil; I don't want the pencil." Test 6, Verbal Imitation, consists of eighteen sentences the child is asked to repeat. Examples are, "Don't use my dough" and "David saw the bicycle and he was happy." The six tests take 20 to 35 minutes to administer, with older children taking less time. The items are ordered in terms of difficulty within each test, and four consecutive failures were the signal for the examiner to move on to the next test. Scores of a subject on each of the tests are transformed into percentage correct scores (that is, the percentage of items passed by the subject on each test). A grammatical ability score is obtained by averaging the percentage correct scores for Tests 2 through 6. Alternately, a linguistic ability score is obtained by averaging the percentage correct scores for all six tests. Separate norms for the vocabulary test, average grammatical ability, and average linguistic ability are given in Mehrabian (1970).

RELIABILITY AND VALIDITY: Interjudge reliabilities ranges for the tests follow: Test 1, .82 to 1.00; Test 2, .70 to 1.00; Test 3, .85 to 1.00; Test 4, .82 to 1.00; Test 5, .81 to 1.00; and Test 6, .75 to .96. For all of the measures, the mean value of interjudge reliability over the items was greater than .90, except for Test 6, where it was .86. Forty children were retested two weeks following the first administration of the tests. Test-retest reliabilities exceeded .82 for all six measures. All the tests exhibited significant intercorrelations among themselves and with age. No significant relationships were obtained in relation to sex. The results of a factor analysis suggest that despite superficial differences these six tests reflect a single linguistic ability dimension. Therefore, a simple average of "percentage correct" scores from these six tests could be considered a satisfactory index of the child's level of verbal skill.

BIBLIOGRAPHY:

Mehrabian, A. "Measures of Vocabulary and Grammatical Skills for Children Up to Age Six." *Developmental Psychology,* 1970, *2,* 439-446.

Prepared by Orval G. Johnson

VOCABULARY USAGE TEST (VUT)

AUTHOR: James E. Nation

AGE: 34 to 63 months

VARIABLE: Vocabulary usage

TYPE OF MEASURE: Test

SOURCE FROM WHICH MEASURE MAY BE OBTAINED: See Nation (1972).

DESCRIPTION OF MEASURE: The VUT involves use of the first seventy plates of the Peabody Picture Vocabulary Test, Form B, but in a different way from their use in the PPVT. The child is instructed to name the objects or concepts he sees when presented with the picture. Two methods of stimulus presentation were used in construction of the measure: confrontation naming—"What is this?"—and sentence completion —"This is a _____." The sentence-completion items elicited correct responses more easily; therefore, the test stimuli were revised using sentence-completion stimuli. In some instances the direct-question stimuli is maintained as an alternative method of obtaining the desired response.

As examples, five selected items from the seventy-item measure are given below.

Word	Plate	Stimulus Sentence	Example Variant Responses
table	1.	This is a _____.	
climbing	11.	This boy is _____. What is this boy doing? _____	11. going to (climb) up the ladder
jacket	14.	This is not a shirt. It is called a _____.	
pulling	15.	This girl is _____. What is the girl doing with the wagon? _____	15. trying to (pull) it
tire	19.	This is not a wheel. It is called a _____.	

RELIABILITY AND VALIDITY: The seventy-item Vocabulary Usage Test was used to obtain test-retest scores from sixteen children ranging in age from 40 to 60 months. All sixteen children were retested within four to seven days. A test-retest reliability coefficient of .91 was obtained (Nation, 1972). An earlier study (Nation, 1970) revealed that vocabulary comprehension and usage develop in a linear fashion as chronological age increases, with significant increases in growth at the 6-month age intervals. Both normal siblings and control normals obtained significantly higher vocabulary comprehension and usage scores than did cleft palate children. Vocabulary comprehension and usage were significantly correlated for all groups.

BIBLIOGRAPHY:

Aram, D. "Developmental Language Disorders: Patterns of Language Behavior." Unpublished doctoral dissertation. Case Western Reserve University, Cleveland, Ohio, 1972.

Chapman, D. "Language Patterns of Certain Primary Level Educable Mentally Retarded

Children." Unpublished doctoral dissertation. Case Western Reserve University, Cleveland, Ohio, 1974.

Nation, J. E. "A Comparative Study of Comprehension and Usage Vocabularies of Normal and Cleft Palate Preschool Children." Unpublished doctoral dissertation. University of Wisconsin, Madison, 1964.

Nation, J. E. "Vocabulary Comprehension and Usage of Preschool Cleft Palate and Normal Children." *The Cleft Palate Journal,* 1970, *7,* 639-644.

Nation, J. E. "A Vocabulary Usage Test." *Journal of Psychology,* 1972, *1,* 221-228.

VOGEL'S SENTENCE REPETITION TEST

AUTHOR: Susan Ann Vogel

AGE: 4 to 10 years

VARIABLE: Syntactic development

TYPE OF MEASURE: Test

SOURCE FROM WHICH MEASURE MAY BE OBTAINED: See Vogel (1975).

DESCRIPTION OF MEASURE: The Vogel Sentence Repetition Test is constructed in such a way as to control three variables: sentence length, vocabulary difficulty, and syntactic complexity. It consists of twenty sentences presented in order of increasing syntactic complexity. Nine of the sentences are eight words in length. Eleven are nine words in length. Contractions are counted as one word. The vocabulary is controlled for level of difficulty so as to include words with which the child should be familiar. Syntactic complexity increases in two ways: (1) developmentally, by incorporating syntactic structures that have been identified as ranging from simple to complex based on studies of language acquisition; and (2) transformationally, by embedding an increasing number of underlying sentences in each sentence. The number of underlying sentences increases from two to four: sentences one to five having *two*, six to fifteen having *three*, and sixteen to twenty having *four* underlying sentences. Examples of items having two, three, and four underlying sentences are given below.

Sentence 2. This is mine, but that one is his.
Sentence 10. He wants to jump higher than everybody else.
Sentence 19. When can someone tell us why it stopped ringing?

This test is administered individually. The examiner tells the child, "I am going to say something to you. When I get all through, you say just what I said." A response is scored as correct if the child repeats the sentence accurately without any additions, substitutions, or changes of word order. Repeating more than once one or more words within a sentence is not considered an error. Likewise if a word such as "it's" is repeated "it is" or vice versa and no other changes are made, the response is scored as correct. An analysis of omissions, substitutions, additions, and repetitions may reveal an individual's specific syntactic competencies and weaknesses. Such information will prove valuable to the special-education teacher and therapist.

RELIABILITY AND VALIDITY: This measure was used to determine if children who were deficient in reading comprehension were also deficient in oral syntactic ability as compared to children with good reading ability. It was found that this test did differentiate between the two groups at statistically significant levels. The original test was administered to forty-five boys between the ages of 7 years, 4 months and 9 years, 5 months. The reliability was estimated by a two-way analysis of variance in which for every item, each child's response was analyzed and compared with his responses to all other items. An estimate of internal consistency, error, and the true variance yielded a reliability coefficient (Hoyt r) of .85. Because the number of words per sentence was held constant, and because in an analysis of covariance it was determined that there was no significant regression due to vocabulary difficulty on the Vogel Test of Sentence Repetition, the reliability coefficient of .85 is mainly a reflection of the syntactic complexity factor.

BIBLIOGRAPHY:

Vogel, S. A. "Syntactic Abilities in Normal and Dyslexic Children." *Journal of Learning Disabilities,* 1974, *7,* 103-109.
Vogel, S. A. *Syntactic Abilities in Normal and Dyslexic Children.* Baltimore, Maryland: University Park Press, 1975.

WIIG-SEMEL TEST OF LINGUISTIC CONCEPTS

AUTHORS: Elisabeth H. Wiig and Eleanor M. Semel

AGE: Middle and upper grades and up

VARIABLE: Auditory comprehension of linguistic concepts

TYPE OF MEASURE: Test

SOURCE FROM WHICH MEASURE MAY BE OBTAINED: ASIS Document NAPS-02252, Microfiche Publications, 440 Park Avenue South, New York, New York 10016. Cost: $3.00.

DESCRIPTION OF MEASURE: The Wiig-Semel Test of Linguistic Concepts has fifty items, ten of each representing comparative, passive, temporal, spatial, and familial relationships. The test was designed to (1) control the length of the majority of the sentences to from five to seven words, (2) limit the relationships to involve only two critical elements, (3) provide a large ethnic variety of proper names, and (4) permit yes/no responses for the majority of the items.

As examples, some representative questions are given below.

1. Comparative relationships: "Are watermelons bigger than apples?"
2. Passive relationships: "Jerry was pushed by Bob. Was Bob pushed?"
3. Temporal relationships: "Does Thursday come after Tuesday?"
4. Spatial relationships: "Hal stood in back of Beth. Was Beth in front."
5. Familial relationships: "Give another name for your mother's father."

RELIABILITY AND VALIDITY: Construct validity was determined by evaluating age differentiation (Wiig and Semel, 1974a). As language comprehension skills are reported to be developmental, test scores were expected to show an increase with age. Grade-school children (N = 210) were randomly selected, thirty each from grades 1 through 7 to 8. Analysis of variance indicated significant differences between grades (F = 92.10, df = 6;203, p < .01). The test was administered to thirty-two learning-disabled children and their academically achieving controls and to thirty learning-disabled adolescents (Wiig and Semel, 1973, 1974b). In both instances learning-disabled youngsters were differentiated from their age peers at statistically significant levels. Concurrent validity has been found to exist between the present test and the Illinois Test of Psycho-linguistic Ability (Wiig and Semel, 1974b). Correlations ranged from r = .43 for Auditory Association to r = .59 for Psycholinguistic Age. The reliability was determined by the split-half method and corrected by the Spearman-Brown formula. The correlation coefficient for thirty children from grades 2 and 3 was .82.

BIBLIOGRAPHY:

Wiig, E. H., and Semel, E. M. "Comprehension of Linguistic Concepts Requiring Logical Operations by Learning-Disabled Children." *Journal of Speech and Hearing Research*, 1973, *16*, 627-636.

Wiig, E. H., and Semel, E. M. "Development of Comprehension of Logico-Grammatical Sentences by Grade School Children." *Perceptual and Motor Skills*, 1974a, *38*, 171-176.

Wiig, E. H., and Semel, E. M. "Logico-Grammatical Sentence Comprehension by Adolescents with Learning Disabilities." *Perceptual and Motor Skills*, 1974b, *38*, 1331-1334.

Prepared by Elisabeth H. Wiig and Eleanor M. Semel

WORD AWARENESS TESTS—TEST I: LISTS; TEST II: SENTENCES; TEST III: HOMOPHONES

AUTHOR: Marjorie H. Holden

AGE: 4 to 8 years

VARIABLE: Recognition and identification of lexical items

TYPE OF MEASURE: Individual oral test

SOURCE FROM WHICH MEASURE MAY BE OBTAINED: See Holden (1972) or write Marjorie H. Holden, Richmond College of City University of New York, 130 Stuyvesant Place, Staten Island, New York 10301.

DESCRIPTION OF MEASURE: The Word Awareness Tests consist of a battery of three progressively more difficult tests, each consisting of ten items. The rationale underlying the battery is based on a theoretical interpretation of language development. It is assumed that during Piaget's preoperational stage the child initially uses words without being aware of them as lexical units, but as the child approaches the stage of concrete operations, words become recognized as lexical items, and the child acquires the ability to analyze higher-order linguistic structures as a function of their lexical components. The battery is assumed to measure the sequential stages in the development of the child's ability to recognize and use lexical items in analyzing language. The tests are administered individually in one sitting of approximately 15 to 20 minutes. The maximum possible score on each test is 20 points, and 60 points is the total for the entire battery. Detailed directions for scoring and administration, together with copies of the entire test, can be found in Holden (1972).

The nature of the task is identical for each of the three tests. Subjects are presented with pairs of stimuli utterances that are identical except for an addition to the second utterance of the pair. After presentation of both utterances, subjects are asked to identify the added segment. In all items the addition is a common English word. In Test I, Lists, the simplest of the three tests, the subject is presented with lists of words: *Dog, up, flower, quiet*; *Dog, up, laugh, flower, quiet.* To receive a perfect score, the child needs only respond *laugh*, after listening to the examiner speak the two lists. In Test II, Sentences, a word is added to a sentence: *The red ball is in the closet*; *The big red ball is in the closet.* In Test III, Homophones, the items are also composed of phonetically identical sentences with one addition to the second of the pair, but each pair is constructed around a pair of homophonous words. On this test only, the addition of a word has the effect of changing the entire meaning of the sentence, because the homophone takes on its alternate meaning, for example, *John leaves after dinner*; *John rakes leaves after dinner.* A preoperational child is expected to be compelled by the semantic aspect of the message and to be unable to shift his focus to the sound of the message.

Norms are available on a sample of 100 white middle-class children from the kindergarten and first grade of the Mount Vernon Woods Elementary School in Alexandria, Virginia. Half of the children in the sample were drawn from the first grade and half from the kindergarten. At each grade level there was an approximately equal division between the sexes.

The study for which these measures were devised was preceded by a study that investigated kindergarten children's conceptions of words in speech and print (Holden and MacGinitie, 1972). A preliminary report of the study for which the Word Awareness Tests were created is in Holden and MacGinitie (1973).

As examples, the first two of the ten items on each of the tests are given below. The respondent answers by repeating to the examiner the word added to the second list of words or the second sentence.

Serial Lists: Test I

1. house, chair
   house, chair, table

2. book, school
   book, pencil, school

Sentences: Test II

1. Jack went swimming.   2. Bob flew like an airplane.
   Jack and Bill went swimming.   Bob flew and buzzed like an airplane

Homophones: Test III

1. The hole is round.   2. There is a big one.
   The whole pig is round.   Their dog is a big one.

RELIABILITY AND VALIDITY: Reliability for the battery of three tests was .93 for the kindergarten and .87 for the first grade. The correlation coefficients for the subtests ranged from .56 for Test II in the first grade to .94 for Test I in the first grade. Complete breakdowns for each test and each grade are given in Holden (1972). These figures reflect internal consistency, which is consistent with the generally high item-test reliabilities. Empirical validation for the increasing difficulty of the three tests and their scalelike character is also presented in Holden (1972). A significant interaction ($p < .01$) between age (grade) and test (list, sentence, homophone) supports the validity of the battery as a developmental measure. Additional validity is provided by the moderate but significant correlations found between the three tests and Piagetian seriation measures, mental age, and a standardized riddle interview. Detailed descriptions of all measures obtained from the normative sample are presented in Holden (1972) and in abbreviated form in Holden and MacGinitie (1973), together with an intercorrelation matrix and the results of a factor analysis.

BIBLIOGRAPHY:

Holden, M. H. "Metalinguistic Ability and Cognitive Performance in Children from Five to Seven." Unpublished doctoral dissertation. Teachers College, Columbia University, New York, 1972.

Holden, M. H., and MacGinitie, W. H. "Children's Conceptions of Word Boundaries in Speech and Print." *Journal of Educational Psychology,* 1972, *63,* 551-557.

Holden, M. H., and MacGinitie, W. H. "Metalinguistic Ability and Cognitive Performance in Children from Five to Seven." Paper presented at the meeting of the American Educational Research Association. New Orleans, February 1973.

Group 1-c

Specific Achievements

BLIND LEARNING APTITUDE TEST (BLAT)

AUTHOR: T. Ernest Newland

AGE: 6 to 16 years possible; 6 to 12 years best

VARIABLE: Learning aptitude (academic)

TYPE OF MEASURE: Test

SOURCE FROM WHICH MEASURE MAY BE OBTAINED: T. Ernest Newland, 702 South Race Street, Urbana, Illinois 61801. The BLAT kit consists of a shipping/storage box, the test booklet (sixty-one items—twelve of them for training), the manual, and a supply of response sheets. Cost: $20 (U.S.) postpaid.

DESCRIPTION OF MEASURE: The BLAT is an individual, untimed test, usually taking from 20 to 45 minutes, for functionally blind children. The only verbal demand is in communicating the tasks. The tactual discrimination of the embossed geometric figures is not as fine as that required for reading Braille. It is based on Spearman theory, heavily sampling his "g," and standardized on 961 residential and day-school functionally blind children in twelve states (two West Coast, two East Coast, five midwestern, three southeastern), socioeconomically and racially representative of the United States. Normative data (learning ages, learning quotients) are available for the age range 6 to 16 but most meaningful in the 6-to-12 range. As of November 1974, it was being used outside of this country in France (being standardized there), Germany, Israel, Ceylon, and Colombia.

RELIABILITY AND VALIDITY: Kuder-Richardson (14) reliability is .93; test-retest reliability (seven-month period, naive retesters, $N = 93$, CA 10-16) is .87. The BLAT correlates higher with measured educational achievement than does either the Hayes-Binet or the WISC Verbal, although from .61 to .91 with them.

BIBLIOGRAPHY:

Newland, T. E. "Prediction and Evaluation of Academic Learning by Blind Children" (I and II). *International Journal for the Education of the Blind,* 1964.

Newland, T. E. *The Blind Learning Aptitude Test.* Final Report to the U.S. Office of Education (Grant No. 3-6-061928-1558). February 1969.

Newland, T. E. "Psychological Assessment of Exceptional Children and Youth." In W. M. Cruickshank (Ed.), *Psychology of Exceptional Children and Youth.* (3rd ed.) Englewood Cliffs, New Jersey: Prentice-Hall, 1971.

Newland, T. E. "Assessing the Cognitive Capability of Exceptional Children." In D. L. Walker and D. P. Howard (Eds.), *Special Education—Instrument for Change in Education for the '70s.* Selected Papers for the University of Virginia Lecture Series, 1970-1971. Charlottesville: University of Virginia, 1972.

Newland, T. E. "Le Test d'Aptitude à l'Apprentissage pour Aveugles (BLAT)." *Bulletin de Psychologie,* 1973-1974, *27,* 398-402.

BODY PARTS NAME INVENTORY (BPNI)

AUTHORS: Alan Coller, Jack Victor, and John Dill

AGE: Preschool

VARIABLE: Knowledge of parts of the body

TYPE OF MEASURE: Nonverbal and verbal identification test

SOURCE FROM WHICH MEASURE MAY BE OBTAINED: Jack Victor, 82-25 218th Street, Hollis Hills, New York 11427.

DESCRIPTION OF MEASURE: The BPNI, one of the Early Childhood Inventories (see Index of Measures), is an individually administered inventory designed to evaluate the child's ability to identify ten parts of his body—chin, stomach, neck, arm, knee, ankle, thigh, cheek, wrist, knuckles. In addition, the child must indicate some understanding of the functions of five other body parts—feet, head, nose, hand, tongue. The items included in the BPNI are a mixture of "easy" and "hard" items. The test is divided into three separate tasks: a nonverbal receptive task, a verbal expressive task, and a verbal identification (of functions) task. In the *nonverbal receptive* task, the child is required to point to designated body parts as they are named by the administrator. In the *verbal* expressive task, the administrator indicates a particular body part, and the child must supply the correct name for it. In the *verbal identification* (of functions) task, the child has to respond to an incomplete sentence with the name of the appropriate body part. The proper sequence for the administration of this inventory is nonverbal receptive task followed by the verbal expressive task, and then the verbal function task.

     As examples, the five items of the verbal function task are given below. If the child gives answers such as "toes" for "feet" or "fingers" for "hands," the administrator should probe for correct response (see last one of the page of BPNI for items).

1. When you get up in the morning you put your shoes on your _____. (Feet)
2. When you go outside, you put your hat on your _____. (Head)
3. When you smell food, you smell through your _____. (Nose)
4. When you put on gloves, you put them on your _____. (Hands)
5. When you lick ice cream, you lick it with your _____. (Tongue)

RELIABILITY AND VALIDITY: None reported.

BIBLIOGRAPHY:

Coller, A., and Victor, J. *Early Childhood Inventories Project.* New York: New York University, Institute for Developmental Studies, 1970.
Ryan, T. J., and Moffitt, A. R. "Evaluation of Preschool Programs." *Canadian Psychologist,* 1974, *15,* 205-219.

Prepared by Alan Coller, Jack Victor, and John Dill

BRYANT-SCHWAN DESIGN TEST

AUTHORS: Antusa S. Bryant and LeRoy B. Schwan

AGE: Elementary-school children and mentally retarded children

VARIABLE: Art design knowledge

TYPE OF MEASURE: Matching and identification test

SOURCE FROM WHICH MEASURE MAY BE OBTAINED: Campus Publishers, Box 1005, Mankato, Minnesota 56001. Cost: Number of sets: 1, $17.50; 2 to 4, $15.00 each; 5 to 9, $13.00 each; 10 or more, $12.50 each. Art Guide only, $4.00. Prices include shipping costs. Canadian orders add $1.00 for handling. (Minnesota residents add 4-percent sales tax.)

DESCRIPTION OF MEASURE: The initial test, which consisted of 120 items, was administered for the first time in 1968. The present test has been developed over a period of six years. The fifty most reliable and valid items from the original test are included in the present test. Five design elements (line, shape, color, value, and texture) are covered. Five items for each of the five elements make up each of the two parts. The first part of each of the elements consists of matching items; the second part consists of identification items. The entire test takes less than 10 minutes to administer individually. The test kit consists of the Design Test, score sheets, Manual of Directions, and Guide for Teaching Art.

RELIABILITY AND VALIDITY: Four separate studies were conducted to obtain data regarding the validity and reliability of the Bryant-Schwan Design Test. Test-retest studies were conducted in Study Two (see below). The correlation between the matching tests and IQ was significant on both Matching 1 (p = .001) and Matching 2 (p = .001). Sex was not significant (p = .651). There was a significant schools effect (p = .001), which resulted mainly from the identification tests (p = .001 in both cases). Study Three, like Study Two, had a retest element. It showed a significant correlation between the tests when compared on a grade-level basis (p = .001). The significance of a grade effect occurred equally on both levels of each test (p = .001). The effect of sex was not significant on this test.

Study One: Ninety-nine subjects were tested by eight examiners. Validity of the matching and identification items was analyzed in relation to IQ, the original Bryant-Schwan Test, matching test, identification test, total test, years of art class attendance, and age. There were noticeable differences between males and females in regard to years of art attendance, age, and IQ on the total test. Examiner effect on scores was also analyzed and found to be significant. These correlations were constructed by pooling the test results obtained by the examiners. Large differences were found between males and females in the correlation of IQ score with matching and identification scores. This may be due partly to the sex-examiner interaction. Study Two: Fifty subjects from two state hospitals were included in this test-retest study. The intercorrelations were rather high, except those in which age was a factor. Study Three: Fifty kindergarteners, fifty first graders, fifty third graders, and fifty fifth graders from a small rural Minnesota elementary school were included in this test-retest study using the final Bryant-Schwan Design Test. Moderately high correlations were obtained. Study Four: One hundred pupils from a fairly large semirural Minnesota public school, ninety-nine from a small rural Minnesota elementary school, and ninety-eight from a large metropolitan public school (grades 1 to 12, including trainable and educable classes) were administered the final Bryant-Schwan Design Test. The scores were analyzed to show how the test factors correlated for each of the three school systems, for all three schools combined, by sex, and with the effect of grade level removed. Years of art and age did not correlate significantly when sex of examinees was considered.

BIBLIOGRAPHY:

Bryant, A. S., and Schwan, L. B. "Art and the Mentally Retarded Child." *NAEA Studies in Art Education*, 1971, *12*, 50-63.

COLOR NAME INVENTORY (CNI)

AUTHORS: Alan Coller and Jack Victor

AGE: Preschool

VARIABLE: Knowledge of colors

TYPE OF MEASURE: Nonverbal and verbal identification

SOURCE FROM WHICH MEASURE MAY BE OBTAINED: Jack Victor, 82-25 218th Street, Hollis Hills, New York 11427.

DESCRIPTION OF MEASURE: The CNI, one of the Early Childhood Inventories (see Index of Measures), is an individually administered inventory designed to evaluate the child's ability to identify twelve common colors—black, blue, brown, gray, green, orange, pink, purple, red, tan, white, and yellow. The CNI consists of two separate tasks—a nonverbal task and a verbal task. In the *nonverbal receptive* task, the child is presented with twelve arrays of four colored squares each. The child is asked to point to specific colors present in the arrays as they are named by the administrator. Each array contains two relatively familiar colors and two relatively unfamiliar colors. In the *verbal expressive* task, the child is presented with each color, one at a time, and is asked to name it. Both tasks use a color wheel to present the stimulus to the child. The nonverbal task is administered first, followed by the verbal task.

Alternate presentation forms of the nonverbal task of the CNI are possible and may be used to evaluate guessing and positional response-set behaviors. If accurate diagnostic information is desired for very young children, *both* nonverbal presentation forms should be administered. The two presentation forms of the CNI differ only in the arrangement of the colored squares in the same array; that is, in Set (or Form) B, position 1 contains the colored squares that were in position 4 in Set A. Positions 1, 2, 3, and 4 in Set A respectively become positions 4, 3, 2, and 1 in Set B.

RELIABILITY AND VALIDITY: Alternate form reliabilities were obtained for a sample of inner-city children in prekindergarten to first grade. The correlations are .81 for prekindergarten, .85 for kindergarten, and .82 for first grade.

BIBLIOGRAPHY:

Coller, A., and Victor, J. *Early Childhood Inventories Project.* New York: New York University, Institute for Developmental Studies, 1970.

Ryan, T. J., and Moffitt, A. R. "Evaluation of Preschool Programs." *Canadian Psychologist,* 1974, *15,* 205-219.

Prepared by Alan Coller, Jack Victor, and John Dill

FAIRVIEW DEVELOPMENT SCALE (FDS)

AUTHORS: Robert T. Ross and Alan Boroskin

AGE: Birth to 5 years, 10 months

VARIABLE: Developmental level

TYPE OF MEASURE: Behavior rating scale

SOURCE FROM WHICH MEASURE MAY BE OBTAINED: Research Department, Fairview State Hospital, 2501 Harbor Boulevard, Costa Mesa, California 92626.

DESCRIPTION OF MEASURE: The FDS is designed for use primarily with the severely and profoundly retarded. It provides numerical equivalents of present behavioral status. The scale is composed of twenty-six items that provide measures of Perceptual and Motor Skills (PM), Self-Help Skills (SH) (Toilet Training, Dressing, Feeding, Grooming), Language (L), Social Interaction (SI), and Self-Direction (SD). The items are stated in terms of what the subject typically "does" and not what he "can do," in order to obtain more objective measures of the individual's behavior(s). The statements start at a level reflecting "no skill" and proceed upward to "mastery." Scores are provided for each skill, and the scale is easily scored. To increase the utility of the scale, it has been constructed so that it is short and can be easily administered and scored by ward personnel, parents, or caretakers.

As examples, one subtest each from the Perceptual and Motor Skills and from the Language sections of the scale are given below. Also included in the scale are Self-Help Skills, Social Interaction, and Self-Direction sections.

I. *Perceptual and Motor Skills*

   3. Perception

     0–Does not react

     1–Stares at window or wall

     2–Startled by sudden sounds

     3–Eyes follow moving objects

     4–Turns head toward a sound source

     5–Reaches for seen objects

     6–Recognizes favorite toys

     7–Spits out distasteful substances

     8–Opens mouth at approach of spoon

     9–Points out objects in a picture

III. *Language*

   A. Articulation

     0–Mute, makes no sounds

     1–Cries or laughs

     2–Differential crying

     3–Single syllables (for example: goo)

     4–Two or more sounds in one breath

     5–Babbles

     6–Uses all vowels

     7–Uses all consonants

RELIABILITY AND VALIDITY: To assess the interrater reliability of scores on the FDS, the ratings (of the same patients) provided by the A.M. shift were compared with those of the P.M. shift for the first administration (April 1973). The same comparison was made using the data from the second administration (June 1973). The averaged coefficients range from .71 to .94 and indicate that scores on the FDS do not vary greatly due to individual differences among raters. To evaluate the stability of FDS scores, the ratings of the A.M. shift for the first and second administrations were compared. The data from the P.M. shift were compared in the same manner. The averaged test-retest reliability coefficients range from .85 to .97.

    The FDS was administered to 127 normal children (sixty-four males, sixty-three females) by their parents. These children ranged in age from 4 months to 71 months, with a mean of 36.5 months (SD = 19.4). The relationship of CA to Total Score was nonlinear and negatively accelerated. The value of *eta* for the regression of CA on total score was .88 and for the regression of total score on CA was .91. The high degree of relationship between CA and total score on the FDS, for the sample of normal children, provides evidence of the validity of scores on the FDS. Giampiccolo and Boroskin (1974) provide additional evidence on validity.

BIBLIOGRAPHY:

Giampiccolo, J. S., Jr., and Boroskin, A. *Manual for the Fairview Developmental Scale.* Costa Mesa, California: Fairview State Hospital, 1974.

Prepared by James S. Giampiccolo, Jr.

FAIRVIEW SELF-HELP SCALE (FSHS)

AUTHOR: Robert T. Ross

AGE: 4 to 9 years

VARIABLE: Self-help skills

TYPE OF MEASURE: Behavior rating scale

SOURCE FROM WHICH MEASURE MAY BE OBTAINED: Research Department, Fairview State Hospital, 2501 Harbor Boulevard, Costa Mesa, California 92626.

DESCRIPTION OF MEASURE: The FSHS is relatively short, easy to fill in by parent or caretaker, easy to score, and capable of assessing various aspects of adaptive behavior so that change can be quickly detected. The first form of the scale was divided into eight sections: Ambulation, Speech, Understanding, Dressing, Grooming, Toilet Training, Eating Skills, and Socialization. This form of the scale was filled out by ward personnel for 341 patients who were systematically selected to be representative of the hospital resident population. A factor analysis of the data indicated that only four factors were represented on the scale instead of eight: Motor Dexterity, Self-Help (Toilet Training, Dressing, Eating, and Grooming), Communication Skills, and Social Interaction. The final form of the FSHS is organized around these four categories plus a fifth one, called Self-Direction. Rating scales for physical handicaps and disruptive behaviors have been added, although they are not scored. The scale itself is composed of thirty-four specific kinds of behavior, each of which is rated as to the level of proficiency demonstrated by the patient. It is essential that the observer be familiar with the patient and that proficiency be rated in terms of present status and not in terms of past performance or potential. A behavioral quotient is computed by dividing the age equivalent score on this measure by the chronological age and multiplying by 100.

As examples, the first subgroup of Motor Dexterity Skills and the fourth subgroup of Self-Direction are given below. Other main categories are Self-Help Skills and Communication Skills, with a total of thirty-four items in the instrument.

1. *Motor Dexterity*
   a. Standing
      0—Does not stand at all—relatively immobile
      1—Does not stand, but crawls
      2—Stands when held by others
      3—Stands alone with support
      4—Stands unsteadily unsupported—falls frequently
      5—Stands well alone
2. *Time Sense*
      0—No sense of time
      1—Recognizes difference of night and day
      2—Knows meaning of "morning," "noon," and "night"
      3—Tells time for morning, noon, and evening meal (8 o'clock, 12 o'clock, and so forth)
      4—Tells time plus or minus one hour

5—Tells time to nearest hour
6—Tells time to nearest quarter hour
7—Tells hours and minutes

RELIABILITY AND VALIDITY: Test-retest reliability (one week interval, $N = 70$) was .91. Measures of stability yielded average correlations of .91 and .87. There was a high significant relationship between chronological age and FSHS scores ($N = 155$ normal children). FSHS and Vineland Social Maturity Scale total scores correlated .97; FSHS and Cain-Levine Social Competency Scale scores correlated .94. Further data are provided in Ross (1970).

BIBLIOGRAPHY:

Ross, R. T. *Manual for the Fairview Self-Help Scale.* Costa Mesa, California: Fairview
    State Hospital, 1970.

Prepared by James S. Giampiccolo, Jr.

FAIRVIEW SOCIAL SKILLS SCALE (FSSS)

AUTHORS: Robert T. Ross and James S. Giampiccolo, Jr.

AGE: 6 to 12½ years

VARIABLE: Social skills

TYPE OF MEASURE: Behavior rating scale

SOURCE FROM WHICH MEASURE MAY BE OBTAINED: Research Department, Fairview State Hospital, 2501 Harbor Boulevard, Costa Mesa, California 92626.

DESCRIPTION OF MEASURE: The FSSS was designed for use primarily with the mildly and moderately retarded, and it provides numerical equivalents of present behavioral status. The scale is composed of thirty-six items that provide measures of Self-Help Skills (SH) (Locomotion, Toilet Training, Dressing, Eating, and Grooming), Communication (COM), Social Interaction (SI), Occupation (OCC), and Self-Direction (SD). The items are stated in terms of what the subject does, and not "can do," in order to minimize the subjective element in filling out the scale. The statements start at a level reflecting "no skill" and proceed upward to "mastery." Scores are provided for each skill, and the scale is easily scored. It is short and can be easily administered and scored by ward personnel, parents, or caretakers as well as by social workers, psychologists, and teachers. Administration of the FSSS, therefore, requires only that the observer or rater know the individual well enough to record his typical behavior. Social age equivalents of total scores are provided, and a social quotient may be calculated for each subject.

As examples, one of five subgroupings in Self-Help Skills and one subgrouping from Occupation are given below. Other main groups of the thirty-six-item instrument are Communication, Social Interaction, and Self-Direction.

I. *Self-Help Skills*
  4. Eating Skills
    a. Use of Tableware
        0—Uses hands only
        1—Uses spoon only
        2—Uses spoon and fork—spills quite a lot
        3—Uses spoon and fork neatly
        4—Uses knife for spreading
        5—Uses knife for cutting
        6—Cares for self at table (uses all available utensils neatly)

RELIABILITY AND VALIDITY: To obtain measures of reliability, every patient on each of two wards was rated by the staff member most familiar with the resident's typical behavior. This sample consisted of 105 individuals (forty-nine males, fifty-six females). All patients were rated by both the A.M. and the P.M. shifts. Each shift was unaware of the ratings provided by the other shifts. No observer rated more than twelve patients. Two months later this process was repeated. Interrater reliabilities ($N = 210$) were .81 for total score and ranged from .68 to .84 for the subscales. Test-retest reliabilities were .89 for the total scale and ranged from .77 to .90 for the subscales. The correlation of FSSS scores with Vineland Social Maturity Scale scores was .53. The value of *eta* for the regression of CA on total score was .89, and for the regression of total score on CA, .94 ($N = 259$ normal children).

BIBLIOGRAPHY:

Giampiccolo, J. S., Jr. *Manual for the Fairview Social Skills Scale.* Costa Mesa, California: Fairview State Hospital, 1974.

Prepared by James S. Giampiccolo, Jr.

GELLERT INDEX OF BODY KNOWLEDGE

AUTHOR: Elizabeth Gellert

AGE: 4½ to maturity

VARIABLE: Children's concepts of their bodily interior

TYPE OF MEASURE: Structured interview and drawing

SOURCE FROM WHICH MEASURE MAY BE OBTAINED: Elizabeth Gellert, Department of Psychology, Hunter College, 695 Park Avenue, New York, New York 10021.

DESCRIPTION OF MEASURE: This measure can be used to tap children's conceptions of the contents and functioning of their bodily interior. The questionnaire is administered individually and filled out by *E*, except for filling in the sketches of body outlines, which is done by the subject. Normative data of subjects' responses, from ages 4.9 to 16.11, are presented in Gellert (1962). Responses are analyzed per question and subcategorized in the following way. The aggregates of explanatory statements given by the subjects in answer to such questions as "What does X (organ) do?" are arranged according to the main ideas expressed therein. Each such "idea" or ideational complex becomes an explanatory category. Explanations of the function of each organ are classified in terms of *all* the ideas represented. For example, the statement "The nerves are (a) to be mad with and (b) to feel pain" implies *two* ideas. Since many subjects include more than one idea in their responses, the total number of "idea units" with respect to each item on the questionnaire usually exceeds the number of subjects sampled. Since publication, the Gellert Index of Body Knowledge has been used in its original form or in adapted form by numerous other investigators.

The questionnaire contains three parts. Part One is one question: "What do you have inside you? Tell me as many things as you can think of that are inside you." Part two has eleven items. The first three are:

1. Show me the head _____ .
   What is in the head? (Tell me all the things that are in the head)
2. Make a circle where, and about how big, the heart is. What does the heart do? (What is it for?) What would happen if we didn't have a heart?
3. Show me some places where you have bones. (Try for minimum of five locations.) What do we have bones for? What would happen if we didn't have bones?

Part Three has two items. They are:

1. What did you think is the most important part of you? (If you picked one part of you as the most important, which one would you pick?) Why? (What makes it the most important?)
2. Are there any parts of you that you could live (get along) without? Yes _____ No _____ Which ones? How come you don't need the . . . ?

RELIABILITY AND VALIDITY: No test for validity. Reliability was measured as follows: Categories were derived from the data by the investigator and one collaborator, independently. The two sets of explanatory categories were then compared. Criteria for classification were sharpened and disagreements ironed out. The resulting system of classification was then used to tabulate the subjects' responses. For the function of each organ, tabulation was done independently by the two persons. Whenever obvious disagreements in categorizing responses occurred, these were discussed. Revisions were made until satisfactory consensus had been attained. Intertabulator reliabilities for the various organ functions were as follows: bone function = .83, heart function = .76, stomach function = .86, lung function = .91, nerve function = .70, rib function = .89, skin function = .69, function of bowel movements = .88, reason for selection of one part as most important = .85. The formula used to compute reliabilities was:

$$\frac{2 \text{ (total number of agreements)}}{\text{total items tabulated by A} + \text{total items tabulated by B}}$$

BIBLIOGRAPHY:

Gellert, E. "Children's Conceptions of the Content and Functions of the Human Body." *Genetic Psychology Monographs,* 1962, *65,* 293-405.

GEOGRAPHICAL CONCEPTS INFORMATION TEST

AUTHORS: Frank L. Franks and Carson Y. Nolan

AGE: Elementary to secondary grade students

VARIABLE: Fundamental geographical concepts

TYPE OF MEASURE: Multiple-choice test

SOURCE FROM WHICH MEASURE MAY BE OBTAINED: See Franks and Nolan (1971) or write Frank L. Franks, American Printing House for the Blind, Box 6085, Louisville, Kentucky 40206.

DESCRIPTION OF MEASURE: The test consists of forty items representing geographical concepts that can be represented on relief maps. The test was developed as a short-form instrument for measuring geographical concept attainment of visually handicapped students. Large-print and braille answer sheets can be used, which enable the student to record his responses independently.

As examples, the first five of the forty items of the test are given below.

1. The largest bodies of water on the earth are called
    (a) seas   (b) lakes   (c) *oceans*   (d) rivers
2. A body of land completely surrounded by water is
    (a) a peninsula   (b) a seashore   (c) *an island*   (d) a cape
3. A body of water surrounded by land is
    (a) an ocean   (b) a bay   (c) a river   (d) *a lake*
4. Land next to the ocean is called
    (a) a channel   (b) *a seashore*   (c) a port   (d) a swamp
5. If the land next to the sea or ocean is flat and sandy it is called a
    (a) marsh   (b) bay   (c) *beach*   (d) peninsula

RELIABILITY AND VALIDITY: A total of forty-eight visually handicapped students, twenty-four braille and twenty-four large-print readers, were selected from grades 6, 8, and 10 in two residential schools for the blind. Analysis of data revealed the same pattern of performance for both braille and large-print students on the forty-item test as was found for braille students on a seventy-item test; that is, sixth-grade performance scores were higher than eighth-grade scores, with tenth-grade performance the highest. Comparison of mean difference through use of the *t* test showed no significant differences between braille and large-print readers for any grade on the forty-item test. A practical application of the forty-item test verified its reliability with the population tested as an instrument for evaluating geographical concept attainment of visually handicapped students in educational programs.

BIBLIOGRAPHY:

Franks, F., and Nolan, C. Y. "Development of Geographical Concepts in Blind Children." *Education of the Visually Handicapped,* 1970, *2,* 1-8.
Franks, F., and Nolan, C. Y. "Measuring Geographical Concept Attainment in Visually Handicapped Students." *Education of the Visually Handicapped,* 1971, *3,* 11-17.

LEARNING POTENTIAL ASSESSMENT DEVICE:
ORGANIZATION OF DOTS

AUTHORS: Andre Rey; LPAD Modification by Reuven Feuerstein

AGE: 8 years to adulthood with normal population; 10 years to adulthood for retarded performers

VARIABLE: Organization of space in complex conditions

TYPE OF MEASURE: Test

SOURCE FROM WHICH MEASURE MAY BE OBTAINED: The dissemination of this test is at this point limited to research and experimental work, and it can be obtained only from the author: Reuven Feuerstein, Hadassah Wizo Canada Research Institute, 6 Karmon Street, Beit Hakarem, Jerusalem, Israel.

DESCRIPTION OF MEASURE: The test is composed of a training sheet and a paper-and-pencil test. The main task consists of connecting discrete dots in order to form the standard geometric figures presented on the page. The task becomes progressively more complex and difficult with the increase in the overlap of two or more geometric figures, creating the need for segregation of the intricate and intertwined lines. The intricacy becomes more accentuated as the figures must be superimposed on one another and the dots are less and less diffuse. The examinee must perceive the standard figure despite changes in its orientation. The training sheet is mainly oriented toward inducing in the examinee the prerequisite behavior for proper problem solving. The entering behavior consists of (1) perception of constancy of figures across the varying orientations in space, (2) capacity to project virtual relationships, (3) planning behavior, (4) summative behavior, (5) segregation of relationships, (6) establishment of criteria permitting the rediscovery of given figures, and (7) comparison of outcome with standard. The test is used both as a power test in which the achievements within a

4-minute time period are measured and as a measurement of the total time required by the examinee to complete the entire sheet. The test is used both as a group test and as an individual test. It provides an insight into the capacity of the child to become involved in a complex task. For a more accurate description of the test and the test procedure, see Feuerstein and others (1972).

RELIABILITY AND VALIDITY: For information on reliability and validity, see Feuerstein and others (1972).

BIBLIOGRAPHY:

Feuerstein, R., and others. *Studies in Cognitive Modifiability.* Vol. 1. Jerusalem, Israel: Hadassah Wizo Canada Research Institute, 1972.
Narrol, H., and Bachor, D. G. *An Introduction to Feuerstein's Approach to Assessing and Developing Cognitive Potential.* Toronto, Canada: Ontario Institute for Studies in Education, 1975.
Rey, A. "About a Procedure for Evaluating Educability." *Archive de Psychologie,* 1934 (in French).
Rey, A., and Dupont, J. B. "Organization de Groupes de Points en Figures Geometriques Simples." *Monographes de Psychologie Appliquee,* 1953, No. 3.

Prepared by Reuven Feuerstein

LEARNING POTENTIAL ASSESSMENT DEVICE: REPRESENTATION STENCIL DESIGN TEST (RSDT)

AUTHOR: Reuven Feuerstein

AGE: 10 years to adulthood

VARIABLE: Representational spatial relations

TYPE OF MEASURE: Individual and group test

SOURCE FROM WHICH MEASURE MAY BE OBTAINED: The distribution of this test at this time is limited to research and experimental work and can be obtained only from the author under specified conditions: Reuven Feuerstein, Hadassah Wizo Canada Research Institute, 6 Karmon Street, Beit Hakarem, Jerusalem, Israel. (The copyright belongs partially to the Psychological Corporation.)

DESCRIPTION OF MEASURE: This test represents a modification of the original Stencil Design Test of Grace Arthur. The original test was a part of the Grace Arthur battery and is very seldom used. One of the major reasons for this seems to be the great difficulty of the test and the rather heavy loading in spatial factors. The modification consists of radical change in the nature of the task, even though the problem as such is kept constant. In the original test the problem consisted of the construction of a standard design by using a set of perforated stencils. In order to construct the design, one had to superimpose a given number of stencils that had to be chosen from those put in front of the examinee. In the original test there was no limitation set on the approaches, techniques, and strategies used by the examinee, and the only criterion was whether or not he was successful in the construction of the design within the time limit of 4 minutes. The majority of the examinees used a trial-and-error approach.

The major modification introduced by the Representation Stencil Design Test lies in the fact that the trial-and-error behavior is totally excluded so that instead of constructing the design manually, the examinee is asked to produce the design in a representational way by pointing out on a poster representing the stencils both the stencils necessary for the construction and the strict order in which the stencils have to be superimposed. The task implies, then, a great variety of functions as the prerequisite for its proper solution. Thus, the perception of size, color, and form, the segregation and completion of forms through segments hinted in the whole, the internalized elaboration of anticipated transformations of the stencil following the superimposition of one stencil upon the other, the internal feedback of these transformations for further appraisal and assessment of the present stage of the design in order to plan further steps, a comparison of the imagined representational design with the perceived one, and the need to keep a very strict order, all make the task a demanding one and lay heavy emphasis on planning ahead and inhibiting impulsive responses. The test is highly attractive and creates strong motivation toward success in normal and high-level functioning adolescents and adults and even in disadvantaged and culturally deprived youth.

The test is made up of the following parts: (1) a colored poster 26 X 38 inches; (2) a training booklet, including twenty training tasks that aim at the familiarization of the examinee with the task, stencils, concept of order, and strategy of approach; and (3) the test, comprising twenty problems and one parallel form for posttesting. The test is used both as part of the individualized clinical battery and as a group test.

RELIABILITY AND VALIDITY: Reliability data were compiled from a group of 150 youngsters who were retested after a month and after a year. The reliability scores range from .51 to .88 on short-period retest and from .35 to .68 on long-period retest. The test is intercorrelated with the LPAD Raven's matrices, measured against school grades and a variety of other criteria of academic progress. The author expects to have validity data on a follow-up study based on results obtained by the examinees on a test given on entering the army. Validity measures on the clinical battery seem to be high and are in process of elaboration by means of follow-up studies.

BIBLIOGRAPHY:

Arthur, G. "A Non-Verbal Test of Logical Thinking." *Journal of Consulting Psychology*, 1944, *8* (1), 33-34.

Boulger, C., and Arthur, G. "Unpublished Design Test." *Journal of Consulting Psychology*, 1944, *8* (2), 31-32.

Feuerstein, R., and others. *Studies in Cognitive Modifiability.* Vols. 1 and 2. Jerusalem, Israel: Hadassah Wizo Canada Research Institute, 1972.

Leiter, R. "The Leiter Adaption of Arthur's Stencil Design Test." *Psychological Service Center Journal*, 1949, *1*, 62-68.

Orgel, A., and Dreger, R. "A Comparative Study of the Arthur/Leiter and Stanford-Binet Intelligence Scales." *Journal of Genetic Psychology*, 1955, *86*, 359-365.

LOCATIONAL AND DIRECTIONAL REFERENTS FOR
MAP READING FOR YOUNG BLIND STUDENTS

AUTHOR: Frank L. Franks

AGE: Kindergarten to fifth grade

VARIABLE: Basic locational and directional referents

TYPE OF MEASURE: Pre- and posttest measure

SOURCE FROM WHICH MEASURE MAY BE OBTAINED: See Franks (1974).

DESCRIPTION OF MEASURE: These diagnostic (pretest) and performance (posttest) instruments consist of sixty items each with two equivalent items for each concept. The concept areas presented are: Location and Direction I (simple referents—near, far; middle, between; left, right); Location and Direction II (cardinal referents—north, south; east, west); Finding Corners I (using simple intermediate referents—near left, far right); Finding Corners II (using cardinal intermediate referents); Diagonal Movement to a Corner from a Reference Point I (using simple intermediate referents); Diagonal Movement to a Corner from a Reference Point II (using cardinal intermediate referents); Vertical Movement (far, near); Horizontal Movement (left, right). These tests are presented using a simple relief map with three areal symbols, three linear symbols, and three point symbols. The map is chromatically coded as well as tactually coded.

As examples, six of the sixty items from the pretest are given below. Each question is repeated twice.

Location:
3. Show me the *right* edge of the map.
14. From the near right corner, move your hand in a straight line to the *far left* corner of the map.
Direction:
27. Find the top of the small hill. Move your hand *east* to the edge of the map.
32. Show me the *north* end of the second road.
Location and Direction:
44. From the far right corner, move your hand in a straight line to the *southeast* corner.
55. Find the *near left* corner of the map.

RELIABILITY AND VALIDITY: The internal consistency of the pretest was estimated using a total of 145 subjects. The Kuder-Richardson formula 20 yielded a coefficient of .94. The internal consistency of the posttest was estimated using a total of 104 subjects. The Kuder-Richardson formula 20 yielded a coefficient of .95. The Pearson product-moment correlation was computed using 104 control subjects to assess the degree of relationship between the pretest and the posttest. A correlation coefficient of .80 ($p < .01$) was obtained.

BIBLIOGRAPHY:

Franks, F. L. "Introduction to Map Study: Teaching Locational and Directional Referents to Young Blind Students." Unpublished doctoral dissertation. George Peabody College for Teachers, Nashville, Tennessee, 1974.

MANIKIN CONSTRUCTION TASK

AUTHOR: Beverly K. Celotta

AGE: 2½ to 11½ years

VARIABLE: Conceptual knowledge of the human figure

TYPE OF MEASURE: Nonverbal puzzle task

SOURCE FROM WHICH MEASURE MAY BE OBTAINED: Beverly K. Celotta, 19015 Stedwick Drive, Gaithersburg, Maryland 20760.

DESCRIPTION OF MEASURE: The test materials consist of sixty white-felt pieces outlined in black, representing parts of the human body. For example, there are several legs (from 8¼ inches to 22 inches long) and several types of arms, eyes, clothing pieces, and so forth. There is also a red felt board (2 X 3 feet) on which to place the body parts. The pieces described above may be reproduced by copying the forms from Celotta (1971) and enlarging them eleven times. The examiner places a head on the board and the child is told to complete the figure with any of the pieces he sees displayed before him. A photograph or checklist may be used to score the thirty-three items. Typical items scored are: neck present, eye proportion, attachment of arms and legs, and clothing present. One point is earned for each item passed. There are also subscale scores for inclusion of parts and knowledge of proportion and integration.

RELIABILITY AND VALIDITY: The test correlated .51 with the Stanford-Binet at the 3-year level and therefore might be considered as a screening device for that age. Eighty boys and eighty girls were tested on the original scale. All children were from a white, middle-class suburb of Denver, Colorado. The Hoyt point-biserial reliability for all ages combined was .94. The separate reliabilities for each age were lower, as expected, but adequate in most cases (Celotta, 1971). When compared to a drawing task derived from the Harris-Goodenough Test of Psychological Maturity (Harris, 1963) the scores on the Manikin Construction Task were significantly higher. The latter task was also superior for measuring inclusion of parts and knowledge of proportion. There were no significant effects due to sex.

BIBLIOGRAPHY:

Celotta, B. K. "Levels of Knowledge of the Human Figure as Measured by Two Tasks." Unpublished doctoral dissertation. University of Colorado, Boulder, 1971.
Celotta, B. K. "Knowledge of the Human Figure as Measured by Two Tasks." *Developmental Psychology*, 1973, *8*, 377-381.
Harris, D. B. *Children's Drawings as Measures of Intellectual Maturity*. New York: Harcourt Brace Jovanovich, 1963.

MEASURES OF MUSICAL APTITUDE

AUTHOR: John B. Davies

AGE: 7 to 12 years

VARIABLE: Tonal memory, pitch location, interval, rhythm

TYPE OF MEASURE: Tape, plus response sheets

SOURCE FROM WHICH MEASURE MAY BE OBTAINED: J. B. Davies, Department of Psychology, University of Strathclyde, 155 George Street, Glasgow, GI IRD, United Kingdom.

DESCRIPTION OF MEASURE: The tests are in the form of a self-administering tape, designed for use with groups. There is no material of a formal musical nature in the battery, so that musically experienced subjects have little advantage over others. Administration takes about 30 minutes, with about 5 minutes of preparation. Scores on all parts of the tests increase with age, though scores are not significantly better than chance with groups younger than 7 years, mainly due to attention/comprehension difficulties. The tests appear to discriminate to a high degree between criterion groups and have been successfully used to screen subjects for experiments in musical cognition. Correlations between the parts of the tests are moderate rather than high. The tests were standardized on two thousand children in the northeastern part of England.

RELIABILITY AND VALIDITY: Test-retest reliability of the total battery with a seventeen-week interval for subjects 9 to 11+ years is .82 and for subjects 7 to 9 years, .70. The correlation with the Bentley tests of musical ability is .66. Differences between groups of musical and nonmusical children and adults were all significant at .001 or better (*t*-test). The measure does not discriminate between nonmusical children and nonmusical adults.

BIBLIOGRAPHY:

Davies, J. B. "New Tests of Musical Aptitude." *British Journal of Psychology*, 1971, *62*, 557-565.

MENSTRUATION KNOWLEDGE TEST

AUTHOR: Janet D. Reese

AGE: Adolescent

VARIABLE: Knowledge and understanding of menstruation

TYPE OF MEASURE: Multiple-choice test

SOURCE FROM WHICH MEASURE MAY BE OBTAINED: Janet D. Reese, 630 North Lincoln, Addison, Illinois 60101.

DESCRIPTION OF MEASURE: The purpose of the instrument is to measure a young girl's knowledge and understanding of menstruation. Content measured by the test was based on the free resource materials made available by three major sanitary napkin companies. A table of specifications was formulated to include four areas of menstruation knowledge with each area weighted in accordance with the findings of the item count. The table of specifications assured that an adequate number of questions in the test form sampled each area of menstruation information. A fifty-item four-option multiple-choice test was constructed.

As examples, four of the fifty items in the test are given below.

1. The flow during any menstrual period usually lasts for
    a. 1-2 days.
    b. 3-4 days.
    c. 6-8 days.
    d. 9-10 days.
5. A visible effect commonly associated with menstruation is
    a. a common cold.
    b. red eyes.
    c. diarrhea.
    d. pimples.
9. The amount of blood lost during the menstrual flow is
    a. much less than one pint.
    b. about one pint.
    c. about one quart.
    d. between one pint and one quart.
14. In some girls, the cause of a let-down or "blue" feeling just before menstruation is usually due to
    a. an unbalance of hormones.
    b. a lack of enzymes.
    c. digestive juices.
    d. diet.

RELIABILITY AND VALIDITY: The experimental test was administered to 225 fifth-, sixth-, and seventh-grade girls. A thorough item analysis was made of the test results, and a reliability coefficient of the test was calculated. The Kuder-Richardson formula 20 produced a reliability of .77. The mean of the raw scores was 30.4, while the standard deviation was 7. Curricular validity was established by making an item count of the free resource materials.

BIBLIOGRAPHY: None reported.

PIAGET-BASED MAP DRAWING MEASURE

AUTHORS: Samuel S. Snyder, David H. Feldman, and Cheryl LaRossa

AGE: 8 years to adult

VARIABLE: Developmental levels and level mixture in spatial reasoning

TYPE OF MEASURE: Map drawing

SOURCE FROM WHICH MEASURE MAY BE OBTAINED: David Feldman, Eliot-Pearson Department of Child Study, Tufts University, Medford, Massachusetts 02155.

DESCRIPTION OF MEASURE: The Map Exercise is an attempt to adapt a Piagetian task for use as a diagnostic instrument covering a common part of the school curriculum. From Piaget and Inhelder (1948), a map drawing task was constructed to assess students' ability to represent space. The content of a drawing is divided into five clusters of similarly difficult elements and then evaluated as to its quality in terms of four capabilities: arrangements of elements, proportional representation of elements, perspective of elements, and symbolization of elements. The five clusters are rated in terms of the four conceptual capabilities to yield twenty separate scores; each score may range from 1 (the most primitive Piagetian level) to 6 (the most sophisticated). The scores are used to compute several indices of spatial reasoning, disequilibrium, and readiness for developmental advance. They may also be used to diagnose specific skill deficits, to investigate hypotheses about the effects of intervention efforts, and so forth.

As examples, the first and last of the six levels of spatial reasoning development assessed by the measure are given below.

Level 1: No spatial correspondence except for a few elementary proximities (about 4 years). Characterized by child's inability to distinguish between spatial proximity and logical resemblance or between spatial separation and logical difference. Yields objects on map which do not appear on model and objects on model which are not represented on map. Arrangement appears virtually arbitrary.

Level 6: The abstract plan with metric coordinates (about 12 to 15 years). Characterized by complete coordination, totally accurate scaling, a consistent 90-degree perspective, and use of abstract symbolization.

RELIABILITY AND VALIDITY: The interrater reliability between two judges was from about .75 to above .90. Correlations of the measure with the following tests of achievement and academic aptitude are: Iowa Map Skills = .54 (N = 38), Iowa composite = .57 (N = 38), personality attribution level = .75 (N = 38), Formal reasoning = .41 (N = 38), Lorge-Thorndike IQ = .40 (N = 199).

BIBLIOGRAPHY:

Feldman, D. H. "Map Understanding as a Possible Crystallizer of Cognitive Structures." *American Educational Research Journal,* 1971, *8,* 485-501.

Feldman, D. H., and Markwalder, W. E. "Systematic Scoring of Ranked Distractors for the Assessment of Piagetian Reasoning Levels." *Educational and Psychological Measurement,* 1971, *31,* 347-362.

Markwalder, W. E. "Susceptibility of Reasoning Level to Change: A Study of Cognitive Stage Transition." Unpublished doctoral dissertation. University of Minnesota, Minneapolis, 1973.

Mates-Druian, P. R. "Attribution Processes in Concrete and Formal Operational Children." Unpublished doctoral dissertation. Yale University, New Haven, Connecticut, 1975.

Piaget, J., and Inhelder, B. *The Child's Conception of Space.* New York: Norton, 1967 (first published in 1948).

Snyder, S. S. "An Experimental Test of the Effects of Internal and External Disequilibrium on Spatial Reasoning Development." Unpublished doctoral dissertation. Yale University, New Haven, Connecticut, 1975.

Snyder, S. S., and Feldman, D. H. "An Experimental Test of the Effects of Internal and External Disequilibrium on Spatial Reasoning Development." Paper presented at Biennial Meeting of the Society for Research in Child Development. Denver, Colorado, April 1975.

Prepared by David H. Feldman

PRIMARY TEST OF ECONOMIC UNDERSTANDING

AUTHORS: Donald G. Davison and John H. Kilgore

AGE: Grades 2 and 3

VARIABLE: Understanding of economic concepts

TYPE OF MEASURE: Test

SOURCE FROM WHICH MEASURE MAY BE OBTAINED: Bureau of Business and Economic Research, College of Business Administration, University of Iowa, Iowa City, Iowa 52242. Cost: $.25 each (ten or more copies, $.10 each).

DESCRIPTION OF MEASURE: The Primary Test of Economic Understanding was constructed to measure the pupil's mastery of certain basic generalizations, understandings, concepts, and subconcepts in economics that might be taught as a part of primary-grade social studies content. The authors ascertained a basic conceptual framework from which the test items to be included in the testing instrument were derived. This framework was based on their experience in working with primary-grade teachers in developing and using materials containing economic concepts and on a careful examination of both textual materials and materials developed by other school systems. The test consists of thirty-two Yes-No matched-pair items and provides persons with a measure of students' growth and a means to assess the effectiveness of existing materials, teaching strategies, and preservice and inservice economic education programs for social studies teachers in the primary grades.

As examples, five of the thirty-two matched-pair items from the test are given below. An item is considered correct only when each of the matched-pair items is correct.

1. Families must choose what goods and services they will buy because their income is limited.
   Since the income of every family is very large, they can buy all the goods and services they want.
2. Most workers receive food and clothing in exchange for their work.
   Most workers receive wages and salaries in exchange for their work.
3. Saving means "buying something on sale."
   Saving means keeping part of your income to spend at a later time.
4. Every family has all kinds of productive resources to sell to businesses.
   Some families have very few resources to sell to businesses.
5. A worker who is a specialist produces most of the things his family needs.
   A worker who is a specialist depends on others to produce most of the things his family needs.

RELIABILITY AND VALIDITY: The PTEU was administered to over four thousand third-grade students in approximately one hundred schools in twenty-one states. The reliability reported for this test is the Kuder-Richardson formula 20 for the thirty-two matched-item pairs comprising the test. The reliability is adequate ($r = .78$) for third-grade students. The reliability of this instrument is such that making decisions about individual students should be done with more information than that provided by this test alone. However, decisions about classroom-size groups (or larger) can be made with a considerable degree of confidence.

BIBLIOGRAPHY:

Brandenburg, D. C., and Whitney, D. R. "Matched Pair True-False Scoring Effect on Reliability and Validity." *Journal of Educational Measurement,* 1972, *9,* 297-302.

Davison, D. G., and Kilgore, J. H. *An Evaluation of Second Grade Economic Materials.* Unpublished manuscript. University of Iowa, Iowa City, 1970.

Davison, D. G., Kilgore, J. H., and Sgontz, L. G. *Workshop and Textbook Effects on the Economic Understanding of Elementary School Students.* Unpublished manuscript. University of Iowa, Iowa City, 1973.

REPERTORY TEST

AUTHORS: Norman F. Watt and Thomas B. Benjamin

AGE: At least fifth- or sixth-grade reading ability

VARIABLE: Semantic meaning

TYPE OF MEASURE: Test

SOURCE FROM WHICH MEASURE MAY BE OBTAINED: Norman F. Watt, Tobin Hall, University of Massachusetts, Amherst, Massachusetts 01002.

DESCRIPTION OF MEASURE: The Repertory Test assesses knowledge of various meanings of homographs, words having two or more possible meanings. It consists of twenty-four multiple-choice items that require the respondent to select from five answers the one closest in meaning to the stem word. The correct answer is often an unusual meaning of the word and not the first meaning that comes to mind. A Homograph Catalogue, containing an exhaustive listing of English homographs with two or more *noun* meanings possible, has also been compiled and can be used as a source for possible additional items.

As examples, ten of the twenty-four items of the test are given below.

1. *vice*	fault	book	fan	squad	band
2. *sound*	craft	horn	term	axe	water
3. *cast*	mold	flow	fly	sail	pull
4. *hail*	vessel	shout	taxi	pen	winter
5. *junk*	hose	pail	file	boat	pet
6. *scope*	batter	court	range	port	pencil
7. *compact*	taps	hole	agreement	organ	spring
8. *board*	meals	song	capital	smoke	hunch
9. *tie*	salt	bank	knot	clothing	deck
10. *match*	earth	meter	opera	swallow	firestick

RELIABILITY AND VALIDITY: None reported.

BIBLIOGRAPHY:

Benjamin, T. B., and Watt, N. F. "Psychopathology and Semantic Interpretations of Ambiguous Words." *Journal of Abnormal Psychology*, 1969, 74, 706-714.
Watt, N. F. "Developmental Changes in the Semantic Interpretation of Ambiguous Words." *Journal of Abnormal Psychology*, 1971, 77, 332-339.

SELF-HELP SKILL ASSESSMENT CHECKLIST (SSAC)

AUTHORS: James M. Gardner (original) and Luke S. Watson, Jr. (revision)

AGE: 6 months to 85 years

VARIABLE: Self-help skills

TYPE OF MEASURE: Rating scale

SOURCE FROM WHICH MEASURE MAY BE OBTAINED: Luke S. Watson, Jr., Behavior Modification Technology, P.O. Box 597, Libertyville, Illinois 60048.

DESCRIPTION OF MEASURE: The Self-Help Skill Assessment Checklist is designed to assess self-help skill proficiency in children. It is a 5-point rating scale consisting of five major subscales: Eating and Drinking, Toileting, Undressing, Dressing, and Personal Hygiene. The SSAC can be used by directly observing and testing a child or by obtaining information from parents, teachers, psychiatric aides, or other persons familiar with the child. While our early research indicated a high degree of correspondence between the actual behavior of the child and information obtained from other people who were familiar with his behavioral characteristics, it is recommended that he be observed directly whenever possible.

Scoring is recorded on the SSAC form (Watson, 1972). Children are assigned one or two types of scores: $A-F$ or $1-5$. $A-F$ is a qualitative type of score. The child's behavior is rated on the basis of quality of response. A score of A indicates the child is negativistic and uncooperative. He refuses to respond at all, even when prompted. B indicates the child is cooperative but responds incorrectly. C indicates the response is a poor approximation of the desired behavior, D indicates the response is of good quality, and E indicates that the behavior exhibited by the child is an excellent approximation of the desired response, and F indicates that the desired behavior is of excellent quality and occurs in a variety of contexts other than the training context. Thus, if he performs fairly well or excellently in the training situation but shows inferior performance in other situations, his score is $C-E$ based on performance in the training situation only. The other scoring system, $1-5$, allows the rater to record the proportion of time the response occurs when the child is observed. A score of 1 indicates the behavior never occurs, 2 indicates it is rarely observed (about one-fourth of the time), 3 indicates it occurs about half the time the child is observed, 4 indicates it occurs nearly all the time (about three-fourths of the time) he is observed, and 5 indicates the behavior occurs every time the child is observed.

All items on all subscales are generally rated. The scale has been arranged so that most severely and profoundly retarded children who have not been in behavior-modification programs will achieve at least a score of E or 5 on the first item of each scale and will receive few ratings of E or 5 on the last item of each scale. Thus the scale is arranged in hierarchical order. The subscale items also are arranged in the same order as the training steps used in the individual training program outlined in Watson (1972). The SSAC is compatible with the accompanying training programs and is designed to be used as the data system for these self-help skill training programs. There is a detailed scoring guide, which provides sufficient guidelines so that the checklist is usable by anyone who can read the scoring criteria. An example of the detail in the scoring guide is the following:

5. Carries own tray.

Child carries tray to and from table before or after meals. Score *A* if he refuses to attempt to carry his tray when prompted. Score *B* if he attempts to carry it but always drops the tray or spills food off of it. Score *C* if he drops some items from the tray or requires assistance holding it. Score *D* if he occasionally drops items from the tray but is able to hold it unassisted. Score *E* if he carries the tray unassisted without spilling food in all cafeteria eating situations. If this item is not relevant to a particular child, for example, a child in a home-training program, score *NA* (not applicable).

RELIABILITY AND VALIDITY: None reported.

BIBLIOGRAPHY:

Gardner, J. M., Brust, D. J., and Watson, L. S. "A Scale to Measure Skill in Applying Behavior Modification Techniques to the Mentally Retarded." *American Journal of Mental Deficiency,* 1970, *74,* 633-636.

Gardner, J. M., and Gaimpa, F. L. "Attendant Behavior Checklist: Measuring On-the-Ward Behavior of Institutional Attendants." *American Journal of Mental Deficiency,* 1971, *75,* 617-622.

Watson, L. S., Jr. *How to Use Behavior Modification with Mentally Retarded and Autistic Children: Programs for Administrators, Teachers, Parents and Nurses.* Libertyville, Illinois: Behavior Modification Technology, 1972.

Prepared by Orval G. Johnson

SHAPE NAME INVENTORY (SNI)

AUTHORS: Alan Coller and Jack Victor

AGE: Preschool

VARIABLE: Knowledge of common shapes

TYPE OF MEASURE: Nonverbal and verbal identification test

SOURCE FROM WHICH MEASURE MAY BE OBTAINED: Jack Victor, 82-25 218th Street, Hollis Hills, New York 11427.

DESCRIPTION OF MEASURE: The SNI, one of the Early Childhood Inventories (see Index of Measures), is an individually administered inventory designed to evaluate the child's ability to identify eight common shapes—circle, cross, diamond, heart, rectangle, square, star, and triangle. The SNI consists of two separate tasks—a nonverbal task and a verbal task. In the *nonverbal receptive* task, the child is presented with eight arrays of four shapes each. The child is asked to point to specific shapes present in the arrays as they are named by the administrator. Each array consists of two relatively familiar shapes and two relatively unfamiliar shapes. In the *verbal expressive* task, the child is asked to name each of the shapes as they are presented to him one at a time on a stimulus presentation dial. The nonverbal task is administered first, followed by the verbal task. Alternate forms of the nonverbal task of the SNI have been developed to aid in the evaluation of guessing and positional set behaviors. If accurate diagnostic information is desired for very young children, *both* nonverbal forms should be administered. The two forms of the SNI differ only in the arrangement of the shapes in the array, that is, in Set B, position 1 contains the shapes that were in position 3 in Set A. Positions 1, 2, 3, and 4 in Set A respectively become positions 3, 4, 1, and 2 in Set B.

RELIABILITY AND VALIDITY: Alternate form reliabilities were obtained for a sample of inner-city children in prekindergarten through first grade. The correlations are .67 for prekindergarten, .76 for kindergarten, and .72 for first grade.

BIBLIOGRAPHY:

Coller, A., and Victor, J. *Early Childhood Inventories Project.* New York: New York University, Institute for Developmental Studies, 1970.
Ryan, T. J., and Moffitt, A. R. "Evaluation of Preschool Programs." *Canadian Psychologist,* 1974, *15,* 205-219.

Prepared by Alan Coller, Jack Victor, and John Dill

SOCIAL AND PREVOCATIONAL
INFORMATION BATTERY (SPIB)

AUTHORS: Andrew S. Halpern, Paul Raffeld, Larry K. Irvin, and Robert Link

AGE: Secondary level EMR

VARIABLE: Knowledge of social and prevocational skills

TYPE OF MEASURE: Test

SOURCE FROM WHICH MEASURE MAY BE OBTAINED: Available on a limited basis from Research and Training Center in Mental Retardation, University of Oregon, Eugene, Oregon 97403.

DESCRIPTION OF MEASURE: The Social and Prevocational Information Battery (SPIB) has been developed to assess the attainment of secondary-school objectives for mildly retarded pupils. This battery consists of nine tests measuring knowledge of social and prevocational competencies. The content of the SPIB reflects pupil knowledge in the areas of job-related behavior, job-search skills, purchasing, budgeting, banking, home management, physical care, personal hygiene, and functional signs (survival reading). Each of the nine tests is designed to be administered in a group setting and requires 15 to 25 minutes for completion. In order to eliminate reading ability as a determinant of performance, the tests contain orally administered true-false items. Initial development of the battery was based on the test results of a sample of 1,100 secondary EMR pupils in Oregon. Final norms and statistical information for the 1974 version of the SPIB are based on approximately nine hundred Oregon pupils.

Examples of items from each test are given below. The respondent answers true or false.

Purchasing Habits:	A TV set that costs $100 in one store may cost less in other stores.
Budgeting:	You should make sure you have enough money for rent, food, and clothes before you buy a dishwasher.
Banking:	You can open a checking account in any department store.
Job-Related Behavior:	If your boss inspects your work, he probably doesn't like you.
Job-Search Skills:	Sometimes an employer will hire you before you actually know how to do the job.
Home Management:	Electrical appliances that are in poor working condition can be used safely if you don't use them too often.
Health Care:	You should not use medicine that is prescribed for other people.
Hygiene and Grooming:	If you wish to have a mole or a wart removed, you should see a doctor.
Functional Signs:	This sign tells you an exit used during an emergency: *Fire Escape.*

RELIABILITY AND VALIDITY: The SPIB was also administered to a group of 220 EMR seniors who graduated in June 1973. Follow-up information on level of community adjustment was then collected on this sample one year after graduation in order to assess the predictive validity of the SPIB. The results of test analyses indicate internal consistency and test-retest reliabilities ranging from .69 to .83 for the nine tests in the battery. Similar indices for the total battery are around .93. The predictive validity study yielded a canonical correlation of .51 between the nine SPIB tests and five measures of community adjustment. These results suggest that the battery can be used appropriately for screening, diagnosis, measuring pupil progress, and program evaluation. Further research on concurrent validity is being conducted.

BIBLIOGRAPHY:

Halpern, A. S., Raffeld, P., Irvin, L., and Link, R. "Measuring Social and Prevocational Awareness in Mildly Retarded Adolescents." Working paper no. 73, Rehabilitation Research and Training Center in Mental Retardation. University of Oregon, Eugene, 1974.

Prepared by Paul Raffeld

SPEED OF VISUAL SCANNING OF PRINTED MATERIAL

AUTHOR: Donald G. Doehring

AGE: 6 years to adult (younger children can complete some subtests)

VARIABLE: Speed of identifying units of print

TYPE OF MEASURE: Test

SOURCE FROM WHICH MEASURE MAY BE OBTAINED: Sample tests may be obtained (until supply is exhausted) from Donald G. Doehring, School of Human Communication Disorders, McGill University, Beatty Hall, 1266 Pine Avenue West, Montreal 112, Quebec, Canada.

DESCRIPTION OF MEASURE: This measure contains ten subtests, each of which is preceded by a practice test. Each subtest consists of a full page of figures, numbers, letters, or combinations of letters, some of which match the criterion stimulus. The subject underlines as rapidly as possible all of the matching responses. Time limits, ranging from 30 to 60 seconds, have been set so that few adults can complete the test within the time limit. Where the test is completed prior to the limit, the time is recorded. The score is mean latency in seconds per correct response. This permits comparison with reaction-time measures. Errors are also recorded. The subject is told to complete the test as rapidly as possible without making errors, to work from left to right and top to bottom of the page, and not to correct errors. Subtest ten, where each item is underlined, provides a control for visual-motor speed. This subtest was devised by John Dudley.

RELIABILITY AND VALIDITY: The author is presently analyzing the test results of normal-reading children, kindergarten to grade 11. Tentative results suggest that the test does not provide a good indication of developmental changes in reading skills.

BIBLIOGRAPHY:

Doehring, D. G. *Patterns of Impairment in Specific Reading Disability.* Bloomington, Indiana: Indiana University Press, 1968.

Doehring, D. G., and Rosenstein, J. "Speed of Visual Perception in Deaf Children." *Journal of Speech and Hearing Research,* 1969, *12,* 118-125.

Dudley, J. G., Doehring, D. G., and Coderre, L. "Speed of Visual Perception in Aphasic and Nonaphasic Patients with Brain Damage." *Cortex,* 1968, *4,* 389-402.

STIMULUS CORRELATES OF EMBEDDED FIGURES

AUTHORS: Stephen K. Reed and A. J. Angaran

AGE: 6 to 12 years

VARIABLE: Embedded-figure parameters

TYPE OF MEASURE: Test

SOURCE FROM WHICH MEASURE MAY BE OBTAINED: See Reed and Angaran (1972). Test forms are not available.

DESCRIPTION OF MEASURE: The test, which consists of four practice and sixteen test embedded-figure patterns, attempts to determine the stimulus variables that correlate with the difficulty of finding a figure hidden in a larger pattern. Previous research using 6- to 12-year-old children found that the number of shared contours, the complexity of the ground, and analysis complexity resulted in significant positive correlations with the difficulty of finding an embedded figure. The complexity of the figure, the complexity of the complete pattern, and the number of overlapping lines resulted in nonsignificant positive correlations with the difficulty in finding the figure.

RELIABILITY AND VALIDITY: None reported.

BIBLIOGRAPHY:

Abercrombie, M. L. *Perceptual and Visuo-Motor Disorders in Cerebral Palsy.* Lavenham, England: Lavenham Press, 1964.
Ghent, L. "Perception of Overlapping and Embedded Figures by Children of Different Ages." *American Journal of Psychology,* 1956, *69,* 574-587.
Gottschaldt, K. "Gestalt Factors in Repetition." In W. D. Ellis (Ed.), *A Sourcebook of Gestalt Psychology.* New York: Humanities Press, 1938.
Reed, S. K., and Angaran, A. J. "Structural Models and Embedded-Figure Difficulty for Normal and Retarded Children." *Perceptual and Motor Skills,* 1972, *35,* 155-164.

TAYLOR-HELMSTADTER PAIRED COMPARISON
SCALE OF AESTHETIC JUDGMENT

AUTHORS: Anne P. Taylor and Gerald C. Helmstadter

AGE: Preschool to adult

VARIABLE: Aesthetic judgment

TYPE OF MEASURE: Paired comparison scale

SOURCE FROM WHICH MEASURE MAY BE OBTAINED: Complete kit of materials available from Gerald C. Helmstadter, Arizona State University, Tempe, Arizona 85281. Cost: $50.00 for thirty-eight pairs of 3 X 5-inch color slides, detailed description of the scale, directions for administering, perforated master score card, and twenty answer sheets.

DESCRIPTION OF MEASURE: This scale consists of thirty-eight pairs of color slides depicting paintings, sculpture, and common household items. One slide of each pair was judged higher than the other on an 11-point successive category scale of aesthetic quality by art experts who independently rated each of 120 original slides. The examinee is asked to choose the one of each pair of slides he likes better. The score is the number of slides chosen that correspond to the preference of the art experts. Response sheets may be filled out directly by the examinee or by an adult listening to oral responses made by a very young child.

RELIABILITY AND VALIDITY: Intrinsic validity of the scale results from the selection of pairs of slides to form each item. A significant difference exists in the scale position of each slide pair as judged by experts. Additionally, whether or not a given slide was judged to be high or low on the scale of aesthetic quality, a substantial proportion of judges selected one slide of the pair as higher than the other. A table providing a complete content description and the two evidences of intrinsic validity of the scale can be obtained from the authors. With one small sample (N = 40) of homogeneous preschool children, a six-week test-retest reliability coefficient was found to be .43.

BIBLIOGRAPHY:

Taylor, A. P., and Helmstadter, G. C. "A Preliminary Pair Comparison Test for Measuring Aesthetic Judgment in Young Children." Paper presented to the annual meeting of the American Educational Research Association. New York, New York, 1971.

Prepared by Gerald C. Helmstadter

TENNESSEE DENTAL HEALTH ACHIEVEMENT TEST

AUTHOR: Division of Dental Health Services, Tennessee Department of Public Health

AGE: Grades 7 to 9

VARIABLE: Dental health knowledge

TYPE OF MEASURE: Test

SOURCE FROM WHICH MEASURE MAY BE OBTAINED: Division of Dental Health Services, Tennessee Department of Public Health, Nashville, Tennessee 37219. Cost:

Sample packet of test forms (A and B), scoring stencil, and manual of instructions, $1.10; test forms (A and B), $.12/copy, fifty or more, $.10/copy; scoring stencil (A and B), $.20/copy; manual of instructions, $.50/copy.

DESCRIPTION OF MEASURE: There are two forms of the test, each of which contains sixty-one items, most of which are four-option multiple choice. Testing time is 40 minutes. Punched-hole scoring stencils are provided for hand scoring. The first seven items are designed to determine dental health habits and attitudes and are not scored; the dental health achievement score is based on the remaining fifty-four questions. Each form of the test includes about the same number of questions on each of seventeen topics, which are tied into a curriculum guide and distributed by the State Division of Dental Health. Norms are provided for eighth graders, based on the scores on 1,438 pupils in thirty-nine Tennessee schools, following instruction in dental health. A manual is provided giving information on materials and directions for administration of the measure, directions for scoring, norms, and evidence on reliability and validity.

RELIABILITY AND VALIDITY: The number of questions on each topic reflects the importance of the topic as determined by a committee of dentists. Every question on the test was passed significantly more often by a group of 127 superior students than by a group of 127 below-average students. The interform reliability of the test, with an interval of one week, was .71. The corrected split-half reliability was .75 for both forms.

BIBLIOGRAPHY:

Collier, D. R. "An Evaluation: Dental Health Guide for Teachers of Tennessee." *Journal of Tennessee State Dental Association*, 1964, *44*, 124-130.

Collier, D. R. "The Use and Evaluation of a Dental Health Guide in an Educational Program." *Journal of Public Health Dentistry*, 1964, *24*, 3-6.

Tennessee Dental Health Achievement Test Manual. Nashville, Tennessee: Division of Dental Health Services, Tennessee Department of Public Health, n.d.

Prepared by Orval G. Johnson

TEST OF ABILITY TO EXPLAIN (ABEX)

AUTHOR: Enoch I. Sawin

AGE: 11 years to adult

VARIABLE: Ability to recognize reasons for events; to identify relevant elements and relationships among the elements and relevant generalizations.

TYPE OF MEASURE: Test

SOURCE FROM WHICH MEASURE MAY BE OBTAINED: See Wallen and others

(1969) or ERIC document no. ED 040 106. Hardbound copies of the study are available in major libraries that are repositories for U.S. government documents.

DESCRIPTION OF MEASURE: The instrument was used as a criterion measure in the Taba Curriculum Development Project in Social Studies (Wallen and others, 1969). The thirty-three items in the test are in multiple-choice format; hence it does not measure explaining behaviors directly. The intent in constructing it was to measure abilities as closely related to the ability to explain as is possible with a machine-scorable test. The test yields a total score and three part scores: (1) Recognition of Events Connected by Causality, (2) Recognition of Principles that Explain Events, and (3) Application of Principles that Explain Cause-and-Effect Relations. The intercorrelations among the part scores (N = 600) ranged from .24 to .42. The correlations between individual part scores and the total score ranged from .62 to .81.

As an example, the first block of practice exercises for the ABEX (+ indicates correct response) is given below. A flowchart of probable cause-and-effect relations leading to an event is the basis for each of the thirty-three blocks of test items. These devices are used for clarifying the reasoning on which the items are based, but they are not presented to the student as part of the test. (No flowcharts are included for practice items.)

Practice Exercise Directions: Read Fact W and Fact X in the boxes below; then answer the question under the boxes.

Fact W	Fact X
A camper started a fire to cook food on a windy day in a forest.	A fire started in dry grass near a campfire in a forest.

1. Both of these facts took place in the same forest. Could one have at least partly caused the other?
   +a. Yes; Fact W could have at least partly caused Fact X.
   b. Yes; Fact X could have at least partly caused Fact W.
   c. No; neither is likely to have caused the other.

Same
facts:

Fact W	Fact X
A camper started a fire to cook food on a windy day in a forest.	A fire started in dry grass near a campfire in a forest.

2. Could any of the following statements be used to explain any of the possible cause-and-effect connections between Facts W and X? If so, which *one* would be best?
   a. The heat from burning trees can set other trees on fire.
   +b. Burning coals from a campfire are hot enough to start a fire in dry grass.
   c. food requires heat for cooking.
   d. None of these

	Fact W		Fact X

Same facts:

Fact W
A camper started a fire to cook food on a windy day in a forest.

Fact X
A fire started in dry grass near a campfire in a forest.

Directions: Here is another fact that happened later the same day in the same forest:

Fact Y
A house in the forest burned down.

   3. Imagine that you have been asked to explain what might have caused the house to burn down in Fact Y. Would Facts W and X be useful as parts of the explanation?

     +a. Yes; both W and X and the possible cause-and-effect relation between them would be useful.

     b. Yes; both W and X would be useful even though neither was likely a cause of the other.

     c. No; because *only one* of Facts W and X was likely a cause of Y.

     d. No; because *neither* W or X was likely a cause.

Read all choices before deciding on your answer.

RELIABILITY AND VALIDITY: Reliability estimates for the total scores obtained by means of Kuder-Richardson formula 20 ranged between .71 for pretest results and .76 for posttest results, based on a sample of about six hundred sixth-grade students. Pretest and posttest correlations (with eight months intervening) for the three part scores and the total score were .45, .62, .36, and .68, respectively. Several methods for checking validity were applied: (1) correlation of scores with scores on a separate *essay* test that measures ability to explain directly, (2) individual oral administration of the test to students in conjunction with intensive interviews to ascertain students' reasoning behind their responses, (3) cluster analyses showing the relative closeness of agreement in the responses of various groups assumed to have differing levels of ability on the variable measured (sixth graders, graduate students, and project staff), and (4) correlations of scores with teacher ratings. The results of these checks on validity were all favorable but not conclusive. For example, the correlation between the total score on the multiple-choice test and that on the essay test was .60.

BIBLIOGRAPHY:

Wallen, N. E., Durkin, M. C., Fraenkel, J. R., McNaughton, A. H., and Sawin, E. I. *The Taba Curriculum Development Project in Social Studies.* Final report, Project No. 5-1314, Grant No. OE-6-10-182, U.S. Department of Health, Education and Welfare. San Francisco State College, California, 1969. ERIC document no. ED 040 106.

TEST OF THE INTEGRAL CONCEPT OF TIME

AUTHOR: K. W. Rogers

VARIABLE: Capacity to solve problems dependent on the conceptualization of time

AGE: 11 years to adult

TYPE OF MEASURE: Questionnaire

SOURCE FROM WHICH MEASURE MAY BE OBTAINED: See Rogers (1967).

DESCRIPTION OF MEASURE: Intended as a measure of cognitive development in a specific content area, this test is essentially a scale with the eighteen items randomly arranged. In cross-sectional use it should reveal a threshold presumed dependent upon the onset of formal operations. Below this threshold the linear correlation with IQ is high (about .6) and above it is low (about .2). In scoring, 1 point is given for each correct response (maximum = 24 points). The time limit for the test is 30 minutes.

As examples, three of the eighteen items on the test are given below.

1. A time machine is featured in a current TV serial. What is a time machine?
   a. A machine which can take you into the past or future.
   b. A machine which measures time.
   c. A machine which can make time go fast or slow.
   d. A machine for making a bomb go off at a certain time.
6. An aeroplane flew around the world from East to West, at such a speed that it arrived back at its starting point after 24 hours. It left at noon on July 3rd. What was the date it arrived back? During the flight of this aeroplane the pilot noticed that:
   a. The sun rose twice.
   b. The sun set twice.
   c. It was noon all the time he was flying.
   d. His day seemed to last 48 hours.
14. It was once said that if the people of China marched ten abreast across a bridge, the procession would never stop.
   a. Could this possibly be true?
   b. Give your reasons for your answer below.

RELIABILITY AND VALIDITY: Split-half reliability is inevitably low (.5). No other reliability measure is available. The items were mostly collected from the literature having face validity only.

BIBLIOGRAPHY:

Rogers, K. W. "Concepts of Time in Secondary School Children of Above-Average IQ." *British Journal of Educational Psychology,* 1967, *37,* 99-109.

TEST TO MEASURE LIFE INSURANCE KNOWLEDGE

AUTHOR: Delbert M. Van Maanen

AGE: High school

VARIABLE: Life insurance knowledge

TYPE OF MEASURE: Multiple-choice test

SOURCE FROM WHICH MEASURE MAY BE OBTAINED: Delbert M. Van Maanen, 526 Georgia Avenue Southwest, Orange City, Iowa 51041.

DESCRIPTION OF MEASURE: This thirty-eight-item instrument is designed to measure the knowledge and understanding high school students have of life insurance. The original test was revised twice, and in the final revision the correct choices of the four-option multiple-choice test were arranged to insure random order for each correct choice of test items.

As examples, the first two of the thirty-eight items on the test are given below.

1. The fee charged by an insurance company for issuing a policy is called a/an: (a) prepayment, (b) rider, (c) endorsement, (d) premium.
2. Which of the following is an insurance company owned by stockholders? (a) mutual company, (b) stock company, (c) endowment company, (d) assessment company.

RELIABILITY AND VALIDITY: The original eighty-four-item test was validated by the faculty of the Insurance Department of the School of Business at the University of Northern Colorado. Forty-six test items were eliminated because they were either insignificant or too difficult for high school students. (The final item of the remaining thirty-eight is a simple demographic item.) Following the administration of the thirty-seven-item test, an item analysis was conducted to determine the difficulty level and the discrimination index of each test item. The point biserial correlation coefficient was used to determine the discrimination index of each test item. The mean score for the 142 high school students who participated in this project was 13.43 with a standard deviation of 3.64. The reliability coefficient of the test, as determined by Kuder-Richardson formula 20, was .45.

BIBLIOGRAPHY:

Van Maanen, D. M. "The Construction of a Test to Measure Life Insurance Knowledge, Understanding, and Application Possessed by Selected High School Students." Unpublished doctoral dissertation. University of Northern Colorado, Greeley, 1974.

TEST OF SOCIAL INFERENCE (TSI)

AUTHORS: Barbara Edmonson, John E. de Jung, Henry Leland, and Ethel M. Leach

AGE: 10 years to adult (mild retardation); 12 or 13 years to adult (moderate retardation); 7 to 13 years (nonretarded)

VARIABLE: Social comprehension

TYPE OF MEASURE: Picture test

SOURCE FROM WHICH MEASURE MAY BE OBTAINED: Educational Activities, Inc., Box 392, Freeport, New York 11520.

DESCRIPTION OF MEASURE: The Test of Social Inference (TSI) was developed in 1964 in a project to demonstrate the remediability of the social comprehension deficit of the retarded. The instrument itself was devised to assess the differences among persons' social interpretations and the relevance of social interpretations to behavior. The test consists of a set of pictures of diverse situations accompanied by standard questions, verbally presented by the examiner, that elicit interpretations. The TSI is not a projective test, as the pictures are relatively unambiguous—in fact they were chosen for their interpretability by nonretarded inner-city eighth and ninth graders of borderline to average intelligence—and the scoring differentiates between less and more probable inferences. It is not a test of social intelligence, as it cannot purport to get at some underlying "potential," but it can be used as an achievement test for the decoding of visual social cues. The test's range of item difficulty permits its use with mildly retarded pupils as young as 9 or 10, presumably with no upward limits for age. Its most useful range for the moderately retarded would be from the age of 12 or 13 and upward. A modified version of the test for use with young children is in process of development. The TSI can also be used to test individuals who are not retarded, the useful range being from about 7 years to 13.

RELIABILITY AND VALIDITY: Interscorer reliability for the TSI in the high .90s has been obtained from experienced scorers (Edmonson and others, 1971). For an intermediate grade group of fifteen pupils tested after a one-week span (Ns of 12, 13, and 20) and a group of institutionalized EMR individuals retested after ten days, all reliability coefficients exceeded .90. Retest coefficients for nonretarded adolescents were less substantial. A group of forty-five eighth and ninth graders retested after a one-week interval provided a reliability estimate of .74 (Edmonson and others, 1971), the skewness of the score distribution suggesting insufficient test ceiling for this population. More recently a subtest of twenty-six of the more difficult TSI items was twice administered to twenty-eight nonretarded junior high school seventh and eighth graders (de Jung and Edmonson, 1972). The test-retest correlation after a one-week interval was .82, more nearly approaching those coefficients reported for poorer-performing, lower-IQ samples. To reliably differentiate among older or higher IQ students, more difficult TSI items or more discriminating scoring procedure are needed.

A considerable body of data regarding validity of the TSI is presented in the manual for the test and is summarized here. TSI performance apparently is unbiased with respect to geographic residence, sex, race, and age. Although related to IQ, particularly to the WISC subtests of Comprehension and Vocabulary, TSI scores have been more closely related than IQs to assessments of acceptance by peers, ease of participation in diverse settings, social skills, independent functioning, and attitude toward work. Two studies independently yielded very similar moderate correlations between TSI scores and social maturity as measured by the Vineland Social Maturity Scale, and correlations with scores on an experimental social problem solving test yielded generally similar coefficients. TSI scores are not related to ratings of appearance, physical development, withdrawal, disruptive behavior, nor to scores of self-concept or locus of control. They are less closely related than IQs to ratings of academic achievement and industriousness in the classroom setting.

BIBLIOGRAPHY:

Charette, A. L. "Age and Sex Differences in Test of Social Inference Responses by Normal Children." Unpublished doctoral dissertation. Ohio State University, Columbus, 1972.

de Jung, J. E., and Edmonson, B. *Measurement and Remediation of Social Competency Deficits of Junior High School Pupils.* Final report, SRS Project RD 15-P-5528. Eugene: University of Oregon, 1972.

de Jung, J. E., Holen, M. C., and Edmonson, B. *Review of Studies Using the Test of Social Inference to Measure Social Cue Perceptions in Retarded Adolescents.* Supplement to final report SRS Project RD 15-P-5529810-03. Eugene: University of Oregon, 1972.

de Jung, J. E., Holen, M., and Edmonson, B. "A Test of Social Inference for Retarded Adolescents." *Psychological Reports,* 1973, *32,* 603-618.

Edmonson, B., de Jung, J. E., and Leland, H. "Social Perceptual (Nonverbal Communication) Training of Retarded Adolescents." *Mental Retardation,* 1965, *3,* 7-9.

Edmonson, B., de Jung, J. E., Leland, H., and Leach, E. M. *Social Inference Training of Retarded Adolescents and the Test of Social Inference.* Eugene: University of Oregon, 1971.

Edmonson, B., de Jung, J. E., Leland, H., and Leach, E. M. *The Test of Social Inference: Teacher's Guide.* Freeport, New York: Educational Activities, 1974.

Edmonson, B., Leach, E., and Leland, H. *Social Perceptual Training for Community Living: Prevocational Units for Retarded Youth.* Kit and Book. Freeport, New York: Educational Activities, 1969.

Edmonson, B., Leland, H., and Leach, E. M. "Social Inference Training of Retarded Adolescents." *Education and Training of Mentally Retarded,* 1970, *5,* (4), 169-176.

Fanning, T. "A Correlational Study of the Test of Social Inference: The Vineland Social Maturity Scale, Behavior Ratings, and Retardate Characteristics." Unpublished master's thesis. University of Wisconsin, Madison, 1970.

Minifie, E. L. "Validation of the Test of Social Inference for Educable Mentally Retarded Adolescents Through the Use of Teacher Ratings." Unpublished doctoral dissertation. Colorado State University, Fort Collins, 1969.

Smith, R. D. "Refinement of Administration and Scoring Procedures for the Test of Social Inference." Unpublished doctoral dissertation. University of Oregon, Eugene, 1968.

TEST SOPHISTICATION SCALE

AUTHORS: James J. Diamond and William J. Evans

AGE: Grade 6 and up

VARIABLE: Test wiseness

TYPE OF MEASURE: Multiple-choice test

SOURCE FROM WHICH MEASURE MAY BE OBTAINED: James J. Diamond, Graduate School of Education (C1), University of Pennsylvania, Philadelphia 19174. Cost: $2.00 for reproduction, postage, and handling payable to Center for Research in Evaluation and Measurement.

DESCRIPTION OF MEASURE: The Test Sophistication Scale consists of thirty four-option multiple-choice items. There are six items for each of five subscales: association between stem and correct alternative, specific determiners, longer correct alternatives, grammatical clues, and overlapping distracters. The items are based upon fictitious material, with each item including only one of the five extraneous clues. The·instrument is in an experimental stage and should be used only for research purposes.

As examples, the first three items from the thirty on the test are given below.

1. The Augustine National Party has its headquarters in
    a. Camden, New Jersey
  X b. St. Augustine, Florida
    c. Palo Alto, California
    d. Dallas, Texas
2. Josef Maruka has been most famous for:
    a. has fought for independence in his country.
    b. was the first man to swim Lake Geneva both ways.
  X c. his invention of the sulfur battery.
    d. has been the main proponent of a "United Europe."
3. The population of Frankton is more than
  X a. 50 million
    b. 60 million
    c. 70 million
    d. 80 million

RELIABILITY AND VALIDITY: Kuder-Richardson estimates of internal consistency range from .22 to .80.

BIBLIOGRAPHY:

Diamond, J. J., and Evans, W. J. "An Investigation of the Cognitive Correlates of Test Wiseness." *Journal of Educational Measurement*, 1972, *9*, 145-150.

TEST OF SPECIFIC DICTIONARY SKILLS

AUTHOR: Marion P. Turkish

AGE: 9 to 11 years

VARIABLE: Dictionary skills

TYPE OF MEASURE: Test

SOURCE FROM WHICH MEASURE MAY BE OBTAINED: Marion P. Turkish, Department of Reading and Language Arts, William Paterson College, Wayne, New Jersey 07470.

DESCRIPTION OF MEASURE: The Test of Specific Dictionary Skills was designed specifically for use with students in grades 4, 5, and 6. The test consists of four major sections: Location, Spelling, Pronunciation, and Meaning. The Location section has four subtests: (1) Finding the Page, (2) Alphabetical Order, (3) Identifying Key Words, and (4) Finding a Definition. The Spelling section has two subtests: (1) Spelling Demons and (2) Spelling Plurals. The Pronunciation section has four subtests: (1) Phonetic Respelling, (2) Pronunciation Using Key, (3) Syllables, and (4) Accentuation. The Meaning section has six subtests: (1) Direct Meaning, (2) Multiple-Meaning Single Entry, (3) Homonyms, (4) Multiple-Meaning Double Entry, (5) Information, and (6) Accent and Meaning. In order to complete all sixteen subtests, students must use and manipulate a dictionary. Directions and samples are given for each subtest, as well as suggested time limits. Because the test is lengthy, it is suggested that it be given by sections.

RELIABILITY AND VALIDITY: A pilot study with sixty-eight students was completed in Union, New Jersey. Reliability and an item analysis were completed on the data collected. Content validity was established by asking three experts to examine the new instrument, and their suggestions were included in the final copy. The major study was conducted in Hillside, New Jersey, on 715 students in five schools. All students completed the Test of Specific Dictionary Skills and the California Reading Test, elementary form.

Reliability coefficients for thirteen to fifteen subtests of the Test of Specific Dictionary Skills were .70 or better for each grade level as well as each of the five schools. With the exception of grades 5 and 6 in two schools, significant differences were found in the performances of students in grades 4, 5, and 6 on the Test of Specific Dictionary Skills. Coefficients of correlation between the Test of Specific Dictionary Skills and the California Reading Test ranged from .72 to .83 for each grade level as well as for the total population. Further coefficients of correlation were computed to find relationships between the subjects of each instrument.

BIBLIOGRAPHY:

Turkish, M. P. "A Study of Dictionary Skills Used by Pupils in Grades Four, Five, and Six." Unpublished doctoral dissertation. Fordham University, New York, New York, 1972.

TESTWISENESS TEST

AUTHOR: Orval G. Johnson

AGE: High school to adult

VARIABLE: Test-taking ability

TYPE OF MEASURE: Four-option multiple-choice test

SOURCE FROM WHICH MEASURE MAY BE OBTAINED: The entire measure is shown below. Readers who are confident of the correct responses to the eight items may reproduce it for use with their students without crediting the source. Others may send a self-addressed, stamped envelope for the scoring key and rationale and will be expected to acknowledge the source in any use of the test. Address correspondence to Orval G. Johnson, 747 12th Street, Boulder, Colorado 80302.

DESCRIPTION OF MEASURE: The test is composed of eight items, each of which is designed to demonstrate one of the pitfalls in item construction. Nonsense words are used to demonstrate that even without meaningful content, the testwise individual can get correct answers. The complete measure is given below. The subject circles the letter preceding the correct response.

1. The purpose of the cluss in furmpaling is to remove
    a. cluss-prags
    b. tremalls
    c. cloughs
    d. plumots
2. Trassig is true when
    a. lusp trasses the vom
    b. the viskal flans, if the viskal is donwil or zortil
    c. the belgo frulls
    d. dissles lisk easily
3. The sigla frequently overfesks the trelsum because
    a. all siglas are mellious
    b. siglas are always votial
    c. the trelsum is usually tarious
    d. no trelsa are feskable
4. The fribbled breg will minter best with an
    a. derst
    b. morst
    c. sortar
    d. ignu
5. Among the reasons for tristal doss are
    a. the sabs foped and the doths tinzed
    b. the kredges roted with the orots
    c. few rakobs were accepted in sluth
    d. most of the polats were thonced

6. Which of the following (is, are) always present when trossels are being gruven?
   a. rint and vost
   b. vost
   c. shum and vost
   d. vost and plone
7. The mintering function of the ignu is most effectively carried out in connection with
   a. a razma tol
   b. the groshing stantol
   c. the fribbled breg
   d. a frally sush
8. a.
   b.
   c.
   d.

RELIABILITY AND VALIDITY: None reported.

BIBLIOGRAPHY: None.

TIME CONCEPT TEST

AUTHORS: William H. Dutton and Lois E. Stephens

AGE: Kindergarten to Grade 3

VARIABLE: Child's ability to tell time to minute and basic concepts related to time (clock)

TYPE OF MEASURE: Test

SOURCE FROM WHICH MEASURE MAY BE OBTAINED: Lois E. Stephens, Oxnard School District, 831 South "B" Street, Oxnard, California 93030.

DESCRIPTION OF MEASURE: The Time Concept Test consists of three divisions: (1) clock drawing, 1 to 7 points; (2) reading clock to hour, 1 point; (3) use of clock in daily activities and telling time from hour to one-minute intervals, 32 points. The total point value is 40 points. Analysis of clock drawings includes eight levels of maturity, each with a point value from 0 to 7. All other test items are scored 1 point each (32 points), making the total of 40 points for the entire test.

As examples, the nine items concerned with time used for daily activities and with understanding the operations of a clock are given below. The second division of the test has nine questions and is divided into two parts. The first part is concerned with time used for daily activities.

2. What time is it by your clock? (in room)
3. What time does school begin?
4. What time do you go home from school?
5. What time do you have lunch?

The second part of this division calls for understanding the operations of a clock.

6. Why does a clock have two hands?
7. What does the long hand tell?
8. What does the short hand tell?
9. How long does it take the long hand to move from 12 to 1?
10. How long does it take the short hand to move from 12 to 1?

RELIABILITY AND VALIDITY: Test-retest reliability was 88. Items in the test were evaluated by a panel of primary-school teachers, and rational and curricular validity were established.

BIBLIOGRAPHY:

Brace, A., and Nelson, L. D. "The Preschool Child's Concept of Number." *The Arithmetic Teacher,* 1965, *12,* 127.
Stephens, L. E. "What Concepts of Telling Time Can Be Developed by Kindergarten Children." Unpublished doctoral dissertation. University of California, Los Angeles, 1964.
Sussman, D. "Number Readiness of Children Entering Kindergarten." Unpublished doctoral dissertation. University of California, Los Angeles, 1962.

TIME QUESTIONNAIRE

AUTHOR: Ruth R. Greenberg Edelstein

AGE: Grades 4 and 5

VARIABLE: Time concepts

TYPE OF MEASURE: Questionnaire

SOURCE FROM WHICH MEASURE MAY BE OBTAINED: Ruth R. Greenberg Edelstein, State University of New York, Upstate Medical Center, 750 East Adams Street, Syracuse, New York 13210.

DESCRIPTION OF MEASURE: The oral Time Questionnaire is divided into two parts. Part A deals with general time concepts involving school happenings, clock time, calendar time, and relationships between events. It consists of twenty-four questions, some of which are based on earlier questionnaires (Farrell, 1953; Sturt, 1925). In most instances the answers are considered either correct or wrong, but in a few instances there is some leeway in obtaining a correct response. For instance, an answer in giving the present clock time is correct if it is not off by more than 30 minutes. Part B consists of thirty questions involving judgments concerning short durations in everyday situations. The first twenty-three questions require judgments of whether a person's described activities are being carried out at either a fast, medium, or slow rate. The next two questions require judgments of events as occurring either early, medium, or late, and the last five items require judgments of various time periods as being either short, medium, or long in duration. For example, one item from Part B was, "A girl drinks a glass of milk in 25 minutes. Is this fast, medium, or slow?"

As examples, the first ten items of Part A are given below.

What day of the week is today?
What day of the month is it?
What month is it?
Name all the months.
What time is it now?
What is the season now?
What day is it in Long Island now?
When you are 12, how much older will you be?
How long is it until school stops for the summer?
How long do you stay in school every day?

The first ten items of Part B are:

A boy gets ready for school in 1 hour. (*Slow*)
A girl takes 10 minutes to eat her supper. (*Fast*)
A boy does his spelling homework in 3 hours. (*Slow*)
A boy finishes high school in 5 years. (*Slow*)
A lady takes 5 minutes ro brush her teeth. (*Slow*)
A man walks one block in 10 minutes. (*Slow*)
A boy washes his face in 5 seconds. (*Fast*)
A girl drinks a glass of milk in 25 minutes. (*Slow*)
A girl takes a message around to all teachers in the school in 4 hours. (*Slow*)
A boy puts on his stockings in 10 minutes. (*Slow*)

RELIABILITY AND VALIDITY: A high degree of internal consistency in Part A is indicated by the fact that those with high total scores (the top 27 percent) did much better than those with low total scores (the bottom 27 percent) in all but three of the twenty-four items. On these three items the low and high scorers did equally well. The Kuder-Richardson formula 21 estimate of the coefficient of reliability for the questionnaire as a whole was .74. This supported the high degree of internal consistency found in the analysis of individual items and indicated that the items as a group had enough in common for the questionnaire to serve as an adequate experimental instrument. Time Questionnaire scores were found to be significantly correlated with intelligence (r = .47) as measured by the Otis Intelligence Test. When age and intelligence were partialed out, there were still significant differences among three reading levels (N = 58 fourth and fifth graders) on the Time Questionnaire scores.

BIBLIOGRAPHY:

Edelstein, R. G. "Time Perception as Related to Reading Achievement." *Perceptual and Motor Skills,* 1971, *33,* 899-905.
Farrell, M. "Understanding of Time Relations of Five-, Six-, and Seven-Year Old Children of High IQ." *Journal of Educational Research,* 1953, *46,* 587-594.
Sturt, M. *The Psychology of Time.* New York: Harcourt Brace Jovanovich, 1925.

TIME UNDERSTANDING INVENTORY

AUTHORS: Ruth K. Forer and Barbara K. Keogh

AGE: Elementary to junior high school grades

VARIABLE: Time understanding

TYPE OF MEASURE: Test

SOURCE FROM WHICH MEASURE MAY BE OBTAINED: Barbara K. Keogh, University of California Graduate School of Education, Los Angeles, California 90024.

DESCRIPTION OF MEASURE: The Time Understanding Inventory is composed of a cognitive section and a perceptual section. The cognitive section is designed to determine children's knowledge and understanding of time within four major areas: subjective, objective, historic, and time judgment. The perceptual section requires a child to demonstrate knowledge of the mechanics of time and includes four subtests: Draw-a-Clock, Clock Matching, Clock Fill-in, and Time Recognition. There are 8 possible points in each subtest, 32 points for the cognitive and perceptual sections, and 64 points possible for a total score. All items were pretested on subsets of 149 normal-achieving children in grades 1 through 6. Items that did not discriminate across grade levels were dropped. This is a research and experimental test and has not been developed for clinical use with individual children.

As examples, selected items from each area of the cognitive section of the test are given below. There are eight items in each area.

Subjective Time
1. When is your birthday?
3. How many hours do you sleep at night?
7. How many more years of school will you have before you graduate from high school?
Objective Time
1. What year is it?
4. How many hours in a day?
7. What is the name of the seventh month of the year?

Historic Time
1. Tell me somebody that was born before our country started.
8. Which happened first: Astronauts fly around the moon; Lincoln became the President; Betsy Ross sewed the flag with 13 stars.
Time Estimation
1. Which would take you longer to go to school every morning, walking or riding a bike?
8. How long do you think you've been sitting here?

RELIABILITY AND VALIDITY: The final inventory was validated on a sample of 142 normal-achieving boys in grades 1 to 6 in public elementary schools. There was steady improvement of time understanding across grade levels, and significant differences favoring perceptual over cognitive scores in five of the six grade groups. There was a significantly high correlation between cognitive and perceptual scores. Further use with educationally handicapped or learning-disabled groups has demonstrated that LD children are less adequate than normal-achieving children of the same age in their mastery of both cognitive and perceptual aspects of time understanding. Learning-disability children in a sample of elementary-age children were found to function approximately three grade levels below the chronological age grade placement equivalent. Poor performance was found for LD children on both the perceptual and cognitive sections.

BIBLIOGRAPHY:

Forer, R. K. "Time Understanding of Normal Achieving and Educationally Handicapped Boys." Unpublished doctoral dissertation. University of California, Los Angeles, 1970.
Forer, R. K., and Keogh, B. K. "Time Understanding of Learning Disabled Boys." *Exceptional Children,* 1971, *37,* 741-743.
Keogh, B. K. "Perceptual Time Understanding of Fourth and Fifth Grade Children." Unpublished technical report. University of California, Los Angeles, 1968.

Prepared by Barbara K. Keogh

TRAINABLE ACHIEVEMENT RECORD (TAR)

AUTHORS: Don Soule and Mallie Stocks

AGE: Any age, mental age 1½ to 8 years

VARIABLE: Academic achievement in trainable class

TYPE OF MEASURE: Individual test

SOURCE FROM WHICH MEASURE MAY BE OBTAINED: Psychology, Research and

Evaluation Section, O'Berry Center, Goldsboro, North Carolina 27530. Cost: Complete set, including 1 manual, 1 set of question cards, 50 answer sheets: $5.00; 1 manual: $.50; 50 answer sheets: $2.00; training videotape on administration procedures on ½" EIAJ-1 Standard or ¾" U-Matic Video Cassette (please state which): $25.00.

DESCRIPTION OF MEASURE: The Trainable Achievement Record (TAR) was developed to measure skills taught in classes for trainable or moderately retarded children. The test is also useful for the older and more able severely retarded and for young educable retarded children. It is an individual test with an administration time of 15 to 20 minutes, yielding an achievement age (AA) score in years and months. From this AA, a ratio achievement quotient (AQ) may be derived for comparison with the subject's IQ score.

The TAR is given through use of verbal directions, but it does not require verbal responses. The test was constructed in this way because many moderately retarded people are subject to rather severe speech defects. The use of nonverbal answers makes it possible for an examiner who is not familiar with the subject's speech to do the testing. Norms were established from a sample of 155 children in institutional and community programs.

As examples, three samples of test items from the subtests Verbal Concepts (A), Numerical Concepts (B), and Spatial Concepts (C) are given below.

(A) 12. See the doors? Which door shows the toilet you would use? Which door would a boy (girl) (opposite sex) use? Which door is the one that says where to go *into* the store? Which door is the one that says where to go *out* of the store?
(B) 10. Place two quarters, two dimes, two nickels, and five pennies on the table in front of the subject. (See manual for further explanation.) See all this money?
a. Put your finger on the
Nickel
Dime
Penny
Quarter
b. Show 5 pennies and ask the subject to show you the coin which is the same as 5 pennies. Show 2 nickels and ask which coin is the same as 2 nickels.
(C) 9. Look at these coffee cups. Some of the cups hold more than others. Which cup holds the least coffee? Which cup holds the most coffee?

RELIABILITY AND VALIDITY: To determine the test-retest reliability of the TAR, a sample of thirty trainable retarded children was selected, given the test, and then retested one month later. The correlation of these scores indicated high test-retest reliability, $r = .97$. Using the same sample, a split-half correlation ($r = .96$) was determined by comparing the total raw score of each individual of odd-numbered test items with the total score on even-numbered test items, corrected to .98 using the Spearman-Brown formula.

BIBLIOGRAPHY:

Snipes, S., and Soule, D. "Some Characteristics of the Trainable Achievement Record." *Research and the Retarded,* Summer 1974.
Stocks, M., and Soule, D. *Trainable Achievement Record.* Research and Evaluation Section, Goldsboro, North Carolina: O'Berry Center, 1973.

UNIVERSITY OF ILLINOIS SMOKING KNOWLEDGE TEST

AUTHORS: William H. Creswell, Jr., Warren J. Huffman, and Donald B. Stone

AGE: Junior and senior high school

VARIABLE: Cognitive aspects of cigarette smoking

TYPE OF MEASURE: Multiple-choice test

SOURCE FROM WHICH MEASURE MAY BE OBTAINED: See Creswell, Huffman, and Stone (1970).

DESCRIPTION OF MEASURE: This test consists of forty-four multiple-choice questions designed to measure knowledge levels of teenagers with respect to cigarette smoking. Each question contains four foils. Content areas include: smoking practices of teenagers; cigarette advertising; physiological, psychological, and social aspects of smoking; and immediate and long-range consequences.

As examples, the first five of the forty-four items of the revised instrument are given below.

1. A study of the smoking habits of American teenagers reveals that
   a. more teenagers than adults smoke cigarettes.
   b. more junior high students smoke than high school students.
   c. approximately 30 percent of all teenagers smoke cigarettes.
   d. more teenage girls than teenage boys smoke cigarettes.
2. Cigarette commercials no longer show professional athletes smoking. Which of the following is *not* true of cigarette advertisements?
   a. Cigarette advertisers sponsor athletic contests on TV.
   b. Some athletes give testimonials against smoking for poster displays.
   c. Cigarette commercials include the health effects of smoking.
   d. Cigarette smoking is associated with participation in recreational activities.
3. The workload of the heart of a cigarette smoker is increased due to
   a. carbon monoxide reducing the oxygen carrying capacity of the blood.
   b. the acceleration of the clotting time of blood.
   c. increased thickening of the walls of the arterioles and small arteries.
   d. all of the above.
4. Surveys indicate that most teenagers smoke because they
   a. like the taste of tobacco.
   b. are rebelling against authority.
   c. want to belong to the group.
   d. say it calms them down.
5. Nicotine, an ingredient in cigarette smoke, is
   a. stimulating to the nervous system.
   b. depressing to the nervous system.
   c. both stimulating and depressing.
   d. neither stimulating nor depressing.

RELIABILITY AND VALIDITY: The instrument has been revised based on previous field trials. The present instrument has not been pilot tested.

BIBLIOGRAPHY:

Creswell, W. H., Jr., Huffman, W. J., and Stone, D. B. *Youth Smoking Behavior Character-istics and Their Educational Implications.* Champaign: University of Illinois Press, 1970.

Irwin, R. P., Creswell, W. H., Jr., and Stauffer, D. J. "The Effect of the Teacher and Three Different Classroom Approaches on Seventh Grade Students' Knowledge, Attitudes, and Beliefs About Smoking." *Journal of School Health,* 1970, *40,* 355-359.

Laoye, J., Creswell, W. H., Jr., and Stone, D. B. "A Cohort Study of 1,205 Secondary School Smokers." *Journal of School Health,* 1972, *42,* 47-52.

Prepared by Donald B. Stone

VERBAL SPATIAL RELATIONSHIPS TEST

AUTHOR: Lawrence C. Hartlage

AGE: 8 years to adult

VARIABLE: Nonvisual spatial reasoning

TYPE OF MEASURE: Test

SOURCE FROM WHICH MEASURE MAY BE OBTAINED: Lawrence Hartlage, De-partment of Neurology, Medical College of Georgia, Augusta, Georgia 30902. Cost: Printing and mailing cost for test, norms, instructions for administration and scoring, and response sheet (no restrictions on reproducing), $2.00.

DESCRIPTION OF MEASURE: The test contains thirty-two items, of which sixteen deal with spatial relationships and sixteen are (balanced) nonspatial items, enabling an isolation of spatial reasoning from general reasoning ability. It was originally normed with children at each grade from 2 through high school, half of whom were blind. Subsequent norms were developed for college students. The test can be given either as a tape recording or read, to either individual subjects or to groups. It has been recently used to compare individuals with lateralized central processing disorders and to predict vocational aptitudes of retarded, blind, and normal subjects.

As examples, two items each of the four categories are given below in order of presentation. Scoring is indicated.

Spatial with Self-Reference
  1. You are in front of Bill
     Bill is in front of Mary
     You are   _____ in back of Mary
                      __X__ in front of Mary
                      _____ can't say

2. You are on the right side of Bill
   Bill is on the right side of Mary
   You are   _____ on the left side of Mary
        __X__ on the right side of Mary
        _____ can't say

Spatial Without Self-Reference
11. John is in front of Mary
    Mary is in front of Bill
    John is   _____ in back of Bill
         __X__ in front of Bill
         _____ can't say

7. John is on the right side of Mary
   Mary is on the right side of Bill
   John is   _____ on the left side of Bill
        __X__ on the right side of Bill
        _____ can't say

Nonspatial with Self-Reference
6. You are bigger than Mary
   Mary is bigger than Bill
   You are   _____ smaller than Bill
        __X__ bigger than Bill
        _____ can't say

2. You are faster than John
   John is faster than Mary
   You are   _____ slower than Mary
        __X__ faster than Mary
        _____ can't say

Nonspatial Without Self-Reference
20. John is bigger than Mary
    Mary is bigger than Bill
    John is   _____ smaller than Bill
         __X__ bigger than Bill
         _____ can't say

12. John is faster than Mary
    Mary is faster than Bill
    John is   _____ slower than Bill
         __X__ faster than Bill
         _____ can't say

RELIABILITY AND VALIDITY: With 100 original subjects, split-half reliability (uncorrected) was in the range of .80 to .86 for each half (spatial/nonspatial). The test's predictive validity for given job successes on tasks requiring spatial conceptualization ranged from .48 to .72.

BIBLIOGRAPHY:

Hartlage, L. C. "The Role of Vision in the Development of Spatial Ability." Unpublished doctoral dissertation. University of Louisville, Kentucky, 1967.

Hartlage, L. C. "Deficit in Space Concepts Associated with Visual Deprivation." *Journal of Learning Disabilities*, 1968, *1*, 21-23.

Hartlage, L. C. "Verbal Tests of Spatial Conceptualization." *Journal of Experimental Psychology,* 1969, *80,* 180-182.

Hartlage, L. C. "Measuring Spatial Aptitudes of the Retarded." *Perceptual and Motor Skills,* 1971, *33,* 1107-1110.

WELCH SCIENCE PROCESS INVENTORY, FORM D

AUTHOR: Wayne W. Welch

AGE: Senior high school students

VARIABLE: Knowledge of scientific processes

TYPE OF MEASURE: Test

SOURCE FROM WHICH MEASURE MAY BE OBTAINED: Wayne W. Welch, 204 Burton Hall, University of Minnesota, Minneapolis, Minnesota 55455. Cost: Fifty tests for $10.00; answer key, $1.00.

DESCRIPTION OF MEASURE: The Welch Science Process Inventory, Form D consists of 135 items pertaining to the assumptions, products, activities, and ethics of science. Students are asked to express agreement or disagreement with each of the statements. The student's response is assumed to indicate his knowledge of the idea contained in the statement. Total scores are obtained by summing the number of agreements with a standard key. The key is based upon the opinions of practicing research scientists.

As examples, five of the 135 items on the inventory are given below. The respondent answers "agree" or "disagree."

1. Surprising or unexpected observations have played an important role in the advance of science.
7. Theories are usually so well established, they do not require experimental testing.
9. If two different hypotheses fit the observed facts, the simpler is accepted.
12. Scientists assume there is order in the universe.
18. Theories suggest new relationships among facts.

RELIABILITY AND VALIDITY: The Kuder-Richardson formula 20 estimate of reliability is .86 on a sample of 171 students. These students were selected randomly from a population of 2,500 students enrolled in physics courses in approximately fifty different high schools throughout the country. Content validity was established by opinion of experts with regard to the original descriptive outline of scientific processes, and the appropriateness of items that sampled the "universe of situations." The inventory discriminates in the expected direction between scientists, science teachers, and students. The test consists only of those items where at least 75 percent of the scientist sample agreed with the keyed response to each item.

BIBLIOGRAPHY:

Walberg, H. J., and Anderson, G. T. "The Achievement-Creativity Dimension and Class-room Climate." *Journal of Creative Behavior,* 1968, *2,* 281-291.
Welch, W. W., and Pella, M. O. "The Development of an Instrument for Inventorying Knowledge of the Processes of Science." *Journal of Research in Science Teaching,* 1967, *5,* 64-68.

WORD AND SENTENCE TEST OF SPEECHREADING

AUTHOR: Mary Rose Costello

AGE: 5 to 14 years

VARIABLE: Speechreading ability

TYPE OF MEASURE: Power test, checklist

SOURCE FROM WHICH MEASURE MAY BE OBTAINED: See Costello (1957).

DESCRIPTION OF MEASURE: This is a test of speechreading consisting of a word section of fifty items and a sentence section of twenty-five items. The test is designed to measure skill in speechreading of words and sentences and not level of vocabulary achievement or grammatical competence.

As examples, five of the twenty-five items from the sentence section of the test are given below.

5. Whose dress is blue?
10. The clock stopped.
15. What color is Bob's suit?
20. Bob fed the dog and the cat.
25. Father said his new hat cost five dollars.

RELIABILITY AND VALIDITY: The correlation between the two sections is high. The validity was evaluated by means of a serial correlation technique between teachers' ratings and scores on the test. Internal reliability is adequate.

BIBLIOGRAPHY:

Costello, M. R. "A Study of Speechreading as a Development Language Process in Deaf and in Hard-of-Hearing Children." Unpublished doctoral dissertation. North-western University, Evanston, Illinois, 1957.
Jeffers, J., and Barley, M. *Speechreading (Lipreading).* Springfield, Illinois: C. C Thomas, 1971.

ZIP TEST

AUTHOR: Norval C. Scott, Jr.

AGE: 6 to 12 years

VARIABLE: Language facility, reading, and math for migrant children

TYPE OF MEASURE: Locator test

SOURCE FROM WHICH MEASURE MAY BE OBTAINED: For a copy of the ZIP Test plus a manual for the instrument, order NAPS Document 00770 from ASIS National Auxiliary Publication Service, c/o CCM Information Science, Inc., 440 Park Avenue South, New York, New York 10016. Cost: $3.00 for microfiche; $6.50 for photocopy.

DESCRIPTION OF MEASURE: The ZIP Test was developed for use with migrant children of elementary-school age and was designed to (1) assess a child's proficiency on a sequence of behaviorally defined reading and mathematics skills so as to determine fairly accurately the learning level (generally and grade-level book) at which his instruction should begin; (2) assess the English language facility of the pupil; (3) be administrable by any adult (teacher, teacher's aide, or clerk); and (4) take no longer than 15 to 25 minutes to administer. The instrument consists of three sections: one for English language facility, using pictures of stick figures for stimuli; a second for reading, containing a word-recognition list, paragraphs for the child to read, and word-opposites list; and a third section for math with graduated computational problems.

In the Language Facility Section the child is shown a picture of an object familiar to him, for example, a chair. He is told in English or Spanish, as necessary, "Tell me, in English, all you can about each picture." The focus here is to determine the child's ability to *conceptualize* in English. The first part of the Reading Section consists of a word-recognition list, which covers the preprimer to the fourth level. The highest level at which a child successfully reads four out of five words on a line is his placement level. Sample: *big, down, blue, have, make* (primer level). The Reading Comprehension Section, covering the preprimer to the third-reader level, was developed specifically for children who read English words but do *not* comprehend their meaning. This situation is identified by a low score on the Language Facility Section. Sample: *Jose lived on a farm. He worked in the fields. Maria was his sister. She milked the cows. When Jose was done he would play near the fence. Then the family would go to town* (level 2). The word-opposites lists range from the third level to beyond the seventh level. The highest level at which a child correctly identifies six or more of ten word-opposites in a set is his placement level. Sample: *slender, broad, glimpse, rely, quit.* The math readiness part of the Math Section consists of numerals to identify and objects to match. The remainder of this section consists of graduated computational problems in the areas of addition, subtraction, multiplication, division, and fractions. At this stage, indications are that most competent adults can administer the test to a migrant child in 10 to 20 minutes.

RELIABILITY AND VALIDITY: The development of the ZIP Test included three types of validity. For content validity, the Language Facility Section of the test was developed using as stimuli pictures of items familiar to the migrant child, for example, a boy eating at a table. The words in the Reading Section were taken from the appropriate levels of the California state-adopted reading texts (Ginn Series). The content of the Math Section was also carefully selected from appropriate levels of the state-adopted texts. Concurrent validity was computed using the independent judgments of experienced migrant teachers against the ZIP Test results. The resulting coefficients were .89 for the Language Facility Section ($N = 126$), .93 for Reading ($N = 69$), and .94 for the Math Section ($N = 69$). Construct validity for the Language Facility Section was determined by comparing the scoring of this section with the methods used by seven credentialed teachers who listened to individual tape recordings of eighteen migrant children who were responding to pictures on the Language Facility Section of the test. The observers were instructed to list the criteria they used to discriminate between the levels of English Language Facility of the children involved in the taping sessions. All seven of the observers reported that a low rating went to a child who gave a one-word answer, a complete sentence obtained a middle rating, and a high rating was given for a longer, more complex sentence. These results agree very closely with the scoring procedure used in the Language Facility Section of the ZIP Test. The split-half reliability for the Language Facility Section with a Spearman-Brown correction was .93. Test-retest reliability coefficients for the Reading and Math Sections were, respectively, .97 and .93 ($N = 125$).

BIBLIOGRAPHY:

Scott, N. C., Jr. "ZIP Test: A Quick Locator Test for Migrant Children." *Journal of Educational Measurement,* 1970, *7,* 49-50.

Group 1-d

Cognitive Style and Cognitive Processes

ADAPTED MODIFIED ROLE REPERTORY TEST

AUTHORS: Nicholas A. Vacc and N. E. Vacc

AGE: 8 to 14 years

VARIABLE: Cognitive complexity; an individual's ability to differentiate among behavioral dimensions

TYPE OF MEASURE: Likert-type scale

SOURCE FROM WHICH MEASURE MAY BE OBTAINED: Nicholas A. Vacc, Thompson Hall, State University College, Fredonia, New York 14063.

DESCRIPTION OF MEASURE: The Adapted Modified Role Repertory Test is similar in format to the Modified Role Repertory Test developed by Bieri (1955). The ten columns of the matrix contain figures selected to represent the people in a child's interpersonal experiences, and the ten rows of the matrix represent the construct dimensions selected to reflect the kind of dimensions commonly invoked when a subject generates his/her own dimensions. The subject designates an individual for each role title and then selects construct dimensions for each individual. Scoring follows the procedure used by Bieri and others (1966, pp. 190-191) with the Modified Role Repertory Test. The highest possible score of 450 indicates that the subject assigns the same ratings to each role type. Accordingly, the subject would be classified as cognitively simple because of the lack of differentiation in constructing the roles. A low score reflects a more cognitively complex individual, while a high score reflects a less cognitively complex individual.

The Adapted Modified Role Repertory Test is appropriate for use by children because (1) the wording of role titles and constructs are comprehensible to a child reading independently on or above a third-grade reading achievement level; (2) the role titles include persons presumed to be of personal importance to a child; and (3) the list of constructs includes direct opposites instead of antonyms, simplifying the instrument for use by children. The selection of the words for a third-grade reading level was based on the Dolch Basic Reading Vocabulary and the reading vocabulary of two basal reading series, those of Houghton Mifflin Company and Scott Foresman Company.

The test is designed as a matrix with the columns labeled as follows:

Someone you find hard to get to know real well	Someone you would like to help
Grownup you do not like	Your mother
Your teacher	Child you do not like
A friend (girl)	Yourself
A friend (boy)	Example B
Your father	Example A

The rows are set up on a 1- to 6-point Likert-type scale with the following characteristics:

all of the time	most of the time	some of the time	some of the time	most of the time	all of the time

Friendly	Not friendly
Gets along well with others	Does not get along with others
Can always decide what to do	Has trouble deciding what to do
Does not get upset quickly	Gets upset quickly
Cares about others	Cares only about himself
Happy	Unhappy
Does all his work	Does not do all his work
Kind to others	Not kind to others
Can work well alone	Needs help with his work
Fun to be with	Not fun to be with

RELIABILITY AND VALIDITY: The test-retest reliability for an interval of four weeks between administrations was significant (rho = .82, $p < .05$). Bieri and others (1966) reported similar correlations for the Modified Role Repertory Test. Correlations reported between the Modified Role Repertory Test and the Adapted Modified Role Repertory Test for two groups were .51 ($p < .05$; $N = 46$) and .55 ($p < .05$; $N = 39$), respectively. The sequential development of cognitive complexity appears linear and indicates that with maturity children become cognitively more complex as demonstrated by the following test results: grade 3, age 8, mean 223.14, standard deviation 67.21, $N = 90$; grade 5, age 10, mean 217.08, standard deviation 65.45, $N = 99$; grade 7, age 12, mean 208.00, standard deviation 52.29, $N = 90$; grade 9, age 14, mean 185.84, standard deviation 58.77, $N = 89$.

BIBLIOGRAPHY:

Bieri, J. "Cognitive Complexity-Simplicity and Predictive Behavior." *Journal of Abnormal and Social Psychology,* 1955, *51,* 163-168.

Bieri, J., Atkins, A. L., Briar, S., Leaman, R. L., Miller, H., and Tripodi, T. *Clinical and Social Judgment: the Discrimination of Behavioral Information.* New York: Wiley, 1966.

Vacc, N., and Greenleaf, W. "The Sequential Development of Cognitive Complexity." Unpublished paper, 1975.

Vacc, N., and Vacc, N. E. "An Adaption for Children of the Modified Role Repertory Test—A Measure of Cognitive Complexity." *Psychological Reports,* 1973, *33,* 771-776.

BIOLOGY FORMAL REASONING TEST

AUTHOR: William Marvin Bart

AGE: 13 years and up

VARIABLE: Formal reasoning ability

TYPE OF MEASURE: Multiple-choice test

SOURCE FROM WHICH MEASURE MAY BE OBTAINED: William M. Bart, Department of Psychological Foundations, College of Education, 330 Burton Hall, University of Minnesota, Minneapolis, Minnesota 55455. Permission for use is required. Cost: Reproduction and handling.

DESCRIPTION OF MEASURE: The Biology Formal Reasoning Test consists of thirty logic items using biological content with six choices for each item. The items in this test have the following specifications: (1) Each item has either imaginary declarative premises or absurd (contrary-to-fact) declarative premises; that is, each premise in each item must be either an imaginary statement that has no concrete referents and that is beyond S's experience or contrary to a fact that S knows to be a fact; (2) each item has logical connectives being used in the premises; (3) the task for each item requires a simple deduction through use of logical rules of inference in order for the validly deducible response to be recognized; and (4) it is indicated to the student in the test that the premises for each item are to be assumed to be true. The correct response for every given item in the test formed the only consistent and valid formula with the premises given. The testing time is 40 minutes.

   As examples, the first two of the thirty items, keyed for the correct response, are given below.

1. Either auxins are proteins or petioles grow on auxins. If auxins are proteins then petioles grow on auxins. Therefore . . .
    X   a. petioles grow on auxins.
         b. either auxins are not proteins or petioles do not grow on auxins.
         c. if petioles grow on auxins then auxins are proteins.
         d. auxins are not proteins.
         e. auxins are proteins.
         f. auxins are proteins and petioles do not grow on auxins.
2. Whelks are more colorful than periwinkles. Whelks are less colorful than abalones. Therefore . . .
         a. whelks are the most colorful of the three animals.
         b. periwinkles are more colorful than abalones.
    X   c. periwinkles are the least colorful of the three animals.
         d. periwinkles are the most colorful of the three animals.
         e. abalones are the least colorful of the three animals.
         f. whelks are the least colorful of the three animals.

RELIABILITY AND VALIDITY: Content validity was indicated as two high school teachers acquainted with the item specifications asserted that the items complied with the specifications. Modest concurrent validity was indicated as the test had correlations of .22, .51, and .48 with composite Piagetian formal reasoning task performance for three different age groups. Three forms of construct validity were examined. The convergent validity of the test was low and the discriminant validity of the test was low, because the test had correlations of only .38, .46, .33, and .33 with four different Piagetian formal reasoning tasks, whereas the test had a correlation of .33 with a vocabulary test. The test appears to comply to a growth pattern different from a vocabulary test. The vocabulary test mean scores for age groups of 13, 16, and 19 years were 15.7, 18.1, and 19.3, whereas the biology test mean scores were 17.4, 20.2, and 19.9. The test has limited construct validity.

BIBLIOGRAPHY:

Bart, W. M. "The Effect of Interest on Horizontal Décalage at the Stage of Formal Operations." *Journal of Psychology,* 1971, *78,* 141-150.
Bart, W. M. "The Factor Structure of Formal Operations." *British Journal of Educational Psychology,* 1971, *41,* 70-77.
Bart, W. M. "Construction and Validation of Formal Reasoning Instruments." *Psychological Reports,* 1972, *30,* 663-670.

BURGART SYMBOL TEST OF ORIGINALITY

AUTHOR: Herbert J. Burgart

AGE: Reading young through adult

VARIABLE: Originality as a component of general creativity

TYPE OF MEASURE: Visual-written test

SOURCE FROM WHICH MEASURE MAY BE OBTAINED: See Burgart (1968).

DESCRIPTION OF MEASURE: This is a simple paper-and-pencil test offering four standardized versions, as well as the opportunity of devising other equally valid original versions by the examiner using the original as base concept. The measure is scored using either established norms or a tested population as base (the latter insures more sensitive sorting for a given group). Items are "nonsense" visual symbols to which *S* responds with one word. Scoring is based on infrequency of response to each item. Original versions contain twenty items each, and group scoring will yield a sensitive ranking of given group from most "original" through least "original."

RELIABILITY AND VALIDITY: Measure and item reliability is based on extensive item analysis and varimax rotation of factors relating to existing "creativity" measures (e.g., E. P. Torrance, K. R. Beittel, J. P. Guilford, S. H. Parnes, L. Welsch, and C. W. Taylor). Results indicate a significant correlation of this measure with measures of general creativity. Utilization of the measure in subsequent projects indicates its usefulness as an early, simple, and easily administered and scored measure for ranking individuals in a given group. The measure has not proved sensitive to short-treatment projects as a pre-post measure.

BIBLIOGRAPHY:

Beittel, K. R. "Factor Analysis of Three Dimensions of Art Judgment Complex: Criteria, Art Objects, and Judges." *Journal of Experimental Education,* 1963, *32,* 167-173.

Burgart, H. J. *The Development of a Visual-Verbal Measure of General Creativity: The Symbol Test of Originality.* U.S. Department of Health, Education and Welfare, Office of Education, Bureau of Research, Washington, D.C. Grant no. OEG 2-7-078168-1534. ERIC document no. 019801. Richmond, Virginia: Richmond Professional Institute, 1968.

Guilford, J. P. "Creativity in Secondary School." *High School Journal,* 1965, *48,* 451-458.

Parnes, S. H. "Can Creativity be Increased?" In W. L. Brittain (Ed.), *Creativity and Art Education.* Washington, D.C.: National Association of Educators in Art, 1964.

Taylor, C. W. "Analysis of Multiple Criteria of Creativity and Productivity of Scientists." Paper presented at Third Research Conference on Identification of Creative Scientific Talent. University of Utah, Salt Lake City, 1959.

Torrance, E. P. *Guiding Creative Talent.* Englewood Cliffs, New Jersey: Prentice-Hall, 1962.

Welsh, L. *Imagination and Human Nature.* London: Kegan Paul, 1935.

"BUTCH AND SLIM": A TEST OF PROPOSITIONAL LOGIC

AUTHOR: James Ward

AGE: 8 years through adolescence

VARIABLE: Operational thinking

TYPE OF MEASURE: Conventional age scale

SOURCE FROM WHICH MEASURE MAY BE OBTAINED: See Ward (1972).

DESCRIPTION OF MEASURE: "Butch and Slim" consists of thirty-two items that directly sample logical operations represented in the calculus of propositional logic (Piaget, 1949). The measure was originally devised to form part of the experimental version of the new British Intelligence Scale. Its likely virtues, in addition to possessing an explicit rationale from developmental theory, were thought to be control over the logical basis of item content, giving opportunities for the construction of parallel forms, and the possibility of clinical inquiry into responses. Preliminary data were obtained from a sample of children aged 8 to 14 ($N = 406$). As might be expected, total scores showed a reasonably linear trend with age, the most promising psychometric aspect of the items being the power of operations using negation to discriminate older subjects. Statements using conditionals were found to be extremely difficult. Analysis of individual response patterns was interesting and instructive.

RELIABILITY AND VALIDITY: Reliability—Kuder-Richardson Formula 20 estimated reliability ranged from .86 to .9. The feasibility of parallel forms is well established (Ward and Pearson, 1973, and several unpublished researches). Validity—Congruent:

Significantly high correlations have been found with the Watson-Glaser Critical Thinking Test, PMA, and AH4. Also, correlations in the .4 to .55 range were found with Piagetian-type measures (pendulum, balance experiments in Inhelder and Piaget's *Growth of Logical Thinking,* translated by A. Parsons and S. Milgram (London: Routledge & Kegan Paul, 1958). Concurrent: Significant correlations with WISC (verbal and performance) and school achievement have been obtained (r_s = .3 to .5). The items have successfully discriminated gifted children in two large-scale researches. Construct: Several analyses suggest that the items do not form a unique dimensional scale although they load substantially upon general factors of intelligence. In terms of probabilistic scaling theory they form a complex hierarchy (Ward, 1974).

A number of improvements for the measure were suggested in the original source, and these have been incorporated into a shortened version (Ward and Pearson, 1973). In practical use the items are most interesting to older and more intelligent subjects, although some users have considered the introductory procedures to be verbose, and the emotional connotations of a format involving truth and falsity can undoubtedly cause difficulties (particularly to penitentiary inmates). Even so the items have been used and developed further in a number of researches, the data from which it is hoped can be collected and issued in summary form at a later date.

BIBLIOGRAPHY:

Piaget, J. *Traité de Logique.* Paris: Armand Colin, 1949.

Ward, J. "Construction of Logic Items for an Individual Test of Intelligence." Unpublished doctoral dissertation. University of Manchester, England, 1971.

Ward, J. "The Saga of Butch and Slim." *British Journal of Educational Psychology,* 1972, *42,* 267-289.

Ward, J. *The Unidimensionality of Formal Operational Thinking.* Unpublished manuscript. University of Victoria, British Columbia, Canada, 1974.

Ward, J., and Pearson, L. "A Comparison of Two Methods of Testing Logical Thinking." *Canadian Journal of Behavioural Science/Revue Canadienne des Sciences du Comportement,* 1973, *5,* 385-398.

CARLSON ANALYTICAL ORIGINALITY SCORING SCALE

AUTHOR: Ruth K. Carlson

VARIABLE: Originality of children's stories

AGE: Elementary and intermediate grades

TYPE OF MEASURE: Rating scale

SOURCE FROM WHICH MEASURE MAY BE OBTAINED: The scale is in *Sparkling Words: 200 Creative and Practical Writing Ideas,* National Council of Teachers of English, 1111 Kenyon Road, Urbana, Illinois 61801.

DESCRIPTION OF MEASURE: This scale was developed by collecting 500 examples of children's writing from published sources, determining original categories from these examples, and then organizing five rating divisions using 5,000 stories collected from twenty-three intermediate-grade classrooms in Contra Costa County, California. The five divisions of the scale are: (1) Story Structure, which includes five items such as unusual title and plot; (2) Novelty, which includes sixteen items such as humor, picturesque speech, and unusual related thinking; (3) Emotion, which includes four items such as unusual ability to identify self with feelings of others; (4) Individuality, which includes four items such as unusual personal experience; and (5) Style of Stories, which includes seven items such as exaggerated tall-tale and fairy-tale type. Stories are rated for originality on a 0-to-5-point scale only on those items pertaining to the story. Rough norms were developed for 217 pupils using four types of stimuli (fantasy directions, personal experience, pictures, and objects).

As examples, two of the five scale divisions are partially given below.

Scale—Division A. *Story Structure*
2. Unusual Beginning—Beginning used which appears with statistical infrequency in stories written by children at this grade level.
   0—Ordinary traditional beginning.
      *Once upon a time or Once.
   1—Fairly usual type of beginning.
      *One day, one night, one afternoon, one evening.
      *It happened this way.
   3—Unusual beginning.
      *July was nine years old. She had blue eyes, red freckles, and golden curls.
      *When I was on my vacation last summer, I had the time of my life.
   5—Beginning which appears rarely.
      *Do you believe in ghosts? Well, I didn't until this happened.
      *The slow, lumbering mule cart came to a stop on a turn of the bumpy road.
      *Clank, Bang, crash, bang! I finished.

Scale—Division C. *Emotional Aspects of Scale*
22. Unusual ability to express emotional depth.
   0—No emotional feeling.
   1—Little emotional feeling shown.
      *The boy was sad.
   3—Some emotional feeling expressed.
      *I stuck myself, and it stung.
   5—Emotional feeling expressed with depth.
      *Gaity—She heard music which put a gay feeling inside her. Finally, it got to her toes and she started to dance.
      *Discomfort—I felt uncomfortable, sticky, and wet. It was a hot day and night. Bugs were flying all around.
      *Anger—I hated everybody in that black moment. Why did they have to watch me? I felt hot anger. Why did everyone come?

RELIABILITY AND VALIDITY: Three judges rated 868 stories written by intermediate-grade children. The Spearman rank correlations for the three possible combinations of judges were .78, .87, and .89.

BIBLIOGRAPHY:

Carlson, R. K. "Seven Qualities of Original Writing." *Elementary English,* 1961, *38,* 576-579.
Carlson, R. K. *Sparkling Words: 200 Creative and Practical Writing Ideas.* Urbana, Illinois: National Council of Teachers of English, 1971.

CHILD SKEPTICISM MEASURE

AUTHOR: Michael D. Berzonsky

AGE: 5 to 9 years

VARIABLE: Child's tendency to say "I don't know"

TYPE OF MEASURE: Test

SOURCE FROM WHICH MEASURE MAY BE OBTAINED: Measure appears below.

DESCRIPTION OF MEASURE: The test was originally designed to assess a child's realization that "no one knows all the answers." When will children admit that they "don't know" in a questioning situation? The keyed test consists of the following five items:

(*Yes*) Do you think your teacher ever makes mistakes?
(*No*)   Do you think I can tell what you are thinking?
(*Yes*) Do you think that there is any question that you can't answer?
(*No*)   Do you think that I can answer every question that you could ask me?
(*Yes*) Who is the smartest grownup person that you know? Do you think that there is anything that he (or she) does *not* know?

The skepticism score is the total number of correct responses. The test has ordinarily been administered orally on an individual basis, especially with kindergarten and first-grade children. It has, however, been group administered to older youngsters, 8- to 10-year-olds.

RELIABILITY AND VALIDITY: Berzonsky (1969) hypothesized that more skeptical youngsters, who were aware that they did not know all the answers, would be less apt to give nonnaturalistic causal explanations than their less-skeptical counterparts. In a factor analysis of thirty variables on eighty-four first graders, the skepticism measure had a loading of .36 on a factor labeled "causal reasoning" (Berzonsky, 1971). In a subsequent study with forty-one 5- to 7-year olds (Berzonsky, 1973b), the skepticism measure loaded .84 on a factor labeled "social judgment." It was suggested that the nature of the skepticism items (that is, they all concern people) might make it more applicable for problem-solving situations involving people. In these studies, the communalities the skepticism measure shared with the other tests in each battery were, respectively, .68 and .71. The skepticism measure has been found to correlate moderately, but significantly, with raw score IQ: Dominion Group Test of Learning Capacity (.44) and California Test of Mental Maturity (.50). The test has also been found to correlate with some measures of social reasoning, namely, a Piaget-type moral reasoning measure (.87) and a Piaget-type justice index (.50) (Durkin, 1959). Scores on the skepticism index, however, have been found to be independent of social desirability, manifest anxiety, and locus of reinforcement control.

BIBLIOGRAPHY:

Berzonsky, M. D. "Factors Influencing Children's Causal Reasoning." Unpublished doctoral dissertation. University of Toronto, Ontario, Canada, 1969.

Berzonsky, M. D. "Interdependence of Inhelder and Piaget's Model of Logical Thinking." *Developmental Psychology,* 1971, *4,* 469-476.

Berzonsky, M. D. "A Factor-Analytic Investigation of Child Animism." *Journal of Genetic Psychology,* 1973a, *122,* 287-295.

Berzonsky, M. D. "Some Relationships Between Children's Conceptions of Psychological and Physical Causality." *Journal of Social Psychology,* 1973b, *90,* 299-309.

Berzonsky, M. D. "Component Abilities of Children's Causal Reasoning." *Developmental Psychology,* 1975, *11,* 111.

Durkin, D. "Children's Acceptance of Reciprocity as a Justice Principle." *Child Development,* 1959, *30,* 289-296.

CHILDREN'S INDIVIDUAL TEST OF CREATIVITY (CITOC)

AUTHORS: N. S. Metfessel, Marilyn E. Burns, J. T. Foster

AGE: Preschool through elementary grades

VARIABLE: Creativity

TYPE OF MEASURE: Individual test

SOURCE FROM WHICH MEASURE MAY BE OBTAINED: Marilyn Burns, 3858 Buena Park Dr., Studio City, CA 91604. Cost: $50.00.

DESCRIPTION OF MEASURE: The test is composed of twelve subtests divided evenly into "Verbal Tests" and "Performance Tests." Subtests, modeled after Guilford's Structure-of-Intellect factor tests found to be related to creativity in adults, bear the same names in the Verbal and the Performance sections: Sensitivity to Problems, Fluency of Thinking, Flexibility, Originality, Redefinition, and Elaboration.

The six Performance subtests, in contrast to Verbal subtests, require minimal verbal response from the child and may be scored on his manipulation of materials and pointing to hidden figures. CITOC is largely untimed and can be individually administered by an experienced person in less than an hour.

Scaled scores are derived from the raw score for each subtest and are summarized into Verbal, Performance, and Total Scores. Preliminary age norms were developed from a sample of 610 boys and girls 4 to 9 years old from schools in California. All of the state's major racial and ethnic groups were represented in the study population.

RELIABILITY AND VALIDITY: Weber (1968) computed test-retest reliabilities, using 100 children in grades 2 and 3 randomly selected from a larger study group, with a 2-week interval between testings. Correlations of .70, .64, .74, .40, .67, and .71 were obtained for the Verbal subtests in the order listed in the description above. For the Performance subtests, in the same order, correlations were .61, .53, .78, .42, .67, and .68. For the same population, Harsh (1967) determined that reliability coefficients for the Verbal, Performance, and Total Scores were .86, .78, and .84.

While it remains to be determined whether CITOC or any other test for children can predict adult creative behavior, CITOC appears to be measuring something distinct from what is measured by intelligence or achievement tests. Burns (1969) found the relationship between Total CITOC scores to be in the slight- to low-positive range often found in correlation studies between intelligence and creativity test scores, ranging from .11 at age 4 to .33 at age 9. In Reid's (1972) sample of grade 2 and 3 pupils the correlation was .14. The relationship between Total CITOC scores and Reading Achievement scores found by Burns (1969) ranged from −.14 at age 7 to .24 at age 9.

BIBLIOGRAPHY:

Burns, M. E. "Selected Characteristics of a Children's Individual Test of Creativity." Unpublished doctoral dissertation. University of Southern California, Los Angeles, 1969.

Harsh, J. R. *Evaluation Report for Orff-Schulwerk Project of Bellflower Unified School District.* Bellflower, California: Orff-Schulwerk Project ESEA, Title III of the Bellflower Unified School District, August 1967.

Reid, I. F. "An Exploratory Study of the Relationship Between Selected Environmental Variables and a Measure of Creativity in Children." Unpublished doctoral dissertation. University of Southern California, Los Angeles, 1972.

Weber, G. McN. "Analysis of the Reliability and Subtest Intercorrelation of the Children's Individual Test of Creativity." Unpublished master's thesis. University of Southern California, Los Angeles, 1968.

Prepared by Marilyn Burns

CHILDREN'S MIRTH RESPONSE TEST (CMRT)

AUTHORS: Edward Zigler, Jacob Levine, and Laurence Gould

AGE: 7 to 15 years

VARIABLE: Cognitive factors in children's humor appreciation

TYPE OF MEASURE: Cartoons and rating scales

SOURCE FROM WHICH MEASURE MAY BE OBTAINED: Edward Zigler, Department of Psychology, Yale University, New Haven, Connecticut 06510. A description of the cartoons and a manual for scoring comprehension are available as Document No. 8837 from Chief, ADI Auxiliary Publications Project, Photoduplication Service, Library of Congress, Washington, D.C. 20540. Cite the document number and remit advance payment of $3.25 for photoprints or $3.55 for 35-mm microfilm. Make checks payable to Chief, Photoduplication Service, Library of Congress.

DESCRIPTION OF MEASURE: The CMRT consists of twenty-five cartoons, which are shown to each child twice. The first time the child's spontaneous facial mirth response to each cartoon and his judgment of how funny each cartoon is are recorded. The mirth response is scored as: 0 = no response, 1 = inhibited to half or slight smile, 2 = full smile, 3 = laugh. Cartoon appreciation is ascertained by asking the child to rate each cartoon on a 5-point scale, which is presented as five size-graduated boxes drawn on a piece of cardboard. The smallest box is number 1 and the largest is number 5. The child either calls the number of, or points to, the box representing his judgment of not funny at all (score of 1), a little funny (2), medium funny (3), quite funny (4), or one of the funniest he has seen (5). On the second presentation of the cartoons the child is asked to explain what he thinks is the point of each cartoon or exactly what is funny about it. The experimenter either writes or tape records these responses, which are later scored for comprehension (0 = no comprehension, 1 = partial comprehension, 2 = full comprehension).

RELIABILITY AND VALIDITY: The twenty-five cartoons were administered to sixteen girls and sixteen boys. Two experimenters each tested four children (two of each sex) in grades 2, 3, 4, and 5. While one experimenter tested the child, the second experimenter sat some distance away and independently scored the child on the rating scales. The correlation between the two experimenter's total mirth response scores for the thirty-two children was .95. For total comprehension scores, the reliability index was .94. The comprehension scoring system was used for a similar set of twelve cartoons administered to ninety-one children. For the twelve cartoons, agreement between two raters ranged from 85 to 100 percent with a median of 92 percent.

BIBLIOGRAPHY:

Zigler, E., Levine, J., and Gould, L. "Cognitive Processes in the Development of Children's Appreciation of Humor." *Child Development,* 1966, *37,* 507-518.
Zigler, E., Levine, J., and Gould, L. "The Humor Response of Normal, Institutionalized Retarded, and Noninstitutionalized Retarded Children." *American Journal of Mental Deficiency,* 1966, *71,* 472-480.

Zigler, E., Levine, J., and Gould, L. "Cognitive Challenge as a Factor in Children's Humor Appreciation." *Journal of Personality and Social Psychology,* 1967, *6,* 332-336.

CHILDREN'S PREFERENCE-FOR-NOVELTY SCALE

AUTHOR: Robert A. Hicks

VARIABLE: Preference for novelty

AGE: 4 years and up

TYPE OF MEASURE: Trimodal test

SOURCE FROM WHICH MEASURE MAY BE OBTAINED: A copy of the thirty stimulus tasks can be obtained without charge. The cost of duplication of stimulus cards of slides will depend on current charges for such services. Write to Dr. Robert A. Hicks, Psychology Department, San Jose State University, San Jose, California 95192.

DESCRIPTION OF MEASURE: These tasks were developed to measure the responses of deprived and nondeprived 4-year-old children to novel stimuli. Three methods of presenting these materials are used, and the nature of the task varies somewhat depending on the mode utilized. It should be noted that the definitions of novelty set forth in Berlyne (1960) have been followed throughout the construction of these tasks.

Hicks and Dockstader (1968) used a seventy-card test. Each card contained a pair of stimuli, that is, a familiar stimulus and a novel representation of that stimulus. The children were shown each card and asked to point to the stimulus they liked best. By this method of presentation, a score was determined by the number of stimuli selected in each category. This method works well unless the child is given or adopts a right-wrong set. This has happened when testing a given group took longer than one day. This set, of course, destroys the meaning of the measure. To overcome this difficulty, Hicks, Dockstader, and Parker (1975) developed a signal-detectionlike procedure. In addition to the seventy cards used in the Preference Method, 140 slides (35 mm) were constructed, one slide for each stimulus appearing on the cards. The slides were projected on a screen tachistoscopically for an exposure period of 4 milliseconds. Specifically, the child was given a card containing a novel and a familiar stimulus pair. Then one of these two stimuli was flashed on the screen and the child was asked to point to the picture that he had seen. For the purposes of this research, the score was the number of errors in detection observed in each stimulus category. The exposure time used was selected to insure an almost random level of response. A significant disproportionality of errors between deprived and nondeprived subjects was considered indicative of a response bias for a given stimulus category. This scoring procedure is comprehensively discussed in Hicks, Dockstader, and Parker (1975).

Hicks and Azamtarrahian (1973) have modified this task for pupillometric assessment of response to novelty. This method presents thirty stimulus items, that is, fifteen novel and fifteen familiar stimulus items, using a pupillometer. The results obtained were consistent with their previous findings. This method has certain advantages: It does not call for a verbal response, it is relatively quick, and it offers an index of emotionality that the other modes do not. However, there are disadvantages: The apparatus is expensive; the stimulus slides are difficult to prepare; and if hand-scored, the pupillary measurements are tedious. Here it should be noted that the two latter methods require the use of apparatus that is novel to young subjects. Great care should be taken to familiarize the subjects with the test situation before proceeding.

RELIABILITY AND VALIDITY: Aside from consistent research findings, no reliability and validity data have been collected.

BIBLIOGRAPHY:

Berlyne, D. E. *Conflict, Arousal and Curiosity.* New York: McGraw-Hill, 1960.

Hicks, R. A., and Azamtarrahian, G. "The Pupillometric Assessment of Fear of Novelty in Deprived and Nondeprived Preschool Children." Paper presented at the meetings of the Western Psychological Association. Anaheim, California, April 1973.

Hicks, R. A., and Dockstader, S. "Cultural Deprivation and Preschool Children's Preferences for Complex and Novel Stimuli." *Perceptual and Motor Skills,* 1968, *27,* 1321-1322.

Hicks, R. A., Dockstader, S., and Parker, M. "Cultural Deprivation and the Response Biases of Preschool Children for Complex and Novel Stimuli." *Perceptual and Motor Skills,* 1975, *34,* 999-1003.

CHILDREN'S STIMULUS-SEEKING SCALE (CSSS)

AUTHORS: Robert A. Hicks, Suzanne L. Decker, and Janet C. Stagnaro

AGE: Grades 4 to 6 (probably useful beyond this range)

VARIABLE: Willingness to seek stimulation

TYPE OF MEASURE: True-false test

SOURCE FROM WHICH MEASURE MAY BE OBTAINED: The factor-analytic data can be obtained without charge by writing Dr. Robert A. Hicks, Psychology Department, San Jose State University, San Jose, California 95192.

DESCRIPTION OF MEASURE: Two sources were used to generate a large pool of items: existing adult measures of stimulus seeking, and items written in conference with teachers and parents to cover children's stimulus-seeking situations. A panel of teachers reworded the items to conform to fourth-grade vocabulary norms. From this pool the 100 most promising items were selected. This step was taken to assure that the children used in the standardization sample would be able to maintain interest throughout the task. The pool of items was administered to 257 fourth, fifth, and sixth graders. On the basis of a factor analysis of these items and an item analysis, the thirty-nine items that make up the CSSS were selected. The test items are keyed in the direction of greater stimulus seeking. Score on the CSSS is determined by simply summing the number of responses that conform to this key.

As examples, twenty keyed items of the thirty-nine-item scale are given below.

1. I like to go exploring (T)
2. I would rather paint with a brush than use my fingers. (F)
3. When I play outside, I do not like to get dirty. (F)
4. I like to ride my bike with no hands. (T)
5. When I grow up, I would like to take a trip to the moon. (T)
6. It is not smart to climb trees because you might fall and get hurt. (F)
7. I get embarrassed when people sing "Happy Birthday" to me. (F)
8. I would like to be the teacher for a day. (T)
9. Children should be allowed to play in the rain. (T)
10. Before I leave our house to go play, I always tell my mother where I am going. (F)
11. I would like to visit the Eskimos and see their igloos. (T)
12. I would like to go to Egypt and climb the pyramids. (T)
13. At home, I like to do the same chores all the time. (F)
14. Riding horses is OK for cowboys, but not for me. (F)
15. You should do something only when you are sure it is right. (F)
16. Sometimes you have to cheat a little to get what you want. (T)
17. Sometimes you have to hurt other people to get what you want. (T)
18. I like to do what the teacher tells me. (F)
19. I would rather play with my friends than hunt lions in Africa. (F)
20. I daydream a lot in class. (T)

RELIABILITY AND VALIDITY: Using an interval of six weeks, the test-retest correlation for 64 fourth, fifth, and sixth graders was found to be .83. The CSSS scores of the 64 Ss used to establish reliability were correlated with a rating scale of classroom activity, filled out for each S by the teacher. This correlation ($r = .39$) was significant ($t = 3.34$). Using thirty Ss, a correlation was computed between the CSSS and a novelty preference task. This correlation ($r = .38$) was also significant ($t = 2.19$). Finally, it should be noted that significant correlations were also obtained between the CSSS and IQ ($r = .20$, $N = 159$, $t = 2.56$) and between the CSSS and overall achievement test score ($r = .21$, $N = 182$, $t = 2.90$). While stimulus seeking should logically be positively related to both IQ and achievement, it is thought that these are not especially crucial to the validation of the CSSS.

BIBLIOGRAPHY:

Hicks, R. A., and Dockstader, S. "Cultural Deprivation and Preschool Children's Preferences for Complex and Novel Stimuli." *Perceptual and Motor Skills,* 1968, *27,* 1321-1322.

CLASSIFICATION TASKS

AUTHOR: Mary Nixon

AGE: 4 to 8 years

VARIABLE: Concrete operations

TYPE OF MEASURE: Test

SOURCE FROM WHICH MEASURE MAY BE OBTAINED: Senior Advisory Officer, Psychological Services, Australian Council for Educational Research, P.O. Box 219, Hawthorn, Victoria, Australia 3122. Cost: $16.50 (Australian) plus overseas postage.

DESCRIPTION OF MEASURE: The Cross-Classification Task deals with class inclusion: the ability to build up mutually exclusive classes. The S is shown two mutually exclusive sets of rods and is required to regroup them using a different criterion. Since the task consists of six similar items, a measure of the consistency with which S can carry out such tasks is obtained. In each item, S is asked to state the basis of the classification after he has regrouped the rods. The material for the tasks may be used for both the Cross-Classification Task and the Equivalence Task. It consists of twenty rods (each numbered on the base), as follows:

	Blue	White	Green	Red	Yellow
Tall thick	1	2	3	4	5
Short thick	6	7	8	9	10
Tall thin	11	12	13	14	15
Short thin	16	17	18	19	20

The testing session is prefaced by introductory exercises, though a child who does both tasks within a reasonably short space of time will not need to do the introductory exercises twice. The items were derived from the attributes of the rods, as follows:

Presented Classes			Required Classes		
1. Dichotomy based on color			Dichotomy based on height		
2.	"	"	height	"	"	color
3.	"	"	color	"	"	diameter
4.	"	"	diameter	"	"	color
5.	"	"	height	"	"	diameter
6.	"	"	diameter	"	"	height

Rods of two colors only are used in each item. In the first four items, the rods that define the required classes are taken from *one* of the presented classes and differ only in the attribute that defines the required classes. In Items 5 and 6, one exemplar rod is taken from each of the presented classes; these two rods differ on *two* attributes—that defining the presented classes and that defining the required classes. The tester should note carefully whether S produces the required classes and should record the occasions on which S simply repeats the presented classes.

The Equivalence Task incorporates recognition of similarities, discrimination of common properties, and recognition of the relationships between such properties. It is based upon Inhelder and Piaget's (1964) matrix items. Each item requires S to produce a pair of rods equivalent to, or ordered in the same way as, a given pair. The task is concerned with children's ability to produce equivalent pairs, using rods rather than material in which the attributes may not be as easily identified. There are six items in the task, and the number of correctly chosen pairs gives a measure of the consistency with which S can operate upon relationships.

In an analogy like this:

> BOY   :   GIRL
>
> : :   MAN   :   WOMAN

two intersecting classes are involved—sex and age (or stage of development). The analogy can also be described as a classification in which there are similarities of age on the horizontal axis and similarities of sex on the vertical axis. Simple analogies have been established using the attributes of the rods, and S's task is to choose a pair from an array of rods. However, since the rods have three attributes (color, diameter, and height) and the matrix has only two axes (vertical and horizontal), each item is necessarily overdetermined, since two attributes will always display similarity in the same direction.

For both tasks, two scores can be obtained. (1) *R Only:* This is the number of items on which S correctly manipulates the rods; the range of possible scores is 0-6. (2) *R+E:* "E" stands for explanation. The basis for this score is the adequacy of the verbal account that S gives to the questions, "How are these rods different from those?" (Cross-Classification) and "How is this pair like the first pair?" (Equivalence). However, S can be given credit for *R+E only if* his *R Only* score is correct. That is, there are three possibilities for each item: (a) S correctly manipulates the rods and adequately explains the basis for classification; he is marked right for *R Only* and right for *R+E*; (b) S correctly manipulates the rods but does not give an adequate explanation; he is marked right for *R Only* and wrong for *R+E*; (c) S does not manipulate the rods correctly; he is marked wrong for *R Only* and wrong for *R+E*. An S's *R Only* score thus places an upper limit on his *R+E* score. Determining whether or not a verbal account is adequate is fairly easy for the Cross-Classification Task. From 4 to 5 years of age children can verbalize color and size differences fairly adequately, though they tend to mix dimensions and to use idiosyncratic terms—"These are big; these are smallies"; "Down lower; up higher"; "Fat-skinny"; "All red-all yellow." By contrast, determining whether or not a verbal account is adequate for the Equivalence Task is difficult. Ss find great difficulty in verbalizing a relationship, which this task requires. An arbitrary criterion has been adopted: If S states two similarities present in an item and indicates the rods involved, he is marked correct for *R+E* (provided, of course, that his score on *R Only* is correct). For instance, the solution to Item 1 is:

> Tall thick blue rod   :   Short thick yellow rod
>
> : :   Tall thin blue rod   :   Short thin yellow rod.

An acceptable explanation would incorporate the vertical similarity in color (or height) and the horizontal similarity in diameter: "Those are blue, and those are fat" or "Same thickness this way, same height that way." Some data, including frequency distributions of scores and mean scores, are provided for 5-, 7-, and 9-year-olds by sex.

RELIABILITY AND VALIDITY: None reported.

BIBLIOGRAPHY:

DeLacey, P. R. "A Cross-Cultural Study of Classificatory Ability in Australia." *Journal of Cross-Cultural Psychology*, 1970, *1*, 293-304.

Inhelder, B., and Piaget, J. *Early Growth of Logic in the Child: Classification and Seriation*. New York: Harper & Row, 1964.

Nixon, M. C. *Children's Classification Skills*. Melbourne: Australian Council for Educational Research, 1971.

Nixon, M. C. "Classification Skills in New Guinea Children." Education in Developing Countries of the Commonwealth: Reports of Research in Education. *Education in the Commonwealth No. 6*. London: Commonwealth Secretariat, 1973.

Nixon, M. C. "Classification Task Performance and Piagetian Theory." *Australian Psychologist*, 1973, *8*, 85-99.

CLASSROOM CREATIVITY OBSERVATION SCHEDULE (CCOS)

AUTHOR: David A. Denny

AGE: Kindergarten to 9 years

VARIABLE: Classroom behaviors fostering pupil creativity

TYPE OF MEASURE: Observation schedule

SOURCE FROM WHICH MEASURE MAY BE OBTAINED: Directions Manual may be obtained from David A. Denny, State University College, Oneonta, New York 13820. With each manual, score sheets which may be reproduced are provided. Cost: $2.00.

DESCRIPTION OF MEASURE: CCOS is designed to record classroom behaviors hypothesized to be related to pupil creativity. It is a revision of the original Denny, Rusch, Ives Classroom Creativity Observation Schedule (Denny, 1966, 1968). Revisions of the eleven-item instrument reduced the number of items in the present schedule to eight. CCOS combines *sign*- and *category*-type observation items. The observer must categorize behavior occurring during a 2-minute interval. Categories indicate frequency or extent of observed behaviors during the interval. Multidimensionality is achieved by using rating-type procedures in which context and content are considered simultaneously with verbal and nonverbal behavior of both teachers and pupils. A low level of observer inference is achieved, however, through a detailed manual of instructions (Denny, 1969) and through a training program for observers. Experience has shown that 10 to 15 hours of observer training will result in acceptable levels of reliability.

Scoring procedures are designed to yield a total score that is positively correlated with pupil gain in creativity. Behaviors hypothesized as negatively related to pupil creativity development contribute to a low total score, while behaviors hypothesized as positively related contribute to a high score. The maximum total score is 32, plus whatever tallies are obtained in Schedule C (see below), an unlimited item. The CCOS score sheet is divided into three Schedules, A, B, and C. At the end of a 2-minute interval, the observer records a code number for each of the items in Schedule A (category-type) that typifies the behavior occurring during that interval. Schedule B consists of four items of the sign-type (Pupil-Interest, Pupil-Pupil Relationship, Teacher-Pupil Relationship, and Teacher Approach). During the 2-minute interval, the observer circles a code number when one of the symptomatic behaviors is observed.

The titles and code numbers of the eight categories of the schedule are: Motivational Climate (AA), Pupil Interest (BA), Teacher-Pupil Relationship (BB), Pupil-Pupil Relationship (BC), Pupil Initiative (AD), Teacher Approach (BD), Encouragement of Pupil Divergency (AC), Unusual Response (CB). The assessment scoring procedure for the first category is as follows: *Motivational Climate:* Assessed on a 5-point scale, each 2-minute period; from continuous threatening or punitive motivational stimuli; (negative = 1); to continuous supportive, positively reinforcing stimuli (positive = 5).

RELIABILITY AND VALIDITY: The studies of Denny (1966, 1968) and Turner and Denny (1969) revealed satisfactory levels of reliability and validity for the original eleven-item schedule. Since the present eight-item instrument was revised to eliminate unreliable items and to improve objectivity, it should show substantial increases in both reliability and validity. Preliminary communications with researchers using the revised schedule appear to support the hypothesis of increased reliability. Draheim (1973) obtained a reliability coefficient of .99 for an adaptation of the CCOS. Branch (1974), using the CCOS with thirty first- and fifth-grade classes, found reliability coefficients of .89 to .98 and further supported the validity of the schedule by high positive correlations (.41 to .58) with her checklist of physical facilities, sensory stimulation, pupil physical activity, and pupil interpersonal activity.

BIBLIOGRAPHY:

Branch, H. M. "A Study of the Relation Between Selected Classroom Conditions and Growth in Creativity." Unpublished doctoral dissertation. Georgia State University, Atlanta, 1974.

Denny, D. A. *Preliminary Analysis of an Observation Schedule Designed to Identify the Teacher-Classroom Variables Which Facilitate Pupil Creative Growth.* U.S. Office of Education, CRP no. 6-8235-2-12-1. Indiana University, Bloomington, 1966. ERIC document no. ED 11257.

Denny, D. A. "Identification of Teacher-Classroom Variables Facilitating Pupil Creative Growth." *American Educational Research Journal,* 1968, *5,* 365-383.

Denny, D. A. *Classroom Creativity Observation Schedule, Directions Manual.* Oneonta, New York: State University College, 1969.

Draheim, D. "The Effect of the Use of a Handbook for Divergency on Classroom Behavior of Student Teachers, Grades Four, Five and Six." Unpublished doctoral dissertation. Boston University, Boston, Massachusetts, 1973.

Turner, R. L., and Denny, D. A. "Teacher Characteristics, Teacher Behavior, and Changes in Pupil Creativity." *The Elementary School Journal,* 1969, *69,* 265-270. ERIC document no. ED 10194.

COGNITIVE ORIENTATION QUESTIONNAIRE OF CURIOSITY

AUTHORS: Shulamith Kreitler and Hans Kreitler

AGE: 4 to 8 years

VARIABLE: Cognitive contents (norms, goals, beliefs) concerning curiosity and its manifestations

TYPE OF MEASURE: Questionnaire

SOURCE FROM WHICH MEASURE MAY BE OBTAINED: Shulamith Kreitler, Department of Psychology, Tel Aviv University, Ramat Aviv, Tel Aviv, Israel.

DESCRIPTION OF MEASURE: The questionnaire does not measure curiosity but measures cognitive contents that orient an individual toward the manifestation of more or less curiosity in his behavior. The questionnaire includes seventy-three questions referring to norms, general beliefs, beliefs about self, and goals. The questions are distributed unequally around ten core themes related to curiosity, for example, curiosity about new games and about asking questions of adults. There are separate forms for boys and for girls. In scoring the questionnaire, an answer reflecting a procuriosity orientation gets 2 points, an answer reflecting anticuriosity orientation gets no points, and an indeterminate answer gets 1 point. All the points for general beliefs, norms, beliefs about self, and goals are summed separately for each belief type. Then a median or mean is computed for the distribution for each belief type separately. A subject gets 1 point for the belief type if the number of points he got in that belief type exceeds the median (or mean), otherwise he gets no points for that belief type. The sum of the points for the four belief types constitute the Cognitive Orientation (CO) score (maximum 4, minimum 0), which is basic for predicting behaviors (see Kreitler and Kreitler, 1976).

    As an example, the item from Part II of the test, with the first four of the ten questions that apply to it, are given below. (BS) is beliefs about self; (Go) is beliefs about goals.

> David and Joe are twins. They have just had a birthday. For his birthday each boy has been given an airplane which can fly by itself. David plays with his airplane a lot because he wants to see all that it can do. Joe does not play with his airplane a lot because he wants to keep his airplane new.

(BS) 1. Who are *you* like? Are *you* like Joe, who does not play with his airplane a lot because he wants to keep his airplane new; or are *you* like David, who plays with his airplane a lot because he wants to see all that it can do?

(Go) 2. Who do you *want* to be like? Do you *want* to be like David, who plays with his airplane a lot; or do you *want* to be like Joe, who does not play with his airplane a lot?

(BS) 3. If a friend gave you a toy for your birthday, like an airplane which can fly by itself, would you, or would you not, take it apart to see how it works?

(Go) 4. Would you, or would you not, *want* to see what is inside the airplane and how it works?

RELIABILITY AND VALIDITY: The reliability and validity studies are performed on children in the United States and Israel. Internal consistency as reflected in split-half reliability coefficients for the four belief types separately ranged from .79 to .93. Test-retest reliability over a two-week period (N = 90) was .91. Interrelations between the four belief types in children 6 to 7 years old ranged from .66 (norms and beliefs about self) to .81 (norms and goals). Content validity was assured by selecting items judged by different judges as representing the belief types and as relevant to curiosity. Predictive validity is evident from the finding that the CO score of curiosity predicted fourteen different behaviors commonly viewed as reflecting curiosity and laden on five different factors of curiosity, as well as six further behaviors identified as reflecting curiosity in the context of probability learning. Examples of behaviors predicted by the CO of curiosity are given below: duration of observing simple stimuli and complex stimuli, number of different manipulations done with toys, choice to play with new rather than with familiar toys, alternating responses and testing hypotheses in the probability learning setup. Strong support for the validity of this measure also derives from the evidence that experimentally induced changes in the CO of curiosity brought about changes in the expected direction in many different curiosity behaviors. The changes remained evident also in the follow-up, two months after termination of the experimental treatment.

BIBLIOGRAPHY:

Kreitler, H., and Kreitler, S. *Cognitive Orientation and Behavior.* New York: Springer, 1976.

Kreitler, S., Kreitler, H., and Zigler, E. "Cognitive Orientation and Curiosity." *British Journal of Psychology,* 1974, *65,* 43-52.

Kreitler, S., Zigler, E., and Kreitler, H. *Curiosity and Probability Learning.* Unpublished manuscript, Department of Psychology, Tel Aviv University, Israel, 1974.

Prepared by Shulamith Kreitler and Hans Kreitler

COGNITIVE PREFERENCE TEST

AUTHOR: Ernest D. McDaniel

AGE: Level 1: 7 to 12 years; Level 2: 13 to 16 years

VARIABLE: Cognitive preference

TYPE OF MEASURE: Test

SOURCE FROM WHICH MEASURE MAY BE OBTAINED: Purdue Educational Research Center, Purdue University, West Lafayette, Indiana 47907.

DESCRIPTION OF MEASURE: This test is designed to measure the preference of students for performing various kinds of intellectual work on instructional material. For each item, students read a brief passage presenting historical information. They then indicate which activity stemming from the material they would most like to do. Students may choose responses that indicate a preference for low-level intellectual activities such as rote recall or for high-level processes such as drawing inferences, questioning sources, forming generalizations, projecting trends, and arriving at value positions. The form for older children has sixty-one three-choice items. The form for younger children has fifteen two-choice items.

RELIABILITY AND VALIDITY: Reliability of a twenty-item preliminary form was computed by test-retest procedure with fifty-six seventh-grade students, one week intervening. This procedure yielded a correlation of .63, and the longer version should be much higher. Validity of the younger children's form is suggested by data collected with inner-city children in Gary, Indiana. With fourth- and sixth-grade children (N's ranging from 100 to 200) the following correlation coefficients were obtained: verbal IQ, .31; logical thinking, .32; and "unity" in written stories, .33.

BIBLIOGRAPHY:

Asher, J. W., Feldhusen, J. F., Gruen, G. E., Kane, R. B., McDaniel, E. D., Stevens, M. I., Towler, J., and Wheatley, G. H. *The Development of New Measures of Cognitive Variables in Elementary School Children.* Contract no. OEC-O-70-4952, Washington, D.C.: U.S. Office of Education, 1971.

McDaniel, E. *The Impact of Multilevel Materials on Teaching Behavior and Learning Outcomes.* Small Grants Contract 2-7-058472-0018. Washington, D.C.: U.S. Office of Education, 1967.

CONCEPTUAL BEHAVIOR BATTERY: CAUSAL QUESTIONS

AUTHOR: Rosemary A. Swanson

AGE: Approximately 3 to 7 years

VARIABLE: Causal question asking

TYPE OF MEASURE: Criterion-referenced measure

SOURCE FROM WHICH MEASURE MAY BE OBTAINED: Office of Child Research, Arizona Center for Educational Research and Development, College of Education, University of Arizona, Tucson, Arizona 85721.

DESCRIPTION OF MEASURE: This test consists of twenty cartoon-type color plates that depict characters and activities based on Papago folklore and culture activities. Upon presentation of each color plate the respondent is directed to ask a question; produced verbalizations are then coded as statements, noncausal questions, or causal questions. Simple answers are provided for both question forms. To date, the test has been employed solely for research purposes in evaluating changes in question production as a result of instruction in question forms.

RELIABILITY AND VALIDITY: Spearman-Brown split-half reliabilities on odd-even halves have all been .99.

BIBLIOGRAPHY:

Henderson, R. W., and Garcia, A. B. "The Effects of a Parent Training Program on the Question-Asking Behavior of Mexican-American Children." *American Educational Research Journal,* 1973, *10,* 193-201.
Henderson, R. W., and Swanson, R. "The Application of Social Learning Principles in a Field Setting: An Applied Experiment." *Exceptional Children,* 1974, *41,* 53-55.
Henderson, R. W., Zimmerman, B. J., Swanson, R., and Bergan, J. R. "Televised Cognitive Skill Instruction for Papago Native American Children." Mimeographed. Tucson: Arizona Center for Educational Research and Development, 1974.

CORNELL CLASS REASONING TEST, FORM X

AUTHORS: Robert H. Ennis, William L. Gardiner, Richard Morrow, Dieter Paulus, and Lucille Ringel

AGE: 10 to 18 years

VARIABLE: Class reasoning ability

TYPE OF MEASURE: Multiple-choice test

SOURCE FROM WHICH MEASURE MAY BE OBTAINED: Illinois Critical Thinking Project, 371 Education Building, University of Illinois at Urbana-Champaign, Urbana, Illinois 61801. Cost: $.30.

DESCRIPTION OF MEASURE: This seventy-two-item test presents one or more premises (including a class statement, e.g., "All Mary's pencils are yellow"), asks the child to suppose them to be true, offers a possible conclusion, and asks whether the conclusion must then be true, can't be true, or might or might not be true because the child was not told enough. A variety of class reasoning patterns are provided, six items to each pattern.

As examples, five selected items from the seventy-two-item test are given below. The reminder is given at the top of each test page.

Here is a reminder of the meaning of the possible answers:
A. *Yes*   It must be true.

B. *No* It can't be true.

C. *Maybe* It may be true or it may not be true. You weren't told enough to be *certain* whether it is "Yes" or "No."

5. Suppose you know that

The pit is inside the mouth of the fox.

The cherry is inside the mouth of the fox.

Then would this be true?

The pit is inside the cherry.

10. Suppose you know that

None of Jane's dolls have hats.

Then would this be true?

None of the dolls that have hats are Jane's.

15. Suppose you know that

All Xs are Ys.

No Zs are Ys.

Then would this be true?

At least some Xs are Zs.

20. Suppose you know that

None of the fifth-grade boys are on the football team.

John is a fifth-grade boy.

Then would this be true?

John is not on the football team.

25. Suppose you know that

At least some of the books on the table are about stars.

None of Bob's books are about stars.

Then would this be true?

All of the books on the table are Bob's.

RELIABILITY AND VALIDITY: The following total-score test-retest reliability estimates were found:

Grade	N	r
4	71	.83
6	78	.88
8	76	.66
10	54	.84
12	50	.86

The argument for content and construct validity is presented in Ennis and Dieter (1965, pp. V-25–V-33).

BIBLIOGRAPHY:

Ennis, R. H., and Dieter, P. *Critical Thinking Readiness in Grades 1-12.* U.S. Office of Education Cooperative Research Project no. 1680. Ithaca, New York: Critical Thinking Project, 1965. ERIC document no. ED 003 818.

Ennis, R. H. "An Alternative to Piaget's Conceptualization of Logical Competence." Paper presented at the Annual Meeting of the Society for Research in Child Development. Denver, Colorado, April 1975.

CORNELL CONDITIONAL REASONING TEST, FORM X

AUTHORS: Robert H. Ennis, William L. Gardiner, John Guzzetta, Richard Morrow, Dieter Paulus, and Lucille Ringel

AGE: 10 to 18 years

VARIABLE: Conditional reasoning ability

TYPE OF MEASURE: Multiple-choice test

SOURCE FROM WHICH MEASURE MAY BE OBTAINED: Illinois Critical Thinking Project, 371 Education Building, University of Illinois at Urbana-Champaign, Urbana, Illinois 61801. Cost: $.30.

DESCRIPTION OF MEASURE: Each item in this seventy-two-item test provides one or more premises (including a conditional "if-then" statement), asks the child to suppose them to be true, offers a possible conclusion, and asks whether the conclusion must then be true, can't be true, or might or might not be because the child was not told enough. A variety of conditional reasoning patterns are provided, six items to each pattern.

As examples, five selected items from the seventy-eight-item test are given below. The reminder is given at the top of each test page.

Here is a reminder of the meaning of the possible answers:
   A. *Yes*   It must be true.
   B. *No*   It can't be true.
   C. *Maybe*   It may be true or it may not be true. You weren't told enough to be *certain* whether it is "Yes" or "No."

10. Suppose you know that
            Harry is on the football team only if he has his mother's permission.
            Harry is on the football team.
   Then would this be true?
            Harry has his mother's permission.

15. Suppose you know that
            There is an X only if there is a Y.
            There is not a Y.
   Then would this be true?
            There is an X.

20. Suppose you know that
            Mary will be in the school play only if she likes plays.
            Mary will be in the school play.
   Then would this be true?
            Mary does not like plays.

25. Suppose you know that
            Jerry was not asked to play ball.
            Jerry is not home only if he was asked to play ball.
   Then would this be true?
            Jerry is not home.

RELIABILITY AND VALIDITY: The following total-score test-retest reliability estimates were found:

Grade	N	r
5	76	.76
7	75	.65
9	64	.78
11	51	.80

The argument for content and construct validity is presented in Ennis and Dieter (1965, pp. V-25–V-33).

BIBLIOGRAPHY:

Ennis, R. H., and Dieter, P. *Critical Thinking Readiness in Grades 1-12.* U.S. Office of Education Cooperative Research Project no. 1680. Ithaca, New York: Critical Thinking Project, 1965. ERIC document no. ED 003 818.

Ennis, R. H. "Children's Ability to Handle Piaget's Propositional Logic: A Conceptual Critique." *Review of Educational Research,* 1974, *45,* 1-4.

Ennis, R. H. "An Alternative to Piaget's Conceptualization of Logical Competence." Paper presented at the annual meeting of the Society for Research in Child Development, Denver, Colorado, April 1975.

Roberge, J. J. "Recent Research on the Development of Children's Comprehension of Deductive Reasoning Schemes." *School Science and Mathematics,* 1972, *72,* 197-200.

CREATIVE WRITING RATING SCALE

AUTHOR: Jack R. McClellan

AGE: 8 to 12 years

VARIABLE: Creative writing of elementary pupils

TYPE OF MEASURE: Rating scale

SOURCE FROM WHICH MEASURE MAY BE OBTAINED: See McClellan (1956).

DESCRIPTION OF MEASURE: This scale, designed to assist teachers in making judgments when evaluating children's written work, is divided into two parts: Effectiveness of the Expression of Ideas and Effectiveness of the Organization of Content. Each part lists from three to thirteen characteristics of creative prose under nine scoring categories ranging from exceptional degree of reader interest and exceptional development of paragraph (9) to No reader interest and No paragraph organization (1). The top three categories are designated Above Average; the middle three, Average; and the lower three, Below Average. The characteristics listed in the first part generally concern the child's ability to handle ideas and language imaginatively, while those in the second part deal with the development of ideas in an orderly way.

   As examples, the highest-rated categories from the two parts of the scale are given below. Eight other categories on the descending scale complete the measure.

Effectiveness of the Expression of Ideas

Above Average

(9) Exceptional degree of reader interest
   Unusual twist in idea
   Imaginative and convincing
   Unique handling of ideas, individuality
   Writer sensitive to environment
   Sincerity of expression; what the child sees and feels
   Keen observation results in feeling, appeal to emotions
   Inferences used
 Use of vocabulary well developed
   Stimulates visualization, mood
   Colorful expression, vivid; picturesque speech
   Genuine use of similies and metaphors; valid comparisons
   Descriptive words appropriately chosen, sparkling
   Words used not usually expected of elementary children
   Ear for language; cadence; rhythm

Effectiveness of the Organization of Content

Above Average

(9) Exceptional development of paragraph
   Two or more paragraphs well organized, well proportioned
   Topic and/or summary sentences evident
   Each paragraph expresses single major idea
   Paragraphs related
 Ideas complete and well organized
   Ideas coordinated and arranged logically
   Main or central idea evident
   Unusual degree of organization
   Ideas clear and related
   Evidence of a beginning, development, and an ending
   No unnecessary or rambling details; organization marked by conciseness
 Fine variety of sentences used effectively
   Shows understanding or use of complex, compound, and simple sentences
   No run-on or fragment sentences
   Sentences clear and well organized

RELIABILITY AND VALIDITY: See McClellan (1956).

BIBLIOGRAPHY:

McClellan, J. R. "Creative Writing Characteristics of Children." Unpublished doctoral dissertation. University of Southern California, Los Angeles, 1956.

Woodfin, M. J. "Correlations Among Certain Factors and the Written Expression of Third-Grade Children." *Educational and Psychological Measurement,* 1968, *28,* 1237-1242.

Woodfin, M. J. "The Quality of Written Expression of Third-Grade Children Under Differing Time Limits." *Journal of Experimental Education,* 1968, *37* (3), 89-90.

CREATIVITY ATTITUDE SURVEY (CAS)

AUTHOR: Charles E. Schaefer

AGE: 8 to 12 years

VARIABLE: Attitudinal aspects of creativity

TYPE OF MEASURE: Questionnaire

SOURCE FROM WHICH MEASURE MAY BE OBTAINED: Psychologists and Educators, Inc., Suite 212, 211 West State Street, Jacksonville, Illinois 62650.

DESCRIPTION OF MEASURE: The Creativity Attitude Survey (CAS) consists of thirty-two statements for each of which the child is asked to indicate his agreement or disagreement. Item construction was based upon a review of the literature for the characteristic attitudes, beliefs, and values of highly creative persons. Two of the thirty-two CAS statements are filler items, which are included to reduce the visibility of the instrument. The remaining thirty items are designed to measure the following dimensions: confidence in my own ideas (eleven items), appreciation of fantasy (seven items), theoretical and aesthetic orientation (five items), openness to impulse expression (four items), and desire for novelty (three items). The CAS can be group-administered in less than 10 minutes. Hand-scoring of each protocol can easily be completed within a few minutes.

As examples, eight items from the thirty-two-item survey are given below.

1. I like to play "make believe" games.
2. I often act on the spur of the moment without stopping to think.
3. I like social studies better than science.
4. I think daydreaming is always a waste of time.
6. I feel that thinking up ideas that are "way out" or "fantastic" is a waste of time.
9. I would rather think up a picture on my own than trace or copy one.
13. I would rather learn strange new games than play games that I know well.
15. Other children have better ideas than I do, and it is best to follow what they do.

RELIABILITY AND VALIDITY: Split-half reliability estimates have ranged from .75 to .81. A five-week test-retest reliability coefficient was found to be .61 for a fifth-grade class. Validity studies have indicated that children who are rated highly creative by their teachers score higher on the CAS than children with low creativity ratings. In addition, pre- and poststudies of children who have received special creativity training programs show they achieve significantly higher scores on the CAS while control children do not.

BIBLIOGRAPHY:

Schaefer, C. E. *Manual for the Creativity Attitude Survey.* Jacksonville, Illinois: Psychologists and Educators, 1971.
Schaefer, C. E., and Bridges, C. I. "Development of a Creativity Attitude Survey for Children." *Perceptual and Motor Skills,* 1970, *31,* 861-862.

CREATIVITY SELF-REPORT SCALE

AUTHOR: John F. Feldhusen

AGE: Junior and senior high school, college, and adults

VARIABLE: Several dimensions of creative and divergent thinking

TYPE OF MEASURE: Self-report questionnaire

SOURCE FROM WHICH MEASURE MAY BE OBTAINED: John F. Feldhusen, Educational Psychology Section, Purdue University SCC-G, West Lafayette, Indiana 47906.

DESCRIPTION OF MEASURE: The Creativity Self-Report Scale (C-R) consists of sixty-seven phrases descriptive of creative persons. The scale yields eight scores applicable to secondary students and seven scores applicable to college students. The eight scores for secondary students are: (1) Total number of self-descriptive items; (2) Factor 1: Socially conforming self-image; (3) Factor 2: Socially nonconforming self-image; (4) Factor 3: Dynamic, energetic aspects of self-image; (5) Factor 4: Diffidence in self-image; (6) Fluency; (7) Flexibility; and (8) Total. The seven scores for college students are: (1) Total number of self-description items; (2) Factor 1-C: Cognitive complexity, innovation, and curiosity; (3) Factor 2-C: Risk-taking, impulsive behavior, and an indifference toward others' views of the respondent; (4) Factor 3-C: Imagination; (5) Fluency; (6) Flexibility; and (7) Total. There are no time limits for administration of the scale. Typical groups take about 10 to 15 minutes. Since the scale has only been used experimentally, norms are not available.

As examples, the first ten of the sixty-seven items of the scale are given below. If the item describes the respondent, he answers "yes", if it does not describe him, he answers "no."

1. Not bothered by mess or disorder.
2. Like adventure.
3. Affectionate.

4. Interested in others.
5. Frequently puzzled by something.
6. Like things which are mysterious.
7. Try to do things which are very difficult.
8. Appear to be bashful.
9. Able to give constructive criticism.
10. Courageous.

RELIABILITY AND VALIDITY: Test-retest reliabilities for a ten-week period for the college level scales are as follows: (1) .73, (2) .68, (3) .72, (4) .61, (5) .64, (6) .68, and (7) .63. A Kuder-Richardson formula 20 estimate of internal consistency for junior and senior high school students yielded a coefficient of .83. As evidence of validity, the scale has been found to be a significant predictor of hypothesized criteria in studies listed below.

BIBLIOGRAPHY:

Bahlke, S. J. "Componential Evaluation of Creativity Instructional Materials." Unpublished doctoral dissertation. Purdue University, West Lafayette, Indiana, 1969.

Best, W. P. "The Prediction of Success in Nursing Education." Unpublished doctoral dissertation. Purdue University, West Lafayette, Indiana, 1968.

Chavers, K., Van Mondfrans, A. P., and Feldhusen, J. F. "Analysis of the Interaction of Student Characteristics with Method in Micro-Teaching." Paper presented at annual meeting of the American Educational Research Association. Minneapolis, Minnesota, 1970.

Denny, T., Starks, D., and Feldhusen, J. F. "Prediction of Divergent Thinking and Creative Performance over a Four-year Period: A Longitudinal Study." Paper presented at the annual convention of the American Psychological Association (Division 5). Washington, D.C., 1967.

Feldhusen, J. F., Denny, T., and Condon, C. F. "Anxiety, Divergent Thinking, and Achievement." *Journal of Educational Psychology,* 1965, *56,* 40-45.

Feldhusen, J. F., Treffinger, D. J., and Elias, R. M. "Prediction of Academic Achievement with Divergent and Convergent Thinking and Personality Variables." *Psychology in the Schools,* 1970, *1,* 46-52.

Owen, S. V. "Predicting Academic Success in Nursing Education with Cognitive, Attitudinal and Adjustment Variables." Unpublished master's thesis. Purdue University, West Lafayette, Indiana, 1968.

Owen, S. V. "The Prediction of Academic Performance in an Associate Degree of Nursing Education Program." Unpublished doctoral dissertation. Purdue University, West Lafayette, Indiana, 1970.

Owen, S. V., and Feldhusen, J. F. "Using Performance Data Gathered at Several Stages of Achievement in Predicting Subsequent Performance." Paper presented at annual meeting of National Council on Measurement in Education. Los Angeles, California, 1969.

Owen, S. V., Feldhusen, J. F., and Thurston, J. R. "Achievement Prediction in Nursing Education with Cognitive, Attitudinal, and Divergent Thinking Variables." *Psychological Reports,* 1970, *26,* 867-870.

Reed, Cheryl L. "The Prediction of Attrition in Nursing Schools Using Cognitive and Noncognitive Variables." Unpublished master's thesis. Purdue University, Lafayette, Indiana, 1970.

CRITICAL READING DIAGNOSTIC TEST

AUTHORS: Joseph M. Scandura, George F. Lowerre, and Alice M. Scandura

AGE: Grade 3 to junior college

VARIABLE: Drawing inferences from detecting inconsistencies in reading material

TYPE OF MEASURE: Diagnostic test

SOURCE FROM WHICH MEASURE MAY BE OBTAINED: Ann Arbor Publishers, Inc., P.O. Box 388, Worthington, Ohio 43085. Cost: Workbook A, one to ten copies, $1.65 each, ten or more, $1.45 each; Workbook B, one to ten copies, $2.00, ten or more, $1.65 each; Workbook C, one to ten copies, $2.50 each, ten or more, $2.00 each; Workbook D, one to ten copies, $2.25, ten or more, $1.40; Answers and manual, $2.00.

DESCRIPTION OF MEASURE: This test, used successfully in diagnostic testing and training for elementary-school children reading from the third- and fourth-grade levels, is designed to measure the student's ability to use three basic logical inference rules: (1) the rule for "or" elimination, (2) the syllogism, and (3) *modus ponens*. These three rules were chosen because they are extremely basic logical inference rules (the syllogism involves the use of a quantifier and the others do not). Based on the test paragraph he reads, the child circles "true" if the statement must be true, "false" if the statement must be false, and "don't know" if the paragraph does not give enough information to determine whether the statement is true or false.

A sample item is given below.

All pro football linemen weigh over two hundred pounds. Tom Smith weighs over two hundred pounds. Fred Jones is a pro football lineman. Paul Franks is a pro football lineman, too.
1. Tom Smith is a pro football lineman.
2. Paul Franks weighs over two hundred pounds.
3. Fred Jones weighs less than two hundred pounds.
4. Tom Smith lives near Paul Franks.
5. Fred Jones weighs over two hundred pounds.

The instructional materials consist of ten workbooks with five carefully sequenced hints for each logical rule. Before moving ahead, the student is required to work problems of a given difficulty level, with diminishing amounts of help as the instruction progresses. Answers are provided for checking. The workbooks contain both diagnostic and instructional materials and are from sixty to eighty pages long. Each test requires from thirty-seven to sixty-two student responses.

The first three test and instruction workbooks each deal with a single logical inference rule. To provide a further challenge after these have been mastered, the fourth test and instruction workbook combine all of the previously learned logical rules and provide an opportunity for the reader to search for missing bits of information that will enable him to find logical answers. Each test determines where the student begins working on the corresponding instruction. If he cannot apply a rule in the simplest settings, he starts at the beginning. If he can use the rule in some settings but not in others, he starts at the point indicated by the test. To show that he has mastered a logical inference rule a student must be able to use it in the following four ways: (1) to make or detect valid deductions; (2) to detect statements that are contrary to other statements; (3) to detect invalid uses of the rule, that is, to detect statements that may or may not be true but that do not follow from the use of the rule; and (4) to identify "missing premises" (important in detecting fallacious reasoning characteristic of much advertising).

RELIABILITY AND VALIDITY: Overall reliabilities on twenty short subtests were almost all above .77 (to .90). Overall performance on single test items yielded correct predictions on other items about 90 percent of the time.

BIBLIOGRAPHY:

Lowerre, G. F., and Scandura, J. M. "Conceptually Based Development and Evaluation of Individualized Materials for Critical Reading Based on Logical Inference." *Reading Research Quarterly*, 1973/1974, *9*, 186-205.

Prepared by Orval G. Johnson

DIAGNOSTIC-DEVELOPMENT MONITORING SYSTEM

AUTHORS: William Fowler and Nasim Khan

AGE: 6 months to 6 years

VARIABLE: Dimensions of personality and cognitive processes

TYPE OF MEASURE: Individual rating scales, case description, and developmental prescription

SOURCE FROM WHICH MEASURE MAY BE OBTAINED: See Fowler and Khan (1973) or the authors at Department of Applied Psychology, Ontario Institute for Studies in Education, 252 Bloor Street West, Toronto, Ontario, Canada.

DESCRIPTION OF MEASURE: This measure consists of a set of bipolar rating scales on personal-social and cognitive processes organized into six categories (cognitive styles, motivation, object relations, social relations with adults, social relations with peers, and physical state), each embracing from two to six characteristics. The ratings are recorded in a format that permits scoring on either a refined 7-point or a quick scoring 3-point (+, 0, −) scale. In either case the format yields a profile of individual characteristics. Below the rating scale profile are spaces for descriptive summaries of a child's functioning for each of the major categories, a space for an overall descriptive summary, and space for listing specific recommendations for improving the child's care and education based on the diagnostic profile and descriptive summaries. The system is designed for individualizing the monitoring, care, and education of young children in group settings (day-care and nursery school) and at home.

As an example, the six items of the Cognitive Styles section of the measure are given below.

		– 0 +	
		1 2 3 4 5 6 7	
1. Analytic	Overlooks signifi-cant details	_____	Focuses on details
2. Integrative	Disorganized	_____	Puts things to-gether
3. Reflective	Impulsive	_____	Thinks before acting
4. Flexible	Rigid	_____	Adaptive
5. Problem-Oriented	Poor awareness of problems	_____	Perceptive of problems
6. Complexity	Likes simple things	_____	Likes complex things

RELIABILITY AND VALIDITY: Interrater reliabilities for the total scale range from .50 to .71, generally improving with increased use of the scale.

BIBLIOGRAPHY:

Fowler, W., and Khan, N. *Diagnostic-Developmental Monitoring System.* Unpublished manuscript. Toronto: Ontario Institute for Studies in Education, 1973.

Prepared by Nasim Khan

DRAWING COMPLETION TASK

AUTHORS: Helen H. Davidson and Judith W. Greenberg

AGE: 8 years to adult

VARIABLE: Creativity and divergent production in figural materials

TYPE OF MEASURE: Drawing completion

SOURCE FROM WHICH MEASURE MAY BE OBTAINED: Judith W. Greenberg, The City College, Convent Avenue and 138 Street, New York, New York 10031.

DESCRIPTION OF MEASURE: The Drawing Completion Task measures several components of intellective and creative behavior in an unstructured nonverbal context. It consists of eight simple, incomplete, ambiguous line drawings and instructs the child to complete them in any way he wishes. After he completes the drawings he is asked to explain what he drew, and his responses are recorded. The instrument is based upon the Franck Incomplete Drawing Test (Franck and Rosen, 1949). The drawings are scored on seven dimensions that measure divergent ability in a nonverbal task and other components of creativity: originality, popularity of subject matter, spontaneous flexibility, asymmetry, dynamism, complexity, and fit to stimulus.

RELIABILITY AND VALIDITY: The percentage of agreement between scorers for four of the incomplete drawings, using a sample of forty children, ranged from 68 percent to 90 percent for the seven dimensions.

BIBLIOGRAPHY:

Davidson, H. H., and Greenberg, J. W. *School Achievers from a Deprived Background.* New York: Associated Educational Services, 1967.

Franck, K., and Rosen, E. A. "A Projective Test of Masculinity-Femininity." *Journal of Consulting Psychology,* 1949, *13,* 247-256.

Greenberg, J. W., Shore, M. S., and Davidson, H. H. "Caution and Creativity as Correlates of Achievement in Disparate Social-Racial Groups." *The Journal of Negro Education,* 1972, *41,* 377-382.

Prepared by Judith W. Greenberg

DRAWING COMPLETION TASK (DCT)

AUTHOR: David Schulman

AGE: Elementary and junior high

VARIABLE: Creativity

TYPE OF MEASURE: Drawing test

SOURCE FROM WHICH MEASURE MAY BE OBTAINED: See Schulman (1966).

DESCRIPTION OF MEASURE: This is an adaptation of the Incomplete Drawing Test designed by Franck and Rosen (1949). It consists of twelve different simple line combinations of two or three lines each, and the subjects are instructed to draw something interesting using the lines given. Thus the subject draws twelve different completions. Creativity is measured by five properties of the drawings: conventionality, theme variability, physical expansion, form initiation, and elaboration. Since 1 point is given for each of the five properties, and there are twelve drawings, the range of possible scores is 0 to 60. The DCT was administered to more than two hundred fourth-grade students, and the results from this sample were used normatively; that is, if no more than two other subjects used the same line combination in the same way, the individual was given 1 point for that line combination. For further scoring details, see Schulman (1964, 1966).

RELIABILITY AND VALIDITY: The corrected split-half reliability coefficient, devised by comparing drawings one to six against seven to twelve, was .83. Using Chi-square, it was found that teachers' predictions of their students' creativity abilities agreed beyond chance with DCT scores, the agreement being significant at the .01 level. A commercial artist and a nurse with artistic and psychological background were individually asked to arrange twenty-seven DCT protocols in order of creativity. The rank order correlations comparing the orders obtained by the two judges with each other and with the order derived from the scoring system were, respectively, .86, .90, and .88.

BIBLIOGRAPHY:

Franck, K., and Rosen, E. A. "A Projective Test of Masculinity-Femininity." *Journal of Consulting Psychology,* 1949, *13,* 247-256.
Frenkel-Brunswik, E. "Intolerance of Ambiguity as an Emotional and Perceptual Variable." *Journal of Personality,* 1949, *18,* 108-143.
Schulman, D. "Objectification and Openness of Perception as Preconditions for Creativity." Unpublished master's thesis. City College of New York, 1964.
Schulman, D. "Openness of Perception as a Condition for Creativity." *Exceptional Children,* 1966, *33,* 89-94.

Prepared by Orval G. Johnson

GROSS GEOMETRIC FORMS (GGF)

AUTHOR: Ruth Brill Gross

AGE: 3 to 10 years

VARIABLE: Visual-pictorial creativity

TYPE OF MEASURE: Standardized, open-ended construction task

SOURCE FROM WHICH MEASURE MAY BE OBTAINED: 1015 Redway Avenue, Cincinnati, Ohio 45229, or Department of Psychology, Xavier University, Cincinnati, Ohio 45207. Cost of mimeographed materials and postage.

DESCRIPTION OF MEASURE: The Gross Geometric Forms (GGF) is an experimental approach to the objective assessment of pictorial creativity. According to a standard procedure, subjects are asked to make ten constructions (anything they can think of) from a layout of forty-eight felt geometric forms (circles, half-circles, squares, rectangles, triangles) in three colors (red, blue, yellow). An open inquiry ("What is it? Tell me about it.") follows each trial. Constructions are scored for form, name, elaboration (action, color, embellishment), and communicability. These components are inter-related. Total possible score is 60. There are no time limits; most children take less than 30 minutes. The GGF was designed to tap elements of creativity stressed by the theoretical literature (productivity, richness of thinking, communicability, ability to maintain an abstract attitude) and to be attractive and fair to children of varying ages (especially the very young) and SES levels.

RELIABILITY AND VALIDITY: Studies to date (some as yet unpublished) indicate interscorer reliability coefficients (Pearson rs) of .87 to .99; generalizability coefficients of .60 for 4-1- to 6-6-year-olds ($N = 42$) for a test-retest interval of sixty to 110 days (median-86) and .55 for a sample of forty 10-year-old children tested a year later. Split-half (corrected) correlation coefficients are in the .80s. Evidence for validity comes primarily from two independent studies of ratings of children's protocols by artistically creative people. In each case averaged ratings correlated .84 with formal scoring. Average rater assessment vs. formal scoring was .75 and .74. Other validation studies yielded a correlation of .46 ($p < .025$, 1-tail) between third-grade GGF per-formance and seventh-grade art grades, and a correlation of .39 ($p < .01$, 1-tail) be-tween first-grade GGF scores and, in second grade, the number of items made at home (self-report). Scores tend to rise with age.

BIBLIOGRAPHY:

Gross, R. B., and Marsh, M. "An Instrument for Measuring Creativity in Young Chil-dren: The Gross Geometric Forms." *Developmental Psychology,* 1970, *3,* 267. An extended report is available from the senior author.

GROUP TEST OF COLOR/FORM PREFERENTIAL BEHAVIOR

AUTHOR: Edward Earl Gotts

AGE: 3 to 7 years

VARIABLE: Selective attention to color, size, and form

TYPE OF MEASURE: Test

SOURCE FROM WHICH MEASURE MAY BE OBTAINED: Edward Earl Gotts, Appa-lachia Educational Laboratory, P.O. Box 1348, Charleston, West Virginia 25325. Cost and handling: $1.00.

DESCRIPTION OF MEASURE: The Group Test consists of thirty-two items that have been constructed to minimize effects of position-preference responding by young chil-dren. The colors blue and red were used to permit most children with color-defective vision to be tested without separate color-vision screening. A reverse color form is available in which the red and blue solids are interchanged. On each item the child is asked to show (by crayon mark or pointing) which two of three printed, solid-color geometric or irregular forms are "most alike." The test allows for equal numbers of color, size, *or* form responses (twenty-four maximum possible for any one), with each appearing equally often in conjunction with all possible of these competing stimulus attributes. It is also possible to make up to twenty-four error responses (an error is a pair whose only shared attribute is also shared by each with the third form, whereas each of the mispaired forms uniquely shares another different attribute with the third form, which provides a satisfactory basis for pairing). Errors provide meaningful data about random behavior and, in a specially constructed subset of items, about conceptual conflict over nonavailability of form, for form-dominant children. Scoring is accomplished by visual inspection using an acetate template. The theoretical rationale is carefully outlined elsewhere (Gotts, 1973). Individual administration is required for prekindergarten-level children; small-group administration is possible after that.

RELIABILITY AND VALIDITY: Two-week test-retest reliability for color-form preference was found to be $r = .92$. Validity has been examined from several perspectives. The preferences are consistently ordered by chronological age; predictable differences are found between groups of children of the same age but of different social class; the preferential behavior is experimentally modifiable; form attending relates to reading readiness ($r = .40$) and is independent of IQ; behavior on the form-conflict frames was orderly and predictable for form dominant children; and in a prospective study first-grade children who were form dominant at the beginning of school were judged five months later by their teachers to be better readers than children who had been color dominant in preference.

BIBLIOGRAPHY:

Gotts, E. E. "Some Determinants of Young Children's Attribute Attending." *Merrill-Palmer Quarterly*, 1973, *18*, 261-273.

HISTORY FORMAL REASONING TEST

AUTHOR: William Marvin Bart

AGE: 13 years and up

VARIABLE: Formal reasoning ability

TYPE OF MEASURE: Multiple-choice test

SOURCE FROM WHICH MEASURE MAY BE OBTAINED: William M. Bart, Department of Psychological Foundations, College of Education, 330 Burton Hall, University of Minnesota, Minneapolis, Minnesota 55455. Permission for use is required. Cost: Reproducing and handling.

DESCRIPTION OF MEASURE: The History Formal Reasoning Test consists of thirty logic items using historical content, with six choices for each item. The items in this test have the following specifications: (1) Each item has either imaginary declarative premises or absurd (contrary-to-fact) declarative premises; that is, each premise in each item must be either an imaginary statement that has no concrete referents and is beyond S's experience or contrary to a fact that S knows to be a fact; (2) each item has logical connectives being used in the premises; (3) the task for each item requires a simple deduction through use of logical rules of inference in order for the validly deducible response to be recognized; and (4) it is indicated to the student in the test that the premises for each item are to be assumed to be true. The correct response for every given item in the test forms the only consistent and valid formula with the premises given. The testing time is 40 minutes.

As examples, the first two of the thirty items, keyed for the correct responses, are given below.

1. Either James II left France or Anne I abdicated. If James II left France, then Anne I abdicated. Therefore . . .
   - X a. Anne I abdicated.
   - b. either James II did not leave France or Anne I did not abdicate.
   - c. if Anne I abdicated then James II left France.
   - d. James II did not leave France.
   - e. James II left France.
   - f. James II left France and Anne I did not abdicate.
2. The Roman Empire was greater than the Napoleonic Empire. The Roman Empire was smaller than the Austrian Empire. Therefore . . .
   - a. the Roman Empire was the greatest of the three empires.
   - b. the Napoleonic Empire was greater than the Austrian Empire.
   - X c. the Napoleonic Empire was the smallest of the three empires.
   - d. the Napoleonic Empire was the greatest of the three empires.
   - e. the Austrian Empire was the smallest of the three empires.
   - f. the Roman Empire was the smallest of the three empires.

RELIABILITY AND VALIDITY: Content validity was indicated as two high school teachers acquainted with the item specifications asserted that the items complied with the specifications. Modest concurrent validity was indicated as the test had correlations of .10, .59, and .48 with composite Piagetian formal reasoning task performance for three different age groups. Three forms of construct validity were examined. The convergent validity of the test was low and the discriminant validity was somewhat high, because the test had correlations of only .40, .39, .22, and .27 with four different Piagetian formal reasoning tasks, but the test had a correlation of .13 with a vocabulary test. The test appears to comply to a growth pattern different from a vocabulary test. The vocabulary test mean scores for age groups of 13, 16, and 19 years were 15.7, 18.1, and 19.3, whereas the history test mean scores were 18.5, 18.4, and 18.7. The test has moderate construct validity.

BIBLIOGRAPHY:

Bart, W. M. "The Effect of Interest on Horizontal Décalage at the Stage of Formal Operations." *Journal of Psychology*, 1971, *78*, 141-150.

Bart, W. M. "The Factor Structure of Formal Operations." *British Journal of Educational Psychology*, 1971, *41*, 70-77.

Bart, W. M. "Construction and Validation of Formal Reasoning Instruments." *Psychological Reports*, 1972, *30*, 663-670.

INQUIRY SKILL

AUTHORS: Daniel Solomon and Arthur J. Kendall

AGE: 9 to 15 years

VARIABLE: Skill at developing a strategy for approaching a problem

TYPE OF MEASURE: Open-ended questionnaire, or interview

SOURCE FROM WHICH MEASURE MAY BE OBTAINED: Daniel Solomon, Psychological Services Section, Montgomery County Public Schools, 850 Hungerford Drive, Rockville, Maryland 20850.

DESCRIPTION OF MEASURE: There are four items, each of which describes a problem situation and asks the child how he would go about solving the problem. Responses are scored for the number of suggestions that would provide useful information, the number that involve going beyond the immediate site of the problem, and the overall completeness of the approach to the problem. The problem situations are: (1) an engineer trying to decide on the best place to build a bridge across a river; (2) a hiker trying to determine why a "ghost town" was deserted; (3) a mayor of a small city trying to decide where to put a new playground; and (4) a child trying to determine whether his room was made messy by the wind, a burglar, or "someone just fooling around."

RELIABILITY AND VALIDITY: The last two of the listed items were used in a pilot study with fifty-six boys and thirty-six girls. Intercoder correlations for the scoring categories mentioned above ranged from .61 to .92 (within items). Reliability coefficients (internal consistency across items) ranged from .41 to .59. In a later study, involving about 1,250 fourth-grade children, internal consistency coefficients (across parallel items) ranged between .13 and .51, while intercoder correlations for the same items, scored for a subsample of 100 children, ranged between .22 and .84 (with median of .62). This study included all of the listed items. In the pilot study, correlations with a teacher rating of "skilled at problem-solving, inquiry" were .30 with the number of informative responses (across items), .18 with the number of "site-extended" responses, and .34 with the rating of the overall completeness of the response.

BIBLIOGRAPHY:

Solomon, D., and Kendall, A. J. "Individual Characteristics and Children's Performance in Varied Educational Settings." Progress report, Spencer Foundation Project, Montgomery County Public Schools, Rockville, Maryland, August 1974.

Solomon, D., and Kendall, A. J. *Individual Characteristics and Children's Performance in Varied Educational Settings.* Final report, Spencer Foundation Project. Montgomery County Public Schools, Rockville, Maryland, Fall 1975.

INSTANCES, ALTERNATE USES, SIMILARITIES, PATTERN MEANINGS, LINE MEANINGS

AUTHORS: Michael A. Wallach and Nathan Kogan

AGE: Approximately 8 years and up

VARIABLE: Ideational fluency

TYPE OF MEASURE: Test

SOURCE FROM WHICH MEASURE MAY BE OBTAINED: See Wallach and Kogan (1965).

DESCRIPTION OF MEASURE: All five tests assess an individual's productivity regarding ideas in response to a specified task constraint. In Instances, he is asked to name as many specific examples of a class concept as he can. Four class concepts are presented one at a time, and, as in all of these tests, the respondent is given as much time as he wishes to answer. In Alternate Uses, he is asked to name as many uses as he can think of for eight objects. In Similarities, he is asked to name as many ways as he can think of in which two specified objects are alike. There are ten items in this test. In Pattern Meanings, he is asked to respond to eight geometric drawings with discrete elements by naming as many possible interpretations as he can of what each drawing represents. He is allowed to turn the drawing in any way he wishes. In Line Meanings, he is asked to respond to nine unstructured line drawings, some of which appear to be scribbles, by giving as many possible interpretations as he can for what each drawing suggests to him. While both output and unusualness measures have been derived, they are interrelated, and the major psychological meaning seems to be carried by output alone.

The first two of the four items in the Instances Test are:

1. "Name all the round things you can think of."
2. "Name all the things you can think of that will make a noise."

The first two of the eight items in the Alternate Uses Test are:

1. "Tell me all the different ways you could use a newspaper."
2. "Tell me all the different ways you could use a knife."

The first two of the ten items in the Similarities Test are:

1. "Tell me all the ways in which a potato and a carrot are alike."
2. "Tell me all the ways in which a cat and a mouse are alike."

RELIABILITY AND VALIDITY: Reliabilities on the order of .7, .8, or .9 by the split-half method have been obtained (Wallach and Kogan, 1965), and further extensive information on reliability questions is available in Wallach and Wing (1969) and Wallach (1970). External validation has been found regarding ecologically meaningful talented attainments in the areas of leadership, creative writing, art, and scientific work, with extensive information on validity, validation criteria, and related issues contained in Wallach and Wing (1969), Wing and Wallach (1971), and Wallach (1971).

BIBLIOGRAPHY:

Wallach, M. A. "Creativity." In P. H. Mussen (Ed.), *Carmichael's Manual of Child Psychology.* Vol. 1 (3rd ed.) New York: Wiley, 1970.
Wallach, M. A. *The Intelligence/Creativity Distinction.* Morristown, New Jersey: General Learning Press, 1971.
Wallach, M. A., and Kogan, N. *Modes of Thinking in Young Children.* New York: Holt, Rinehart and Winston, 1965.
Wallach, M. A., and Wing, C. W., Jr. *The Talented Student.* New York: Holt, Rinehart and Winston, 1969.
Wing, C. W., Jr., and Wallach, M. A. *College Admissions and the Psychology of Talent.* New York: Holt, Rinehart and Winston, 1971.

INTENSITY OF INVOLVEMENT SCALE

AUTHORS: Walter L. Hodges and Boyd R. McCandless

AGE: Unlimited

VARIABLE: Degree of task involvement

TYPE OF MEASURE: Rating scale

SOURCE FROM WHICH MEASURE MAY BE OBTAINED: Walter L. Hodges, Department of Early Childhood Education, Georgia State University, Atlanta, Georgia 30303.

DESCRIPTION OF MEASURE: This is an event-sampling instrument based on seven categories of behavior exhibited by a subject. These categories range from "unoccupied" to "complete" involvement. Classrooms or other groupings of children have been the usual subjects of Intensity of Involvement observations. Usually two observers observe the same child for 5 seconds, then the next child, and so on until all children in the group have been observed. The sweep of the children is repeated four times so that there are four observations per child. Percentage of involvement can be derived as a general variable for use in studies of various influences on child involvement.

As examples, descriptions of the first two lowest involvement categories are given below.

1. Unoccupied (*Un*): The *S* exhibits no evidence of attention to anything that is going on in the room, e.g., apparent 'inward looking'; aimless wandering behavior, perhaps picking up and putting things down; sitting passively, looking at nothing, staring into space.
2. Onlooking (*On*): Watching the activities of others (including observers) but not involved in any tasks of his own. Watching apparently purposeless—i.e., no indicating of watching in order to learn. Attention to a story being read or told by the teacher is not included here, nor is watching, which is judged to be for the purpose of modeling, imitation, or to determine when his own turn is coming up. Closely akin to *Un*, except that at least some curiosity can be inferred, even though it may be idle.

RELIABILITY AND VALIDITY: Interrater agreements after two hours of training were .56 to .96. These data are typical of those obtained in the study "The Development and Evaluation of a Diagnostically Based Curriculum for Preschool Psychosocially Deprived Children" conducted by Walter L. Hodges, Boyd R. McCandless, and Howard H. Spicker at Indiana University from 1963 through 1967. Brief mention is made of the instrument in Hodges, McCandless, and Spicker (1971).

BIBLIOGRAPHY:

Hodges, W. L., McCandless, B. R., and Spicker, H. H. *Diagnostic Teaching for Preschool Children.* Arlington, Virginia: Council for Exceptional Children, 1971.

INTEREST AND FREE WRITING FORM SB (1966) AND
INTEREST AND FREE WRITING FORM SB (1967)

AUTHOR: Joan C. Barker-Lunn

AGE: 9 to 11 years

VARIABLE: Interests and creativity or divergent thinking

TYPE OF MEASURE: Questionnaire and test

SOURCE FROM WHICH MEASURE MAY BE OBTAINED: Copies of the Interest and Free Writing Forms SB and manual (photocopy only at present) are available from the Principal Research Officer, Guidance and Assessment Service, National Foundation for Educational Research in England and Wales, The Mere, Upton Park, Slough, Bucks, England. Estimated costs are £7.50 for 100 copying forms and 72 pence for photocopy of the manual.

DESCRIPTION OF MEASURE: The purpose of these instruments is to establish whether certain types of school do much more to foster and stimulate creative interest and talent than do others. Each instrument is in two parts: Part I is an Interest Questionnaire consisting of thirty items. The items fall under two factor scales, Creative Interests and Logical/Analytic Interests. The response to each item is recorded on a 3-point scale. Part II is a "creativity" or "divergent thinking" test of six items. The items are deliberately designed to present a new and unfamiliar situation to the child— *similar objects, consequences,* and *unusual uses*—types of items common in creativity tests. Below are examples of an item from *consequences* from the 1967 version and an item from *unusual uses* from the same test; the answers are scored for flexibility, fluency, and originality:

"Just suppose that everybody looked alike. Write down all the things that might happen because of this. You can have two minutes."
"This is a picture of a toy dog." (A child is given 8 minutes to write on unusual ways of changing the toy to get the most fun out of it).

RELIABILITY AND VALIDITY: A subsample of initial Interest Questionnaires of 400 boys and 400 girls was drawn and the responses were factor analysed. This revealed nine first-order factors and three second-order factors. Only two of the second-order factor scales, Creative Interest and Logical/Analytical Interests, were used. Their internal consistencies (Cronbach's *alpha* coefficients) are .70 and .63, respectively, for both versions. The Free Writing part of the instrument has not been fully validated, but Barker-Lunn (1970) gives some evidence that the instrument differentiates contrasted groups of schools (on the basis of teaching methods as well as teacher-pupil relationships) in fostering development of creative interests and talent among children.

BIBLIOGRAPHY:

Barker-Lunn, J. C. *Streaming in the Primary School.* Windsor, England: National Foundation for Educational Research in England and Wales, 1970.

Prepared by Staff of National Foundation for Educational Research

INTERVIEW TEST OF CRITICAL THINKING

AUTHORS: Norman E. Wallen and R. Garry Shirts

AGE: High school and older

VARIABLE: Critical thinking

TYPE OF MEASURE: Structured interview

SOURCE FROM WHICH MEASURE MAY BE OBTAINED: See Wallen and Shirts (1966).

DESCRIPTION OF MEASURE: This measure consists of twelve questions pertaining to a specific topic—sleep learning—of which ten are scored. Scoring is done by comparing responses on each question to examples. The scoring system was developed by having three sophisticated judges rate each of seventy responses on a 6-point scale. These responses were selected by the authors as representative of those given by a sample of fifty-nine high school juniors. The interview requires approximately 5 minutes. The questions can be modified to apply to other topics.

As examples, the first four of the twelve questions of the interview are given below.

Question 1: We are interested in student opinions about sleep learning, you know, the technique where you listen to a record while you sleep. Have you ever tried it? (This answer is not scored.)

Question 2: Advertisements say that you can use this device to improve your mind, lose weight, learn a foreign language, learn to play the piano. What do you think about this?

Weight	Answer
1	Yes, I think it can be done because it is advertised over the radio all the time.
2	I believe it will work because it works on your subconscious.
4	It might be OK; it depends on whether or not your subconscious can be active while you are asleep.
5	I would have to know more about it before I could say.

Question 3: Suppose I were to tell you that this technique is endorsed or approved by the head of General Motors. Would this make any difference to you? Why?

Weight	Answer
1	Yes, the president of General Motors knows what he is talking about.
2	If he has endorsed it, then he has tried it and it obviously worked.
3	It might make a difference.
5	It might; he is smart enough in his field, but sleep learning isn't his field.

Question 4: One argument in favor of sleep learning is as follows: We know that all learning results from information we get through our senses—our eyes, ears, etc. Since this device provides us with information through our ears, it follows that we must learn, does it not?

Weight	Answer
1	Yes it does.
2	Yes, this is a good argument because I have heard of studies that they have done where the person learned through the senses while he was asleep.
3	No, because your mind is not alert when you are asleep as when you are awake.
5	If it can be proved that these senses can learn while you are asleep, then I'll accept it.
6	No, it can go through our ears but we might not learn or remember all we hear.

RELIABILITY AND VALIDITY: The interview was administered to fifty-nine Caucasian middle-class high school juniors and then tape recorded. Two judges independently scored forty-seven interviews with a resultant correlation of .85. The split-half Spearman-Brown reliability was .64. Content validity is supported by the degree of agreement of judges in rating items; a range of 3 or less on all but four of seventy responses. Concurrent validities with the Watson-Glaser and Ennis tests of critical thinking, based on the above sample, were .58 and .54 respectively. The correlation with teachers' ratings after a one-year course in critical thinking in American history was .60.

BIBLIOGRAPHY:

Wallen, N., and Shirts, R. "An Interview Test of Critical Thinking." *Journal of Educational Research*, 1966, *59*, 198-200.

KANSAS REFLECTION-IMPULSIVITY SCALE FOR PRESCHOOLERS (KRISP)

AUTHOR: John C. Wright

AGE: Approximately 3 to 5½ years

VARIABLE: Reflection-impulsivity

TYPE OF MEASURE: Test

SOURCE FROM WHICH MEASURE MAY BE OBTAINED: KRISP, score sheets (Forms A and B), and User's Manual are available from CEMREL, Inc., 3120 59th Street, St. Louis, Missouri 63139.

DESCRIPTION OF MEASURE: The KRISP (Wright, 1972) is an individually administered test designed to identify those young children who are unusually reflective or impulsive in their cognitive style or tempo (Kagan, 1966). It was developed initially as a research instrument but may now be used by teachers of preschoolers and other child-care specialists without extensive formal training in mental tests and measurements, as well as by psychologists. Age and sex norms are given. A revised set is in preparation.

There are two comparable forms of the KRISP, Forms A and B, each consisting of five practice items followed by ten test items. (The practice items for the two forms are the same). Each item is a match-to-sample problem requiring the child to find in an array of similar figures the one that is an exact copy of the standard stimulus appearing above the array. The child's total errors and mean time to first response on the ten test items are recorded as his scores. The KRISP is published with a set of instructions for administration to the child. The procedure is very simple and requires only the use of a stopwatch and the appropriate score sheet. Users of the KRISP are cautioned that the stability of reflection-impulsivity, while fairly well established for older populations, has *not* been proved for children at the preschool level. It would therefore be risky to try to predict from KRISP scores at age 4 the cognitive style expected of a child at age 8 or 10. Nevertheless, it appears useful to attempt to identify those preschoolers who are exceptionally impulsive or reflective, so that preschool teachers and others can select appropriate learning materials and settings for such children.

RELIABILITY AND VALIDITY: Interform reliability *r*s ranged from .61 to .80, using children ages 2 years, 10 months to 6 years, 8 months. While there was no practice effect for time scores, a significant practice effect was noted for the error score (error reduction).

BIBLIOGRAPHY:

Kagan, J. "Developmental Studies in Reflection and Analysis." In A. H. Kidd and J. H. Rivoire (Eds.), *Perceptual Development in Children.* New York: International Universities Press, 1966.

Siegel, A. W., Kirasic, K. C., and Kilburg, R. R. "Recognition Memory in Reflective and Impulsive Preschool Children." *Child Development,* 1973, *44,* 651-656.

User's Manual for the Kansas Reflection-Impulsivity Scale for Preschoolers (KRISP). St. Ann, Missouri: CEMREL, Inc., 1973.

Wright, J. C. "Technical Report on the KRISP." Annual Report of the Kansas Center for Research in Early Childhood Education. Lawrence: University of Kansas, 1972.

LEARNING BEHAVIOR GUIDE (LBG)

AUTHOR: D. H. Stott

AGE: 5 to 10 years

VARIABLE: Behavior of the child in a learning situation

TYPE OF MEASURE: Checklist

SOURCE FROM WHICH MEASURE MAY BE OBTAINED: Brook Educational Publishing Limited, P.O. Box 1171, Guelph, Ontario, Canada. Cost: Single copies $.35; 25 for $8.50; 100 for $15.00. Or see Stott (1972) or Stott and Morgan (n.d.). Cost of Stott and Morgan is $2.00.

DESCRIPTION OF MEASURE: The LBG is designed first for the identification of students who are currently not making optimum use of their potential owing to inappropriate learning strategies. Its format allows it to be used for screening in the primary grades with minimal call on the teacher's time. On the front page are seven descriptions of good learning style. If the teacher can unreservedly check all of these for a pupil, there is no necessity (in a screening program) to complete the whole form. The second purpose of the LBG is to diagnose faulty learning styles with a view to remediation and the prevention of future learning failure.

The LBG was evolved as a result of five years of systematic observation and recording of inappropriate learning styles in young children. Fourteen such styles were identified. Each is embodied in a one-sentence description. If the teacher considers that it aptly describes the child, she is asked to check one or more of three further descriptions that indicate its severity. These may be entered in clinical or special education records on a Profile Form, or on punch cards from the coding provided.

As an example, the first item of the guide is given below.

(A) *He/she is afraid to commit himself to an answer*
   Somewhat: Needs encouragement not to be afraid of a new task, but overcomes his fear if given time.
   Definite: You have to coax every answer out of him; afraid to say the answer.
   Severe: "Freezes" and you can hardly get an answer out of him. Very frightened of anything new or supposedly difficult.

RELIABILITY AND VALIDITY: In a survey covering 250 kindergarten children, good agreement was registered between learning style as recorded on the LBG and teachers' general expectations of learning progress. (Stott and Morgan, no date). O'Neill (1975) found the guide a valid and reliable instrument for assessing improvement in learning style as a result of a remedial program among kindergarten children.

BIBLIOGRAPHY:

O'Neill, M. J. "An Evaluation of a Method for Developing Learning Strategies in Kindergarten Children with Potential Learning Disabilities." Unpublished doctoral dissertation. University of Toronto, Ontario, Canada, 1975.

Stott, D. H. *Behavioral Aspects of Learning Disabilities: Assessment and Remediation.* APA Experimental Publication System, 1971.

Stott, D. H. *The Flying Start Learning-to-Learn and Extension Kits.* Guelph, Ontario, Canada: Brook Educational Publishing Ltd., 1972.

Stott, D. H. "A Preventive Programme for the Primary Grades." *Elementary School Journal,* 1974, *74*, 299-308.

Stott, D. H., and Morgan, G. A. V. *Inappropriate Cognitive Styles as Immediate Causes of Learning Failure.* Guelph, Ontario, Canada: Center for Educational Disabilities, University of Guelph, n.d.

LITERATURE FORMAL REASONING TEST

AUTHOR: William Marvin Bart

AGE: 14 years and up

VARIABLE: Formal reasoning ability

TYPE OF MEASURE: Multiple-choice test

SOURCE FROM WHICH MEASURE MAY BE OBTAINED: William M. Bart, Department of Psychological Foundations, College of Education, 330 Burton Hall, University of Minnesota, Minneapolis, Minnesota 55455. Permission for use is required. Cost: Reproduction and handling.

DESCRIPTION OF MEASURE: The Literature Formal Reasoning Test consists of thirty logic items using literary content, with six choices for each item. The items in this test have the following specifications: (1) Each item has either imaginary declarative premises or absurd (contrary-to-fact) declarative premises; that is, each premise in each item must be either an imaginary statement that has no concrete referents and is beyond S's experience or contrary to a fact that S knows to be a fact; (2) each item has logical connectives being used in the premises; (3) the task for each item requires a simple deduction through use of logical rules of inference in order for the validly deducible response to be recognized; and (4) it is indicated to the student in the test that the premises for each item are to be assumed to be true. The correct response for every given item in the test forms the only consistent and valid formula with the premises given. The testing time is 40 minutes.

As examples, the first two of the thirty items, keyed for the correct response, are given below.

1. Either Laertes dueled or Claudius conspired against Laertes. If Laertes dueled then Claudius conspired against Laertes. Therefore . . .
   X a. Claudius conspired against Laertes.
   b. either Laertes did not duel or Claudius did not conspire against Laertes.
   c. if Claudius conspired against Laertes then Laertes dueled.
   d. Laertes did not duel.
   e. Laertes dueled.
   f. Laertes dueled and Claudius did not conspire against Laertes.
2. Homer was more poetic than Seneca. Homer was less poetic than Ovid. Therefore . . .
   a. Homer was the most poetic of the three men.
   b. Seneca was more poetic than Ovid.
   X c. Seneca was the least poetic of the three men.
   d. Seneca was the most poetic of the three men.
   e. Ovid was the least poetic of the three men.
   f. Homer was the least poetic of the three men.

RELIABILITY AND VALIDITY: Content validity was indicated as two high school teachers acquainted with the item specifications asserted that the items complied with the specifications. Modest concurrent validity was indicated, as the test had correlations of .40, .52, and .52 with composite Piagetian formal reasoning task performance for three different age groups. Three forms of construct validity were examined. The convergent validity of the test was moderate and the discriminant validity was low, because the test had correlations of .42, .54, .46, and .38 with four different Piagetian formal reasoning tasks, whereas the test had a correlation of .40 with a vocabulary test. The test clearly complies to a growth pattern different from a vocabulary test. The literature test mean scores were 15, 19.8, and 19.8 for age groups of 13, 16, and 19 years respectively, whereas the vocabulary test mean scores were 15.7, 18.1, and 19.3. The test has moderate construct validity.

BIBLIOGRAPHY:

Bart, W. M. "The Effect of Interest on Horizontal Décalage at the Stage of Formal Operations." *Journal of Psychology,* 1971, *78,* 141-150.
Bart, W. M. "The Factor Structure of Formal Operations." *British Journal of Educational Psychology,* 1971, *41,* 70-77.
Bart, W. M. "Construction and Validation of Formal Reasoning Instruments." *Psychological Reports,* 1972, *30,* 663-670.

MATCHING FAMILIAR FIGURES TEST (MFF)

AUTHOR: Michael Lewis

AGE: 36 to 70 months

VARIABLE: Impulsivity and reflectivity

TYPE OF MEASURE: Test

SOURCE FROM WHICH MEASURE MAY BE OBTAINED: Educational Testing Service, Princeton, New Jersey 08540.

DESCRIPTION OF MEASURE: The test consists of two practice items and eighteen test items. On each item the child is shown one standard and four comparison figures. Figures are simple line drawings done in black on a white background; five items show animals, five show humans, seven use common objects, and three use geometric designs. In each case one of the comparison figures is identical to the standard, while each of the remaining figures differs from the standard in some detail. The child is first shown the set of comparison figures and is asked to look in turn at each figure. He is then given the standard and must point to the one figure among the four that is identical to it. Latency to first choice and number of errors (to a maximum of two per item) are recorded. Feedback on errors is given after the first error for an item, but the child's second choice is accepted regardless of accuracy. Testing time is about 10 minutes. The test is not difficult to administer but requires accurate use of a stopwatch, careful avoidance of giving the child cues as to which of the alternatives is correct, and establishment of a rhythm in item presentation, which assures that the instruction is completed, the standard presented, and the stopwatch started, all simultaneously.

RELIABILITY AND VALIDITY: Matching Familiar Figures test errors showed significant relations to measures of intellectual competence and achievement, in other words, correlating −.42 with scores on a preschool inventory. They were associated with both verbal and nonverbal indices, correlating, for example, −.43 with both the Peabody Picture Vocabulary Test, Form A, and the Johns Hopkins Perceptual Test (whose format is virtually identical to that of MFF). These correlations fall within the range previously reported for error-IQ association in other studies (Ward, 1972).

BIBLIOGRAPHY:

Lewis, M., Rausch, M., Golberg, S., and Dodd, C. "Error Response Time and IQ: Sex Differences in the Cognitive Style of Preschool Children." *Perceptual and Motor Skills,* 1968, *26,* 563-568.

Ward, W. C. Matching Familiar Figures Test. Technical Report 11 in the series, "Disadvantaged Children and Their First School Experiences," prepared for Project Head Start. Washington, D.C.: U.S. Office of Education, Department of Health, Education and Welfare, 1972.

Prepared by Michael Lewis and William A. Ward

MAWS' ABOUT MYSELF SCALE

AUTHORS: Wallace H. Maw and Ethel W. Maw

AGE: Grades 4 to 6

VARIABLE: Curiosity

TYPE OF MEASURE: Rating scale

SOURCE FROM WHICH MEASURE MAY BE OBTAINED: See Maw and Maw (1968).

DESCRIPTION OF MEASURE: The Maws' About Myself Scale consists of forty-one items that were found to differentiate between high- and low-curiosity children. The items were selected to give information on behavior and attitudes that logically seemed related to curiosity. The children are told that there are no right or wrong answers, and that the best answer for any item is what they believe is true about themselves. Each response category has been rated so that the scoring for "never," "sometimes," "often," and "always" may vary from item to item.

As examples, the first ten of the forty-one items with their score weights are given below.

1. I like to explore strange places.
2. If a grownup says something, I believe it.
3. When I see a neighbor digging in his yard, I wonder what he is doing.
4. When someone talks about strange things, I want to know more about them.
5. I question things that I read or see.
6. When there is something new in the room, I notice it right away.
7. I like to find out how things work.
8. I make up my mind very quickly.
9. I keep my hands clean.
10. I keep away from strange and unusual things.

RELIABILITY AND VALIDITY: An estimate of reliability of the self-rating instrument was obtained with 158 white suburban fifth-grade public-school children. The split-half reliability was .91, using the first forty items and the Spearman-Brown correction formula. Using the same sample, which had been divided into high- and low-curiosity groups according to combined teacher and peer ratings, the Maws' About Myself Scale discriminated between the two groups at the .005 level.

BIBLIOGRAPHY:

Maw, W. H., and Maw, E. W. "Self-Appraisal of Curiosity." *Journal of Educational Research,* 1968, *61*, 462-466.

MEANS-ENDS PROBLEM-SOLVING (MEPS) PROCEDURE

AUTHORS: Jerome J. Platt and George Spivack

AGE: Short scale: grade 6 to adult; full scale: high school to adult

VARIABLE: Problem-solving cognition

TYPE OF MEASURE: Content-analysis system

SOURCE FROM WHICH MEASURE MAY BE OBTAINED: Division of Research and Evaluation, Department of Mental Health Sciences, Hahnemann Medical College and Hospital, 314 North Broad Street, Philadelphia, Pennsylvania 19102. Copy of 1971 manual and scoring procedure available without charge until supply is exhausted. Copy of 1974 revision: $3.50 per copy (approximately 125 pages). Both include copy of instrument and score recording sheets.

DESCRIPTION OF MEASURE: The Means-Ends Procedure is a measure of the extent to which the subject, when presented with a story situation involving an aroused need and the resolution of the problem (satisfying that need), is capable of conceptualizing appropriate and effective means of reaching the problem resolution stage of the story. There are separate forms for males and females. Each of the nine stories is designed to represent a real-life problem situation. The stories deal with a number of different content areas. Although most stories deal with interpersonal themes, some also represent impersonal themes. Each story has a beginning in which a need is aroused for the protagonist and an ending in which the hero succeeds in satisfying his need, but no middle. The child is instructed that the examiner is interested in his imagination, that the child is going to be given the beginning and the end of each of a number of stories, and that the task is to make up the middle of each story. The first story is as follows: "Mrs. A. was listening to the people speak at a meeting about how to make things better in her neighborhood. She wanted to say something important and have a chance to be a leader, too. The story ends with her being elected leader and presenting a speech. You begin the story at the meeting where she wanted to have a chance to be a leader."

The stories are scored for the number of instrumental acts (means) given by the subject that enable the hero to reach the stated goal or to overcome obstacles to his doing so. Individual story scores are summed to provide a single total score. A second score, in the form of a ratio, is derived by dividing the total number of relevant problem-solving means by the total number of responses given by an individual. The latter number includes responses irrelevant to the problem or ineffective in reaching the resolution stage of the problem, as well as relevant means.

RELIABILITY AND VALIDITY: In several studies, MEPS scores have consistently differentiated criterion groups of adjusted and disturbed preadolescents, adolescents, and adults. The MEPS is not a measure of adjustment, however, since it has only minimal relationship to paper-and-pencil tests of this variable. Rather, it measures an important cognitive antecedent of adjustment. The nine MEPS stories have been factor-analyzed and shown to have a single underlying dimension. Spearman-Brown and Kuder-Richardson formula 20 coefficients of reliability averaged .82. Test-retest reliability coefficients range from .43 for delinquent adolescents to .64 for college males. Substantial validational and background data and norms, together with the scoring procedure, are available in the 1975 revision of the manual (Platt and Spivack, 1975).

BIBLIOGRAPHY:

Platt, J. J., and Spivack, G. "Real-Life Problem-Solving Thinking in Neuropsychiatric Patients and Controls." Paper presented at the Eastern Psychological Association meeting. Atlantic City, New Jersey, April 1970.

Platt, J. J., and Spivack, G. "Content Analysis of Real-Life Problem-Solving Thinking in Psychiatric Patients and Controls." Paper presented at Eastern Psychological Association meeting. Boston, Massachusetts, 1972.

Platt, J. J., and Spivack, G. "Problem-Solving Thinking of Psychiatric Patients." *Journal of Consulting and Clinical Psychology,* 1972, *39,* 148-151.

Platt, J. J., and Spivack, G. "Social Competence and Effective Problem-Solving Thinking in Psychiatric Patients." *Journal of Clinical Psychology,* 1972, *28,* 3-5.

Platt, J. J., and Spivack, G. "Studies in Problem-Solving Thinking of Psychiatric Patients: (I) Patient-Control Differences; (II) Factorial Structure of Problem-Solving Thinking." Paper presented at American Psychological Association meeting. Montreal, Quebec, Canada, 1973. In *Proceedings, 81st Annual Convention of the American Psychological Association,* 1973, *8,* 461-62.

Platt, J. J., and Spivack, G. *Factor Analytic Dimensions of Real-Life Problem-Solving Thinking.* Unpublished manuscript. Department of Mental Health Sciences, Hahnemann Medical College and Hospital, Philadelphia, Pennsylvania, 1973.

Platt, J. J., and Spivack, G. "Performance in Important Areas of Life as a Source of Positive Self-Regard." Paper presented at American Psychological Association meeting. Montreal, Quebec, Canada, 1973. In *Proceedings, 81st Annual Convention of the American Psychological Association,* 1973, *8,* 235-236.

Platt, J. J., and Spivack, G. "Means of Solving Real-Life Problems: I. Psychiatric Patients Versus Controls, and Cross-Cultural Comparisons of Normal Females." *Journal of Community Psychology,* 1974, *2,* 45-48.

Platt, J. J., and Spivack, G. *Means-Ends Problem-Solving Procedure Manual,* 1975 revision. Philadelphia, Pennsylvania: Hahnemann Medical College and Hospital, 1975.

Platt, J. J., and Spivack, G. "Unidimensionality of the Means-Ends Problem-Solving (MEPS) Procedure." *Journal of Clinical Psychology,* 1975, *43,* 279.

Platt, J. J., Spivack, G., Altman, N., Altman, D., and Peizer, S. B. "Adolescent Problem-Solving Thinking." *Journal of Consulting and Clinical Psychology* (in press).

Platt, J. J., Spivack, G., and Bloom, M. *Means-Ends Problem-Solving Procedure (MEPS): Manual and Tentative Norms.* Department of Mental Health Sciences, Hahnemann Medical College and Hospital, Philadelphia, Pennsylvania, 1971.

Platt, J. J., Scure, W. C., and Hannon, J. R. "Problem-Solving Thinking of Youthful Incarcerated Heroin Addicts." *Journal of Community Psychology,* 1973, *1,* 278-281.

Platt, J. J., and Siegel, J. M. *MMPI Characteristics of Good and Poor Social Problem-Solvers Among Psychiatric Patients.* Unpublished manuscript.

Platt, J. J., Siegel, J. M., and Spivack, G. "Do Psychiatric Patients and Normals See the Same Solutions as Effective in Solving Interpersonal Problems?" *Journal of Consulting and Clinical Psychology,* 1975, *43,* 279.

Siegel, J. M., Platt, J. J., and Spivack, G. "Means of Solving Real-Life Problems: II: Do Professionals and Laymen See the Same Solutions as Effective in Solving Problems?" *Journal of Community Psychology,* 1974, *2,* 49-50.

METAPHORIC CAPACITY: THE ABILITY
TO MAKE CROSS-MODAL MATCHES

AUTHOR: Howard Gardner

AGE: 3½ to 19 years

VARIABLE: Metaphoric capacity

TYPE OF MEASURE: Test

SOURCE FROM WHICH MEASURE MAY BE OBTAINED: See Gardner (1974).

DESCRIPTION OF MEASURE: Metaphoric capacity is operationalized as the ability to project in an appropriate manner sets of antonymous or "polar" adjectives whose literal denotation within a *domain* (sensory modality or other coherent system) is known onto a domain where they are not ordinarily employed. By drawing from a variety of domains, a large collection of potential metaphors was obtained. This procedure ensured that the subjects' capacities to appreciate "fresh" (as opposed to "established") metaphors would be ascertained. The domains include a verbal description (metaphor strictly construed) and elements drawn from various sense modalities (metaphor defined as above). Five pairs of polar adjectives are mapped onto diverse domains by the subjects: (1) visual (color); (2) visual-physiognomic (facial expressions), auditory (pitches), tactile (objects felt while blindfolded), verbal-kinesthetic (a general bodily feeling expressed in words); and (3) abstract lines. Subjects were always probed for the reasons for their selections. The table below presents the stimuli used in the test.

Stimuli in Metaphor-Modality Test

Modalities	Target Words				
	Cold/Warm	Hard/Soft	Happy/Sad	Loud/Quiet	Light/Dark
Visual-color	Blue/red	Raw umber (brown)/ blue-gray	Yellow-orange/ violet/blue	Lemon-yellow/spring green	Literal
Visual-physiognomic (face)	Blank/angry	Frown/smile	Literal	Upset/pensive	Happy/eyes looking down
Visual-abstract	Rectangular/ ovoid	Triangle of straight lines/triangle of loops	Soft wavy curves ("birds flying")/ jagged curves (three-cornered hats)	Dense thick lines/sparse thin lines	Upside-down tripod/ tripod
Auditory	Staccato/ legato	Triangle/ recorder	Major triad/ minor triad	Literal	High C/ low C
Tactile	Metal/wood	Literal	Small pieces of clay/one lump of clay	Jacks/Ping-Pong ball	Mild sandpaper/ abrasive sandpaper
Verbal-kinesthetic	Literal ("ice/ fire")	"In bed with a tummy ache"/ "sleeping soundly"	"A bright morning"/ "a cloudy afternoon"	"Playing on a jungle gym"/ "painting at an easel"	"Getting lots of presents on your birthday"/ "getting no presents on your birthday"

Source: Gardner (1974). Reprinted by permission of The Society for Research in Child Development, Inc.

RELIABILITY AND VALIDITY: A 2×4 analysis of variance indicated that there was significant effect of sex and no interaction but that there was a significant difference across ages, $F(3,93) = 44.6$, $p < .01$. With the exception of three preschool subjects who scored at or below the chance level, subjects received relatively high scores. There were significant differences in the number of correct answers among all the age groups except for the oldest two groups, whose scores were virtually identical.

BIBLIOGRAPHY:

Asch, S., and Nerlove, H. "The Development of Double Function Terms in Children: An Exploratory Study." In B. Kaplan and S. Wapner (Eds.), *Perspectives in Psychological Theory*. New York: International Universities Press, 1960.

Chukovsky, K. *From Two to Five*. Berkeley: University of California Press, 1963.

Clark, E. "On the Child's Acquisition of Antonymns in Two Semantic Fields." *Journal of Verbal Learning and Verbal Behavior*, 1972, *11*, 750-758.

Gardner, H. *The Arts and Human Development*. New York: Wiley, 1973.

Gardner, H. "Metaphor and Modalities: How Children Project Polar Adjectives onto Diverse Domains." *Child Development*, 1974, *45*, 84-91.

Gardner, H., Kircher, M., Winner, E., and Perkins, D. "Children's Metaphoric Productions and Preferences." *Journal of Child Language*, 1975, *2*, 125-141.

Prepared by Ellen Winner

NEURO-DEVELOPMENTAL OBSERVATION (NDO)

AUTHORS: Mark N. Ozer and H. Burtt Richardson, Jr.

AGE: 5 to 8 years

VARIABLE: Learning problems

TYPE OF MEASURE: Structured interaction

SOURCE FROM WHICH MEASURE MAY BE OBTAINED: For information concerning training: Mark N. Ozer, Director, Program for Learning Studies, 2125 13th Street N.W., Washington, D.C. 20009.

DESCRIPTION OF MEASURE: Prototype tasks have been selected to serve as a context for demonstration and involvement of child, parents, and teachers in exploring a number of strategies by which a child with learning problems may experience success. The strategies include the use of programing a variety of input modes and the use of focusing to limit the number of stimuli available at any one time. The feedback aspects illustrated deal with the quality of affinity with the child, the intensity or frequency of feedback on the part of the adult, and the degree to which power is increasingly shared in the interaction. The principle is to simulate the process of child development in this 15-minute interaction in order to highlight and enhance awareness of some simple approaches that are directly applicable by the individuals involved.

RELIABILITY AND VALIDITY: The specific training of the individual carrying out this diagnostic procedure is accomplished in about 16 hours to the point of 90 percent reliability in administration and scoring.

BIBLIOGRAPHY:

Ozer, M. N. "The Use of Operant Conditioning in the Evaluation of Children with Learning Problems." *Clinical Proceedings, Children's Hospital of the District of Columbia*, 1966, *22*, 235.

Ozer, M. N. "The Neurological Evaluation of School-Age Children." *Journal of Learning Disabilities*, 1968, *1*, 84.

Ozer, M. N., and Richardson, H. B., Jr. "The Diagnostic Evaluation of Children with Learning Problems: A Communication Process." *Journal of Childhood Education International*, 1972, *48*, 244-247.

ORDERING TASKS

AUTHORS: Barbara J. Brandes and Susan Rindler

AGE: 10 to 14 years

VARIABLE: Ability to logically sequence tasks leading to a goal

TYPE OF MEASURE: Performance test

SOURCE FROM WHICH MEASURE MAY BE OBTAINED: Research for Better Schools, Inc., Public Information Office, 1700 Market Street, Philadelphia, Pennsylvania 19103. Provided at cost.

DESCRIPTION OF MEASURE: Ordering Tasks tests the student's ability to place in correct time sequence the tasks that must be performed to attain a specified goal. The student is given a set of four envelopes. Each envelope has printed on it a statement of a hypothetical goal. Inside each envelope is a set of six cards, each describing one task that would have to be accomplished to attain the goal. The student is instructed to arrange the cards in the correct sequence for performing the tasks. The test is scored by comparing the student's order with the correct order. A perfect match between the student's order and the correct order earns a maximum score of zero. Discrepancies between the two orders are penalized by the total number of position deviations for each card. An example is given below.

Correct Order: A   B   C   D   E   F

Student's Order: B   A   C   F   E   D

The student places card A one position away from its correct position. This carries a penalty of 1 point. The same is true for card B. Card C is in the correct position and carries no penalty. Card F is penalized by 2 points because the student places it two positions away from its correct position. In this example, the student would be penalized a total of 6 points. Penalty points are summed over the four goals to yield the student's total score.

RELIABILITY AND VALIDITY: None reported.

BIBLIOGRAPHY:

Brandes, B. J. *Achievement Competence Training: Field Test and Evaluation.* Philadelphia, Pennsylvania: Research for Better Schools, Inc., 1974.

PAULUS CONDITIONAL-REASONING TEST, FORM Z (ASSESSING)

AUTHOR: Dieter H. Paulus

AGE: 12 to 16 years (approximate)

VARIABLE: Conditional (deductive) reasoning

TYPE OF MEASURE: Multiple-choice test

SOURCE FROM WHICH MEASURE MAY BE OBTAINED: Dieter H. Paulus, U-64, Department of Educational Psychology, University of Connecticut, Storrs, Connecticut 06268.

DESCRIPTION OF MEASURE: This test evaluates knowledge of six principles of conditional (if . . . then) reasoning over three content dimensions. Each principle is evaluated by ten items; on each item the subject is presented with some information he is to assume to be true. The subject must then determine if a conclusion necessarily follows from this information. Operational definitions for "mastery" of a principle are provided. Content included is neutral, abstract, and suggestive. A subscale score for "negation" may also be obtained.

As examples, six items illustrating in order the six principles of conditional reasoning are given below.

1. Suppose you know that
   If Joan goes to the museum, then she will meet her friend Sue.
   Today, Joan is going to the museum.
   Then would this be true?
   Today, Joan will meet her friend Sue.
2. Suppose you know that
   If the shirt is green, then I will not wear it.
   I will not wear the shirt.
   Then would this be true?
   The shirt is not green.

22. Suppose you know that
   If the shoes are brown, then they belong to Mary.
   The shoes are not brown.
   Then would this be true?
   The shoes do not belong to Mary.
23. Suppose you know that
   If the car is black, then it is a police car.
   The car is not a police car.
   Then would this be true?
   The car is not black.
24. Suppose you know that
   If there is a flook, then there is a rkonk.
   If there is a rdonk, then there is an utillop.
   Then would this be true?
   If there is a flook, then there is not an utillop.
32. Suppose you know that
   If there is an X, then there is a Y.
   Then would this be true?
   If there is not a Y, then there is an X.

RELIABILITY AND VALIDITY: Kuder-Richardson formula 20 reliability estimates for the six principle subscales range from .64 to .72. Reliability estimates increase with the chronological age of subjects. Item difficulty and discrimination indices fall within acceptable ranges. Original test construction procedures assure a very high level of content and/or face validity. Correlations of test scores with other familiar measures strongly support the instrument's construct validity. Some supportive factor-analytic data are also available.

BIBLIOGRAPHY:

Berzonsky, M. D., and Ondrako, M. A. "Cognitive Style and Logical Deductive Reasoning." *Journal of Experimental Education,* 1974, *43,* 18-24.

Diffley, W. J. "Deductive Reasoning in the Inner City: A One-Hundred Classroom Experiment." Unpublished doctoral dissertation. University of Connecticut, Storrs, 1971.

Paulus, D. H. "A Study of Children's Abilities to Deduce and to Judge Deductions." Unpublished doctoral dissertation. Cornell University, Ithaca, New York, 1967.

Roberge, J. J., and Paulus, D. H. "Developmental Patterns for Children's Class and Conditional Reasoning Abilities." *Developmental Psychology,* 1971, *4,* 191-200.

PENNSYLVANIA ASSESSMENT OF
CREATIVE TENDENCY (PACT)

AUTHOR: Thomas J. Rookey

AGE: 9 to 14 years

VARIABLE: Creative tendency

TYPE OF MEASURE: Likert-type scale

SOURCE FROM WHICH MEASURE MAY BE OBTAINED: Norms-Technical Manual available from Thomas J. Rookey, Educational Development Center, East Stroudsburg State College, East Stroudsburg, Pennsylvania 18301.

DESCRIPTION OF MEASURE: The Pennsylvania Assessment of Creative Tendency (PACT) is an attitude inventory. Subjects respond on a 5-point scale from "strongly agree" to "strongly disagree" with each item. Conceptually, PACT is based upon three assumptions: (1) There is such a thing as a student potential for creative output, (2) there are events that affect creativity, and (3) there are characteristics that are common to creative production, whether the product be tangible or ideational. To utilize or define a mode of measurement, creativity was defined as the conception by an individual of an event or relationship which, in the experience of that individual, did not previously exist. To construct items that concur with this definition, a profile of the creative child was drawn. This profile yielded nine traits that became the criteria for item construction. These traits were self-direction, evaluative ability, flexible thinking, original thinking, elaborative thinking, willingness to take risks, ease with complexity, curiosity, and fluent thinking ability. In 1968, 244 fifth-grade pupils were tested with the original sixty-three-item PACT. The pupils in this study were a heterogenous mixture of racial and socioeconomic groups. Eighteen of the sixty-three items failed to discriminate at the .01 level between the bottom and top 27 percent. The remaining forty-five items were collated for use as PACT (Form-45). In 1969, 2,820 fifth-grade pupils were tested with the forty-five-item PACT. These pupils were randomly selected from the Commonwealth's fifth grades using stratification to insure adequate representation. The average interitem correlation was .08 and the reliability coefficient was .80. The six weakest items were deleted from the scale and the data were reanalyzed. The interitem correlation of the thirty-nine-item PACT was .10. The reliability coefficient was raised to .81. In 1972, 2,048 pupils in grades 4, 5, and 6 were administered PACT 39. The group was also divided into 648 fourth and 470 sixth graders. In all cases the item analysis was satisfactory and did not deviate from the previous item analyses.

As examples, ten selected items from the forty-five-item form of the PACT are given below. An asterisk denotes negative scoring.

*1. If the last page of a book is missing, the book is not worth reading.
 2. I would like to make up a new song.
*4. TV news shows are boring.
14. Learning how to do things is more important than getting excellent marks.
16. I like to make things without following directions.
19. I think I could make up stories as good as those in books.

24. I enjoy learning how to do something in a new and different way.

31. The more pieces in a puzzle, the better I like it.

*32. The best friends are the ones who like the same things as I do.

*38. Singing a song that nobody else knows is silly.

RELIABILITY AND VALIDITY: In 1968, a test-retest of thirty-nine fifth graders with a thirty-day interval yielded a reliability coefficient of .89. In 1968, PACT was administered to 1,214 randomly selected fifth graders. The Kuder-Richardson formula 20 internal consistency coefficient was .87. In 1969, a Kuder-Richardson formula 20 coefficient computed on 550 fifth-grade pupils was .92. In 1970, PACT was administered to 19,513 fifth-grade pupils from 355 randomly selected schools. Cronbach's coefficient *alpha* was .79. In 1972 (Rookey and Valdes, 1972), 2,048 fourth-, fifth-, and sixth-grade pupils from schools in eight states were administered PACT 39. The *alpha* coefficient was .78. In 1972, a sample of twenty Pennsylvania schools was tested at the seventh-grade level with PACT 39. The *alpha* coefficient was .87. In 1972 (Rookey, 1972), a sample of 932 fifth-grade pupils from a small central Pennsylvania city was tested. The *alpha* coefficient was .82. The items for PACT were judged by a group of educators as relevant to creative behavior. Winners ($N = 84$) of a national fourth-grade creative writing contest were on the average one standard deviation above the fifth-grade population mean on PACT, and eighty-three of the eighty-four individuals were above the population mean. Hyer (1972) found that PACT scores were significantly related (.01 level) with the three subscores and the composite score of the Minnesota Tests of Creative Thinking, when both were administered to 288 seventh and eighth graders. He found significant relationships of PACT and two of three cognitive styles.

BIBLIOGRAPHY:

Beers, J. *The Ten Goals of Quality Education.* Harrisburg: Pennsylvania Department of Education, 1970.

Hyer, L., and Rookey, T. J. "Cognitive Style and Creativity." Paper presented at the National Meeting of the American Educational Research Association, Chicago, April 1972. ERIC document no. ED 060 063.

Rookey, T. J. "Validation of a Creativity Test." *Journal of Creative Behavior,* 1974, *8,* 211-213.

Rookey, T. J., and Valdes, A. "A Study of Individually Prescribed Instruction and the Affective Domain." Unpublished paper, 1972. ERIC document no. ED 069 723.

PERCEPTUO-CONCEPTUO DEVELOPMENTAL TEST BATTERY

AUTHORS: James E. Wise, Franklin R. Jones, and Paul Renz

AGE: 5 to 11 years

VARIABLE: Information processing ability

TYPE OF MEASURE: Channel capacity

SOURCE FROM WHICH MEASURE MAY BE OBTAINED: For information, write James E. Wise, School of Education, University of South Carolina, Columbia, South Carolina 29208. Copyright obtained.

DESCRIPTION OF MEASURE: The assumption is made here that children with normal perceptuo-conceptuo development would have maximum channel capacity approximating that of the normal adult, while those of lesser developmental levels would reach saturation in terms of load more rapidly. Their lesser-developed channel capacity would approach maximum at 4, 5, or 6 information lead points. The test battery consists of five sections for tachistoscope presentation at 40 milliseconds. Each section is designed to investigate perceptual responses of either form or color, or both. The five parameters are: (1) transitive form—changes in the number of inflections in the contour of a shape (sides or vertices); (2) transposition form parameter—changes in the spatial position of a shape from the typical viewing angle (e.g., rotation of the form by 45 or 90 degrees); (3) intransitive form parameter—changes in the distribution of area of a shape from its characteristic or learned values (e.g., reducing or enlarging the area); (4) absence of color parameter—change in the color cue of a learned shape by removing the cue (e.g., changing the color to black); and (5) noncharacteristic color parameter—change in the color cue from the characteristics or learned hue to a different hue (e.g., blue or red). Geometrically shaped figures of 3, 4, 5, 6, or 7 sides are used as the stimulus objects for each parameter. The overall test battery consists of twenty-five slides (35 mm) for tachistoscope presentation.

RELIABILITY AND VALIDITY: None reported.

BIBLIOGRAPHY:

Wise, J. E. "An Investigation of the Effects of Varying Color on Perceptual Recognition: With Implications for Educational Psychology and Guidance and Counseling." Unpublished master's thesis. Old Dominion University, Norfolk, Virginia, 1968.

Wise, J. E. "The Effects of Varying Color on Perception Recognition." Paper presented to Institute of Electrical and Electronic Engineers' Ninth Annual Symposium on Human Factors in Electronics. Washington, D.C., May 1968.

Wise, J. E. "Development and Pretest of a Visual Perceptual Screening Test for Use in Preschool Education." Unpublished doctoral dissertation. Old Dominion University, Norfolk, Virginia, 1974.

Wise, J. E., Jones, F. R., and Renz, P. "Development of Visual Perceptual Tests for Normal and Neurologically Handicapped Children." *Perceptual and Motor Skills,* 1972, *34,* 429-430.

Prepared by Franklin Ross Jones

PICTORIAL CLASS INCLUSION PROBLEMS

AUTHORS: Giyoo Hatano and Keiko Kuhara

AGE: 5 to 7 years

VARIABLE: Concrete reasoning

TYPE OF MEASURE: Test

SOURCE FROM WHICH MEASURE MAY BE OBTAINED: A complete manual of the test can be obtained without charge from Giyoo Hatano, 7-12, Honkomgome–6, Bunkyo-ku, Tokyo, 113, Japan.

DESCRIPTION OF MEASURE: This is a simple test of class inclusion, using both pictures of familiar objects and geometric figures, and asking "fewer" as well as "more." Each of the four critical questions is preceded by a few Smedslund-type preparatory questions (Smedslund, 1964), any wrong responses to be corrected. For example, before being asked the critical question, "Are there more sunflowers or flowers?" a child is required to give the names of "tulip" and "sunflower," to collect all "flowers," and to compare tulips and sunflowers in number. Although this test takes less than 5 minutes, it can be effectively used for assessing this aspect of concrete reasoning, except where the child has been extensively trained. Among the 123 5-to-6-year-old subjects attending day-care centers, only 7.3 percent answered all four critical questions correctly (mean = .99, SD = 1.19).

RELIABILITY AND VALIDITY: The coefficient of internal consistency by the Kuder-Richardson formula 20 was .63.

BIBLIOGRAPHY:

Hatano, G., and Kuhara, K. "Training on Class Inclusion Problems." *Japanese Psychological Research*, 1972, *14*, 61-69.
Smedslund, J. "Concrete Reasoning: A Study of Intellectual Development." *Monographs of the Society for Research in Child Development*, 1964, *29* (93).

PRESCHOOL CREATIVITY RATING SCALE (PCRS)

AUTHOR: Robert M. Dowling

AGE: 1 to 6 years

VARIABLE: Extent of constructive environmental manipulation

TYPE OF MEASURE: Rating scale

SOURCE FROM WHICH MEASURE MAY BE OBTAINED: Robert M. Dowling, Psychology Department, Edinboro State College, Edinboro, Pennsylvania 16444.

DESCRIPTION OF MEASURE: The PCRS is an adaptation of the Creativity Subscale of the Preschool Attainment Record (Doll, 1966). The adaptation was done to make the ratings applicable to hearing-impaired children and to make possible direct ratings by teachers or others with observational knowledge of the child. The scale was originally used in a research project as one of several behavioral, psychological, and social history measures obtained on a group of hearing-impaired preschool children who were showing differential responses to an intensive language stimulation and training program. The scale attempts to measure the extent of a child's creativelike response to his environment by providing a 5-point rating of the degree to which a child is actually displaying the following ten relatively specific behaviors (which are defined and exemplified on the scale itself): Tests, Questions, Transfers, Explores, Tears, Builds, Paints, Individualizes, Solos, and Experiments.

As examples, the first three of the ten items on the scale are given below. The 5-point scoring scale ranges from 0 (not at all) to 4 (very frequently or to a great extent).

1. *"Tests"*
Tries things out as if searching, e.g., takes things apart, piles things together or otherwise explores as if "to see what will happen if . . ."
2. *"Questions"*
Shows an inquisitive interest in his surroundings by gesture or action, e.g., pulls open drawers, looks into bags, asks "why."
3. *"Transfers"*
Moves things about, rearranges objects, carries objects in containers purposefully and with some constructiveness and originality (not merely as a way of being negative or destructive).

RELIABILITY AND VALIDITY: The original study was conducted over a two-year period (1969-1970), and on both occasions the Creativity Rating Scale measures were found to be significantly and positively correlated with the criterion measure of responsiveness to the language stimulation and training program. Test-retest as well as interrater reliability appeared satisfactory based on measures made on the same children by multiple observers one year apart. (The exact data are available in Monsees, 1971). Additional data are also available in that the instrument has been used by the author of the original research (Edna Monsees) to monitor the progress of hearing-impaired children in special infant and preschool programs in the Montgomery County (Maryland) Public Schools.

BIBLIOGRAPHY:

Doll, E. A. *Preschool Attainment Record.* (Research ed.) Circle Pines, Minnesota: American Guidance Service, 1966.
Monsees, E. K. *Predicting Language Performance in Hearing Impaired Children.* Upper Marlboro, Maryland: Prince George's County Public Schools, 1971. ERIC document no. 082 436.

PUPIL SITUATIONAL INVENTORY (PSI)

AUTHOR: George S. C. Cheong

AGE: 8 to 13 years

VARIABLE: Experimental attitude

TYPE OF MEASURE: Rating scale

SOURCE FROM WHICH MEASURE MAY BE OBTAINED: George S. C. Cheong, Mount St. Vincent University, Halifax, Nova Scotia, Canada.

DESCRIPTION OF MEASURE: The twenty-five-item PSI was designed to measure the degree of experimental attitude of children in grades 4 to 6 in accord with John Dewey's philosophy of experimentalism. More explicitly, Brown's theoretical framework (Brown, 1962) and two forms of his Teacher Practices Inventory were used in constructing items for the PSI, along with material based on Dewey's *Democracy and Education* (1916) and *Experience and Education* (1938), plus several items developed by the author.

As examples, eight of the twenty-five items to be answered on a YES, yes, no, NO continuum are given below.

1. Miss P. B. often asks her children to make guesses and try them out. Would you like a teacher like her?
3. Miss B. P. is only interested in giving her children facts and information. Would you like a teacher like her?
5. Mrs. B. A. tells her class that what is good and what is bad should not be questioned. Would you like a teacher like her?
7. Mrs. K. I. is interested in giving her children a wide choice in how they answer questions. Would you like a teacher like her?
9. Miss R. P. usually tells all her children to work on the same page of the same book at the same time. Would you like a teacher like her?

RELIABILITY AND VALIDITY: The PSI has an internal consistency coefficient of .92, a test-retest reliability coefficient of .81, and a validity coefficient of .82 with creativity as a correlate. University faculty in education and philosophy judged the relevance of items to Dewey's philosophy. Agreement by six of the eight judges was required before an item was included.

BIBLIOGRAPHY:

Brown, B. B. "The Relationships of Experimentalism to Classroom Practices." Unpublished doctoral dissertation. University of Wisconsin, Madison, 1962.
Cheong, G. S. C. "Pupil Situational Inventory: A Measure of Experimental Attitude." *Journal of Experimental Education,* 1969, *38* (2), 24-30.
Dewey, J. *Democracy and Education: An Introduction to the Philosophy of Education.* New York: Macmillan, 1916.
Dewey, J. *Experience and Education.* New York: Macmillan, 1938.

PURDUE ELEMENTARY PROBLEM-SOLVING INVENTORY

AUTHORS: John F. Feldhusen, John C. Houtz, and Susan Ringenbach

AGE: Kindergarten to grade 6

VARIABLE: Problem-solving abilities

TYPE OF MEASURE: Test

SOURCE FROM WHICH MEASURE MAY BE OBTAINED: John F. Feldhusen, Educational Psychology Section, Purdue University SCC-G, West Lafayette, Indiana 47906. Cost: $25.00 per set including audio cassette, filmstrip, and booklet.

DESCRIPTION OF MEASURE: The Purdue Elementary Problem-Solving Inventory was designed to measure problem-solving abilities of socioeconomically disadvantaged children of different ethnic backgrounds in grades 1 to 6 using real-life tasks. The test consists of forty-nine problems, which are presented as slides portraying children in cartoon form in real-life situations. Ss respond by listening to a tape recording of directions, problem descriptions, and alternatives and then drawing an "X" in a test booklet over the alternative of their choice, which may be a picture or a verbal description. The inventory is designed to measure the following abilities: sensing that a problem exists, defining the problem, asking questions, guessing causes, clarifying the goal of the problem situation, judging if more information is needed, analyzing details, redefining familiar objects for unusual uses, seeing implications, solving single- and multiple-solution problems, and verifying solutions. Two alternative forms are available: (1) a picture-book form, in which all the pictures are presented in a booklet but a tape recording is used to present the items; and (2) an all-verbal form, in which all item content must be read by the examinee, and printed verbal descriptions replace the pictures.

RELIABILITY AND VALIDITY: Kuder-Richardson Formula 20 reliability of the inventory is .79. Analyses of variance demonstrated that ethnic background accounted for only 3 percent of the variance and SES only 5 percent while grade level accounted for 37 percent. A principal factor analysis demonstrated that six of the cognitive operations are indeed assessed. Another investigation was designed to determine interrelationships between the inventory and measures of several other cognitive skills. The Purdue Elementary Problem-Solving Inventory and tests of logical thinking, concept formation, language development, perceptual skills, response style, as well as measures of reading, IQ, and school achievement were administered to 1,071 second, fourth, and sixth graders from different ethnic and socioeconomic backgrounds. Significant correlations between all of the measures and problem solving were obtained. A principal components analysis demonstrated a distinct problem-solving factor, separate from measures of school achievement and language abilities but related to logical thinking and conceptual ability.

BIBLIOGRAPHY:

Asher, J. W., Feldhusen, J. F., Gruen, G. E., Kane, R. B., McDaniel, E., Stephens, M. I., Towler, J., and Wheatley, G. H. "The Development of New Measures of Cognitive Variables in Elementary School Children." (Phase I). Unpublished technical report. Washington, D.C.: U.S. Office of Education, 1970.

Asher, J. W., Feldhusen, J. F., Gruen, G. E., Kane, R. B., McDaniel, E., Stephens, M. I., Towler, J., and Wheatley, G. H. "The Development of New Measures of Cognitive Variables in Elementary School Children." (Phase II). Unpublished technical report. Washington, D.C.: U.S. Office of Education, 1971.

Feldhusen, J. F. "Problem Solving and the Concrete-Abstract Dimension." *Gifted Child Quarterly*, 1975, *19*, 122-129.

Feldhusen, J. F., Houtz, J. C., and Ringenbach, S. "Development of a New Measure of Problem-Solving Abilities of Disadvantaged Children." *Proceedings, 80th Annual Convention, American Psychological Association*, 1972, 55-56.

Feldhusen, J. F., Houtz, J. C., and Ringenbach, S. "The Purdue Elementary Problem-Solving Inventory." *Psychological Reports*, 1972, *31*, 891-901.

Houtz, J. C., and Feldhusen, J. F. "Problem-Solving Ability of Disadvantaged Elementary School Children Under Four Testing Formats: A Replicated Experiment." *Psychology in the Schools*, 1975, *12*, 26-33.

Houtz, J. C., Ringenbach, S., and Feldhusen, J. F. "Relationship of Problem Solving to Other Cognitive Variables." *Psychological Reports*, 1973, *33*, 389-390.

Speedie, S. M., Houtz, J. C., Ringenbach, S., and Feldhusen, J. F. "Abilities Measured by the Purdue Elementary Problem-Solving Inventory." *Psychological Reports*, 1973, *33*, 959-963.

REACTION SCALE AND INVENTORY OF PRACTICE

AUTHOR: Roy W. Otte

AGE: Teachers and principals of elementary schools

VARIABLE: Belief and practice regarding or affecting creativity in teaching

TYPE OF MEASURE: Likert-type scale

SOURCE FROM WHICH MEASURE MAY BE OBTAINED: See Otte (1964).

DESCRIPTION OF MEASURE: The Otte belief and practice scale provides a method of measuring the strength of teacher and principal opinion on each of twenty-two different factors that foster or hamper creativity in teaching and a method of measuring the actual practice of these same twenty-two factors. By using a 5-point Likert-type scale to answer each statement, a comparison of percentages can be made between what people actually believe fosters and hampers creativity in teaching and what they actually perceive the practice to be within a school. The measure is composed of a Reaction Scale of twenty-two statements and a related Inventory of Practice of twenty-two statements. The Inventory of Practice may be used without the Reaction Scale, or the latter could be used with known outstanding creative teachers and authorities in creativity in order to provide a base from which actual comparisons could be made with the results of the actual practice inventory.

As examples, eight of the twenty-two items of the Reaction Scale and two of the twenty-two items of the Inventory of Practice are given below. The two scales are constructed so that the items of the first correspond to those of the second (item 1 corresponds to item 23, and so forth). On the first scale the respondent answers according to what he actually believes, using a 5-point response format ranging from "Strongly agree" to "Strongly disagree." On the second scale the respondent answers according to what is the actual practice in the school, using a 5-point response format ranging from "Very often" to "Never."

Reaction Scale

2. Creativity in teaching is fostered by providing assistance for teachers in making teaching aids.
4. When teachers are fearful because their ideas are in conflict with those in authority, creativity in teaching is hampered.
7. When teachers are expected to "cover" the textbooks closely, creativity in teaching is hampered.
9. When teachers are expected to follow specific methods of teaching, creativity in teaching is hampered.
12. When instructional materials are inadequate, creativity in teaching is hampered.
16. Good architectural design of a school building will foster creativity in teaching.
17. Creativity in teaching is fostered by having available instructional space in addition to that of the classroom.
20. Creativity in teaching is fostered by planning lessons carefully.

Inventory of Practice

25. In our school, the principal is skillful in releasing the creative potential of teachers so that they encourage and stimulate each other.
32. In our school, teachers, in general, have small class enrollments.

RELIABILITY AND VALIDITY: None reported.

BIBLIOGRAPHY:

Otte, R. W. "The Reactions of Elementary School Teachers and Principals in Indiana Public School Study Council School Systems to Various Factors that Hamper Creativity in Teaching." Unpublished doctoral dissertation. University of Colorado, Boulder, 1964.

Otte, R. W. "Creativity in Teaching." *Childhood Education,* 1966, *43,* 40-43.

SAMPLING ORGANIZATION AND RECALL
THROUGH STRATEGIES

AUTHOR: R. Hunt Riegel

AGE: 4 to 8 years

VARIABLE: Classification of meaningful material; recall

TYPE OF MEASURE: Sorting and interview

SOURCE FROM WHICH MEASURE MAY BE OBTAINED: R. Hunt Riegel, Department of Special Education, College of Education, Western Michigan University, Kalamazoo, Michigan 49001.

DESCRIPTION OF MEASURE: This measure uses children's sorting responses, interview techniques, and recall protocols in order to derive three basic scores for each subject. The first is a sorting-level score based on the groups the child forms by sorting an array of twenty pictures of inanimate concrete objects. Each picture is 8.75 centimeters square, belonging to one of five categories (things that grow, things that make noise, furniture, houses, and vehicles). In addition each picture is colored either red, yellow, blue, or white so that no two category members are of the same color. The pictures are presented one at a time as the child names each, until all twenty are in a rectangular array of four rows of five cards each. No two category members are adjacent to each other, and no two adjacent pictures are the same color.

The sorting level for each child corresponds to one of the following four levels, with an interrater reliability coefficient of .93 between two coders on thirty subject protocols. *Level 1: Syncretic Strategies.* Grouping at this level reflects a general failure to generate relations between items on the basis of an attribute or set of attributes. Grouping items by their spatial contiguity ("because they were next to each other") or subordinating the sorting task to an unrelated manipulative operation ("I wanted to make a square with the pictures") are examples of this level. Also included are instances of no strategy for grouping at all, such as the case of a subject simply pulling all items into a single pile or not moving them at all. *Level 2: Perceptual Strategies.* Groupings at this level are sorted on the basis of characteristics of attributes related to color, shape, or size. When color, for example, is introduced as an attribute of the stimulus materials, younger children tend to sort items on that basis, rather than attending to more intrinsic characteristics of the items such as function or category membership. *Level 3: Low Associative Strategies.* This level includes associations for which intrinsic or semantic attributes of the items constitute the basis for grouping. Such groups as thematic collections (formed by creating a story about the items) and complexes (collections of items for which interitem associations were formed but for which no overall defining attribute is available) are examples of Level 3 strategies. *Level 4: Superordinate and Categorical Strategies.* Groupings at this level include superordinate groupings, in which all items in a group are subsumed under a single intrinsic attribute or attribute set. Examples of groupings at this level include groups based on items having similar function (e.g., they all are for eating; you can live in them) or on category membership (they are furniture).

Recall scores are calculated by totaling the number of items named during recall and subtracting all repetitions and intrusions. Thus the subject's recall score is the total number of correct items recalled from the array of twenty. The clustering of recall is computed for each subject using the statistic described by Frankel and Cole (1971). Each recall protocol is coded such that each item recalled is assigned a number corresponding to the group in which it had been placed (excluding repetitions and intrusions). An analysis of runs of items is then conducted. Clustering is assumed if the resulting z score is greater than 1.96, indicating significantly fewer runs than random recall would have yielded.

RELIABILITY AND VALIDITY: Thirteen percent of eighty-six preprimary educable mentally retarded subjects (mean CA = 97 months) sorted the items into groupings classified as associative (Levels 3 and 4 combined). By contrast, 55 percent of a non-retarded sample ($N = 31$) produced groupings at this level. The difference in proportion of each sample generating associative grouping was significant ($z = 4.70$, $p < .001$), as calculated with a proportion test (Bruning and Kintz, 1968). In addition, a comparison of the proportion of subjects in each sample producing superordinate grouping (Level 4 only) was made. The difference between 7 percent of the EMR subjects and 26 percent of the nonretarded subjects was also found to be significant ($z = 2.77$, $p < .01$). Comparison between the two groups on recall scores showed the nonretarded sample to have remembered an average of nearly four items more than the EMR sample, the two means being 9.55 and 5.65 respectively, the difference being significant at the .001 level.

BIBLIOGRAPHY:

Bruning, J. L., and Kintz, B. L. *Computational Handbook of Statistics.* Glenview, Illinois: Scott, Foresman, 1968.

Frankel, F., and Cole, M. "Measures of Organization in Free Recall." *Psychological Bulletin,* 1971, *76,* 39-44.

Riegel, R. H. *Sampling Organization and Recall Through Strategies: Administration and Scoring Manual.* Research, Development, and Demonstration Center in Education of Handicapped Children. University of Minnesota, Minneapolis, 1973.

Riegel, R. H., Danner, F. W., and Donnelley, L. J. *Developmental Trends in the Generation and Utilization of Associative Relations for Recall by EMR and Nonretarded Children: The SORTS Test.* Research, Development, and Demonstration Center in Education of Handicapped Children. University of Minnesota, Minneapolis, 1973.

Riegel, R. H., Danner, F. W., Johnson, L. S., and Kjerland, L. K. *Improving Organization and Memory.* Research, Development, and Demonstration Center in Education of Handicapped Children. University of Minnesota, Minneapolis, 1973.

Prepared by Orval G. Johnson

SANTOSTEFANO LEVELING-SHARPENING HOUSE TEST

AUTHOR: Sebastiano Santostefano

AGE: 4 years to adult

VARIABLE: Management of information changing over time—memory organization

TYPE OF MEASURE: Individually administered test

SOURCE FROM WHICH MEASURE MAY BE OBTAINED: Sebastiano Santostefano, Director of Child Psychology, McLean Hospital Children's Center, 115 Mill Street, Belmont, Massachusetts 02178. Cost: Test cards, manual and fifty protocols, $40.00.

DESCRIPTION OF MEASURE: The construction of the test was based upon the operational definition of the cognitive control leveling-sharpening, which concerns the unique style with which an individual maintains, in memory, images of information over time. The test consists of sixty cards, each containing a line-drawn black-and-white picture of a house scene. The first three of the sixty displays contain all elements; with the fourth display, the doorknob on the front door of the house drops out and remains absent for the remainder of the test. With the seventh display, part of the fence drops out and remains absent during the rest of the test. In this manner nineteen elements are omitted from the scene accumulatively, each scene representing some combination of omissions. Each card is displayed for 5 seconds. The individual is asked to look at each picture as carefully as time permits and to say "stop" if he notices a change in terms of the previous picture. When the individual asks the examiner to stop the presentation, the examiner conducts a brief inquiry to establish what looks different about the picture. The examiner continues the presentation until all sixty pictures have been displayed. Testing time is approximately 15 minutes.

RELIABILITY AND VALIDITY: Validity has been established primarily through factor analysis studies. Comparison of age groups has shown a developmental progression from leveling (maintaining global, diffuse memory images of information) to sharpening (maintaining discrete, articulated memory images). The procedure has been used to investigate various clinical problems (such as the effects of glue sniffing on memory functioning, the relationship between memory organization and reading disability, and the early detection of learning disability in kindergarten children at risk). It is recommended that the test be used as part of a battery assessing cognitive controls.

BIBLIOGRAPHY:

Santostefano, S. "A Developmental Study of the Cognitive Control Leveling-Sharpening." *Merrill-Palmer Quarterly*, 1964, *10*, 343-360.
Santostefano, S. "Cognitive Controls Versus Cognitive Styles: An Approach to Diagnosing and Treating Cognitive Disabilities in Children." *Seminars in Psychiatry*, 1969, *1*, 291-317. Also in S. Chess and A. Thomas (Eds.), *Annual Progress in Child Psychiatry and Child Development*. New York: Brunner/Mazel, 1970.

SCALE OF ACADEMIC CURIOSITY

AUTHORS: Derek C. Vidler and Hashim R. Rawan

AGE: Grade 8 and up

VARIABLE: Curiosity in educational settings

TYPE OF MEASURE: Self-report scale

SOURCE FROM WHICH MEASURE MAY BE OBTAINED: Derek Vidler, Box 1661, Hunter College of City University of New York, New York, New York 10021.

DESCRIPTION OF MEASURE: The Scale of Academic Curiosity is a true-false self-report scale consisting of forty-five items selected from eighty items on the basis of point-biserial correlations and factor analysis. The eighty items were the survivors of an original one hundred items submitted to a group of five judges for determination of content validity. Considerable research is needed, though some has already been undertaken, to show that this scale is related to other measures of curiosity and academic performance. The factors of the scale have not yet been clearly identified, but they appear to be similar to those of other measures of academic curiosity.

As examples, the first ten of the forty-five items of the scale are given below. Each statement is to be answered "true" or "false."

1. I like to look up new words in a dictionary.
2. I like to try to solve problems that present a mental challenge.
3. I am always eager to know more about the universe we live in.
4. When I hear about a new subject I like to find out more about it.
5. When I hear about events that happened in the past, I like to find out more about them.
6. I read little outside school unless I have to.
7. I like to experiment with new kinds of ways of solving familiar problems.
8. I like things which make me think rather than just entertain me.
9. I prefer to read for pleasure than just for the sake of learning.
10. I don't like to take courses in areas that I know little about.

RELIABILITY AND VALIDITY: Some evidence for reliability and validity is contained in Vidler (1974) and Vidler and Rawan (1974). Split-half reliability coefficients are in the .80s. The scale has been found to correlate significantly with teacher ratings of curiosity and with some performance indices in a study of more than six hundred college students.

BIBLIOGRAPHY:

Vidler, D. C. "Relationships Between Convergent and Divergent Thinking, Test Anxiety, and Curiosity." *Journal of Experimental Education,* 1974, *43,* 86, 79-85.
Vidler, D. C., and Karan, V. E. "A Study of Curiosity, Divergent Thinking, and Test Anxiety." *Journal of Psychology,* 1975, *90,* 237-243.
Vidler, D. C., and Rawan, H. R. "Construct Validation of a Scale of Academic Curiosity." *Psychological Reports,* 1974, *35,* 263-266.

Vidler, D. C., and Rawan, H. R. "Further Validation of a Scale of Academic Curiosity." *Psychological Reports,* 1975, *37,* 115-118.

SCALE FOR RATING BEHAVIORAL CHARACTERISTICS OF SUPERIOR STUDENTS (SRBCSS)

AUTHORS: Joseph S. Renzulli and Robert K. Hartman

AGE: Elementary to high school

VARIABLE: Learning, motivation, creativity, leadership

TYPE OF MEASURE: Rating scale

SOURCE FROM WHICH MEASURE MAY BE OBTAINED: See Renzulli and others (1971).

DESCRIPTION OF MEASURE: The SRBCSS is designed to obtain teacher estimates of student characteristics on the four variables listed above. The items are derived from the research literature dealing with the characteristics of gifted and creative persons. The scales are intended primarily for use in the process of screening and selecting students for special programs or experiences that are designed to enhance the development of high potential. Guided teacher judgment has been found to be a valuable means of supplementing psychometric information in the process of identifying students for special educational experiences.

Given below as examples are one item from each of the four parts of the thirty-seven-item measure, each item to be rated on a scale from 1 to 4: (1) "if you have *seldom* or *never* observed this characteristic" to (4) "if you have observed this characteristic *almost all of the time.*"

Part I: Learning Characteristics
4. Has rapid insight into cause-effect relationships; tries to discover the how and why of things; asks many provocative questions (as distinct from informational or factual questions); wants to know what makes things (or people) "tick."

Part II: Motivational Characteristics
1. Becomes absorbed and truly involved in certain topics or problems; is persistent in seeking task completion. (It is sometimes difficult to get him to move on to another topic.)

Part III: Creativity Characteristics
1. Displays a great deal of curiosity about many things; is constantly asking questions about anything and everything.

Part IV: Leadership Characteristics
1. Carries responsibility well; can be counted on to do what he has promised and usually does it well.

RELIABILITY AND VALIDITY: Coefficients of stability were obtained by administering the instrument to groups of fifth- and sixth-grade students before and after a three-month interval. The coefficients for the four scales ranged between a low of .77 and a high of .91 (all significant beyond the .01 level). Interjudge reliability ranged from .67 to .91 ($p < .01$). Validity studies using ANOVA techniques indicated that the scales significantly discriminated between known groups of gifted and average students. Correlational data showed moderate relationships between each scale and tests of intelligence, achievement, and creativity. The leadership scale was generally significantly related to sociometric data. The items of the test have been selected and developed from the writing and research of leading researchers in the field of the gifted.

BIBLIOGRAPHY:

Plowman, P. D. "Programming for the Gifted Child." *Exceptional Children*, 1969, *35*, 547-551.
Renzulli, J. S. "Identifying Key Features in Programs for the Gifted." *Exceptional Children*, 1968, *35*, 217-221.
Renzulli, J. S., Harman, R. K., and Callahan, C. M. "Teacher Identification of Superior Students." *Exceptional Children*, 1971, *38*, 211-214.

SCHEMATIZING TEST

AUTHOR: Philip S. Holzman

AGE: 11 years to old age

VARIABLE: Cognitive control of leveling-sharpening

TYPE OF MEASURE: Psychophysical judgment

SOURCE FROM WHICH MEASURE MAY BE OBTAINED: Philip S. Holzman, Department of Psychiatry, University of Chicago, 950 East 59th Street, Chicago, Illinois 60637. Cost: Nominal.

DESCRIPTION OF MEASURE: The subject judges the size of 150 blank squares (fourteen different sizes from 1 inch to 18 inches) that are projected one at a time on a screen. At first the five smallest squares are presented three times each in haphazard order. Then without the subject's knowledge the smallest square is removed and the next larger one is inserted into the series, which is again presented three times. In this way the entire range of fourteen squares is traversed. The test measures the degree to which subjects make accurate discriminations between temporally juxtaposed squares and the degree to which subjects lag behind the progressive increase in sizes. Both measures are assumed to tap the degree to which persons assimilate new stimuli to previous memory traces. Two scores, percent accuracy and lag score, represent the extent to which subjects are inaccurate in discriminating successive squares and in keeping track of the changing series.

RELIABILITY AND VALIDITY: The relationship to specific defensive preferences of repression, qualities of memory organization, time-error performance, and affect organization have been established in a series of papers. The test is stable over time. It has been found that ninety presentations give results as reliable as 150 presentations.

BIBLIOGRAPHY:

Gardner, R. W., Holzman, P. S., Klein, G. S., Linton, H., and Spence, D. "Cognitive Control." *Psychological Issues,* 1959, *1* (4).

Holzman, P. S. "The Relation of Assimilation Tendencies in Visual, Auditory, and Kinesthetic Time-Error to Cognitive Attitudes of Leveling and Sharpening." *Journal of Personality,* 1954, *22,* 375-394.

Holzman, P. S. "Repression and Cognitive Style." *Bulletin of the Menninger Clinic,* 1962, *26,* 273-282.

Holzman, P. S., and Gardner, R. W. "Leveling and Repression." *Journal of Abnormal and Social Psychology,* 1959, *59,* 151-155.

Holzman, P. S., and Gardner, R. W. "Leveling-Sharpening and Memory Organization." *Journal of Abnormal and Social Psychology,* 1960, *61,* 176-180.

Holzman, P. S., and Rousey, C. "Disinhibition of Communicated Thought: Generality and Role of Cognitive Style." *Journal of Abnormal Psychology,* 1971, *77,* 263-274.

Staines, J. W. "Leveling-Sharpening and Academic Learning in Secondary School Children." *Australian Journal of Psychology,* 1968, *20,* 123-127.

SENSORY-PSYCHOMOTOR TEST

AUTHOR: Robert E. Lowell

AGE: 5 to 12 years

VARIABLE: Learning style preference

TYPE OF MEASURE: Test

SOURCE FROM WHICH MEASURE MAY BE OBTAINED: Learning Associates, Inc., Stillwater, Maine 04489.

DESCRIPTION OF MEASURE: This is a test of learning style to the extent that the pupil test behaviors are very much like those required for pupil success in school. The styles of learning are defined by the methods of presenting stimuli and taking responses. For example, in this test digits and letters are shown (visual) or spoken (auditory) to pupils. Pupils respond by either naming or writing a duplicate of the stimulus. Processing in this test means to hear or see (but not both) digits or letters and to name or say them in the same order of presentation. The Sensory-Psychomotor Test measures a child's performance in speaking and writing sets of digits and letters presented by visual memory, visual copy, and auditory memory, and it is designed to show a child's learning preference on a profile of abilities. It can be used with individual children of any age whose reading, writing, and spelling on standardized tests indicate they are achieving within primary-grade levels. The test can be varied to be used with groups by requiring only the written responses.

The following are condensed directions for Test 1. In this test, the examiner names digits and letters one at a time at the rate of approximately one per second. As the subject responds, the examiner must write the responses on the answer sheet exactly as given by the subject.

Examiner says:	Subject listens and speaks:
I am going to say some numbers.	
When I tell you to, say them after me.	
Listen, two-four, you say them—	two-four
Listen, three-one-six, say them—	three-one-six
Next, four-seven-five-two—	four-seven-five-two
Nine-one-eight-four-three—	nine-one-eight-four-three
Four-two-four-one-five-seven—	four-two-four-one-five-seven
Now I am going to say some letters	
and you are to say them after me.	
Listen, a-t, say them	a-t
n-o-t	n-o-t
p-a-c-k	p-a-c-k
h-o-u-s-e	h-o-u-s-e
m-o-t-h-e-r	m-o-t-h-e-r

RELIABILITY AND VALIDITY: Reliability computed with data from ninety-two subjects (age range 7½ to 8½ years), using Kuder-Richardson formula 21 is .91. Correlations of the Sensory-Psychomotor Test with subtests of the Metropolitan Achievement Test were as follows: word knowledge, .65; total reading, .64; spelling, .63; total math, .62.

BIBLIOGRAPHY: None reported.

SOMETHING ABOUT MYSELF (SAM)

AUTHOR: Joe Khatena

AGE: Adolescent to adult

VARIABLE: Creativity

TYPE OF MEASURE: Self-report checklist

SOURCE FROM WHICH MEASURE MAY BE OBTAINED: Joe Khatena, Department of Educational Foundations, Marshall University, Huntington, West Virginia 25701.

DESCRIPTION OF MEASURE: Something About Myself (Khatena, 1970, 1971a, 1971b) is a creativity checklist based upon the rationale that creativity is reflected in the personality characteristics of the individual, in the kind of thinking strategies he employs, and in the products that emerge as a result of his creative strivings. The selection of items for the biographical self-report was based on previous research findings of other investigators and hypotheses relative to correlates of creativity (Khatena, 1969; MacKinnon, 1962; Taylor, 1964; Torrance and Khatena, 1970). One hundred items were identified and later reduced to seventy-four. These items were then administered to 180 college adults and intercorrelated. When items were found to correlate .30 or better, or if one item appeared to provide the same information as another, they were combined to make single items. In this way seventy-four items were reduced to fifty on the final form of the checklist. The items included represent three categories of creative functioning: personality traits, use of creative thinking strategies, and creative productions. Item order is randomized. As a check on the appropriateness of these items, each of the fifty items was correlated with the total score by the point-biserial method using the responses of 773 male and female adults and 304 male and female adolescents. The correlations for all fifty items obtained from the adult responses ranged from .11 to .54 ($p < .01$), and for the children's responses correlations ranged from .12 to .45, where forty-seven of the items were significant at the .01 level and three at the .05 level.

The checklist can be easily administered to groups and individuals. Most subjects complete the checklist in 10 to 15 minutes. The test can be easily scored by counting the number of affirmative responses and giving each of the responses a credit of 1. The total possible score is 50. A factor-analytic study of the measure (Bledsoe and Khatena, 1973) has identified six creative orientations: environmental sensitivity, initiative, self-strength, intellectuality, individuality, and artistry.

Six sample items reported in a recent paper on the measure (Khatena, 1971a) are given below.

1. I am an imaginative person, a dreamer, or visionary.
2. When I think of an idea I like adding to it to make it more interesting.
3. I have improvised in dance, song, or instrumental music.
4. I like making guesses, testing them, and if I am proved wrong will make new guesses.
5. I am not afraid to take risks should a need arise.
6. I have invented a new product.

RELIABILITY AND VALIDITY: Internal consistency of the test was determined by the split-half and equivalence methods. The responses of sixty adolescent and sixty college adult subjects were used, and the odd and even items were correlated and corrected by the Spearman-Brown prophecy formula to give rs of .92, .95, and .94 for adolescent and adult groups and the two groups combined. When the responses of 773 adult and 304 adolescent subjects were analyzed by the equivalence method to determine further the internal consistency of the checklist, rs of .85, .79, and .68 were found for the adult and adolescent groups and the two groups combined. Test-retest reliability coefficients were also computed, using the responses of thirty-eight and forty-three adult subjects with a varying time interval of one day and four weeks, and rs of .98 and .77 were obtained, respectively ($p < .01$).

Subjects who report themselves as high creatives on the checklist should also produce more original responses than their less creative peers, as measured by two tests of verbal originality using either sound or onomatopoetic word stimuli now published as a test battery entitled *Thinking Creatively with Sounds and Words* (Khatena and Torrance, 1973) and on another creative personality measure entitled *What Kind of Person Are You?* (Torrance and Khatena, 1970). The responses of fifty-two and 102 subjects on the checklist and the two measures of originality were analyzed as follows: Originality scores of fifty-two subjects were available on Form 1 of the adult version of *Sounds and Images* and *Onomatopoeia and Images* (Torrance, Khatena, and Cunnington, 1973). These subjects were divided into two groups of equal number—high and low creatives—according to their self-reports on *Something About Myself*. The mean originality score of the high group on *Sounds and Images* was found significantly superior to those of the low group ($M = 32.61$, $SD = 6.93$; $M = 28.92$, $SD = 8.07$). This was also found to be the case with *Onomatopoeia and Images* ($M = 90.57$, $SD = 21.79$; $M = 81.69$, $SD = 21.22$). The mean differences on both tests of originality were found to be significant ($t = 2.19$, $t = 2.15$). When 102 adult subjects were divided into three groups of equal number according to their scores on *Something About Myself*—high, moderate, and low creative groups—it was found that high creatives showed a mean originality score superior to the moderate and low creatives ($M = 102.00$, $SD = 26.25$; $M = 90.70$, $SD = 25.70$; $M = 94.91$, $SD = 23.49$), with low creatives somewhat superior to the moderate creatives ($F = 4.55$, $df = 2.99$, $p < .05$). Another study attempting to determine construct validity of the measure with the *Runner Studies of Attitude Patterns* (III) as criterion using 120 college adults as subjects found creative subjects exhibiting experimental, intuitive, and power orientations (Khatena, 1972). When SAM scores of groups of fifty-two and 102 subjects were compared with scores on two creativity measures (*Sounds and Images* and *Onomatopoeia and Images*), significant relationships were found.

Using the total score of *Something About Myself* as a creative index, the scores of 144 subjects were correlated with verbal originality scores on Form II of the children's version of *Sounds and Images* as criterion to find an r of .18 ($p < .05$). When the scores of 159 and 144 subjects on the checklist were correlated with Forms I and II of the children's version of *Onomatopoeia and Images* as the second criterion, rs of .22 ($p < .05$) and .15 ($p < .05$) were found. The scores of 405 adult and adolescent subjects on this measure and on the *What Kind of Person Are You?* test were correlated and an r of .46 ($p < .01$) was obtained.

BIBLIOGRAPHY:

Bledsoe, J. C., and Khatena, J. "A Factor-Analytic Study of Something About Myself." *Psychological Reports*, 1973, *32*, 1176-1178.

Khatena, J. "Autobiography and the Creative Potential." *Gifted Child Quarterly*, 1969, *13*, 255-238.

Khatena, J. *Something About Myself: A Creativity Checklist.* Unpublished manuscript. Marshall University, Huntington, West Virginia, 1970.

Khatena, J. "Something About Myself: A Brief Screening Device for Identifying Creatively Gifted Children and Adults." *Gifted Child Quarterly*, 1971a, *15*, 262-266.

Khatena, J. *Something About Myself: Norms Technical Manual.* (Research ed.) Unpublished manuscript. Marshall University, Huntington, West Virginia, 1971b.

Khatena, J. "Attitude Patterns as Providing Validity Evidence on Something About Myself." *Psychological Reports*, 1972, *31*, 565-566.

Khatena, J., and Torrance, E. P. *Thinking Creatively with Sounds and Words: Norms Technical Manual.* (Research ed.) Lexington, Massachusetts: Personnel Press, 1973.

MacKinnon, E. W. (Ed.) *The Creative Person.* Berkeley, California: University of California General Extension, 1962.

Schaefer, C. E., and Anastasi, A. "A Biographical Inventory for Identifying Creativity in Adolescent Boys." *Journal of Applied Psychology*, 1968, *52*, 42-48.

Taylor, C. W. *Creativity: Progress and Potential.* New York: McGraw-Hill, 1964.

Torrance, E. P., and Khatena, J. "What Kind of Person Are You?: A Brief Screening Device for Identifying Creatively Gifted Adolescents and Adults." *Gifted Child Quarterly*, 1970, *14*, 71-75.

Torrance, E. P., Khatena, J., and Cunnington, B. F. *Thinking Creatively With Sounds and Words (Adult and Children's Versions).* Lexington, Massachusetts: Personnel Press, 1973.

STANDARD EDUCATIONAL INTELLIGENCE TEST (SEIT)

AUTHORS: Malcolm J. Slakter and Roger A. Koehler

AGE: Grade 5

VARIABLE: Four aspects of test-wiseness and risk taking

TYPE OF MEASURE: Test

SOURCE FROM WHICH MEASURE MAY BE OBTAINED: Directions for administration are available from Malcolm J. Slakter, Department of Educational Psychology, 7 Foster Annex, State University of New York, Buffalo, New York 14214. For copies of the test or similar measures for grades 7, 9, and 11, and other supporting data, order

NAPS document no. 00808 from ASIS National Auxiliary Publication Service, c/o CCM Information Sciences, 440 Park Avenue South, New York, New York 10016. Cost: $3.00 for microfiche; $6.50 for photocopy.

DESCRIPTION OF MEASURE: SEIT is a disguised measure of test-wiseness and risk taking on objective examinations. It consists of five "nonsense" items and sixteen content-free items embedded in thirty-three legitimate items. Four aspects of test-wiseness are measured. The examinee should be able to: (1) select the option that resembles an aspect of the stem; (2) eliminate options known to be incorrect and choose from among the remaining options; (3) eliminate similar options, that is, options that imply the correctness of each other; and (4) eliminate those options that include specific determiners.

As examples, four selected items from the fifty-four items on the test are given below.

22. The Flying Spider is known for its ability to
    a. blend in with its surroundings.
    b. glide through the air.
    c. kill its prey with poison.
    d. make very large webs.
25. The greatest advantage of using slent in the manufacture of steel is that slent makes the steel
    a. transparent.
    b. stainless.
    c. heavy.
    d. bulky.
28. When Bestor crystals are added to water,
    a. heat is given off.
    b. the temperature of the solution rises.
    c. the solution turns blue.
    d. the container becomes warmer.
33. The stridule principle of arithmetic is useful when you
    a. add.
    b. divide.
    c. sum.
    d. total.

RELIABILITY AND VALIDITY: For the four-item measures of test-wiseness, Kuder-Richardson formula 20 values are in the vicinity of .15 for "similar-options" and "specific-determiners," .25 for "stem-option," and .40 for "absurd-options." Reliabilities for the first two dimensions generally run low, probably because there is evidence that fifth-grade students have not yet mastered these aspects of test-wiseness and tend to respond on what appears to be a chance basis. The Kuder-Richardson formula 20 value for the five-item risk-taking measure is generally about .85. More information about reliability and validity is provided in the references below.

BIBLIOGRAPHY:

Crehan, K. D., Koehler, R. A., and Slakter, M. J. "Longitudinal Studies of Test-Wiseness." *Journal of Educational Measurement,* 1974, *11,* 209-212.

Slakter, M. J. "Generality of Risk Taking on Objective Examinations." *Educational and Psychological Measurement,* 1969, *29,* 115-128.

Slakter, M. J., Koehler, R. A., and Hampton, S. H. "Grade Level, Sex, and Selected Aspects of Test-Wiseness." *Journal of Educational Measurement,* 1970, *7,* 119-122.

Prepared by Malcolm J. Slakter

STARKWEATHER ORIGINALITY TEST
FOR YOUNG CHILDREN

AUTHOR: Elizabeth K. Starkweather

AGE: 3½ to 6½ years

VARIABLE: Originality

TYPE OF MEASURE: Test with visual aids

SOURCE FROM WHICH MEASURE MAY BE OBTAINED: Information about the availability of the Starkweather Originality Test can be obtained from E. K. Starkweather, Family Relations and Child Development Department, Oklahoma State University, Stillwater, Oklahoma 74074.

DESCRIPTION OF MEASURE: The Starkweather Originality Test is designed to measure the creative potential of young children. In the test, no attempt is made to differentiate the closely related factors of creative ability that have been identified in older children and adults, such as originality, flexibility, fluency, and elaboration. It is possible that all of these factors contribute to a high score on the Originality Test, and it is possible that strength in one factor alone may be sufficient to produce a high test score. The Originality Test requires verbal responses; nevertheless, the originality scores are independent of verbal ability. The test materials .are simple three-dimensional shapes made of plastic foam. In the pretest there are eight pieces, two each of four different shapes and in the test proper there are forty pieces, four each of ten different shapes. The purpose of the pretest is to determine whether the child has the ability and the freedom to communicate verbally to the extent necessary for taking the Originality Test and to be sure that he understands that any response he makes is acceptable. The test proper offers the child four opportunities to respond to each of the ten different shapes. He examines the pieces one at a time and tells what each might be. Each child's score is the number of different responses he gives, with a maximum possible score of 40.

RELIABILITY AND VALIDITY: Two forms of the Originality Test (Form A and Form B) have been developed, and the comparability of the two forms has been demonstrated in test-retest research with seventy-six children, two groups of thirty-eight children matched on initial test scores. For one group of children, Form A was administered first, and for the other group, Form B was given first. Statistical analyses indicated that the children in the two groups had similar retest scores, that changes in test-retest scores of individual children in the two groups were similar, and that the number of different responses given to the items in Form A was similar to the number given to the items in Form B. The internal consistencies of the two forms of the test (split-half with Spearman-Brown correction) were .86 for Form A and .81 for Form B, both significant beyond the .01 level. Interjudge reliability in scoring was demonstrated in a comparison of two sets of scores. (1) The responses of 144 children were scored jointly by two judges who participated in the development of the test; and (2) the same responses were scored by another person, trained in child development, but who had no experience with the test and who had no instructions other than the written directions for scoring. The correlation (r) between the two sets of judges' scores was +.99 ($p < .01$). The use of the scoring directions as written should assure reliable scoring. The validity of the Originality Test was demonstrated in terms of a quality that is accepted as a pervasive characteristic of the creative person—freedom of expression. Children's Originality Test scores were compared with scores indicating the freedom with which they expressed themselves in exploring and manipulating objects in their environment. A Spearman rank correlation between these two sets of scores yielded a coefficient of +.69 ($p < .02$).

BIBLIOGRAPHY:

Starkweather, E. K. "Problems in the Measurement of Creativity in Preschool Children." *Journal of Educational Measurement,* 1964, *1,* 109-113.
Starkweather, E. K. "Potential Creative Ability and the Preschool Child." In *First Seminar on Productive Thinking in Education.* Creativity Project, Macalester College, St. Paul, Minnesota, January 1966.
Starkweather, E. K. "Creativity Research Instruments Designed for Use with Preschool Children." *Journal of Creative Behavior,* 1971, *5,* 245-255.
Starkweather, E. K., and Azbill, P. "An Exploratory Study of Preschool Children's Freedom of Expression." *Proceedings of the Oklahoma Academy of Science,* 1964, *45,* 176-180.

STARKWEATHER TARGET GAME FOR PRESCHOOL CHILDREN

AUTHOR: Elizabeth K. Starkweather

AGE: 3 to 6 years

VARIABLE: Willingness to try difficult tasks

TYPE OF MEASURE: Target game

SOURCE FROM WHICH MEASURE MAY BE OBTAINED: Details for construction of the instrument can be obtained from E. K. Starkweather, Family Relations and Child Development Department, Oklahoma State University, Stillwater, Oklahoma 74074.

DESCRIPTION OF MEASURE: The Starkweather Target Game is designed to measure preschool children's willingness to try difficult tasks and to measure this characteristic independent of ability. The game consists of a box-shaped target that responds somewhat like a jack-in-the-box. When a bull's-eye at the front of the target is hit, the lid opens and a surprise picture appears. The picture can be removed, and when it has been seen by the child, it is replaced by another picture. The ability of each child is determined in a pretest, and the difficulty of the game is then adjusted so that the midpoint in the target range is a distance at which the child has approximately a 50-percent chance of success. During the game the child shows his willingness to try difficult tasks (WD) as he chooses between relatively easy and relatively difficult target distances. Five target distances are provided in the game, and these are paired in the manner of a paired-comparisons test. The scoring of the Target Game takes into consideration the skill with which the child actually plays the game, and thus provides an additional adjustment for ability. The score is calculated from the number of balls the child uses (B) and the number of times he chooses the more difficult target distance (D) in relation to the number of successes (S) he experiences while playing the game. (WD = B + D − S.)

RELIABILITY AND VALIDITY: The Target Game is adjusted for the ability of each child on the basis of a pretest. This adjustment has been evaluated in terms of the skill demonstrated during the game by fifty-two children whose pretest scores placed them in three different ability groups. An ability score, the distance in feet at which each child actually had a 50-percent chance of success, was calculated. A comparison of these scores indicated that the abilities of the children in the three groups were significantly different (Kruskal-Wallis, $H = 11.675$; $p < .01$). When the children's abilities were expressed in terms of the target range rather than in feet, the point of 50-percent success for all three groups was approximately the same, indicating that a reliable adjustment for ability had been made ($H = 0.983$; n.s.). The Target Game measures children's willingness to try difficult tasks independent of their ability. Statistical evidence for this was obtained by correlating WD scores with ability scores, using a Spearman rank order correlation ($rho = .12$; n.s.). The internal consistency of the target game was demonstrated by means of a split-half correlation (Spearman-Brown formula), which yielded a coefficient of .88 ($p < .01$), indicating that the instrument is reliable.

BIBLIOGRAPHY:

Starkweather, E. K. *Preschool Children's Willingness to Try Difficult Tasks.* Cooperative Research Project no. 5-0333. Washington, D.C.: U.S. Department of Health, Education and Welfare, Office of Education, 1966.
Starkweather, E. K. "Creativity Research Instruments Designed for Use with Preschool Children." *Journal of Creative Behavior,* 1971, *5,* 245-255.

TEST OF CAUTION

AUTHORS: Helen H. Davidson and Judith W. Greenberg

AGE: 9 to 14 years

VARIABLE: Caution in cognitive domain

TYPE OF MEASURE: Test

SOURCE FROM WHICH MEASURE MAY BE OBTAINED: Judith W. Greenberg, City College of the City University of New York, Convent Avenue and 138th Street, New York, New York 10031.

DESCRIPTION OF MEASURE: The Test of Caution measures cautiousness as an aspect of cognitive control in a school-related task, defined here as the capacity to withhold checking an item if the child does not know the right answer. The test consists of thirty four-choice items, with the number of correct choices varying from none to four. Eighteen items are informational and vary in difficulty. The remaining twelve items are "impossible" to answer, since each contains a fabricated key word; for example, "A *lemis* is like a hammer, drill, screwdriver, saw." The child is instructed to check all the choices that he thinks are correct answers, from none to four for each question. The "impossible" items control for differences in amount of information, since no one could know the fabricated word. The test is self-administered in a group setting. The score is the number of choices to fabricated items the child does *not* check. Possible range of scores is 0 to 48; the higher the score the more "cautious" the behavior. The eighteen informational items serve merely to disguise the real purpose of the test and are not scored.

As examples, three of the twelve fabricated items of the test are given below.

5. A dramb is
   a. an animal.
   b. a flower.
   c. a rock.
   d. a fish.
8. A kiroscope is used to
   a. look inside the body.
   b. see the stars.
   c. enlarge a picture.
   d. show a movie.
13. Wishbone Day comes in
   a. March.
   b. August.
   c. the Spring.
   d. the Winter.

RELIABILITY AND VALIDITY: The split-half reliability coefficient for the twelve fabricated items was .81.

BIBLIOGRAPHY:

Davidson, H. H., and Greenberg, J. W. *School Achievers from a Deprived Background.*
   New York: Associated Educational Services, 1967.
Greenberg, J. W., Shore, M. S., and Davidson, H. H. "Caution and Creativity as Corre-
   lates of Achievement in Disparate Social-Racial Groups." *The Journal of Negro
   Education,* 1972, *41,* 377-382.
Grossman, N. S. "Achievement and Social Class Related to Caution, Creativity, and
   Middle-Class Values." *Graduate Research in Education and Related Disciplines,*
   1966, *2,* 100.

Prepared by Judith W. Greenberg

TEST OF LEARNING PROCESS (TLP)

AUTHOR: Richard H. Bloomer

AGE: Grades 1 to 12

VARIABLE: Learning processes

TYPE OF MEASURE: Test

SOURCE FROM WHICH MEASURE CAN BE OBTAINED: Richard H. Bloomer, Box U-7, University of Connecticut, Storrs, Connecticut 06268.

DESCRIPTION OF MEASURE: The Test of Learning Process (TLP) measures the developmental state of a pupil's learning ability for verbal material. The test gives measures of imitative visual rate, short-term memory both simple and complex, auditory short-term memory simple and complex, apprehension span, serial learning, long-term memory, relearning, paired associate learning and interference, analytic concepts, and synthetic concepts. The scores can be used to determine the most appropriate learning pattern for a particular child, and thus not only teach content but also method of presentation can be specified. The TLP is standardized for a normal school population. The scores from the test are directly translatable into appropriate teaching behavior for effective teaching of either individuals or classroom groups. The instrument is currently being used with learning-disabled and emotionally disturbed populations as a prescriptive teaching methodology device. The test requires two 40-minute sittings spaced two days apart and may be administered to groups as well as individually. The test is available in two equated forms for pre- and posttesting.

RELIABILITY AND VALIDITY: Split-half reliabilities of individual variables range from .69 to .93, and correlations between forms for individual subtests range between .74 and .92.

BIBLIOGRAPHY: None reported.

Prepared by Orval G. Johnson

TICK-TACK-TOE TEST

AUTHORS: Brian Sutton-Smith, John M. Roberts, and Robert Kozelka

AGE: 5 to 15 years

VARIABLE: Elementary strategic competence

TYPE OF MEASURE: Test

SOURCE FROM WHICH MEASURE MAY BE OBTAINED: See Sutton-Smith, Roberts, Kozelka, and others (1967).

DESCRIPTION OF MEASURE: The Tick-Tack-Toe Test, designed to measure elementary strategic competence by use of the familiar children's game, contains six items, each of which represents a game of tick-tack-toe at different stages of completion. The respondent is asked to make only the next move, or play. The items were picked to illustrate standard situations in the game. Items one to four represent situations in which the respondent indicates by his opening moves the type of game he is likely to play, whether it be to win, to draw, or to lose. Items five and six are rather like chess problems, in which the player must cross to win in a minimum number of moves. The assumptions about moves, of course, imply familiarity with the game and do not follow if the player does not understand the game as a whole. Scores are attached to item responses according to probabilities of that response's leading to a win, to a draw, or to a loss. Scoring, norms, and testing procedures are contained in Sutton-Smith, Roberts, Kozelka, and others (1967). Administration of the instrument takes about 5 minutes.

RELIABILITY AND VALIDITY: Reliabilities over a three-week and a three-month period were satisfactory only at the sixth-grade level and on the X score (winning) axis. Validities of the test as against real play at tick-tack-toe were significant (.55) only for boys on the X axis.

BIBLIOGRAPHY:

Roberts, J. M., Hoffman, H., and Sutton-Smith, B. "Pattern and Competence: A Consideration of Tick Tack Toe." *Palacio*, 1965, *72 (3)*, 17-30.
Sutton-Smith, B., Roberts, J. M., Kozelka, R., and others. "Studies of an Elementary Game of Strategy." *Genetic Psychology Monographs*, 1967, 76, 3-42.

TRIPLE MODE TEST OF CATEGORIZATION

AUTHOR: Toby R. Silverman-Dresner

AGE: 7 to 15 years

VARIABLE: Modes of categorization

TYPE OF MEASURE: Pair comparisons test

SOURCE FROM WHICH MEASURE MAY BE OBTAINED: Sample copy available from Toby R. Silverman-Dresner, 35 Anderson Drive, Wayne, New York 07470.

DESCRIPTION OF MEASURE: The test consists of fifty pictorial stimuli and three hundred pictorial backgrounds, and it measures the preferred mode of categorization: associative, functional, or superordinate. Directions for each of the test items say to the child: "Look at the picture. Put an 'X' in the box where the picture belongs." For each picture (pictorial stimulus) there are three sets of alternative pictorial backgrounds, the child's choice indicating mode of classification (associative, functional, or superordinate). For example, a pictorial stimulus of a child's sled presents two alternative backgrounds in which to place the picture of the sled: background of ice-skate, roller skate, bicycle (superordinate); or background of a decorated Christmas tree (associative). The sled will appear two more times in the test—in an associative vs. functional context and in a functional vs. superordinate context. This test was administered, along with the Stanford Achievement Reading Tests, to 313 hearing children, 225 typically deaf children, and twenty-seven deaf children in special classes to determine whether the deaf exhibit similar modes of categorization at the same or different developmental levels as hearing children. The modes of categorization were similarly studied at different achievement levels to determine whether these modes contribute to differential scholastic achievement. Different developmental patterns were observed in the categorization modes of deaf and hearing children, with both age and scholastic achievement. When deaf and hearing children were matched exactly on reading achievement scores, all differences in categorization behavior disappeared.

RELIABILITY AND VALIDITY: The split-half correlations between superordinate choices, parts 1 and 2, were .78 for the deaf and .66 for the hearing group. The correlations between functional choices, parts 1 and 2, were .81 for the deaf group and .52 for the hearing group. The correlations between associative choices, parts 1 and 2, were .41 for the deaf and .45 for the hearing group. All the correlations were significant beyond the .01 level. The item analysis resulted in correlations ranging from poor (.02) to excellent (.80). Sixty-five superordinate discriminating items remained out of eighty-four (fifty-eight out of eighty-four functionals and only twenty-five out of eighty-four associatives), calling for fairly extensive revision of the test, especially for the associative category.

BIBLIOGRAPHY:

Kates, S. L., Kates, W. W., Michael, J., and Walsh, T. M. "Categorization and Related Verbalizations in Deaf and Hearing Adolescents." *Journal of Educational Psychology,* 1961, *52,* 188-194.

Silverman, T. R. "Categorization Behavior and Achievement in Deaf and Hearing Children." *Journal of Exceptional Children,* 1967, *34,* 241-250.

Silverman, T. R. "Categorization Behavior and Achievement in Deaf and Hearing Children." Final report, Project No. S-8024, Grant No. 0-5553-029, U.S. Department of Health, Education and Welfare. School of Education, New York University, 1967.

Group 1-e

Miscellaneous

ANIMISM QUESTIONNAIRE

AUTHOR: Paul M. Smeets

AGE: 6 to 11 years

VARIABLE: Attribution of life and life traits to animate and inanimate objects

TYPE OF MEASURE: Questionnaire

SOURCE FROM WHICH MEASURE MAY BE OBTAINED: Paul M. Smeets, Department of Psychology, University of Leiden, Rijnsburgerweg 157, Leiden, Holland.

DESCRIPTION OF MEASURE: The Animism Questionnaire consists of seventy items, that is, seven questions about each of ten objects. The objects were selected from the following categories: (1) nonmoving objects (table, bottle); (2) objects moving, but not "on own accord" (clock, automobile); (3) objects moving "on own accord" (cloud, river); (4) plants (tree, flower); and (5) animals (fish, cat). The questions were designed to assess the opinion of retarded and normal children on the presence of life and specific life traits (growing, dying, hearing, feeling, talking, and knowing) in each of the ten objects. Examples of some test items are given below.

Q: Is a table alive?
Q: Can an automobile die?
Q: Does a cloud hear things?
Q: Does a tree feel things?
Q: Does the fish know he is a goldfish?

Each question is followed by at least one supplementary question (such as, "What makes you think so?"), and, if necessary, by one or more counter questions. Examples:

Q: Does the fish know he is a goldfish?
A: No.
Q: What makes you think so?
A: Because he cannot see himself; he cannot turn his head like we do.
Q: Would the fish know if we put a mirror in the fish tank?
A: Sure he would, because he would see himself.

RELIABILITY AND VALIDITY: Test-retest reliability was established using twenty-five randomly selected retarded (IQ 50 to 80) children. The *phi* coefficient was used to assess the reliability on the first part of each test item (yes = 1, no = 0) separately. The correlations varied from .46 to 1.00. In addition, the proportion of subjects who did not change their opinion (*C* percent) during the retest was determined for each test item. The *C* percent ranged from 84 percent to 100 percent. The correlation (product-moment) between the subjects' total score (maximum score: 70) on the pretest and posttest was .93.

BIBLIOGRAPHY:

Smeets, P. M. "The Animism Controversy Revisited: A Probability Analysis." *Journal of Genetic Psychology,* 1973, *123,* 219-225.
Smeets, P. M. "The Influence of MA and CA on the Attribution of Life and Life Traits to Animate and Inanimate Objects." *Journal of Genetic Psychology,* 1974, *124,* 17-27.

BACKWARD SPEECH

AUTHORS: William R. Tiffany and B. R. Witkin

AGE: Upper elementary to college

VARIABLE: Speech sound awareness

TYPE OF MEASURE: Test

SOURCE FROM WHICH MEASURE MAY BE OBTAINED: See Tiffany (1963).

DESCRIPTION OF MEASURE: The subject is given a word, which may be real or nonsensical, and is asked to reverse the sounds to produce a sensible word. Thus it requires an oral presentation and a written response. The subject is given 5 seconds in which to respond with the word that represents a backward pronunciation of the stimulus word. Examples of items from the twenty-four-item test are given below.

Test Items	Answers
mate	tame
tyke	kite
Cal	lack
enough	funny
seal	lease

There was a wide variation in scores among a group of sixty-one college students who took the test. The correct answers varied from one to twenty-four in this group, with a mean of 11.7 and a standard deviation of 6.25.

RELIABILITY AND VALIDITY: The Backward Speech test scores of college students correlated .43 with final grade in the speech course, .60 with teacher ratings of phonetic ability, and .63 with scores on a spelling test. Correlations with grade-point averages were positive but low and were not statistically significant. Backward Speech test scores correlated .26 with the quantitative score of the ACE College Entrance Examination Test and .46 with the linguistic score of the same measure.

BIBLIOGRAPHY:

Tiffany, W. R. "Sound Mindedness: Studies in the Measurement of 'Phonetic Ability.' "
Western Speech, 1963, Winter, 5-15.
Witkin, B. R. "An Analysis of Some Dimensions of Phonetic Ability." Unpublished
doctoral dissertation. University of Washington, Seattle, 1962.

Prepared by Orval G. Johnson

CONCEPT OF DEATH IN
MIDWESTERN CHILDREN AND YOUTHS

AUTHORS: Matilda S. McIntire, Carol R. Angle, and Lorraine J. Struempler

AGE: 5 to 18 years

VARIABLE: Concept of death

TYPE OF MEASURE: Structured interview

SOURCE FROM WHICH MEASURE MAY BE OBTAINED: Carol R. Angle, University
of Nebraska, College of Medicine, Department of Pediatrics, 42nd and Dewey Avenues,
Omaha, Nebraska 68105.

DESCRIPTION OF MEASURE: This structured interview was first utilized in the out-
patient department of the University of Nebraska Hospital, Omaha. Development of
the final questions was made after consultation with leading clergymen representing the
Roman Catholic, Congregational, Protestant, and conservative Jewish faiths. Design of
the questionnaire focuses on simple phrasing of each question and coding of responses
to avoid ambiguity. Both direct and indirect questions are used. Through the cooperation of the clergy and their congregations, 548 children, ages 5 to 16 years, of middle
and upper-middle socioeconomic background, were interviewed. Information on exact
family status was not available, but the majority were intact. The interviews were conducted by the church school teachers after an orientation and training session given by
the investigators. A random sampling (8 percent) of the interviews was conducted by
the nurse suicidologist. Each church school sent home a letter of explanation and a
form for parental consent; interest and cooperation were extremely high, and the limitations of time led each teacher to a random selection of subjects for interview by
pinstick of the class list. Interview of fifty University of Nebraska clinic patients, ages
5 to 16 years (control group one), was conducted by the suicidologist. Subjects were
all lower and low-middle in socioeconomic status. A briefer interview concerning only
the avowed concept of death was also asked of fifty subjects (control group two), ages
6 to 17 years, interviewed at their schools by public health nurses as controls for a
study on self-poisoning. The interviewer writes down verbatim the subject's response.
This gives a check on coding and ambiguity, provides a good insight into age-related
responses, and also lends itself to content analysis by standard procedures.

As examples, five items from the Concept of Death section of the interview are given below.

17. If you die, what happens to you?
18. Is dying like going to sleep; can you wake up again?
19. Can people who die sometimes return to life?
20. If the body is dead, does a spirit or soul live on?
21. Can the spirit or soul think just as the living person did?

RELIABILITY AND VALIDITY: None reported.

BIBLIOGRAPHY:

LaVoie, J., McIntire, M. S., and Angle, C. R. "Children's Animistic Thought and Their Concept of Death." Paper presented at the meeting of American Academy of Pediatrics. Chicago, Illinois, October 1973.

McIntire, M. S., and Angle, C. R. "The Taxonomy of Suicide as Seen in Poison Control Centers." *Pediatric Clinics of North America,* 1970, *4,* 697-706.

McIntire, M. S., and Angle, C. R. "Is the Poisoning Accidental?" *Clinical Pediatrics,* 1971, *10,* 414-417.

McIntire, M. S., and Angle, C. R. "The Psychological Biopsy in Adolescent Self-Poisoning." *American Journal of Diseases of Children,* 1973, *126,* 42-46.

Prepared by Carol R. Angle

INTERPERSONAL AWARENESS TEST

AUTHOR: Helene M. Borke

AGE: 3 to 5 years

VARIABLE: Children's perceptions of emotional responses

TYPE OF MEASURE: Test

SOURCE FROM WHICH MEASURE MAY BE OBTAINED: For a copy of the stories and pictures, write: Helene M. Borke, Hay Associates, 3 Gateway Center, Pittsburgh, Pennsylvania 15222. Cost: $3.00 to cover reproduction and mailing.

DESCRIPTION OF MEASURE: The Interpersonal Awareness Test consists of two parts. Part I contains eleven stories describing general situations that might make a youngster feel happy, afraid, sad, or angry. Part II consists of twelve stories that describe the subject as behaving toward another child in ways that might make the other child feel happy, afraid, sad, or angry. Before hearing the stories, the subjects are shown drawings of faces representing the four emotions and are helped to identify them. Each story in Part I is accompanied by a picture of a child with a blank face engaged in the described activity. The subject is asked to complete the picture by selecting the face that best shows how the child in the story feels. The faces are presented in random order, and the examiner identifies the emotions for the subjects with each presentation. The same procedure is used for all the stories. There are two sets of faces, one for Caucasian subjects and one for black subjects.

This instrument was originally developed for a cross-cultural study on the early development of emotional awareness. Kindergarten children from two cultures were asked to describe the kinds of situations they perceived as making them feel happy, afraid, sad, or angry. The situations mentioned spontaneously by both groups of children were made into stories and administered to second-grade youngsters from each culture. Only those stories were selected to which the majority of children from both cultures responded in a similar manner. The distribution of stories for each of the four emotions in Parts I and II of the test are:

	Part I	Part II
Happy	1 and 11	1 and 12
Afraid	5 and 9	5 and 8
Sad	6 and 10	4 and 6
Angry	4 and 7	7 and 10

The children's responses to the remaining stories either showed a high degree of ambivalence about whether someone would react by being sad or angry (Part I, Story 2; Part II, Stories 3 and 9) or reflected marked cultural differences in the choice of sad or angry as the appropriate response (Part I, Stories 3 and 8; and Part II, Stories 2 and 11). The research done thus far with this instrument indicates that while subjects can differentiate between happy and afraid responses, sad and angry responses appear to be equally acceptable reactions to frustrating situations. Consequently, when testing individual youngsters an item should be scored correct if the child gives "happy" as a response to the happy situations, "afraid" as a response to the fearful situations, and either "angry" or "sad" as a response to all of the remaining situations. Since there were no statistically significant differences between Part I and Part II, the scores for happy, afraid, and unhappy reactions can be combined for both parts of the test. It has generally been found advisable to administer the test twice to subjects between 3 and 3½ years of age. The task is sufficiently new to those younger subjects that even when the children know the examiner, they frequently "freeze" the first time around. Since there is no learning involved, the double presentation simply insures greater validity of results.

As examples, five items from Part I of the test are given below.

1. Show me how Nancy (Johnny) would feel *if her mother was going to take her some place she liked to go.* Would she feel (examiner names emotions according to sequence)? Pick up the face you think and put it on the picture. Why do you think Nancy (Johnny) would feel _____?

2. Show me how Nancy (Johnny) would feel *if she wanted to do something and her mother said, "No."* Would she feel (examiner names emotions according to sequence)? Pick up the face you think and put it on the picture. Why do you think Nancy (Johnny) would feel _____?

4. Show me how Nancy (Johnny) would feel *if her mother forced her to eat something she didn't like.* Would she feel (examiner names emotions according to sequence)?

Pick up the face you think and put it on the picture. Why do you think Nancy (Johnny) would feel _____?

5. Show me how Nancy (Johnny) would feel *if she dreamed that a tiger was chasing her.* Would she feel (examiner names emotions according to sequence)? Pick up the face you think and put it on the picture. Why do you think Nancy (Johnny) would feel _____?

6. Show me how Nancy (Johnny) would feel *if she fell and hurt herself.* Would she feel (examiner names emotions according to sequence)? Pick up the face you think and put it on the picture. Why do you think Nancy (Johnny) would feel _____?

RELIABILITY AND VALIDITY: None reported.

BIBLIOGRAPHY:

Borke, H. M. "Interpersonal Perception of Young Children." *Developmental Psychology*, 1971, *5*, 263-269.

Borke, H. M. "The Development of Empathy in Chinese and American Children Between Three and Six Years of Age: A Cross-Culture Study." *Developmental Psychology*, 1973, *9*, 102-108.

Category 2

Personality and Emotional Characteristics

This category includes measures of personality and specific emotional characteristics, classified into four groups.

Group 2-a. Personality–General. *The measures in this group are designed to sample across several or many aspects of personality. This group is composed of a large proportion of rating scales, personality checklists, and projective tests. It includes specific measures of autism.*

Group 2-b. Personality Variables. *Most of these measures are concerned with one or just a few aspects of personality. Generally the name of the measure indicates the variable involved. Measures of motivation and reinforcement preference measures are also included here.*

Group 2-c. Personality Adjustment. *The effectiveness of the child's efforts to adjust to his environment, and in particular his adjustment to school, is emphasized by these measures. Some of them measure learning problems not based primarily on perceptual processes.*

Group 2-d. Anxiety. *These measures could be classified logically in Group 2-b, but we judged that they warranted a separate group because of their number and because of the important role of the anxiety construct in research.*

Group 2-a

Personality - General

ADJECTIVE INVENTORY DIAGNOSTIC (AID)

AUTHORS: Robert E. Peck and J. E. Everson

AGE: Children and adults

VARIABLE: Psychiatric diagnosis

TYPE OF MEASURE: Self-rating scale

SOURCE FROM WHICH MEASURE MAY BE OBTAINED: Test forms and other material may be obtained from Computer Paramedics Inc., 175 Jericho Turnpike, Syosset, New York 11791. Cost: $5.00 per test. Test forms are supplied free, and the fee of $5.00 is payable only after a finished report is received by the user.

DESCRIPTION OF MEASURE: The AID test consists of a list of 100 common, self-descriptive adjectives, each one rated on a 0-to-10 scale. The resulting matrix is then compared by computer with matrices made up of twelve different psychiatric conditions and also with a matrix of psychiatrically normal persons. The highest correlation coefficient between the groups is taken as a tentative psychiatric diagnosis. Besides giving a diagnosis the test gives an estimate of degree, and it can also estimate certain personality traits such as type of personality and relative intelligence level. The tests on children may be filled out by parents or other knowledgeable persons.

As examples, the first fifteen of the 100 items on the scale are given below. The respondent answers on a scale of 1 (least) to 10 (most), describing how much the word applies to him.

1. Active	6. Anxious	11. Careful
2. Adaptable	7. Bitter	12. Careless
3. Affectionate	8. Blaming	13. Cheerful
4. Aggressive	9. Calm	14. Cold
5. Alert	10. Carefree	15. Compulsive

RELIABILITY AND VALIDITY: The reliability of the different diagnostic categories varies considerably from a high of about 93 percent at the present time to a low of 40 percent. The overall average correct diagnosis is over 85 percent. The test is constantly being improved by introduction of new material into the criterion matrices.

BIBLIOGRAPHY:

Peck, R. E. "Automated Psychiatric Screening." *American Family Physician*, 1974, *9*, 134-138.

Peck, R. E., and Everson, J. E. "Similarities Between Parents and Offspring on a Personality Inventory." *American Journal of Psychiatry*, 1975, *132*, 453-454.

Peck, R. E., and Everson, J. E. "The 'AID'—Watergate Game." Unpublished paper, n.d.

Peck, R. E., and Everson, J. E. "The Effects of Randomization on the AID Test." Unpublished paper, n.d.

Peck, R. E., and Fogel, M. L. "Incidence of Psychiatric Illness in a Mensa Sample." *Mensa Research Journal*, 1975, *5*, 33-38.

Peck, R. E., and Pearlmutter, F. "A Note on the AID Test and the Youthful Drug Abuser." *Nassau County Psychology Association Letter* (in press).

AUTISM PERFORMANCE SCALE

AUTHOR: Donald T. Saposnek

AGE: 2½ years to adulthood

VARIABLE: Degree of autistic withdrawal

TYPE OF MEASURE: Rating scale

SOURCE FROM WHICH MEASURE MAY BE OBTAINED: Donald T. Saposnek, Pediatric Treatment Center, County of Santa Cruz, 290 Pioneer Street, Santa Cruz, California 95060.

DESCRIPTION OF MEASURE: The Autism Performance Scale consists of eleven main behavioral categories, which are broken down into eighteen behavioral items used for rating. Within each item, behavior is rated before and after a treatment procedure in terms of strength of response. Rating marks are chosen from a simple ordinal scale: 0 = no response, 1 = slight or minimal, 2 = moderate, and 3 = intensive or strong. The difference scored from pre- to posttreatment indicates the degree of change from autistic withdrawal to normalcy of behavior. The measure was originally developed and used to test the treatment effects of what is called rage-reduction therapy of autistic children, but it seems applicable to other treatment approaches for autism as well.
     The eighteen behavioral items on the scale are given below.

1. Gives Eye Contact
   a. Spontaneously
   b. Upon command
   c. Upon command during
      physical contact
2. Gives Face-to-Face Contact
   a. Spontaneously
   b. Upon command
3. Approaches
   a. Spontaneously
   b. Upon command
4. Embraces
   a. Spontaneously
   b. Upon command

5. Tasks: Performs Simple Tasks upon Command.
   (List tasks in spaces)
   a. _____
   b. _____
   c. _____
6. Shows Directed Aggression
   a. Hits hand upon command
   b. Hits face upon command
7. General Approach Behavior
8. Vocalization Normalcy
9. Normalcy of Behavior
10. Relaxed Muscle Tonus
11. Shows Startle Response to:
    a. Sound
    b. Touch

RELIABILITY AND VALIDITY: When two raters observed twenty-two children, it was found that both judges agreed exactly on 42 percent of the ratings. On 55 percent of the ratings the judges differed by one rating category. For all ratings on which the two raters differed by one category, the ratings were in the same direction from the pre- to the posttreatment rating. On 3 percent of the ratings there was a difference of two rating categories, in opposite directions from the pre- to the posttreatment rating.

BIBLIOGRAPHY:

Saposnek, D. T. "An Experimental Study of Rage-Reduction Treatment of Autistic Children." *Child Psychiatry and Human Development,* 1972, *3,* 50-62.

BEHAVIOR-RATING CHECKLIST FOR AUTISTIC CHILDREN

AUTHOR: Victor Lotter

AGE: Prepubertal children

VARIABLE: Austistic behavior

TYPE OF MEASURE: Checklist

SOURCE FROM WHICH MEASURE MAY BE OBTAINED: See Lotter (1966).

DESCRIPTION OF MEASURE: The checklist includes twenty-four items in five areas of behavior (speech, social behavior, movement peculiarities, responses to sound, and repetitive/ritualistic behavior) used in an epidemiological survey to identify children with autistic behavior. Ratings were based upon developmental and contemporary behavioral descriptions of 8- to 10-year-old handicapped children, all of whom had been selected in preliminary screening as having some such behaviors. Items were rated 0, 1, or 2 according to severity. Summed scores of speaking and nonspeaking children were ranked separately, and cut-off points were determined by inspection. In the original survey a score of 11 was used to distinguish between autistic and nonautistic children. Nonspeaking, severely mentally retarded (usually institutionalized) children were included in preliminary selection only when relevant behaviors were evident also in categories other than speech and social behavior. The instrument may be a useful screening device; the cutoff score between autistic and other children will depend on the composition of the screened population and interpretation of the individual items. Basically what the device achieves is a systematic and fairly reliable distinction between groups of children according to "how much" autistic behavior they exhibit. It is important to note that developmental descriptions should be included, as autistic manifestations change with age.

As examples, the items from the third behavior area are given below.

Movement Peculiarity:
10. Self-spinning.
11. Jumping.
12. Flapping.
13. Toe walking.
14. Other marked mannerisms.

RELIABILITY AND VALIDITY: From a pool of fifty-four cases, of whom thirty-two were classed as autistic by one rater, an independent rater agreed on twenty-eight of the thirty-two.

BIBLIOGRAPHY:

Demyer, M. K., Churchill, D. W., Pontius, W., and Gilkey, K. "Comparison of Five Diagnostic Systems for Childhood Schizophrenia and Infantile Autism." *Journal of Autism and Childhood Schizophrenia*, 1971, *1*, 175-189.
Gair, D. S. "A Commentary." *Schizophrenia Bulletin*, 1972, *5*, 55-61.
Lotter, V. "Epidemiology of Autistic Conditions in Young Children, I: Prevalence." *Social Psychiatry*, 1966, *1*, 124-137.
Wing, L., Yeates, S. R., Brierley, L. M., and Gould, J. "The Epidemiology of Early Childhood Autism: A Comparison of Surveys Using Different Methodologies." *Psychological Medicine* (in press).

BIOGRAPHICAL INVENTORY (BI) (HIGH SCHOOL FORM)

AUTHOR: Donald E. Super (in collaboration with Martha B. Heyde and Winthrop R. Adkins)

AGE: Grades 11 and 12

VARIABLE: Personality traits

TYPE OF MEASURE: Inventory

SOURCE FROM WHICH MEASURE MAY BE OBTAINED: Donald E. Super, Department of Psychology, Teachers College, Columbia University, New York, New York 10027.

DESCRIPTION OF MEASURE: The Biographical Inventory (BI) was developed as a measure of personality traits revealed through life experiences. This form of the test was designed for adolescents in the last two years of high school; there are two forms for older subjects. The traits measured by the inventory and the number of items devoted to each are as follows: achievement motivation (25), achievement competence (22), independence (40), cultural participation (33), and social participation (30). The five traits tested by the present forms are considered educationally and vocationally relevant, socially acceptable, appropriate at adolescent and adult age levels, reliably measured, and relatively independent. The BI contains 150 items, each in multiple-choice form. Of these 150 items, 112 permit selection of only one answer from the three to five alternatives, while thirty-eight permit as many answers as apply. There is no time limit, but most high school juniors or seniors finish in less than 40 minutes if instructed to work rapidly. The content and scoring of the BI make it an urban and suburban middle-class measure, and the authors suggest that its use at the present be restricted to that population. The measure is equally usable with both sexes, but scores should be interpreted only with the help of sex norms. Hand-scoring can be done using two stencils and takes from 10 to 15 minutes per subject.

As examples, selected items from Part I and Part II are given below. Each of questions 1 to 112 in Part I is to be answered by the one of several alternatives that best describes the statement. Questions 113 to 150 in Part II may be answered by one or more of the alternatives given.

22. The number of people I have dated is
    + a. a great many.
    + b. a number.
    0 c. a few.
    − d. one.
    − e. none.
27. While growing up I
    − a. took little part in family conversation.
    0 b. talked about as much as anyone else.
    + c. probably did more than my share of talking at home.
34. I usually read
    + a. a book or more a week.
    + b. a book every two weeks to a month.
    + c. a book every two to six months.
    0 d. a book every six months to a year or longer.
    − e. I don't read books.
49. My usual reaction to competition has been that I
    + a. enjoyed it.
    0 b. neither liked nor disliked it.
    + c. disliked but participated in it.
    − d. tried to avoid it.
    0 e. none of the above.
51. When some member of my family needs help, the person he is most likely to turn to is my
    0 a. father or mother.
    0 b. spouse.
    0 c. brother or sister.
    + d. self.
    0 e. none of the above.
94. When I have some free time on my hands, I usually
    0 a. know how to fill it up.
    0 b. find it difficult to decide among the many things I'd like to do.
    − c. find it difficult to think of things to do.

— d. welcome the chance just to relax and take it easy.

0 e. I never have free time on my hands.

119. I read regularly

+ a. travel magazines like *Holiday, National Geographic.*

+ b. consumer magazines like *Consumer Reports.*

0 c. fashion and society magazines like *Vogue, Town and Country, Harper's Bazaar.*

0 d. girls' magazines like *Seventeen.*

0 e. None of the above.

126. I have visited the following kinds of places:

+ a. a scientific laboratory.

+ b. an observatory or planetarium.

+ c. a broadcasting studio (radio or TV).

+ d. a motion picture studio.

— e. None of the above.

143. I have worked especially hard to become good at

+ a. keeping my temper.

+ b. being reasonable with unreasonable people.

+ c. school work or studies.

+ d. something in spite of a physical, cultural, or social handicap.

0 e. None of the above.

RELIABILITY AND VALIDITY: Rabinowitz (1965) reported Kuder-Richardson formula 21 reliabilities ranging from .71 to .82 at age 18 and from .65 to .87 at age 25, with seventy subjects of heterogeneous social and intellectual status. Test-retest reliabilities for upper high school boys range from .67 to .93 with a median of .86. For girls, the test-retest reliabilities range from .75 to .88 with a median of .79. Stability over a longer period was studied by Rabinowitz (1965), from twelfth grade to age 25, on seventy boys. Achievement competence had a seven-year test-retest correlation of .41; independence, .51; and social participation, .33—all significant at the .05 level or better.

The preliminary manual for the BI provides tables of intercorrelations of the five trait scales, by sex, and a table of correlations of trait scales with other basic traits. The data on validity of the BI are provided in the form of tables of intercorrelations of BI scale traits with school-related achievement variables and vocational variables. The validity data may be summarized as follows: The five scales of the BI tend to show expected types of validity when checked against the appropriate educational and vocational criteria. The numbers are small, some scales have not been studied against some criteria, and the results are not always consistent or in line with expectations.

BIBLIOGRAPHY:

Rabinowitz, M. "The Relationship of Self-Regard to the Effectiveness of Life Experiences." Unpublished doctoral dissertation. Teachers College, Columbia University, New York, 1965.

Super, D. E. "The Biographical Inventory as a Method of Describing Adjustment and Predicting Success." *Bulletin of the International Association of Applied Psychology,* 1960, *9,* 19-39.

Super, D. E., and Overstreet, P. L. *The Vocational Maturity of Ninth-Grade Boys.* New York: Teachers College Press, 1960.

Super, D. E., Kowalski, R. S., and Gotkin, E. H. "Floundering and Trial After High School." Mimeographed. New York: Teachers College, Columbia University, n.d.

Prepared by Orval G. Johnson

BUTLER CHILD HEALTH QUESTIONNAIRE–FORM A (CHQ)

AUTHOR: Alan C. Butler

AGE: Teachers of children aged 6 to 9 years

VARIABLE: Psychological health

TYPE OF MEASURE: Questionnaire

SOURCE FROM WHICH MEASURE MAY BE OBTAINED: See Butler (1975).

DESCRIPTION OF MEASURE: The Butler Child Health Questionnaire–Form A (CHQ) consists of twenty item descriptions of child behavior that can be evaluated by teachers. A version of the scale is also available for parents, but because of greater parental bias it requires further refinement. Weights of 2, 1, and 0 are given to the teacher's appraisal of whether a statement "certainly applies," "applies somewhat," or "doesn't apply." While a stringent cutoff point of 34 without any zero ratings is established as the point identifying the psychologically healthy child, caution must be taken to avoid labeling children below that point as unhealthy, since they may also be demonstrating many psychological health traits. The CHQ approaches the behavior of a child not from an abnormal point of view but rather with the assumption that each child is a special unique individual who possesses a variety of psychological health characteristics. This conceptual model of health as a creative growth-oriented process distinguishes between the so-called normal child, who may or may not be healthy, and a psychologically healthy child. The scale may be particularly useful to teachers as a screening and remedial instrument.

As examples, the first ten items of the twenty-item questionnaire are given below.

1. Has good physical health (few colds).
2. Rarely complains of aches and pains.
3. Speech is clear for age.
4. Demonstrates appropriate use of intelligence.
5. Is unique, original, or creative.
6. Demonstrates a wide range of interests.

7. Is intellectually curious.
8. Relates well with other children.
9. Relates well with teachers.
10. Can quickly establish a trusting relationship.

RELIABILITY AND VALIDITY: The CHQ was administered to teachers of fifty middle-class urban children and to teachers of twenty lower-class rural children. Inter-rater reliability coefficients of .76 and .79, respectively, were obtained by having current first-grade teachers and past kindergarten teachers rate each child. Odd-even internal consistency coefficients ranged from .82 to .89. The validity of the scale is supported by the capacity of it to discriminate between psychologically healthy children and children who are "normal" or who have emotional problems. *Phi* coefficients of −.76 and −.81 were obtained when the scale was correlated with Rutter's Behavior Questionnaire (Rutter, 1967). Construct validity is further supported by the finding that high CHQ children are evaluated as functioning in a psychologically healthy manner both at home and at school. A discrimination index of 84 percent for all high CHQ children suggests that the health characteristics of the scale are actually mirroring the daily lives of healthy children.

BIBLIOGRAPHY:

Butler, A. C. "The Child Health Questionnaire: Preliminary Data." *Psychology in the Schools*, 1975, *12*, 153-160.
Rutter, M. "A Children's Behavior Questionnaire for Completion by Teachers: Preliminary Findings." *Journal of Child Psychology and Psychiatry*, 1967, *8*, 1-11.

CHILD BEHAVIOR CHARACTERISTICS (CBC) FORM

AUTHORS: Edgar F. Borgatta and David Fanshel

AGE: Infancy to 17+ years

VARIABLE: Child behavior

TYPE OF MEASURE: Rating scale

SOURCE FROM WHICH MEASURE MAY BE OBTAINED: David Fanshel, Columbia University School of Social Work, 622 West 113th Street, New York, New York 10025.

DESCRIPTION OF MEASURE: This instrument is based upon prior studies of foster children, children in residential treatment settings, and children known to psychiatric out-patient clinics. The form has been designed so that it is possible to engage in longitudinal assessment of children from infancy to late adolescence. It consists of 109 items. A child can be rated as exhibiting the behavior conveyed by "never," "rarely," "sometimes," "often," and "almost always." A minimal set of items is identified as appropriate for infants, and these items are also included in the scales to be created for older children. Further specific content is identified with early childhood (2 to 6 years of age) and for the age group 7 to 17+. A series of factor analyses carried out for each age group has been used to develop a scoring scheme to emphasize othogonal content. The items can be summed into twenty-seven component scores, and these can be further consolidated into sixteen component scores. The sixteen component scales include: alertness-intelligence, learning difficulty, responsibility, unmotivated-laziness, agreeableness, defiance-hostility, likeability, emotionality-tension, infantilism, withdrawal, appetite, sex precociousness, overcleanliness, sex inhibition, activity, and assertiveness.

As examples, ten of the 109 items are given below.

1. Is physically active, vigorous.
2. Is alert.
3. Is friendly.
4. Is interested in what goes on.
5. Is gloomy or sad-looking.
6. Is likeable.
7. Is cheerful.
8. Is smart.
9. Is moody.
10. Has a good appetite.

RELIABILITY AND VALIDITY: The scales are based upon a number of factor-analytic studies including a major study of over six hundred foster children. Normative data for these children are available. Cronbach *alpha* coefficients have been reported for all component scales according to age groupings; 90 percent of these are .70 or over. Interjudge reliability coefficients are reported for each scale. Regarding validity, Fanshel and Shinn (1975) have reported correlations with scores achieved by children in intelligence tests, figure drawing tests, and with teacher ratings. Stability of scores over time is also reported.

BIBLIOGRAPHY:

Borgatta, E. F., and Cautely, P. W. "Behavioral Characteristics of Children: Replication Studies with Foster Children." *Multivariate Behavioral Research,* 1966, *1,* 399-424.

Borgatta, E. F., and Fanshel, D. *Behavioral Characteristics of Children Known to Psychiatric Out-Patient Clinics.* New York: Child Welfare League, 1965.

Borgatta, E. F., and Fanshel, D. "The Child Behavior Characteristics (CBC) Form: Revised Age-Specific Forms." *Multivariate Behavioral Research,* 1970, *5,* 49-82.

Fanshel, D., Hylton, L., and Borgatta, E. F. "A Study of Behavior Disorders in Children in Residential Treatment Centers." *Journal of Psychological Studies,* 1963, *14,* 1-23.

Fanshel, E., and Shinn, E. B. *Children in Foster Care.* New York: Columbia University Press, 1975.

Prepared by David Fanshel

CHILD BEHAVIOR CHECKLIST

AUTHOR: Richard N. Walker

AGE: Parents of preschool children

VARIABLE: Eight temperament variables

TYPE OF MEASURE: Rating scale (in checklist format)

SOURCE FROM WHICH MEASURE MAY BE OBTAINED: See Walker (1963).

DESCRIPTION OF MEASURE: The checklist consists of sixty-eight adjectives and brief phrases for use by an informant. Since the rater cannot only underline characteristic traits but also circle traits clearly uncharacteristic, and double underline or double circle for emphasis, the list can be scored as a 5-point rating scale. Individual items are summed to give eight cluster scores: energetic, active; curious, thoughtful; aggressive, assertive; fearful, anxious; social, friendly; excitable, tense; cooperative, conforming; and cheerful, expressive. These were determined by cluster analysis. Their composition is given in Walker (1963). No representative norms are available. Mean scores are available for two nonrepresentative groups: a sample of bright American preschoolers, aged 2 to 5 years (Walker, 1963) and a sample of disturbed Dutch children, aged 6 to 14, in a residential treatment institute (Verdonck, 1972). Circumplex order of the traits (loadings on the two principal factors) for the two very dissimilar samples was strikingly similar (Verdonck and Walker, in press).

　　As examples, the first twenty of the sixty-eight items are given below. The parent underlines those items that describe his child, or, if they are especially apt, underlines them twice. He circles those items that do not describe his child, or, if they are particularly inappropriate, circles them twice. Traits that are not outstanding one way or another are not marked.

1. Good appetite.	11. Jealous.
2. Tires easily.	12. Cries easily.
3. Cautious.	13. Enthusiastic.
4. Affectionate.	14. Mischievous.
5. Worries.	15. Sympathetic.
6. Bashful, shy.	16. Competitive.
7. Unpredictable.	17. Orderly, neat.
8. Destructive.	18. Talkative.
9. Well-mannered.	19. Teases.
10. Energetic.	20. Fearful.

RELIABILITY AND VALIDITY: Coefficients of reliability ranged from .44 to .81 with a median of .74, in the American nursery school sample. For nineteen preschool boys and seventeen girls rated one year later by the same raters (mothers), correlations ranged from .39 to .83, with a median of .62. Correlations with ratings by nursery-school teachers on variables bearing the same names (but different item composition and format) ranged from near zero to just .47; most were significant but low. Teachers' and parents' views showed little similarity, in part, perhaps, because the children behaved differently at home and at school.

BIBLIOGRAPHY:

Walker, R. N. "Body Build and Behavior in Young Children: II. Body Build and Parents' Ratings." *Child Development,* 1963, *34,* 1-23.

Verdonck, P. F. *Lichaamsbouw en Gedrag (Body Build and Behavior).* Haarlem, The Netherlands: Uitgerverij de Toorts, 1972.

Verdonck, P. F., and Walker, R. N. "Body Build and Behavior in Emotionally Disturbed Dutch Children." *Genetic Psychology Monographs* (in press).

CHILD DEVELOPMENT CENTER Q SORT (CDCQ)

AUTHORS: Frances Fuchs Schachter, Allan Cooper, and Rona Gordet

AGE: Toddler to maturity

VARIABLE: Personality development

TYPE OF MEASURE: Q-sort

SOURCE FROM WHICH MEASURE MAY BE OBTAINED: Society for Research in Child Development, Business Office, 5801 Ellis Avenue, Chicago, Illinois 60637. Cost: Monograph, $3.00; test materials, $2.00 per kit; additional Q-sort decks, $1.00. Test materials are available from Frances F. Schachter, Barnard College, Columbia University, New York, New York 10027.

DESCRIPTION OF MEASURE: The CDCQ involves a novel application of Q-sort, a developmental sort covering five age levels: toddler, preschool, kindergarten, school age, adolescent-maturity. New items are added at each age level from forty-one at the toddler level to 113 at maturity. Block's comprehensive California Q-sort formed the basis of the CDCQ. Sorting is done by mental health workers, including specially trained teachers. Comprehensive clinical or research protocols, or a comprehensive familiarity with the child, forms the basis for sorting. Age-ideal sorts based on the consensus of mental health experts are available at age levels toddler, preschool, and kindergarten. The discrepancy between real and ideal sorts provides a general index of deviation in personality development.

As examples, the items (1-13) covering Independence-Dependence are given below. There are 113 items covering the eight variables: Affect (14-19); Relations-People (20-47); Relations-Self (48-60); Relations-Inanimate Objects (61-68); Relations-Heterosexual Matters (69-72); Ego (73-106); Superego (107-113).

1. Has an urge for independence and autonomy, is basically independent, whether conscious or not, whether obvious to the observer or hidden.—Lacks urge for independence and autonomy, is basically dependent, whether conscious or not, whether obvious to the observer or hidden. (T)

2. Seeks out physical contact.—Avoids physical contact. (T)

3. Unable to fulfill bodily needs and perform bodily functions by self (feeding, toileting, etc.).—Able to fulfill bodily needs and perform bodily functions by self (feeding, toileting, etc.). (T)
4. Seeks attention from others.—Is not likely to seek attention from others. (T)
5. Seeks reassurance from others.—Is not likely to seek reassurance from others. (P)
6. Tends to initiate activities for self or others.—Needs others to initiate activities for self. (T)
7. Takes active steps in fulfilling own desire.—Fails to take the steps that are necessary for own benefit. (T)
8. Is turned to for advice and reassurance.—Is not likely to be turned to for advice and reassurance. (A-M)
9. Requires structure and direction; is uncomfortable with ambiguity.—Is not likely to require structure and direction; takes ambiguity in stride. (P)
10. Makes others want to help and protect self.—Makes others feel can take care of self. (T)
11. Behaves in a submissive manner at home.—Behaves in a domineering, bossy manner at home. (T)
12. Behaves in a submissive manner outside the home.—Behaves in a domineering, bossy manner outside the home. (T)
13. Creates and exploits dependency in people, regardless of the technique employed.—Respects and encourages the independence and individuality of others. (SA)

RELIABILITY AND VALIDITY: Reliability: The sample consisted of sixteen Ss, eight clinical and eight control, matched for age, socioeconomic factors, and sorters. Sorting was carried out on comprehensive protocols, including interviews with mothers, teachers' interviews or reports, psychological tests, and reports of direct observation and interviews of Ss. The results indicate that high levels of reliability can be obtained both from protocols typical of longitudinal studies of normals and from clinical records. Intersorter reliability based on composites of three sorters was .83 for clinical cases and .83 for controls. The mean intersorter correlation was .62, so that only two sorters are needed to obtain a mean of .77 for the reliability of the composite. Specially trained teachers were found to be as reliable as clinicians. Inconsistent or meager protocols yielded significantly lower intersorter reliabilities, with the obvious implication that reliable Q-sorts cannot be expected from unreliable data. Validity: Real sorts for each of the sixteen preschoolers were correlated with "normal" sorts; the real-normal sort similarity was then correlated with clinical rankings of adjustment based on the protocols. Three kinds of normal sorts were used: an age-ideal conceptual sort of the ideal preschooler relative to the typical preschooler (reliability of the composite sort of six sorters = .93); an age-typical conceptual sort of the typical preschooler relative to the typical child of another age (reliability of the composite sort of five sorters = .80); and a statistically normal sort based on the eight control Ss. Clinical rankings, age-ideal, and age-typical sorts were all carried out independently of each other. Validity correlations were .75, .77, and .47, respectively. A comparison of the three "normal" sorts shows the age-ideal to be superior.

BIBLIOGRAPHY:

Schachter, F. F., Cooper, A., and Gordet, R. "A Method for Assessing Personality Development for Follow-up Evaluation of the Preschool Child." *Monographs of the Society for Research in Child Development*, 1968, *33* (3) (serial no. 119).

CHILDREN'S AUTONOMY QUESTIONNAIRE (MC-3)

AUTHOR: Ron Shouval

AGE: 8 to 14 years

VARIABLE: Four types of children's autonomies in face of parental pressure, peer pressure, task completion pressure, and traumatic pressure

SOURCE FROM WHICH MEASURE MAY BE OBTAINED: Ron Shouval, Psychology Department, Tel-Aviv University, Tel-Aviv, Israel.

DESCRIPTION OF MEASURE: The questionnaire includes twenty-eight items, each with three possible answers reflecting different levels of autonomy. The sentence stems present conflict situations that can be resolved by answers reflecting self-help and self-determination, or by seeking help and yielding to the pressures of others. The technique yields four independent factor scores, two focusing on autonomy from specific socializing agents (parents and peers) and two focusing on autonomy in specific situations (traumatic and task completion).
    One example from seven for each factor is given below.

1. *Obstacle Press*   If a button on my shirt is torn . . .
                          I'll change the shirt.
                          I'll sew it on again.
                          I'll ask my mother to fix it.

2. *Parental Pressure*   If I want to go on a trip and my parents won't let me go . . .
                          I try to persuade them, but if they won't let me, I won't go.
                          I stay home and don't go on the trip.
                          I go on the trip without their permission.

3. *Trauma or Anxiety*   If I get a small cut on my hand . . .
                          I put more medicine on it.
                          I go to my mother.
                          I go to a nurse.

4. *Peer Pressure*   My friends and I went out to see a movie. I very much wanted to see a certain movie and my friends did not agree with me . . .
                          I tried to persuade them, but when they didn't agree I went to the movie they wanted.
                          I went to the movie they wanted.
                          I went alone to the movie I wanted to see.

RELIABILITY AND VALIDITY: The items were selected from a large pool of questions administered to more than one thousand urban children aged 8 to 14. The twenty-eight items of the present measure (MC-3) were selected according to item analysis and factor analysis. In all the replications that were done, it was found significantly that the older the child, the higher the autonomy score in each factor. No significant differences in autonomy were found between boys and girls. In two studies, low but significant correlations were found between autonomy scores and peer nomination of autonomy ($N = 34, r = .56; N = 33, r = .25$). Children raised in children's homes in the kibbutz were found to be more autonomous of parent pressure than were children raised in a cooperative village (Moshav) who lived in the parents' home. Conversely, kibbutz children were less autonomous of peer pressure than were Moshav children.

The four factors were found to be consistent in several replications: ($N = 430$, $N = 499$, $N = 1,461$, $N = 823$). The factors of parental pressure and obstacle press are clear and strong. The factors of trauma and peer pressure are less clear. Kuder-Richardson formula 20 ($N = 823$) computed separately on four groups (boys—eastern ethnic, boys—western ethnic; girls—eastern ethnic, girls—western ethnic) yields similar results. The average Kuder-Richardson coefficients are: factor parental pressure, .65; factor trauma, .53; factor obstacle press, .54; factor peer pressure, .27; total score, .62. The average intercorrelation between the four factor scores was close to zero.

BIBLIOGRAPHY:

Shouval, R., Bronfenbrenner, U., Kav-Venaki, S., Devereux, E. C., and Kiely, E. "The Anomalous Reactions to Social Pressure of Israeli and Soviet Children Raised in Family vs. Collective Settings." *Journal of Personality and Social Psychology*, 1975, *32*, 477-489.

Shouval, R. and Duek, E. "Children's Autonomy: A Sentence-Completion Measure." Mimeographed. Tel-Aviv University, Tel-Aviv, Israel, 1973.

Shouval, R., Duek, E., and Ginton, A. "A Multiple-Choice Version of the Sentence-Completion Method." *Journal of Personality Assessment*, 1975, *38*, 41-49.

Shouval, R., Zakai, D., and Halfon, Y. "Autonomy or Autonomies?: Trait Consistency and Situation Specificity." Mimeographed. Tel-Aviv University, Tel-Aviv, Israel, 1975.

CHILDREN'S CLASSROOM ACTIVITY RATING SCALE

AUTHORS: Robert A. Hicks, Suzanne L. Decker, and Janet C. Stagnaro

AGE: 6 to 12 years

VARIABLE: Teacher's rating of child's activity level

TYPE OF MEASURE: Rating scale

SOURCE FROM WHICH MEASURE MAY BE OBTAINED: Robert A. Hicks, Psychology Department, San Jose State University, San Jose, California 95192.

DESCRIPTION OF MEASURE: A substantial number of items were written and pooled from various sources to measure classroom activity. This pool was submitted to a sample of teachers who rated their students, and the data were factor analyzed. One of the three factors that emerged was labeled a normal activity factor. The items that made up this normal activity factor served as the basis of this scale. These items were submitted to a panel of teachers who screened them for wording and suggested certain additional items that seemed consistent with this normal activity factor. This procedure resulted in the forty-item instrument. On the basis of conversations with teachers, a 3-point rating scale was adopted—the item does not apply (weighted 0), applies sometimes (1), or applies frequently (2). Total activity score is the sum of the weighted responses to each item. However, since no norms are available, this scale, while deemed convenient by teachers, should be considered discretionary.

As examples, the first fifteen items of the scale are given below.

Disruptiveness; tendency to annoy and bother others.
2. Restlessness, inability to sit still.
3. Shows difficulty in paying attention.
4. Unnecessarily touches and handles objects.
5. Does not know how to have fun; behaves like a little adult.
6. Passivity, suggestibility; easily led by others.
7. Social withdrawal, preference for solitary activities.
8. Crying over minor annoyances and hurts.
9. Hangs around with delinquent friends.
10. Uncooperativeness in group situations.
11. Actions are unpredictable.
12. Reads books or stories not assigned.
13. Fights.
14. Sluggishness, lethargy.
15. Jitteriness, jumpiness; easily startled.

RELIABILITY AND VALIDITY: The reliability of this measure has not been established. Scores on this scale were found to be significantly correlated, for example, $r = .39$, $df = 63$, $t = 3.34$, with the Children's Stimulus-Seeking Scale. (see p. 000 and Hicks and Dockstader, 1968).

BIBLIOGRAPHY:

Hicks, R. A., and Dockstader, S. "Cultural Deprivation and Preschool Children's Preference for Complex and Novel Stimuli." *Perceptual and Motor Skills,* 1968, *27,* 1321-1322.

CHILDREN'S TEMPERAMENT QUESTIONNAIRE

AUTHOR: Richard N. Walker

AGE: Grades 3 to 7

VARIABLE: Six traits of temperament: energy, aggressiveness, fearfulness, socialness, stability, cheerfulness

TYPE OF MEASURE: Questionnaire

SOURCE FROM WHICH MEASURE MAY BE OBTAINED: See Walker (1967).

DESCRIPTION OF MEASURE: *Format.* The questionnaire consists of ninety-six items, sixteen for each of six scales. Each trait is scored by the subject's agreement or disagreement with self-descriptive statements of relatively obvious import. (No items are intended to be subtle.) The test is orally administered; items are read aloud by the examiner and the child responds on an answer sheet. *Composition.* Items were chosen from a larger number (154 candidate items) intended to measure the traits, by correlation of each item with the total score for the proposed cluster. Many items were chosen from existing scales (Sarason's GASC, Guilford and Zimmerman's Temperament Survey, Buss and Durkee's Hostility Inventory, Sutton-Smith and Rosenberg's Impulsivity Scale, Thurstone's Temperament Schedule, Cattell's Junior P Quiz), and others were original. The six traits were used to derive two factor scores: active and controlled. *Norms.* Sten scores are provided for boys and girls separately for each grade from 3 to 6. The normative sample was 406 public school children.

As examples, the first ten of the ninety-six items are given below.

1. I often hurry to get places, even when there is plenty of time.
2. I like to fight.
3. When I am alone in a room and I hear a strange noise, I get a frightened feeling.
4. I like to play with both boys and girls.
5. People often say I'm too noisy.
6. Someday I'd like a job that lets me travel around and have many new experiences, even if the pay isn't good.
7. I enjoy it when I play so hard that I really get worn out.
8. When someone makes me mad, I almost always let him know it.
9. When my mother is away from home, I worry about whether she is going to come back.
10. I would like to belong to lots of different clubs.

RELIABILITY AND VALIDITY: *Internal consistency.* Split-half reliability coefficients were determined for 257 boys and girls in grades 3 through 6. Corrected correlations for the six traits ranged from .62 to .88; correlations for the factor scores were .82 and .83. *Retest correlations.* For 368 subjects retested a year after their first testing, correlations for the whole sample ranged from .42 to .65 for the six traits, .59 and .60 for the two factor scores. *Correlations with other measures.* The scores of 390 subjects were correlated with corresponding variables as rated by their teachers and as evaluated by their classmates in "Guess-who" sociometric ratings. All the correlations for the total group were significant, but all were quite low. Correlations were higher with peers' evaluations (.12 to .30) than with teachers' (.11 to .21).

BIBLIOGRAPHY:

Walker, R. N. "Some Temperament Traits in Children as Viewed by Their Peers, Their Teachers, and Themselves." *Monographs of the Society for Research in Child Development,* 1967, *32* (6).

CHILD'S BEHAVIOR TRAITS (CBT)

AUTHORS: Phyllis Levenstein and staff, Verbal Interaction Project

AGE: 2 to 12 years

VARIABLE: Socioemotional development

TYPE OF MEASURE: Likert-type scale

SOURCE FROM WHICH MEASURE MAY BE OBTAINED: Available for research purposes from Phyllis Levenstein, Verbal Interaction Project, 5 Broadway, Freeport, New York 11520.

DESCRIPTION OF MEASURE: The CBT consists of twenty items, each of which rates on a 5-point scale the degree of presence of behavior considered to be socioemotional, thus indicating the child's emotional well-being and social adjustment. The item score range is from 1 to 5, so that the total summative score ranges from 20 to 100. The twenty items are classified under five subscales as follows, with examples of items:

1. Responsible Independence: Seems self-confident, not timid.
2. Social Cooperation: Refrains from physically aggressive behavior toward others.
3. Cognitively Related Skills: Is well organized in work or play.
4. Emotional Stability: Is spontaneous without being explosive.
5. Task Orientation: Is attentive and concentrates on tasks.

The scale was developed to evaluate the socioemotional status of low-income children at age 2 and 4 years in the Mother-Child Home Program of the Verbal Interaction Project, and in subsequent school years. During the program, ratings are based on the global evaluations of home interveners ("toy demonstrators") who have observed the child in home sessions. In school years, teachers rate the children from observations of classroom behavior.

RELIABILITY AND VALIDITY: The CBT's development began in 1970 and reached final form in 1974, when the coefficient *alpha* for its internal reliability (Nunnally, 1967) for 390 children, 2 to 10 years of age, was .95. A multigroup factor analysis indicated that .48 of the variance among items was accounted for by the total-score factor. For fifty-five untreated 8- to 10-year-old school children rated by their teachers, the CBT was age independent ($r = -.03$), but not for program 2- to 4-year olds rated by their home interveners ($r = .36$). Evidence for validity derives from three sources: (1) the coefficient of $-.70$ ($N = .75$) resulting from correlation of CBT total score with the presence of school problems indicated by the same teachers who rated the CBT; (2) for fifty-nine children, the coefficients of .58 and .58 respectively for math teachers' CBT scores correlated with classroom teachers' indication of school problems, and vice versa; and (3) the correlation of .43 between the CBT scores and the IQs of 273 children (in follow-up and those just completing the program), aged about 4 to 10 years.

BIBLIOGRAPHY:

Levenstein, P. "Learning Through (and From) Mothers." *Childhood Education,* 1971,
    48, 130-134.
Nunnally, J. *Psychometric Theory.* New York: McGraw-Hill, 1967.

COLOR SYMBOLISM PERSONALITY TEST

AUTHORS: Torao Obonai and Takeshi Matsuoka

AGE: Junior high to adult

VARIABLE: Abnormality, masculinity, femininity, types of personality

TYPE OF MEASURE: Projective

SOURCE FROM WHICH MEASURE MAY BE OBTAINED: The Nippon Seihan Company, 5-25-16 Otsuka, Bunkyo-ku, Tokyo, Japan. (Price unfixed.)

DESCRIPTION OF MEASURE: This test consists of forty-one stimulus words (e.g., horror, anxiety, confidence, friendship, and so forth) and the color list of sixteen colors. The examinee is given the forty-one stimulus words, one word per 15 seconds, and chooses one of the colors among the color list that he feels to be the most suitable to the affective meaning caused by the stimulus words. As these chosen colors (response colors) prove to reflect the examinee's personality as is shown by the research results, the examinee's personality is diagnosed as follows: (1) abnormality of personality: Response colors are picked out that have significantly less frequency than theoretical value in each stimulus word, based on the test results of many examinees, and these response colors are called deviation colors. Deviation colors have some relation to the abnormality of personality in the area of social adaptability, and the examinee's personality is classified and diagnosed into five types—morbid discord, discord, balance, concord, and overconcord—by the number of deviation colors in all the response colors. (2) Masculinity and femininity in personality: The colors chosen significantly more frequently by men than women to each stimulus word are called male-color and the opposites are called female-color. The masculinity and femininity of the examinee is classified and diagnosed into nine types according to the frequency of these colors in all the response colors. (3) Diagnosis of each type of personality by predominant response color (PRC): PRCs are response colors most frequently chosen by the examinee without any relation to the stimulus words and are determined by the average choice of colors by people in general. As PRCs represent the characteristics of each examinee's personality, the type of the examinee's personality is diagnosed by his PRC.

RELIABILITY AND VALIDITY: Test-retest reliabilities for three groups were: junior high students, .53; senior high students, .60; and college students, .68.

BIBLIOGRAPHY:

Obonai, T., and Matsuoka, T. *Color Symbolism Personality Test.* Nakaym Nakayama Shten, Tokyo, 1956 (in Japanese).
Obonai, T., and Matsuoka, T. *Principles and Method of Color Symbolism Personality Test.* Nippon Seihan Company, Tokyo, 1966 (in English).

Prepared by Takeshi Matsuoka and Kenzo Marumo

THE COLUMBUS: PICTURE ANALYSIS OF GROWTH TOWARDS MATURITY

AUTHOR: M. J. Langeveld

AGE: 5 to 18 years

VARIABLE: Personality development and problems in growing up

TYPE OF MEASURE: Projective test

SOURCE FROM WHICH MEASURE MAY BE OBTAINED: S. Karger Publishing Company, 4000 Basel, Arnold-Bocklin Str. 25, Switzerland.

DESCRIPTION OF MEASURE: The Columbus consists of twenty-four pictures or picture situations, of which twenty-one are in black and white and three in color. The artwork, while uneven in style, is appealing, and the color pictures, especially, are whimsical and captivating. The author suggests a grouping of the cards according to four age groups. The pictures were composed for projective communication with children from 5 to 18 years and were used experimentally with European, South African, Egyptian, and Israeli children. They are useful for the analysis of personality structure and history as well as for therapeutic communication with the normal, neurotic, or difficult child. A seventy-two-page manual accompanies the test. No specific administration instructions are provided, the author suggesting that age and resistance to the examination should be taken into consideration in determining the approach to be used by the examiner.

The author suggests evaluation of the responses in terms of at least two basic frames of reference. The first includes four categories: affectivity-emotionality, material of the problems, structural form, and quality. These are divided into subcategories. The other basic frame of reference has to do with the following three variables: (1) relationship to the present, which includes relationship to persons, degree of integration in milieu and community, and socioeconomical cultural background; (2) relationship to oneself, others, and the world of objects, which includes relationship to instinctual drives, relationship to resistances encountered, relationship to existing conscience, sense of identity, relationship to others, and relationship to the world of objects; and (3) relationship to the future, which includes outlook on the future, mode of approach to the future, relationship to the incompletely known, and relationship to the formless.

RELIABILITY AND VALIDITY: The manual offers a number of categories for analysis of personality development but no quantitative analysis or scales. The author mentions forty unpublished research papers in the Dutch language.

BIBLIOGRAPHY:

Garbers, J. G. *Pedi Adolescence. The Educational Situation and Image of the Pedi School Child.* Port Elizabeth, Union of South Africa: University Press, 1971.

Langeveld, M. J. *The Columbus: Picture Analysis of Growth Toward Maturity; A Series of 24 Pictures and a Manual.* New York: S. Karger, 1969.

Nildriks, G. *Social Disadvantage and Educational Opportunity: A Study of 50 Individual Cases from Two Working-Class Neighborhoods in Holland.* Ghent, Belgium: University of Ghent, Laboratory of Psychology, 1972.

Prepared by Orval G. Johnson

DIAGNOSTIC CHECKLIST FOR BEHAVIOR DISTURBED CHILDREN, FORM E2

AUTHOR: Bernard Rimland

AGE: 3 years and up

VARIABLE: Autism in children (classification of childhood psychoses)

TYPE OF MEASURE: Checklist

SOURCE FROM WHICH MEASURE MAY BE OBTAINED: Institute for Child Behavior Research, 4758 Edgeware Road, San Diego, California 92116. Cost: Less than 5 copies, no charge; 10 copies, $1.00; 50 copies, $3.00.

DESCRIPTION OF MEASURE: Diagnostic Checklist for Behavior Disturbed Children, Form E2, was especially designed to identify cases of classical infantile autism (Kanner's Syndrome) from undifferentiated psychotic children loosely diagnosed as autistic. It is also used, through computer cluster analytic techniques, in the detection of other syndromes among the childhood psychoses. It is designed to be completed by the child's parents and asks questions concerning pregnancy and delivery, early postnatal life, speech, behavior, and behavior patterns through age 5, with particular emphasis on the symptomatology of classical infantile autism.

As examples, eleven selected items from the eighty-item checklist are given below.

8. Unusual conditions of birth and infancy (check only one number in left-hand column):

    _____*1* Unusual conditions (Indicate which: blindness _____, cerebral palsy _____, birth injury _____, seizures _____, blue baby _____, very high fever _____, jaundice _____, other _____

    _____*2* Twin birth (identical _____, fraternal _____)

    _____*3* Both 1 and 2

    _____*4* Normal, or don't know

9. Concerning baby's health in first 3 months:

    _____*1* Excellent health, no problems

    _____*2* Respiration (frequent infections _____, other _____)

    _____*3* Skin (rashes _____, infection _____, allergy _____, other _____)

    _____*4* Feeding (learning to suck _____, colic _____, vomiting _____, other _____)

    _____*5* Elimination (diarrhea _____, constipation _____, other _____)

    _____*6* Several of above (indicate which: 2 _____, 3 _____, 4 _____, 5 _____, 6 _____)

11. In the first year, did the child react to bright lights, bright colors, unusual sounds, etc.?

    _____*1* Unusually strong reaction (pleasure _____, dislike _____)

    _____*2* Unusually unresponsive

    _____*3* Average, or don't know

13. (Age 4-8 months) Did the child reach out or prepare himself to be picked up when mother approached him?

    _____*1* Yes, or I believe so

    _____*2* No, I don't think he did

    _____*3* No, definitely not

    _____*4* Don't know

14. Did the child rock in his crib as a baby?

    _____*1* Yes, quite a lot

    _____*2* Yes, sometimes

    _____*3* No, or very little

    _____*4* Don't know

29. (Age 2-5) Is he cuddly?

    _____*1* Definitely, likes to cling to adults

    _____*2* Above average (likes to be held)

    _____*3* No, rather stiff and awkward to hold

    _____*4* Don't know

45. (Age 3-5) Does child get very upset if certain things he is used to are changed (like furniture or toy arrangement, or certain doors which must be left open or shut)?

    _____*1* No

    _____*2* Yes, definitely

    _____*3* Slightly true

51. (Age 3-5) Is it possible to direct child's attention to an object some distance away or out a window?

    _____*1* Yes, no special problem

    _____*2* He rarely sees things very far out of reach

    _____*3* He examines things with fingers and mouth only

56. (Age 3 and 5) Is the child extremely fearful?

_____1 Yes, of strangers or certain people

_____2 Yes, of certain animals, noises or objects

_____3 Yes, of 1 and 2 above

_____4 Only normal fearfulness

_____5 Seems unusually bold and free of fear

_____6 Child ignores or is unaware of fearsome objects

67. (Before age 5) Can the child answer a simple question like "What is your first name?" "Why did Mommy spank Billy?"

_____1 Yes, can answer such questions adequately

_____2 No, uses speech, but can't answer questions

_____3 Too little speech to tell

70. (Before age 5) Has the child used the word "Yes"?

_____1 Has used "Yes" fairly often and correctly

_____2 Seldom has used "Yes," but has used it

_____3 Has used sentences, but hasn't used word "Yes"

_____4 Has used a number of other words or phrases, but hasn't used word "Yes"

_____5 Has no speech, or too little speech to tell

RELIABILITY AND VALIDITY: A number of studies have shown that the E2 Checklist is effective in differentiating children with classical autism from the remainder of the children loosely diagnosed as autistic. Among these analyses are included a comparison of the scores of children diagnosed as autistic by Leo Kanner and those diagnosed otherwise by Dr. Kanner; construct validity studies conducted through item-analysis techniques; biochemical studies performed on a double-blind basis, which showed the children scored high on the E2 Checklist; and, almost uniformly, a biochemical abnormality in the blood platelets that was not found in psychotic children who scored low on the E2 Checklist. Other studies cited in some of the publications listed below also demonstrate Form E2 to be valid for its purpose.

BIBLIOGRAPHY:

Boullin, D. J., Coleman, M., O'Brien, R. A., and Rimland, B. "Laboratory Predictions of Infantile Autism, Based on 5-Hydroxytryptamine Efflux from Blood Platelets and Their Correlation with the Rimland E2 Score." *Journal of Autism and Childhood Schizophrenia,* 1971, *1,* 63-71.

Cameron, J. R. "Background Variables Related to the Various Forms of Childhood Autism." Unpublished doctoral dissertation. University of California, Berkeley, 1969.

Douglas, V. I., and Sanders, F. A. "A Pilot Study of Rimland's Diagnostic Checklist with Autistic and Mentally Retarded Children." *Journal of Child Psychology and Psychiatry,* 1968, *9,* 105-109.

Judd, L. J., and Mandell, A. J. "Chromosome Studies in Early Infantile Autism." *Archives of General Psychiatry,* 1968, *18,* 450-457.

Rimland, B. *Infantile Autism.* New York: Appleton, 1964.

Rimland, B. "On the Objective Diagnosis of Infantile Autism." *Acta Paedopsychiatrica,* 1968, *35,* 146-161.

Rimland, B. "Recent Research on Infantile Autism." *Journal of Operational Psychiatry,* 1972, *3,* 35-39.

Rimland, B. "The Effect of High Dosage Levels of Certain Vitamins on the Behavior of Children with Severe Mental Disorders." In D. R. Hawkins and L. Pauling (Eds.), *Orthomolecular Psychiatry*. San Francisco: Freeman, 1973.

Rimland, B. "Infantile Autism: Status and Research." In A. Davids (Ed.), *Child Personality and Psychopathology: Vol. I, Current Topics*. New York: Wiley, 1974.

DRAW-A-PERSON TEST AS A MEASURE
OF EGO-STAGE DEVELOPMENT

AUTHOR: Alan D. Entin

AGE: Kindergarten

VARIABLE: Ego-stage development and adjustment

TYPE OF MEASURE: Projective technique

SOURCE FROM WHICH MEASURE MAY BE OBTAINED: Alan D. Entin, 1406 Park Avenue, Richmond, Virginia 23220.

DESCRIPTION OF MEASURE: Four ego-stage scales, each consisting of nine points, were constructed from the Harris-Goodenough DAP items and projective interpretations of drawings to measure the Ericksonian concepts of personality development and adjustment in kindergarten children. The points earned on each scale are summed to obtain a score on each ego-stage scale. The DAP total score represents the child's level of intellectual maturity (Harris, 1963). The DAP items for each scale are given below. Numbers in parentheses refer to the Harris scoring guide.

Trust vs. Mistrust
1. Head present (1).
2. Eyes present (4).
3. Eyes: detail—brow or lashes (6), pupil (7).
4. Nose present (9).
5. Mouth present (11).
6. Both chin and forehead shown (14).
7. Hair I (any indication of hair) (18).
8. Ears present (22).
9. Happy, pleasant, smiling expression.
Autonomy vs. Shame and Doubt (Dependency)
1. Arms present (30).
2. Arms at side or engaged in activity (33).
3. Legs present (35).
4. Feet I: any indication (39).
5. Trunk present (46).

6. Trunk in proportion, two dimensions (47).
7. Clothing I (any clear representation) (55).
8. Clothing II (at least two articles of clothing present) (56).
9. Drawing larger than 2" tall.

Initiative vs. Guilt (Passivity)
1. Neck present (2).
2. Fingers present (24).
3. Correct number of fingers shown (25).
4. Details of fingers correct (26).
5. Attachment of arms and legs I (both attached to trunk at any point) (44).
6. Attachment of arms and legs II (at correct point) (45).
7. Movement: arms (72), legs (73).
8. Motor coordination: lines (63).
9. Sex differentiation (by clothes, by hair).

Industry vs. Inferiority (Nonindustry)
1. Hands present (28).
2. Joints (wrist, ankle, shoulders, elbows, hip I, II, knee) (29, 31, 34, 36, 37, 38).
3. Proportion: feet II (40).
4. Proportion: head I (48).
5. Proportion: arms I (51).
6. Proportion: legs (53).
7. Proportion: limbs in two dimensions (54).
8. Additional items included in the drawing: 1-2 items.
9. Additional items included in the drawing: 3+ items.
   (Score any item scored in the Harris-Goodenough system not included above, score for an additional person drawn, sun, pockets, grass, etc.)

RELIABILITY AND VALIDITY: Pearson product-moment correlations of interjudge reliability of DAP scorings were trust, .87; autonomy, .89; initiative, .89; industry, .93; and total score, .93. DAP ego-stages test-retest stability over a two-month period were trust, .13; autonomy, .47; initiative, .54; industry, .60; and total score, .63. The low-to-moderate test-retest stability of the DAP ego-stage scales limits their correlations with the other measures. Significant but low correlations were obtained between the patterns of DAP ego-stage scales and behavioral ratings; the correlations were near the upper bounds set by the reliability of the instruments. The DAP ego scales are highly interrelated. Moderate relationships were demonstrated between the DAP total score and teachers' (.42) and an observer's (.45) ratings of adjustment; teachers' and observer ratings of adjustment correlated .67. The total score of the DAP is highly correlated with the total score of the Metropolitan Readiness Test (.56). The interrelatedness of the various dimensions of ego development obtained may reflect the interrelatedness of the ego stages. The high correlations among DAP total score, teachers' and observer ratings, and the total score of the Metropolitan Readiness test indicate that all the indices are focusing on the social, emotional-cognitive, intellectual maturity of the children.

BIBLIOGRAPHY:

Entin, A. D. "Personality Development and Adjustment in Kindergarten Children." Unpublished doctoral dissertation. University of Chicago, 1967.

Harris, D. B. *Children's Drawings as Measures of Intellectual Maturity.* New York: Harcourt Brace Jovanovich, 1963.

Henry, W. E., and Entin, A. D. *Personality Development and Adjustment in Children.* Research Grant NIH 1 RO3 MH 13, 146-01, National Institute of Health, Washington, D.C., 1967.

GUMPGOOKIES

AUTHORS: Bonnie L. Ballif and Dorothy C. Adkins

AGE: 3½ to 8 years

VARIABLE: Motivation to achieve in school in young children

TYPE OF MEASURE: Objective-projective test

SOURCE FROM WHICH MEASURE MAY BE OBTAINED: Curriculum Research and Development Group, College of Education, University of Hawaii, 1776 University Avenue, Honolulu, Hawaii 96822. Cost: $10.00.

DESCRIPTION OF MEASURE: This is a test consisting of seventy-five dichotomous items, each depicted by two pictures of amorphous characters called Gumpgookies. The examiner describes each gumpgookie orally, and the child decides which one is his or is most like him. The test was constructed to test five hypothetical components of motivation—school or work enjoyment, self-confidence, purposiveness, instrumental activity, and self-evaluation. In the initial format, problems in interpretations of extensive factor analyses revealed that some factors were dominated by response sets, depending on the position of the answer (left vs. right and up vs. down) and order of presentation of the textual material. A method of factoring was developed that would partial out these response sets and lead to substantively interpretable factors. The intent of the factoring was to substantiate a claim of content validity, not to lead to highly dependable measures of each factor. The problem of response sets does not affect the total score, since answer position and order or presentation can be controlled in advance, as is also true of factors for later tests based on the original data. Examples of two items are given below.

This gumpgookie does what it wants to.
This gumpgookie does things well.
   Which is your gumpgookie?
Learning to count makes this one feel good.
Learning to count makes this one feel bad.
   Which is yours?

This test is a precursor of a new improved sixty-item test called Animal Crackers, on which the California Test Bureau is currently collecting normative data by a device of combining data from groups who administered the test in different forms, which negates the response-set problem faced heretofore with only one form. The Gumpgookies test has been individually administered for preschool and kindergarten children, and the Animal Crackers test is designed to be individually administered for pre-schoolers, individually or group administered for kindergarteners, and group administered for older children. Unlike Gumpgookies, Animal Crackers is designed for either hand or machine scoring.

Age norms for Gumpgookies were obtained in terms of transformed Z-scores for the total score and each factor score, based on a total of 1,588 children ranging in age from 39 to 76 months. Age had been computed to the nearest month for this purpose, and the norms were extrapolated to cover the range 31 to 80 months, with a mean of 100 and a standard deviation of 15. Since then, data based on perhaps two thousand additional children have been analyzed in various ways. Some study has been made of similarities and differences of ten ethnic groups. Individual items have also been studied intensively from the standpoints of their difficulties, item test correlations, and factor loadings for various solutions. The total score for a given age or grade group tends to correlate positively but low with both age and Stanford-Binet IQ.

RELIABILITY AND VALIDITY: The total score typically has shown Kuder-Richardson reliability coefficients in the .80s for children aged 3½ to 4½ or 5. (Those for the separate factors have ranged from about .35 to .65.) For one group of first and second graders, the test-retest reliability was .65. No similar estimates are available for younger children. The test has been used extensively as a pretest and posttest in comparing effects of various curricular modules, including some experimental ones on motivation. In general, these have confirmed the validity of the test, although clearly much depends on the teacher. Test results have also been compared with teacher ratings on a specially prepared rating scale by Adkins and Ballif (1972) and on selected rating items from the Behavior Inventory, a scale originally used in Head Start programs. Again, results were positive although not uniformly high for all teachers. When ten preschool teachers indicated the three most and the three least motivated children, seventeen of the highest thirty were above the test median and three at the median. Of the thirty ranked lowest, ten were above the median, one at the median, and nine below it. Such findings and additional data for first and second graders yield differences significant at the .05 level. Much more data on Gumpgookies are available in the annual reports of the former Center for Research in Early Childhood Education of the University of Hawaii, which had a phasing out date of June 30, 1974, by legislative decree. These may still be available at cost through the College of Education, University of Hawaii, 1776 University Avenue, Honolulu, Hawaii 96822.

BIBLIOGRAPHY:

Adkins, D. C., and Ballif, B. L. "A New Approach to Response Sets in Analysis of a Test of Motivation to Achieve." *Educational and Psychological Measurement,* 1972, *32,* 559-577.

Adkins, D. C., Apayne, F. D., and Ballif, B. L. "Motivation Factor Scores and Response Set Scores for Ten Ethnic-Cultural Groups of Preschool Children." *American Educational Research Journal,* 1972, *9,* 557-571.

Horst, P. "Factor Scores Independent of Item Traits." *Educational and Psychological Measurement,* 1972, *32,* 601-612.

Prepared by Dorothy C. Adkins and Bonnie L. Ballif

HYPERACTIVITY-WITHDRAWAL RATING SCALES FOR PRESCHOOLERS

AUTHORS: Richard Q. Bell, Mary F. Waldrop, and George M. Weller

AGE: 2 to 3 years

VARIABLE: Fast-moving, impulsive behavior and play; inhibited play and overcontrolled behavior

TYPE OF MEASURE: Ratings

SOURCE FROM WHICH MEASURE MAY BE OBTAINED: Users should reproduce scales for their own use from Bell, Waldrop, and Weller (1972). The scales are not available from any other source. The federal government retains the copyright.

DESCRIPTION OF MEASURE: Six teachers' or observers' ratings scales for fast-moving, impulsive play and social behavior, and three for withdrawal were developed from a series of studies on 202 early preschool-age children. The six hyperactivity scales are: frenetic play; induction of intervention; inability to delay; emotional aggression; nomadic play; and spilling, throwing. The three withdrawal scales are: vacant staring, closeness to adult base, and chronic fearfulness. On most of the nine 11-point scales, four scale positions have been defined concretely to provide anchors for judgments. A factor scoring system is provided that teachers or observers can apply periodically to keep track of hyperactive and withdrawn behavior in the usual preschool setting. Some scale positions may be specific to the research nursery school (small number of children, large number of observers and teachers), but most scale positions and all overall ratings should be applicable to most preschool settings.

As examples, two of the nine categories on the two rating scales are given below. Definitions of the behavior corresponding to anchor positions on the 11-point scale for each category are included.

Frenetic Play   (Hyperactivity)
11. Much more than others, shows impulsive, fast-moving, ineffective, incomplete play.
 9. During play and transitions shows behavior with only two or three of the components listed in number 11, or play showing all components but with less intensity.
 6. Only during transitions or in vehicle shows frenetic behavior.
 4. During transitions shows mild frenetic behavior.

Scale	11	10	9	8	7	6	5	4	3	2	1
Percentage distribution	0	.2	.2	1	1	2	2	4	8	16	64

Vacant Staring   (Withdrawal)
11. Is immobile and staring without apparent focus much more than others.
 9. Spends a large amount of time staring in a single direction, at a single object, setting, or area, or occasionally shows staring without focus. (This can accompany relatively disorganized or aimless play.)
 3. Seldom shows fixed or vacant staring and then as a reaction to some specific or fearful incident.
 1. Never shows fixed or vacant staring.

Scale	11	10	9	8	7	6	5	4	3	2	1
Percentage distribution	0	.1	1	1	2	6	10	14	20	24	24

RELIABILITY AND VALIDITY: Interobserver agreement is reported in Bell, Waldrop, and Weller (1972) and is quite adequate for all scales. Split-half reliability assessments were not practicable and short-term tests of stability inappropriate, because of evidence of substantial change occurring in children in periods as short as one month. Individual scales have been validated against an index of congenital contributors, which has in turn shown a strong relationship to hyperactivity (Waldrop and Halverson, 1971).

BIBLIOGRAPHY:

Bell, R. Q., and Waldrop, M. F., and Weller, G. M. "A Rating System for the Assessment of Hyperactive and Withdrawn Children in Preschool Samples." *American Journal of Orthopsychiatry*, 1972, *42*, 23-34.

Waldrop, M. F., and Halverson, C. F. "Minor Physical Anomalies and Hyperactive Behavior in Young Children." In J. Hellmuth (Ed.), *Exceptional Infant: Studies in Abnormalities.* Vol. 2. New York: Brunner/Mazel, 1971.

INFANT TEMPERAMENT QUESTIONNAIRE

AUTHOR: William B. Carey

AGE: 4 to 9 months

VARIABLE: Temperament

TYPE OF MEASURE: Questionnaire

SOURCE FROM WHICH MEASURE MAY BE OBTAINED: See Carey (1973), or write to Educational Testing Service, Princeton, New Jersey 08540, or to William B. Carey, 319 West Front Street, Media, Pennsylvania 19063. Cost (from author): $5.00 per copy.

DESCRIPTION OF MEASURE: This questionnaire is based directly on the research interview of Thomas, Chess, and Birch (1968) and yields similar results but can be completed by the mother in 20 minutes and scored in about 10. It consists of seventy statements, each having three choices for completion, describing specific behavior of the baby in certain situations, such as reactions to new foods or strangers. The questionnaire is rated on a separate scoring sheet into the nine categories of temperament: activity, rhythmicity, adaptability, approach, sensory threshold, intensity, mood, distractibility, and persistence. Babies are then designated as "difficult" if they are irregular, low in adaptability and approach, or intense and predominantly negative. "Easy" babies have the opposite characterisitcs. The measure has been standardized on 200 infants in a single pediatric practice. The questionnaire was designed as a screening device for difficult temperament for use in pediatric practice and teaching but has also been used for research by pediatricians and psychologists.

As examples, six of the seventy items on the questionnaire are given below. The respondent circles the choice that correctly describes the baby.

Sleep
  1. a. Generally goes to sleep at about same times (within half hour), night and naps.
     b. Partly the same times, partly not.
     c. No regular pattern at all. Times vary 1-2 hours or more.

Feeding
  6. a. Generally wants and takes milk at about same time. Not over 1 hour variation.
     b. Sometimes same, sometimes different times.
     c. Hungry times quite unpredictable.

Soiling and Wetting
 26. a. When having bowel movement, generally cries.
     b. Sometimes cries.
     c. Rarely cries though may get red in face. Generally happy (smiles, etc.) in spite of having bowel movement.

Diapering and Dressing
 34. a. Squirms and kicks much at these times.
     b. Moves some.
     c. Generally lies still during these procedures.

Bathing
 37. a. Usual reaction to bath—smiles or laughs.
     b. Variable or neutral.
     c. Usually cries or fusses.

Procedures: Nail Cutting, Hair Brushing, Washing Face and Hair, Medicines
 43. a. Initial reaction to any new procedure is generally acceptance.
     b. Variable.
     c. Generally objects; fusses or cries.

RELIABILITY AND VALIDITY: Reliability was determined by asking a randomly selected group of twenty mothers to complete the questionnaire, and complete it again two weeks later. For the five categories used in the difficult/easy designations there was a 90-percent agreement as to rating above or below the mean. For all nine categories, the agreement was 87 percent. The problem of establishing validity is discussed in Carey (1970).

BIBLIOGRAPHY:

Carey, W. B. "A Simplified Method for Measuring Infant Temperament." *Journal of Pediatrics,* 1970, *77,* 188-194.

Carey, W. B. "Measuring Infant Temperament." *Journal of Pediatrics,* 1972, *81,* 414.

Carey, W. B. "Clinical Applications of Infant Temperament Measurements." *Journal of Pediatrics,* 1972, *81,* 823-828.

Carey, W. B. "Measurement of Infant Temperament in Pediatric Practice." In J. C. Westman (Ed.), *Individual Differences in Children.* New York: Wiley, 1973.

Carey, W. B. "Night Waking and Temperament in Infancy." *Journal of Pediatrics,* 1974, *84,* 756-758.

Carey, W. B., Lipton, W. L., and Myers, R. A. "Temperament in Adopted and Foster Babies." *Child Welfare,* 1974, *53,* 352-359.

Thomas, A., Chess, S., and Birch, H. G. *Temperament and Behavior Disorders in Children.* New York: New York University Press, 1968.

INTERVIEW FOR EVALUATION OF
EGO DEVELOPMENT AND PREFERENTIAL JUDGMENT

AUTHOR: Leland van den Daele

AGE: Birth through adulthood

VARIABLE: Stages of ego development and preferential judgment

TYPE OF MEASURE: Structured interview

SOURCE FROM WHICH MEASURE MAY BE OBTAINED: Leland van den Daele, Box 119, Teachers College, Columbia University, New York, New York 10027. Write for *Manual for Codification of Ego Development and Preferential Judgment.* Cost: $20.00.

DESCRIPTION OF MEASURE: A stage scheme is described, which permits the evaluation of ego development through codification of preferential judgment. Discursive justifications obtained through a semistructured interview are coded for level of interpretation and discursive reference. Levels of interpretation range from preinterpretive to metatheoretical constructions. Discursive reference is either subjective, objective, or coordinative. The intersection of a level of interpretation and a discursive reference yields a set of fifteen stages of preferential judgment: A. Homeostatic-tropistic; B. Action-efficacious; C. Objectal-interactional; A. Voluntaristic; B. Functional-attributive; C. Categorical-regulatory; A. Preferential-hierarchical; B. Pragmatic-utilitarian; C. Instrumental-normative; A. Individual-relativistic; B. Definitional-deductive; C. Consensual-valuative; A. Existential-reflective; B. Systematic-constructive; and C. Ontotelic-paradigmatic.

As examples, one of the five categories of goals and one of the six categories of scoring criteria are given below.

Section 2: Material Goals. When you are grown up, what kind of house would you like to live in? Why would you like that kind of house? Where would you find a house like that? (Or, what would you have to do to find such a house?) (B) What would you like to see out the window? Why? How? (See the above questions for the general form of the why and how questions.) (C) When you are grown up, what kind of things would you like to own? Why? How?

Purpose of Choice
Level 1. Control others through overt power assertion. Choose objects for their speech, motion, and glamour. Generalized excitation.

Level 2. Incorporate controllers through being good as the controllers demand. Choose objects to manipulate or operate. Play.

Level 3. Be nice or good. Do or act like same-sex parent to avoid conflict or "trouble." Choose objects to have "fun."

Level 4. Conform to externalized aspects of sex role or occupation. Choose the accouterments of sex role or occupation.

Level 5. Be liked by others. Objects chosen to satisfy personal needs (in the material, not the psychological sense) or to satisfy interest.

Level 6. Be adult. Conform to general social expectations and group opinions. Objects chosen to fulfill functional needs related to interpersonal role.

Level 7. Fulfill social duty and responsibility.

RELIABILITY AND VALIDITY: Interrater reliability varies from $r = .69$ to $r = .88$. Stages of preferential judgment and ego development correlate moderately with measures of intelligence, moral judgment, and alternative measures of ego development.

BIBLIOGRAPHY:

van den Daele, L. D. "Ego Development and Preferential Judgment in Lifespan Perspective." In N. Datan and H. Ginsburg (Eds.), *Lifespan Developmental Psychology IV: Normative Life Crises.* New York: Academic Press, 1975.

van den Daele, L. D. "Ego Development in Dialectical Perspective." *Human Development* (in press).

van den Daele, L. D. "Form and Rationale." In L. D. van den Daele, J. Pascual-Leone, and K. Witz (Eds.), *Neo-Piagetian Perspectives in Cognition and Development.* New York: Academic Press (in press).

MANNERISM CHECKLIST

AUTHORS: Mary R. Haworth and Frank J. Menolascino

AGE: 2 to 9 years

VARIABLE: Deviant, stereotyped mannerisms

TYPE OF MEASURE: Checklist

SOURCE FROM WHICH MEASURE MAY BE OBTAINED: Mary R. Haworth, Research Scientist Development Section, Division of Extramural Research Programs, National Institute of Mental Health, 5600 Fishers Lane, Rockville, Maryland 20852.

DESCRIPTION OF MEASURE: The checklist consists of thirty deviant behaviors frequently observed in autistic, psychotic, or retarded children. Typical items include finger tapping, drooling, licking objects, hand flapping, and toe walking. The checklist was developed for use when analyzing videotapes of standardized play interviews but can also be used during direct observations of children's play. The presence of each separate "sequence" of a specific behavior is noted, up to a maximum of six sequences for any one item in a 15-minute play period.

As examples, the first ten of the thirty-two item checklist, along with instructions to the examiner, are given below.

Check each sequence of observed behavior up to a maximum of *six*. If a checked behavior recurs after some intervening activity or change of toy, give successive checks up to the maximum. (For example, if a child "taps" on a car [one check], then plays with some other toy, then returns to tapping the car or another toy, give a second check for tapping.)

1. Stares away from E or toys.   _____ _____ _____ _____ _____ _____
2. Stares at ceiling.
3. Hands over eyes.
4. Slight mouth movements.
5. Grimacing.
6. Nose twitching.
7. Tics.
8. Drools.
9. Spits.
10. Grinds teeth.

RELIABILITY AND VALIDITY: Rank ordering of the number of mannerism sequences per child yielded a *rho* of .80 for two judges. The checklist effectively discriminates psychotic-autistic and childhood schizophrenics (mean scores of 28.0 and 15.0) from normals, retardates, and brain-damaged groups. (Mean scores ranged from 2.5 to 6.5.)

BIBLIOGRAPHY:

Haworth, M. R., and Menolascino, F. J. "Videotape Observations of Disturbed Young Children." *Journal of Clinical Psychology,* 1967, *23*, 135-140.

Haworth, M. R., and Menolascino, F. J. "Some Aspects of Psychotic Behavior in Young Children: Thoughts on Etiology." *Archives of General Psychiatry,* 1968, *18*, 355-359.

MISSOURI CHILDREN'S BEHAVIOR CHECKLIST

AUTHORS: Jacob O. Sines, Jerome D. Pauker, Lloyd K. Sines, and David R. Owen

AGE: 5 to 16 years

VARIABLE: Six clinically relevant dimensions of behavior

TYPE OF MEASURE: Checklist

SOURCE FROM WHICH MEASURE MAY BE OBTAINED: J. O. Sines, Department of Psychology, University of Iowa, Iowa City, Iowa 52240.

DESCRIPTION OF MEASURE: These are internally consistent, relatively independent scales relating to aggression (A), inhibition (withdrawal) (I), activity level (H), sleep disturbance (Sl), somatic complaints (Ps), and sociability (So) as rated by a parent or responsible adult. Norms are available on a clinical population of boys (N = 404), on middle-class boys 7 and 9 years of age (N = 165), and on girls 7 and 9 years of age (N = 137).

As examples, two selected checklist items and the scored responses from each of the six behavior dimensions are given below.

A-3   Says "Others are to blame" for own actions. (Y)

A-11   Destroys or defaces property. (Y)

I-3   Does not try new situations, "hangs back," is considered by others as fearful or shy. (Y)

I-11   Has few close friendships. (Y)

H-6   Becomes more active or more talkative in groups, becomes noisier and more excited than usual when he is in a group. (Y)

H-9   Is said to be distractable, turns away quickly from what he is doing when something else moves, when someone speaks, or other sounds are made. (Y)

Sl-3   Complains of bad dreams. (Y)

Sl-8   Has difficulty going to sleep. (Y)

Ps-2   Worries a great deal, is said to be a worrier, expresses worry or concern about bad grades, health, etc. (Y)

Ps-5   Complains of pains in limbs or back (muscle aches and pains). (Y)

So-2   Expresses appreciation for others' acts. (Y)

RELIABILITY AND VALIDITY: Interjudge reliability (mother-father) is 68 percent to 93 percent. Scale scores discriminate between groups of boys seen in clinics and normal boys matched for age and IQ.

BIBLIOGRAPHY:

Sines, J. O., Pauker, J. D., Sines, L. K., and Owen, D. R. "Identification of Clinically Relevant Dimensions of Children's Behavior." *Journal of Consulting and Clinical Psychology,* 1969, *33,* 728-734.

MISSOURI CHILDREN'S PICTURE SERIES

AUTHORS: Jacob O. Sines, Jerome D. Pauker, and Lloyd K. Sines

AGE: 5 to 16 years

VARIABLE: Eight personality variables

TYPE OF MEASURE: Objective, nonverbal test

SOURCE FROM WHICH MEASURE MAY BE OBTAINED: Psychological Assessment and Services, Inc., P.O. Box 1031, Iowa City, Iowa 52240. Cost: Specimen set, $15.00.

DESCRIPTION OF MEASURE: The series consists of 238 numbered simple line drawings, each on a 3 X 5 card. The pictures show a child of indefinite age and of sometimes unclear sex engaged in a variety of activities in several different situations. In some pictures this child is the sole person, in other pictures there are additional people. In some the child is with other children, in some with adults. Sometimes the child is involved in what is in progress in the picture, sometimes not. Sometimes he is part of a group, sometimes apart from it. The pictures are sorted by the subject and scored on eight scales: conformity, masculinity-femininity, maturity, aggression, inhibition, activity level, sleep disturbance, and somatization. These are criterion-keyed scales and are normed on 3,877 school children between the ages of 5 and 16 years. Elevations on single scales and patterns of scale scores have been shown to relate to several clinically important behaviors in children.

RELIABILITY AND VALIDITY: Test-retest reliability coefficients vary with scale, sample, and interval; they range from .41 to .67 in the most recent study with clinic boys (Willis and Gordon, 1974).

BIBLIOGRAPHY:

Pauker, J. D., Sines, J. O., and Sines, L. K. "An Objective Nonverbal Test of Personality for Children." Paper presented at meeting of clinical psychologists in Children's Bureau Mental Retardation Clinics. New York, September 1966.

Register, M., and L'Abate, L. "An Objective Nonverbal Personality Test for Children." *Psychology in the Schools,* 1972, *9,* 378-387.

Willis, J. W., and Gordon, D. "The Missouri Children's Picture Series: A Validation Study with Emotionally Disturbed Children." *Journal of Clinical Psychology,* 1974, *30,* 213-214.

NURSERY SCHOOL BEHAVIOR INVENTORY

AUTHOR: Richard N. Walker

AGE: 2 to 5 years

VARIABLE: Teacher judgments of sixty-six behavior traits, summarized in nine temperament variables

TYPE OF MEASURE: Rating scale

SOURCE FROM WHICH MEASURE MAY BE OBTAINED: See Walker (1962), or write to Richard N. Walker, Gesell Institute of Child Development, 310 Prospect Street, New Haven, Connecticut 06511.

DESCRIPTION OF MEASURE: The inventory consists of sixty-six behavior traits to be rated on 7-point scales. The end points of each trait are described in some detail. The format resembles that of Conrad's *California Behavior Inventory* (1933), from which many of the items were drawn. Scores for individual items were summed to give nine cluster scores: energetic, active; alert, curious; aggressive, assertive; fearful, anxious; social, friendly; unstable, excitable; cooperative, conforming; cheerful, expressive; and sensitive, easily hurt. Their composition is given in Walker (1962). Mean scores and standard deviations are available for cluster scores of seventy-three boys and fifty-two girls attending a private nursery school, each child rated by four or five teachers independently (Walker, 1962). Means are given by sex for ages separately (2, 3, and 4 years) and together. Subjects were not a representative sample; their parents had predominantly professional and managerial occupations. Circumplex order of the nine cluster scores was very similar for boys and girls, and similar also to structures of ratings by other raters and for other ages (Walker, 1967).

As examples the first five of the sixty-six descriptions of behavior traits on the inventory are given below.

1. *Tempo or Speed*
   1. Always quick; darts and scurries. Child would rather run than walk.
   7. Slow; plods or just takes his time. Child would rather walk than run.
2. *Energy Level*
   1. Outstandingly vigorous; has great stores of energy to burn.
   7. Little motor energy. Never does things energetically or vigorously.
3. *Tenseness*
   1. Child is high-strung, tense, intense, hectic, taut. Child continually seems keyed up. Very difficult to relax at rest time.
   7. Child is relaxed, calm, untense. Relaxes completely at rest time.
4. *Expressiveness of Posture, Gesture, Voice*
   1. Free, flexible, fluid expressive patterns of voice, face, body.
   7. Tight, constrained, rigid, unexpressive response. Can't let himself go during music, dancing, games.
5. *Dreaminess*
   1. An outstandingly dreamy child; can get lost in reverie for long periods, losing contact with those around him.

7. Never stops in order to daydream. Child gives no hint that he is engaged in an inner life apart from what is concerned with right here and right now.

RELIABILITY AND VALIDITY: Horst's index for reliability of measures from multiple scores (four to five judges) for separate age-sex groups ranged from .75 to .92, two-thirds of them falling above .85, in the norm sample. For twenty-three boys and eighteen girls rated one year later by different raters, correlation coefficients by sex ranged from .29 to .78, with a median of .65. Relations of the items and the cluster scores to external variables of physique, judged by other raters from photographs, ranged from none to moderate with a ceiling around .50 (r of aggressiveness rating with physique).

BIBLIOGRAPHY:

Conrad, H. S. *The California Behavior Inventory for Nursery School Children.* Berkeley: University of California Press, 1933.
Walker, R. N. "Body Build and Behavior in Young Children: I. Body Build and Nursery School Teachers' Ratings." *Monographs of the Society for Research in Child Development,* 1962, *27,* 3.
Walker, R. N. "Some Temperament Traits in Children as Viewed by Their Peers, Their Teachers, and Themselves." *Monographs of the Society for Research in Child Development,* 1967, *32,* 6.

OHIO STATE PICTURE PREFERENCE SCALE (OSPPS)

AUTHOR: Jack R. Frymier

AGE: 12 years and up

VARIABLE: Creativity, delinquency processes

TYPE OF MEASURE: Picture preference scale

SOURCE FROM WHICH MEASURE MAY BE OBTAINED: Jack R. Frymier, College of Education, The Ohio State University, 29 West Woodruff Avenue, Columbus, Ohio 43210. Cost: $5.00.

DESCRIPTION OF MEASURE: The OSPPS is a 100-item instrument consisting of 100 pairs of pictures. Respondents are asked to "study both pictures carefully and select the one picture you prefer." Responses are made by drawing a circle around the number on the answer sheet corresponding to the number beneath the preferred picture. The OSPPS is still very much an experimental measuring device. A very limited number of instruments are available to researchers for experimental processes.

RELIABILITY AND VALIDITY: Several analyses have been accomplished comparing "known groups" of respondents item by item. This research is still continuing. No norms are available. The author is interested in securing raw data from persons interested in using the scale experimentally.

BIBLIOGRAPHY:

Frymier, J. R. "Development and Validation of a Nonverbal Measure of Personality." Mimeographed. Columbus: College of Education, Ohio State University, 1974.

PRESCHOOL MENTAL HEALTH ASSESSMENT

AUTHOR: Dorothy A. Millichamp

AGE: 3 to 4 years

VARIABLE: Behavior response patterns

TYPE OF MEASURE: Checklist or structured interview

SOURCE FROM WHICH MEASURE MAY BE OBTAINED: The Brora Centre, 164 Eglinton Avenue East, Suite 106, Toronto, Canada M4P 1G4. Cost: $1.00 per copy for mailing and duplicating expenses.

DESCRIPTION OF MEASURE: There are two assessment forms, one applying to home and one to nursery school. The home assessment consists of 139 behavior responses to recurring life situations divided into "x" items (fifty-eight) indicating adjustment and "y" items (eighty-one) indicating adjustment difficulties. The nursery-school assessment has fifty-two "x" items and ninety-one "y" items. The caretaker (parent or teacher) checks those items characteristic of the child's behavior. The gross scoring formula used is:

$$\frac{x \text{ items endorsed} - y \text{ items endorsed}}{x + y \text{ applying}} \times 100 =$$

Practically, the results provide objective information concerning a child for clinical appraisal and guidance. Theoretically, the assessment is designed as a projective measure of mental health. Based on Blatz' security theory (1966) the assembly of items is planned to assess the child's psychological potential for dependent interaction with adults and for independent self-effort reflecting sense of trust and confidence (security state) and/or uncertainty, conflict, and emotional distress (insecurity state). Items have been classified accordingly as acceptance or refusal of dependent and independent opportunity. The assessment is not concerned with ability level.

As examples, ten selected "x" and "y" items from 139 on the home form of the measure are given below. The items on the nursery school form are sufficiently different that a potential user should examine both forms.

x items	*y items*
3. Can maintain own rights with other children.	3. Usually gives in to other children in play, routine, conversation.
9. Can accept shared adult attention with sibling(s).	9. Disturbed by parent attention to sibling(s). —plays for attention to self. —withdraws. —shows emotion—protests, whines, cries, temper tantrums, excited, hits, pushes adult or child.
10. Venturesome physically.	12. Avoids venturesome play. —shows emotion—runs away, protests, cries.
18. Can amuse self happily for reasonable length of time with play things.	23. Settles to play only when given attention continually.
19. Content to play alone routinely. —outdoors. —indoors.	24. Refuses to play alone—shows emotion —protesting, crying, temper tantrums, sulking.

RELIABILITY AND VALIDITY: Because the instrument was developed initially for use in a longitudinal study of 100 normal children, analysis of data is incomplete. Factor analysis has yielded results meaningful in terms of the theoretical construct. Individual differences emerged using the assessment for clinical appraisal of normal and psychologically disturbed groups. This assessment is similar in design to the *Flint Infant Security Scale* (1974), a description of which appears elsewhere in this *Handbook*.

BIBLIOGRAPHY:

Blatz, W. E. *Human Security.* Toronto, Canada: University of Toronto Press, 1966.

Flint, B. M. *The Security of Infants.* Toronto, Canada: University of Toronto Press, 1959.

Flint, B. M. *The Child and the Institution.* Toronto, Canada: University of Toronto Press, 1966.

Flint, B. M. *The Flint Infant Security Scale.* Guidance Centre, Faculty of Education, University of Toronto, Canada, 1974.

PROJECT *TALENT* STUDENT ACTIVITIES INVENTORY

AUTHOR: Project TALENT Staff

AGE: Grades 9 to 12

VARIABLE: Job-related personality traits of normal individuals

TYPE OF MEASURE: Rating scale

SOURCE FROM WHICH MEASURE MAY BE OBTAINED: Project TALENT tests and inventories are available to researchers as Project TALENT Specimen Set, which may be ordered from American Institutes for Research, P.O. Box 1113, Palo Alto, California 94302. Cost: $3.00. The Project TALENT battery is not to be used for nonresearch testing.

DESCRIPTION OF MEASURE: The Project TALENT Student Activities Inventory consists of a total of 150 statements related to the following ten scales: sociability, social sensitivity, impulsiveness, vigor, calmness, tidiness, culture, leadership, self-confidence, and mature personality. (Number 10, mature personality, is a composite of productivity, persistence, and responsibility.) A statement that contributes to the impulsiveness scale is, for example, "I often do things on the spur of the moment." Students are asked to indicate how well such statements would describe them and their own behavior by checking one of the following: extremely well, quite well, fairly well, slightly, or not very well.

RELIABILITY AND VALIDITY: No reliability data are available. Predictive validity is demonstrated by Project TALENT's one-, five-, and eleven-year follow-up studies. *Five Years After High School, Appendix II* (Flanagan, Shaycoft, Richards, and Claudy, 1971) presents means and standard deviations for SAI variables grouped by occupation.

BIBLIOGRAPHY:

Cooley, W. W., and Lohnes, P. R. "Predicting Development of Young Adults." Interim report no. 5 to the U.S. Office of Education, Cooperative Research Project No. 3051. Palo Alto, California: Project TALENT Office, American Institutes for Research and University of Pittsburgh, 1968.

Cureton, E. E. "A Factor Analysis of Project TALENT Tests and Four Other Test Batteries." Interim report no. 4 to the U.S. Office of Education, Cooperative Research Project No. 3051. Palo Alto, California: Project TALENT Office, American Institutes for Research and University of Pittsburgh, 1968.

Flanagan, J. C., Shaycoft, M. F., Richards, J. M., Jr., and Claudy, J. G. *Five Years After High School: Appendix II.* Palo Alto, California: Project Talent Office, American Institutes for Research and University of Pittsburgh, 1971.

Flanagan, J. C., Tiedeman, D. V., Willis, M. B., and McLaughlin, D. H. *The Career Data Book: Results from Project TALENT's Five-Year Follow-up Study.* Palo Alto, California: American Institutes for Research, 1973.

Prepared by Wendy Yen

PRIOR SAMENESS BEHAVIOR QUESTIONNAIRE

AUTHOR: Margot R. Prior

AGE: Autistic children 2 to 18 years

VARIABLE: Obsessive behavior or the desire for sameness

TYPE OF MEASURE: Questionnaire

SOURCE FROM WHICH MEASURE MAY BE OBTAINED: See Prior and MacMillan (1973).

DESCRIPTION OF MEASURE: The Prior Sameness Behavior Questionnaire is made up of twenty-eight items concerning obsessive and stereotyped behavior exhibited by autistic and psychotic children. The questions are read to the parents and their replies noted verbatim. Where necessary, probe questions may be used, and parents are encouraged to give details about the child's behavior at any age. For each item a score of 2 is given if the behavior is severe, marked, or frequent; a score of 1 is given if the behavior is present but not marked; and 0 is scored if the behavior is not present. Total possible score is 56. Previous data have shown that a score of 21 or above indicates a marked degree of "sameness" behavior. Scores on this questionnaire can be used as an aid for the diagnosis of early infantile autism. Studies carried out in diagnosis and classification in childhood psychosis (Prior and MacMillan, 1973; Prior, Gajzago, and Perry, 1975) have confirmed the importance of sameness behavior in subclassification.

As examples, the first eight of the twenty-eight items of the questionnaire are given below.

1. Does he insist on furniture remaining in the same place, windows or doors open or shut, blinds up or down, etc.?
2. Does he insist on creating and maintaining patterns of toys, objects, furniture, etc.?
3. Does he insist on eating the same foods or only a particular kind of food?
4. Does he object to visiting new places?
5. Does he refuse to allow anyone to teach him anything new?
6. Does he become very upset if interrupted in what he is doing?
7. Does he make a ritual out of (a) going to bed, (b) eating meals, (c) having a bath, (d) getting dressed?
8. Is he extremely attached to a particular toy or object?

RELIABILITY AND VALIDITY: None reported.

BIBLIOGRAPHY:

Prior, M. R., and MacMillan, M. B. "Maintenance of Sameness in Children with Kanner's Syndrome." *Journal of Autism and Childhood Schizophrenia*, 1973, *3*, 154-167.

Prior, M. R., Gajzago, C. C., and Perry, D. "Kanner's Syndrome or Early Onset Psychosis: A Taxonomic Analysis of 142 Cases." *Journal of Autism and Childhood Schizophrenia*, 1975, *5*, 71-80.

PSYCHIATRIC BEHAVIOR SCALE (PBS)

AUTHORS: William F. Barker, Louise Sandler, Agnes Bornemann, Gail Knight, Frederick Humphrey, and Steven Risen

AGE: 2½ to 6½ years

VARIABLE: Emotional development

TYPE OF MEASURE: Rating scale

SOURCE FROM WHICH MEASURE MAY BE OBTAINED: William Barker, Center for Preschool Services, Room 469, Franklin Institute Research Laboratories, 20th and The Parkway, Philadelphia, Pennsylvania 19103. No cost at present.

DESCRIPTION OF MEASURE: The Psychiatric Behavior Scale (PBS) consists of five bipolar items, one unipolar item, and eight yes-no questions that purport to assess a preschool child's emotional development. The scale can be used for children 2½ to 6½ years old. The subscales assessed by the five bipolar items (six or eight choices) are: expression of aggression, relationships, independence-dependence, impulse control, and reaction to stress. The unipolar item is intended to assess the need for communication. The eight yes-no questions concern two areas in which almost all children receive a "yes" answer—appropriate coordination and appropriate feeling; and six bizarre behaviors in which almost all children receive a "no" answer—spinning in circles, head banging, and so forth. Ratings are provided by the day-care worker based upon his perceptions derived from at least one month of continuous contact with the child. The item choices are behaviorally specific and avoid the use of technical jargon as much as possible. Based upon the experience of at least fifty child-care workers, it seems clear that (1) the scale is easy to use, (2) useful information is provided to both the researcher and the day-care worker, and (3) the day-care worker is forced to consider each child in useful ways, which he may not have done in the past.

Norms are available for six 6-month age groups from 36 to 71 months of age, based upon a total sample of 1,040 children. The norms were developed from both urban and suburban advantaged and disadvantaged males and females. Results from extensive statistical analysis indicate that separate norms are appropriate for all four groups, advantaged and disadvantaged males and females. Although the data are cross-sectional in nature, the norm scores across all four groups follow a U-shape developmental trend.

The PRS was developed as an evaluation instrument to assess longitudinally emotional development of preschool children with problems. Experience gained over the past three years would seem to indicate that it can be used as follows: (1) for screening, (2) for program evaluation, (3) to act as a guide to the day-care worker in identifying specific areas of development that may need remediation, (4) to alert day-care workers to areas of development of which they should be aware, and (5) to assess day-care workers' effectiveness.

As an example, the first of the six bipolar items on the revised scale is given below. Other items are relations, dependency, impulse, reaction to stress, and need for communication.

I. *Expression of Aggression—General Pattern of Behavior*

( ) Overly aggressive   The child demands his own way in virtually all situations. He often takes toys from other children while refusing to share his own. The child often persists despite the teacher's intervention.

( )   The child will generally take toys for himself without sharing with other children but will change his behavior on the teacher's insistence.

( ) Tendency toward   The child is able to stand up for his own rights but is also able to share with others without the need for the teacher to intervene.

Typical

( ) Tendency toward   The child is able to stand up for his own rights but is also able to share with others without the need for the teacher to intervene.

( )   The child is able to stand up for himself when supported by the teacher or another child.

( ) Overly withdrawn   The child is unable to stand up for himself in virtually all situations even when encouraged to do so by the teacher.

RELIABILITY AND VALIDITY: Based upon the ratings of 250 children by two groups of raters (pairs of raters rated fifteen to twenty children each independently), the average of interrater correlation coefficient estimates was .71. Further work is in progress to improve the reliability of the scale. Some item choices are being reworded, and more detailed and specific rating procedure directions are being developed.

    The usual types of judgmental validity (constructor, user, and face) have been obtained. The constructor validity was obtained via comparison between the item choices and the original scale. The user validity was obtained via discussion with at least sixty-five day-care workers who used the scale. Finally, the face validity was obtained via discussions with users as well as with other kinds of day-care, mental-health, and psychometric professionals. More sophisticated statistical procedures have been used to indicate the predictive, factorial, and congruent validity. The predictive validity was determined through the use of a discriminant analysis. This analysis indicates that the PBS can classify children as typical or nontypical with a high degree of accuracy. Factorial validity was determined by examining the factor structure of the PBS. As expected, expression of aggression, impulse control, and reaction to stress load on the first factor, and expression of aggression was determined by examining the factor structure of an analysis of the combination of the Preschool Rating Scale (see pp. 114-116) and the PBS. The almost complete lack of overlap in factor loadings for the two scales suggests that the assessment of emotional development is possibly separate from personal-social factors. Information that will allow the determination of concurrent and inferential validity is now being gathered.

BIBLIOGRAPHY: None reported.

PUPIL BEHAVIOR RATING SCALE (PBRS)

AUTHOR: Nadine Lambert

AGE: Elementary school

VARIABLE: Noncognitive classroom behavior

TYPE OF MEASURE: Rating scale

SOURCE FROM WHICH MEASURE MAY BE OBTAINED: Nadine Lambert, School of Education, University of California, Berkeley, California 94720.

DESCRIPTION OF MEASURE: The PBRS was developed to provide an interval scale for eleven attributes selected from an extensive review of measurement of classroom behavior. To reduce rater bias through precise specification of scale criteria, teacher-assigned scale values for descriptive anchors were developed. Teachers were initially asked to rate students in the eleven attributes on a 7-point scale and then provide behavioral descriptions for each point on the scale. To establish descriptor validity, first graduate student psychologists and then teachers assigned each descriptor to one of the eleven attributes with 80-percent agreement among raters required for acceptance. This reduced the 1,700 original descriptors to 300, of which fifteen were selected for each attribute. Then a new set of sixty teachers in grades 1, 3, and 5 scaled the items by assigning values from 0.0 (least like the attribute) to 3.0 (most like the attribute). After elimination of statements inconsistently rated, six to nine descriptors were retained for each attribute.

Items defining cluster 1 describe the child who displays difficulties in achievement, following directions, independent work, and motivation, and indicate a "learning problem behaviors" dimension (LPB). Definers of cluster 2 depict the child who is pugnacious, dangerous, easily distracted, but not failing. This suggests an aggressive or "acting out behaviors" dimension (AOB). Items defining cluster 3 describe the child who is sick, immature, unhappy, and friendless, and indicate a "withdrawn behaviors" dimension (WB). LPB accounted for 68 percent of the communality among scores, AOB accounted for 20 percent, and WB accounted for 12 percent.

As an example, one of the eleven attributes with the behavioral descriptions for various points on the scale is given below.

3.00

_____
_____
_____
_____

These pupils generally have considerable difficulty disregarding even the slightest distraction in carrying out assigned tasks.

2.75
_____
_____
_____ ←This pupil flits from thing to thing.
_____

2.50 ←This pupil usually looks around a lot while working and has trouble focusing on one project at a time.

——

——

——

2.25

——

—— ←This pupil often talks or looks at children near him.

——

——

2.00

——

—— ←This pupil is easily distracted by friends and likes to distract others but will do his work.

——

These pupils can ignore most classroom disturbances and concentrate on assigned work or activity.

1.75

——

——

——

—— ←This pupil must be reminded occasionally to pay attention and to do his work.

1.50

——

——

—— ←This pupil usually pays attention but will be distracted if something unusual happens.

1.25

——

——

——

1.00

——

——

——

Even with the most distracting situation, these pupils continue to persevere at assigned work or activity.

0.75 ←This pupil chooses to sit alone so as not to be distracted.

——

——

——

0.50

——

—— ←This pupil wastes little time even with many distractions.

——

—— ←This pupil can spend a whole hour concentrating.

0.25

——

——

——

——

0.00

RELIABILITY AND VALIDITY: Nicoll (1973) found scaling reliabilities ranging from .70 to .995 with only two values below .95. Lambert (1974) provides detailed validity information for each of eight of the items, including concurrent validity using summary clinical judgment and multiple correlation of clinical factor scores with the items as the criteria. Predictive validity data are given for each of eight items using high school factor scores and successful vs. unsuccessful high school status as criteria.

BIBLIOGRAPHY:

Hartsough, C. S. *Classroom Adaptation of Elementary School Children Varying with Respect to Age, Sex and Ethnic Status.* Berkeley: University of California, 1973.

Lambert, N. M. *The Prediction of School Adjustment.* U.S. Office of Education, Cooperative Research Project No. 1980. Sacramento: California State Department of Education, 1964.

Lambert, N. M. "Intellectual and Nonintellectual Predictors of High School Status." *Journal of Special Education,* 1972, 6(3), 247-259.

Lambert, N. M. *Technical Report Supplement: The Development of Instruments for the Nonintellectual Assessment of Effective School Behavior.* Berkeley: University of California, 1974.

Lambert, N. M., and Bower, E. M. *A Process for In-School Screening of Emotionally Handicapped Children.* Atlanta: Educational Testing Service, 1961, 1974.

Lambert, N. M., and Hartsough, C. S. *Teacher Assigned Scale Values for Descriptive Anchors Defining Behavior Attributes of Elementary School Pupils.* Project Report, the Stress of School Project, 1971, University of California, Berkeley, Grant No. MH14605, National Institute of Mental Health.

Lambert, N. M., and Hartsough, C. S. "Scaling Behavioral Attributes of Children Using Multiple Teacher Judgments of Pupil Characteristics." *Educational and Psychological Measurement,* 1973, 33(4), 859-874.

Lambert, N. M., Hartsough, C. S., and Zimmerman, I. L. "The Comparative Predictive Efficiency of Intellectual and Nonintellectual Components of High School Functioning." *American Journal of Orthopsychiatry,* 1976, 46(1), 109-122.

Nicoll, R. C. *Classroom Behavior Ratings as Predictors of First and Second Grade Reading Achievement.* Berkeley: University of California, 1973.

Swain, C. "The Relationship between Classroom Adjustment and Decentering of Thought in Fourth Grade Children." Unpublished doctoral dissertation, University of California, Berkeley, 1975.

Urbanski, C. "The Relationship of School Achievement and Peer Ratings to Behavioral Profiles Determined from Teacher Ratings of Pupil Behavior." Unpublished master's thesis, University of California, Berkeley, 1974.

ROSENZWEIG PICTURE-FRUSTRATION (P-F) STUDY, FORM FOR ADOLESCENTS

AUTHOR: Saul Rosenzweig

AGE: 12 to 18 years

VARIABLE: Modes of response to frustration

TYPE OF MEASURE: Projective technique

SOURCE FROM WHICH MEASURE MAY BE OBTAINED: Saul Rosenzweig, 8029 Washington Avenue, St. Louis, Missouri 63114. Cost: Minimum order: 25 examination blanks (test booklets), 25 scoring blanks, 1 examiner's manual—$11.00 plus transportation. Specimen set not available.

DESCRIPTION OF MEASURE: The study consists of twenty-four cartoonlike pictures, each of which represents an everyday frustrating situation involving two persons. The individual on the left of the item is shown saying something that either frustrates or helps to describe the frustration of the other character. The other individual is drawn with a blank balloon or caption box above his head, which the subject is instructed to fill. He is to do so by writing the very first words that occur to him, which the character might say in that situation. Facial features are purposely left vague in the drawings to facilitate projective structuring by the subject. Mean administration time is 15 minutes. The normative population was made up of 813 subjects consisting of 383 males and 430 females, with an age range of 12 through 18 years. Responses are scored according to a two-dimensional matrix: direction of aggression (extraggression, introgression, and imagression) and type of aggression (obstacle-dominance, need-persistence, and ego-defense).
 As examples, two of the twenty-four items are given below.

1. A mature woman and an adolescent boy are standing beside the closed door of an automobile. She is saying, "This is a fine time to have lost the keys!"
2. A male attendant is shown behind the checkout desk of a library. A young girl with a pile of several books in her arms is standing in front of the desk. He is saying, "The library rules permit you to take only *two* books at a time."

RELIABILITY AND VALIDITY: Interscorer reliability is in the range of 80 to 90 percent. Retest correlations range .40 to .70, depending on the particular scoring category. The validity can be inferred from numerous investigations of validity of the parallel children's and adult forms. Construct, concurrent, and predictive validity have been demonstrated on the basis of experimental work (intervening frustration), criterion groups, ratings by teachers, and so forth, correlated with test scores. The validity of the adolescent form itself has not yet been directly investigated.

BIBLIOGRAPHY:

Bjerstedt, A. "The Rosenzweig Picture-Frustration Study." In O. K. Buros (Ed.), *The Sixth Mental Measurements Yearbook.* Highland Park, New Jersey: Gryphon Press, 1965.
Rosenzweig, S. "The Picture-Association Method and Its Application in a Study of Reactions to Frustration." *Journal of Personality,* 1945, *14,* 3-23.
Rosenzweig, S. "Levels of Behavior in Psychodiagnosis with Special Reference to the Picture-Frustration Study." *American Journal of Orthopsychiatry,* 1950, *20,* 63-72.
Rosenzweig, S. "The Rosenzweig Picture-Frustration Study, Children's Form." In A. I. Rabin and M. Haworth (Eds.), *Projective Techniques with Children.* New York: Grune & Stratton, 1960.
Rosenzweig, S. "Sex Differences in Reaction to Frustration Among Adolescents." In J. Zubin and A. M. Freedman (Eds.), *The Psychopathology of Adolescence.* New York: Grune & Stratton, 1970.
Rosenzweig, S., and Braun, S. H. "Adolescent Sex Differences in Reaction to Frustration as

Explored by the Rosenzweig P-F Study." *Journal of Genetic Psychology,* 1970, *116,* 53-61.

Rosenzweig, S., and Kogan, K. L. *Psychodiagnosis.* New York: Grune & Stratton, 1949.

Rosenzweig, S., Ludwig, D. J., and Adelman, S. "Fidelité Test-Retest du Test de Frustration de Rosenzweig et de Techniques Semiprojectives Analogues." *Revue de Psychologie Appliquée,* 1974, *24,* 181-196.

Rosenzweig, S., Ludwig, D. J., and Adelman, S. "Retest Reliability of the Rosenzweig Picture-Frustration Study and Similar Semiprojective Techniques." *Journal of Personality Assessment,* 1975, *39,* 3-12.

SEIKEN CHECKLIST FOR AUTISTIC CHILDREN (CLAC)

AUTHORS: Kosaku Umetsu, Kiyoshi Makita, Issei Takamura, and others

AGE: 1 to 10 years

VARIABLE: Behavioral characteristics

TYPE OF MEASURE: Checklist

SOURCE FROM WHICH MEASURE MAY BE OBTAINED: See Makita and Umetsu (1972).

DESCRIPTION OF MEASURE: CLAC aims at such purposes as (1) determining the individual characteristic of the autistic child at the beginning of his treatment, (2) helping to establish a therapeutic program, (3) providing materials for parental interviews, (4) evaluating sequential therapeutic effectiveness, (5) predicting symptomatology and therapeutic efficacy of the child in other facilities, and (6) the subclassification of autistic manifestations. CLAC is comprised of a 5-point rating scale checklist covering such areas as food intake, elimination, sleep, activities of daily living, play, human relationships, speech and language, expression, manipulations of hand and fingers, behavioral autonomy, and abnormal emotional expressions. The checklist is filled in by professional observers. Parents will be able to fill in the checklist when the manual for CLAC is completed. The results are transcribed on a radiating psychogram by plotting each rating level, thereby illustrating each individual feature of the child visually on the polygonal gestalt. This gestalt is formed by connecting the rating points on the psychogram.

As examples, selected items from the checklist are given below.

I. *Eating Behaviors*
 3. Mealtime
  1. is daily inconsistent in frequency and time.
  2. is daily consistent in frequency but eats at his own time.
  3. eats more or less at a fixed time of his own.
  4. eats with other family members but walks around.
  5. eats correctly with other family members.

V. *Play*
   10. Varieties of play
       b. Check the child's favorite maneuver among the following and describe it con-
          cretely between the parentheses.
          1. plays with a part of his own body.
          (   )
          2. likes to climb up high.
          (   )
          3. likes to place things in order.
          (   )
          4. likes to spin objects.
          (   )
          5. absorbed in writing or drawing.
          (   )

VI. *Interpersonal Relationships*
   13. Relationships with family members
       a. with adults
          (1) is indifferent or ignores.
          (2) evades.
          (3) will make intervention based on his own demands.
          (4) will interact when invited by some particular person.
          (5) can interact with all adults in the family.
       b. with siblings
          (1) is indifferent or ignores.
          (2) evades.
          (3) will make intervention based on his own demands.
          (4) will interact when invited by some particular person.
          (5) can interact with all siblings.

IX. *Manipulation of Hand and Fingers of Others*
   19. Use of other's hands and fingers
       a. uses other's hand and fingers as a manipulator for doing things he can do for
          himself.
       b. uses other's hand and fingers partially for the above-mentioned purpose.
       c. uses his own hand and fingers when instructed to do for himself.
       d. uses other's hand and fingers for doing things he cannot do for himself.
       e. does not use other's hand and fingers at all.

RELIABILITY AND VALIDITY: Statistical analysis not yet complete regarding the
reliability and validity. The comparison thus far was made on the basis of studies with
control groups of 254 normal (age 1 to 6), forty-two mentally retarded (age 4 to 6),
and forty-four deaf (age 3 to 6) children. The results clarify the characteristic profile
of developmental arrest in each autistic child and contribute to differential diagnosis
from other kinds of disturbances. The shortcomings of the present CLAC lie in that
the questionnaire items are a mixture of developmental (increasing with chronological
age) and nondevelopmental (unrelated to chronological age) factors, and also in that
age patterns could not be determined because of the overwhelming variety of deviations among the autistic group. Studies are now under way to address these problems.

BIBLIOGRAPHY:

Makita, K., and Umetsu, K. "An Objective Evaluation Technique for Autistic Children: An Introduction of CLAC Scheme." *Acta Paedopsychiatrica*, 1972, *39*, 237-253.

Umetsu, K., Makita, K., and others. "The Study of Autistic Children with Behavior Therapy —V." *Bulletin of the Seishin-Igaku Institute*, 1970, *17*, 61-70 (in Japanese).

Umetsu, K., Takamura, S., Makita, K., and others. "The Study of Autistic Children with Behavior Therapy—VII." *Bulletin of the Seishin-Igaku Institute*, 1974, *18*, 75-116 (in Japanese).

Prepared by Kiyoshi Makita, Kosaku Umetsu,
and Issei Takamura

SELF-REPORT INVENTORY (SRI)

AUTHOR: Oliver H. Bown

AGE: High school and up

VARIABLE: Self-reported attitudes

TYPE OF MEASURE: Likert-type scale

SOURCE FROM WHICH MEASURE MAY BE OBTAINED: Oliver H. Bown, Research and Development Center for Teacher Education, University of Texas, Education Annex, Austin, Texas 78712. Cost: $1.50 per 100.

DESCRIPTION OF MEASURE: The SRI consists of forty-eight items, each consisting of a statement followed by a 5-point scale ranging from "like me" to "unlike me." Items are weighted from 0 to 4. Half of the items are expressed in the positive mode and half in the negative. The forty-eight items are classified into eight areas, each of which is measured by the sum of an independent set of six scores. The eight areas are: self, others (peers), children, authority, work (and accomplishment), reality, parents, and hope (optimism regarding the future). Scores are also derived to provide indices of relative positiveness of attitude toward self vs. others and intensity of response (tendency to use end vs. middle scale points in responding). Form R-3 has been used most extensively with prospective teachers but has also been used successfully with many populations of young adults. Form R-4 (adult) is recommended for all populations other than prospective teachers and has been used occasionally with high school students. Adaptations have been made for use with mentally retarded and for geriatric populations. The instrument R-3 is also available in Spanish and French translations.

As examples, the first seven of the forty-eight items of Form R-3 are given below.

1. The way I get along with my friends is extremely important to me.

2. I resist getting down to work and often have to drive myself to get it done.

3. In their relationship with me, my parents were always basically kind, considerate, and understanding.

4. I really look forward to the time when I will be settled down to my life's work.

5. I have almost always resented people who were in a position to tell me what to do.

6. I'm very comfortable and happy when I am with children.

7. I don't seem to have very much basic respect for myself.

RELIABILITY AND VALIDITY: The item pool was developed in 1958 and subjected to expert judgments on item clarity, linearity, and face validity. Through administration of the instrument to relatively large populations of undergraduates, three major revisions of the instrument were accomplished using item and factor analysis along with other psychometric refinement techniques. The self, children, and hope scales meet the criterion of factorial purity. The remaining factors, although not independent of one another, each load their own hypothesized scale factor more strongly than do others in the set, and they are thus consistent with this less restrictive concept of factorial separation. Internal consistency reliability indices, provided by *alpha* coefficients, range from .65 to .85 with the exception of the authority (.53) and reality (.28) scales. The reality scale has been retained in spite of its unacceptable reliability to maintain the integrity of the instrument. Test-retest reliabilities for one-week ($N = 48$) and two-week ($N = 30$) intervals ranged from .72 (reality) to .90 and from .64 to .93, respectively. Content validity was established by selecting from the original item pool only those items that 100 percent of expert judges classified on the scale intended. Concurrent, construct, and predictive validity evidence has been accumulated through more than fifty research studies in which the instrument has successfully discriminated or predicted in hypothesized directions.

BIBLIOGRAPHY:

Bown, O. H. "The Development of a Self-Report Inventory and Its Function in a Mental Health Assessment Battery." Paper presented before the annual meeting of the American Psychological Association. New York, September 1961.

Bown, O. H. "Self-Perception and Attitudes of Freshmen English Students with Different Patterns of Verbal and Quantitative Ability." Report to the Department of English and the administration of the University of Texas at Austin. Mimeographed. The Personality Research Center, University of Texas, Austin, 1963.

Bown, O. H., and Richek, H. G. "Phenomenal Correlates of Jung's Typology." *Journal of Analytical Psychology,* 1963, *8,* 57-65.

Bown, O. H., and Richek, H. G. "The Bown Self-Report Inventory (SRI): A Quick-Screening Instrument for Mental Health Professionals." *Comprehensive Psychiatry,* 1967, *8,* 45-65.

Bown, O. H., and Richek, H. G. "The Mental Health of Commuter Students: A Partial Test of Kysar's Hypothesis." *Mental Hygiene,* 1968, *52,* 354-359.

Veldman, D. J., and Bown, O. H. "Relationships of Cigarette Smoking to Academic Achievement, Cognitive Abilities, and Attitudes Toward Authority." *Multivariate Behavioral Research,* 1968, *3,* 513-516.

SOUND-APPERCEPTION TEST

AUTHOR: Kenneth L. Bean

VARIABLE: Personality dynamics

AGE: Grade 1 to adult

TYPE OF MEASURE: Projective technique

SOURCE FROM WHICH MEASURE MAY BE OBTAINED: Kenneth L. Bean, Sound Apperception Test Distributor, 3505 Oakdale, Temple, Texas 76501. Cost: Complete set including manual, disc, and durable mailing container, $20.00.

DESCRIPTION OF MEASURE: This is a clinical instrument in which the stimuli are two series of unstructured and semistructured sounds. Series 1 is composed of unstructured sounds, and these ten items are like the auditory equivalent of inkblots. Responses are scored on a Reality-Orientation Scale much like form level accuracy on the Rorschach test. Responses to these sounds are also rated on a Like-Indifferent-Dislike scale. Series 2 consists of sixteen sound-effect sequences that are semistructured stimuli comparable to TAT pictures. Noises are usually identifiable, but the situation is intentionally ambiguous. Stories much like TAT narratives are elicited, with inquiry on omitted feelings, thoughts, or endings. Thematic emphases and endings are scored on a checklist sheet, but qualitative aspects may suggest useful hypotheses. The material includes a manual describing the development of the test and its norms, reliability, validity, and so forth. Instructions for administering, scoring, and interpretation are provided. Guidelines for qualitative content analysis are included, with case illustrations and references. A disc recording (LP, monaural) provides the stimuli that must be played on good quality high fidelity equipment. Only thirty young children were included in the original standardization group, but subsequent testing of more children has supported the author's belief that the Sound Apperception Test is useful from elementary school age on.

As an example, a description of the first one of the ten sounds in Series 1, followed by examples of responses that are scored on the Reality-Orientation Scale, is given below.

Sound 1. Opening and closing screen door, lowered one octave.
Score 0: Moving furniture or heavy objects over floor. Door opening or closing.
Score 1: Animal growl or roar. Orchestra tuning up or musical instruments. Airplane. Record going too slow.
Score 2: Music. Cows in stall crying. Tuning a P.A. system. Aircraft taking off, engine failing. Fog horn. Shot fired from distance, explosion. Storm coming up. Saw. Car. Diesel train.

RELIABILITY AND VALIDITY: Evidence for the validity of the Sound-Apperception Test has been found through different approaches. Two experienced clinical psychologists attempted to identify as "normal" or "schizophrenic" each of ten randomly selected normal cases and ten randomly selected schizophrenic cases who had taken the test. Each of the two clinicians made only one error. A second method of validating the Sound-Apperception Test involving the comparison of test results with case histories of college students and mental patients was inconclusive. The third validating technique involved an attempt to differentiate clinical groups statistically. Raw scores for each series of stimuli were determined, and mean scores for populations of normals and psychotics were computed. Psychotics were found to be significantly different ($p < .01$) from normals on reality orientation (Series 1). Psychotics showed a statistically significant trend toward liking sounds usually disliked by normals, and toward more indifferent reactions ($p < .02$). Of 154 hospitalized psychotics, thirty-eight were known to have some organic brain damage. On Series 1, these thirty-eight patients gave responses that differed in no significant way from those given by the remaining patients. Further, paranoid schizophrenics did not distinguish themselves from the rest of the hospital population on the unstructured sounds, except for quality. College students (N = 131) stood out as significantly different from Air Force normals in that more of them gave multiple interpretations (rather than a single interpretation) for any given stimulus. Further validity evidence is provided by Bean (1965).

BIBLIOGRAPHY:

Bean, K. L. "The Sound-Apperception Test: Origin, Purposes, Standardization, Scoring, and Use." *Journal of Psychology*, 1965, *59*, 371-412.

Bean, K. L., and Moore, J. R. "Music Therapy from Auditory Ink Blots." *Journal of Music Therapy*, 1964, *1*, 143-147.

STATEN ISLAND BEHAVIOR SCALE (SIBS)

AUTHORS: Wallace Mandell, Richard M. Silberstein, and Allan Cooper

AGE: 1 to 17 years

VARIABLE: Behavior disorder signs and symptoms

TYPE OF MEASURE: Checklist

SOURCE FROM WHICH MEASURE MAY BE OBTAINED: Wallace Mandel, School of Hygiene and Public Health, Johns Hopkins University, 615 North Wolfe Street, Baltimore, Maryland 21205.

DESCRIPTION OF MEASURE: The long form of the SIBS contains 295 items descriptive of children's behavior reported in the literature as used to evaluate children's adjustment by mental health center clinicians and researchers. The short form contains ninety-six items that were rated by several leading senior child psychoanalysts as representing pathology when seen in a child at any age. The correlation between the short form and long form was .96 for a sample of thirty-eight psychotic children.

As examples, the first ten of the 295 items on the scale are given below. The rater checks "yes" or "no" in two columns: "Ever" and "Last 3 months."

1. Responds to social stimulation by smiling, babbling, reaching, etc.
2. Is slow in his movements.

3. Maintains a rigid posture when standing, sitting, lying, or being held.
4. Grits or grinds teeth.
5. Voice is flat and monotonous.
6. Appears indifferent to toys or other objects around him.
7. Keeps falling alseep on and off during the day.
8. Bangs head on wall or other hard surface.
9. Holds breath until face changes color.
10. Responds to physical contact with limpness.

RELIABILITY AND VALIDITY: The test-retest product-moment reliability after one week for ratings of thirty-eight psychotic or latently psychotic children by their mothers was .79. The retest reliability of the short form, pathological items only, was .72.

BIBLIOGRAPHY:

Mandel, W., and Silberstein, R. M. "Children's Psychopathology Behavior Rating Scale." Paper presented at meeting of Eastern Psychological Association, Atlantic City, New Jersey, April 1965.

Tolor, A., Scarpetti, W. L., and Lane, P. A. "Teachers' Attitudes Toward Children's Behavior Revisited." *Journal of Educational Psychology*, 1967, *58*, 175-180.

SYMPTOMS AND CONDITIONS OF EMOTIONAL STRESS: CLASS SUMMARY SHEET

AUTHOR: Paul Hurewitz

AGE: Elementary to college

VARIABLE: Emotional stress

TYPE OF MEASURE: Behavior inventory

SOURCE FROM WHICH MEASURE MAY BE OBTAINED: Paul Hurewitz, Education Department, Herbert H. Lehman College of the City University of New York, Bedford Park Boulevard West, Bronx, New York 10468. Send a self-addressed stamped envelope.

DESCRIPTION OF MEASURE: The instrument allows the teacher to identify twenty symptoms of emotional stress for the entire classroom in approximately 15 to 20 minutes, and it allows each child to be rated in a number of different behavior categories on a quick, easily ratable scale. With the use of this instrument, the teacher, psychologist, or guidance counselor will have a fact sheet of the entire classroom providing a graphic picture of children in need of follow-up and special help. Another use of the instrument is to collect demographic data about the incidence and intensity of emotional stress and to clarify the degree of awareness a teacher has of certain kinds of disturbances.

As examples, the first ten of the twenty items of behavior to be rated for each member of the class are given below.

1. Exceedingly shy, timid, withdrawn.
2. Has no friends.
3. Overaggressive, quarrelsome, antagonistic.
4. Works far below capacity.
5. Little or no motivation to learn.
6. Needs constant attention.
7. Daydreams frequently.
8. Serious health problem.
9. Nervous mannerisms, tics, excessive use of lavatory, enuresis.
10. Stuttering.

RELIABILITY AND VALIDITY: The categories were selected from the literature and from clinical observation as indices of emotional stress. The scale has been tested by more than one thousand teachers and student teachers.

BIBLIOGRAPHY: None reported.

Group 2-b

Personality
Variables

ABERDEEN ACADEMIC MOTIVATION INVENTORY

AUTHOR: N. J. Entwistle

AGE: 12 to 14 or 15 years

VARIABLE: Motivation toward academic success

TYPE OF MEASURE: Likert-type scale

SOURCE FROM WHICH MEASURE MAY BE OBTAINED: N. J. Entwistle, School of Education, University of Lancaster, University House, Bailrigg, Lancaster, England.

DESCRIPTION OF MEASURE: This scale was designed to assist in the prediction of school attainment from noncognitive dimensions. Twenty-four items relate to drive, school attitudes, and scholastic expectations, and these items are all individually related to attainment. Scoring is by "agree," "disagree" responses without differential weightings. The dimension measured is too specific to be picked up in general personality measures and is thus a useful adjunct to such measures in investigations of the correlates of school attainment. It is unlikely that the scale is unidimensional.

The complete measure is given below.

	"Correct" Response
1. Do you like being asked questions in class?	Yes
2. Does your mind often wander off the subject during lessons?	No
3. Do you enjoy most lessons?	Yes
4. Do your parents want you to start work when you are 15?	No
5. Do you think school is rather a waste of time?	No
6. Do you like to leave your homework to the last minute?	No
7. If you were given lower marks than usual in a test, would this make you unhappy?	Yes
8. Do you expect school to provide you with good qualifications for a job?	Yes
9. Is it important to you to do well at school?	Yes
10. Are you happier working with your hands?	No
11. When you are given a difficult problem, do you enjoy trying to find the answer?	Yes
12. Do your parents expect you to go to university or college?	Yes
13. Do you generally find lessons rather dull?	No
14. Do you dread being given a test on your homework?	No
15. Do your friends think that you never take work seriously?	No
16. Would you like to leave school as soon as possible?	No
17. Do your parents tell you to enjoy yourself and not to worry about school?	No
18. Do you work hard most of the time?	Yes
19. Do your parents think that you must do well at school if you are to succeed in later life?	Yes
20. Do your teachers think that you misbehave too much?	No
21. Do you worry about not doing well in class?	Yes

	"Correct" Responses
22. Are you more interested in games than school work?	No
23. Do you find it difficult to keep your mind on your work?	No
24. Do you always try your hardest to get your homework right?	Yes

RELIABILITY AND VALIDITY: Test-retest reliability was .83 after an interval of ten weeks. Scores on the test correlated more highly with attainment measures (.46) than with verbal reasoning tests (.36). The inventory discriminated effectively between "improving" and "deteriorating" pupils within each social class. The test was used with a sample of 2,700 Scottish children and has since been used in England.

BIBLIOGRAPHY:

Entwistle, N. J. "The Transition to Secondary Education: The Age of Transfer and Correlates of Academic Success in the First Year at Secondary School." Unpublished doctoral dissertation. University of Aberdeen, Scotland, 1967.

Entwistle, N. J. "Academic Motivation and School Attainment." *British Journal of Educational Psychology,* 1968, *38,* 181-188.

Entwistle, N. J., and Bennett, S. N. "The Interrelationships Between Personality, Divergent Thinking and School Attainment." Report to the S.S.R.C. London, 1973.

Nisbet, J. D., and Entwistle, N. J. *The Transition to Secondary Education.* London: University of London Press, 1969.

ACHIEVEMENT MOTIVATION TEST FOR CHILDREN— *PRESTATIE MOTIVATIE TEST VOOR KINDEREN* (PMT-K)

AUTHOR: Hubert J. M. Hermans

AGE: 9 to 15 years

VARIABLE: Anxiety, social desirability, achievement motives (debilitating and facilitating)

TYPE OF MEASURE: Questionnaire

SOURCE FROM WHICH MEASURE MAY BE OBTAINED: Swetz and Zentlinger, Keizersgracht 487, Amsterdam, Netherlands. Cost: Test booklet, answer form, scoring keys, and manual, $30.00.

DESCRIPTION OF MEASURE: The PMT-K consists of ninety-four multiple-choice items constituting four scales: achievement motive, debilitating anxiety, facilitating anxiety, and social desirability. Norms are based on a representative sample of 10- to 12-year-old Dutch boys and girls. Decile norms are used for each scale.

As examples, four selected items from the twenty-nine-item achievement motive subscale are given below.

63. Working is something:
    I would rather not do.
    I don't like doing very much.
    I would rather do now and then.
    I like doing.
    I like doing very much.
 7. To prepare yourself a long time for an important task:
    really is senseless.
    often is rather rash.
    can often be useful.
    testifies to a sense of reality.
    is necessary to succeed.
26. When I am working, the demands I make upon myself are:
    very high.
    high.
    pretty high.
    not so high.
    low.
    very low.
39. At high school I thought perseverance was:
    very unimportant.
    rather unimportant.
    important.
    very important.

RELIABILITY AND VALIDITY: Kuder-Richardson formula 20 reliabilities of between .80 and .90 were found for the scales in several investigations. There are a number of validity studies, with criteria such as performance in school, behavior ratings from teachers, underachievement, dropout, pleasure in study, and psychological well-being (see Hermans, 1970, 1971; and Hermans and others, 1972).

BIBLIOGRAPHY:

Hermans, H. J. "A Questionnaire Measure of Achievement Motivation." *Journal of Applied Psychology*, 1970, *54,* 353-363.
Hermans, H. J. *Prestatiemotie en Faslangst in Gezin en Onderzüg.* Amsterdam, Netherlands: Swetz and Zentlinger, 1971.
Hermans, H. J., Laak, J. J., and Maes, P. C. "Achievement Motivation and Fear of Failure in Family and School." *Developmental Psychology*, 1972, *6,* 520-528.

ACHIEVEMENT MOTIVE QUESTIONNAIRE

AUTHOR: W. P. Robinson

AGE: 13 years and up

VARIABLE: Achievement motive (Q Ach), motive to achieve (Q Ach +), motive to avoid failure (Q Ach −)

TYPE OF MEASURE: Questionnaire

SOURCE FROM WHICH MEASURE MAY BE OBTAINED: W. P. Robinson, MacQuare University, North Ryde, N. S. W., Australia 2113; or Michael Argyle, Institute of Experimental Psychology, Oxford University, Oxford, England.

DESCRIPTION OF MEASURE: This instrument can be used for intergroup comparisons and studies of individual differences. There are no age-group norms. For Q Ach +, sum items 1, 5, 7, 10, and 12. For Q Ach −, sum items 2, 6, 8, 9, and 13. For the probability of a person's entering achievement-related situations, see (Q Ach +) minus (Q Ach −). For a general measure allegedly equivalent to TAT need-achievement, sum all items. The rationale for the questionnaire is based on Atkinson's (1957) theory of risk-taking behavior.

      The questionnaire is reproduced below.

1. In how many activities do you wish to do your very best?
       as many as possible   many   some   few   very few
2. Would you hesitate to undertake something that might lead to your failing?
       nearly always   frequently   about half the time   seldom   hardly ever
3. In how many areas are you personally concerned about how well you do?
       most   many   some   few   very few
4. Success brings relief or further determination and not just pleasant feelings. Do you agree?
       strong agreement   agreement   neutral   disagreement   strong disagreement
5. How much effort do you use to reach the goals you set yourself?
       almost 0 percent   25 percent   50 percent   75 percent   100 percent
6. How often do you lack confidence when you have to compete against others?
       hardly ever   seldom   about half the time   frequently   nearly always
7. How hard do you feel you have to try in seemingly trivial tasks?
       not at all   not very   medium   fairly   very
8. How strong is your desire to avoid competitive situations?
       very   fairly   medium   not very   none
9. How true is it to say that your efforts are directed toward avoiding failure?
       quite untrue   not very true   unsure   fairly true   quite true
10. In how many spheres do you think you will succeed in doing as well as you can?
        most   many   some   few   very few
11. How far do you agree that effort rather than success is what is important?
        strong agreement   agreement   neutral   disagreement   strong disagreement
12. How often do you seek opportunities to excel?
        hardly ever   seldom   about half the time   frequently   most of the time

13. How many situations do you avoid in which you may be exposed to evaluation?
     very few   few   some   many   most
14. Do you ever do better if you are worried about failing?
     hardly ever   seldom   about half the time   frequently   most of the time
15. The stronger the chance of failing the more determined you are to succeed. Do you agree?
     strong disagreement   disagreement   neutral   agreement   strong agreement

RELIABILITY AND VALIDITY: There are no reliability coefficients per se, but correlations and factor analyses in combination with examinations of concurrent validity confirm the utility of the measure (Robinson, 1961).

BIBLIOGRAPHY:

Argyle, M., and Robinson, W. P. "Two Origins of Achievement Motivation." *British Journal of Social and Clinical Psychology,* 1962, *1,* 107-120.
Atkinson, J. W. "Motivational Determinants of Risk-Taking Behavior." *Psychological Review,* 1957, *64,* 359-372.
Robinson, W. P. "The Measurement of Achievement Motivation." Unpublished doctoral dissertation. Oxford University, Oxford, England, 1961.

ACHIEVEMENT-RELATED AFFECT SCALE

AUTHORS: Daniel Solomon and Judy Yaeger

AGE: 8 to 15 years

VARIABLE: Achievement motivation

TYPE OF MEASURE: Questionnaire

SOURCE FROM WHICH MEASURE MAY BE OBTAINED: Daniel Solomon, Psychological Services Section, Montgomery County Public Schools, 850 Hungerford Drive, Rockville, Maryland 20850. No charge, but only one copy per request.

DESCRIPTION OF MEASURE: On the assumption that achievement motivation contains elements of behavioral striving for success and of affect associated with both success and failure, items were constructed that tap each of these. In order to get a measure that might be generalized across situations, some of the items deal with school, some with peer competition in games and sports, and others with individual achievement efforts, some involve externally defined achievement standards, while others involve internal standards. The final scale includes twenty items, counterbalanced for agreeing response tendencies.
     The scale with key is given below.

No   1. If I have done my best, losing a game doesn't bother me.
Yes 2. If I can't learn something easily, I feel bad and want to try harder.
No   3. When I play a game with a friend, it doesn't matter to me if I win.
Yes 4. I get very disappointed when I don't get a high grade on a test.
Yes 5. I like trying to learn a new sport better than playing one I already know.
No   6. If I have a good time making something, I don't care how well it turns out.
Yes 7. When I play a game, I don't enjoy it much unless I am winning.
No   8. When I work a puzzle, I don't mind stopping even if I haven't figured it out.
Yes 9. When my friends and I are telling jokes, I'm happiest if mine are the funniest.
No 10. In school, I don't care much if my answer is better than someone else's.
No 11. When something I make turns out badly, I don't want to try it again.
Yes 12. I feel very unhappy when I hand in school work that I know isn't very good.
No 13. When I can't understand something my teacher explains, I don't worry about it much.
Yes 14. When I draw a picture, I enjoy trying ways of improving it.
Yes 15. When I play a game and don't win, I sometimes get angry.
No 16. When a friend beats me at a game, I don't mind because he is a friend.
Yes 17. If I can't understand something in a book, I want to keep working until I do.
Yes 18. I get pleased and excited when I get good grades.
No 19. When I can do something as well as my friends, I'm satisfied.
No 20. If a gym teacher told me I wasn't very good at a sport, I would want to give it up.

RELIABILITY AND VALIDITY: Internal consistency reliability (*alpha*) with a sample of ninety-six fourth-grade suburban boys was .47. With the same sample, the following correlations with other measures were found: social desirability (Crandall), −.02; locus of control (IAR, Crandall), .24; IQ, .11; anxiety (CMAS), .06; lie scale, .02; and grade point average, −.02. In addition, correlations with several achievement test subscores ranged from .13 (for word knowledge) to −.13 (computation).

BIBLIOGRAPHY:

Crandall, V. C., Crandall, V. J., and Katkovsky, W. "A Children's Social Desirability Questionnaire." *Journal of Consulting Psychology,* 1965, *29,* 27-36.

Solomon, D. and Yaeger, J. "Determinants of Boys' Perceptions of Verbal Reinforcers." *Developmental Psychology,* 1969, *1,* 637-645.

Solomon, D. and Kendall, A. J. *Individual Characteristics and Children's Performance in Varied Educational Settings.* Final report, Spencer Foundation Project. Montgomery County Public Schools, Rockville, Maryland, Fall 1975.

CHABASSOL ADOLESCENT STRUCTURE INVENTORY (CASI)

AUTHOR: David J. Chabassol

AGE: Adolescence, 13 to 18 years

VARIABLE: Structure needs and perceptions in adolescence

TYPE OF MEASURE: Rating scale

SOURCE FROM WHICH MEASURE MAY BE OBTAINED: David J. Chabassol, Faculty of Education, University of Victoria, Victoria, British Columbia, Canada V8W 2Y2. No cost for one copy of the scale and scoring key.

DESCRIPTION OF MEASURE: The CASI attempts to measure the extent to which adolescents want structure and perceive themselves as having structure. It yields two separate scores, WS (wants structure) and HS (has structure), each of which is determined by the subject's answers to twenty items. "Structure" is here defined as guidance, advice, information, clarity, or direction as offered to the adolescent by some adult authority figure. The CASI contains forty-seven items, to which the subject responds on a Likert-type format, checking one of: strongly agree, mildly agree, mildly disagree, and strongly disagree. Seven of these items are not involved in the computation of the HS and WS scores and relate to the subject's dealings with his parents, especially as influenced by peer pressures. An item analysis of the scales reveals a strong general WS factor in all of the twenty items in the WS scale, as well as the presence of four other factors of varying strengths. In the HS scale, a general factor is reflected in seventeen of the twenty items, and an additional four factors are also noted in varying degrees of strength. The CASI has now been given to about three thousand adolescents in school settings.

As examples, every fifth item of the forty-seven-item inventory, scored on a 4-point scale from "strongly agree" to "strongly disagree," is given below.

1. I sometimes worry about the number of decisions a person my age has to make and wish I had more guidance and advice from an older person.
6. I feel that I am being "bossed" too much in this school, and I would like to see students have a bigger say in the making of decisions here.
11. My parents want to know in advance what I am going to do when I go out with friends.
16. I believe my ability to make decisions and to accept responsibility is being hindered because the adults with whom I come into contact won't accept me as a mature person.
21. I think people my age sometimes make demands on their parents that they really don't expect their parents to agree to.
26. I think parents should be very clear as to what time their teenage daughter should be in the house at night.
31. I wish that I had some suggestions from an older person as to how I could improve my appearance so that I could make a better impression on people.
36. I would like to have some advice from some adult on making money, budgeting money, saving money, and using money to the best advantage.

41. There is no limit placed at home on the number of times I am permitted to go out with friends throughout the week.
46. I feel adults don't trust me to make sensible decisions.

RELIABILITY AND VALIDITY: Reliability for the WS and HS subscales was determined to be .92 and .91, respectively, using the odd-even method, as corrected by the Spearman-Brown formula. Evidence of construct validity is offered in the 1973 Chabassol study, in which a number of hypotheses relating to the correlation between WS and HS scores for males and females in grades 8 through 11 were supported. Correlations ranging from .30 (eighth-grade boys) through .41 (eleventh-grade girls) were noted between HS scores and scores on Rotter's I-E scale, these being significant at the .01 and .001 levels, respectively. A correlation of −.28, significant at the .01 level, was determined for WS scores and I-E scores in Chabassol (1975). The Adjective Check List (ACL) was compared with the CASI subscale scores in the same study. Eighteen predictions were made regarding expected relationships among twelve of the appropriate ACL scale scores and the WS and HS scores. Fourteen of these were found to be significant and in the direction indicated. Further attempts to provide validity evidence are currently underway. Validation of the CASI is made difficult by the fact that the concept, as here isolated, is a novel one and other external measures of structure are scarce, if not absent entirely.

BIBLIOGRAPHY:

Chabassol, D. J. "A Scale for the Evaluation of Structure Needs and Perceptions in Adolescence." *Journal of Experimental Education,* 1971, *40,* 12-16.
Chabassol, D. J. "The Measurement of Some Aspects of Structure in Adolescence." *Journal of Educational Research,* 1973, *66,* 247-250.
Chabassol, D. J. "An Attempt to Validate a Measure of Structure in Adolescence." *Journal of Experimental Education,* 1975, *43,* 46-50.

CHECKLIST OF CHILDREN'S FEARS

AUTHORS: James W. Croake and Nancy Catlin

AGE: 8 to 16 years

VARIABLE: Children's self-reported fears

TYPE OF MEASURE: Checklist

SOURCE FROM WHICH MEASURE MAY BE OBTAINED: James W. Croake, Virginia Polytechnic Institute and State University, Blacksburg, Virginia 24060.

DESCRIPTION OF MEASURE: This scale consists of seventy-one items, which make up eleven categories of fears (animals, school, supernatural, home, personal relations, future, political, drugs, safety, natural phenomena, ecological). Since there is an unequal number of fears in the various categories, each item is weighted in the scoring so that the categories receive equal consideration. Each item is further scored for intensity so that categories carry a frequency and intensity score. The checklist can be administered to individuals or to groups. Directions for administration are uniform.

As examples, the first thirty-five of the seventy-one item scale, including directions for administering, are given below.

Circle 0 if you never worry about or are afraid of this.
Circle 1 if you hardly ever worry about or are afraid of this.
Circle 2 if you sometimes worry about or are afraid of this.
Circle 3 if you often worry about or are afraid of this.
Circle 4 if you almost always worry about or are afraid of this.

1. Animals on farms.
2. Bugs.
3. The dark.
4. Ghosts or monsters.
5. My friend's problems.
6. War.
7. Being nervous.
8. People driving too fast.
9. Earthquakes.
10. How to act in class.
11. Wild animals.
12. Going crazy from taking drugs.
13. Getting on the team in sports.
14. My pet getting hurt.
15. Mathematics.
16. Getting sick or dying from pollution.
17. School tests.
18. Not getting help with school work.
19. Flunking.
20. Not getting my school work done.
21. Not getting my jobs at home done.
22. Getting hurt while playing games.
23. Swimming.
24. Strange noises.
25. Not doing school work right.
26. Not doing jobs at home right.
27. People I don't know.
28. Being hungry.
29. Falling from high places.
30. Falling into the water.
31. Getting lost.
32. College.
33. Our house on fire.
34. Getting bad grades.
35. Too many people in the world (overcrowded).

RELIABILITY AND VALIDITY: The items for the original checklist (1965) resulted from interviews with 156 children from stratified socioeconomic levels, sex, age, and geographic location. The checklist was originally grouped into ten categories that were unanimously agreed upon as to category and item inclusion by five psychologists. The checklist was then administered to 2,600 children throughout the United States. An item analysis resulted in deleting several items and one category. Subsequently, fifty additional children were interviewed, which resulted in the inclusion of two additional categories: ecology and drugs. The additional items and categories were unanimously agreed upon by three child psychologists. The revised checklist (1973) is the one described above.

BIBLIOGRAPHY:

Croake, J. W. "Fears of Adolescence." *Adolescence,* 1967, *2,* 459-468.
Croake, J. W. "Dissonance Theory and Fear Retention." *Psychology,* 1969, *6,* 19-22.
Croake, J. W. "Fears of Children." *Human Development,* 1969, *12,* 239-247.

CHILDREN'S ACHIEVEMENT MEASURE (CACHM)

AUTHOR: Margaret M. Clifford

AGE: Grades 3 to 8

VARIABLE: Tendency toward personal achievement

TYPE OF MEASURE: Questionnaire

SOURCE FROM WHICH MEASURE MAY BE OBTAINED: Margaret M. Clifford, Department of Educational Psychology, University of Iowa, Iowa City, Iowa 52242.

DESCRIPTION OF MEASURE: This measure consists of twenty-six paired statements, each of which first requires S to choose the one that best describes him, and secondly requires S to indicate (on a 3-point scale) how sure he is that the chosen statement describes him better than the other. The items are designed to assess several aspects of achievement tendency: preference for (1) individual vs. group credit, (2) difficult vs. easy tasks, (3) enjoying success vs. fearing failure, (4) high vs. low persistence, and (5) skill vs. chance tasks. Items one, four, five, eight, nine, ten, twelve, fifteen, eighteen, nineteen, twenty-two, twenty-three, and twenty-six are scored 1 to 6 from "positive" on the first statement to "positive" on the second statement. All others are scored in the reverse. Item scores are totaled to obtain CACHM score. The measure is designed for group administration with the administrator reading each item aloud. It has only recently been designed, and reliability and validation data are currently being collected.

   The first ten items are given below, with the example item.

EXAMPLE:

I like dessert.   I hate to do dishes.

positive   pretty sure   think so   think so   pretty sure   positive

The rest of the items are presented below without the six response categories.

1. I worry about getting bad grades.   I think about getting good grades.
2. I like to work on tasks I can do my-   I like to work on tasks done by groups.
   self.
3. I like to try difficult tasks.   I like to do easy tasks that I'm sure I can
                                                  do.
4. I like to do things that are very safe.   I like things that are risky.
5. If I'm not very good at something, I   If I'm not good at something, I like to get
   like to try something else.   better at it.
6. I like a book with good information.   I like a movie that's good.
7. I like important jobs that are difficult   I like jobs that are not too important and
   even if I might fail at them.   not very difficult.
8. I like to learn to do things others can   I like to learn things very few people can
   do.   do.
9. I like card games that are easy.   I like card games that take a lot of
                                                  thought.
10. I like to race or compete with people   I like to race or compete with people who
    I can usually beat.   are about as good as I am even if I don't
                                                  win.

RELIABILITY AND VALIDITY: None reported.

BIBLIOGRAPHY: None reported.

CHILDREN'S ACHIEVEMENT MOTIVATION SCALE

AUTHOR: Bernard Weiner

AGE: 6 to 14 years

VARIABLE: Achievement motivation

TYPE OF MEASURE: Forced-choice questionnaire

SOURCE FROM WHICH MEASURE MAY BE OBTAINED: Bernard Weiner, Department of Psychology, University of California, 405 Hilgarde Avenue, Los Angeles, California 90024.

DESCRIPTION OF MEASURE: The items on the scale were derived from a theory of achievement motivation and from empirical findings that have been shown to differentiate individuals high and low in achievement needs. The items tap, in part, the kind of affect (hope or fear), the direction of behavior (approach or avoidance), and the preference for risk (intermediate vs. easy or difficult) expressed in achievement situations. Data have shown that individuals high in achievement needs are "hope" oriented, approach achievement tasks, and prefer intermediate risk, while those low in achievement needs are "fear" oriented, avoid achievement activities, and prefer easy to difficult tasks. The appropriate psychometric work has not yet been conducted, and investigators should be cautious in their use of the scale. At the same time, other validated measures of achievement motivation among children are not in existence.

As examples, the first ten items from the measure are given below.

1. I prefer
    a. working with others.
    b. working by myself.
2. I prefer jobs
    a. that I might not be able to do.
    b. which I'm sure I can do.
3. I would rather learn
    a. fun games.
    b. games where I would learn something.
4. I prefer a game
    a. where I'm better than anyone else.
    b. where everyone is about the same.
5. I would rather
    a. play a team game.
    b. play against just one other person.
6. I would rather
    a. wait one or two years and have my parents buy me one big present.
    b. have them buy me several smaller presents over the same period of time.
7. When I am sick, I would rather
    a. rest and relax.
    b. try to do my schoolwork.
8. I
    a. like giving reports before the class.
    b. don't like giving reports before the class.
9. Before class tests I am
    a. often nervous.
    b. hardly ever nervous.
10. When I am playing in a game or sport I am
    a. more interested in having fun than with winning.
    b. more interested in winning.

RELIABILITY AND VALIDITY: Reliability data have not been collected. There have been two studies of empirical validity relating achievement motivation to causal ascriptions and to self-reward for achievement accomplishments. Males in the fifth and sixth grades scoring high on the scale ascribe success internally (to ability and effort) more frequently than low-scoring males. This pattern is not exhibited by the fifth- and sixth-grade females. In addition, males in these grades scoring high on the achievement scale reward themselves more in a self-reinforcement operant setting than males scoring low on the achievement scale.

BIBLIOGRAPHY:

Cook, R. E. "Relation of Achievement Motivation and Attribution to Self-Reinforcement." Unpublished doctoral dissertation. University of California, Los Angeles, 1970.
Weiner, B., and Kukla, A. "An Attributional Analysis of Achievement Motivation." *Journal of Consulting and Clinical Psychology,* 1970, *15,* 1-20.

CHILDREN'S AFFILIATION MEASURE (CAFFM)

AUTHOR: Margaret M. Clifford

AGE: Grades 3 to 8

VARIABLE: Affiliative tendency

TYPE OF MEASURE: Rating scale

SOURCE FROM WHICH MEASURE MAY BE OBTAINED: Margaret M. Clifford, University of Iowa, Department of Educational Psychology, Iowa City, Iowa 52242.

DESCRIPTION OF MEASURE: There are twenty-six statements, each requiring S to indicate agreement or disagreement on an 8-point scale. Items one, four, seven, nine, eleven, twelve, fifteen, eighteen, nineteen, twenty, twenty-one, twenty-three, and twenty-five are scored from "very strong disagreement" to "very strong agreement." All other items are scored in the reverse. Item scores are totaled, and high scores indicate a strong affiliative tendency. This is a newly designed instrument; reliability and validation data are currently being collected. It is intended for group administration with the administrator reading each item aloud.

As examples, the first ten items of the measure are given below. Each item is answered on an 8-point scale as follows: (1) very strong agreement, (2) strong agreement, (3) moderate agreement, (4) slight agreement, (5) slight disagreement, (6) moderate disagreement, (7) strong disagreement, (8) very strong disagreement.

1. When I meet new people, I don't try to make them my friends.
2. I like a leader who is friendly and easy to talk to, better than one who is very quiet and doesn't say much.
3. When I'm not feeling well, I would rather be with others than alone.
4. I'd rather be smart than well liked or popular.
5. Having friends is very important to me.
6. I like to thank people publicly for the good things they do.
7. I enjoy a good movie more than a good party.
8. I like to make as many friends as I can.
9. I would rather take a bicycle ride alone than with one or two friends.

10. When I meet someone I don't like very well, I try to plan another get-together so we can become better friends.

RELIABILITY AND VALIDITY: None reported.

BIBLIOGRAPHY: None reported.

CHILDREN'S DEPENDENCY SCALE

AUTHORS: Carole Golightly, Don Nelson, and James Johnson

AGE: 8 to 12 years

VARIABLE: Dependency

TYPE OF MEASURE: Questionnaire

SOURCE FROM WHICH MEASURE MAY BE OBTAINED: Carole Golightly, McGuire Veterans Administration Hospital, Psychology Service (183), Richmond, Virginia 23249.

DESCRIPTION OF MEASURE: Most items on the Children's Dependency Scale are based on intuitive notions of instrumental and emotional dependency situations. A few items were suggested by questions on Doll's Vineland Social Maturity Scale. In the main, questions are representative of home, school, and play situations. The questions are written in the form of true-false statements and are worded to be commensurate with the vocabulary and attention span of fourth-, fifth-, and sixth-grade children. The scale consists of sixty-five items arranged in a booklet entitled *Grade School Attitude Questionnaire*. Because children often have difficulty with separate answer sheets, questions are answered on the booklet itself by circling a *T* or an *F* appearing in front of each item.
    As examples, the first ten of the sixty-five items are given below.

1. When I was little, I had an invisible friend.
2. My mother lets me choose the clothes she buys for me.
3. I like to be just a little sick so I can have meals in bed.
4. I often telephone my friends.
5. I don't like to have my face washed.
6. I ask my teacher a lot of questions.
7. My parents like all my friends.
8. When my toys break, I try very hard to fix them.
9. My mother brings me to school.
10. I like to have my mother hug me a lot.

RELIABILITY AND VALIDITY: A scale designed to measure dependency in fourth-, fifth-, and sixth-grade children was constructed by means of internal consistency item analysis procedures. Sixty-five true-false items were administered to 219 elementary-school children. The analysis yielded thirty-three cross-validated items. With a new sample, test-retest reliability (two weeks) was .67 for fourth graders, .87 for fifth graders, and .82 for sixth graders. In subsequent concurrent validity studies, scores on the Children's Dependency Scale were found to decrease with the increasing age of children, to be higher for girls than for boys, and to be higher for children in dependent families. A slight relationship was obtained between scale scores and teacher ratings of dependency.

BIBLIOGRAPHY:

Golightly, C., Nelson, D., and Johnson, J. "Children's Dependency Scale." *Developmental Psychology,* 1970, *3,* 114-118.

CHILDREN'S HUMOR TEST

AUTHORS: Priscilla V. King and James E. King

AGE: 4 to 8 years

VARIABLE: Hostile and nonsensical humor

TYPE OF MEASURE: Two-alternative drawing completion

SOURCE FROM WHICH MEASURE MAY BE OBTAINED: James E. King, Department of Psychology, University of Arizona, Tucson, Arizona 85721. Photographs of the five figures are available at cost.

DESCRIPTION OF MEASURE: This test consists of five pictures, each with a missing section. The subject is provided with two alternatives to complete the missing section. One of the alternatives gives the picture a nonsensical and humorous meaning; the other alternative gives the picture a more hostile and humorous meaning. For example, in one drawing two witches are stirring a boiling pot, and the object in the pot is either a large soup can or a boy.

RELIABILITY AND VALIDITY: King and King (1973) found that 4-year-olds preferred hostile-aggressive alternatives more often than 5-year-olds ($p < .001$). Boys preferred hostile-aggressive alternatives more often than girls ($p < .05$). The age-by-sex interaction was not significant. There were significant differences in hostile-aggressive responses elicited by the five drawings ($p < .001$), but the drawings did not significantly interact with age or sex.

BIBLIOGRAPHY:

King, P. V., and King, J. E. "A Children's Humor Test." *Psychological Reports,* 1973, *33,* 632.

Prepared by James E. King

CHILDREN'S PREFERENCE, ORIENTATION, AND MOTIVE SCALES

AUTHORS: Daniel Solomon and Arthur J. Kendall; Mark I. Oberlander (coauthor of the measure of intrinsic motivation)

AGE: 8 to 15 years

VARIABLE: Several preferences, orientations, and motives related to achievement

TYPE OF MEASURE: Questionnaire

SOURCE FROM WHICH MEASURE MAY BE OBTAINED: Daniel Solomon, Psychological Services Section, Montgomery County Public Schools, 850 Hungerford Drive, Rockville, Maryland 20850. No charge, but only one copy per request.

DESCRIPTION OF MEASURE: This is a set of six measures. The following are descriptions and one example of each one. (1) Personal expression vs. structured role orientation (twelve items): A measure of the child's preference for situations that are clearly structured and highly organized as opposed to those that are less structured and provide freer vent to the child's feelings, dispositions, and so forth. "I would rather: (a) play in a game where everyone knows the rules, (b) make up a new game." (2) Fear of failure (ten items): A measure of the child's tendency to avoid situations of possible failure. "I would rather: (a) work a puzzle I know I can do, (b) work a hard puzzle I've never done before." (3) Intrinsic motivation (twelve items): A measure of the motive to strive for the sake of the pleasure derived directly from the activity rather than for rewards from external sources. "John is painting a picture. Why? (a) He wants to get a good grade in his art class, (b) He enjoys painting pictures." (4) Class characteristics preferences (twenty-six items): A measure of children's preferences for different kinds of classrooms, centering on the distinction between "open" and "traditional" classrooms. "I would most like a class where (a) the kids choose what they want to do, (b) the teacher and kids together plan what to do, (c) the teacher plans what the kids will do." (5) Locus of instigation (fifteen items): A measure of the child's belief that he is responsible for initiating his own activities, actions or situations (as opposed to having them initiated by other persons or forces, or by chance). This is differentiated from "locus of control" in that the latter refers to the causes of the *outcomes* of actions, while locus of instigation refers to the causes of their *initiation.*

"When I read a difficult book, it is usually because (a) I was told to, or had to; (b) I was asked to, and agreed; (c) I decided to; (d) I just happened to pick it up." (6) Task preference generality-specificity (twelve items): A measure of the degree to which a child's liking for striving tasks tends to be generalized across a broad variety of task types or narrowly focused on a small number. The number of *a* responses (see below) are summed over the items; those with many are considered "generalizers," those with few are considered "specifiers." "Practicing dart-throwing to become a better shot—(a) I would like doing this very much, (b) I would like doing this fairly well, (c) I would like doing this a little, (d) I would dislike doing this a little, (e) I would dislike doing this pretty much, (f) I would hate doing this."

RELIABILITY AND VALIDITY: Internal consistency (*alpha*) reliability coefficients on preliminary versions of these measures used in a pilot study with ninety-two fourth-grade children were as follows: personal expression vs. structured role orientation, .61; fear of failure, .34; intrinsic motivation, .63; locus of instigation, .59; task preference generality-specificity, .69. Overall reliability was not assessed for the class characteristics preferences items, but the reliability of a 14-item subscale (which included items referring to characteristics observed to actually differentiate the "open" and "traditional" classes in the pilot study) was .66 (this subscale was called "preference for open classes").

Convergent validity correlations in the pilot study were: −.35, between personal expression orientation and a measure of "bureaucratic orientation" (Gordon, 1968; see also p. 526); −.23 between fear of failure and a measure of achievement motivation (Weiner and Kukla, 1970); .29 between generality-specificity and the achievement motivation measure; and .24 between locus of instigation and locus of control (Crandall, Katkovsky, and Crandall, 1965). Correlations with a social desirability measure (Crandall, Crandall, and Katkovsky, 1965) were low and nonsignificant with the exception of personal expression vs. structured role orientation (−.28) and locus of instigation (−.20).

Reliability coefficients obtained in a later study with 1,250 fourth-grade children were as follows: personal expression vs. structured role orientation, .54; fear of failure, .46; intrinsic motivation, .66; locus of instigation, .53; task preference generality-specificity, .69. In this study, three subscales were derived from the "class characteristics preferences" items. These subscales were called "Preference for free and unrestricted vs. controlled classrooms," "Preference for classrooms with child autonomy and decision-making opportunities," and "Preference for classrooms in which children are involved in teaching activities vs. teacher monopolization of such activities." The respective reliability coefficients for these three scales were .62, .70, and .49.

BIBLIOGRAPHY:

Crandall, V. C., Crandall, V. J., and Katkovsky, W. "A Children's Social Desirability Questionnaire." *Journal of Consulting Psychology,* 1965, *29,* 27-36.
Crandall, V. C., Katkovsky, W., and Crandall, V. J. "Children's Beliefs in Their Own Control of Reinforcement in Intellectual-Academic Achievement Situations." *Child Development,* 1965, *36,* 91-109.
Gordon, L. V. *School Environment Preference Schedule.* Albany, New York: SUNY at Albany, 1968.
Solomon, D. *Perceptions of Similarity Between Striving Tasks and the Generality of Task Preferences.* Unpublished manuscript, 1972.

Solomon, D., and Kendall, A. J. "Individual Characteristics and Children's Performance in Varied Educational Settings." Progress report, Spencer Foundation Project. Montgomery County Public Schools, Rockville, Maryland, 1974.

Solomon, D., and Oberlander, M. I. "Locus of Control in the Classroom." In R. H. Coop and K. White (Eds.), *Psychological Concepts in the Classroom.* New York: Harper & Row, 1971.

Weiner, B., and Kukla, A. "An Attributional Analysis of Achievement Motivation." *Journal of Personality and Social Psychology,* 1970, *15,* 1-20.

CHILDREN'S REINFORCEMENT SURVEY SCHEDULE (CRSS)

AUTHORS: Joseph R. Cautela and Linda Meisels

AGE: Forms A and B: kindergarten through grade 3; Form C: grades 4 through 6

VARIABLE: Reinforcing stimuli and their relative reinforcing values

TYPE OF MEASURE: Likert-type scale

SOURCE FROM WHICH MEASURE MAY BE OBTAINED: Joseph R. Cautela, Department of Psychology, Boston College, Chestnut Hill, Massachusetts 02167.

DESCRIPTION OF MEASURE: The Children's Reinforcement Survey Schedule (CRSS) was developed as three forms. The two CRSS forms for kindergarten through third grade, Forms A and B, each contain twenty-five items. The child is asked to rate his preference for each item according to a 3-point, multiple-choice scale with the following categories: dislike, like, like very much. An answer sheet requiring no reading by the participant consists of twenty-five numbered answer blanks. After the test administrator reads a question aloud, the child need only circle his preference on a 3-point scale designated by pictures. Items comprising the multiple-choice questions of the CRSS include some discrete objects and activities that can be presented to a child in most conventional settings. The CRSS also includes some items that for most practical purposes can be presented only through facsimile or imagination. Individual items for all three forms were chosen according to their age-appropriateness for the children and their usefulness as overt as well as covert reinforcers. Form C of the CRSS was developed for children in the fourth through sixth grades. This form consists of seventy-five multiple-choice questions in which the child is asked to rate his preference on the same 3-point scale used in Forms A and B. There are five-open-ended questions at the end of Form C. These questions are included to identify possible high probability behaviors, highly reinforcing environmental settings, and specific reinforcers.

Examples from each form of the CRSS are given below. The respondent replies "dislike," "like," or "like very much" to the first nine questions.

Form A
Do you like candy?

Do you like kickball?
Do you like people to tell you that you did a good job?
Form B
Do you like apples?
Do you like cartoons and comic books?
Do you like your parents to ask you what you did in school today?
Form C
Do you like to play with model cars and trains?
Would you like to have sports equipment of your own?
Do you like to stay overnight at a friend's house?
What do you daydream?
What would you like for your birthday?

RELIABILITY AND VALIDITY: Test-retest reliabilities (N = 141 elementary-school-aged children) obtained on Forms A, B, and C were, respectively, .48, .48, and .72. All the correlations were significant at the .02 level for a two-tailed test. The female responses were consistently more stable over time than the male responses on all three forms.

BIBLIOGRAPHY:

Cautela, J. R. "Reinforcement Survey Schedule: Evaluation and Current Application." *Psychological Reports,* 1972, *30,* 683-690.

Cautela, J. R., and Kastenbaum, R. "A Reinforcement Survey Schedule for Use in Therapy, Training and Research." *Psychological Reports,* 1967, *20,* 1115-1130.

Cautela, J. R., and Kastenbaum, R. "A Reinforcement Survey Schedule for Use in Therapy, Training and Research." In E. T. Thomas (Ed.), *Behavior Modification Procedure: A Sourcebook.* Chicago: Aldine, 1974.

Cautela, J. R., Kastenbaum, R., and Wincze, J. P. "The Use of the Fear Survey Schedule and the Reinforcement Survey Schedule to Survey Possible Reinforcing and Aversive Stimuli Among Juvenile Offenders." *Journal of Genetic Psychology,* 1972, *121,* 255-261.

Cautela, J. R., Steffan, J., and Wish, P. "Covert Reinforcement: An Experimental Test." *Journal of Clinical and Consulting Psychology* (in press).

Cautela, J. R., and Wisocki, P. A. "The Use of the Reinforcement Survey Schedule in Behavior Modification." In R. Rubin (Ed.), *Advances in Behavior Therapy.* New York: Academic Press, 1969.

Keehn, J. D., Bloomfield, F. F., and Hug, M. A. "Uses of the Reinforcement Survey Schedule with Alcoholics." *Quarterly Journal of Studies on Alcoholism,* 1970, *31,* 602-615.

Kleinknecht, R. A., McCormick, C. E., and Thorndike, R. M. "Stability of Stated Reinforcers as Measured by the Reinforcement Survey Schedule." *Behavior Therapy,* 1973, *4,* 407-413.

Mermis, B. J. "Self-Report of Reinforcers and Looking Time." Unpublished doctoral dissertation. University of Tennessee, Knoxville, 1971.

Steffan, J. "Covert Reinforcement with Hospitalized Patients." Paper presented at the annual convention of the Association for the Advancement of Behavior Therapy. Washington, D.C., September 1971.

Thorndike, R. M., and Kleinknecht, R. A. "Reliability of Homogeneous Scales of Reinforcers: A Cluster Analysis of the Reinforcement Survey Schedule." *Behavior Therapy,* 1974, *5,* 58-63.

CHOICE DILEMMAS QUESTIONNAIRE (CDQ)

AUTHORS: Nathan Kogan and Michael A. Wallach

AGE: Approximately 17 years and up

VARIABLE: Self-described risk-taking attitudes

TYPE OF MEASURE: Questionnaire

SOURCE FROM WHICH MEASURE MAY BE OBTAINED: See Appendix E in Kogan and Wallach (1964).

DESCRIPTION OF MEASURE: The CDQ is a twelve-item instrument in which each item represents a choice dilemma between a risky and a safe course of action. The procedure reflects a person's attitudes with regard to risk taking. He is asked in each of the twelve situations, which involve such areas as business, sports, and marriage, how he would advise someone who had to make a decision involving some risk. In answering he is allowed to choose one of six alternatives ranging from taking no risk to taking a risk where the chances are 1 in 10 that the person advised will succeed. The other alternatives represent varying intermediate odds.

As an example, the first of twelve items of the questionnaire is given below.

Mr. A, an electrical engineer, who is married and has one child, has been working for a large electronics corporation since graduating from college five years ago. He is assured of a lifetime job with a modest though adequate salary and liberal pension benefits upon retirement. On the other hand, it is very unlikely that his salary will increase much before he retires. While attending a convention, Mr. A is offered a job with a small, newly founded company which has a highly uncertain future. The new job would pay more to start and would offer the possibility of a share in the ownership if the company survived the competition of the larger firms.

Imagine that you are advising Mr. A. Listed below are several probabilities or odds of the new company's proving financially sound. Please check the lowest probability that you would consider acceptable to make it worthwhile for Mr. A. to take the new job.

The chances are 1 in 10 that the company will prove financially sound.
The chances are 3 in 10 that the company will prove financially sound.
The chances are 5 in 10 that the company will prove financially sound.
The chances are 7 in 10 that the company will prove financially sound.
The chances are 9 in 10 that the company will prove financially sound.

Place a check here if you think Mr. A should *not* take the new job no matter what the probabilities.

RELIABILITY AND VALIDITY: See Wallach and Mabli (1970) and Wallach and Wing (1968).

BIBLIOGRAPHY:

Harntnett, J. J., and Barber, R. M. "Fear of Failure in Group Risk Taking." *British Journal of Social and Clinical Psychology,* 1974, *13,* 125-129.

Kogan, N., and Wallach, M. A. *Risk Taking.* New York: Holt, Rinehart and Winston, 1964.

Kogan, N., and Wallach, M. A. "Risk Taking as a Function of the Situation, the Person, and the Group." In *New Directions in Psychology III.* New York: Holt, Rinehart, and Winston, 1967.

Wallach, M. A., Kogan, N., and Bem, D. J. "Group Influence on Individual Risk Taking." *Journal of Abnormal and Social Psychology,* 1962, *65,* 75-86.

Wallach, M. A., and Mabli, J. "Information Versus Conformity in the Effects of Group Discussion on Risk Taking." *Journal of Personality and Social Psychology,* 1970, *14,* 149-156.

Wallach, M. A., and Wing, C. W., Jr. "Is Risk a Value?" *Journal of Personality and Social Psychology,* 1968, *9,* 101-106.

Prepared by Michael A. Wallach and Orval G. Johnson

COLLETT-LESTER FEAR-OF-DEATH SCALE

AUTHORS: David Lester and Lora Jean Collett

AGE: Grade 6 and up

VARIABLE: Fear of death

TYPE OF MEASURE: Self-report inventory

SOURCE FROM WHICH MEASURE MAY BE OBTAINED: David Lester, Department of Psychology, Stockton State College, Pomona, New Jersey 08240.

DESCRIPTION OF MEASURE: This is a self-report inventory that assesses the fear of death. Its advantage over other fear-of-death scales is that it includes four subscales, as follows: (1) the fear of death of self (nine items), (2) the fear of dying of self (sixteen items), (3) the fear of death of others (ten items), and (4) the fear of dying of others (eleven items). Each subscale contains items keyed positively and items keyed negatively. Thus although the scale is scored as any conventional Likert-type scale, care is needed in distinguishing the items of each scale and in distinguishing the positively keyed and the negatively keyed items. The scores have meaning only in relation to the scores of other subjects. The items have not been constructed so that a score of, say, +A means that the subject has a fear of death, while a score of −A means that the subject has no fear of death. The only kind of statement that is logically possible with this scale is that subject X has a higher (or lower) score than subject Y. There are no adequate norms for the scales. Several of the studies that have been published, however, do report mean scores on each of the subscales for a variety of subject populations.

As examples, eighteen of the thirty-six item scale are given below, to be scored as follows: +1, slight agreement; +2, moderate agreement; +3, strong agreement; −1, slight disagreement; −2, moderate disagreement; −3, strong disagreement.

1. I would avoid death at all costs.
2. I would experience a great loss if someone close to me died.
3. I would not feel anxious in the presence of someone I knew was dying.
4. The total isolation of death frightens me.
5. I am disturbed by the physical degeneration involved in a slow death.
6. I would not mind dying young.
7. I accept the death of others as the end of their life on earth.
8. I would not mind visiting a senile friend.
9. I would easily adjust after the death of someone close to me.
10. If I had a choice as to whether or not a friend should be informed he/she is dying, I would tell him/her.
11. I would avoid a friend who was dying.
12. Dying might be an interesting experience.
13. I would like to be able to communicate with the spirit of a friend who has died.
14. I view death as a release from earthly suffering.
15. The pain involved in dying frightens me.
16. I would want to know if a friend were dying.
17. I am disturbed by the shortness of life.
18. I would not mind having to identify the corpse of someone I knew.

RELIABILITY AND VALIDITY: Reliability studies have not yet been reported. The scale has obvious face validity. It was derived using interitem analyses. The authors provide correlations between scores on the four subscales and correlations of each of the four subscales with the original (1967) Lester Fear-of-Death Scale.

BIBLIOGRAPHY:

Alexander, M., and Lester, D. "Fear of Death in Parachute Jumpers." *Perception and Motor Skills,* 1972, *34,* 338.

Collett, L. J., and Lester, D. "The Fear of Death and the Fear of Dying." *Journal of Psychology,* 1969, *72,* 179-181.

Ford, R. E., Alexander, M., and Lester, D. "Fear of Death in a High Stress Occupation." *Psychological Reports,* 1971, *29,* 502.

Lester, D. "Fear of Death and Nightmare Experiences." *Psychological Reports,* 1969, *25,* 437-438.

Lester, D. "Correlates of 'Animism' in Adults." *Psychological Reports,* 1970, *27,* 806.

Lester, D. "Relation of Fear of Death in Subjects to Fear of Death in Their Parents." *Psychological Record,* 1970, *20,* 541-543.

Lester, D. "Religious Behavior and the Fear of Death." *Omega,* 1970, *1,* 181-188.

Lester, D. "Attitudes Toward Death Held by Staff of a Suicide Prevention Center." *Psychological Reports,* 1971, *28,* 650.

Lester, D. "Attitudes Toward Death in a Nondisturbed Population." *Psychological Reports,* 1971, *29,* 386.

Lester, D. "Studies in Death Attitudes: Part Two." *Psychological Reports,* 1972, *30,* 440.

Lester, D., and Collett, L. J. "Fear of Death and Self-Ideal Discrepancy." *Archives of the Foundation of Thanatology,* 1970, *2,* 130.

Lester, D., Getty, C., and Kneisl, C. "Attitudes of Nursing Students and Nursing Faculty Toward Death." *Nursing Research,* 1974, *23,* 50-53.

Lester, G., and Lester, D. "The Fear of Death, the Fear of Dying, and Threshold Differences for Death Words and Neutral Words." *Omega,* 1970, *1,* 175-179.

COMPREHENSIVE SOCIAL DESIRABILITY SCALE FOR CHILDREN (CSDC)

AUTHOR: James A. Walsh

AGE: 2½ to 6½ years

VARIABLE: Tendency to give the socially desirable response

TYPE OF MEASURE: True-false scale

SOURCE FROM WHICH MEASURE MAY BE OBTAINED: James A. Walsh, Department of Psychology, University of Montana, Missoula, Montana 59801.

DESCRIPTION OF MEASURE: The CSDC is composed of twenty-eight true-false items of the objective personality type covering a very wide range of content. They are nonpathological and are distributed uniformly over the entire social desirability range. The items were selected so that sex differences in responding were eliminated at all age levels. The items from Form A of the CSDC, their social desirability scale values, keying, and sequence are given below.

SDSV (combined male and female)	Key	Sequence	
1.59	N	10	Do you write with crayons on the wall?
1.89	N	19	Do you hit other children?
2.08	N	26	Would you hit a boy or girl who was smaller than you are?
2.31	N	11	Do you play with your food?
2.54	N	25	Do you get angry when you don't get your way?

SDSV (combined male and female)	*Key*	*Sequence*	
2.74	N	6	Do you get mad easily?
3.18	N	18	Do you yell in the house?
3.39	N	13	Do you forget things you are supposed to do?
3.78	N	9	Do you tease people?
3.79	N	15	Are you shy?
4.34	N	5	Do you run too much?
4.41	N	24	Are you afraid of being hurt by a dog?
4.80	N	21	When you are alone in a room and you hear a strange noise, do you get a frightened feeling?
4.86	N	12	Can other people get you to do what they want you to?
5.05	Y	14	Do you do the things others do?
5.22	Y	27	Do you feel that you have to be the best in everything?
5.56	Y	20	Would you like to be older?
5.69	Y	7	Do you like being quiet?
6.12	Y	8	When you are sick, are you glad to see the doctor?
6.21	Y	17	Do you ask a lot of questions?
6.90	Y	4	Do you like to take a bath?
6.90	Y	22	Are you strong?
7.15	Y	3	When are riding in a car, do you sit down in your seat?
7.21	Y	28	(Does your mother do things for you), or do you do things for yourself?
7.58	Y	2	Do you pick up your toys when you're through playing?
7.82	Y	23	Are you usually happy?
8.22	Y	16	Are you polite?
8.26	Y	1	Are you friendly?

Norms for the scale were obtained for every six-month interval from calendar age 2.51 to 6.50 years, a total of 167 females and 168 males comprising the normative group. The trend in social desirability responding to the CSDC was shown to increase linearly from 2.51 to 6.50 years and to be related to vocabulary, calendar age, and joint effects of vocabulary and calendar age. Trends of social desirability responding to items in different ranges of scale values are different and are taken to support a social-reinforcement theory of the social desirability response.

RELIABILITY AND VALIDITY: Alternate-form reliability of the CSDC was shown to be .92 for twenty-five subjects from 3.01 to 3.50 years of age and .91 for twenty-five subjects from 3.51 to 4.00 years of age. Convergent and discriminant validity, respectively, were demonstrated by correlations of .81 with Cruse's social desirability scale and .36 with the Crandall and others (1965) social approval scale. An empirical study involving fifty first graders showed that the CSDC more accurately distinguished between pupils requiring consultation with a speech therapist, school psychologist, or disciplinary counselor than did a group intelligence test.

BIBLIOGRAPHY:

Crandall, V. C., Crandall, V. J., and Katkovsky, W. "A Children's Social Desirability Questionnaire." *Journal of Consulting Psychology*, 1965, *29*, 27-36.

Klieger, D. M., and Walsh, J. A. "A Pictorial Technique for Obtaining Social Desirability Ratings from Young Children." *Psychological Reports*, 1967, *20*, 295-304.

Walsh, J. A., Tomlinson-Keasey, C., and Klieger, D. M. "Acquisition of the Social Desirability Response." *Genetic Psychology Monographs*, 1974, *89*, 241-272.

CONCERNS ABOUT SUCCESS AND FAILURE

AUTHOR: Roy C. Herrenkohl

AGE: 15 years and up

VARIABLE: Achievement orientation

TYPE OF MEASURE: Questionnaire

SOURCE FROM WHICH MEASURE MAY BE OBTAINED: Roy C. Herrenkohl, Center for Social Research, Lehigh University, Bethlehem, Pennsylvania 18015.

DESCRIPTION OF MEASURE: This 160-item measure is designed to assess an individual's attitudes toward or orientation to achievement. Item content was suggested by existing measures and by issues considered relevant to achievement orientation. The content of the items focuses on success and failure in academic undertakings, vocation, marriage, and interpersonal relations. The measure is a self-description type, involving true-false responses. Ten dimensions, defined by factor analysis, with sample items, are as follows: Test anxiety: *I get upset before exams.* Threat of failure: *Even when I do something well my efforts are not recognized.* Parental expectations: *My parents encouraged me to be above average in whatever I undertook.* Unwillingness to risk failing: *I would avoid a course in which I might do poorly, even if it were very interesting.* Dislike of persons who do better than oneself: *I dislike people who do better than I do.* Concern about failing in primary roles: *There are times I worry about being a successful husband (or wife).* Desire to excel: *I have a strong desire to be above average.* Sensitivity to others knowing of one's failure: *Even if I were to fail in something important, I could still face my friends.* Exerting effort to do well: *I attempt to learn everything I can from a course.* Valuation of competition: *I like competition.*

The measure was administered to 2,774 students (grades 10 to 12) from nine public high schools and 2,328 students from sixteen colleges of different entrance standards. Respondents were from a diversity of social and economic backgrounds The measure can be administered to groups and is scored using unit-weighted summative scores.

As examples, the first fifteen of the 160 items of the measure are given below.

1. I sometimes think about being successful.
2. When my friends talk about their successes, I feel like a failure.
3. My parents expected the highest possible level of achievement from their children.
4. I refuse to put a book aside before I know almost every detail, even though I am not responsible for learning the details.
5. I could still face my family if I failed in school.
6. After examinations I feel confident I have done well.
7. There are times when I worry that I may not know the answers on an examination.
8. I would be upset if my friends were doing better than I in something important.
9. I don't mind getting average grades.
10. My parents didn't encourage me to be competitive.
11. To avoid failing I must work longer and harder than other people.
12. It is easy for me to set aside an important project I am working on.
13. My parents encouraged me to do better than others in whatever I undertook.
14. It would be difficult to feel friendly toward someone who won a prize I was working for.
15. My parents wanted me to be friends with the smartest or most popular children in school.

RELIABILITY AND VALIDITY: The reliability of the dimensions defined by the factor-analytic procedure was determined by splitting the respondent sample, doing a factor analysis on each half of the sample, and then determining the congruence between factors from the two samples using Burt's unadjusted correlation coefficient (also called Tucker's *phi*). Ten factors rotated for both halves of the respondent sample gave the highest congruence, .90 or greater for each pair. The Spearman-Brown estimate of Cronbach's *alpha* ranged from .71 to .84. Finally, test-retest reliability coefficients were computed and ranged from .78 to .88. Validity of each dimension on the measure is as yet unclear. There is evidence that there is a statistically significant relationship between a respondent's score on several of the dimensions (threat of failure, unwillingness to risk failing, desire to excel, and valuation of competition) and self-reported grade average; a statistically significant relationship between respondents' sex and their scores on nine out of ten of the dimensions; and weak (mostly not statistically significant) relationships between indicators of a respondent's social status and scores on the dimensions.

BIBLIOGRAPHY:

Herrenkohl, R. C. "A Comparison of Criteria for Determining the Number of Factors to Rotate Using Real Data." Unpublished, mimeographed, n.d.

Herrenkohl, R. C. "Concerns About Success and Failure: Scoring Manual." Unpublished, mimeographed, n.d.

Herrenkohl, R. C. "Factor-Analytic and Criterion Study of Achievement Orientation." *Journal of Educational Psychology*, 1972, *63*, 314-326.

Herrenkohl, R. C., and Farris, E. "The Influence of Interdependence, Task Difficulty, Voice Quality and Performance Similarity on Interpersonal Attraction." Unpublished, mimeographed, n.d.

DEAN'S COMPOSITE EMOTIONAL MATURITY SCALE

AUTHOR: Dwight G. Dean

AGE: Adolescence to adulthood

VARIABLE: Perceived emotional maturity

TYPE OF MEASURE: Likert-type (certainty method)

SOURCE FROM WHICH MEASURE MAY BE OBTAINED: Dwight G. Dean, Department of Sociology, Iowa State University, Ames, Iowa 50010. Keyed copy at no cost. Reprint or abstract requested.

DESCRIPTION OF MEASURE: This twenty-two-item composite scale includes items from nearly all fourteen dimensions of original emotional maturity scales containing 183 items. The mature person: (1) is able to handle stress, (2) is able to handle anger, (3) relates well to authority (neither rebellious nor dependent), (4) moves toward integration, (5) exercises self-control, (6) exercises good judgment, (7) progresses toward a mutually satisfying heterosexuality, (8) has an open attitude toward learning, (9) has achieved an adult level of intellectual maturity, (10) is drawing toward responsibility, (11) is growing from egocenteredness toward sociocenteredness, (12) utilizes communication effectively, (13) possesses relative emotional security, and (14) has social poise. The scale has been utilized primarily with married couples (hence the score represents each spouse's perception of the other's maturity).

As examples, six of the twenty-two items on the scale are given below. The respondent, who is asked to pretend that he is someone else describing himself, answers on a 5-point frequency scale ranging from "very frequently" to "practically never."

1. When upset by being frustrated, resorts to crying, fussing, feeling hurt, being peevish.
5. Tries to avoid unpleasant but necessary tasks.
8. Seems emotionally secure; seldom exhibits anxiety.
12. Plans his time, adapting if necessary.
13. Feels uneasy and apprehensive in the presence of his superiors.
20. May resent reasonable rules and regulations (on the job, traffic laws, etc.).

RELIABILITY AND VALIDITY: Validity of the original fourteen scales was determined by the following procedures and results: (1) face validity, since thirty-one of the 183 items were taken almost verbatim from Eilbert (1957), who validated with fourteen psychiatrists; (2) freshman men were assumed to be less mature than freshman women—thirteen of the fourteen scales were in the right direction, twelve significantly so; (3) freshman women were assumed to be less mature than senior women—all scales were in the right direction, four significantly; (4) housemothers in a small liberal arts college were asked to rank the girls in their cottages on a 5-point continuum—ten of the fourteen scales were in the predicted direction. Reliability by Spearman split-half method varied from a minimum of .70 for authority to .87 for communication. Reliability of the composite twenty-two-item scale was .75. A recent study ($N = 44$ married couples, general population) yielded an *alpha* of .90 (scoring by the certainty method format).

BIBLIOGRAPHY:

Dean, D. G. "Romanticism and Emotional Maturity." *Marriage and Family Living*, 1961, *23*, 44-45.

Dean, D. G. "Romanticism and Emotional Maturity: A Further Exploration." *Social Forces*, 1964, *42*, 298-303.

Dean, D. G. "Emotional Maturity and Marital Adjustment." *Journal of Marriage and the Family*, 1966, *28*, 454-457.

Dean, D. G. "Maturity—It's Essential." *The Long Island Catholic*, 1967, *8*, 22.

Dean, D. G. "Improving Marital Prediction: A Model and a Pilot Study." Paper presented at the National Council on Family Relations. St. Louis, Missouri, October 1974.

Eilbert, L. "A Tentative Definition of Emotional Immaturity Utilizing the Critical Incident Technique." *Personnel and Guidance Journal*, 1957, *35*, 554-567.

DEPENDENCE-INDEPENDENCE OBSERVATION FRAMEWORK

AUTHOR: Glen Heathers

AGE: Preschool children (2 to 5 years)

VARIABLE: Socialization (emotional dependence)

TYPE OF MEASURE: Observation frame of reference

SOURCE FROM WHICH MEASURE MAY BE OBTAINED: See Heathers (1955).

DESCRIPTION OF MEASURE: This measure requires the collection of a verbatim running account of 3-minute samples of a child's behavior. Within the 3-minute period the child's activities are recorded in detail, including such behavior as watching other children, ignoring or noticing extraneous stimuli, wandering about, approaching or leaving others, playing alone, interacting with children, and interacting with adults. The data are then scored in terms of fourteen categories, four involving emotional dependence, six for emotional independence, and four for amount or type of play. The four emotional-dependence categories measure two general modes of dependence: a relatively passive, infantile mode (clinging or seeking affection) and a relatively active mode (seeking attention, affection, or approval). The six emotional-independence categories include three measures of self-reliance as manifested by nondistractibility or persistence and three measures of self-assertion or dominance in social interaction. The play categories measure the opportunities the child's play provides for making different sorts of responses. Thus a child who is inactive or plays alone almost all the time has few occasions to express dominance over other children.

As examples, three of the fourteen categories are given below.

Emotional Dependence Categories

1. *Clings to or seeks affection from teacher.* Hangs around teacher, seeks to enter into play with her, touches or leans against her, wants her to hold self in lap, asks her if she likes self. Don't score when child approaches teacher for information, for permission, for necessary help, to invite attention, or to show an accomplishment. Score each instance.

5. *Ignores stimuli from teacher.* A teacher stimulus is scored when the teacher talks, approaches, or goes by the child, provided the child is not interacting with the teacher nor the teacher seeking the child's attention. Score an instance of ignoring if the child doesn't look up or watch the teacher.

Play Categories

11. *Not playing.* Score once for each minute during which the child sits or stands unoccupied for 15 seconds or so. Do not score if child is waiting to play or performing any role related to initiating or continuing any play activity. Also do not score if child is interacting with teacher.

RELIABILITY AND VALIDITY: Heathers (1955) reports data on forty middle-class children, twenty 2-year-olds, and twenty 4- or 5-year-olds. When observers scored each others' observations and their own (N = 38 children aged 2 to 5), interscorer reliabilities (*rho*) for the eight categories requiring judgment by the scorer ranged from .63 to .98, median .85. The comparability of two samples of observational data for each of two age groups was obtained by correlating the scores yielded by the two samples, category by category. In the 2-year-old group, the correlations range from .45 to .90, with one exception (r = 10). One r of .45 approached significance; the other twelve correlations were significant at the .04 level or less. In the 4 to 5 age group, all fourteen correlation coefficients were significant at the .04 level or less, ranging from .50 to .93. Comparing the two age groups, key findings were that seeking affection from the teacher declined with age (.01 level), while seeking attention or approval from the teacher increased (.05 level) and also increased in responses to other children (.01 level).

BIBLIOGRAPHY:

Heathers, G. "Emotional Dependence and Independence in Nursery School Play." *Journal of Genetic Psychology,* 1955, *87,* 37-57.

Prepared by Orval G. Johnson

DEVELOPMENTAL SURVEY OF RISK-TAKING BEHAVIOR

AUTHOR: John W. Hollender

AGE: 10 years to adult

VARIABLE: Impulsivity

TYPE OF MEASURE: Questionnaire

SOURCE FROM WHICH MEASURE MAY BE OBTAINED: Manuscript referred to below contains the scales and other data and is available without cost from John W. Hollender, Department of Psychology, Emory University, Atlanta, Georgia 30322.

DESCRIPTION OF MEASURE: The survey ranges in length from seventy-six core items to 134 items and is available in three forms. The shortest form is used with younger students (aged 10 to 15), twenty-seven items are added for older high school students (aged 16 to 18), and the college student and adult form adds another thirty-one items. Items indicate age-relevant risky behavior and are grouped according to developmental time periods. Older subjects respond to the earlier items retrospectively. Thirty-one items are currently scorable on an impulsivity scale for male elementary students, and thirty-three items are scorable for female students. For college students and adults there are sixty-four items scorable on an impulsivity scale for males and sixty-nine items scorable for females. Most of the items (75 percent or more) are behavioral in nature and are responded to with a 3- or 5-point frequency scale, depending on the age of the subject. Item selection was a combination of judges' ratings of content for the selection of the initial pool, item-criterion correlation, factor analysis, and item-factor correlation. The impulsivity scales as behavioral scales are global measures reflecting various personal characteristics, including self-concept, learned skills, and cognitive factors.

As examples, twenty items from the measure are given below. The first ten items refer to behavior during elementary school, and items 41 to 50 refer to behavior during high school. Additional items not listed refer to college and adult years.

1. I was sent to the principal's office for punishment, by the teacher.
2. I couldn't pay attention to the teacher.
3. I made my friends laugh in class.
4. I took fruit from trees without permission.
5. I threw rocks at friends.
6. I waded barefoot in dirty water.
7. I climbed up high in tall trees.
8. I played outside in thunderstorms.
9. I broke a window.
10. I threw things at passing cars.
41. I rode on a motorcycle (or minibike) even though I felt it was not safe.
42. I didn't do important homework assignments.
43. I studied for exams well in advance of the tests.
44. I studied for exams early in the morning on the day of the exam.
45. I stayed home to avoid difficult tests.
46. I cheated on tests.
47. I was in physical fights with classmates.
48. My sexual activity was risky.
49. I drank beer or wine.
50. I did things which I knew were wrong.

RELIABILITY AND VALIDITY: An earlier twenty-four-item scale composed of items all selected by empirical criteria had an internal consistency of .88 (Gulliksen formula). It is assumed that the lengthier scales with items selected on the additional criteria of consistent and high factor loadings will have greater reliability. Validity data vary from scale to scale. The validity data are probably poorest for the female scale for elementary students, where less than half of the items had a significant relationship to external criteria of delay of gratification and to Kagan's Matching Familiar Figures test of reflectivity-impulsivity. All items on the college student scales have statistically significant relationships with both the elementary school factor-analytic scales and with various external validity criteria.

BIBLIOGRAPHY:

Hollender, J. W. *The Development of Questionnaire Measures of Impulsivity.* Unpublished manuscript. Emory University, Atlanta, Georgia, November 1974.

DRAW-A-GROUP TEST

AUTHOR: Norman J. Ferin

AGE: 6 to 14 years

VARIABLE: Dominance, aggression, dependency, and isolation in group behavior

TYPE OF MEASURE: Test

SOURCE FROM WHICH MEASURE MAY BE OBTAINED: See Ferin (1954).

DESCRIPTION OF MEASURE: (A) Developmental scales: The child is instructed to draw a picture of a group to include at least five children. His pencil drawing depicts his idiosyncratic perception of a group. Each age level from 6 to 12 exhibits unique features of group structure and activity. The development of the group concept is thus graphically portrayed in children's group drawings, from the 6-year-old who may have no understanding of group formation, to the autocratic and tightly controlled 9-year-old's group, to the democratically oriented group of the 12-year-old. (B) Prediction of children's group behavior (dominance, aggression, dependency, isolation): The child is instructed to draw a picture of a group of which he is a member. By the relative size of the figures, the placement of the figures in the group setting, the order in which figures are drawn, the attitude of the figures portrayed, and by spontaneous comments, children reveal the role they play in a group. The drawings of other group members generally confirm the individual's role projection of himself.

RELIABILITY AND VALIDITY: To validate the prediction of group role behavior made from the children's drawings, a rating scale was devised that would measure four variables: dominance, aggression, dependency, and isolation. Since the children belonged to organized groups with adult leaders, each leader was asked to rate the child on these four variables. These results generally confirmed the predictions made from the drawings of role behavior.

BIBLIOGRAPHY:

Ferin, N. J. "The Development of a Figure Drawing Method for the Study of the Concepts of Dominance, Aggression, Dependency, and Isolation as They Relate to Group Behavior in Children." Unpublished doctoral dissertation. Case Western Reserve University, Cleveland, Ohio, 1954.

ELEMENTARY SCHOOL FORM OF THE DOGMATISM SCALE

AUTHOR: Russell L. Figert, Jr.

AGE: 10 to 12 years

VARIABLE: Open/closedmindedness

TYPE OF MEASURE: Self-rating scale

SOURCE FROM WHICH MEASURE MAY BE OBTAINED: See Figert (1965, 1968)

DESCRIPTION OF MEASURE: The scale consists of fifty forced-choice items (agree, uncertain, disagree) adapted from among sixty-six items developed by Rokeach (1960). His scale and the elementary-school form are designed to help identify persons whose belief-disbelief systems may be so organized as to place them near either end of an open-minded-closedminded continuum. Those so identified can be grouped for comparisons of other behaviors in experimental studies designed to test the validity of Rokeach's theory on the organization of belief-disbelief systems. In his theory, Rokeach postulates dimensions such as isolation and differentiation of beliefs and disbeliefs, a hierarchy of their importance to individuals, and the breadth of an individual's orientation to the past, present, and future. In composing and testing items to delineate belief-disbelief system dimensions, Rokeach takes into account such factors as a person's tolerance level, views of authority, existence of contradictions within subsystems, "party-lining," and outlook for the future. Typical items from the elementary-school form that are related to these and other factors are given below.

It is good when all people can have their say. But we cannot let some people do that yet.
Most people just do not care about others.
I cannot stand some people because of the way they think about things.
We must believe our leaders if we are to know what is going on in the world.
Lots of people are not happy now. This will change in the future.

RELIABILITY AND VALIDITY: Reliability of the instrument as determined by use of the split-half method and the Spearman-Brown formula was determined to be .67 when responses of a sample of 458 subjects were compared. The subjects were pupils in grades 4, 5, and 6 in a small rural midwestern United States city. A jury of psychologists, reading specialists, and Rokeach studied, commented on, and eventually approved the adaptations of items. Comparisons of scale data with other data available on the subjects provided evidence that the scale was measuring many of the same factors among children as the adult form of the scale was measuring among adults.

BIBLIOGRAPHY:

Felker, D. W., and Treffinger, D. J. "Elementary School Form of the Dogmatism Scale." *Journal of Experimental Education,* 1971, *39* (2), 24-26.

Figert, R. L., Jr. "An Elementary School Form of the Dogmatism Scale." Unpublished doctoral dissertation. Teachers College, Ball State University, Muncie, Indiana, 1965.

Figert, R. L., Jr. "An Elementary School Form of the Dogmatism Scale." *Journal of Experimental Education,* 1968, *37* (2), 19-23.

Rokeach, M. *The Open and Closed Mind.* New York: Basic Books, 1960.

EXPLORATION PREFERENCES QUESTIONNAIRES
(FORMS D AND E)

AUTHORS: Daniel W. Edwards and James G. Kelly

AGE: Grade 8 to adult

VARIABLE: Coping (exploration) preference

TYPE OF MEASURE: True-false questionnaire

SOURCE FROM WHICH MEASURE MAY BE OBTAINED: Daniel W. Edwards, University of California at Davis, Sacramento Medical Center, 4430 "V" Street, Sacramento, California 95817.

DESCRIPTION OF MEASURE: This measure has two thirty-item parallel forms developed to assess the coping preference of exploration in male high school students. The scales evolved out of an item pool of over one thousand items and have gone through three major empirically based revisions. Items judged to be socially desirable or having item difficulties below .20 or above .80 were eliminated. The scales are balanced with equal numbers of positive and negative items to control for acquiescence. Mean item difficulty (eighth graders) is .56 for Form D and .57 for Form E. Mean item total-score correlation is .33 (Form D) and .34 (Form E). These scales were major selection criteria for a longitudinal study of the social and emotional development of high school boys (Edwards, 1971b). The scales were designed to assess one component of the person side of person-environment transactions, which determine the varied adaptations made to the high school experience. Sample items are: "I often have new ideas for class projects" and "I go out of my way to take part in different activities."

RELIABILITY AND VALIDITY: Internal consistency as estimated by coefficient *alpha* is .75 for both forms, with a value of .85 for the total sixty items. Parallel-form reliability is estimated at .77 and can be taken as a direct estimate of the common variance between forms. Test-retest reliability after two weeks (seventy-nine ninth-grade boys) is .82, while test-retest stability after a year is .67 ($N = 219$). These exploration questionnaires have good reliabilities for research instruments measuring personal preferences. Convergent validity has been assessed through three methods. Significant positive relationships were found between questionnaire scores and peer nominations of high, medium, and low explorer preference individuals in two samples. Significant positive relationships were found between the questionnaire scores and a self-report multiple-choice thematic measure of exploration preferences. Finally, significant and positive relationships ($r = .67$) were found with an alternative self-report questionnaire of preferences (fourteen 7-point scales) but not with an alternative self-report questionnaire measure of exploration behavior ($r = .33$, fourteen 13-point frequency scales). Divergent validity was estimated through correlational studies between Forms D and E and more than fifteen common personality and achievement measures. These studies indicated low relationships between exploration preference and intelligence (.35), need for social approval (.23), or internal-external control ($-.31$).

BIBLIOGRAPHY:

Edwards, D. W. "The Development of a Questionnaire Measure of Measuring Exploration Preferences." *Buffalo: Studies in Psychotherapy and Behavioral Change* (Buffalo, New York: State University of New York), 1971a, *2*, 99-107.

Edwards, D. W. "Exploration and the High School Experience: A Study of Tenth-Grade Boys' Perceptions of Themselves, Their Peers, and Their Schools." Unpublished doctoral dissertation. University of Michigan, Ann Arbor, 1971b.

Edwards, D. W. "Blacks Versus Whites: When Is Race a Relevant Variable?" *Journal of Personality and Social Psychology*, 1974, *29*, 39-49.

Edwards, D. W. "Coping Preference, Adaptive Roles, and Varied High School Environments: A Search for Person-Environment Transactions." In D. Adelson (Ed.), *Community Psychology Series.* New York: Behavioral Publications (in press).

FESHBACH AND ROE AFFECTIVE SITUATION TEST FOR EMPATHY (FASTE)

AUTHORS: Norma Deitch Feshbach and Kiki Roe

AGE: 6 to 10 years

VARIABLE: Empathy

TYPE OF MEASURE: Slides with narration

SOURCE FROM WHICH MEASURE MAY BE OBTAINED: Norma D. Feshbach, Department of Education, University of California, 405 Hilgard Avenue, Los Angeles, California 90024. Cost: In United States, $30.00; outside United States, $35.00.

DESCRIPTION OF MEASURE: In this measure, children are individually administered a series of slide sequences depicting a boy or girl in different affective situations. Two of these sequences involve happy events (having a birthday party, winning a contest for tickets to Disneyland); other sequences convey sadness (child's dog runs away, child with no one to play with), fear (child lost in woods, child attacked by strange dog), and anger (child is falsely accused, child stealing another's toy). Each sequence consists of three slides accompanied by appropriate narration in which the use of affective terms is completely avoided. There are two such sequences for each of the four affects, with separate sets prepared for male and female stimulus persons. The two slide sequences for each affect are presented consecutively, with a short task interposed between any two affects. Immediately following each slide sequence the child is asked simply to state how he or she felt. In order for empathy to be scored, the affect reflected in the response has to be a specific match with the affective situation observed. A separate assessment is made of the child's comprehension of these affective situations, the child being asked at a later point to indicate how the stimulus person in the slides feels.

RELIABILITY AND VALIDITY: The test-retest reliability of the FASTE was conducted over a one-week period with twenty middle-class kindergarteners (mean age 71 months) and first graders (mean age 82 months). Using the general scoring procedure in which the child's empathic response must be of the same valence as the story, the correlation between times I and II was .91 ($p = .01$). Using the specific scoring procedure in which the child's empathic response must specifically match the story content, the correlation between times I and II was .84 ($p = .01$). Kindergarteners and first graders have similar reliabilities using the general scoring procedure ($K = .92$, first = .86, $p = .01$) and the specific scoring procedure ($K = .77$, first = .94, $p = .01$). Although the difference between the means of boys and girls was not significant using the general scoring, the specific scoring procedure yielded mean scores that were significantly higher for girls than boys at both testings ($p = .05$). Correlation coefficients for the general scoring procedure for boys was .86; girls, .94 ($p = .01$); and for the specific scoring procedure, .74 for boys and .89 for girls ($p = .01$).

BIBLIOGRAPHY:

Feshbach, N. D. "Empathy: An Interpersonal Process." Paper presented as part of a Symposium on Social Understanding in Children and Adults: Perspectives on Social Cognition, at the American Psychological Association meeting. Montreal, Quebec, Canada, August 1973.

Feshbach, N. D. "Empathy in Children: Some Theoretical and Empirical Considerations." *The Counseling Psychologist,* 1975, 5 (2), 25-30.

Feshbach, N. D. "Studies on Empathic Behavior in Children." In B. A. Maher (Ed.), *Progress in Experimental Personality Research,* Vol. 8. New York: Academic Press (in press).

Feshbach, N. D., and Kuchenbecker, S. L. "A Three-Component Model of Empathy." Paper presented at the American Psychological Association meeting. New Orleans, Louisiana, September 1974.

Feshbach, N. D., Kuchenbecker, S. L., and Pletcher, G. "The Effects of Age, Sex, and Modality upon Social Comprehension and Empathy." Paper presented at the Western Psychological Association meeting. San Francisco, California, April 1974.

Feshbach, N. D., and Roe, K. "Empathy in Six- and Seven-Year-Olds." *Child Development,* 1968, *39,* 133-145.

FINLAYSON'S CONFORMITY SCALE

AUTHOR: Douglas S. Finlayson

AGE: 12 to 18 years

VARIABLE: Conformity and dependence

TYPE OF MEASURE: Questionnaire

SOURCE FROM WHICH MEASURE MAY BE OBTAINED: D. S. Finlayson, Educational Research, The University of Liverpool, 19-23 Abercromby Square, P.O. Box 147, Liverpool, England L69 3BX.

DESCRIPTION OF MEASURE: The items of this scale were derived from the forty-five items of Flanders' Dependent Proneness Scale (1961), some of which was modified to suit the English context. The items had as their themes positive and negative instances either of seeking help, approval and affection, or of conformity and compliance. The final thirty-two items were selected following item analysis of the responses of 302 secondary-school boys of average and above-average ability. The normally distributed scores had a mean of 8.68 and a standard deviation of 4.36.

As examples, the first ten items of the thirty-two items are given below. The subject responds either "agree" or "disagree."

1. I do not like to ask for help from others.
2. It's fun to try out ideas that others think are crazy.
3. I like working with boys who get good marks.
4. I like to ask people to help me when I find things difficult.
5. I never argue with my parents.
6. My folks usually have to ask me twice to do something.
7. I seldom do "little extra things" at home just to please my parents.
8. I want my friends to leave me alone when I am sad.
9. I often disagree with my parents.
10. I never do anything at home until I find out if it's all right.

RELIABILITY AND VALIDITY: The split-half reliability, corrected by the Spearman-Brown formula, was .67. In the full scale, items referring to dependencies on and conformity to parents and peer groups are both included. In subsequent research, these two sets of items have been scored separately and, though highly correlated, showed differential relationships with measures of a number of parental variables including their emotional warmth toward their boy and their approval of and pride in their boy.

BIBLIOGRAPHY:

Finlayson, D. S., and Banks, O. *Success and Failure in the Secondary School: An Interdisciplinary Approach of School Achievement.* London: Methuen, 1973.
Flanders, N. A., Anderson, J. P., and Amidon, E. J. "Measuring Dependence Proneness in the Classroom." *Educational and Psychological Measurement,* 1961, *21,* 575-587.

GAMES CHECKLIST (WALKER REVISION OF ROSENBERG AND SUTTON-SMITH CHECKLIST)

AUTHOR: Richard N. Walker

AGE: Grades 3 to 6

VARIABLES: Masculinity-femininity

TYPE OF MEASURE: Checklist

SOURCE FROM WHICH MEASURE MAY BE OBTAINED: Richard N. Walker, Gesell Institute of Child Development, 310 Prospect Street, New Haven, Connecticut 06511.

DESCRIPTION OF MEASURE: The measure consists of an alphabetical list of 136 games, which children check for those they play and like and those they play but dislike. All but two games were taken directly from Rosenberg and Sutton-Smith's (1959) 180-item list. Each "like" choice is scored 3, 2, 1, or 0 for masculinity and femininity (weights determined in a sample of 419 Connecticut school children). The principal feature of this revision is introduction of a corrector for total number of choices. On Rosenberg and Sutton-Smith's original scales, the Connecticut subjects showed positive correlations of around .45 between masculinity and femininity (because of their r with the third variable, total choices); on the corrected scales, rs ranged from $-.54$ to $-.75$. Sten scores for the revised scales for 419 Connecticut public school children, by grade (3 to 6), are available (through ADI document listed in Walker, 1964).
　　The first thirty of the 136 items are given below.

Baseball	Bingo
Bandits	Blind man's buff
Basketball	Boating
Bike riding	Bowling

Bows and arrows	Clay modeling
Boxing	Climb trees
Build fort or huts	Clue
Build snowmen	Cooking
Camping	Cops and robbers
Capture the flag	Cowboys
Cards	Crack the whip
Cars	Dancing
Cartwheels	Darts
Checkers	Doctors
Chess	Dodgeball

RELIABILITY AND VALIDITY: Point-biserial correlation within the Connecticut sample was .73 between tthe original (Rosenberg and Sutton-Smith) scoring for masculinity and subjects' actual sex, .68 for femininity and sex. For the revised scale, point-biserial rs were .85 and .90 for masculinity and sex, .82 and .86 for femininity and sex.

BIBLIOGRAPHY:

Rosenberg, B. G., and Sutton-Smith, B. "The Measurement of Masculinity and Femininity in Children." *Child Development*, 1959, *30*, 373-380.
Walker, R. N. "Measuring Masculinity and Femininity by Children's Games Choices." *Child Development*, 1964, *35*, 961-971.

GENDER-PROBLEM RATING SCALE

AUTHORS: John E. Bates, William M. Skilbeck, Katherine Smith, and Peter M. Bentler

AGE: 4 to 13 years

VARIABLE: Characteristics of gender-problem referrals and their families

TYPE OF MEASURE: Rating scale

SOURCE FROM WHICH MEASURE MAY BE OBTAINED: See Bates and others (1974).

DESCRIPTION OF MEASURE: The Gender-Problem Rating Scale was developed as a means for clinicians to rate the characteristics of gender-problem referrals and their families. Although it proved useful in differentiating extreme gender-problem boys from lesser gender-problem boys in our sample, it should be regarded merely as an instrument for formalizing clinical observations. It is not a rigorously constructed test, although it did show some interpretable internal structure when used by clinicians. It is suggested that users of this set of scales use the items listed in the factor loadings table (Table II) in Bates and others (1974). The response scales that correspond with the information in the table are as follows: 2-point scale: No (0), Yes (1); 3-point scale: No (0), Yes, seldom (2), Yes, often (3); 5-point scale: Assign rating of 1 to 5: 1 corresponding to the first end of the scale, and 5 corresponding to the opposite end (described in parentheses with the item). To compute a score for each factor, which can be compared with the means for the samples, (1) add scores on all positively loaded items; (2) subtract all scores for negatively loaded items from a constant 1, 2, or 6 for 2-point, 3-point, and 5-point scale items respectively; (3) add all these reversed-keyed scores; and (4) add the scores obtained in (1) and (3).

As examples, eight of the fifty-five items in the measure are given below.

Factor I: Effeminacy
Speaks with feminine inflections when excited.
Moves in feminine way when excited.
Has fantasies more characteristic of girls than boys.
Speaks with feminine inflections normally.
Has a high interest in playacting.
Factor II: Family Normalcy
Father is more masculine than normal.
No father or stepfather.
Has a high interest in mother's appearance.

RELIABILITY AND VALIDITY: The rating scale was analyzed into an interpretable set of principal components. Regarding validity, in a small sample three of the four factors showed significant or trend differences between children who had been a priori classified as highly effeminate and those classified as mildly effeminate or noneffeminate. For better validated, parent-report instruments concerning gender problems in boys, see Bates, Bentler, and Thompson (1973) or Bates and Bentler (1973).

BIBLIOGRAPHY:

Bates, J. E., and Bentler, P. M. "Play Activities of Normal and Effeminate Boys." *Developmental Psychology,* 1973, *9,* 20-27.

Bates, J. E., Bentler, P. M., and Thompson, S. K. "Measurement of Deviant Gender Development in Boys." *Child Development,* 1973, *44,* 591-598.

Bates, J. E., Skilbeck, W. M., Smith, K., and Bentler, P. M. "Gender Role Abnormalities in Boys: An Analysis of Clinical Ratings." *Journal of Abnormal Child Psychology,* 1974, *2,* 1-16.

GENERALIZED CONTENTMENT SCALE (GCS)

AUTHOR: Walter W. Hudson

AGE: 12 years and up

VARIABLE: Nonpsychotic depression

TYPE OF MEASURE: Rating scale

SOURCE FROM WHICH MEASURE MAY BE OBTAINED: Walter W. Hudson, George Warren Brown School of Social Work, Washington University, St. Louis, Missouri 63130.

DESCRIPTION OF MEASURE: This scale was designed for use in repeated administrations to monitor and evaluate client responses to treatment over time. Positively worded items are reverse-scored, all item scores are then summed, and a constant of 25 is subtracted from the total to produce a possible range from 0 to 100. Scores below 30 give little evidence of a problem with depression, while those above 30 indicate the client is depressed. A history of scores exceeding 30 over several time periods is much more indicative of a clinically relevant depressive syndrome than is a single score at one point in time. The scale is sensitive to transient or temporary depressive reactions, and it is this sensitivity that makes the scale useful in monitoring a client's response to treatment. Age and sex differences appear thus far to be second-order disturbances, but the scale has not yet been normed on a sufficiently large sample to disregard second-order effects. The scale was not designed as a classification tool and should not be used for that purpose. Rather, it was intended as a means of measuring the magnitude of nonpsychotic depression over time, and as such it responds well regardless of the "type" of depression encountered. The scale should not be factored into subscales, as it was not designed as a multidimensional measure of depression.

As examples, the first ten of the twenty-five items on the scale are given below. The respondent answers on a 5-point frequency scale ranging from "rarely or none of the time" to "most or all of the time."

1. I feel powerless to do anything about my life.
2. I feel blue.
3. I am restless and can't keep still.
4. I have crying spells.
5. It is easy for me to relax.
6. I have a hard time getting started on things that I need to do.
7. I do not sleep well at night.
8. When things get tough, I feel there is always someone I can turn to.
9. I feel that the future looks bright for me.
10. I feel downhearted.

RELIABILITY AND VALIDITY: Based on a sample of 281 persons, seven estimates of split-half and test-retest reliability ranged from .92 to .98 with a mean of .94. The scale has been shown to have high face, discriminant, and construct validity with a discriminant validity coefficient of .76. Additional statistical details are reported in Hudson and Proctor (1975).

BIBLIOGRAPHY:

Hudson, W. W., and Proctor, E. K. "Assessing Nonpsychotic Depression in Social Work Practice." Mimeographed. George Warren Brown School of Social Work, Washington University, St. Louis, Missouri, 1975.

GORDON PRENATAL AND POSTNATAL SCALES

AUTHORS: Richard E. Gordon and Katherine K. Gordon

AGE: Childbearing women

VARIABLE: Emotional outcome of pregnancy

TYPE OF MEASURE: Questionnaire

SOURCE FROM WHICH MEASURE MAY BE OBTAINED: Richard E. Gordon and Katherine K. Gordon, 1625 SW 6th Terrace, Gainesville, Florida 32601. Cost: $1.00 for the pair of instruments, plus postage.

DESCRIPTION OF MEASURE: The Gordon Prenatal Scale uses fifty-three questions that have been selected for their proven discriminatory power between women who enjoy an emotionally satisfying postpartum experience and those who develop emotional distress ranging from mild postpartum crying to severe psychosis requiring hospitalization. This questionnaire is used to predict which pregnant women are likely to develop abnormal emotional and psychosomatic complications of pregnancy in the postpartum period. The kinds of items used include the following: (1) multiple questions dealing with the personal and social history of the patient; (2) items from the Leighton scale (Leighton, Harding, Maslin, and others, 1963) that have been shown to be useful in this setting; and (3) items from the Holmes and Rahe scale (1967), which also have been validated.

     The Postnatal Scale (thirty-six items) is similar to the Prenatal Scale except that it takes into account events that have occurred during the woman's pregnancy and childbirth experience. It is administered while the woman is still in the hospital after delivering the baby and also functions to predict postpartum emotional outcome of childbearing. Since events can change in a woman's life during pregnancy that can influence her emotional adjustment, the postnatal questionnaire is needed to modify the scores obtained in the prenatal instrument. The prenatal questionnaire can be administered in the first trimester and is scored either simply by counting the numbers of abnormal items or by using a slightly more complicated weighting process: the higher the score the greater the likelihood of distress and the more serious the disorder that develops. It has been used in research settings for selecting patients for research but has not been disseminated to obstetricians and family physicians for screening out women with a high risk for postpartum emotional distress. Data from the research suggest that it can be used for this purpose. Initially the research was done on over four hundred expectant mothers and about seventy-five postpartum psychiatric patients. The work was cross-validated successfully and reported in Larsen and others (1968).

As examples, two selected questions of the fifty-three total number on the Prenatal Scale are given below.

14. My family:
    0—I am an only child.
        1—I am the oldest daughter of two or three children.
        2—I am the oldest daughter of four or more children.
            3—I am the youngest daughter of two or three children.
            4—I am the youngest daughter of four or more children.
                5—I am the middle daughter of three or more children.
15. Husband's family:
    0—He is an only child.
        1—He is the oldest son of two or three children.
        2—He is the oldest son of four or more children.
            3—He is the youngest son of two or three children.
            4—He is the youngest son of four or more children.
                5—He is the middle son of three or more children.

Three selected questions of the thirty-six total number on the Postnatal Scale are given below.

12. Feeding problems
    0—None   1—Colic   3—Diarrhea
                    2—Food allergies   4—Constipation
                    5—Other_____
15. Who helped you with the baby when you came home from the hospital?
    0—No one
        1—No one but husband
        2—Mother
        3—Mother-in-law
        4—Other female relative
        5—Friends
        6—Baby nurse
17. Did you have enough help?
    0—No   1—Rarely   2—Usually

RELIABILITY AND VALIDITY: The coefficient of validity is .59 and of reliability, .87.

BIBLIOGRAPHY:

Gordon, R. E. *Prevention of Postpartum Emotional Difficulties.* Ann Arbor, Michigan: University Microfilms, 1961.

Gordon, R. E., and Gordon, K. K. "Social Factors in the Prevention of Postpartum Emotional Adjustment." *Obstetrics and Gynecology,* 1960, *15,* 443-448.

Gordon, R. E., and Gordon, K. K. "Social Factors in the Prevention of Postpartum

Emotional Problems." In G. V. Coelho and others (Eds.), *Coping and Adaptation.* Chevy Chase, Maryland: Public Health Service Education No. 2087, NIMH, 1970.

Gordon, R. E., Kapostins, E. E., and Gordon, K. K. "Factors in Postpartum Emotional Adjustment." *Obstetrics and Gynecology,* 1965, *2,* 156-166.

Holmes, T. H., and Rahe, R. H. "The Social Readjustment Rating Scale." *Psychosomatic Research,* 1967, *11,* 213-218.

Larsen, V. L., and others. *Prediction and Improvement of Postpartum Adjustment.* Final report. Children's Bureau Research Grant H-66. Fort Steilacoom, Washington: Division of Research, 1968.

Leighton, D. C., Harding, J. S., Maslin, D. B., and others. *The Character of Danger.* New York: Basic Books, 1963.

GREENBERG-ROSENBERG MATERNAL POSTPARTUM SURVEY AND ROOMING-IN QUESTIONNAIRE

AUTHORS: Martin Greenberg and Ingrid Rosenberg

AGE: Primiparous mothers

VARIABLE: Maternal self-confidence, competence, and related variables

TYPE OF MEASURE: Multiple-choice questionnaire

SOURCE FROM WHICH MEASURE MAY BE OBTAINED: See Greenberg and others (1973) or write: Martin Greenberg, 2366 Snowden Avenue, Long Beach, California 90815. Cost: $3.00.

DESCRIPTION OF MEASURE: The multiple-choice questionnaire consists of fifty general questions given to both nonrooming-in and rooming-in mothers. The exam was originated in Swedish and has been translated into English. Some of the areas of focus of this descriptive questionnaire include the experiences of the hospital, attitude toward hospital personnel, adequacy of hospital care, and how adequate the hospital was in providing contact with the child. It also includes a survey of the mother's general attitude toward breastfeeding and toilet training and also elaboration of any particular problem that developed in breastfeeding. The questionnaire was first administered to twenty-five Swedish mothers and was then subsequently revised after this pilot study.

As examples, three selected items from the fifty on the questionnaire are given below.

5. After having been in the hospital for about one week, I now feel that my self-confidence on the question of child care is
    a. very large.

    b. rather large.

    c. neither large nor small.

    d. rather small.

    e. very little.

14. How do you feel about your coming role of being a mother?

    a. I am happy about it and feel confident in myself.

    b. I am happy but a little bit uneasy.

    c. I am a little anxious.

    d. I am a little anxious and uncertain.

16. Many mothers don't develop a strong feeling toward the baby right away. This is completely normal. When did you first get the feeling that the baby was all yours?

    a. Immediately after the birth.

    b. After the first 3 days.

    c. After the first week.

    d. It's coming, but I don't quite have it yet.

RELIABILITY AND VALIDITY: Greenberg and others (1973) administered the questionnaire to 100 primiparous Swedish mothers, who were subdivided into two equal groups: fifty mothers who roomed in with their children and fifty mothers who did not room in with their children. The two groups were similar in age, socioeconomic characteristics, and in age and education of husbands. In addition, various characteristics of the infants such as birth weight were compared, and there was essentially no difference in the two groups. There were no significant differences with respect to rooming-in vs. conventional mothers in (1) how much they thought the baby would restrict their normal activities, (2) the number of future children they wanted, (3) how great a responsibility they considered their infant, (4) how anxious they were about its care, (5) how much of a hurry they were in to go home, (6) how tired they judged themselves to be immediately after delivery and one day prior to discharge, (7) how much rest or sleep and medication they received, (8) breastfeeding problems, and (9) how many fathers were in the delivery room prior to delivery. There was also no significant difference between rooming-in and conventional mothers in attitudes on child-rearing, toilet training, crying, feeding, presence of obstetrical or pediatric paternal factors, or socioeconomic data. There was no difference in the two groups in how they planned to have their baby, how many had had prepartum instruction, or in how mothers had heard about or requested rooming-in.

BIBLIOGRAPHY:

Greenberg, M., Rosenberg, I., and Lind, J. "First Mothers Rooming-in with Their Newborns: Its Impact upon the Mother." *American Journal of Orthopsychiatry,* 1973, *43,* 783-788.

Jackson, E. "General Reactions of Nurses and Mothers to Rooming-in." *American Journal of Public Health,* 1948, *38,* 689.

Jackson, E., and others. "Hospital Rooming-in Unit for Newborn Infants and Their Mothers: Descriptive Account of Background, Development, and Procedures with Few Preliminary Observations." *Pediatrics,* 1948, *1,* 28.

Levy, P. "Advice and Reassurance." *American Journal of Public Health,* 1954, *44,* 1113-1118.

Montgomery, T., Stewart, R., and Shenk, E. "Observations on Their Rooming-in Program of Baby with Mother in Ward and Private Service." *American Journal of Obstetrics and Gynecology,* 1944, *57,* 176.

Paris, J., McLendon, P., and Kelly, M. "Optional Nursery Facilities for the Care of Mothers and Newborn Infants." *American Journal of Obstetrics and Gynecology,* 1953, *66,* 938.

GUILT SCALE

AUTHOR: Michael Argyle

AGE: 11 years and up

VARIABLE: Guilt

TYPE OF MEASURE: Checklist

SOURCE FROM WHICH MEASURE MAY BE OBTAINED: See Argyle and Robinson (1962).

DESCRIPTION OF MEASURE: The measure consists of twenty Likert-type items designed to provide a quickly obtained index of the intensity and extensity of guilt. Intensity of guilt is derived by adding the scores of all items, while greater extensity is indicated by the wider scattering of higher scores among the twenty items.

The items of the scale are given below. The respondent answers to what extent he feels guilt or worry on a 5-point scale ranging from "not at all" to "considerable guilt."

1. Untidiness.
2. Wasting money.
3. Greed.
4. Laziness.
5. Being unkind.
6. Not telling the truth.
7. Cheating.
8. Not being punctual.
9. Selfishness.
10. Cowardice.
11. Not going to church.
12. Disobedience.
13. Not working hard enough.
14. Bad temper.
15. Causing suffering.
16. Not keeping promises.
17. Stinginess.

18. Lack of persistence.
19. Not washing.
20. Boasting.

RELIABILITY AND VALIDITY: None reported.

BIBLIOGRAPHY:

Argyle, M., and Robinson, W. "Two Origins of Achievement Motivation." *British Journal of Social and Clinical Psychology*, 1962, *1*, 107-120.

Prepared by W. P. Robinson

HOWARD MAZE TEST

AUTHOR: Kenneth I. Howard

AGE: 3+ years

VARIABLE: Stimulus seeking (exploration)

TYPE OF MEASURE: Test

SOURCE FROM WHICH MEASURE MAY BE OBTAINED: See Howard and Diesenhaus (1965a).

DESCRIPTION OF MEASURE: The Maze Test is a practical experimental technique for measuring spontaneous variation in behavior. It consists of repeated presentations of a simple paper-and-pencil maze, where each presentation is completed by drawing a line along any clear pathway from the starting point to the goal. The two forms of the test have a number of alternate paths to one or several goals. There are no blind alleys, and all paths are equally "correct" so that the mazes themselves do not constitute "a problem situation." The subject has the opportunity, and option, to vary his routes through the maze on each successive presentation or to repeat his initial route. The direct paths to the goal each have ten linear segments that must be traversed to reach a goal. This makes it possible to quantify the amount of change from one maze to the next when only partially different routes are chosen. Change is defined as the number of segments traversed on a particular presentation of the maze differing from the segments traversed on the maze immediately preceeding. The total change score is a function of the changes for each adjacent pair of mazes in a single series. The higher the change score (the greater the difference in paths traversed), the more "stimulus-seeking" behavior the individual exhibits.

RELIABILITY AND VALIDITY: Test-retest reliabilities were .70+, with alternate form reliability about .70. Howard and Diesenhaus (1965b), using a sample of sixty psychiatric and medical patients, found consistent correlations between maze change and three personality factors on the 16 Personality Factor Questionnaire (Cattell, Saunders, and Stice, 1957) that parallel the theoretical analysis of the Maze Test.

BIBLIOGRAPHY:

Bottrill, J. H. "Difference in Curiosity Levels of Blind and Sighted Subjects." *Perceptual and Motor Skills,* 1968, *26,* 189-190.
Cattell, R. B., Saunders, D. R., and Stice, G. *Handbook for the 16 Personality Factor Questionnaire.* Champaign, Illinois: Institute for Personality and Ability Testing, 1957.
Domino, G. "A Validation of Howard's Test of Change-Seeking Behavior." *Educational and Psychological Measurement,* 1965, *25,* 1073-1078.
Howard, K. I. "A Test of Stimulus-Seeking Behavior." *Perceptual and Motor Skills,* 1961, *13,* 416.
Howard, K. I., and Diesenhaus, H. I. "Handbook for the Maze Test." *Research Reports of the Institute for Juvenile Research, Chicago,* 1965a, *2* (4).
Howard, K. I., and Diesenhaus, H. I. "Personality Correlates of Stimulus-Seeking Behavior." *Perceptual and Motor Skills,* 1965b, *21,* 655-664.

IMAGINATIVE ENDINGS

AUTHOR: R. Sumner

AGE: Students 13 to 18 years

VARIABLE: Awareness of temperament and character

TYPE OF MEASURE: Written free projective response

SOURCE FROM WHICH MEASURE MAY BE OBTAINED: Copies of test, manual, and scoring guide available from R. Sumner, Guidance and Assessment Service, N.F.E.R., The Mere, Upton Park, Slough, Berkshire, England SL1 2DQ. Cost of photocopying and postage: approximately $2.00.

DESCRIPTION OF MEASURE: A projective response is elicited by inviting subjects to finish in their own words a set of incomplete paragraphs that describe a personal reaction to a variety of situations. Only brief responses are requested, but there are twenty items intended to evoke the following traits: self-reliance, integrity, self-respect, honesty, sense of responsibility, determination, acting from principle, observing duties and rights, courtesy, poise, fairness, conscientiousness, self-control, independence of thought, and respect for property. These traits are not scored separately, but the scheme provides three scales for (1) general awareness of character; (2) quality in terms of a positive buoyant outlook vs. a depressed, negative view of people; and (3) sensitivity to particular situations. Scoring is by appraisal in accordance with the test rationale; a comprehensive scoring guide, with illustrations and a practice example, is provided. The measure is experimental and not intended for individual counseling use at this stage.

As examples, five selected items of the twenty are given below.

1. Jane was known as an awkward type. Whatever was going on she just had to do things her own way, whether it was saddling a horse at riding school or doing homework. The upshot was that she did some peculiar _____.
3. "Jumbo" lumbered toward the larder, treading softly through the kitchen lit only by the dim skylight. As his hand touched the doorknob he felt again the rising thrill of pleasure as he thought of the treat to come in the privacy of his darkened room. "Of course," he told himself, "I'm not doing anything wrong. No one has forbidden _____."
10. "Will I crawl into my shell again?" thought Pen, as she slid off the pillion, "or will it be alright this time? Girls are too vulnerable; hair wrong, dress wrong, eyes wrong, clumsy hands, no style . . . ugh! Shivers." "Come on, girl," yelled Bill, leaping the steps toward the party sound _____.
11. "Fifteen cars at four bob a time; four of us on the job—should be fifteen bob each" Sally protested. "Who set up the car-wash service and had to take on assistance on account of too much business?" demands Mary hotly. "You get ten bob each and like it." Jim shouted, "_____."
20. The fishing rod lay across my track. As I drew nearer I could see that it was an expensive make though this concerned me less than did my bicycle, which suddenly began to _____.

RELIABILITY AND VALIDITY: Two judges scored the items. With $N = 379$ of almost equal numbers of 16-year-old boys and girls, intermarker agreement was high; for example, overall scores correlated .92. Pooled scores from two independent judges are recommended. Kuder-Richardson formula 20 reliability for the twenty-item version was .83. Responses were factor analyzed and interpreted in terms of the traits posted initially; only 55 percent of the common variance was accounted for by the major first-order components. Interpretative labels for the four second-order (varimax) factors are responsible principle vs. personal allegiance, pertinacity, resolution, and self-sustained conviction. Third-order factors were interpreted as probity and dedication. The factor analyses and item data were used as a basis for recommending two shortened versions for further experimental work.

BIBLIOGRAPHY: None reported.

INSOLENCE-IMPULSIVENESS SCALE

AUTHOR: David Kipnis

AGE: 15 years and up, males only

VARIABLE: Impulsiveness

TYPE OF MEASURE: Questionnaire

SOURCE FROM WHICH MEASURE MAY BE OBTAINED: See Kipnis (1971).

DESCRIPTION OF MEASURE: The Insolence-Impulsiveness Scale is a forty-one-item scale consisting mainly of biographical-type items that ask the respondent to describe childhood and present activities in terms of relations with school authority, interest in thrill-seeking and risk-taking behavior, and interest in sex, gambling, and drinking. Unit weights are assigned to the scored items. Items included in the scale were selected on the basis of their correlations with various school and work adjustment criteria.

As examples, ten selected items of the fifty-six on the scale are given below (there are fifteen filler items).

When you were a boy, did you engage in the following activities fairly often? (Answer "yes" or "no")
1. Football (filler item)
2. Diving
3. Skiing

Do you remember doing the following things as a child before you were 15? (Answer "yes" or "no")
9. Playing with snakes
10. Being interested in sex
11. Being afraid of the dark
12. Arguing with parents and teachers fairly often about your rights
13. Reading a great deal
45. In grade school how many times a year were you sent to the principal for fooling around in class?
    a. Usually not sent.
    b. Once or twice.
    c. Three or four times.
    d. Fairly often.
50. When you are with a group of friends deciding what to do for the evening, what do you usually do?
    a. Make a suggestion and try to get the others to accept it.
    b. Make a suggestion and let it go at that.
    c. Wait for others to make suggestions and express your opinion about their suggestions.
    d. Say nothing and go along with the others.
    e. Leave the group if you do not like the decision.

RELIABILITY AND VALIDITY: The scale is homogeneous in makeup, as indicated by a split-half reliability of .84, computed among 222 university students. The validity of the scale has been examined in a variety of field and experimental settings concerned with five aspects of impulsive behavior: (1) degree of acceptance of conventional values, (2) threshold of responsiveness to anxiety and shame-provoking situations, (3) responsiveness to social influence, (4) responsiveness to sensory stimulation, and (5) level of achievement at school and at work. The first four areas are considered to represent differing sources of inhibition upon impulsive behavior. A general finding has been that intelligence moderates the validity of the Insolence-Impulsiveness Scale in that the scale predicts behavior among more intelligent subgroupings.

BIBLIOGRAPHY:

Kipnis, D. "Studies in Character Structure." *Journal of Personality and Social Psychology,* 1968, *8,* 217-227.

Kipnis, D. *Character Structure and Impulsiveness.* New York: Academic Press, 1971.

Kipnis, D., and Goodstadt, B. "Character Structure and Friendship Relations." *British Journal of Social and Clinical Psychology,* 1970, *9,* 201-211.

JUNIOR INDEX OF MOTIVATION (JIM SCALE)

AUTHOR: Jack R. Frymier

AGE: 12 to 18 years

VARIABLE: Academic motivation

TYPE OF MEASURE: Questionnaire

SOURCE FROM WHICH MEASURE MAY BE OBTAINED: See Frymier (1970) or write: Publications Sales Office, Ohio State University, 20 Lord Hall, 124 West 17th Avenue, Columbus, Ohio 43210. Cost: $3.75 per 100 copies; $1.50 per manual.

DESCRIPTION OF MEASURE: The Junior Index of Motivation measures objectively students' desires to do good work in school. It is a pencil-and-paper measure that takes about 30 minutes for all students to complete. Research involving more than twenty thousand junior and senior high school students throughout the United States has supported the validity of the JIM Scale. Normative studies have been completed, and repeated validation studies have indicated that it consistently differentiates among secondary-school students according to grades received, standardized achievement scores, and teachers' judgments of motivation to learn in school. Eighty items requiring a Likert-type response make up the measure. Normative data are available by sex and grade levels 7 to 12.

 As examples, the first fifteen items of the eighty-item questionnaire are given below. The subject is requested to indicate one of the following: +1, slight support, agreement; +2, strong support, agreement; −1, slight opposition, disagreement; −2, strong opposition, disagreement.

1. Late afternoon is the best time of day.
2. Many children have often been punished without cause.
3. Students should be made to go to school until they are 18 years old.
4. Being right is more important than being kind.
5. School is more fun when teachers let students do things they want to.
6. Pupils who try should get good grades even if they make mistakes.
7. Successful people are those who make the most money.
8. The best way to spend a free evening is with a good book.
9. Most young people do not want to go to school.
10. Some new ideas are interesting, but most of them are not.
11. Practical people are usually highly respected.
12. Knowing the answer is more important than knowing where to get the answer.
13. Many young people feel grouchy.
14. The best people refuse to depend on other persons.
15. Some teachers make school more interesting than others.

RELIABILITY AND VALIDITY: See Frymier (1970).

BIBLIOGRAPHY:

Frymier, J. R. "Development and Validation of a Motivation Index." *Theory into Practice,* 1970, *9,* 56-88.
White, W. F., and McConnell, J. "Affective Responses and School Achievement Among Eighth-Grade Boys and Girls." *Perceptual and Motor Skills,* 1974, *38,* 1295-1301.

KEELE ACADEMIC MOTIVATION QUESTIONNAIRE

AUTHORS: James Hartley, Janet Holt, and F. W. Hogarth

AGE: 12 to 16 years

VARIABLE: Academic motivation

TYPE OF MEASURE: Questionnaire

SOURCE FROM WHICH MEASURE MAY BE OBTAINED: See Hartley and others (1971).

DESCRIPTION OF MEASURE: The Keele Academic Motivation Questionnaire consists of fifteen items, arrived at by carrying out item-whole correlations with an original pool of forty-four items. In the final stages of this procedure, a sample of 500 school children was used.

The questionnaire and the scale, with item-whole correlations indicated in parentheses are given below. The items are answered on a 5-point scale: very true of me, partly or usually true of me, cannot say—no feelings one way or other, partly or usually untrue of me, very untrue of me.

(.61) I enjoy most lessons.
(.59) I work hard most of the time.
(.66) I feel school is largely a waste of time.
(.60) I leave my homework to the last minute.
(.76) I generally find lessons rather dull.
(.69) I hate to miss school because I enjoy it so much.
(.61) I try my hardest to get my homework right.
(.62) I am quiet in the classroom and get on with my work.
(.72) I think homework is a bore.
(.69) I find it difficult to keep my mind on my work.
(.64) Often I'm just not in the mood for work and then I don't do it.
(.59) I try hard to please my teacher with my work.
(.67) I never take work seriously.
(.74) I don't like school.
(.66) I like homework because in that way I am sure I learn more.

RELIABILITY AND VALIDITY: Test-retest correlations over a five-month interval were calculated with an intermediate version of the scale containing twenty-one items. For two groups of 13-year-old children and two groups of 14-year-old children, the correlations were .85, .80, .52, and .72, respectively. To assess validity, correlations were calculated between position in class and the motivation test scores. In addition, the scores of pupils who were promoted were compared with those who were demoted across sets. All these data indicated a fair degree of validity. Correlations with three other questionnaire methods of assessing academic motivation were high (.74, .81, and .84).

BIBLIOGRAPHY:

Hartley, J., Holt, H., and Hogarth, F. W. "Academic Motivation and Programmed Learning." *British Journal of Educational Psychology*, 1971, *41*, 171-183.

KOHN PROBLEM CHECKLIST

AUTHOR: Martin Kohn

AGE: 3 to 6 years

VARIABLE: Two dimensions of emotional disturbance

TYPE OF MEASURE: Rating scale

SOURCE FROM WHICH MEASURE MAY BE OBTAINED: Martin Kohn, William Alanson White Institute, 20 West 74th Street, New York, New York. Cost: $5.00.

DESCRIPTION OF MEASURE: The Kohn Problem Checklist is a teacher rating instrument designed to measure emotional disturbance in preschool- and kindergarten-age children. The checklist consists of forty-nine items of clinically significant behavior. The scale measures two unipolar dimensions of emotional disturbance, apathy-withdrawal and anger-defiance. Examples of items are given below.

Apathy-withdrawal: Keeps to himself; remains aloof, distant. Stares blankly into space.
Anger-defiance: Screams, bangs objects, etc. when angry, inhibited, or frustrated. Child treats other children with deliberate cruelty; bullies other children, hits or picks on them.

Each item is rated on a 3-point scale, from "not at all typical" to "very typical." Four hundred and seven children aged 3 to 5 in public day-care centers were rated by their full-time day-care teachers. Only the first two of nine rotated factors were retained; they accounted for more than 50 percent of the communal variance. These two factors are relatively independent of each other ($r = .81$). Approximately 5 to 10 minutes are required to complete the instrument. Scoring is greatly facilitated by use of a scoring key and requires less than 2 minutes per child. A rating and scoring manual is available from the author.

RELIABILITY AND VALIDITY: Interrater reliability (Spearman-Brown corrected) was found to be .73 for both dimensions of the instrument. The corresponding factors of the Social Competence Scale (Kohn and Rosman, 1972a; see also p. 1181) and the Problem Checklist were found to be highly correlated. The correlation between interest-participation vs. apathy-withdrawal in the Social Competence Scale and apathy-withdrawal in the Problem Checklist was −.75; the correlation between cooperation-compliance vs. anger-defiance on the Social Competence Scale and anger-defiance in the Problem Checklist was found to be −.79; the cross-factor correlations were relatively low ($r = -.25$ and $r = -.13$, respectively).

The major difference between the Problem Checklist and the Social Competence Scale is that the former differentiates between presence or absence of emotional disturbance, while the latter allows for differentiation within the whole spectrum ranging from health to disturbance. The Problem Checklist shows the same relationship to validity criteria as the Social Competence Scale; because of the fewer items it is a somewhat less reliable instrument. It is a relatively simple, economical screening device for emotionally disturbed children.

BIBLIOGRAPHY:

Kohn, M. "The Social Systems Meaning of the Two-Factor Model of Social-Emotional Competence." Paper presented at the meeting of the American Educational Research Association. Washington, D.C., April 1975.

Kohn, M., and Cohen, J. "Emotional Impairment and Achievement Deficit in Disadvantaged Children—Fact or Myth?" *Genetic Psychology Monographs,* 1975, *92,* 57-78.

Kohn, M., and Parnes, B. "Social Interaction in the Classroom—A Comparison of Apathetic-Withdrawn and Angry-Defiant Children." *Journal of Genetic Psychology,* 1974, *125,* 165-175.

Kohn, M., and Rosman, B. L. "Therapeutic Intervention with Disturbed Children in Day Care: Implications of the Deprivation Hypothesis." *Child Care Quarterly,* 1971, *1,* 21-46.

Kohn, M., and Rosman, B. L. "A Social Competence Scale and Symptom Checklist for the Preschool Child: Factor Dimensions, Their Cross-Instrument Generality, and Longitudinal Persistence." *Developmental Psychology,* 1972a, *6,* 430-444.

Kohn, M., and Rosman, B. L. "Relationship of Preschool Social-Emotional Functioning to Later Intellectual Achievement." *Developmental Psychology,* 1972b, *6,* 445-452.

Kohn, M., and Rosman, B. L. "Cognitive Functioning in Five-Year-Old Boys as Related to Social-Emotional and Background-Demographic Variables." *Developmental Psychology,* 1973, *8,* 277-294.

Kohn, M., and Rosman, B. L. "A Two-Factor Model of Emotional Disturbance in the Young Child: Validity and Screening Efficiency." *The Journal of Child Psychology and Psychiatry,* 1973, *14,* 31-56.

Kohn, M., and Rosman, B. L. "Cross-Situational and Longitudinal Stability of Social-Emotional Functioning in Young Children." *Child Development,* 1973, *44,* 721-727.

Kohn, M., and Rosman, B. L. "Social-Emotional, Cognitive and Demographic Determinants of Poor School Achievement: Implications for a Strategy of Intervention." *Journal of Educational Psychology,* 1974, *66,* 267-276.

LANYON'S INCOMPLETE SENTENCES TASK (IST)

AUTHOR: Barbara J. Lanyon

AGE: Grades 7 to 9

VARIABLE: Hostility, anxiety, and dependency

TYPE OF MEASURE: Sentence-completion test

SOURCE FROM WHICH MEASURE MAY BE OBTAINED: Barbara J. Lanyon, 1855 East Aspen Drive, Tempe, Arizona 85282.

DESCRIPTION OF MEASURE: The Lanyon Incomplete Sentences Task consists of thirty-nine items that predict seventh- through ninth-grade teachers' ratings of their students' hostility (eighteen items), anxiety (ten items), and dependency (eleven items). Using a rationally developed scoring manual, each item response is scored either 2, 1, or 0 according to whether the response *definitely* indicates the personality variable in question, *suggests* it, or *does not* indicate it. The initial seventy-five-item pool from which the final thirty-nine items were selected was designed to reflect the content of a factored teacher checklist that was developed (from the responses of expert judges) to serve as a criterion measure for the construction of each sentence-completion variable. The criterion checklist was based on overt behaviors, and the three sentence-completion variables are defined behaviorally rather than psychodynamically. Each of the final items was selected for its statistical significance in predicting the criterion measure, based on responses of 328 children for whom either two or three sets of criterion ratings had been returned by the teachers. These data were collected from junior high schools in greater Pittsburgh, with socioeconomic class about equally middle and lower-middle class. About 5 to 7 percent of the students were black. Boys and girls were equally represented. Percentile norms were computed separately for 557 new subjects (267 boys and 290 girls).

As examples, the first ten items of the task are given below.

1. When I am bored, _____ .
2. If I find it hard to say what I mean, _____ .
3. When the teacher calls on me in class, _____ .
4. If I feel I am not good at something, _____ .
5. When I feel like "mouthing off" in class, _____ .
6. Being the "boss" over other children _____ .
7. If the teacher is not available to help me, _____ .
8. If I feel like just sitting around, _____ .
9. When things go wrong for me, _____ .
10. If the teacher gives us too much homework, _____ .

RELIABILITY AND VALIDITY: No reliability data are currently available for the three sentence-completion variables. Scorer reliability in using the manual (correlations between two trained scorers) was found to be .97 and .95 for two different samples. All items have obvious content validity for the variable that they were designed to predict. The Lanyon IST was administered to 100 subjects classified as either high or low on one or more of the three variables according to teacher criterion ratings. Each of the three sentence-completion variables continued to separate the high and low groups on the relevant criterion variable beyond the .01 level of significance, thus providing evidence of concurrent validity. Intercorrelations among the scales were: hostility/anxiety, .19; hostility/dependency, .36; anxiety/dependency, .29. Modest negative correlations were found for hostility and dependency with both IQ and grade-point average, ranging from −.22 to −.29.

BIBLIOGRAPHY:

Lanyon, B. J. "Development of a Sentence Completion Test for Children. I: Construction of Criterion Measures." Unpublished master's thesis. University of Pittsburgh, Pennsylvania, 1969.

Lanyon, B. J. "Development of a Sentence Completion Test to Assess Hostility, Anxiety, and Dependency in Children. II: Sentence Stems, Scoring Procedures, and

Cross-Validity." Unpublished doctoral dissertation. University of Pittsburgh, Pennsylvania, 1970.

Lanyon, B. J. "Empirical Construction and Validation of a Sentence Completion Test for Hostility, Anxiety and Dependency." *Journal of Consulting and Clinical Psychology,* 1972, *39,* 420-428.

LOUISVILLE FEAR SURVEY SCALES FOR CHILDREN

AUTHORS: Lovick C. Miller, Helen Noble, Edward Hampe, and Curtis Barrett

AGE: 4 to 18 years

VARIABLE: Parent ratings of children's fears

TYPE OF MEASURE: Checklist

SOURCE FROM WHICH MEASURE MAY BE OBTAINED: Lovick C. Miller, Child Psychiatry Research Center, 608 South Jackson Street, Louisville, Kentucky 40202.

DESCRIPTION OF MEASURE: Form B of this instrument contains 104 items describing situations that are known to elicit fear reactions in children. The items are rated by parents on a 5-point scale from "not at all" to "very much." Three factor scales have been developed to describe the major dimensions of children's fears: natural events, physical injury, and social stress. General population norms are available. Excessive fear in the general population is rare, usually occurring less than 5 percent on most variables. The basic structure of fear is similar for boys and girls, although the intensity level is higher for girls. Other demographic variables have little effect on manifest fear.

As examples, the first ten of the 104 items on the checklist are given below. The parent rates his child for each item on a 5-point scale ranging from *frightens me* "not at all" to "very much."

1. The ocean.
2. Getting a serious illness.
3. People of the opposite sex.
4. Being touched by others.
5. Going to sleep at night.
6. Someone in the family getting a serious illness.
7. Getting a shot.
8. Bats.
9. Going crazy.
10. Monsters.

RELIABILITY AND VALIDITY: Reliability for each scale ranges around .80, and one validity study indicated that the main difference between a clinically phobic group and a general population group was on the social stress scale. This finding reflected the high incidence of school phobia in the phobic group.

BIBLIOGRAPHY:

Miller, L. C., Barrett, C., Hampe, E., and Noble, H. "Factor Structure of Childhood Fears." *Journal of Consulting and Clinical Psychology,* 1972, *39,* 264-268.
Miller, L. C., Barrett, C., Hampe, E., and Noble, H. *Louisville Fear Survey Scales for Children.* Unpublished manuscript. Child Psychiatry Research Center Bulletin no. 1, Louisville, Kentucky, 1974.

MICHIGAN STATE M-SCALES

AUTHOR: William W. Farquhar

AGE: Grades 7 to 12

VARIABLE: Academic motivation

TYPE OF MEASURE: Likert-type scale and forced choice

SOURCE FROM WHICH MEASURE MAY BE OBTAINED: William W. Farquhar, 439 Erickson Hall, Michigan State University, East Lansing, Michigan 48824.

DESCRIPTION OF MEASURE: The Michigan State M-Scales is a battery of four tests designed to measure academic motivation. Separate forms were developed for males and females. All items were validated and cross-validated on a sample of underachieving and overachieving high school students.

   The Generalized Situational Choice Inventory (forty-six items) is essentially a forced-choice objective measure of McClelland's *n-ach* construct. There are two forms, male and female. The Preferred Job Characteristics Scale (fifty-nine items), also of a forced-choice format, is designed to measure the *n-ach* components of work aspiration. The Word Rating List (ninety-two items) is a measure of reflected self-concept consisting of words and phrases typically employed by teachers to describe students. The Human Trait Inventory (sixty items) is a personality inventory designed to measure such constructs as compulsivity, agitation, and emotional stability. The item that loaded highest on the varimax factors of each of the four tests follows:

Generalized Situational Choice Inventory
I would prefer to
   a. study for an exam one night and know that I would receive an "A", or
   b. go to a party on this night and take a chance on a lower grade.
Preferred Job Characteristics Scales
I prefer
   a. a job that does not tie me down.
   b. a job that has high work standards.

Word Rating List

Teachers feel that I am (never   sometimes   usually   always)

   a. an achiever.

   b. a person who postpones.

Human Trait Inventory

I have a hard time concentrating on the subject during class period: (never   sometimes   usually   always)

Even though a 4-point Likert scale is used for two of the tests, all items are weighted 0, 1. Replication studies have been done with favorable results down through seventh grade. Attempts to validate the scales beyond twelfth grade have failed. *The measures are strictly for research purposes.* Replication studies have been done on black, Indian, Jewish, and foreign samples.

     As examples, three selected items from the female form and three from the male form of the M-Scales are given below.

Female Form

I would prefer to

1. a. work hard for what I get, or

   b. just get what I want.

4. a. have the best teachers in the state in my school, or

   b. have a large recreation center in my school.

7. a. pass a usual classroom examination, or

   b. pass a college entrance examination.

Male Form

I would prefer to

1. a. avoid failing in school, or

   b. do well in school

4. a. buy a car, or

   b. continue my education.

7. a. develop a new product that may or may not be good, or

   b. make a product as good as the best one available.

RELIABILITY AND VALIDITY: All four measures were validated and cross-validated on criterion groups of underachievers and overachievers. For the total scale, Hoyt's analysis of variance reliability based on samples of 240 males was .94, and based on 240 females, .93. Subscale estimates of reliability ranged from .68 to .92 for males and .60 to .93 for females. The validity estimates for 254 males and 261 females for the total-scale prediction of grades were .56 and .40, respectively, in the original battery. Cross-validation values were .49 for females and .32 to .51 for males. The many replication studies on various samples have resulted in similar validity findings with the exception of the negative findings on post high school students.

BIBLIOGRAPHY:

Farquhar, W. W. *Motivation Factors Related to Academic Achievement.* U.S. Office of Health, Education and Welfare Cooperative Research Project no. 846 ER 9. Office of Research and Publications, College of Education, Michigan State University, East Lansing, Michigan, 1963.

Farquhar, W. W., and Payne, D. "Factors in the Academic-Occupational Motivations of

Eleventh Grade Under- and Overachievers." *Personnel and Guidance Journal,* 1963, *42,* 245-251.

Farquhar, W. W., and Payne, D. "A Classification and Comparison of Techniques Used in Selecting Under- and Overachievers." *Personnel and Guidance Journal,* 1964, *42,* 874-884.

Green, R. L., and Farquhar, W. W. "Negro Academic Motivation and Scholastic Achievement." *Journal of Educational Psychology,* 1965, *56,* 241-243.

McDonald, K. H. "The Relationship of Socioeconomic Status to an Objective Measure of Motivation." *Personnel and Guidance Journal,* 1964, *42,* 997-1002.

Payne, D., and Farquhar, W. W. "The Dimensions of an Objective Measure of Academic Self-Concept." *Journal of Educational Psychology,* 1962, *53,* 187-192.

Taylor, R. G., and Farquhar, W. W. "Personality, Motivation, and Achievement: Theoretical Constructs and Empirical Factors." *Journal of Counseling Psychology,* 1965, *12,* 186-191.

Taylor, R. G., and Farquhar, W. W. "The Validity and Reliability of the Human Trait Inventory Designed to Measure Under- and Overachievement." *Journal of Educational Research,* 1966, *59,* 227-230.

Thweatt, R. C. *Development of a K Scale for a Motivational Test Battery.* U.S. Office of Health, Education and Welfare Cooperative Research Project no. 1594. Western State College, Gunnison, Colorado, 1965.

(The above are in addition to eighteen doctoral dissertations involving the use and development of the M-Scales.)

MORRISON'S PASSIVE AGGRESSION SCALE FOR PUPILS

AUTHOR: Evelyn Morrison

AGE: Middle grades to high school

VARIABLE: Passive-aggressive behavior

TYPE OF MEASURE: Likert-type rating scale

SOURCE FROM WHICH MEASURE MAY BE OBTAINED: Evelyn Morrison, Special Services Department, Edison Township Public Schools, 2825 Woodbridge Avenue, Edison, New Jersey 08817.

DESCRIPTION OF MEASURE: The Morrison Scale consists of fifteen items designed to measure passive aggression on the part of the pupil as perceived by the teacher. The passive-aggressive personality uses such behavioral traits as obstructionism, pouting, procrastination, intentional inefficiency, and stubbornness. The teacher rates the pupil on each item under one of four categories.

As examples, the first five of the fifteen items of the scale, to be rated on a 4-point scale from "very much like" (4) to "not at all like" (1), are given below.

1. He will do what he is asked to do but takes a long time.
2. He often argues a point for the sake of argument.
3. He will often do the opposite of what is asked.
4. He always tries to follow directions closely.
5. He would rather say, "I can't" than try to do.

RELIABILITY AND VALIDITY: Every item in the scale is designed to measure passive aggression in the classroom. The scale is considered functionally homogeneous. Teacher ratings were obtained for 164 boys. By random sampling, seventy-five ratings, or almost 50 percent of the total, were selected for a test of split-half reliability ($r =$ .87). Criteria used to devise the instrument included attitudes reflecting quiet rebellion, negativism, obstinacy, lack of responsibility toward rules and demands, and tendency to undermine authority. Sixteen items were developed by the author and submitted to two psychologists for critical judgment. As a result, one item was deleted and two were modified. The final scale was considered to have face validity.

BIBLIOGRAPHY:

Morrison, E. "Underachievement Among Preadolescent Boys Considered in Relationship to Passive Aggression." *Journal of Educational Psychology*, 1969, *60*, 168-173.

NEED SATISFACTION SCHEDULE (NSS)

AUTHOR: Donald J. Lollar

AGE: Late childhood to adolescence

VARIABLE: Perceived need satisfactions

TYPE OF MEASURE: Forced-choice interview schedule

SOURCE FROM WHICH MEASURE MAY BE OBTAINED: Donald J. Lollar, Rockdale County Mental Health Services, 951 Railroad Street, Conyers, Georgia 30207.

DESCRIPTION OF MEASURE: The Need Satisfaction Schedule consists of thirty-two items to assess perceived need satisfactions. The basis of the items is the lower four levels of the Maslow need hierarchy—physiological, physical safety and security, affection/belonging, and self-esteem/worth. Each level is represented by a subscale of eight items. The items are administered in an interview setting and in the form of a forced-choice questionnaire. The interviewer asks the randomly ordered questions, and S responds either "yes" or "no." Administration time is approximately 10 minutes. Scoring of each level is obtained by adding together the number of responses indicating satisfaction of a particular need area. For each level the possible range for each individual's responses is 0 to 8-0 indicating a perception of low satisfaction, and 8 indicating a perception of high satisfaction of the need. The instrument was constructed for use with delinquent adolescents to assess perceived need satisfactions across differing environments—basically institutional and noninstitutional. Use has been made for assessing and establishing priorities of needs in delinquency institutions. Also the measure has been used in clinical evaluation of adolescents' need strengths and deficits.

As examples, the first eight of the thirty-two items of the schedule are given below.

1. Are you getting enough sleep here?
2. Have you been getting enough to eat during the last two weeks?
3. Do you have a chance around here to see the person you think is your closest or best friend?
4. If you do something for somebody else, do you get credit for it?
5. Is there anyone around here who would wake you up if a fire broke out while you were asleep?
6. Do you get enough exercise around here?
7. Are you in good health?
8. Have you missed a meal during the last week because there wasn't enough food for you?

RELIABILITY AND VALIDITY: The NSS went through two pilot testings with delinquent adolescents to establish clarity and simplicity of questions, and to determine if adequate differentiation could be made by the items. The second revision (forty-eight questions) was presented to twenty-nine judges to assess if the items appeared to tap the appropriate Maslow need level. To insure initial subscale homogeneity, each subscale was reduced to eight questions. Percentage of agreement among judges for the final thirty-two items ranged from a low of 85 percent for Level II to a high of 95 percent for Level IV. Total agreement for the items was 91 percent. Two hundred delinquent adolescents were then administered the NSS by the researchers. Test-retest reliability was established (*phi* coefficients yielding *chi*-square < .001). Internal consistency using the coefficient *alpha* ranged from .40 for Level II to .78 for the total schedule. Internal consistency was relatively higher for the upper levels of the hierarchy. A correlation matrix (item by each subscale) was used to determine convergent and discriminant validity. Convergent validity was demonstrated by the significant relationship found between each subscale item and its assigned need level by the judges. Using the sign test, the chance probability of such an occurrence is .0039. A binomial test was used with the matrix to establish discriminant validity of the NSS; that is, the relative positions of correlations in the matrix showed the low probability of such occurrences by chance. Finally, validation through one-way ANOVA by levels for the total sample was calculated. A significant difference ($F = 8.95$, $p < .001$) was found among the levels.

BIBLIOGRAPHY:

Lollar, D. "Institutionalization: A Viable Alternative in the Treatment of Delinquent Adolescents?" *Journal of Research in Crime and Delinquency,* 1973, *10* (2), 195-202.

Lollar, D. "An Operationalization and Validation of the Maslow Need Hierarchy." *Educational and Psychological Measurement,* 1974, *34,* 639-651.

PERSONALITY TRAIT: GAMBLING

AUTHOR: Frances Swineford

AGE: Secondary school, college

VARIABLE: Tendency to take a chance

TYPE OF MEASURE: Indirect measure

SOURCE FROM WHICH MEASURE MAY BE OBTAINED: See description below.

DESCRIPTION OF MEASURE: Any objective test may be used for this measure. It is important that the test be a relatively difficult one, in order that even the best students will make enough errors to provide a reliable "gambling" measure, G. The student is told in test instructions that he may claim credit up to 4 points for each item, with the understanding that twice the amount of credit claimed will be subtracted from his score if the answer is wrong. This method was first reported by Soderquist (1936). G is calculated by the following formula:

$$G = \frac{\text{Errors marked "4"}}{\text{Total errors} + \frac{1}{2} \text{ omissions}} \times 100$$

RELIABILITY AND VALIDITY: The reliability of G computed on the basis of a seventy-five-item true-false test at the graduate-school level was .80. The correlation of G with the achievement score on the same test was .08. There are no validity data in the usual sense.

BIBLIOGRAPHY:

Soderquist, H. O. "A New Method of Weighting Scores in a True-False Test." *Journal of Educational Research*, 1936, *30*, 290-292.
Swineford, F. "The Measurement of a Personality Trait." *Journal of Educational Psychology*, 1938, *29*, 295-300.
Swineford, F. "Analysis of a Personality Trait." *Journal of Educational Psychology*, 1941, *32*, 438-444.

PLAYFULNESS SCALE (A FORMAT)

AUTHOR: J. Nina Lieberman

AGE: Adolescence

VARIABLE: Playfulness

TYPE OF MEASURE: Rating scale

SOURCE FROM WHICH MEASURE MAY BE OBTAINED: See Lieberman (1967).

DESCRIPTION OF MEASURE: The sample for formulation of the rating scale consisted of 115 junior high school and high school teachers. Four psychologists reviewed the data obtained from the teachers' observations and produced the rating instrument. Factor analysis of results from 610 adolescents in grades 9 to 12 yielded a "social-emotional" and an "academic" factor. The Playfulness Scale consists of twelve items, on each of which the student is rated along a 5-point scale.

As an example, scale item IA is given below.

How consistently does the student show spontaneous physical movement and activity in class?

Physically on the move   Physically rigid

5	4	3	2	1

This is the student who moves around a lot, likes to change his seat, has trouble settling down, fidgets with things, mischievously throws objects.

This is the student who sits stiffly, with a tense facial expression, and a rigid manner.

RELIABILITY AND VALIDITY: Kuder-Richardson internal consistency coefficients were .87 on test and .90 on retest. The quantity (A) and quality (B) scales were considered equivalent, so split-half reliabilities could be computed. The coefficients were .84 on test and .86 on retest, uncorrected, and .91 and .92, respectively, when corrected by the Spearman-Brown formula. A stability coefficient for the total test was .82. Test-retest coefficient for the A-scale was .80, for the B-scale, .75. Interrater reliabilities, however, were quite low, which may have been due to an overly homogeneous subsample. Correlations of the ratings with teachers' rankings were .69 on test and .76 on retest, with mean item validities of .47 and .56 on test and retest, respectively.

BIBLIOGRAPHY:

Lieberman, J. N. *Personality Traits in Adolescents: An Investigation of Playfulness-Nonplayfulness in the High School Setting.* 1967. ERIC document no. ED 032584.

Lieberman, J. N. *Playfulness: A Quality of Play and Its Relationship to Imagination and Creativity.* New York: Academic Press (in press).

POSITIVE REINFORCEMENT OBSERVATION SCHEDULE (PROS)

AUTHORS: Donald N. Bersoff and Dale Moyer

AGE: Unrestricted

VARIABLE: (1) Reinforcement preferences; (2) reinforcement emission

TYPE OF MEASURE: (1) Paired comparisons scale; (2) observation schedule

SOURCE FROM WHICH MEASURE MAY BE OBTAINED: Donald N. Bersoff, 274 Sherman Avenue, New Haven, Connecticut 06511. Cost: $1.00 per copy.

DESCRIPTION OF MEASURE: The PROS consists of ten categories of positive consequences that may be emitted by mediators. The instrument is adaptable as a mediator reinforcement preference scale and as an observation schedule to obtain frequency and rate of positive reinforcement emission in a variety of settings. The authors make no claim for the transsituational nature or generalized effectiveness of the categories. An assumption of the PROS is that reinforcement is relational rather than an absolute property of an activity. The schedule merely represents ten diverse consequential events that may potentially serve a reinforcing function in a given situation. As a preference scale the PROS can be used to measure disparity of reinforcement preferences between behavior modifiers and teachers. It has served to assess attitude change before, during, and at the completion of training for those undergoing instruction in behavior modification. It is most useful as a schedule to guide observation in training and research and as a clinical tool for assessing teacher/parent-child interaction. It can be used to train student-teachers to increase rate of reinforcement emission, to provide clues to parental responses to children's behavior, and to identify the most effective reinforcers for any one child.

As examples, the ten categories for observation defined in the set of instructions are given below.

Aiding by Example: Demonstration of appropriate behavior by teacher/tester when the child is either nonresponsive or incorrect in exhibiting expected response.
Positive Facial Attention: Looking at a child when teacher/tester is smiling or attending to what the child is doing or what the child has to say (teacher/tester might nod head, wink, or give other indication of approval while smiling). Concerned looking or attending to a child also belongs in this category.
Accepts Feelings: Teacher/tester accepts and clarifies the feeling tone of the child in a nonthreatening manner. Feelings or student emotions may be positive or negative. Predicting or recalling feelings is included. The teacher/tester accepts feelings when he says he/she understands how the child feels, that he has a right to these feelings, and that he will not punish the child for his feelings.
Positive Physical Contact: Actual physical contact such as patting, embracing, holding arm, taking hand, etc.
Accepts Ideas: Clarifying, building, or developing ideas suggested by the child. Teacher/ tester may paraphrase the student's statement, restate the idea more simply, or summarize what the student has said. The key teacher/tester behaviors are clarifying and developing ideas. Simple restatement without building such as when teacher/tester verbalizes student answer during recording on blackboard or test booklet is not scored.

Rapport-Praise: Evaluative reactions that go beyond the teacher/tester's level of simple affirmation or positive feedback by verbally complimenting the child. Rapport-Praise communicates a positive evaluation or a warm personal reaction to the child and not merely an impersonal communication. Teacher/tester responses are considered RP if the verbal content (Yes, Um-hmm, Fine, Good, Right) or nonverbal content (headnod) is accompanied by nonverbal communication of warmth, joy, or excitement.

Affirmation of Appropriate Behavior: Verbal contact indicating approval, commendation to a child that his responses are correct or acceptable, or that his behavior is appropriate. Verbal affirmation may either be loud or soft, and consists of such examples as "That's good," "Fine," "You're studying well."

Administration of Concrete Rewards (Direct): Giving of direct concrete rewards such as candy, money, or free time. This category also consists of those instances when the teacher/tester gives concrete but symbolic rewards (such as giving flashcard to a child contingent upon correct answer to that card) that have no backup or other value.

Administration of Concrete Rewards (Token): Giving of symbolic rewards that will be redeemed for direct concrete rewards at some future time. Common examples are poker chips, tallies, colored sticks, stars, stickers, etc.

Adjuvant Mastery: Urging, prompting, fostering, promoting confidence and success, providing encouragement for response production. When the child refuses to answer, the teacher/tester may suggest guessing, give encouragement ("You just got the last one") or systematically employ a graded series of suggestions.

RELIABILITY AND VALIDITY: As a preference scale the stability of preference was .88 on test-retest after fifteen days. As an observation scale, three different data-collection programs with seven pairs of observers provided evidence that categories could be reliably observed and recorded. Agreement averaged 95 percent, and when PPM was calculated, mean r was .95. In one test of validity, two categories were added that were considered punishments, and two that were considered neutral were added to the ten considered positive. Using a paired-comparison format, 147 Ss unaware of the authors' designation ranked the ten reinforcers 1 to 10, the two neutral stimuli 11 and 12, and the negative stimuli 13 and 14. To demonstrate that the PROS behaviors could actually accelerate predesignated behavior, arithmetic achievement was significantly increased in third-grade students by systematically increasing teachers' use of PROS categories. A four-time increase in teacher emission of PROS categories led to a two-time increase in arithmetic rate correct on progressively harder material.

BIBLIOGRAPHY:

Bersoff, D. N., and Moyer, D. "Positive Reinforcement Observation Schedule (PROS): Development and Applications to Educational Settings" Summary in *Proceedings of the 81st Annual Convention of the American Psychological Association,* 1973, *8,* 713-714.

Byalick, R., and Bersoff, D. N. "Reinforcement Practices of Black and White Teachers in Integrated Classrooms." *Journal of Educational Psychology,* 1974, *66,* 473-480.

Martin, F. "The Effect of Grade Level Upon Teacher Reinforcement Preferences." *Journal of School Psychology,* 1974, *12,* 199-203.

Rigsby, M. B., and Bersoff, D. N. "Reinforcement Emission in Clinical and Classroom Settings." Paper presented at annual meeting of American Psychological Association. New Orleans, Louisiana, September 1974.

Tillman, M., Bersoff, D. N., and Dolly, J. P. *Learning to Teach.* Lexington, Massachusetts: Heath (in press).

RATING FORM FOR FEAR OR DISCOMFORT AND SURPRISE

AUTHOR: Rheta DeVries

AGE: 3 to 6 years

VARIABLE: Emotional reactions to a live event

TYPE OF MEASURE: Emotional concomitant of cognitive experience

SOURCE FROM WHICH MEASURE MAY BE OBTAINED: See DeVries (1969) Appendix B; also available from the Society for Research in Child Development, University of Chicago Press, 5750 South Ellis Avenue, Chicago, Illinois 60637.

DESCRIPTION OF MEASURE: This rating form is designed to measure children's emotional reactions to an apparent transformation in the generic identity of a living animal. The transformation is accomplished by putting rabbit and dog masks on a cat. In the development of the measure, seven levels of fear or discomfort are distinguished in terms of specific observable behaviors, such as "screams," "quavering voice," and "uncomfortable smile." The levels range from Terror (Level 1) to No Fear or Discomfort (Level 7). In order to decrease the reliance upon clinical judgment, a standard petting procedure is followed before and after the identity change. Based on the work of Jersild and Holmes (1935), the child is invited to pet the animal, then is urged, reassured, and finally supported and helped if he refuses. Behaviors specified include petting, vocalization, and facial and body movements. Four levels of surprise are similarly distinguished, such as "verbalizes surprise and puzzlement," ranging from Strong Surprise (Level 1) to No Surprise (Level 4). These behaviors are derived by describing the actions of a small sample of children clinically judged as belonging at each of the levels. For all children, then, raters check the behaviors observed from videotaped interviews of the Live Form of the Generic Identity Task (DeVries, 1969). The rater then makes a global rating from 1 to 7 (in the case of fear) and from 1 to 4 (in the case of surprise). In the case of fear, children sometimes show increases or decreases during the time period being rated, for example, during the first introduction to the live animal. Therefore, the rater should make both maximum and minimum ratings of fear or discomfort. Surprise is rated at the particular defined moments when the situation tends to elicit it, such as upon presentation of the animal whose identity has apparently changed.

RELIABILITY AND VALIDITY: The assessment of emotional response was intended as a validity check on children's verbal responses to the Live Form of the Generic Identity Task. Changes in fear or discomfort did correspond to children's beliefs about the animal's identity constancy. The surprise rating was also useful in validating children's cognitive beliefs, depending on when they showed surprise and what they were surprised about. The validity of the global, clinical judgments was checked by studying the agreement between raters on the behavioral items. Agreement between E and a graduate student ranged from 80 to 90 percent on these specific behaviors, and product-moment correlations on overall ratings ranged from .74 to .94 on a randomly selected group of twenty cases.

BIBLIOGRAPHY:

DeVries, R. "Constancy of Generic Identity in the Years Three to Six." *Society for Research in Child Development Monographs,* 1969, *34* (127), 1-67.
Jersild, A. T., and Holmes, F. B. "Children Fears." *Society for Research in Child Development Monographs,* 1935 (20).

RATING SCALE FOR SELF-DISCLOSURE
IN PREADOLESCENTS

AUTHORS: Sarah I. Vondracek and Fred W. Vondracek

AGE: Elementary to junior high school

VARIABLE: Content and intimacy of self-disclosures

TYPE OF MEASURE: Content scoring system

SOURCE FROM WHICH MEASURE MAY BE OBTAINED: Rating scale and scoring instructions available from Fred W. Vondracek, Beecher House, Pennsylvania State University, University Park, Pennsylvania 16802.

DESCRIPTION OF MEASURE: The essential stimulus for eliciting self-disclosure statements is "Tell me things about yourself" or "Tell me things about yourself that you would usually tell only a few special people" or "Tell me some things that you think people your age would tell to only a few special people." Self-disclosure statements of a pretest sample of preadolescents (N = 73) were classified into eight content categories: family, friends, self, activities, evaluation of own performance, transgressions, tastes and attitudes, and expression of feelings. Each content category was made up of either one, two, or three levels of rated intimacy, based primarily on the relative frequency of occurrence in pilot interview sessions. Scoring weights for the different levels of intimacy have not been standardized. Until further experience is gained in the use of the procedure, it is recommended that a weight of 1 be assigned to statements scored in intimacy level I, a weight of 2 to intimacy level II, and a weight of 3 to intimacy level III. Entire thought sequences rather than individual bits of information form the basic rating unit.

As examples, three sample disclosure protocols are given below.

1. I was sort of jealous one day when my neighbor's rabbit had four little ones, and I just have one rabbit and he had about eight all together. I was jealous 'cause I just had one rabbit.

    Scored as: Expression of Feeling, Level II
2. There's this little kid in my neighborhood. He's a lot younger than I am. Sometimes I play with him 'cause I don't have anything better to do, but I sure wouldn't want my friends to find out about that.

    Scored as: Activities, Level II

3. There's this pool up at the playground—just a little wading pool and my friends and I, we had Coke bottles and we smashed them in there. A cop came up and told us the lady across from the playground told him we were doing this and he wanted everybody's name. He said we had to clean up the glass or else we'd get hauled down.

   Scored as: Transgressions, Level III

RELIABILITY AND VALIDITY: Interscorer agreement was .96 (N = 80). Some evidence for the validity of the scoring procedure was obtained when subjects in a "disclosing" interview condition obtained significantly higher disclosure scores than subjects in a "nondisclosing" interview condition.

BIBLIOGRAPHY:

Vondracek, S. I. "The Measurement and Correlates of Self-Disclosure in Preadolescents." Unpublished doctoral dissertation. Pennsylvania State University, University Park, 1969.

Vondracek, S. I., and Vondracek, F. W. "The Manipulation and Measurement of Self-Disclosure in Preadolescents." *Merrill-Palmer Quarterly of Behavior and Development*, 1971, *17*, 51-58.

Prepared by Fred W. Vondracek

REINFORCEMENT SURVEY SCHEDULE

AUTHORS: Joseph R. Cautela and Robert Kastenbaum

AGE: Adolescents and adults

VARIABLE: Reinforcing stimuli and their relative reinforcing values

TYPE OF MEASURE: Likert-type scale

SOURCE FROM WHICH MEASURE MAY BE OBTAINED: See Cautela and Kastenbaum (1967).

DESCRIPTION OF MEASURE: The Reinforcement Survey Schedule is divided into four major sections. The first three sections ask the respondent to rate items on a 5-point scale representing the degree to which the stimuli give joy or other pleasurable feelings. The response categories are: *not at all, a little, a fair amount, much,* and *very much.* Section I consists of thirty-three items that actually can be presented to a client in many conventional settings. Section II consists of 106 items which, for most practical purposes, can be presented only through facsimile or imagination. Section III presents six situations rather than discrete objects and activities as presented in the preceding two sections. In Section IV the individual completing the measure is asked to list the things he does or thinks about more than certain designated frequencies from five to twenty per day.

Examples from the first three sections of the Reinforcement Survey Schedule are given below. The respondent answers on a 5-point scale ranging from "Not at all" to "Very much."

Section I
Eating
   Ice cream   Pastry
   Candy   Nuts
   Fruit   Cookies
Section II
Looking at beautiful scenery
Like to sing
   Alone
   With others
Section III
How much would you enjoy being in the following situation?

You are at a lively party. Someone walks across the room to you, smiles in a friendly way and says, "I'm glad to meet you. I've heard so many good things about you. Do you have a moment to talk?"

RELIABILITY AND VALIDITY: The internal consistency for the population of undergraduate college students used in the development of the Reinforcement Survey Schedule (Cautela and Kastenbaum, 1967) was found to be reliable with a correlation of .89 when the percentage of favorable responses from the themes in Section III were correlated with the discrete items and activities in Sections I and II (Keehn, Bloomfield, and Hug, 1970). This study, using the same measure of internal consistency, found a correlation of .96 using a sample of alcoholic subjects. The Reinforcement Survey Schedule was found to be reliable over time periods of one, three, and five weeks with median test-retest correlation coefficients of .73, .67, and .71, respectively, with a nonclinical population of college students (Kleinknecht, McCormick, and Thorndike, 1973). Median correlation coefficients for each S were generally higher than those found for the items. They were .83 for the one-week interval group, .78 for the three-week group, and .80 for the five-week group. Kleinknecht, McCormick, and Thorndike (1973) concluded that the data indicated sufficient stability over time intervals of up to five weeks to warrant use of the schedule as a clinical and research instrument. Cautela, Steffan, and Wish (in press) found the Reinforcement Survey Schedule to show validity when they used it to determine reinforcers used in a covert reinforcement paradigm in which the task was to judge circle size. The study used a nonclinical sample. Employing another nonclinical sample, Mermis (1971) tested validity by correlating self-reported reinforcers on the Reinforcement Survey Schedule with the amount of time spent looking at slides of items represented on the Reinforcement Survey Schedule. Steffan (1971) did a validity study using the Reinforcement Survey Schedule with a sample of psychiatric patients labeled schizophrenic.

BIBLIOGRAPHY:

Cautela, J. R. "Reinforcement Survey Schedule: Evaluation and Current Application." *Psychological Reports,* 1972, *30,* 683-690.
Cautela, J. R., and Kastenbaum, R. "A Reinforcement Survey Schedule for Use in Therapy, Training and Research." *Psychological Reports,* 1967, *20,* 1115-1130.

Cautela, J. R., Kastenbaum, R., and Wincze, J. P. "The Use of the Fear Survey Schedule and the Reinforcement Survey Schedule to Survey Possible Reinforcing and Aversive Stimuli Among Juvenile Offenders." *Journal of Genetic Psychology,* 1972, *121,* 255-261.

Cautela, J. R., Steffan, J., and Wish, P. "Covert Reinforcement: An Experimental Test." *Journal of Clinical and Consulting Psychology* (in press).

Cautela, J. R., and Wisocki, P. A. "The Use of the Reinforcement Survey Schedule in Behavior Modification." In R. Rubin (Ed.), *Advances in Behavior Therapy.* New York: Academic Press, 1969.

Keehn, J. D., Bloomfield, F. F., and Hug, M. A. "Uses of the Reinforcement Survey Schedule with Alcoholics." *Quarterly Journal of Studies on Alcoholism,* 1970, *31,* 602-615.

Kleinknecht, R. A. McCormick, C. E., and Thorndike, R. M. "Stability of Stated Reinforcers as Measured by the Reinforcement Survey Schedule." *Behavior Therapy,* 1973, *4,* 407-413.

Mermis, B. J. "Self-Report of Reinforcers and Looking Time." Unpublished doctoral dissertation. University of Tennessee, Knoxville, 1971.

Steffan, J. "Covert Reinforcement with Hospitalized Patients." Paper presented at the annual meeting of the Association for the Advancement of Behavior Therapy. Washington, D.C., September 1971.

Thorndike, R. M., and Kleinknecht, R. A. "Reliability of Homogeneous Scales of Reinforcers: A Cluster Analysis of the Reinforcement Survey Schedule." *Behavior Therapy,* 1974, *5,* 58-63.

RELEVANT ASPECTS OF POTENTIAL (RAP)

AUTHORS: Thomas E. Grant and Joseph S. Renzulli

AGE: 12 years to adult

VARIABLE: Potential of minorities for college success

TYPE OF MEASURE: Structured interview inventory

SOURCE FROM WHICH MEASURE MAY BE OBTAINED: RAP Researchers, c/o Thomas E. Grant, Sandy Lane, Marlborough, Connecticut 06424. Cost: Specimen Kit includes manual, inventory booklet, price lists, and reprint of research, $10.00 payable in advance; $11.00 if invoice is requested.

DESCRIPTION OF MEASURE: The inventory consists of items that help identify students from low socioeconomic or minority-group backgrounds who express talents and interests relevant to success in future educational programs. An item pool of 145 questions was developed and field-tested. The final instrument consists of thirty items appropriate for individuals or groups. The inventory is researched to provide valid questions of a structured and standard interview procedure that may be utilized with other forms of testing and interviewing for the purpose of improving selection processes.

RAP contains thirty items, all of the following type, to which the student responds on a 5-point scale from "strongly disagree" to "strongly agree." Three examples are given below.

1. Davis had organized a successful campaign, which has insured the integration of the history of minority groups into the curricula of his high school. Bill would never organize such a movement but would support the campaign. Byron sees no reason why people should bother about changing what is taught in school.
   _____I am more like Davis than like either Bill or Byron.
2. Raymond, one of the dudes of the group, was busted by the police. Charles went right down to the police station to help Raymond. David volunteered to go along and support Charles. Daniel felt there was nothing he could do to help Raymond. He did not go.
   _____I am more like Charles than like either David or Daniel.
3. Bill Johnson reads a great deal about things that interest him and finds satisfaction in thinking and rapping about what he has read with others.
   _____I am often like Bill.

RELIABILITY AND VALIDITY: Construct validation was investigated through three procedures: item analysis, factor analysis, and known-groups method for determining validity. Experimental and control groups were compared. Thirty items, which comprise the final published inventory, were found to be significant indicators of students with the highest abilities and motivation for future educational opportunities.

BIBLIOGRAPHY:

Grant, T. E., and Renzulli, J. S. "Identifying Achievement Potential in Minority Group Students." *Exceptional Children,* 1975, *41,* 255-259.

SCALE-FOR-PARENTS' RATING

AUTHOR: Richard N. Walker

AGE: Parents of school-aged children

VARIABLE: Ten temperament traits in children, as judged by their parents

TYPE OF MEASURE: Q-sort

SOURCE FROM WHICH MEASURE MAY BE OBTAINED: See Walker (1968).

DESCRIPTION OF MEASURE: The test materials are eighty-four descriptive statements, each on a separate card. (Items and format are partly derived from Medinnus, 1961). The informant's task consists of ordering two sets of forty-two items—one set favorably phrased, one unfavorably—into seven piles of six items apiece, ranging from least to most descriptive of the child. Each set contains four items for each of ten traits; ratings of the eight items in the two sets are summed for a total score. The traits measured are energy, surgency, socialness, stability, cooperativeness, fearfulness, sensitivity, aggressiveness, dominance, competence. Two additional scores, derived from factoring the above traits, are activity and control. Sten-score equivalents for raw sums for the ten traits and two factor scores are given for mothers' and fathers' ratings, based on responses of sixty mothers and thirty fathers of fourth-grade school children. Circumplex structure of interrelations among the traits (loadings on first and second factors) was very similar for fathers' and mothers' ratings and closely resembled structures of descriptions of children by teachers, classmates, and themselves (Walker, 1967).

As examples, eight of the eighty-four items on the scale, those constituting the energetic trait measure, are given below. The parent first sorts the favorable items into three piles representing "yes," "no," and "maybe" or "can't say." He then further sorts these items into seven piles on a 7-point scale ranging from "most like this" to "least like this." The same procedure is repeated with the unfavorable set of items. Items with (—) are negatively scored.

Favorable Set
1. Has a lot of energy and pep; doesn't get tired very quickly.
2. Loves exercise; plays hard.
3. Often sits quietly at an activity for a long time (—).
4. Is quiet and gentle in actions (—).

Unfavorable Set
1. Is noisy and loud.
2. Is always on the go; restless.
3. Is sort of a slow mover; takes his time (—).
4. Is a daydreamer (—).

RELIABILITY AND VALIDITY: Split-half correlations, corrected, ranged from .49 to .93, with a mean of .73 for the ten traits, in the ratings of thirty fathers and sixty mothers. For thirty parent pairs, ipsative correlations across the individual items were computed; parent pairs ranged from little agreement in viewing their child to high agreement, with a mean r close to .50. Ipsative correlations across the ten traits, in sten-score form, averaged about .60. Normative correlations for the ten traits ranged from .17 to .83 for the same thirty parent pairs and were .65 and .71 for the factor scores. Scores on six of the ten cluster traits and the two factor scores were available for the thirty children on a peer nomination ("guess-who") device, a teacher's rating, and a temperament questionnaire. Though correlation values for mothers' and fathers' ratings against all other measures ranged up to .63, most were small and only about 13 percent were significant.

BIBLIOGRAPHY:

Medinnus, G. R. "Q-Sort Descriptions of Five-Year-Old Children by Their Parents." *Child Development*, 1961, *32*, 473-489.

Walker, R. N. "Some Temperament Traits in Children as Viewed by Their Peers, Their Teachers, and Themselves." *Monographs of the Society for Research in Child Development*, 1967, *32* (6), 1-36.

Walker, R. N. "A Scale for Parents' Ratings: Some Ipsative and Normative Correlations." *Genetic Psychology Monographs*, 1968, *77*, 95-133.

SCHOOL ENVIRONMENT PREFERENCE SCHEDULE (SEPS)

AUTHOR: Leonard V. Gordon

AGE: 9 to 18 years

VARIABLE: Endorsement of bureaucratic values

TYPE OF MEASURE: Likert-type scale

SOURCE FROM WHICH MEASURE MAY BE OBTAINED: Leonard V. Gordon, Education Building 114, State University of New York, Albany, New York 12222. Cost: Specimen set, $2.00.

DESCRIPTION OF MEASURE: The SEPS is designed to measure at the student level a personality construct "bureaucratic orientation" that reflects a commitment to the values, attitudes, and behaviors characteristically fostered and rewarded in bureaucratic environments. High scores typify the student who is accepting of and acquiescent to authority, who would prefer to have specific rules and guidelines to follow, who is disinclined to question expert judgment, and who seeks the security of institutional and group identification. The SEPS is a parallel instrument to the adult test, Work Environment Preference Schedule or WEPS (Gordon, 1973). Both instruments are derived from the descriptive schema of Max Weber (1946). The WEPS uses the organization and the SEPS the school as the frames of reference. The SEPS contains twenty-four items, is self-administered (except at the lowest level), requires about 12 minutes to complete, and yields a single score. Norms based on broad regional sampling are available for grades 4 through 12.

As examples, the first four statements of the twenty-four item SEPS are given below. Responses are on a scale from "strongly agree" to "strongly disagree" with midpoint "undecided."

1. A student should always do what his teacher wants him to.
2. A teacher should know the answer to any question in the subject he teaches.
3. In school, a student should never do anything that might be considered wrong.
4. What a student says about his school should agree with what most of the other students say.

RELIABILITY AND VALIDITY: The median coefficient *alpha* reliability for grades 4 through 12 was .86; the median long-range stability was .66. A monotonic decrease in SEPS means with grade level was noted in studies in the United States, Japan, and India. SEPS scores were consistently found to be negatively correlated with academic achievement in the United States (median $r = -.37$), in Japan (median $r = -.36$), and in Norway ($r = .27$). The more bureaucratically oriented student did more poorly in school. SEPS scores were positively related to ratings of conduct in the United States ($r = .18$) and absence of truancy in India ($r = .38$), and to attitude toward school in the United States (median $r = .35$) and in Japan (median $r = .48$). The more bureaucratic student was better behaved and had more favorable attitudes toward his school.

SEPS scores were found to be positively related to authoritarianism, dogmatism, and valuing conformity and orderliness, and negatively related to valuing independence and variety. The latter four relationships, obtained with the author's Survey of Interpersonal Values and Survey of Personal Values (Gordon, 1960, 1967) were also found in Japan and India. Corresponding findings were obtained with measures of dogmatism and conservatism in Great Britain. Among other research findings were negative relationships with rated or measured indices of creativity, noted in both the United States and Great Britain, and positive relationships with the students' preferences for traditional classroom environments, structured roles, and extrinsic rewards.

BIBLIOGRAPHY:

Cohen, L., and Harris, R. "Personal Correlates of Bureaucratic Orientation." *British Journal of Educational Psychology,* 1972, *42,* 300-304.

Danelz, R., and Kennon, M. L. *Relationships of Children to Bureaucratic Organization.* Unpublished manuscript. Memphis State University, Tennessee, 1972.

Gordon, L. V. *Survey of Interpersonal Values.* Chicago: Science Research Associates, 1960.

Gordon, L. V. *Survey of Personal Values.* Chicago: Science Research Associates, 1967.

Gordon, L. V. "The Measurement of Bureaucratic Orientation." *Personnel Psychology,* 1970, *23,* 1-11.

Gordon, L. V. "Weber in the Classroom." *Journal of Educational Psychology,* 1971, *62,* 60-66.

Gordon, L. V. *Work Environment Preference Schedule and Manual.* New York: Psychological Corporation, 1973.

Gordon, L. V., and Kikuchi, A. "The Measurement of Bureaucratic Orientation in Japan." *International Revue of Applied Psychology,* 1970, *19,* 133-140.

Haipt, M. "A Study of the Relationships Among Perceptions of the School, Bureaucratic Orientation Levels and Satisfaction-Dissatisfaction Measures of Secondary School Students." Unpublished doctoral dissertation. University of Maryland, College Park, 1972.

Kakkar, S. B. "Bureaucratic Orientation of Indian Students." *Panjab University Research Bulletin,* 1971, *2,* 83-97.

Kennon, M. L. *A Study of Student's Behavior and Attitudes as Related to Environment.* Unpublished manuscript. Memphis State University, Tennessee, 1973.

Khalique, N. *The Bureaucratic Orientation of Truants and Nontruants.* Unpublished manuscript. Patna University, Bihar, India, 1969.

Kikuchi, A., and Gordon, L. V. "Bureaucratic Orientation of the Japanese Adolescent." *Japanese Annals of Social Psychology,* 1970, *11,* 217-229.

Kurtz, B. *Correlations Between the SEPS and Attitude and Intelligence.* Unpublished manuscript. State University of New York, Albany, 1972.

Lindner, P. A. "Relationships Among Children's Bureaucratic Orientation, Parental Bureaucratic Orientation, and Child-Rearing Attitudes." Unpublished master's thesis. Illinois Institute of Technology, Chicago, 1974.

Lyden, M. *A Comparison of Anonymous and Identifiable Responses to a Measure of Bureaucratic Values.* Unpublished manuscript. State University of New York, Albany, 1973.

Miller, O. V. "The Effects and Relationships of a Self-Evaluation Project on Student Skill in Self-Evaluating Written Compositions." Unpublished doctoral dissertation. Fordham University, New York, New York, 1970.

Moran, W. F. "Effect of the Middle School Program upon the Academic Achievement and Attitudes of Fifth-Grade Students in the Valley Central School District."

Unpublished doctoral disssertation. Fordham University, New York, New York, 1969.

Solomon, D. "Individual Characteristics and Children's Performance in Varied Educational Settings." Progress report. Montgomery County Public Schools, Rockville, Maryland, 1974.

Weber, M. *Essays in Sociology.* (Translated by H. H. Garth and C. W. Mills.) New York: Oxford University Press, 1946.

SCHOOL MOTIVATION TEST

AUTHOR: Ivan L. Russell

AGE: 12 years and up

VARIABLE: Achievement motivation in terms of school-oriented items

TYPE OF MEASURE: Paper-and-pencil test

SOURCE FROM WHICH MEASURE MAY BE OBTAINED: See Russell (1969).

DESCRIPTION OF MEASURE: This test is a self-report instrument of thirty short questions to which the responses are "Yes" or "No." Test time is approximately 10 minutes, with scoring time about 2 minutes. Data from two doctoral dissertations indicate test results to be relatively independent of socioeconomic and racial factors.

As examples, the keyed first ten items from the thirty-item test are given below.

No 1. Students should set their goals only as high as they can easily reach.
Yes 2. Does it bother you if another student makes better grades than you do?
Yes 3. Would you rather be a leader in a small school than to be just another student in a large school?
No 4. Does failure discourage you from trying as hard the next time?
Yes 5. You should select your friends from among those whose goals are generally as high as your own.
No 6. Would you like to take a school subject in which no tests were to be given?
Yes 7. Do you often compare your work with the work of others?
Yes 8. Are you usually on time with written assignments?
No 9. Do you believe, "Win or lose, who cares?"
Yes 10. Do you try to make better grades than other students in your classes?

RELIABILITY AND VALIDITY: Split-half reliability of the instrument, corrected with the Spearman-Brown formula, was .96. Students in general mathematics and in algebra classes were asked to volunteer for an academic type of contest. Later the mean motivation score of volunteers exceeded the mean for nonvolunteers significant at the .01 level of confidence. Algebra students' mean score was significantly higher than the mean for general mathematics students ($p < .001$). Three months after the motivation scores were obtained, scores on the California Achievement Test were collected. Product-moment correlations between motivation scores and achievement scores ranged from .60 to .72 (Russell, 1969). Validity information is presented also in Fox (1968).

BIBLIOGRAPHY:

Fox, R. B. "The Relationship of Achievement Motivation to Sex, Achievement, Intelligence, Socioeconomic Status, and Level of Educational Aspiration for an Eighth Grade Group." Unpublished doctoral dissertation. University of Kentucky, Lexington, 1968.
Russell, I. L. "Motivation for School Achievement: Measurement and Validation." *Journal of Educational Research*, 1969, *62,* 263-266.

SELF-ADMINISTERED DEPENDENCY QUESTIONNAIRE (SADQ)

AUTHOR: Ian Berg

AGE: Mothers of school-aged children, 7 to 15 years

VARIABLE: Four kinds of dependency

TYPE OF MEASURE: Questionnaire

SOURCE FROM WHICH MEASURE MAY BE OBTAINED: Ian Berg, 7 Stone Rings Close, Harrogate, Yorkshire, England.

DESCRIPTION OF MEASURE: The SADQ consists of twenty-one questions concerned with task-oriented and person-oriented dependency, mainly shown in the mother-child relationship. Correlation and principal component analyses, on results of applying the questionnaire to mothers of children from the general population of a part of England, suggest that four kinds of dependency can be measured, called, respectively, affection, communication, assistance, and travel. Each question is scored on a 5-point rating scale, from 0 to 4. A simple summation of the raw scores on several different questions produces the subscale scores. A scoring card is provided.

    As examples, six of the twenty-one items of the questionnaire are given below. The mother answers each question by marking a 5-point frequency scale ranging from "less than once a week or not at all" to "more than once a day (several times a day)."

1. Did you wash or bath him/her? (not including hair washing)
2. Did he/she go shopping or on visits with you? (not for you but actually in your company)

3. Did he/she either make his/her own bed or clear up his/her room? (indicate frequency of either)
4. Did he/she either clear off the table or wash the dishes at home? (indicate frequency of either)
5. Did he/she come into your bed for company at night or in the early morning?
6. Did he/she come close to you for affectionate contact? (for example, sitting on knee or putting arm round; do not include kissing)

RELIABILITY AND VALIDITY: The administered form of the questionnaire was used on 116 randomly selected mothers of children from the general population stratified for age, sex, social class, and type of school (Berg, McGuire, and Whelan, 1973). The self-administered form was given to a similar group of 256. Test-rest reliability of actual scores was satisfactory: assistance, $r = .94$; travel, $r = .92$; affection, $r = .77$; communication, $r = .63$. Pairs of subscale scores did not differ significantly using t tests for correlated means. Composite r was .80 for total randomly selected groups of retests, $N = 60$. Thirty-nine phobic youngsters were more dependent than fifty-eight other psychiatrically disturbed youngsters as far as assistance and travel were concerned. This confirmed work with the administered version (Berg, McGuire, and Whelan, 1973). Preference scores were used to measure maternal attitudes in these cases. Mean preference subscale scores were significantly raised in school phobics but not in other cases, indicating overprotection on the part of mothers.

BIBLIOGRAPHY:

Berg, I. "A Self-Administered Dependency Questionnaire (SADQ) for Use with the Mothers of School Children." *British Journal of Psychiatry,* 1974, *124,* 1-9.
Berg, I., and McGuire, R. "Are Mothers of School Phobic Adolescents Overprotective?" *British Journal of Psychiatry,* 1974, *124,* 10-13.
Berg, I., McGuire, R., and Whelan, E. "The Highlands Dependency Questionnaire (HDQ): An Administered Version for Use with the Mothers of School Children." *Journal of Child Psychology and Psychiatry,* 1973, *14,* 107-121.

SELF-FOCUS SENTENCE COMPLETION (SFSC)

AUTHOR: John E. Exner, Jr.

AGE: 13 years to adult (experimental form, 8 to 12 years)

VARIABLE: Egocentricity

TYPE OF MEASURE: Sentence completion

SOURCE FROM WHICH MEASURE MAY BE OBTAINED: See Exner (1973).

DESCRIPTION OF MEASURE: This measure is a thirty-item sentence-completion blank, in which most of the stems contain a self-reference (I, me, or my). Responses are scored for one of four basic categories: (1) those focusing on the self (S); (2) those focusing on the external world (E); (3) those that are ambivalent, that is, focusing on both the self and the external world (A); and (4) those that are neutral with regard to focus (N). There are also two scoring subcategories: (1) when the self-focus answer is negative (Sn), and (2) when the external world focus answer is distinctly affective (Ea). The data derived may be used to study the extent of "egocentric balance," that is, the extent to which a balance exists between the amount of self-focus and the amount of external world focus. The data also appear to provide a useful index of egocentricity as a form of response style.

As examples, the first two of the thirty items of the sentence completion, together with examples of scoring for the different categories, are given below.

1. I think
   - S: best when I'm alone; I am creative; therefore I am.
   - Sn: I am very nervous; I'm unhappy; I will die.
   - E: people are fun; about teaching children; about my children.
   - Ea: my dad is the greatest; everyone is beautiful; this country is an evil place.
   - A: of what to do about myself and my family; my wife is terrible but she loves me so.
   - N: sometimes; when I'm awake; when I think about it.
2. I was happiest when
   - S: I was alone; I succeeded; I was well; I was loved.
   - Sn: I went crazy; I was unhappy.
   - E: I was with Mary; I was home; my children graduated.
   - Ea: we went on our honeymoon; I told her I loved her; my mother finally died.
   - A: I became an adult and had friends.
   - N: school was out; the sun was shining; I was outside.

RELIABILITY AND VALIDITY: The SFSC was standardized on 2,592 nonpsychiatric subjects representing five different kinds of populations and 273 psychiatric patients from nine different diagnostic groups. Interscorer reliabilities have been shown to range from .81 to .97 depending on the score and the level of training of the scorer. Validation studies show that specific scores and scoring configurations are significantly related to evaluations of successful outcome in psychotherapy and to successful completion of service in the Peace Corps. High S scores have been demonstrated to be significantly related to "mirror viewing" time and to the number of personal pronouns used by nonpatients during an interview situation.

BIBLIOGRAPHY:

Exner, J. E., Jr. "The Self Focus Sentence Completion: A Study of Egocentricity." *Journal of Personality Assessment,* 1973, *37,* 437-455.

SIMILARITY OF CHILD TO PARENTS

AUTHOR: Arlene H. Morgan

AGE: 5 to 18 years

VARIABLE: Personality variables thought to be related to hypnotizability

TYPE OF MEASURE: Rating scale

SOURCE FROM WHICH MEASURE MAY BE OBTAINED: Arlene H. Morgan, Department of Psychology, Stanford University, Stanford, California 94305.

DESCRIPTION OF MEASURE: The scale was derived as an attempt to find personality correlates with hypnotizability ("degree to which child possesses this trait") and then to find similarities between the child and either parent on these personality variables. It was part of a study that investigated the possibility of a genetic component in hypnotizability and involved assessing the hypnotic susceptibility of a sample of twins (both identical and fraternal), their siblings, and their parents.

As examples, the first five of the eleven items on the scale are given below. The person rating the subject checks "most like father," "most like mother," "like both equally," or "like neither." He also rates the subject as either "high" or "low" on possession of each trait.

1. Sensitivity to criticism or punishment
2. Sense of humor
3. Curiosity
4. Pride in accomplishing tasks
5. Cautiousness

RELIABILITY AND VALIDITY: None reported.

BIBLIOGRAPHY:

Hilgard, E. R. *Hypnotic Susceptibility.* New York: Harcourt Brace Jovanovich, 1965.
Hilgard, E. R. *Personality and Hypnosis.* Chicago: University of Chicago Press, 1970.
Morgan, A. H. "The Heritability of Hypnotic Susceptibility in Twins." *Journal of Abnormal Psychology,* 1973, *82,* 55-61.
Morgan, A. H., Hilgard, E. R., and Davert, E. C. "The Heritability of Hypnotic Susceptibility of Twins: A Preliminary Report." *Behavior Genetics,* 1970, *1,* 213-223.

SUMMER CAMP TEST

AUTHOR: Barbara J. Brandes

AGE: 10 to 14 years

VARIABLE: Self-directedness

TYPE OF MEASURE: Multiple-choice test

SOURCE FROM WHICH MEASURE MAY BE OBTAINED: Research for Better Schools, Inc., Public Information Office, 1700 Market Street, Philadelphia, Pennsylvania 19103.

DESCRIPTION OF MEASURE: The Summer Camp Test is a multiple-choice test that assesses the child's ability to apply concepts of self-direction. It is useful primarily for purposes of program evaluation in which a major program objective is to enhance self-directedness in children. In the test, students are presented with hypothetical problem situations in which fictional characters must select self-directed or other-directed solutions to problems pertaining to personal goal striving. The test is scored for the number of times that the student selects the most self-directed option. The test is considered to measure the child's understanding of and ability to apply self-directed solutions rather than the child's own disposition to behave in a self-directed manner.

The introduction of this test is a description of a fictional summer camp where children are allowed to choose their own activities. The respondent is asked to pretend that he is a counselor at the camp and to answer the fourteen items on the scale. As examples, two of the items are given below.

6. Gwen: "I've been playing the guitar like mad for the past two weeks. I can play ten chords now and I've learned several new songs. I've even helped a couple of kids learn how to play 'C' and 'G7.' I think when I get home I'll put an ad in the paper and start giving guitar lessons." As Gwen's counselor, what would you do?
   a. _____ Tell her to find out how well a person should be able to play the guitar before she starts giving lessons.
   b. _____ Tell her that it's a silly idea.
   c. _____ Tell her to go ahead and give guitar lessons.
7. Tom: "I've been doing a few things in crafts which I like, and I decided that I want to make a boat using a piece of bark. I want to get lots of other kids to also make boats so we can put candles on them and float them on the lake and see whose candle stays lighted the longest. Maybe we could float our boats tomorrow night or so." As Tom's counselor, what would you do?
   a. _____ Tell him that sounds like a fine idea.
   b. _____ Tell him to think about all the things he must do to get ready for the activity. He should find other kids who want to do it and get the necessary supplies.
   c. _____ Tell him that the baseball team still needs another outfielder, and he'd be better off doing that.

RELIABILITY AND VALIDITY: An estimate of the reliability of the instrument is based on a sample of 387 10- to 12-year-old children representing primarily the middle and upper-middle economic classes in a large metropolitan area. An internal consistency reliability of .76 was computed for the scale using Kuder-Richardson formula 20. A correlation of .24 was obtained between the Summer Camp Test and a measure of internal locus of control.

BIBLIOGRAPHY:

Brandes, B. J. *Achievement Competence Training: Field Test and Evaluation.* Philadelphia, Pennsylvania: Research for Better Schools, Inc., 1974.

SYMBOLIC MEASURE OF AUTHORITARIANISM (SF-TEST)

AUTHOR: H. Wayne Hogan

AGE: 5 years and up

VARIABLE: Authoritarianism, tolerance for ambiguity

TYPE OF MEASURE: Forced-choice projective test

SOURCE FROM WHICH MEASURE MAY BE OBTAINED: H. Wayne Hogan, Department of Sociology, Tennessee Technological University, Cookeville, Tennessee 38501.

DESCRIPTION OF MEASURE: The Hogan Symbolic Measure of Authoritarianism consists of fifteen pairs of line drawings and number arrangements. The instructions ask the respondent to check the one drawing or arrangement in each pair that he (she) likes best. In each pair, one drawing or arrangement is less complete, more ambiguous, or less symmetrical, that is, less "normative," than the other. Selection of the less normative drawing and arrangement is scored 1 point, selection of the more normative item is scored 2 points. Scores thus range from 15 (least authoritarianism) to 30 (most authoritarianism). When first developed and tested in June 1968, the measure's fifteen pairs of drawings and number arrangements were distributed over five pages of an accompanying questionnaire booklet. As presently used, all pairs of stimuli are reduced in size and appear on just one sheet of paper.

RELIABILITY AND VALIDITY: Use of the split-half method corrected by the Spearman-Brown formula has resulted in coefficients of .93 and .91 for two groups of American undergraduates numbering seventy-three and seventy-two, respectively; .88 and .84, respectively, for 285 German soldiers and eighty-three German law students; and an atypical coefficient of .15 for fifty-five American prison guards (a coefficient attenuated by a mean SF-score of 29 of a possible 30). Validity is indicated by "known-group" scores of 29.0 for American prison guards, 28.5 for deaf American grade-school and college students, 26.5 for American police cadets, 24.1 for American undergraduates, 23.0 for American social-work students, and 21.6 for German drug users. Convergent validity is suggested by correlation coefficients between the non-verbal SF-score and verbal measures of authoritarianism of .64 for American students and .27 for New Zealand borstal boys.

BIBLIOGRAPHY:

Hogan, H. W. "Authoritarianism Among White and Black Deaf Adolescents: Two Measures Compared." *Perceptual and Motor Skills*, 1970, *31*, 195-200.

Hogan, H. W. "Reliability and Convergent Validity of the Symbolic Test for Authoritarianism." *Journal of Psychology*, 1970, 76, 39-43.

Hogan, H. W. "A Symbolic Measure of Authoritarianism: An Exploratory Study." *Journal of Social Psychology*, 1970, *82*, 215-219.

Hogan, H. W. "A Symbolic Measure of Authoritarianism: A Replication." *Journal of Social Psychology*, 1970, *80*, 241-242.

Hogan, H. W. "Authoritarianism Among Nursing Students: Two Measures Compared." *American Psychological Association Experimental Publication System*, 1971, *12*, 399-412.

TEENAGE PICTURE STUDY (TAPS)

AUTHOR: James O. Palmer

AGE: 12 to 17 years

VARIABLE: Subjective response to social frustration

TYPE OF MEASURE: Structured projective technique

SOURCE FROM WHICH MEASURE MAY BE OBTAINED: James O. Palmer, Neuro-psychiatric Institute, University of California at Los Angeles, 760 Westwood Plaza, Los Angeles, California 90024.

DESCRIPTION OF MEASURE: The TAPS is made up of twenty-four cartoon-form situations socially frustrating to adolescents. Each cartoon depicts an adolescent being challenged verbally in a frustrating situation by an adult or a peer. An approximately equal number of situations depict each sex. Similarly, an attempt is made to show boys and girls frustrated by mothers, fathers, youths of the same sex, and youths of the opposite sex in about the same proportions. For example, TAPS item 21 shows mother standing in the doorway as the adolescent male is about to leave with a friend of the same sex. Mother says, "Going out? You haven't put your things away!" There are two forms of the test. In the open-end Form C, the subject writes his own responses. In the multiple-choice version, Form D, the subject chooses among four given responses. The test is scored by categorizing the responses using a modification of the schema of Rosenzweig and others (1947, 1948). Norms are available, based on administration of the test to 200 public-school children.

RELIABILITY AND VALIDITY: See Palmer (1972).

BIBLIOGRAPHY:

Palmer, J. O. "Patterns of Perceived Reactions to Frustration Among Adolescents." *Genetic Psychology Monographs,* 1972, *85,* 133-153.
Rosenzweig, S., Fleming, E., and Clarke, H. "Revised Scoring Manual for the Rosenzweig Picture-Frustration Study." *Journal of Psychology,* 1947, *24,* 165-208.
Rosenzweig, S., Fleming, E., and Rosenzweig, R. "The Children's Form of the Rosenzweig Picture-Frustration Study." *Journal of Psychology,* 1948, *26,* 141-191.

VISUAL JUDGMENT SCALE

AUTHOR: Thomas L. Pasternack

AGE: Elementary school to adult

VARIABLE: Conformity (yielding behavior)

TYPE OF MEASURE: Test

SOURCE FROM WHICH MEASURE MAY BE OBTAINED: Educational Testing Service, Princeton, New Jersey 08540. Xerox copies at no cost; $2.00 for microfiche when available through *Tests in Microfiche.*

DESCRIPTION OF MEASURE: The Visual Judgment Scale enables the examiner to distinguish between *compliant* (public but not private acceptance of group norms) and *conformant* (private as well as public acceptance of group norms) behavior in individuals who yield in a group. It consists of three pages, each of which contains drawings of ten pairs of partially obscured cubes. The cubes in each pair are labeled, and space is provided for the respondent to indicate which of the two he believes is larger. Although the two forms of the scale appear the same to the respondent, Form 110 and Form 550 differ from each other on six of the ten pairs. As a result, when all subjects but one have Form 110, the subject who has Form 550 will experience a discrepancy between the verbal reports of others and what he sees on twelve of twenty trials. The scale is designed to be used in groups of six, in which everyone except the fifth subject, sequentially, will have Form 110. On the first page of the test, everyone responds to each of the pairs verbally. On the second page, two subjects respond verbally to each of the pairs before everyone indicates his choice for that pair with a check mark. The two subjects who respond verbally do so on a rotating basis. Page three, on which all persons privately mark their responses without any verbal reports, is identical for both forms of the scale.

RELIABILITY AND VALIDITY: None reported.

BIBLIOGRAPHY:

Pasternack, T. L. "The 'Naive Majority' Technique: A New Method for Conformity Studies." *Psychological Record,* 1972, *22,* 555-558.

Pasternack, T. L. "Qualitative Differences in Development of Yielding Behavior by Elementary School Children." *Psychological Reports,* 1973, *32,* 883-896.

WERRY-WEISS-PETERS ACTIVITY SCALE

AUTHORS: John S. Werry, G. Weiss, and John E. Peters

AGE: 5 to 12 years

VARIABLE: Activity level and related behavior

TYPE OF MEASURE: Parent rating scale

SOURCE FROM WHICH MEASURE MAY BE OBTAINED: See Werry (1968).

DESCRIPTION OF MEASURE: This thirty-one-item symptom checklist/rating scale is designed to assess the activity level of children in seven areas: during meals, television, doing homework, play, sleep, behavior away from home (except school), and school behavior. The parents are interviewed, and the interviewer checks one of three frequencies as descriptive of the child's behavior on each item.

As examples, ten of the thirty-one items are given below. The interviewer checks "No," "Yes—a little bit," or "Yes—very much" for each item.

During Meals
1. Up and down at table.
2. Interrupts without regard.
3. Wriggling.
4. Fiddles with things.
5. Talks excessively.
Television
1. Gets up and down during program.
2. Wriggles.
3. Manipulates objects or body.
4. Talks incessantly.
5. Interrupts.

RELIABILITY AND VALIDITY: No reliability data are reported. Drug-sensitive scores decline with age but do not differ by sex. As shown by factor analysis, the measure is not a homogeneous activity scale but consists of seven distinct factors.

BIBLIOGRAPHY:

Conners, C., and Rothschild, G. "Drugs and Learning in Children." In *Learning Disorders*, Vol. 3. Seattle: Special Child Publications, 1968.

Routh, D. K., Schroeder, C. S., and O'Tuama, L. A. "Development of Activity Level in Children." *Developmental Psychology,* 1974, *10,* 163-168.

Werry, J. S. "Developmental Hyperactivity." *Pediatric Clinics of North America,* 1968, *15,* 581-599.

Werry, J. S., Weiss, G., Douglas, V., and Martin, J. "Studies on the Hyperactive Child: III. The Effect of Chlorpromazine upon Behavior and Learning Ability." *Journal of the American Academy of Child Psychiatry,* 1966, *5,* 292-312.

WRAY BEHAVIOR SCALE

AUTHOR: Grace A. Wray

AGE: 3 to 10 years and up

VARIABLE: Behavior factors

TYPE OF MEASURE: Rating scale

SOURCE FROM WHICH MEASURE MAY BE OBTAINED: Grace A. Wray, Research and Development Center in Educational Stimulation, University of Georgia, Athens, Georgia 30601. Cost: Duplication and mailing.

DESCRIPTION OF MEASURE: The Wray Behavior Scale was designed to include fifteen behavior symptoms and their opposites that seem to be particularly indicative of certain characteristics observable in early childhood and that can be followed as the child grows and develops. Each child is observed on each symptom and a check made to indicate where he stands on a 5-point scale on each pair of characteristics. A description of the terminal traits on the scale is given in Wray (1969).

The fifteen items on the scale are given below.

1. Aggressive-Submissive
2. Social-Nonsocial
3. Independent-Dependent
4. Cooperative-Uncooperative
5. Eager-Dull
6. Talkative-Uncommunicative
7. Attentive-Nonattentive
8. Active-Still
9. Happy-Sad
10. Leads-Follows

11. Imaginative-Prosaic
12. Persistent-Nonpersistent
13. Gregarious-Lone
14. Obedient-Disobedient
15. Courteous-Rude

RELIABILITY AND VALIDITY: None reported.

BIBLIOGRAPHY:

Wray, G. A. "Wray Behavior Scale." Unpublished report prepared for the Research and Development Center in Educational Stimulation. University of Georgia, Athens, 1969.

Group 2-c

Personality Adjustment

A-M-L BEHAVIOR RATING SCALE

AUTHOR: Phyllis P. Van Vleet

AGE: Preschool through high school

VARIABLE: Classroom behavior and learning symptoms

TYPE OF MEASURE: Rating scale

SOURCE FROM WHICH MEASURE MAY BE OBTAINED: Phyllis P. Van Vleet, 243 Asilomar Boulevard, Pacific Grove, California 93950.

DESCRIPTION OF MEASURE: The A-M-L Behavior Rating Scale is a simple, economical, reliable eleven-item screening device for identifying children with learning and/or behavior problems. The school classroom provides an opportunity for direct observation of children over a period of time and under a variety of circumstances. The A-M-L Scale serves the purpose of helping the teacher record, in an orderly fashion, various kinds of observed behavior in children. The frequency with which these behavior characteristics occur is checked on a 5-point scale. The five odd-numbered items comprise subscale A (aggressive, outgoing behavior). The five even-numbered items comprise subscale M (moody, withdrawn, internalized behavior). Item eleven comprises subscale L (degree of learning difficulty). The range in total A-M-L score is 11-55 points, with lower scores indicating more acceptable behavior. Subscale scores can also be derived for A, M, and L. For effective use of the scale, it is recommended that the teacher observing and rating children shall have been their classroom teacher for a period of not less than three consecutive months. The scale is essentially a screening instrument that has been successfully used in identifying children from very high-risk families and children from families with beginning symptoms—potentially high-risk families. Depending on the purpose for screening, from 10 to 25 percent of the high-scoring children will require some intervention.

The eleven items of the scale are given below. They are responded to on a 5-point scale from "seldom or never" to "all of the time."

This pupil
 1. Gets into fights or quarrels with other pupils.
 2. Has to be coaxed or forced to work or play with other pupils.
 3. Is very restless.
 4. Is unhappy or depressed.
 5. Enjoys disrupting class discipline.
 6. Becomes sick when faced with a difficult school problem or situation.
 7. Is very obstinate.
 8. Is overly sensitive to criticism.
 9. Is very impulsive.
10. Can be very moody.
11. Has difficulty learning.

RELIABILITY AND VALIDITY: The eleven-item A-M-L Scale was derived by factor analysis from two existing behavior rating scales. These scales were used by classroom teachers (120), in thirty-eight schools in twelve school districts, kindergarten through fifth grade. In each classroom were one or more children from families known to more than one county social adjustment agency (multiproblem families). One hundred children from these families and under 10 years of age comprised the experimental group. A control group of 100 children was selected from the same school population and met the same criteria except that their families were not known to be multiproblem. Eighty percent of the multiproblem families were identified by teachers rating their children on the items included in the two scales. The Kuder-Richardson 21 reliability formula, when applied to the total population studied (2,872), showed an r of .74 for one scale and .92 for the other scale. A factor analysis of the two scales undertaken simultaneously resulted in three substantial factors: A, M, and L. The most significantly differentiating items comprise the A-M-L Behavior Rating Scale.

BIBLIOGRAPHY:

Beisser, P., and Van Vleet, P. *Early Identification of Behavior-Problem Children and Multiproblem Families.* Redwood City, California: Office of San Mateo County Superintendent of Schools, 1962.

Cowen, E. L. "Some Correlates of Early Detected Emotional Dysfunction in the Schools." *American Journal of Orthopsychiatry,* 1969, *39,* 619-626.

Cowen, E. L., and others. "Interrelation Among Screening Measures for Early Detection of School Dysfunction." *Psychology in the Schools,* 1971, *36,* 56-61.

Cowen, E. L., and others. "The A-M-L: A Quick-Screening Device for Early Identification of School Maladaption." *Journal of Community Psychology,* 1973, *1,* 12-35.

Van Vleet, P., and Kannegieter, R. *Investments in Prevention: the Prevention of Learning and Behavior Problems in Young Children. Evaluation Report. 1966-1969.* Redwood City, California: Pace I.D. Center. South San Francisco Unified School District (Title III-ESEA).

Van Vleet, P., and others. "Young Children at Risk: A Three-Year Research and Demonstration Project Concerned with Early Intervention and Prevention of Learning and Behavior Problems." *American Journal of Orthopsychiatry,* 1970, *40,* 320-322.

BEHAVIOR CHECKLIST

AUTHOR: Eli Rubin

AGE: Elementary age

VARIABLE: Behavioral adjustment in classroom

TYPE OF MEASURE: Checklist

SOURCE FROM WHICH MEASURE MAY BE OBTAINED: Eli Z. Rubin, 13440 East Warren Avenue, Detroit, Michigan 48215. Cost: $1.00.

DESCRIPTION OF MEASURE: The Behavior Checklist is a thirty-two-item checklist useful to teachers and others who have reasonable knowledge of children in a group situation. Observation over at least a two weeks' to a month's period increases the reliability. The items relate to usual and common observable classroom misbehaviors capable of being reported by the teacher. The items cluster according to seven factors, the first three of which are (1) behaviors related to poor spatial orientation and poor motor control, (2) antisocial behaviors, and (3) unassertive behaviors. The checklist can be useful in identifying children considered behaviorally maladjusted and in need of further evaluation or remediation.

As examples, ten selected items from the thirty-two-item checklist are given below. The rater is instructed to use *one* checkmark if the item is representative of the child's typical behavior, *two* checkmarks for behavior shown more frequently, and *three* checkmarks if the behavior is outstanding by its frequency.

1. Very sensitive to criticism.
4. Is excessively neat or finicky about work or possessions.
9. Can't work independently.
13. Seems to fear being assertive even in ordinary ways (asking to go to toilet, defending self, making legitimate messes, joining in allowable noisy play).
15. Poor coordination (trouble with buttoning, tying shoes, getting shoes on correct feet).
16. Can't take turns; "Me first."
17. Lacks responsibility for self, always has excuse for shortcomings.
18. Resists limits or rules in group games.
25. Displays infantile behavior (crawling, whining, clinging, sucking, chewing, and so forth).
29. Is disoriented in space; is confused as to directions given.

RELIABILITY AND VALIDITY: None reported.

BIBLIOGRAPHY:

Rubin, E., Simson, C., and Betwee, M. *Emotionally Handicapped Child and Elementary School.* Detroit: Wayne State Press, 1966.

BEHAVIOR RATING SCALES FOR SCHOOL BEGINNERS

AUTHORS: Barbara H. Long and Edmund H. Henderson

AGE: 3 to 8 years

VARIABLE: Adjustment to school

TYPE OF MEASURE: Rating scales

SOURCE FROM WHICH MEASURE MAY BE OBTAINED: Barbara H. Long, Goucher College, Baltimore, Maryland 21204.

DESCRIPTION OF MEASURE: These are twenty-four 7-point scales describing class-room behaviors, with positive and exemplifying behavior considered more mature. Items are partially derived from Medinnus's (1961) First Grade Adjustment Scale. Examples follow: Shy with teacher/Friendly with teacher; Does not complete tasks/Completes tasks.

RELIABILITY AND VALIDITY: Correlates and factor analyses are presented in the studies listed below. Total ratings are positively related to Otis IQs and Metropolitan Readiness and predict promotion from grade 1 and Metropolitan Reading scores in grade 2. Corrected split-half reliability is .95.

BIBLIOGRAPHY:

Henderson, E. H., and Long, B. H. "Correlates of Reading Readiness Among Children of Varying Backgrounds." *The Reading Teacher*, 1968, *22*, 40-44.
Henderson, E. H., and Long, B. H. "Personal and Social Correlates of Academic Success Among Disadvantaged School Beginners." *Journal of School Psychology*, 1971, *9*, 101-113.
Long, B. H., and Henderson, E. H. "Teachers' Judgments of Black and White School Beginners." *Sociology of Education*, 1971, *44*, 358-368.
Medinnus, G. R. "The Development of a First-Grade Adjustment Scale." *Journal of Experimental Psychology*, 1961, *30*, 243-248.

BEHAVIOR IN SCHOOL INVENTORY (BSI)

AUTHOR: M. B. Youngman

AGE: 9 to 13 years

VARIABLE: Adjustment to school

TYPE OF MEASURE: Questionnaire/checklist

SOURCE FROM WHICH MEASURE MAY BE OBTAINED: M. B. Youngman, School of Education, University of Nottingham, Nottingham, England.

DESCRIPTION OF MEASURE: Being an inventory of behavioral items, the BSI can be used in two forms, either by the child himself or by a teacher for completion. The thirty-four items break down into three subscales: studiousness (twelve items), compliance (fifteen items), and teacher contact (seven items). The scales are additive, producing an overall adjustment to school score if required. Early analyses (Youngman, 1969; Brennan and Youngman, 1971) showed that normal school children could be classified into behavioral types that related to school achievement. A subsequent analysis (Bennett and Youngman, 1973) confirmed this finding and further showed the BSI's value in identifying aspects of school behavior outside the scope of traditional methods of personality assessment. Currently the scale is being used in delinquency research and in the evaluation of teaching systems aimed at preventing failure later in school life.

As examples, seventeen of the thirty-four items, with scale allocation indicated, are given below.

1. Do you often look out of the classroom window?	1
2. Have you had things taken from you by the teacher?	2
3. Is your work usually neat?	2
4. Do you nearly always answer if teacher asks you a question?	3
5. Do you often talk to the person next to you in class?	1
6. Do you sometimes run errands for the teacher?	3
7. Do you find it difficult to sit still for a long time?	1
8. Is your writing easy to read?	2
9. Do your books get scruffy quickly?	2
10. Are you often late for your lessons?	2
11. Are you usually quiet in class?	1
12. Do you nearly always put your hand up if a teacher asks a question?	3
13. Do you sometimes daydream?	1
14. Have you nearly always got a pen or biro with you?	2
15. Have you been punished by a teacher quite often?	2
16. Do you always do your homework?	2
17. Have you been in any fights in school?	2

RELIABILITY AND VALIDITY: The validity of the scale was established by comparing scale scores with an overall assessment of school adjustment supplied by teachers. When the same children were assessed by different teachers, the scores showed a correlation of .53. Considering the inevitable differences that would occur anyway, this can be assumed to be an underestimate of the reliability. Scale definition was carried out by factor analyzing a sample of 274 children. Internal consistencies (measured by Cronbach's *alpha*) for the three subscales and the total scale obtained on a replicate sample (N = 288) were, respectively, .77 (studiousness), .77 (compliance), .60 (teacher contact), and .86 (total adjustment score).

BIBLIOGRAPHY:

Bennett, S. N., and Youngman, M. B. "Personality and Behavior in School." *British Journal of Educational Psychology,* 1973, *43,* 228-233.

Brennan, T., and Youngman, M. B. "Numerical Taxonomy: A New Technique for the Study of the Classroom—and an Illustrative Example." Paper presented at the British Psychological Society annual conference. Exeter, England, April 1971.

Youngman, M. B. "Behavior Assessments and Their Relation to School Performances." Unpublished master's thesis. University of Lancaster, England, 1969.

CHECKLIST FOR THE CLASSIFICATION
OF SCHOOL-AGED MALADJUSTED CHILDREN

AUTHOR: Ted L. Christiansen

AGE: Grades 1 to 12

VARIABLE: Maladjustment

TYPE OF MEASURE: Checklist

SOURCE FROM WHICH MEASURE MAY BE OBTAINED: See Christiansen (1967).

DESCRIPTION OF MEASURE: The thirty-seven items of the checklist are statements of behavior that may be judged to be negative in nature. It is intended for use by the classroom teacher to identify cases of serious maladjustment in the classroom and to identify those children who can profit from psychological evaluation. It serves as an appropriate screening device for identifying maladjustment when the teacher uses certain criteria as guides. The most important criteria to consider are the number, kind, and frequency of negative behaviors exhibited by the child.

As examples, the first twenty items of the checklist are given below.

1. Underachievement in school that is not related to physiologic or other logical causes.
2. Chronic displays of unhappiness or depression.
3. Destroys the property of others.
4. Frequently lies or boasts.
5. Often steals things.
6. Disrupts normal classroom procedures constantly.
7. Frequent absence or tardiness for which no physiologic or other sound reason can be found.
8. Relates poorly to peers in cooperative situations.
9. Shows withdrawal characteristics such as excessive timidity or quietness.
10. Daydreams frequently.
11. Shows unusual anxiety, fearfulness, or tenseness.
12. Shows a preference for working and playing alone.
13. Highly sensitive to the reactions and criticisms of others.
14. Tires easily or appears to be drowsy much of the time.
15. Has an unkempt or slovenly appearance.
16. Tries too hard to please others.
17. Constantly strives to gain the attention and approval of others.
18. Overly concerned with a sense of order and consistency. Tends to resist change.
19. Shows fear of getting dirty.
20. Displays facial or other bodily twitchings or tics.

RELIABILITY AND VALIDITY: None reported.

BIBLIOGRAPHY:

Christiansen, T. L. "A Method of Identifying Maladjusted Children in the Classroom." *Mental Hygiene,* 1967, *51,* 574-575.

COPING ANALYSIS SCHEDULE FOR
EDUCATIONAL SETTINGS (CASES)

AUTHOR: Robert L. Spaulding

AGE: Preschool through high school

VARIABLE: Classroom behavior of students and preschoolers

TYPE OF MEASURE: Behavior category system

SOURCE FROM WHICH MEASURE MAY BE OBTAINED: Robert L. Spaulding, Room 201, Education Building, San Jose State University, 125 South Seventh Street, San Jose, California 95192. Cost: $2.50 for materials, postage, and handling.

DESCRIPTION OF MEASURE: The Spaulding Coping Analysis Schedule for Educational Settings (CASES) was designed to measure the process of normal personality development and socialization occurring in the school environment. The original categories were couched in terms reflective of ego psychology. The work of Lois Murphy and her associates was basic to the category system in its first form (Murphy, 1956). The ego terminology was eventually replaced by behavioral descriptions, and the system was augmented to include references to the values and goals of the classroom teacher or the school authority in charge. In its present form it consists of thirteen basic categories with six of them subject to considerations of teacher expectation or values. The more active coping categories are grouped at one end and the more passive at the other, but the numerals do not represent a scale. The categories identify specific types of behaviors such as "hitting," "kicking," "annoying," "directing," "manipulating," "resisting," "delaying," "thoughtful," "helping," "task-oriented," "distracted," "daydreaming," and so on. The nineteen categories are grouped for scoring. By means of case studies augmented by factor analysis, eight "styles" of coping behavior were identified. The eight coping styles are identified by letters and descriptive terms as follows: A—aggressive, manipulative; B—nonconforming, resistant; C—withdrawn; D—distractible; E—adult dependent; F—socially integrative; G—self-directed, task-oriented; and H—other-directed, conforming. Percentage scores or standard scores are obtained for each coping style, as well as an overall score based on weights assigned to percentage scores.

The brief form of CASES is given below.

1. *Aggressive Behavior*
   Direct attack: grabbing, pushing, hitting, pulling, kicking, name-calling; destroying property; smashing, tearing, breaking.
2. *Negative (Inappropriate) Attention-Getting Behavior*
   Annoying, bothering, whining, loud talking (unnecessarily), attention-getting, aversive, noise-making, belittling, criticizing.
3. *Manipulating, Controlling, and Directing Others*
   Manipulating, bossing, commanding, directing, enforcing rules, conniving, wheedling, controlling.
4. *Resisting*
   Resisting, delaying; passive-aggressive behavior; pretending to conform, conforming to the letter but not the spirit; defensive checking.

5. *Self-Directed Activity*
   Productive working; reading, writing, constructing with interest; self-directed dramatic play (with high involvement).

6. *Paying Close Attention; Thinking, Pondering*
   Listening attentively, watching carefully; concentrating on a story being told, a film being watched, a record played; thinking, pondering, reflecting.

7. *Integrative Sharing and Helping*
   Contributing ideas, interests, materials, helping; responding by showing feelings (laughing, smiling, etc.) in audience situations; initiating conversation.

8. *Integrative Social Interaction*
   Mutual give and take, cooperative behavior, integrative social behavior; studying or working together where participants are on a par.

9. *Integrative Seeking and Receiving Support, Assistance and Information*
   Bidding or asking teachers or significant peers for help, support, sympathy, affection, etc., being helped; receiving assistance.

10. *Following Directions Passively and Submissively*
    Doing assigned work without enthusiasm or great interest; submitting to requests; answering directed questions; waiting for instructions as directed.

11. *Observing Passively*
    Visual wandering with short fixations; watching others work; checking on noises or movements; checking on activities of adults or peers.

12. *Responding to Internal Stimuli*
    Daydreaming; sleeping; rocking or fidgeting (not in transaction with external stimuli).

13. *Physical Withdrawal or Passive Avoidance*
    Moving away, hiding; avoiding transactions by movement away or around; physical wandering avoiding involvement in activities.

Note: Categories *3, 5, 6, 7, 8,* and *9* are further coded as *a* or *b* in structured settings to indicate appropriate or inappropriate timing or location of activity (based on the teacher's expectations for the setting). Example: *5a* would be recorded when a child was painting during art period (when painting was one of the expected activities). Painting during "story time" or in an academic setting would normally be coded *5b*. The code *b* represents behaving in a certain coping category at the "wrong" time or place. What is "right" or "wrong" is based on the values and goals of the teacher or authority responsible in a given situation. A child might be sharing with another child in an integrative manner (7) some bit of information the teacher regarded as highly inappropriate. It would be coded as *7b* since it was an integrative act of sharing occurring at the "wrong" time in the "wrong" place, from the point of view of the teacher.

RELIABILITY AND VALIDITY: The reliability of the data is based upon several factors, such as the number of observations made per subject and the range of school setting covered by the sampling plan. Observer bias is another factor to be considered. In studies completed in the past, observer reliability was estimated by *in situ* observations of a single subject by two observers with synchronized stop watches. The number of exact agreements was used as an index of observer reliability. These estimates ranged from the low 80s to 100-percent agreement, depending upon the complexity of the setting and the subject's activity. Settings were selected to represent the full range of school environments in most studies, and data were gathered over a ten-day period with a minimum of fifty tallies (observations) per pupil. Content validity was indicated in most studies to date by the extent of agreement (regarding the behavior styles) among teachers trained in clinical psychology and teachers knowledgeable regarding the school settings observed and the subjects involved. Additional validity is suggested by correlational studies in which specific behavior styles were found significantly related to academic achievement (Spaulding and Papageorgiou, 1972; Papageorgiou, 1973).

BIBLIOGRAPHY:

Murphy, L. *Personality in Young Children. Vol. I: Methods for the Study of Personality in Young Children.* New York: Basic Books, 1956.
Palmo, A. J., and Kunzniar, J. "Modification of Behavior Through Group Counseling and Consultation." *Elementary School Guidance and Counseling,* 1972, *6,* 258-262.
Papageorgiou, M. R. "Using CASES in Measuring Effects of Compensatory Education." Article based on a paper presented at the annual meeting of the American Educational Research Association, New Orleans, Louisiana, February 1973.
Sibley, S. A., Abbott, M. S., and Cooper, B. P. "Modification of the Classroom Behavior of a Disadvantaged Kindergarten Boy by Social Reinforcement and Isolation." *Journal of Experimental Child Psychology,* 1969, *7,* 203-219.
Spaulding, R. L. *Classroom Behavior Analysis and Treatment.* San Jose, California: San Jose State College, 1970.
Spaulding, R. L., and Papageorgiou, M. R. *Effects of Early Educational Intervention in the Lives of Disadvantaged Children.* Final report, California State University, San Jose, Project No. 1-I-124, Contract No. OEC-9-72-0005(057), National Center for Educational Research and Development, June 1972.

DEGREE OF INCAPACITATION SCALE

AUTHOR: Phyllis F. Herson

AGE: Elementary and secondary school teachers

VARIABLE: Psychological incapacitation of children

TYPE OF MEASURE: Thurstone scale

SOURCE FROM WHICH MEASURE MAY BE OBTAINED: Phyllis F. Herson, M.A.T. Program, Trinity College, Washington, D.C. 20017.

DESCRIPTION OF MEASURE: Scoring weights on the eighteen agree-disagree items comprising the scale range from 1 to 7, so that together they comprise a Thurstone equal-appearing interval scale. A subject's score is the arithmetic mean of the scale weights of the items with which he agrees. Incapacitation is conceptualized as including the degree to which the statement implies a condition in which the behavior is "sick" or abnormal, the prognosis is poor, the person is in need of specialist-type help, and the person has adverse effects upon his peers.

The eighteen items of the scale, with scale weights, are given below.

4.88 1. A pupil like this would require too much of a regular teacher's time and attention.

5.23 2. A pupil like this will probably get worse without special help.

2.29 3. What this pupil needs most are new learning experiences or new approaches to solving his/her problems.

2.38 4. A pupil like this is probably immature or having problems in growing up.

5.13 5. A pupil like this will have a bad effect upon the progress or well-being of the other members of the class.

5.13 6. Most regular classroom teachers do not have enough training to handle a pupil like this.

7.00 7. A pupil like this should be institutionalized.

5.71 8. A pupil like this will probably have trouble throughout the rest of his/her schooling.

1.42 9. It isn't very unusual for pupils of this age to act like this.

1.92 10. There is a good chance that this problem will be overcome even if nothing is done about it.

5.40 11. A pupil like this should be seeing a specialist regularly.

5.83 12. A pupil like this should be in special classes or in some special type of school.

3.42 13. The kind of training or experiences this pupil has had are probably the cause of the problem.

4.13 14. The regular teacher should consult with a specialist about the best way to handle a pupil like this.

5.13 15. A pupil like this will probably have trouble in later life.

5.25 16. A teacher would probably do more harm than good if he/she attempted to help this pupil himself/herself.

3.20 17. A pupil like this needs special help from the teacher.

3.25 18. A pupil like this probably needs help through a difficult period.

RELIABILITY AND VALIDITY: The scale was developed by presenting the statements to a group of expert judges (eleven Ph.D.-level professional counselors at the University of Maryland) who were asked to rank each of the items along a 7-point continuum on degree of incapacitation implied. Reliability was supported by a pilot study involving nineteen graduate students enrolled in a course in remedial reading. A reliability coefficient of .88 was obtained by the test-retest method with a one-week interval. Further validity was established through another pilot study in which nineteen students in a graduate-level mental-health class rated a hypothetical paranoid schizophrenic significantly higher on the scale than a depressed neurotic. In the author's study, the scale yielded significant differences between students described by mental-health diagnostic labels and those described by behavioral descriptions.

BIBLIOGRAPHY:

Herson, P. F. "Biasing Effects of Diagnostic Labels and Sex of Pupil on Teachers' Views of Pupils' Mental Health." *Journal of Educational Psychology*, 1974, *66*, 117-122.

FEHRENBACH SENTENCE-COMPLETION TEST

AUTHOR: Alice R. Fehrenbach

AGE: Grades 7 to 12

VARIABLE: Personality adjustment

TYPE OF MEASURE: Sentence-completion test

SOURCE FROM WHICH MEASURE MAY BE OBTAINED: Alice R. Fehrenbach, 3232 S. Josephine Street, Denver, Colorado 80201. Duplicating and mailing costs.

DESCRIPTION OF MEASURE: The Fehrenbach Sentence-Completion Test consists of 100 sentence stems. The type of completion discriminates between students with potential leadership qualities in terms of outstanding adjustment, those within the average range, and those who may become troublesome in the classroom. Scores are weighted in terms of omissions, evasions, reverse identifications, and other specific responses discussed in the manual accompanying the test. These "specific responses" were based upon statistical frequency, not clinical opinion. The instrument is designed to be used with groups as well as with individuals and by teachers as well as psychologists, social workers, and other personnel with clinical background. It is directed as much to classroom management based on knowledge of emotional responses of students in a class as it is to differentiating among the three groups named above. Spanish-language versions of both the child and adolescent forms of the test are also available.

As examples, the first twenty of the 100 sentence stems are given below.

1. Gary was happiest when
2. She likes nothing better than to
3. When caught behind the enemy lines
4. Nothing annoyed Bob more than
5. Mike's fondest ambition
6. When Kay saw her teacher coming
7. Bill got irritated when they
8. My greatest fear is
9. When told to keep in his place, Harry
10. What Emily regretted most was
11. I admire
12. Nothing made Harry more furious than
13. She was uneasy because
14. John thought that his future
15. If I were a teacher, I
16. A person's life
17. When he saw that the others were doing better than he, John
18. Every time she wasn't invited, Ruth
19. When I was little, I
20. I try hard

RELIABILITY AND VALIDITY: The test was administered to three separate groups of students in three schools of differing socioeconomic and cultural backgrounds. The children were not randomly drawn but chosen by school personnel because of a wide range of intellectual ability and control problems in two schools. In the third group, the experimental school, 100 students were randomly drawn from a total seventh-grade population. *Chi*-square was used as a test of the null hypothesis. Scores above 35 and below 35 served as categories. The judgments of administrators regarding "troublesome" and "adjusted" determined the other two categories. Yates correction for continuity was used. *Chi*-square was equal to 27.3, significant at the 1-percent level. Since the decision of administrators was forced, a *phi* coefficient was employed as a measure of association. *Phi* was found to be .74. Maximal *phi* was computed as an aid to interpretation; it was .95 in the standardization group. Of the 100 stems, thirty-six were found to have discriminatory power. The remainder were retained in order to provide an emotional cushion for the student.

BIBLIOGRAPHY:

Thompson, A. "The School Psychologist Goes into the Classroom." *School Psychologist,* 1973, *28* (2), 20-22.
Schubert, D. G., and Togerson, T. L. *Improving the Reading Problem.* (3rd ed.) Dubuque, Iowa: Brown, 1972.

THE FLINT INFANT SECURITY SCALE

AUTHOR: Betty Margaret Flint

AGE: Birth to 2 years

VARIABLE: Mental health of infants

TYPE OF MEASURE: Checklist

SOURCE FROM WHICH MEASURE MAY BE OBTAINED: The Guidance Center, Faculty of Education, University of Toronto, 1000 Yonge Street, Toronto, Canada.

DESCRIPTION OF MEASURE: The Flint Infant Security Scale is a revision of the measure appearing under the title Toronto Infant Scale on page 232, Handbook I. This revised scale as a total of seventy-four items descriptive of the behavior of infants. The items have been selected from more than a hundred original behavioral descriptions. Gradual elimination through repeated trial runs and evaluations has led to the present selection of items that seem to be the most highly significant for the measurement of security. The test items describe a range of behavior embracing a variety of life experiences. These experiences encompass the life space of most infants. However, some infants are more protected from experiences than are others. Hence the life space of some infants is more restricted than the range covered by the scale. In such cases, not all the items on the scale would necessarily apply. The assessment is made through interview with a mother (or caretaker) while the baby is informally observed as he plays in the same room. In administering the test, the examiner encountering an item that does not describe some aspect of the child's present experience or life space deletes that item. In this way the child who has limited experiences is not unfairly penalized in the scoring.

As examples, two of the seventy-four items are given below.

	Secure	*Deputy Agent and Regression*

Eating

Accepts new foods readily	Protests when new foods are offered
eats them with enjoyment	refuses to taste
eats them with caution	turns away
eats them despite dislike of them	pushes mother's hand
	spits out
	cries

Unfamiliar Situation

Cooperates when unfamiliar person is in charge at meal time (baby-sitter, visitor)	Uncooperative unless familiar person is in charge at meal time
eats with caution	refuses to eat
eats with usual appetite	whines and protests

RELIABILITY AND VALIDITY: Validity of the scale was established by measurement of a group of babies whose dramatic changes in living arrangements through time would be likely to effect measurable changes in their security. These children, comprising a group of young babies in foster care and awaiting transfer to their adoptive homes, were assessed three times. It was anticipated that the security scores were likely to reflect a pattern: on the first test, relatively high scores; a drop in the second test as the result of change to the adoptive home; and a return to something approximating the first scores on the third test after five to six months' residence in their adoptive homes. The anticipated pattern was demonstrated. An analysis of variance showed a significant difference among the three groups of scores, and the least significant difference range test showed that scores in the foster home differed from the two adoptive-home scores. Reliability was tested by two sophisticated testers with an extensive knowledge of infants who assessed the same infants simultaneously. Nineteen infants were assessed three times each. Each test had seventy-four items that provided an opportunity for agreement or disagreement, and beyond this was the possibility of two other patterns of endorsement. Out of the four thousand opportunities for agreement or disagreement, only nine disagreements appeared. Hence reliability between testers is extremely high.

BIBLIOGRAPHY:

Flint, B. M. *The Security of Infants*. Toronto, Canada: University of Toronto Press, 1959.

Flint, B. M. *The Flint Infant Security Scale Manual*. Toronto, Canada: Guidance Center, Faculty of Education, University of Toronto, 1974.

HAHNEMANN HIGH SCHOOL BEHAVIOR
RATING SCALE (HHSB)

AUTHORS: George Spivack and Marshall Swift

AGE: Grades 7 to 12

VARIABLE: Achievement-related classroom behavior

TYPE OF MEASURE: Rating scale for use by teachers

SOURCE FROM WHICH MEASURE MAY BE OBTAINED: George Spivack and
Marshall Swift, Hahnemann Community Mental Health/Mental Retardation Center, 314
North Broad Street, Philadelphia, Pennsylvania 19102. Cost: Manual, $2.00; Scale, 25
at $.20 each; 50 at $.15 each; 200 at $.13 each; 500 at $.11 each.

DESCRIPTION OF MEASURE: The Hahnemann High School Behavior Rating Scale
(HHSB) was developed to measure overt classroom behaviors that reflect a student's
overall adaptation to the demands of the classroom setting and his subsequent academic achievement in that classroom. Separate factor analyses were carried out following the rating of a large pool of behaviors of normal and special-education (emotionally
disturbed) junior and senior high school students by their teachers. The separate
analyses revealed twelve factors common to both the normal and special class samples,
a thirteenth factor emerging only in the special class sample (verbal negativism). The
final HHSB scale consists of forty-five items. The teacher is asked to make each behavior rating based upon his subjective "norm" of what the average, normal child of the
same sex and age behaves like in the classroom. Teachers report no difficulty in carrying out the task. The scale takes an average of 8 minutes to complete, and a scoring
profile is attached for calculating factor scores and graphing them in standard score
units. The profile includes norms. A manual is available.

Five of the thirteen factors relate positively to academic success, describing the
degree to which the student demonstrates thoughts, work habits, and interpersonal behaviors suggesting a "producer" orientation. The factors are reasoning ability (the ability to apply principles, make inferences, and grasp concepts in the day-to-day classroom environment); originality (the youngster brings up unique or original ideas and
materials to be explored or discussed by the class); verbal interaction (positive verbal
involvement in class discussion); rapport (friendliness and responsibleness when interacting with the teacher); and anxious producer (the youngster who does more work
than assigned and exhibits an inner pressure to master each task before being satisfied
with his efforts). Eight factors negatively relate to academic success, suggesting certain
negative or disturbing feelings and behaviors. These factors include general anxiety (the
extent of display of outward nervousness during class, and flustering and "blocking"
when expressing ideas verbally); quiet-withdrawn (the degree to which the student is
uncommunicative, oblivious, and lacking in social interaction); poor work habits (for-
getting or misplacing of materials, and poor organization of work); lack of intellectual
independence (the youngster tends to quit when work is difficult, and reliance upon
the teacher and peers in order to complete work); dogmatic-inflexible (the degree to
which the youngster is closed to the opinions of others and shows a desire for quick
"black and white" answers); verbal negativism (the degree of negative and critical

verbal behavior exhibited in class); disturbance-restless (the level of restlessness, interference with the work of others, and the extent to which reprimand or control of the student's behavior is called forth in the teacher); and expressed inability (the degree to which the youngster says that too much work has been assigned or that he is not capable of doing the work assigned). Separate norms are available on a suburban group, derived from the initial factor-analytic study involving 882 ratings, and a center-city urban sample of 602 youngsters equally distributed over grades 7 to 12.

RELIABILITY AND VALIDITY: Both the original factor-analytic studies and subsequent urban studies revealed consistent and significant relationships between factor scores and teacher grades, this relationship independent of the issues of measured IQ. Factor scores have been found to significantly differentiate between different diagnostic groups of disturbed youngsters but bear no relationship to sex of student. No data on test-retest or rater reliability are available on the HHSB.

BIBLIOGRAPHY:

Spivack, G., and Swift, M. *Patterns of Disturbed Classroom Behavior.* Project no. 2165. Final report to U.S. Office of Education, Washington, D.C., 1967.

Spivack, G., and Swift, M. "The Classroom Behavior of Children: A Critical Review of Teacher-Administered Rating Scales." *Journal of Special Education,* 1972, *7,* 55-89.

Spivack, G., Swift, M., and Prewitt, J. "Syndromes of Disturbed Classroom Behavior: A Behavioral Diagnostic System for Elementary Schools." *Journal of Special Education,* 1971, *5,* 269-292.

Swift, M., and Back, L. "A Method for Aiding Teachers of the Troubled Adolescent." *Adolescence,* 1973, *29,* 1-16.

Swift, M., and Spivack, G. "Achievement-Related Classroom Behavior of Secondary School Normal and Disturbed Students." *Exceptional Children,* 1969, *36,* 99-104.

Swift, M., and Spivack, G. "Academic Success and Overt Classroom Behavior in Urban Secondary Schools." *Exceptional Children,* 1973, *39,* 392-399.

Swift, M., and Spivack, G. "Patterns of Disturbed Classroom Behaviors of Normal and Delinquent Girls." *Journal of Crime and Delinquency,* 1973, *32,* 31-45.

Swift, M., and Spivack, G. *Alternative Teaching Strategies: Helping Behaviorally Troubled Children Achieve.* Champaign, Illinois: Research Press, 1974.

Prepared by Marshall Swift

HUREWITZ QUICK-SCORING BEHAVIOR RATING SCALE

AUTHOR: Paul Hurewitz

AGE: Prekindergarten to college

VARIABLE: (1) Social habits, (2) relationship with adults, (3) relationship with parents, (4) emotional response, (5) work habits and achievement, (6) general physical appearance and health, (7) use of crafts and creative media

TYPE OF MEASURE: Rating scale

SOURCE FROM WHICH MEASURE MAY BE OBTAINED: Send a self-addressed stamped envelope to Paul Hurewitz, Education Department, Herbert H. Lehman College, Bedford Park Boulevard West, Bronx, New York 10468.

DESCRIPTION OF MEASURE: Each of the seven factors or areas of adjustment is measured by several items. This scale assumes that each rater is internally consistent in rating a child's behavior. This verifiable assumption allows each rater to decide the degree of intensity of a behavior symptom without having to read a long list of qualifications. The bias of the rater becomes an important part of the rating, as the bias may reflect the actual reactions of the rater to the child. If the observer does not have sufficient information about a category, it is left blank. One can thus note if an area has insufficient data to make the category a reliable one. This scale reflects changes in behavior in a positive or negative way, since the rater is asked to note specifically if there have been any changes in behavior. The instrument is also self-ratable by the parents. This allows for a multidimensional view of the child by people who know or work with the child. The scale takes about 5 to 10 minutes to complete. The author and colleagues have used this measure to evaluate programs and intervention services. It has also been used in education programs for school professionals to develop observation skill and understanding of adjustment problems.

As examples, the first eight items of the social habits category and the total eight items of work habits and achievements are given below. They are to be rated from −1 to +3 "behavior deteriorating (extreme response)" to "excellent improvement (almost always)."

A. Social Habits
1. Desire to relate to others and be accepted.
2. Acceptance by others.
3. Level of social maturity.
4. Response to social group controls and norms.
5. Degree of self-confidence in social relationships.
6. Sharing things, bringing things to class.
7. Accepting social and work responsibilities.
8. Social leadership.

E. Work Habits and Achievement
1. Degree of organization in work and study habits.
2. Completion of work.

3. Degree of self-confidence in trying new work.
4. Attitudes toward work.
5. Subject improvement.
6. General attention span.
7. Response to special attention and help.
8. Use of potential

RELIABILITY AND VALIDITY: Over one thousand students and teachers have used these scales. The categories were developed with teachers and other professionals, and they were found to be observable and ratable. Each item had to meet a test of face validity in order to be included. The validity and reliability of a category in this test should be questioned if half the items in the category are not ratable by that person. An index of validity may be obtained for each rater by determining the percentage of items the rater is able to observe.

BIBLIOGRAPHY: None reported.

LEVEL OF ANALYSIS BATTERY
FOR HIGH SCHOOL STUDENTS

AUTHORS: Daniel W. Edwards and Richard Rice

AGE: Junior high and high school students

VARIABLE: Social and emotional development

TYPE OF MEASURE: Varied self-report formats: 5-point scales, 7-point scales, and semantic differential scales

SOURCE FROM WHICH MEASURE MAY BE OBTAINED: Daniel W. Edwards, University of California at Davis, Sacramento Medical Center, 4430 "V" Street, Sacramento, California 95817.

DESCRIPTION OF MEASURE: This battery involves twelve composite scores: Organizational Level—school change, perceived opportunity, school identification, positiveness of principal, counselors, and teachers; Social Level—positiveness of other students, change social self; Personality Level—change physical self, initiative, depression, and social problems. These twelve measures represent half of the major dependent variables used in a longitudinal study of the social and emotional development of high school boys (Edwards, 1971). They are designed to allow annual assessment of major adaptational changes that occur through the interaction of varied explorational preferences and varied high school environments.
　　Examples of items are given below.

School Change: "How important is it to change the classes I'm in?" (7-point response format)

Perceived Opportunity: "How much chance does this school give you to be with friends and enjoy each other's company?" (5-point response format)

School Identification: "How much do you feel part of this school?" (5-point response format)

Positiveness of School Authorities: "The principal of this school is" (7-point semantic differential, for example, 1, strict; 7, easygoing)

Positiveness of Other Students: "The students in this school are" (7-point semantic differential, for example, 7, friendly; 1, unfriendly)

Change Social Self: "How important is it to change myself as a student?" (7-point response format)

Change Physical Self: "How important is it to change how tall I am?" (7-point response format)

Initiative: "I take risks where I might fail." (7-point never-often continuum)

Depression: "I have trouble concentrating on something until it's finished." (7-point never-often continuum)

Social Problems: "I have a hard time making friends" (7-point never-often continuum)

A total of seventy-two items are used to create the twelve composite scores.

RELIABILITY AND VALIDITY: The twelve scales are composed of highly intercorrelated items (average item-total rs range from .59 to .79). Internal consistency as assessed by coefficient *alpha* ranges from .66 to .87. The primary use of these scales as dependent measures has precluded convergent and divergent validity studies, although some analysis is currently under way on the longitudinal data on high school students.

BIBLIOGRAPHY:

Edwards, D. W. "Exploration and the High School Experience: A Study of Tenth Grade Boys' Perceptions of Themselves, Their Peers, and Their Schools." Unpublished doctoral dissertation. University of Michigan, Ann Arbor, 1971.

Edwards, D. W. "Coping Preference, Adaptive Roles, and Varied High School Environments: A Search for Person-Environment Transactions." In D. Adelson (Ed.), *Community Psychology Series.* New York: Behavioral Publications (in press).

Edwards, D. W. "Persons and Environments." In D. Adelson (Ed.), *Community Psychology Series.* New York: Behavioral Publications (in press).

LOUISVILLE BEHAVIOR CHECK LIST

AUTHOR: Lovick C. Miller

AGE: Form E1, 3 to 6 years; Form E2, 7 to 13 years

VARIABLE: Parent ratings of children's deviant and prosocial behaviors

TYPE OF MEASURE: Checklist

SOURCE FROM WHICH MEASURE MAY BE OBTAINED: Lovick C. Miller, Child Psychiatry Research Center, 608 South Jackson Street, Louisville, Kentucky 40202. Cost: Test booklets, $5.00 per 100; manual, $6.00; plus postage and handling.

DESCRIPTION OF MEASURE: This measure contains 164 yes/no items in each form covering the entire range of deviant behavior occurring in children between ages 3 and 13. Eight scales constructed from a factor analysis of a clinic population sample, three summary scales from a second-order factoring, and eight additional clinical scales are available for special purposes. General population norms and clinic norms are provided in terms of standard scores. Family income has a decided effect on amount of deviant behavior reported, as well as IQ of child, but age, sex, and race have minimal effects. Interpretations can be based on ideographic scanning or multidimensional profile analysis. The instrument can be scored by hand or optical scan. The manual provides administrative and scoring procedures as well as a summary of research.

As examples, the first ten of the 164 items from Form E1 of the checklist are given below. The parent answers each item "true" or "false."

 1. Cries easily.
 2. Whines and complains.
 3. Shy.
 4. Dependent; leans heavily on others.
 5. Generally considerate and able to share.
 6. Demands that parents do what wants done.
 7. Cruel with animals or people in a shocking way.
 8. Refers to his (her) things as "mine" or "my. . . ."
 9. Finds it hard to talk with others.
10. Wets the bed at night at least once a month.

RELIABILITY AND VALIDITY: Split-half and test-retest reliabilities of factor scales range from .80 to .97. Validity studies indicate that scales separate general population samples from clinic samples as well as samples of phobic, aggressive, learning disability, and autistic children from one another. Discriminant analysis indicates that each of these syndromes is defined by multiple dimensions. A special scale, School Disturbance Predictor Scale, has a predictive validity of .44.

BIBLIOGRAPHY:

Bloch, J. P. "Agreement Between Parents' and Teachers' Ratings of Childhood Emotional Adjustment." Unpublished master's thesis. University of Louisville, Kentucky, 1971.

Byassee, J. "Interaction Patterns of Autistic Family Triads." Unpublished master's thesis. University of Louisville, Kentucky, 1973.

Hampe, E., Miller, L. C., Noble, H., and Barrett, C. L. "Phobic Children One and Two Years Posttreatment." *Journal of Abnormal Psychology,* 1973, *82,* 446-453.

Miller, L. C. "Dimensions of Psychopathology in Middle Childhood." *Psychological Reports,* 1967, *21,* 897-903.

Miller, L. C. "Louisville Behavior Check List for Males, 6-12 Years of Age." *Psychological Reports,* 1967, *21,* 885-896.

Miller, L. C. "School Behavior Check List: An Inventory of Deviant Behavior for Elementary School Children." *Journal of Consulting and Clinical Psychology,* 1972, *38,* 134-144.

Miller, L. C., Barrett, C. L., Hampe, E., and Noble, H. "Revised Anxiety Scales for the Louisville Behavior Checklist." *Psychological Reports,* 1971, *29,* 503-511.

Miller, L. C., Barrett, C. L., Hampe, E., and Noble, H. "Comparison of Reciprocal Inhibition, Psychotherapy, and Waiting List Control for Phobic Children." *Journal of Abnormal Psychology,* 1972, *79,* 269-279.

Miller, L. C., Hampe, E., Barrett, C. L., and Noble, H. "Children's Deviant Behavior Within the General Population." *Journal of Consulting and Clinical Psychology,* 1971, *37,* 16-22.

Miller, L. C., Hampe, E., Barrett, C. L., and Noble, H. "Test-Retest Reliability of Parent Ratings of Children's Deviant Behavior." *Psychological Reports,* 1972, *31,* 249-250.

Miller, L. C., Hampe, E., Barrett, C. L., and Noble, H. *Method Factors Associated with Assessment of Child Behavior: Fact or Artifact?* Unpublished manuscript. Child Psychiatry Research Center Bulletin no. 1, 1973.

OFFER SELF-IMAGE QUESTIONNAIRE FOR ADOLESCENTS

AUTHOR: Daniel Offer

AGE: 12 to 19 years

VARIABLE: Adjustment

TYPE OF MEASURE: Self-administered questionnaire

SOURCE FROM WHICH MEASURE MAY BE OBTAINED: Daniel Offer, Michael Reese Hospital, 2959 South Ellis Avenue, Chicago, Illinois 60616. Cost: $.50.

DESCRIPTION OF MEASURE: This is a self-descriptive personality test of adjustment for teenage boys and girls between the ages of 12 and 19. The questionnaire has 130 items that cover eleven important areas in the psychological world of the teenager. The subjects are asked to rate themselves on a 6-point scale on each item from "Describes me very well" to "Does not describe me at all." The eleven scales are: impulse control, emotional tone, body- and self-image, social attitudes, morals, sexual attitudes, family relations, external mastery, vocational and educational goals, psychopathology, and superior adjustment.

As examples, the first ten of the 130 items of the boys' form of the questionnaire are given below.

1. I carry many grudges.
2. When I am with people I am afraid that someone will make fun of me.
3. Most of the time I think that the world is an exciting place to live in.
4. I think that I will be a source of pride to my parents in the future.
5. I would not hurt someone just for the "heck of it."
6. The recent changes in my body have given me some satisfaction.
7. Most people my age have scary dreams once in a while.
8. I "lose my head" easily.
9. My parents are almost always on the side of someone else, e.g., my brother or sister.
10. The opposite sex finds me a bore.

RELIABILITY AND VALIDITY: The questionnaire has been administered to over ten thousand subjects including male and female, younger and older teenagers, normal vs. psychiatrically disturbed and delinquent adolescents, urban and suburban, in fifteen different communities in the United States and Australia. The questionnaire discriminates effectively between the above groups. There was a high degree of consistency across samples for any specific item and scale. The interclass correlations (*alphas*) were consistent with those for the item-total analysis, suggesting the internal consistency of the scales (with the exception of the sexual attitudes scale). Analysis of variance and *t*-test showed that the questionnaire discriminated well between the various samples tested.

BIBLIOGRAPHY:

Offer, D. *The Psychological World of the Teenager.* New York: Harper & Row, 1973.
Offer, D., and Howard, K. I. "An Empirical Analysis of the Offer Self-Image Questionnaire for Adolescents." *Archives of General Psychiatry,* 1972, *27,* 529-533.

PERSONAL-SOCIAL BEHAVIOR RATING SCALE

AUTHOR: Walter Emmerich

AGE: Preschool

VARIABLE: Personal-social behavior

TYPE OF MEASURE: Rating scales

SOURCE FROM WHICH MEASURE MAY BE OBTAINED: See Emmerich (1971).

DESCRIPTION OF MEASURE: The instrument consists of twenty-one bipolar scales, 127 unipolar scales, and a manual of unipolar scale definitions and examples. The bipolar scales assess broad personality dimensions. Despite some overlap in their meanings, this rather large number of general dimensions was included to help clarify the structure of the personal-social domain at its more abstract levels. The unipolar scales assess more specific categories of behavior, including social motives (e.g., aggression), coping mechanisms (e.g., ignores frustration), and activities or interests (e.g., gross motor behavior). Each bipolar scale contains 7 points and calls for a judgment on the relative strengths of the attributes defining each pole. Each unipolar scale calls for an estimate of a behavior's frequency of occurrence during a specified period of observation, based upon the following 4-point scale: 0, totally absent; 1, occurred once; 2, occurred more than once, but not continuously; 3, continuous during the observation period. There are important advantages to including both bipolar and unipolar scales in the same system of measurement. This strategy provides empirical links between the more global dimensions of personality and specific behavioral cues. Bipolar scales are not explicitly defined by the manual, but judges are instructed to rate a given child on the unipolar scales immediately prior to rating the child on the bipolar scales and to use information contained in the unipolar ratings when making bipolar judgments. Thus correlations between these two types of scales indicate which behavioral cues (unipolar scale definitions) are utilized by judges in arriving at each bipolar rating.

The typical procedure for rating a child is as follows. A pair of raters simultaneously observes a target child continuously for 25 to 30 minutes during a "free play" period when adults in the classroom minimally structure the child's activities. Immediately after this observation period the two observers leave the classroom and independently rate the child on the complete set of scales. The manual of scale definitions and examples provides guidelines for rating the behavior of the child on each of the 127 unipolar scales.

Scale definitions and examples for the first two scales are given below.

Attribute: 1. Seeks physical affection from adult.
                  2. Seeks physical affection from other child.
Definition: Actively seeks physical affection from another.
Examples: a. Child hangs onto teacher.
                  b. Child goes to teacher and clearly wants to be picked up or hugged.
                  c. Child seeks to hold teacher's hand.
                  d. Target child hangs onto another child.
Qualifications: Merely being receptive to affection initiated by others is not included
                  here.

RELIABILITY AND VALIDITY: Pearson correlations were computed on all scales for rater pairs who observed at least twenty children simultaneously within the same period (fall or spring). These interrater reliability estimates are reported for each site and period in Emmerich (1971), Appendix E. For the twenty-one bipolar scales as a set, the median of the medians across pairs, sites, and periods was .63. For the 127 unipolar scales as a set, this overall median was .74.

BIBLIOGRAPHY:

Emmerich, W. "Continuity and Stability in Early Social Development." *Child Development,* 1964, *35,* 311-332.

Emmerich, W. "Continuity and Stability in Early Social Development: II. Teacher Ratings." *Child Development,* 1966, *37,* 17-27.

Emmerich, W. "Personality Development and Concepts of Structure." *Child Development,* 1968, *39,* 671-690.

Emmerich, W. "Children's Personal and Social Development." In *Disadvantaged Children and Their First School Experiences: Theoretical Considerations and Measurement Strategies.* 2 Vols. Princeton, New Jersey: Educational Testing Service, 1968. Prepared under Contract OEO 4206 and Grant CG-8256, U.S. Office of Economic Opportunity, Washington, D.C. ERIC document no. ED 037 486.

Emmerich, W. "Models of Continuity and Change in Development." In *Disadvantaged Children and Their First School Experiences: From Theory to Operations.* Princeton, New Jersey: Educational Testing Service, 1969. Prepared under Grant H-8256, U.S. Department of Health, Education and Welfare, Washington, D.C. ERIC document no. ED 043 397.

Emmerich, W. "Structure and Development of Personal-Social Behaviors in Preschool Settings." In *Disadvantaged Children and Their First School Experiences: From Theory to Operations.* Princeton, New Jersey: Educational Testing Service, 1971. Prepared under Grant H-8256, U.S. Department of Health, Education and Welfare.

Emmerich, W., and Wilder, G. "Classroom Observation Rating Scale (Personality)." In *Disadvantaged Children and Their First School Experiences: From Theory to Operations.* Princeton, New Jersey: Educational Testing Service, 1969. Prepared under Grant H-8256, U.S. Department of Health, Education and Welfare. ERIC document no. 043 397.

Prepared by Orval G. Johnson

PRESCHOOL BEHAVIOR QUESTIONNAIRE (PBQ)

AUTHORS: Lenore Behar and Samuel Stringfield

AGE: 3 to 6 years

VARIABLE: Behavior patterns

TYPE OF MEASURE: Rating scale

SOURCE FROM WHICH MEASURE MAY BE OBTAINED: The Learning Institute of North Carolina, Durham, North Carolina 27705. Cost: Manual and 50 questionnaires, $4.00.

DESCRIPTION OF MEASURE: The Preschool Behavior Questionnaire (PBQ) is designed to be a quick screening instrument for the detection of emotional problems in children aged 3 to 6. The scale can be used by preschool or day-care teachers or others who have familiarity over time with a child in a group setting. The PBQ consists of thirty items. For each item, a rater is given three response choices: "Does not apply," "Applies sometimes," or "Applies frequently." The choices are weighted 0, 1, or 2, respectively. Summing the thirty item scores yields a total score on the behaviorally disturbed scale. In addition, the PBQ contains three factor-analytically derived subscales: Hostile-aggressive, Anxious-fearful, and Hyperactive-distractible, each of which is readily calculated on the PBQ sheet itself.

As examples, the first ten of the thirty items of the rating scale are given below.

1. Restless. Runs about or jumps up and down. Doesn't keep still.
2. Squirmy, fidgety child.
3. Destroys own or others' belongings.
4. Fights with other children.
5. Not much liked by other children.
6. Is worried. Worries about many things.
7. Tends to do things on his own, rather solitary.
8. Irritable, quick to "fly off the handle."
9. Appears miserable, unhappy, tearful, or distressed.
10. Has twitches, mannerisms, or tics of the face and body.

RELIABILITY AND VALIDITY: In the replication study interrater reliability (Pearson's r) was computed between teachers and their aides. This procedure yielded scores of .84, .81, .71, and .67 on the total scale and the three factors respectively. A test-retest reliability study over four months yielded scores of .87, .93, .60, and .94 for the total scale and three respective factors. Using a thirty-six-item scale, the authors arranged for the administration of the scale to 496 children in seven preschools intended for normal children in North Carolina and Oregon, and 102 preschoolers from across the United States who had been previously diagnosed as emotionally disturbed. On a Chi-square test, thirty-two of the thirty-six items discriminated significantly ($p \leqslant$ .01) between the groups. To further determine which items of those that differentiated between the groups would account for the greatest amount of between-group variance, a stepwise multiple regression was performed on the data. Next the data were factor analyzed and the three previously mentioned factors emerged. The scale was then shortened to thirty items by deleting items that did not (1) differentiate significantly on the Chi-square and (2) either rank in the highest twenty-five items on the stepwise multiple regression or have a loading of .55 or higher on one of the three varimax rotated factors. Using the shortened PBQ, a replication study was initiated. In this study all three factors differentiated between normal and disturbed groups ($p \leqslant$ .001), as did the overall scale ($p \leqslant$ .0001).

BIBLIOGRAPHY:

Behar, L., and Stringfield, S. "A Behavior Rating Scale for the Preschool Child." *Developmental Psychology,* 1974, *10,* 601-610.
Beuttel, S. H. "A Study of Mental Health Criteria and Indicators and a Program Eval-

uation Model." Unpublished doctoral dissertation. University of North Carolina, Chapel Hill, 1974.

Runquist, M. P. "Mental Health Consultation to Daycare Centers: An Experiment in Primary Prevention." Unpublished doctoral dissertation. University of Nebraska, Lincoln, 1975.

Prepared by Leonore Behar and Samuel Stringfield

PRESCHOOL INTERPERSONAL PROBLEM-SOLVING (PIPS) TEST

AUTHORS: Myrna B. Shure and George Spivack

AGE: 4 to 5 years

VARIABLE: Interpersonal problem-solving thinking skills

TYPE OF MEASURE: Test

SOURCE FROM WHICH MEASURE MAY BE OBTAINED: Myrna B. Shure, Head, Child Development Studies; George Spivack, Director, Division of Research and Evaluation, Community Mental Health/Mental Retardation Center, Department of Mental Health Sciences, Hahnemann Medical College and Hospital, Philadelphia, Pennsylvania 19102. Cost: Manual, $3.50; score sheets and test forms, $1.00 per package of 25; pictures, $2.50.

DESCRIPTION OF MEASURE: The Preschool Interpersonal Problem Solving (PIPS) Test measures the child's ability to conceptualize alternative solutions to real-life interpersonal problem situations and differentiates young children who differ in overt behavioral adjustment. The PIPS Test has two parts. The first presents a series of stories describing a problem between peers, each story depicting one child wanting to play with a toy another child has; for example, "Here is Johnny (show picture) and this is Jimmy (show picture). Johnny is playing with this truck (show picture) and has been playing with it for a long time. Now Jimmy wants a chance to play with this truck. What can Jimmy do (or say) so he can have a chance to play with the truck?" In the second part, each story depicts a child having damaged property, for example, a broken window. In each instance the child is asked, "What can (Peter) do so his Mommy will not be mad at him?" In both the peer-problem and the mother-problem situations, new characters are presented (with a new toy or act of damage to property) after each new relevant solution has been offered by the child, in order to maintain interest in the stories. Examples of the pictures are shown and the size and mounting described in the manual (Shure and Spivack, 1974b). Although the PIPS score of a child consists of the total number of different *solutions* given to peer- and mother-problem stories (the two correlate significantly), it is easier to first code them into categories. Spivack and Shure (1974) have used PIPS to evaluate their program to enhance interpersonal thinking skills of four-year-olds. (A similar kindergarten program is available from the authors.)

The examples given below are a portion of the twenty-seven categories (sixteen peer and eleven mother) and forty-four different, relevant solutions (twenty-six peer and eighteen mother) described in the scoring section of the manual.

Peer Problem

Category	*Solution*
Ask	"Can I hold it"
Fair, share, turns	"Play together"
Trade, bribe	"I'll give you my toys"
Force-grab	"Snatch it"
Force-attack	"Hit him"
Manipulate affect	"I won't be your friend"
Finagle	"Only us can play, no one else"

Mother Problem

Category	*Solution*
Truth-apology	"I'm sorry"
Manipulate affect	"Hug her and kiss her"
Replace	"Buy a new one"
Repair	"Fix it"
Authority-aid	"Get the window-fixer"
Finagle	"Pretend he's asleep and mother can't yell"

RELIABILITY AND VALIDITY: The most extensive research has been done with 4-year-old inner-city youngsters. Means, standard deviations, and cumulative percentages by behavior groups are presented in a manual for 469 4-year-old inner-city children, 220 boys and 249 girls over a four-year period. Consistently, adjusted youngsters offered a greater number and a wider range of alternative solutions to real-life problems than did their more impulsive or inhibited classmates. Further validity of the PIPS Test is evidenced by its relationship to socioeconomic status (comparing lower SES with middle SES group) and its relationship to specific interpersonal behaviors. Research findings also indicate the PIPS does not measure general cognitive "power" or IQ and is independent of general language skill. Subsequent data also show test validity in 5-year-old inner-city kindergarten children with respect to behavior-adjustment group, IQ, and language skills. One-week test-retest reliability for fifty-seven randomly selected youngsters yielded a reliability coefficient of .72 and a standard error of 1.27.

BIBLIOGRAPHY:

Shure, M. B., and Spivack, G. *A Mental Health Program for Kindergarten Children: Training Script.* Philadelphia, Pennsylvania: Community Mental Health/Mental Retardation Center, Department of Mental Health Services, Hahnemann Medical College and Hospital, 1974a.

Shure, M. B., and Spivack, G. *The PIPS Test: Manual.* Philadelphia, Pennsylvania: Community Mental Health/Mental Retardation Center, Department of Mental Health Sciences, Hahnemann Medical College and Hospital, 1974b.

Shure, M. B., Spivack, G., and Jaeger, M. A. "Problem-Solving Thinking and Adjustment Among Disadvantaged Preschool Children." *Child Development*, 1971, *42,* 1791-1803.

Spivack, G., and Shure, M. B. *Social Adjustment of Young Children: A Cognitive Approach to Solving Real-Life Problems.* San Francisco: Jossey-Bass, 1973.

PUPIL BEHAVIOR INVENTORY (PBI): EARLY EDUCATION VERSION

AUTHORS: Rosemary Sarri and Norma Radin

AGE: 3 to 8 years

VARIABLE: Behavior in class setting

TYPE OF MEASURE: Rating scale

SOURCE FROM WHICH MEASURE MAY BE OBTAINED: Norma Radin, School of Social Work, University of Michigan, Ann Arbor, Michigan 48104.

DESCRIPTION OF MEASURE: The inventory, a modification of a rating scale developed for secondary-school students (Vinter, Sarri, Vorwaller, and Schaefer, 1966) contains fifty-four behaviors rated on a 5-point scale from "Very frequently" to "Very infrequently." A factor analysis of the instrument was performed based on 279 students, 4 to 8 years of age, at least half of whom were lower class. The name given to each factor and the items with the highest loadings are as follows: (1) Classroom Misconduct—"Influences other toward troublemaking"; (2) Creative Inquisitiveness—"Asks questions"; (3) Good Student Behavior—"Shows flexibility"; (4) Teacher Dependence —"Seeks teacher's approval"; (5) Poor Physical Condition—"Inappropriate personal appearance"; (6) Academic Motivation—"Positive concern for own education"; (7) Antisocial Behavior—"Steals"; (8) Problematic Socioemotional State—"Appears depressed." A scoring mask for each factor is available to facilitate the scoring procedure if a computer is not available. The mean factor score is then readily calculated.

The PBI has been used to evaluate intervention programs when administered before and after the intervention to the same teachers (Radin, 1972). In addition, the inventory has been used to assess the child's school performance in studies relating parent socialization practices to child behavior in school (Radin, 1970, 1971, 1974). The PBI has also been used by school personnel to identify problems visible to the teacher and to reveal changes in teacher's attitudes over time in the absence of specific intervention programs (Vinter, Sarri, Vorwaller, and Schaefer, 1966). The fact that some factors, but not others, have shown change over time suggests that teachers can and do discriminate student behaviors and do not give merely global evaluations to the youngsters.

As examples, the first ten of the fifty-four items of the inventory are given below.

1. _____ Shows initiative
2. _____ Uses materials in a variety of ways
3. _____ Blames others for trouble
4. _____ Late for school
5. _____ Resistant to teacher
6. _____ Seeks teacher's approval
7. _____ Alert and interested in school work
8. _____ Can stay with one activity for some time
9. _____ Attempts to manipulate adults
10. _____ Asks questions

RELIABILITY AND VALIDITY: The instrument's reliability has not been assessed, but there is evidence of concurrent and construct validity. The factor Academic Motivation correlated significantly with independent measures of this predisposition assessed by trained psychologists (Radin, 1970, 1971). The same factor also correlated significantly with measures of the child's Binet IQ and observations of maternal nurturant behavior (Radin, 1970, 1971, 1974). When used as a pre- and posttest in a cognitively oriented preschool program, the factors Creative Inquisitiveness, Good Student Behavior, and Academic Motivation showed significant increases over the school year. These changes would have been hypothesized given the goals of the program.

BIBLIOGRAPHY:

Radin, N. "Childrearing Antecedents of Cognitive Development in Lower-Class Preschool Children." Unpublished doctoral dissertation. University of Michigan, Ann Arbor, 1970.

Radin, N. "Maternal Warmth, Achievement Motivation, and Cognitive Functioning in Lower-Class Preschool Children." *Child Development,* 1971, *42,* 1560-1565.

Radin, N. "Three Degrees of Maternal Involvement in a Preschool Program: Impact on Mothers and Children." *Child Development,* 1972, *43,* 1355-1364.

Radin, N. "Observed Maternal Behavior with Four-Year-Old Boys and Girls in Lower-Class Families." *Child Development,* 1974, *45,* 1126-1131.

Radin, N., and Sonquist, H. *The GALE Preschool Program: Final Report.* Ypsilanti Public Schools, Michigan, 1968.

Sarri, R., and Radin, N. "Development of a Pupil Behavior Assessment Inventory for Preschool and Early Elementary Students." Mimeographed. School of Social Work, University of Michigan, Ann Arbor, 1973.

Vinter, R., Sarri, R., Vorwaller, D., and Schaefer, W. *Pupil Behavior Inventory: A Manual for Administration and Scoring.* Ann Arbor, Michigan: Campus Publisher, 1966.

RHODE ISLAND PUPIL IDENTIFICATION SCALE (RIPIS)

AUTHORS: Harry S. Novack, Elisa Bonaventura, and Peter Merenda

AGE: Kindergarten to grade 2

VARIABLE: Learning problems

TYPE OF MEASURE: Rating scale

SOURCE FROM WHICH MEASURE MAY BE OBTAINED: RIPIS, P.O. Box 9311, Providence, Rhode Island 02904. Cost: Box of 35 scales, $6.00; manual, $6.00.

DESCRIPTION OF MEASURE: The Rhode Island Pupil Identification Scale is a pupil behavior observation scale for use by classroom teachers. The primary functions of the instrument are (1) to help the classroom teacher identify children with learning problems; (2) to help the classroom teacher indicate more readily, using the scale language, the specific aspects of the school problem requiring attention; and (3) to permit the classroom teacher or receiving specialist to address himself more efficiently to the resolution of the specific school problem as observed in its natural surroundings. The scale consists of forty items scored according to a Likert scale and is divided into two parts. Part I contains twenty-one items dealing with behavior that is quite readily observable through regular classroom activity. The nineteen items in Part II deal with behavior that may be evaluated through a review of the pupil's written work. The standardization sample was comprised of 851 subjects drawn from three school districts. Each district furnished subjects in kindergarten through grade 2 and was selected so as to yield generally representative samples of children in terms of age, sex, in-state geographic location, race distribution, and ethnic origin.
        Examples from each part are given below.

Part I
a. Has difficulty cutting.
    ( ) never   ( ) rarely   ( ) occasionally   ( ) frequently   ( ) always
b. Bumps into objects.
    ( ) never   ( ) rarely   ( ) occasionally   ( ) frequently   ( ) always
c. Trips over self.
    ( ) never   ( ) rarely   ( ) occasionally   ( ) frequently   ( ) always
Part II
a. Has difficulty writing within lines.
    ( ) never   ( ) rarely   ( ) occasionally   ( ) frequently   ( ) always
b. Has difficulty completing written work in the time alloted.
    ( ) never   ( ) rarely   ( ) occasionally   ( ) frequently   ( ) always
c. Runs words or parts of words together in copying.
    ( ) never   ( ) rarely   ( ) occasionally   ( ) frequently   ( ) always

RELIABILITY AND VALIDITY: The reliability of the RIPIS has been established by use of the Pearson product-moment correlation formula for eight observations, October through May. The coefficients derived by this method reveal substantially high reliabilities reported between adjacent months (range .53 to .99). While correlations are lower for those for which the time interval is relatively great (e.g., October vs. May), they are nevertheless significantly positive (r = .53). Concurrent validity was determined by computing coefficients between the May observation scale scores and the individual test scores on the CTMM and SAT administered in June. All of the correlations were found to be negative and statistically significant at least at the .05 level of significance.

BIBLIOGRAPHY:

Engleman, S. "Relationship Between Psychological Theories and the Act of Teaching." *Journal of School Psychology,* 1967, *2,* 93-100.
Fine, M. J. "Consideration in Educating Children with Cerebral Dysfunction." *Journal of Learning Disabilities,* 1970, *3,* 132-142.
Haring, N. G., and Ridgway, R. W. "Early Identification of Children with Learning Disabilities." *Exceptional Children,* 1967, *6,* 387-395.
Lovitt, T. C. "Assessment of Children with Learning Disabilities." In R. H. Bradfield (Ed), *Behavior Modification of Learning Disabilities.* San Rafael, California: Academic Therapy Publications, 1971.
Myklebust, H. R. *Manual for the Pupil Rating Scale.* New York: Grune & Stratton, 1971.
Novack, H. S., Bonaventura, E., and Merenda, P. F. "A Scale for Early Detection of Children with Learning Problems." *Exceptional Children,* 1973, *39,* 98-106.

SCHOOL ADJUSTMENT SCALE (SAS)

AUTHOR: Timothy M. Flynn

AGE: 6 to 13 years

VARIABLE: School adjustment

TYPE OF MEASURE: Rating scale

SOURCE FROM WHICH MEASURE MAY BE OBTAINED: Timothy M. Flynn, Department of Child and Family, Southern Illinois University, Carbondale, Illinois 62901.

DESCRIPTION OF MEASURE: The School Adjustment Scale (SAS) was constructed to provide an objective method to obtain the teachers' previous observations of the child. The multiple-choice format used by the SAS accomplishes this by defining the possible behavior as unambiguously as possible. This approach also eliminates the need for the teacher to weigh behaviors on a quantitative scale. She merely selects the behavior that best describes the child's usual mode of behavior in the presented thirty situations.

As examples, three selected items of the thirty situations are given below, with choice "a" receiving a weight of 5 and choice "e" a weight of 1.

5. In dealing with adults on a one-to-one basis, this child is
    a. confident and courteous.
    b. well-mannered, but tension is evident.
    c. embarrassed and halting, but does make an effort to be courteous.
    d. somewhat flippant, but not insulting.
    e. loud and boisterous, and occasionally insulting.
8. If involved in a competitive game with others, this child takes defeat by
    a. remaining calm.
    b. becoming somewhat angry with self.
    c. making excuses, along with a tendency to blame others for his defeat.
    d. crying.
    e. having a tantrum.
15. In class activities that require the child to work with other children this child
    a. takes a leadership role, and contributes more than his share.
    b. contributes many ideas.
    c. is an infrequent contributer, but does follow suggestions.
    d. is very passive, only contributing as a result of urging.
    e. hinders the group's activities.

RELIABILITY AND VALIDITY: To obtain validity and reliability information, 122 teachers were asked to rate 122 children. In validating the SAS, two different criteria were used. The first criterion was promotion to the next grade. The total SAS correlation with promotion was .49 (.001); however, with fourteen items from the SAS it was possible to classify the child as promoted or retained with 85-percent accuracy using discriminant analysis. The second criterion was whether the child was retarded or normal. The full SAS correlation with this criterion was .46 (.001) with eight items classifying children as retarded or normal with 84-percent accuracy. The estimate of inter-rater reliability was obtained by correlating the special-class and regular-class teachers' ratings of part-time special-class retarded students. The obtained correlation was .74 (p < .001), while an internal consistency measure (Kuder-Richardson formula 20) was .93.

BIBLIOGRAPHY:

Flynn, T. M. "Development of a Multiple-Choice Behavioral Observation Scale." Paper presented at annual meeting of the American Educational Research Association. Minneapolis, Minnesota, March 1970.

Flynn, T. M. "The Effectiveness of a Part-Time Special Education Program on the Adjustment of EMR Students." *Exceptional Children,* 1970, *36,* 680-681.

Flynn, T. M. "Implicit Criteria Used to Determine Promotion for Normal and Retarded Students." *Psychology in the Schools,* 1971, *8,* 204-208.

SCHOOL BEHAVIOR PROFILE

AUTHORS: Bruce Balow and Rosalyn A. Rubin

AGE: 5 to 18 years

VARIABLE: Problem behavior, personal adjustment

TYPE OF MEASURE: Rating scale

SOURCE FROM WHICH MEASURE MAY BE OBTAINED: Bruce Balow or Rosalyn Rubin, Department of Special Education, University of Minnesota, Minneapolis 55455.

DESCRIPTION OF MEASURE: The School Behavior Profile is a fifty-eight-item experimental scale on which the classroom teacher or other observer rates a child's behavior as observed in routine school activities. It provides a functional (practical) measure of problem behavior or personal-adjustment difficulties in the environment of the school. A total score is obtained reflecting the general level of problem behavior shown by the child. Additionally, three subscale or factor scores may be obtained to indicate the particular type of problem the child may be showing—specifically, poor control, development immaturity, and anxious-neurotic behavior.

As examples, ten selected items from the fifty-eight-item SBP, are given below. They are to be rated "almost always," "often," "seldom," or "almost never."

1. Sluggishness, lethargy.
6. Although able to speak, uses mime or demonstration.
11. Talkative, chatterbox.
18. Preoccupied with certain aspects of things (e.g., their shininess, texture, or color).
22. Self-consciousness; easily embarrassed.
27. Examines things in odd ways (e.g., by sniffing or biting them).
31. Temper tantrums (complete loss of temper with shouting or angry movements, etc.).
35. Boisterousness, rowdiness.
50. Jealousy over attention paid other children.
57. Generally unnoticed by others.

RELIABILITY AND VALIDITY: Two methods of estimating reliability have been used. A split-half reliability coefficient of .96, with Spearman-Brown correction, was obtained on nearly twelve hundred subjects. Estimates of stability over time with different raters (between first grade ratings and those obtained at grades 2, 3, and 4) ranged from .42 to .46. Validity has been assessed by completing SBP ratings at grade 1 with fourth-grade teacher ratings of attitude and behavior and with the aggregate of special services received by subjects through grade 4. These correlations center around .40. Concurrent validity has been found in that girls consistently score better than do boys and handicapped groups such as those receiving speech therapy, remedial reading, special classes, and so forth, all score significantly worse than the general population of school children.

BIBLIOGRAPHY:

Balow, B., and Rubin, R. A. *Manual of Directions for the School Behavior Profile.* Minneapolis: University of Minnesota, Department of Special Education, 1970.

Rubin, R. A., and Krus, P. H. "Validation of a School Behavior Rating Scale." Paper presented at the annual meeting of the American Educational Research Association. New Orleans, Louisiana, February 1973.

Rubin, R. A., and Krus, P. H. "Predictive Validity of a School Behavior Rating Scale." Paper presented at the annual meeting of the American Educational Research Association. Chicago, April 1974.

SCHOOL BEHAVIOR RATING SCALE

AUTHORS: Helen H. Davidson and Judith W. Greenberg

AGE: 9 to 14 years

VARIABLE: Teachers' perceptions of children's behaviors and traits relevant to school achievement

TYPE OF MEASURE: Rating scale

SOURCE FROM WHICH MEASURE MAY BE OBTAINED: See Davidson and Greenberg (1967).

DESCRIPTION OF MEASURE: This scale of twenty-six items asks teachers to rate the frequency of certain specific behaviors that occur in the school setting. It was developed for a large project that assessed differences between high and low achievers on a large number of cognitive, affective, motivational, and background variables hypothesized to be related to achievement. Subjects were lower-class black children attending fifth grade in urban ghetto schools. Teachers rated high achievers more favorably; mean total ratings (based on a possible range of 26 to 130) were 104.5 for high achievers and 81.1 for low achievers. A factor analysis of the scale yielded three factors that accounted for 59 percent of the variance: academic effort, conformity to authority demands, and personal qualities. Significant differences between high and low achievers were obtained for all three factors.

As examples, the first five of the twenty-six items of the scale are given below. Extreme score values are indicated.

For each item below check the space that best describes how this child typically behaves.

	Almost always	Usually	Some-times	Seldom	Almost never
1. Careful and neat in doing his home-work and class work.	5				1
2. Well-liked by other children; chosen as playmate or partner.	5				1
3. Listless; tired; easily fatigued.	1				5
4. Cheerful; friendly; laughs easily when appropriate.	5				1

	Almost always	Usually	Some-times	Seldom	Almost never
5. Shows concern about how well he is doing in his work (but is not over-anxious).	5				1

RELIABILITY AND VALIDITY: None reported.

BIBLIOGRAPHY:

Davidson, H. H., and Greenberg, J. W. *School Achievers from a Deprived Background.* New York: Associated Educational Services Corporation, 1967.

SCHOOL NOMINATIONS DEVICE (GROUP)
SCHOOL BEHAVIOR CHECKLIST (INDIVIDUAL)

AUTHORS: Edward Earl Gotts (earlier version, Beeman N. Phillips)

AGE: 5 to 14 years

VARIABLE: Social aspect of child personality; selected intrapsychic characteristics

TYPE OF MEASURE: Checklist (individual); nominations (group)

SOURCE FROM WHICH MEASURE MAY BE OBTAINED: Edward Earl Gotts, Appalachia Educational Laboratory, Inc., P.O. Box 1348, Charleston, West Virginia 25325. Cost: $1.00 for postage and handling.

DESCRIPTION OF MEASURE: The 140 items are checked on the individual form, or the adult writes in the names of children to whom the labels apply on the group form. Items have been assigned to scales by a group of clinical judges. The social aspect of child personality is linked to a sixteen-vector, concentric-circles model originally developed for adults by Leary and Coffey (1955). Some of the 140 behavior items have been assigned weights on these sixteen interpersonal vectors (here arranged in bipolar pairs): blunt-overconventional, responsible-distrustful, overgenerous-skeptical, autocratic-modest, aggressive-cooperative, competitive-dependent, exploitative-docile, managerial-self-effacing. These vectors can further be collapsed into a four-quadrant interpersonal typology: Aggressives, Self-effacing dependents, Responsible conformers, and Manipulative controllers. These four types are differentiated from one another along two dimensions: interpersonally coping/noncoping and active/passive style. This interpersonal scoring system was first validated using an earlier seventy-two-item version of the scale. It has since been expanded to 140 items to strengthen its sampling of the social domain of behavior, in terms of the Leary-Coffey model. Three intrapsychic (nonsocial) scales have also been developed and weights assigned in a similar manner.

These scales are: Personal disorganization, Anxiety symptoms, and Symptoms of depression. An eighth scale, Defensiveness, is still in more tentative form. Computer scoring is used. Hand-scoring is possible but is time consuming. This procedure has been used to screen normal school populations for those children who may be experiencing social and emotional difficulties. The procedure has provided a useful corroborative type of data for the case study of the individual child.

As examples, selected items from the three scales comprising the measure are given below.

1. Carelessness in work.
2. Cheating.
3. Cruelty, bullying.
4. Daydreaming.
5. Destroying school materials.
41. Clings to teacher and seeks to be near him (her) and hold his (her) hand.
42. Habitually pulls his (her) hair, picks at his (her) nose, pulls his (her) ears, bites his (her) nails.
43. Uses real or imagined inferiorities as an excuse for not really trying.
44. Fights with little provocation.
45. Exhibits righteousness, snobbishness.
101. Gets others to do work for him (her).
102. Usually does the ordinary or expected thing.
103. Upset by small setbacks.
104. Willingly includes others in activities.
105. Is disorganized in his (her) thinking.

RELIABILITY AND VALIDITY: Stability coefficients were computed for the eight bipolar dimensions listed above for 224 fourth-grade children from fall to spring of a school year. These coefficients were, in the above order, .57, .43, .58, .55, .57, .58, .55, and .57. Validity was examined by comparing children classified as A, B, C, or D types, using a variety of measures as dependent variables. The coping groups of children (C and D) compared with the A and B groups were higher in school motivation, grade-point average, verbal and nonverbal achievement, and verbal and nonverbal intelligence. The only exceptions were that B children sometimes appeared more capable of coping than A children and thus were not as debilitated in comparison to C and D children. Further, C and D children were more socially accepted than A and Bs, whereas only As were highly peer rejected. These and other tested differences showed that classification from only seventy-two nominations was congruent with all of these other variables. In terms of the active-passive distinction, the A group showed the most conventional masculine sex-typing. Similar validation work has been carried out for children classified into the intrapsychic groups E and F. Personally disorganized children (E) compared to non-Es are lower in school motivation, higher on feelings of inferiority and on social and academic symptoms of neuroticism, higher on active forms of withdrawal from the environment, less peer accepted and more peer rejected. Children with anxiety symptoms (F) compared to non-Fs are lower in school motivation, more self-devaluating, higher in feelings of inferiority and on social and academic symptoms of neuroticism, higher on active forms of withdrawal from the environment, less peer accepted and more peer rejected. Children with anxiety symptoms (F) compared to non-Fs are lower in school motivation, more self-devaluating, higher in feelings of

inferiority and on social and academic symptoms of neuroticism, higher on active withdrawal, less peer accepted and more peer rejected, and lower in grade-point average.
The *G* scale of depression is still being validated.

BIBLIOGRAPHY:

Dil, N. "Sensitivity of Emotionally Disturbed and Emotionally Nondisturbed Elemen-
        tary School Children to Emotional Meanings of Facial Expressions." Unpub-
        lished doctoral dissertation. Indiana University, Bloomington, 1971.
Evans, J. H. "The Influence of Teacher Personality and Pupil Misbehavior upon
        Teacher Impressions of Pupils." Unpublished doctoral dissertation. Indiana Uni-
        versity, Bloomington, 1971.
Gotts, E. E., Adams, R. L., and Phillips, B. N. "Personality Classification of Discrete
        Pupil Behaviors." *Journal of School Psychology,* 1969, *7* (3), 54-62.
Gotts, E. E., and Dil, N. "A Scale of Children's Personal Disorganization: Validity and
        Application." *Journal of School Psychology* (in press).
Leary, T., and Coffey, H. S. "Interpersonal Diagnosis: Some Problems of Methodology
        and Validation." *Journal of Abnormal and Social Psychology,* 1955, *50,*
        110-124.

SCHOOL RECORDS CODING MANUAL
AND PUPIL RATING FORM

AUTHOR: Norman F. Watt

AGE: Teachers of children 5 to 18 years

VARIABLE: Classroom behavior

TYPE OF MEASURE: Coding system and rating scale

SOURCE FROM WHICH MEASURE MAY BE OBTAINED: Norman F. Watt, Tobin
Hall, University of Massachusetts, Amherst, Massachusetts 01002. No cost at this time.

DESCRIPTION OF MEASURE: Though based on extensive preliminary research, these
instruments are still intended primarily for pilot use. The Coding Manual offers a
highly specific system for coding the ad lib remarks about children's classroom behavior, as recorded in cumulative school records. The Pupil Rating Form is an adaptation
of the Coding Manual, which permits concurrent assessment of classroom behavior
through quantified ratings.
        As examples, the first five of the twenty-eight behavioral dimensions of the
Pupil Rating Form are given below. The teacher rates the child from 1 to 5.

1. Orderliness: orderly   careless.
2. Confidence: insecure   confident.

3. Loquaciousness: silent   talkative.
4. Leadership: leader   follower.
5. Cooperation: compliant   negativistic.

RELIABILITY AND VALIDITY: The interjudge reliabilities for the separate scales of the Coding Manual fluctuate widely, from .40 to .98, with an average around .60 to .70. When combined into five rational factors, the factor scores show reliability from .61 to .90 with a median of .81. Preliminary analyses also show very promising validity, even longitudinally.

BIBLIOGRAPHY:

Watt, N. F. *Psychological Conceptions of High Risk for the Development of Schizophrenia.* Washington, D.C.: National Institute of Mental Health, June 1969.

Watt, N. F. "School-Age Children at Risk by Genetic and Behavioral Criteria." Paper presented at the Conference on Risk for Schizophrenia. Dorado Beach, Florida, October 1972.

Watt, N. F. "Childhood and Adolescent Routes to Schizophrenia." In D. F. Ricks, M. Roff, and A. Thomas (Eds.), *Life History Research in Psychopathology.* Vol. 3. Minneapolis: University of Minnesota Press, 1974.

Watt, N. F. "Longitudinal Changes in the Social Behavior of Children Hospitalized for Schizophrenia as Adults." *Journal of Nervous and Mental Disease,* 1972, *155,* 42-54. Reprinted in R. Cancro (Ed.), *Annual Review of the Schizophrenic Syndrome.* Vol. 4. New York: Brunner/Mazel, 1974.

Watt, N. F. "Patterns of Childhood Social Development in Adult Schizophrenics." *Journal of Abnormal Psychology,* (in press).

Watt, N. F., and Lubensky, A. W. "Childhood Roots of Schizophrenia." *Journal of Consulting and Clinical Psychology* (in press).

Watt, N. F., Stolorow, R. D., Lubensky, A. W., and McClelland, D. C. "School Adjustment and Behavior of Children Hospitalized for Schizophrenia as Adults." *American Journal of Orthopsychiatry,* 1970, *40,* 637-657. Reprinted in R. Cancro (Ed.), *The Schizophrenic Syndrome: An Annual Review.* New York: Brunner/Mazel, 1972.

STUDENT ROLE BEHAVIOR SCALE

AUTHOR: Laura Weinstein

AGE: Elementary school

VARIABLE: Social and achievement-related behavior

TYPE OF MEASURE: Rating scale

SOURCE FROM WHICH MEASURE MAY BE OBTAINED: Office of Liaison and

Information Services, John F. Kennedy Center for Research on Education and Human Development, Box 40, George Peabody College, Nashville, Tennessee 37203.

DESCRIPTION OF MEASURE: The Student Role Behavior Scale is a twenty-seven-item instrument for rating school behavior and achievement. The items, in the form of specific questions, are answered "yes," "?," or "no." Items *a* through *p* are scored 1 point for each check in the "yes" column, while items *q* through *zz* are scored 1 point for each check in the "no" column. Any check in the "?" column or any item left blank is scored .5. The top possible score is 27. If the number of blanks plus the number of checks in the "?" column sum to more than 6, the scale is considered unscorable.

As examples, six selected items of the twenty-seven are given below. The respondent answers "yes," "?," or "no."

1. Is the student willing to come to school?
3. Does he have as much self-control as needed in the school situation?
7. Does he usually listen well enough to understand directions?
12. Is he willing to let other students share the teacher's attention?
20. Does he get easily discouraged and quit before a task is completed?
22. Does he seem to have an unusual need to win, be first, get the largest share?

RELIABILITY AND VALIDITY: Scores (mean, 13.1; standard deviation, 5.3) of 127 boys in grades 1 through 6, defined by their schools as having behavioral or emotional problems requiring special help, differed significantly from scores (mean, 25.9; *SD,* 1.8) of 128 matched children not seen by the schools as having such problems. For the combined group of 255 children, scores correlated .72 with scores from different teachers one year later and .64 with scores from a third set of teachers two years later. Scores the first year correlated .85 with the same teacher's global rating of the child's behavioral-emotional adjustment based on a 4-point scale (in the normal range, mild problems, fairly severe problems, very severe problems), .69 with the next year's teacher's global rating, and .64 with the following year's teacher's global rating. Correlations with teacher global ratings of academic performance, based on the same 4-point scale for the same years, were .74, .56, and .46, respectively. The Student Role Behavior Scale score also correlated .86 with the sum of the teacher's ratings of the child on five items relating to the extent the child's school achievement measured up to his potential for learning, the child's disruptiveness in class, his feelings of personal distress, his ability to face new or difficult situations, and his relationship with his classmates. In addition, Student Role Behavior Scale scores correlated .40 with positive nominations and −.68 with rejections on sociometric questionnaires filled out by classmates. Correlations with age (−.11), IQ (.16), father's education (.12), and father's occupation (.04) were low.

BIBLIOGRAPHY:

Weinstein, L. "Project Re-Ed Schools for Emotionally Disturbed Children: Effectiveness as Viewed by Referring Agencies, Parents, and Teachers." *Exceptional Children,* 1969, *35,* 703-711.

Group 2-d

Anxiety

CHILDREN'S FORM OF THE ALPERT-HABER
ACHIEVEMENT ANXIETY SCALE

AUTHORS: Diane Stanford, William N. Dember, and L. Bradley Stanford

AGE: 8 years and perhaps older

VARIABLE: Anxiety about academic achievement

TYPE OF MEASURE: Questionnaire

SOURCE FROM WHICH MEASURE MAY BE OBTAINED: William N. Dember, Department of Psychology, University of Cincinnati, Cincinnati, Ohio 45221.

DESCRIPTION OF MEASURE: Eighteen of the nineteen items in the Alpert-Haber Achievement Anxiety Scale were recorded for use with third graders. A "Yes" or "No" response is required for each item; items are presented orally.
    The items of the scale are given below.

1. If you get worried while you are taking a hard test, does it make you do worse on it?
2. Do you do your best job when you know the test is very important?
3. If you made a bad grade on the last test in class, does it worry you so that you may make an even worse grade on the next test?
4. When you haven't studied for a test do you get worried and miss the questions that you really know the answers to?
5. When your teacher says a test is very important do you do worse on it?
6. After you start on a test, do you forget about being worried?
7. Do you sometimes find that you can't remember the answer to a question until just after the test is over?
8. If you get worried while you are taking a test, do you do a better job on it?
9. Once you start working on a test do you feel that nothing else bothers you?
10. Do you feel a lot of the time that at the start of a test you can't think of anything to put down, and it takes a few minutes for you to start answering the questions?
11. Do you mind taking tests?
12. Do you sometimes get so tired from worrying about a test that you almost don't care how well you do on it?
13. If you are worried about finishing a test on time, do you do worse on the test than the other kids do?
14. Can you do just as well on a test if you wait until right before the test to study for it?
15. Do you like hard tests better than easy ones?
16. Do you usually need to read a question more than once before you understand it?
17. Do you do better on a test when the teacher says it is a very important one?
18. If you have a hard time answering the first question on a test, does it worry you so much that you have a lot harder time answering the rest of the questions?

RELIABILITY AND VALIDITY: The questionnaire was administered to sixty-one third graders. No sex difference was found and no relation of anxiety score to IQ (California Test of Mental Maturity). Anxiety scores were significantly related to grade in reading. Classifying children as Low Anxiety-High IQ or High Anxiety-Low IQ (median split on both variables) allowed accurate prediction of reading grade for thirty-three of thirty-six children.

BIBLIOGRAPHY:

Stanford, D., Dember, W. N., and Stanford, L. B. "A Children's Form of the Alpert-Haber Achievement Anxiety Scale." *Child Development,* 1963, *34,* 1027-1032.

Prepared by William N. Dember

COMPLIANT, AGGRESSIVE, DETACHED (CAD) INTERPERSONAL ANXIETY INVENTORY

AUTHOR: Spencer F. Tinkham

AGE: Adolescence and up

VARIABLE: Compliant, aggressive, and detached anxiety

TYPE OF MEASURE: Rating scale

SOURCE FROM WHICH MEASURE MAY BE OBTAINED: See Tinkham (1973).

DESCRIPTION OF MEASURE: The CAD Interpersonal Anxiety Inventory is a twenty-seven-item satisfaction-with-self rating scale designed to measure three areas of salient interpersonal anxiety. Empirical contributions of Cattell and others (1970), Sarason (1960), and others indicate that high-anxiety subjects tend to be more self-deprecatory, lower in ego control, and generally less content with themselves than subjects lower in the distribution of anxiety scores. These findings suggest that dissatisfaction with self in the interpersonal sphere should be a valid indicant of interpersonal anxiety.

The CAD Interpersonal Anxiety Inventory can be used in conjunction with Cohen's (1967) CAD Interpersonal Inventory, thus providing measures of both trait possession and trait salience. Cohen's CAD instrument assesses the degree to which an individual possesses the compliant, aggressive, and detached interpersonal orientations. The CAD Interpersonal Anxiety Inventory, on the other hand, measures the relative salience or arousal of each interpersonal area, in the sense that interaction in salient areas is most desired or most avoided. As in the case of Cohen's CAD instrument, the three construct categories of the Interpersonal Anxiety Inventory are derived from Horney's (1945) tripartite interpersonal model. Twenty-seven interpersonal trait terms are rated in terms of how satisfied or dissatisfied the individual is with respect to his possession of each trait. Traits appear on the test form in repeated C, D, and A order. While trait terms with clearly negative connotations are not included in the list of traits, the twenty-seven items encompass a range of meaning broad enough to tap the multidimensional nature of each of Horney's interpersonal categories.

As examples, the first ten of the twenty-seven items on the inventory are given below. The respondent answers on a 6-point scale ranging from "completely satisfied" to "completely dissatisfied."

How satisfied or dissatisfied are you with yourself, with respect to each of the following characteristics?

Considerate   Active
Independent   Adaptable
Self-controlled   Unique
Helpful   Enterprising
Intellectual   Cooperative

RELIABILITY AND VALIDITY: Sixty-three trait terms were rated in terms of self-satisfaction by fifty-seven junior college students and were correlated with raw scores on Cattell and others' (1970) 16 PF (Form C). Criteria for selection of twenty-seven potential test items included: (1) significant ($p < .05$) correlations with one or more of the six 16 PF factors related to anxiety; (2) nonsignificant correlations with other personality factors on the 16 PF; (3) high interjudge agreement as to proper item categorization, employing responses by seven expert judges familiar with Horney's theory; and (4) breadth of item meaning, consistent with the scope of Horney's definitions of the three response modes. A second sample of forty-eight junior college students completed the twenty-seven-item test, as well as Cattell's 16 PF (Form C) and Cohen's CAD Interpersonal Inventory. Significant correlations were found between dissatisfaction scores and four of the six anxiety factors on the 16 PF—Factors C, H, O, and Q4. Significant negative correlations were found between dissatisfaction scores and the 16 PF motivational distortion (lie) scale, consistent with Cattell's observation that subjects low in anxiety tend to score higher on motivational distortion. Low but significant negative correlations were also found between dissatisfaction scores on the compliant and aggressive traits and scores on the compliant and aggressive dimensions of Cohen's CAD instrument. Discriminant validity of the CAD Interpersonal Anxiety Inventory is supported by the fact that no significant relationships were found between dissatisfaction scores and the ten factor scores of the 16 PF not related to anxiety.

Five persuasive communication studies in the area of police recruitment, employing student and police trainee samples, found significant negative relationships between interpersonal anxiety scores and response to persuasive appeals. A significant ($p < .001$) interaction was found between compliant scores and compliant anxiety scores as they affect preference for persuasive appeals. High-compliant subjects who were also high in compliant anxiety strongly preferred compliant appeals to aggressive appeals.

The CAD Interpersonal Anxiety Inventory was administered to a national quota sample of one thousand housewives in an advertising study for a new hair-coloring product. Significant ($p < .001$) negative correlations were found between each of the three interpersonal anxiety scores and housewives' reported self-confidence in their ability to judge hair-color brands. In addition, low compliant anxiety scores were associated with greater likelihood of hair-color use ($p < .05$) and with more positive attitudes toward hair-color products and advertising ($p < .01$). Housewives with low aggressive anxiety scores tended to have smaller families ($p < .10$), and those with lower levels of detached anxiety reported higher levels of formal education ($p < .05$). These findings contribute to the predictive validity of the instrument and suggest the value of trait-specific, rather than general, anxiety measures for predicting interpersonal behavior.

Thirty-six junior college students completed the Interpersonal Anxiety Inventory twice, with a one-week interval between administrations. Test-retest correlations for the three interpersonal anxiety dimensions were .76, .85, and .83. Internal consistency estimates were calculated using the Kuder-Richardson coefficient *alpha* formula, yielding *alpha* scores of .68, .75, and .67 for anxiety items associated with the compliant, aggressive, and detached dimensions.

BIBLIOGRAPHY:

Cattell, R. B., and others. *Handbook for the Sixteen Factor Questionnaire (16 PF).* Champaign, Illinois: Institute for Personality and Ability Testing, 1970.
Cohen, J. B. "An Interpersonal Orientation to the Study of Consumer Behavior." *Journal of Marketing Research,* 1967, *4,* 270-278.
Horney, K. *Our Inner Conflicts.* New York: Norton, 1945.
Sarason, I. G. "Empirical Findings and Theoretical Problems in the Use of Anxiety Scales." *Psychological Bulletin,* 1960, *57,* 403-415.
Tinkham, S. F. "Interpersonal Traits, Interpersonal Anxiety, and Response to Need-Oriented Communications." Unpublished doctoral dissertation. University of Illinois, Urbana-Champaign, 1973.

DEATH ANXIETY SCALE

AUTHOR: Donald I. Templer

AGE: 12 years to old age

VARIABLE: Death anxiety

TYPE OF MEASURE: True-false test

SOURCE FROM WHICH MEASURE MAY BE OBTAINED: See Templer (1970).

DESCRIPTION OF MEASURE: For the initial step in the construction of the scale (Templer 1969, 1970) forty items were devised on a rational basis, with the intention of tapping death anxiety as it permeates a variety of life experiences. Judges' ratings of face validity and subsequent determination of internal consistency reduced the scale number to fifteen. One point is scored for every answer in the death anxiety direction, so that a score can be as low as 0 or as high as 15. Details of administration and normativelike data are presented by Templer and Ruff (1971).

The items and the direction in which they are keyed are given below.

T   1. I am very much afraid to die.
F   2. The thought of death seldom enters my mind.
F   3. It doesn't make me nervous when people talk about death.
T   4. I dread to think about having to have an operation.

F   5. I am not at all afraid to die.

F   6. I am not particularly afraid of getting cancer.

F   7. The thought of death never bothers me.

T   8. I am often distressed by the way time flies so very rapidly.

T   9. I fear dying a painful death.

T 10. The subject of life after death troubles me greatly.

T 11. I am really scared of having a heart attack.

T 12. I often think about how short life really is.

T 13. I shudder when I hear people talking about a World War III.

T 14. The sight of a dead body is horrifying to me.

F 15. I feel that the future holds nothing for me to fear.

RELIABILITY AND VALIDITY: The scale was found to have satisfactory reliability and to be relatively free of response sets. The determination of validity employed a diversity of procedures. In one of these, it was found that psychiatric patients who had spontaneously verbalized death concern in counseling sessions had significantly higher Death Anxiety Scale scores than control patients. Subsequent research has related the scale to an array of variables. In one study, with over twenty-five hundred subjects from 13 to 85 years of age, there was no relationship between death anxiety and age. In this study, the death anxiety of adolescents resembled that of their parents, with the correlations being significantly higher with the parent of the same sex.

BIBLIOGRAPHY:

Lester, D., and Templer, D. I. "Parent-Child Death Anxiety Resemblance as a Function of Age of Adolescent." *Psychological Reports,* 1972, *31,* 750.

Pandley, R. E., and Templer, D. I. "Use of the Death Anxiety Scale in an Interracial Setting." *Omega,* 1972, *3,* 127-130.

Tarter, R. E., Templer, D. I., and Perley, R. L. "Death Anxiety in Suicide Attempters." *Psychological Reports,* 1974, *34,* 895-897.

Templer, D. I. "Death Anxiety Scale." *Proceedings of the 77th Annual Convention of the American Psychological Association,* 1969, *4,* 737-738.

Templer, D. I. "The Construction and Validation of a Death Anxiety Scale." *Journal of General Psychology,* 1970, *82,* 165-177.

Templer, D. I. "The Relationship Between Verbalized and Nonverbalized Death Anxiety." *Journal of Genetic Psychology,* 1971, *112,* 211-214.

Templer, D. I. "Relatively Nontechnical Description of the Death Anxiety Scale." *Archives of the Foundation of Thanatology,* 1971, *3,* 91-93.

Templer, D. I. "Death Anxiety in Religiously Very Involved Persons." *Psychological Reports,* 1972, *31,* 361-362.

Templer, D. I., and Dotson, E. "Religious Correlates of Death Anxiety." *Psychological Reports,* 1970, *26,* 895-897.

Templer, D. I., Lester, D., and Ruff, C. F. "Fear of Death and Femininity." *Psychological Reports,* 1974, *35,* 530.

Templer, D. I., and Ruff, C. F. "Death Anxiety Scale Means, Standard Deviations, and Embedding." *Psychological Reports,* 1971, *29,* 173-174.

Templer, D. I., Ruff, C. F., and Ayers, J. "Alleviation of High Death Anxiety with Symptomatic Treatment of Depression." *Psychological Reports,* 1974, *35,* 216.

Templer, D. I., Ruff, C. F., and Franks, C. M. "The Relationship of Age and Sex to Death Anxiety." *Developmental Psychology,* 1971, *4,* 108.

FROST SELF-DESCRIPTION QUESTIONNAIRE

AUTHOR: Barry P. Frost

AGE: 8 to 14 years

VARIABLE: Personality problem areas

TYPE OF MEASURE: Questionnaire

SOURCE FROM WHICH MEASURE MAY BE OBTAINED: RESCON, Alberta Behavioral Resource Consultants, Mrs. S. Bundi, Secretary-Treasurer, Department of Education Psychology, The University of Calgary, Alberta, Canada. Cost: Booklets, $12.50/50; answer sheets, $5.00/50; scoring keys, $3.00/set; manual, $1.00 each.

DESCRIPTION OF MEASURE: This true-false questionnaire in its revised (1970) version consists of 107 items, including twenty-five buffer items. It is divided into fourteen scales (mostly of five items each): test anxiety, social anxiety, worry and tension, concentration anxiety, separation from family anxiety, spatial separation anxiety, body damage anxiety, free-floating anxiety, externalized aggression, internalized aggression, projective aggression, affiliation, denial, and submissiveness. The questionnaire is intended to be used as a selective device to pinpoint areas in which an individual child is experiencing problems. Norms are available on 1,415 boys and 1,327 girls, aged 8 to 14, from eleven schools in Calgary, Alberta. Japanese and Spanish versions also exist.

As examples, the first eight of the 107 true-false items are given below.

1. I like to play with model trains.
2. When I was younger I was never scared of anything.
3. I find it hard to keep my mind on a test.
4. I like hit parade music.
5. I feel that I don't do enough for my parents.
6. I would like to be an electrician when I leave school.
7. I don't remember ever being afraid of anything at school.
8. I am always pleasant and agreeable when playing with other children.

RELIABILITY AND VALIDITY: Construct validity has been demonstrated by means of biserial correlations of items with scale totals, factor analysis of items, and replication of factor structure. No reliability data are yet available, and internal consistency measures would be inappropriate.

BIBLIOGRAPHY:

I. *Original (1967) version:*

Frost, B. P. "Anxiety and Educational Achievement." *British Journal of Educational Psychology,* 1968, *38,* 293-301.

Frost, B. P. "Extraversion and Educational Achievement." *Western Psychologist,* 1969, *1,* 5-18.

Frost, B. P. "A Note on Extraversion and Aggression." *Western Psychologist,* 1970, *1,* 81-88.

II. *Revised (1970) version:*

Frost, B. P. *Frost Self-Description Questionnaire Manual.* Calgary, Alberta, Canada: RESCON, 1973.

Frost, B. P., Iwawaki, S., and Fogliatto, H. "Argentinian, Canadian, Japanese, and Puerto Rican Norms on The Frost Self-Description Questionnaire." *Journal of Cross-Cultural Psychology,* 1972, *3,* 215-218.

HARDY ANXIETY SCALE FOR THE BLIND (HASB)

AUTHOR: Richard E. Hardy

AGE: 12 years and up

VARIABLE: Manifest anxiety

TYPE OF MEASURE: True-false questionnaire

SOURCE FROM WHICH MEASURE MAY BE OBTAINED: American Foundation for the Blind, 15 West 16th Street, New York, New York 10011. Cost: $2.00.

DESCRIPTION OF MEASURE: The Hardy Anxiety Scale for the Blind (HASB) consists of seventy-eight true-false items judged by psychologists working with the blind to be effective measures of manifest anxiety among blind persons (both totally blind and partially sighted). Scoring is done by hand. Anyone using the scale should read the entire booklet, which is available from the American Foundation for the Blind.

    As examples, the first ten items of the seventy-eight-item scale and the responses that indicate anxiety are given below.

True   1. I often worry about losing my hearing.
False   2. I almost always trust the people who guide me.
True   3. I frequently get upset because I feel closed in.
True   4. Crowds often make me nervous.
True   5. I am frequently embarrassed by my clothes.
True   6. I am uncomfortable when I must eat with sighted persons.
False   7. I don't worry about making friends.
False   8. I don't think people see me blush very often.
True   9. I am usually at ease at social get-togethers.
True 10. I would say that blindness has completely ruined my life.

RELIABILITY AND VALIDITY: Reliability was evaluated in two ways. The odd-even split-half method yielded an *r* of .79 for the scores of 122 students of high school age. The test-retest *r* over a three-week period was .75. Validity: The HASB is an experimental instrument. Empirical validity of the scale has been indicated by the correlation of .74 with the Taylor Manifest Anxiety Scale. This correlation held over a three-week period. In addition, HASB scores were correlated with ratings of teachers who used a clinically evaluated rating scale of manifest anxiety developed by Hardy (1967) to judge manifest anxiety levels of students. Each student was rated by two teachers. Correlations between the HASB and the teacher ratings were .28 for the first teacher and .29 for the second teacher. The correlations were significant at the .005 level. The items were chosen by psychologists who were asked to evaluate them in terms of their meaningfulness as measures of manifest anxiety with both totally blind students and students with some useful vision who met the criteria of legal blindness.

BIBLIOGRAPHY:

Hardy, R. E. "Prediction of Manifest Anxiety Levels of Blind Persons Through the Use of a Multiple-Regression Technique." *International Journal for the Education of the Blind,* 1967, *17,* 51-55.

Hardy, R. E. *The Anxiety Scale for the Blind.* New York: American Foundation for the Blind, 1968.

Hardy, R. E. "A Study of Manifest Anxiety Among Blind Residential School Students." *The New Outlook for the Blind,* 1968, *63,* 173-180.

JUNIOR MANIFEST ANXIETY SCALE

AUTHOR: Ram Tirath Joshi

AGE: 9 to 16 years

VARIABLE: Manifest anxiety

TYPE OF MEASURE: Test

SOURCE FROM WHICH MEASURE MAY BE OBTAINED: See Joshi (1974).

DESCRIPTION OF MEASURE: The Junior Manifest Anxiety Scale consists of forty items, of which six are filler or lie items. A "yes" answer for each anxiety item counts toward the anxiety score, and the maximum possible anxiety score on the scale is 34. The test can be administered individually as well as in groups. In order to overcome any reading disability, which is more difficult to detect in group testing, the tester should read the test aloud. Each of the first ten items should be read at an interval of 5 seconds, after which the interval may be reduced to 3 seconds.

As examples, twenty of the forty statements to be answered "yes" or "no" are given below.

1. I often have stomach upsets.
2. I cannot keep on one task for a long time.

3. I often worry over things I cannot do.

4. I get tired quickly.

5. My hands shake when I am annoyed.

6. I try not to annoy people.

7. I am not more nervous than anybody else.

8. I cannot wait long for anything I want.

9. I often feel anxious about pleasing my friends.

10. I get excited easily when things go wrong.

11. I am confident that I can complete anything I undertake.

12. I wish I could be as happy as some of my friends are.

13. At times I become nervous.

14. Life often seems a drag to me.

15. When upset I find it hard to go to sleep.

16. Sometimes I feel shattered at the end of a school day.

17. Most of the teachers are satisfied with my work.

18. I avoid making my mother angry.

19. I do not play games in which I might get hurt.

20. Sometimes I feel that I am good at nothing.

RELIABILITY AND VALIDITY: The original scale was administered to 200 school children. The test-retest reliability after a two-week interval was found to be .86. The content validity of .88 was obtained on the basis of the agreement level of two professionals. Evidence of concurrent validity is apparent from the highly significant correlations of .4 and .23 between anxiety scores and the neuroticism scores measured on the Eysenck Junior Personality Inventory and the Maudsley Junior Personality Inventory, respectively. Means and standard deviations for various age groups are available from the author.

BIBLIOGRAPHY:

Joshi, R. T. "Field-Dependence, Anxiety and Personality." *Perceptual and Motor Skills,* 1974, *38,* 1328.

MODIFIED BOXALL TEST OF ANXIETY IN SCHOOL

AUTHORS: Jean Boxall (original) and Reginald R. Dale (modified)

AGE: Approximately 10 to 16 years

VARIABLE: Anxiety in school

TYPE OF MEASURE: Questionnaire

SOURCE FROM WHICH MEASURE MAY BE OBTAINED: See Dale (1969, 1971).

DESCRIPTION OF MEASURE: This measure is a twenty-three-item questionnaire in which the child responds on a "yes" or "no" basis. The items sample broadly from school experiences and situations. The test is modified from Boxall (1961).

As examples, the first ten of the twenty-three statements to be answered "yes" or "no" are given below.

1. I feel all funny inside if I have to stand up and speak in front of the class.
2. I get very worried if I see a new kind of sum on the blackboard and I do not know how to do it.
3. It worries me if some of my sums are wrong.
4. My teacher makes me frightened when he or she is cross with the class.
5. At home I often worry about school.
6. I am very worried if I promise to bring a book to school and then forget.
7. I dread making a mistake when reading aloud to the class.
8. I don't like other children to know if I get a bad mark for arithmetic.
9. I do not like having new teachers.
10. Shivers go up and down my spine if I hear that a child in school is to be severely punished.

RELIABILITY AND VALIDITY: The original Boxall Test correlated with the Children's Manifest Anxiety Scale (Castaneda and others, 1956) as follows: .66 (boys) and .83 (girls). It correlated with Test Anxiety Scale for Children (Sarason and others, 1960) as follows: .49 (boys) and .77 (girls). Boxall applies item discrimination by the upper- and lower-third technique, and Dale (1969) reduced the test to twenty-three items by the elimination of those low in discriminatory powers by removing a clearly ambiguous question and by the consensus of three psychologists scrutinizing all items. The modified test (at 11+) has corrected split-half reliability coefficients of .70 (boys) and .80 (girls). The correlation with the Mooney Problem Checklist (1941-1950) as a measure of general anxiety is .42.

BIBLIOGRAPHY:

Boxall, J. "A Study of Some of the Relationships Between Anxiety and Failure in Learning to Read." Unpublished doctoral dissertation. University of Birmingham, England, 1961.

Castaneda, A., McCandless, B. R., and Palermo, D. C. "The Children's Form of the Manifest Anxiety Scale." *Child Development,* 1956, *27,* 317-326.

Dale, R. R. "Anxiety About School Among First-Year Grammar School Pupils and Its Relations to Occupational Class and Coeducation." *British Journal of Educational Psychology,* 1969, *39,* 21-26.

Dale, R. R. *Mixed or Single-Sex School?* Vol. 2. London: Routledge & Kegan Paul, 1971.

Mooney, R. *Problem Check List.* New York: Psychological Corporation, 1941-1950.

Sarason, S. B., Davidson, K. S., Lighthall, F., Waite, R. R., and Ruebush, B. K. *Anxiety in Elementary School Children.* New York: Wiley, 1960.

Prepared by Reginald R. Dale

MULTIFACTORIAL SCALE OF ANXIETY

AUTHORS: Walter D. Fenz and S. Epstein

AGE: Adolescent to adult

VARIABLE: Muscle tension, autonomic arousal, feelings of insecurity

TYPE OF MEASURE: Subjective rating scale

SOURCE FROM WHICH MEASURE MAY BE OBTAINED: Walter D. Fenz, Psychology Department, University of Waterloo, Waterloo, Ontario, Canada.

DESCRIPTION OF MEASURE: This anxiety scale consists of a total of fifty-three items, comprising three subscales: Muscle Tension (eighteen items), Autonomic Arousal (sixteen items), and Feelings of Insecurity (nineteen items). The scale distinguishes between two kinds of somatic symptoms and a third symptom of fear and insecurity. The somatic symptoms are either descriptive of the effect of sustained contraction of striated or voluntary muscles, or refer to visceral symptoms associated with activation of the autonomic nervous system. By using an overall score of anxiety some information is lost, especially in the case of highly anxious subjects, who manifest greater specificity of symptoms than normals. The personality data derived from the use of this scale indicate that psychological mediating processes account for some of the specificity in a somatic response to anxiety. Autonomic arousal is related to a more inward expression of energy, to needs for dependency and succorance, and to inhibition, and is more highly related to conflict over hostility than to hostility itself and acting-out ideation. Furthermore, autonomic arousal is more clearly a feminine symptom than one manifested by males, at least in the western cultures. Striated muscle tension is negatively related to inhibition and positively related to need aggression, and to the ideation to act out in a hostile manner, especially in delinquent males. Generally, it is more characteristic of males.

As examples, the first five items from each of the three subscales are given below. (R) refers to an item on which the scoring must be reversed.

Autonomic Arousal
I am troubled by discomfort in the pit of my stomach.
I have pounding headaches in which I can feel a definite beat.
I am bothered by dizziness.
I notice my heart pounding.
I am afraid that I am going to blush!
Muscle Tension
I am troubled with backaches.
The muscles in my neck ache as if they were tied in knots.
The top of my head feels tender.
I have a hard time swallowing.
I have trouble with my hand shaking while I write.
Feelings of Insecurity
My feelings are easily hurt.
I am an easy-going person. (R)

I have a tendency to worry.
I am a nervous person.
I have frightening dreams.

RELIABILITY AND VALIDITY: Test-retest reliability coefficients at six-week intervals (N = 188) were .63 for MT, .70 for AA, and .62 for FI; respective values for odd-even reliability (N = 98) were .84, .83, and .85. Centroid patterns in a normal population revealed a general factor and a specific factor, the latter associated with muscle tension. Neurotic subjects manifested more specificity in factor loadings associated with the three scales than did normals. Relationships with physiological recordings of autonomic measures and measures on the three scales were also noted. Personality correlates to specific somatic complaints are documented.

BIBLIOGRAPHY:

Brandt, K., and Fenz, W. D. "Specificity in Verbal and Physiological Indicants of Anxiety." *Perceptual and Motor Skills*, 1969, *29*, 663-675.

Epstein, S., and Fenz, W. D. "Habituation to a Loud Noise as a Function of Manifest Anxiety." *Journal of Abnormal Psychology*, 1970, *75*, 189-194.

Fenz, W. D. "Specificity in Somatic Responses to Anxiety." *Perceptual and Motor Skills*, 1967, *24*, 1183-1190.

Fenz, W. D., and Dronsejko, K. "Effects of Real and Imagined Threat of Shock on GSR and Heart Rate as a Function of Trait Anxiety." *Journal of Experimental Research in Personality*, 1969, *3*, 187-196.

Fenz, W. D., and Epstein, S. "Manifest Anxiety: Unifactorial or Multifactorial Composition." *Perceptual and Motor Skills*, 1965, *20*, 773-780.

Horvath, S., and Fenz, W. D. "Specificity in Somatic Indicants of Anxiety in Psychoneurotic Patients." *Perceptual and Motor Skills*, 1971, *33*, 147-162.

SCHOOL ANXIETY QUESTIONNAIRE

AUTHORS: James A. Dunn and John R. Bergan

AGE: Grades 4 to 12

VARIABLE: Five dimensions of school anxiety

TYPE OF MEASURE: Self-rating questionnaire

SOURCE FROM WHICH MEASURE MAY BE OBTAINED: James A. Dunn, American Institute for Research, P.O. Box 1113, Palo Alto, California 94302.

DESCRIPTION OF MEASURE: The School Anxiety Questionnaire is a 5-point scale, 105-item multiple-choice questionnaire. A large item pool was initially reduced to 160 items and subsequently to 105 through factor analysis of results from two elementary school groups, using unit-weighted factor scores computed through use of a special ipsative scoring procedure developed for the SAQ by Bergan (1966, 1968). Five factors, representing 58 percent of the items in the battery, accounted for 54 percent of the common variance. They were: Report Card Anxiety, 12 percent; Failure Anxiety, 12 percent; Test Anxiety, 11 percent; Achievement Anxiety, 12 percent; and Recitation Anxiety, 7 percent (this last scale had only six items). The balance of the common variance was accounted for by the forty-four items comprising the Response Bias Adjustment Scale.

As examples, selected items from the designated sections of the SAQ are given below. The subject responds on a 5-point Likert scale from "frequently" to "seldom," or "a lot" to "not much."

Report Card Anxiety
1. How much does it bother you when you think about having to show your report card to your parents?
2. How much do you wish that the teacher would never hand out report cards?
3. How much does it bother you when you know report cards will be coming out soon?
4. How nervous do you feel when you start to look at your report card?
5. How often do you worry that your parents won't like your report card?

Failure Anxiety
1. How often do you worry about being too lazy in school?
2. How often do you worry that the teacher has so many rules you won't be able to remember them all?
3. How often do you worry that a substitute teacher might give you work you can't do?
4. How often do you worry that your pencil might break while you are taking a test?
5. How nervous do you get when everything you do in school seems to go wrong?

Achievement Anxiety
1. How much does it bother you when the teacher is not clear about what she wants you to do?
2. How much does it bother you when the teacher collects papers before you have finished?
3. How nervous do you get when you forget an answer to a question on a test?
4. How much does it bother you when there isn't enough time for you to finish your school work?
5. How nervous do you get when you come back to school after you have been absent for a while?

Test Anxiety
1. How much does it bother you when the teacher tells you that you are going to have a test tomorrow?
2. How nervous do you get when you know you are going to have a test?
3. How often do you worry about doing poorly when the teacher says there is going to be a test?
4. How often do you wish you didn't worry so much about tests?
5. How nervous do you get when the teacher hands out tests?

Recitation Anxiety
1. How nervous do you get when you have to make a speech in class?

2. How nervous do you get when you have to read out loud to the class?

3. How nervous do you get when you know everyone is watching you?

RELIABILITY AND VALIDITY: The reliability estimates for the thirteen-item scales ranged from .82 to .88. The estimates for the fourteen-item scales ranged from .84 to .91. The estimates for the six-item scale ranged from .69 to .80. Multiple correlations between the SAQ scale and academic achievement are on the order of .45. Multiple correlation with IQ as measured by the California Test of Mental Maturity is .28. The factor structure of the SAQ is relatively well defined and replicates across age groups in the upper-elementary-school grades. From grades 3 to 6, there is a significant and pronounced increase with age in Recitation Anxiety. The only sex difference in SAQ scores was in Report Card Anxiety—girls reported less. There is a significant relationship between teacher behavior and children's school anxiety. Children's school anxiety levels are generally lower in classes where teachers emit positive reinforcement cues. There appears to be a trend toward predictable variation in children's school anxiety as a function of the school year.

BIBLIOGRAPHY:

Bergan, J. R. "Visual Imagery and Reading Achievement." Paper presented at the American Educational Research Association meeting. Chicago, Illinois, February 1966.

Bergan, J. R. "A Special Scoring Procedure for Minimizing Response Bias on the School Anxiety Questionnaire." *Psychology in the Schools*, 1968, *5*, 210-216.

Dunn, J. A. "The Theoretical Rationale Underlying the Development of the School Anxiety Questionnaire." *Psychology in the Schools*, 1968, *5*, 204-210.

Schelkun, R. F., and Dunn, J. A. "School Anxiety and the Facilitation of Performance." Paper presented at the meeting of the Midwest Psychological Association. Chicago, Illinois, May 1967.

Prepared by Orval G. Johnson

SEPARATION ANXIETY TEST

AUTHOR: Henry G. Hansburg

AGE: Approximately 10 to 15 years

VARIABLE: Response to separation experiences

TYPE OF MEASURE: Clinical test

SOURCE FROM WHICH MEASURE MAY BE OBTAINED: See Hansburg (1972a). For forms and other supplementary material, write Henry G. Hansburg, Jewish Child Care Association, 345 Madison Avenue, New York, New York 10017. Cost of book: $15.75.

DESCRIPTION OF MEASURE: This is a clinical instrument that is easy to administer, consisting of twelve separation-situation pictures ranging from mild and usual ones to more serious and traumatic ones. Each picture has a subtitle, which the child reads. His attention is then called to a set of mental set questions: "Did this ever happen to you?" (*yes* or *no*). "If not, can you imagine how you would feel if it did happen?" (*yes* or *no*). Following this the child is told to select as many phrases out of seventeen that he feels will tell how the child in the picture feels. The child reads each statement and tells the examiner the statements he feels represents the feelings of the child. The examiner has a recording sheet on which he circles the number of the selected phrases. The phrases are similar for each picture but arranged in different order and with some variability in phraseology. The responses in each of the seventeen areas are summed, as is the total for each picture. The responses are then organized into patterns that have been found to be of unusual clinical interpretive use. Separate forms are available for girls and boys.

As examples, a description of Picture 1 and the first three of the seventeen statements to be checked by the respondent are given below.

Picture 1. (The boy is sitting on the porch of his grandmother's house, watching his mother and father depart.) *The boy will live permanently with his grandmother and without his parents.*
1. Did this ever happen to you? Yes _____   No _____
2. If it never happened to you, can you imagine how this child feels? Yes _____   No _____

3. Check off below as many statements as you think will tell how the boy feels. The boy feels
   a. that he will be much happier now.
   b. that his parents don't love him any more.
   c. like curling up in a corner by himself.
   d. a terrible pain in his chest.
   e. alone and miserable.

RELIABILITY AND VALIDITY: Reliability data for most patterns on 250 children aged 10 to 15 run in the .70s and .80s, when using the Spearman-Brown split-half method. Validation was achieved largely through theoretical and clinical means, that is, comparisons of cases seen in residential care with normative populations as well as with psychiatric opinion, case histories, and psychological tests. Statistical tables are provided in the text. The method is in process of continuous clinical validation in the Psychiatric Clinic of the Jewish Child Care Association in New York City. It is used to determine the child's degree of attachment need, capacity to utilize it, its balance with self-initiative and self-sufficiency, degree of affect response and type, and diagnostic and dynamic indications.

BIBLIOGRAPHY:

Bowlby, J. *Separation: Anxiety and Anger.* New York: Basic Books, 1973; and London: Hogarth Press, 1973.
Hansburg, H. G. *Adolescent Separation Anxiety: A Method for the Study of Adolescent Separation Problems.* Springfield, Illinois, C. C Thomas, 1972a.
Hansburg, H. G. "Adolescent Separation Hostility: A Prelude to Violence." *Proceedings*

of the Twentieth International Congress of Psychology. Tokyo: Science Council of Japan. August 1972b.

Hansburg, H. G. "Separation Problems of Displaced Children." In R. Parker (Ed.), *The Emotional Stress of War, Violence and Peace.* Pittsburgh, Pennsylvania: Stanwyx House, 1972c.

Hansburg, H. G. "A Study of Adolescent Separation Stress." *Journal of Clinical Issues in Psychology,* 1972d, *4,* 30-37.

Hansburg, H. G. "A Study of Adolescent Separation Stress." *American Journal of Orthopsychiatry,* 1972e, *42,* 330-331.

Hansburg, H. G. "The Use of the Separation Anxiety Test in the Detection of Self-Destructive Tendencies in Early Adolescence." In D. V. Sankar (Ed.), *Mental Health in Childhood.* Vol. I (in press).

SHORT-FORM CHILDREN'S SCHOOL QUESTIONNAIRE (CSQ)

AUTHOR: Beeman N. Phillips

AGE: Upper-elementary school

VARIABLE: School anxiety and self-disclosure coping styles

TYPE OF MEASURE: Questionnaire

SOURCE FROM WHICH MEASURE MAY BE OBTAINED: Beeman N. Phillips, Department of Educational Psychology, University of Texas, Austin, Texas 78712.

DESCRIPTION OF MEASURE: The original CSQ was designed to measure a number of variables related to school stress and anxiety. The conceptualization and measurement of these variables is described in detail in the bibliographic references. One of these is school anxiety, which has as its conceptual basis the widely shared view that anxiety is consciously experienced affect, including fear, worry, and their physiological concomitants. Further, anxiety is at least partly a response to stressful situations, which for school anxiety would be school itself or school-related situations. Anxious responses to stressful peer and authority relationships, test and testlike situations, individual differences of an invidious nature (e.g., the belief that one's clothes aren't as nice as those of others), and other in-school anxiety arousing transactions were included in the original effort to measure school anxiety.

The original CSQ had 198 items, including items from the Test Anxiety Scale for Children, the Achievement Anxiety Scale, the Audience Anxiety Scale, and the Defensiveness Scale for Children, with the remainder originating in the Child Development in School Project (Phillips, 1966). Factor analyses of responses of combined samples of white, black, and Mexican-American upper-elementary school-aged children produced a replicated seventy-item school anxiety factor. Further factoring of these seventy items produced four major factorial dimensions, and the short form of the

CSQ contains the six items that best represented each of these factors, plus twenty-four other items. In addition to a school anxiety score, the following dimensions can be scored: (1) rejection by others, especially peers and teachers; (2) tests and test taking; (3) meeting expectations of others, especially teachers and parents; and (4) stress of reactivity.

The conceptual basis of coping styles in relation to self-disclosure is described by Phillips (1966, 1971). Briefly, coping style is a function of the meaning and threat of the *content* of the self-disclosure instrument responded to and/or of the *context* in which a person responds to a self-disclosure instrument. In identifying coping styles, two types of items are used. Type A items describe behaviors, events, and so forth that have a socially desirable connotation but that would be applicable to only a few children. Type B items describe behaviors, events, and so forth that have a socially undesirable connotation but that would be applicable to most children. When the context dominates in responding, acquiescent or negativistic coping may occur. Acquiescent coping is indicated by a strong tendency to agree with both types of items, while negativistic coping is indicated by a strong tendency to disagree with both types of items. On the other hand, when content dominates in responding, self-enhancing or self-derogating coping may occur. Self-enhancement is indicated by a strong tendency to agree with Type A items and disagree with Type B items, while in self-derogation the opposite tendency occurs. Although cutoff points are somewhat arbitrary, the use of these items on an exploratory basis is recommended, since coping styles in relation to self-disclosure are intrinsically important, as well as being useful in evaluating the anxiety results.

As examples, the first eight of the forty-eight items on the questionnaire are given below. The respondent replies on an answer sheet by checking either "yes" or "no" (odd-numbered items) and "no" or "yes" (even-numbered items).

1. Do you sometimes dream at night that the teacher is angry because you do not know your lessons?
2. Are you frequently afraid you may make a fool of yourself?
3. Do you pay close attention to what the teacher says when she explains something?
4. Is it hard for you to have as good a report card as your parents expect you to have?
5. Is it hard for you to do as well as the teacher expects you to do in class?
6. Do your knees shake when you are asked to recite in class?
7. Has anyone ever been able to scare you?
8. Do you feel terrible if you break something which belongs to somebody else?

RELIABILITY AND VALIDITY: School anxiety has a moderate degree of stability over the school year, with stability coefficients of the order of .60 to .70 for total scores, while coefficients for the four school anxiety dimensions range from .40 to .50. The following are evidence of validity: (1) School anxiety correlates higher with teacher grades, achievement tests, and underachievement in elementary school than general anxiety does; in addition, indices of early school adjustment are more predictive of school anxiety than general anxiety in the later elementary years. (2) As predicted from Schachter's theory, high school-anxious children have a greater tendency to pick popular peers and to reject unpopular peers than low school-anxious children; and, as expected from developmental theory, masculinity-femininity is significantly related to the school anxiety of boys but not girls. (3) The degree of socialization into middle-class school culture is negatively related to school anxiety; child personality variables, as evidenced in classroom coping and disruptive behaviors, are related to levels of school anxiety; and it has been shown that some school anxiety phenomena have cross-cultural invariance of uniformity.

BIBLIOGRAPHY:

Adams, R. L., and Phillips, B. N. "Factors Associated with Under- and Overachievement Among Socioeconomically and Racial-Ethnically Different Elementary School Children." *Psychology in the Schools,* 1968, *5,* 170-174.

Gotts, E. E., and Phillips, B. N. "The Relation Between Psychometric Measures of Anxiety and Masculinity-Femininity." *Journal of School Psychology,* 1967, *6,* 123-130.

McNeil, K. A., and Phillips, B. N. "Scholastic Nature of Responses to the Environment in Selected Subcultures." *Journal of Educational Psychology,* 1969, *60,* 79-85.

Phillips, B. N. *An Analysis of Causes of Anxiety Among Children in School.* Final report, project no. 2616, U.S. Office of Education. University of Texas, Austin, 1966.

Phillips, B. N. "Anxiety as a Function of Early School Experience." *Psychology in the Schools,* 1967, *4,* 335-340.

Phillips, B. N. "The Nature of School Anxiety and Its Relationship to Children's School Behavior." *Psychology in the Schools,* 1968, *5,* 195-204.

Phillips, B. N. "Problem Behavior in the Elementary School." *Child Development,* 1968, *39,* 895-903.

Phillips, B. N. "School Stress as a Factor in Children's Responses to Tests and Testing." *Journal of Educational Measurement,* 1971, *8,* 21-26.

Phillips, B. N., Harris, C., Ahuja, S. L., and Ng, S. N. "School Anxiety Among Malaysian and Indian Children." Submitted for publication.

Phillips, B. N., Martin, R. P., and Meyers, J. "Interventions in Relation to Anxiety in School." In C. D. Spielberger (Ed.), *Anxiety: Current Trends in Theory and Research,* Vol. 2. New York: Academic Press, 1972.

SIMON'S WORRY RESPONSE SURVEY

AUTHOR: Allen Simon

AGE: 11 to 16 years

VARIABLE: Children's worries

TYPE OF MEASURE: Questionnaire

SOURCE FROM WHICH MEASURE MAY BE OBTAINED: See Simon and Ward (1974) or write Allen Simon, Glamorgan Polytechnic, Buttrills Road, Barry, CF6 6SE, Wales; or L. O. Ward, Department of Education, University College, Swansea, South Wales.

DESCRIPTION OF MEASURE: The measure comprises two questionnaires, Worry List Questionnaire A and Worry List Questionnaire B. The former seeks data relating to frequency of worry, while the latter is designed to determine intensity of worries reported by pupils. Each questionnaire consists of the same 100 items derived mainly from a pilot study or worries reported spontaneously by 1,070 boys and girls in the age range 11 to 16 years. A small number of items were drawn from adult sources. Items were classified as belonging to one of eight categories of worry: family, school, economic, social, personal adequacy, personal health, animal, and imagination. Worry List Questionnaire A requires the pupil to put the letter "M" in the answer column opposite items that worry him often, while in Worry List Questionnaire B the subject is requested to put the letter "D" opposite items that worry him deeply. In both questionnaires the pupil is told to draw lines through any items that do not worry him and to put "No" opposite such items. Tentative norms exist for age groups 12+, 13+, and 14+ years for grammar and modern secondary-school pupils (N = 336 grammar school pupils and 336 secondary modern school pupils). Each age group had 224 pupils, and the sex ratio within each age group was the same. The questionnaires can be administered individually or to groups. Simple addition of items ticked gives the total of different types of worry responses for individual categories and all categories combined for individual pupils.

As examples, the first ten of the 100 items on the two forms of the questionnaire are given below. The respondent replies either "No" or "M" (many times) to each item on Form A, and either "No" or "D" (deeply) to each item on Form B.

Do you worry about:
1. Failing a test or exam.
2. Witches.
3. Choking when eating.
4. Being late for school.
5. Having bad dreams.
6. Getting the cane.
7. Parents punishing you.
8. Strange people following you.
9. Making your parents sad.
10. Not finding a job after leaving school.

RELIABILITY AND VALIDITY: The reliability of the survey was checked by determining the coefficient of correlation between pupils' negative responses to the 100 items on WLQ1A and WLQ1B. The reliability coefficient was .93. Evidence of validity comes in several forms. First, in classifying the items according to the various categories, six experienced judges reached agreement levels of 88 percent, suggesting content validity. However, the main criteria used to test the validity of responses made to questionnaire items were teachers' opinions or estimates of their pupils' worries. Teachers were asked to mark the responses of pupils according to the following instructions: (1) responses with which they fully agreed; (2) responses with which they partially agreed; (3) responses with which they disagreed; and (4) responses, the correct answers of which were unknown to them. If unknown responses are deducted, a very close agreement exists between pupils' reports of their worries and teachers' ratings of their accuracy, suggesting that the responses, in general, are valid. Agreement levels for frequency and intensity were 92 and 94 percent. Response validity was also tested by asking teachers to rank groups of thirty pupils in each age group according to frequency and intensity worry questionnaire scores. The p coefficients for frequency ranged from .89 to .91 and for intensity ranged from .86 to .89. Finally, the validity of a number of pupils' responses was studied by comparing their responses with conclusions reached concerning their troubles by clinicians employing psychiatric and other procedures. Responses to questionnaires in the number investigated were in close accord with the findings obtained by using clinical criteria.

BIBLIOGRAPHY:

Simon, A., and Ward, L. O. "Variables Influencing the Source, Frequency, and Intensity of Worry in Secondary School Pupils." *British Journal of Social and Clinical Psychology*, 1974, *13*, 391-396.

S-R INVENTORY OF ANXIOUSNESS, FORMS EY-L-64A and SA-66

AUTHORS: Norman S. Endler and J. McV. Hunt

AGE: Adolescents

VARIABLE: Anxiety

TYPE OF MEASURE: Self-report questionnaire

SOURCE FROM WHICH MEASURE MAY BE OBTAINED: Norman S. Endler, Department of Psychology, York University, 4700 Keele Street, Downsview, Ontario, Canada M3J 1P3.

DESCRIPTION OF MEASURE: The S-R Inventory of Anxiousness is a self-report questionnaire measuring trait anxiety. The original form of the inventory sampled fourteen modes of response and eleven situations, thus yielding a scale of 154 items. For each situation the subject rates his degree of anxiousness for each mode of response on a 5-point scale ranging from "not at all" to "very much." Using this format, it is possible to analyze the amount of variance attributable to subjects, situations, and modes of response, as well as the various interactions among these.

Form E-YL-64A of the scale, which was designed for adolescents, samples fourteen situations and ten modes of response and was administered to six samples of normal adolescents (404 males and 358 females). In addition, the inventory was administered to a sample of normal adolescents and to a sample of disturbed adolescents who were receiving psychiatric treatment. Form SA-66, which was also designed for adolescents, samples twelve situations and ten modes of response. The inventory was administered to two samples of adolescents (147 males and 142 females).

As examples, the first five of the ten response items to the first situation on Form EY-L-64A of the inventory are given below.

You are just starting off on a long automobile trip.
1. Heart beats faster.
2. Get an "uneasy feeling."
3. Emotions disrupt action.
4. Feel exhilarated and thrilled.
5. Want to avoid situation.

RELIABILITY AND VALIDITY: Reliability and validity data are available on the original form of the inventory.

BIBLIOGRAPHY:

Endler, N. S. "Estimating Variance Components from Mean Squares for Random and Mixed Effects Analysis of Variance Models." *Perceptual and Motor Skills,* 1966, *22,* 559-570.

Endler, N. S., and Bain, J. M. "Interpersonal Anxiety as a Function of Social Class." *Journal of Social Psychology,* 1966, *70,* 221-227.

Endler, N. S., and Hunt, J. McV. "Sources of Behavioral Variance as Measured by the S-R Inventory of Anxiousness." *Psychological Bulletin,* 1966, *65,* 336-346.

Endler, N. S., and Hunt, J. McV. "Triple Interaction Variance in the S-R Inventory of Anxiousness." *Perceptual and Motor Skills,* 1968, *27,* 1098.

Endler, N. S., and Hunt, J. McV. "Generalizability of Contributions from Sources of Variance in the S-R Inventories of Anxiousness." *Journal of Personality,* 1969, *37,* 1-24.

Endler, N. S., Hunt, J. McV., and Rosenstein, J. A. "An S-R Inventory of Anxiousness." *Psychological Monographs,* 1962, *76* (536), 1-33.

Endler, N. S., and North, C. "Changes in Adolescents' Self-Report Anxiety During Psychotherapy." *Psychotherapy: Theory, Research, and Practice,* 1973, *10,* 253-255.

Prepared by Marilyn Okada

Category 3

Perceptions
of Environment

The measures in this category are concerned with the ways in which children perceive different aspects of their environment. Some direct measures of the environment are also included.

Group 3-a. Perceptions of Adults. *These are primarily measures of children's perceptions of the influential adults in their lives—parents and teachers. Some school attitude measures (Group 8-a) also include a section on perception of teachers. Sex-role measures are included here simply because of the assumption that sex identification is closely tied to perceptions of parents or parent substitutes.*

Group 3-b. Perceptions of Peers. *These are primarily sociometric-type measures.*

Group 3-c. Other Environmental Perceptions and Characteristics. *These are miscellaneous measures, including locus-of-control measures.*

Group 3-a

Perceptions
of Adults

AUTHORITY FIGURE PERCEPTION TEST (AFP)

AUTHORS: Ben Ferguson and Kevin Kennelly

AGE: 13 years to adult

VARIABLE: Perceptions of authority figures

TYPE OF MEASURE: Test

SOURCE FROM WHICH MEASURE MAY BE OBTAINED: Kevin Kennelly, Department of Psychology, North Texas State University, Denton, Texas 76203.

DESCRIPTION OF MEASURE: The revised AFP consists of five scales, each of which contains fifteen forced-choice-type items. Each item provides the subjects with two alternative views of authorities: one representing a positive perception and the other representing a negative perception. The individual scales are designed to measure perception of authority figures as: Encouraging vs. Discouraging Constructive Environmental Manipulations, Supporting vs. Rejecting When Difficulty Encountered, Positive vs. Negative Reinforcers, Having Predictable vs. Unpredictable Standards, and Acting Upon Issue-Oriented Reason vs. Arbitrary Rule.
Examples of items in each scale are given below.

Encouraging vs. Discouraging
26. a. If given the choice, most teachers would tell parents that the best way to help teenagers become mature adults is to closely control their behavior.
   b. If given the choice, most teachers would tell parents that the best way to help teenagers become mature adults is to provide them with the freedom to learn what it's like to be an adult.

Supportive vs. Rejecting
42. a. Employers expect their employees to make mistakes and are eager to help them solve the problems they encounter.
   b. Employers expect their employees to make mistakes and usually ignore them when they have problems.

Positive vs. Negative Reinforcers
23. a. Most of the rules a high school student must obey are designed to make sure the student knows who is in control.
   b. High school rules are enforced in order to help the school provide an adequate learning environment.

Predictable vs. Unpredictable Standards
39. a. Unfortunately, many policemen are inconsistent law enforcers.
   b. Fortunately, most policemen consistently enforce the law.

Issue-Oriented vs. Arbitrary Reason
54. a. When an employee has difficulty meeting a deadline, most employers are willing to listen to reason.
   b. Unfortunately, most employers will not listen to reason when an employee has difficulty meeting a deadline.

RELIABILITY AND VALIDITY: The AFP has been administered to 307 preparatory high school students in grades 7 through 12. Ninety-five of these students received global classroom behavior ratings. The internal consistency of the AFP scales was determined by means of the coefficient *alpha*. The alpha coefficients obtained were: Encouraging vs. Discouraging, .53; Supportive vs. Rejecting, .64; Positive vs. Negative Reinforcer, .61; Predictable vs. Unpredictable Standards, .56; Issue-Oriented vs. Arbitrary Reason, .50; and total test, .88. The teachers' global ratings of classroom behaviors correlated .27 with total test scores, providing some validity for the AFP.

BIBLIOGRAPHY:

Ferguson, B., and Kennelly, K. "Internal-External Locus of Control and Perception of Authority Figures." *Psychological Reports,* 1974, *34,* 1119-1123.

BIRTHDAY TEST

AUTHOR: Mary L. Northway

AGE: 4 to 12 years

VARIABLE: Degree of children's preference for adults or children

TYPE OF MEASURE: Sociometric-type

SOURCE FROM WHICH MEASURE MAY BE OBTAINED: Mary L. Northway, 267 Rosedale Heights Drive, Toronto, Ontario, Canada M4T 1C7. Cost: $1.00 per set to cover handling and postage. Only one set supplied. If reproducing additional copies for use, please obtain permission from author.

DESCRIPTION OF MEASURE: The Birthday Test was created to assess children's preferences for adults or children as companions. It was developed to supplement other measures used in the longitudinal study of the Institute of Child Study, University of Toronto, introduced in 1962 and projected until 1974. The plan was to follow the six groups of children entering nursery school in 1962 and subsequent years until their graduation from grade 6. Sociometric tests of peer-group relations were given twice annually as a standard part of the measurement program. The Birthday Test was introduced in 1963 to gain further information on the children's social relations, namely those with adults *and* peers. It was anticipated that with increasing age, children would show increased preference for children; that at any age level, there would be wide individual differences; and that children showing greatest preference for children would receive higher sociometric scores.

  There are two forms of the test: Primary and Elementary. On each, the subject is asked to select three children and three adults whom he would like to have go with him on a birthday outing. This becomes an imaginary but basic sociometric group from which he makes his choices. Having established this basic group, he then follows a story describing six situations that occur during this outing; for each situation he selects three of the six members of the original group. The Primary form is an individual test, adapted to 4- to 8- or 9-year olds (nursery school to grade 3). It can be used with individual older children if the situation or children warrant it. A set of fourteen dolls (three representing men, three women, four boys, four girls, and an extra boy and girl to serve as the subject's self) is recommended for use with the primary form. Pipe cleaner dolls differing in size and dress, with weighted feet, have been used to advantage, adding interest and a focus for the subject's attention during test time. More realistic dolls have also been used, and which type served the test better is yet to be determined. The Elementary form is adapted to groups of 8- or 9- to 12-year-olds (grades 4 to 6) and is probably not suited to groups younger than 8. Both the Primary and Elementary forms of the test have been used in school settings, but the test is seen as applicable as well to other groupings of children such as in day-care centers and camps and has been found useful in clinical practice with individuals.

RELIABILITY AND VALIDITY: Northway and others (1969) in a study involving 539 children from nursery school to grade 6, found that choices of children (as against choosing adults) increased with age. Increases of choices to children, as indicated by differences between succeeding means, were significant at least at the .05 level for the following comparisons: nursery school with all other grades; kindergarten with grades 5 and 6; grade 1 with grades 4, 5, and 6; grade 2 with grades 4, 5, and 6; grade 3 with grades 4, 5, and 6; and grade 4 with grade 6.

BIBLIOGRAPHY:

Northway, M. L. (Ed.) *Primer of Sociometry.* (2nd ed.) Toronto, Canada: University of Toronto Press, 1967.

Northway, M. L. "The Sociometry of Society: Some Facts and Fancies." *Canadian Journal of Behavioral Science,* 1971, *3,* 18-36.

Northway, M. L., Davis, M., and Weld, L. "Sociometric Differences Between Two Groups of Children." *Educational Research,* 1969, *11,* 113-118.

BODY IMAGE IDENTIFICATION TEST

AUTHOR: Eleanor Bell Gottesman

AGE: Boys, 8 to 12 years; girls and boys, 13 to 17 years

VARIABLE: Feelings of masculinity-femininity as they relate to body image

TYPE OF MEASURE: Quantitative projective test

SOURCE FROM WHICH MEASURE MAY BE OBTAINED: See Gottesman and Caldwell (1966).

DESCRIPTION OF MEASURE: This test consists of seven outline drawings of the anterior view of the human body, seven drawings of faces, seven of shoulders, and seven of hips (a total of twenty-eight drawings), each on a 4 X 7 white card and each drawing differing from the next in the series on a continuum according to an exact scale. The drawings differentiate qualities thought to be feminine and masculine physical attributes: curve of eyebrow, direction of eye glance, amount of eyelash, shape and fullness of lips, width of shoulders, waist size, and hip size. There are no genitalia. The only changes in the figures from most masculine to most feminine are those described above. Questions asked are: "Which is most nearly like you?" "Which would you rather be like?" and others related to the separate body parts using objective methods to evaluate subjective feelings. Additional qualitative material is obtained through observing nonverbal language and spontaneous verbal language. This quickly administered and interpreted test is given to one person at a time but could be group-administered.

RELIABILITY AND VALIDITY: The test was administered to and validated on four groups or samples: (1) emotionally disturbed males, aged 8 to 11 (in special schools and in residential centers); (2) normal males, aged 8 to 11 (attending regular classes in public schools); (3) slow-learner males, aged 13 to 17 (in special classes for slow learners); and (4) slow-learner females, aged 13 to 17 (in special classes for slow learners). Differences were found between normal males and disturbed males at the .02 and .05 levels using *chi*-square. Male slow learners differed from female slow learners on the .05, .02, .01, and .001 levels. There were significant differences on eight criteria measuring body image feelings unconsciously or consciously but subjectively experienced and on an exact scale.

BIBLIOGRAPHY:

Gottesman, E. B., and Caldwell, W. E. "The Body-Image Identification Test: A Quantitative Project Technique to Study an Aspect of Body Image." *Journal of Genetic Psychology*, 1966, *108*, 19-33.

CHILDREN'S LOCUS-OF-CONTROL SCALE

AUTHORS: Irv Bialer and Rue L. Cromwell

AGE: 6 to 14 years

VARIABLE: Children's conception of locus of control

TYPE OF MEASURE: Questionnaire

SOURCE FROM WHICH MEASURE MAY BE OBTAINED: See Bialer (1960, 1961) and Gozali and Bialer (1968).

DESCRIPTION OF MEASURE: The construct "locus of control" is seen as reflecting the individual's ability to conceptualize the relationship between his own behavior and the outcome of events. The Children's Locus of Control Scale (Bialer, 1960, 1961; Cromwell, 1963) is designed to measure the extent to which a child characteristically construes event outcomes (positive and negative) as being due to his own actions (internally controlled) or to the whims and/or manipulations of fate, chance, or others (externally controlled). The scale contains twenty-three questions. These are verbally administered and so worded that for some a "yes" answer and for others a "no" answer indicate internal control. In the administration of the scale, the child is asked to say "yes" or "no" to each item as it is read to him, and the scale is scored in terms of the total number of responses in the direction of internal control. The higher the score, the more internal the orientation. Gozali and Bialer (1968) developed a reverse form of the scale, which may serve as an alternate form. An earlier version of this measure is described in Johnson and Bommarito (1971).

As examples, the first five items each from the regular form and from the reverse form are given below. The letter "f" following item number indicates that an answer of "yes" is scored as internal control; the letter "p" signifies that an answer of "no" is scored as internal control.

Regular Form

1p. When somebody gets mad at you, do you usually feel there is nothing you can do about it?

2f. Do you really believe a kid can be whatever he wants to be?

3f. When people are mean to you, could it be because you did something to make them be mean?

4f. Do you usually make up your mind about something without asking someone first?

5f. Can you do anything about what is going to happen tomorrow?

Reverse Form

1f. When somebody gets mad at you, do you usually feel that you can do something about it?

2p. Is it impossible for a person to be whatever he wants to be?

3p. Are people mean to you even if you do not do anything to make them be mean?

4p. Do you usually ask someone first before you make up your mind about something?

5p. Is it impossible for you to do anything about what is going to happen tomorrow?

RELIABILITY AND VALIDITY: The scale was standardized with a combined group of mentally retarded and normal children, ranging in chronological age from 6 to 14 years, in mental age from 4 to 16 years, and in IQ from 51 to 110. With this sample, an adjusted split-half reliability coefficient of .86 was derived. In later studies, Miller (1960) obtained an adjusted split-half reliability of .87, and McConnell (1962) found a test-retest reliability of .73. Gozali and Bialer (1968) obtained test-retest reliabilities (Pearson) of .84 and .87 with the original and reverse forms of the scale, respectively, as well as significant indications that the scales were independent of response-set bias among retarded youth ranging in age from 17 to 28 years, and in IQ from 59 to 87. Validity is demonstrated in numerous studies reviewed by Cromwell (1963), Lefcourt (1966), McConnell (1965), and in the original study (Bialer, 1960), by significant correlations with MA and CA, delay of gratification, and response to cues of success and failure.

BIBLIOGRAPHY:

Bartel, N. R. "Locus of Control and Achievement in Middle-Class and Lower-Class Children." Unpublished doctoral dissertation. Indiana University, Bloomington, 1968.

Battle, E., and Rotter, J. B. "Children's Feelings of Personal Control as Related to Social Class and Ethnic Group." *Journal of Personality,* 1963, *31,* 482-490.

Bialer, I. *Conceptualization of Success and Failure in Mentally Retarded and Normal Children.* Ann Arbor, Michigan: University Microfilms, 1960. (Also in brief in *Journal of Personality,* 1961, *29,* 303-320.)

Cromwell, R. L. "A Social Learning Approach to Mental Retardation." In N. R. Ellis (Ed.), *Handbook of Mental Deficiency.* New York: McGraw-Hill, 1963.

Gozali, J., and Bialer, I. "Children's Locus-of-Control Scale: Independence from Response-Set Bias among Retardates." *American Journal of Mental Deficiency,* 1968, *72,* 622-625.

Johnson, O. G., and Bommarito, J. W. *Tests and Measurements in Child Development: A Handbook.* San Francisco: Jossey-Bass, 1971.

Lefcourt, H. M. "Internal Versus External Control of Reinforcements: A Review." *Psychological Bulletin,* 1966, *65,* 206-220.

McConnell, T. R. "The Effects of Failure on Locus of Control in Retardates." *Abstracts of Peabody Studies in Mental Retardation,* 1962, *2* (11).

McConnell, T. R. *Locus of Control, Examiner Presence, and Source of Reinforcement as Factors in Visual Discrimination Learning with Mental Retardates.* Ann Arbor, Michigan: University Microfilms, 1965.

Miller, M. B. "Reliability of the Bialer-Cromwell Locus-of-Control Scale in an Institutionalized Mentally Retarded Sample." *Abstracts of Peabody Studies in Mental Retardation,* 1960 (73).

Rotter, J. B. "Generalized Expectancies for Internal Versus External Control of Reinforcement." *Psychological Monographs,* 1966, *80* (1) (Whole Number 609).

Shipp, D. "Impulsivity and Locus of Control as Predictors of Achievement and Adjustment in Mildly Retarded and Borderline Youth." *American Journal of Mental Deficiency,* 1971, *76,* 12-22.

Shore, M. F., Milgram, N. A., and Malasky, C. "The Effectiveness of an Enrichment Program for Disadvantaged Young Children." *American Journal of Orthopsychiatry,* 1971, *41,* 442-449.

FAMILY RELATIONS INVENTORY

AUTHOR: Richard J. Brunkan

AGE: High school and older

VARIABLE: Perceived parental attitudes

TYPE OF MEASURE: True-false questionnaire

SOURCE FROM WHICH MEASURE MAY BE OBTAINED: Richard J. Brunkan, Humber, Mundie, and McClary, 2021 Marine Plaza, Milwaukee, Wisconsin 53202.

DESCRIPTION OF MEASURE: The FRI is a 202-item questionnaire designed to measure the perceived attitudes of the subject's mother and father. Items are assigned to one of six scales: mother avoidance, mother acceptance, mother concentration, father avoidance, father acceptance, father concentration. The number of items in each scale varies from thirty to thirty-seven. The items are designed to measure the individual's perceptions of his parent's attitudes toward him in childhood and adolescence. A standard IBM answer sheet can be used, and scoring can be done by hand. The measure was originally designed to evaluate Roe's theory that vocational choice is related to the person's perception of his parent being either avoiding, accepting, or concentrating. Since its development, it has been used in a variety of other applications, which can be found in the literature.

As examples, the first twenty of the 202 forced-choice statements of the inventory, to be answered "true" or "false," are given below.

1. My father was often "too busy to listen" to me.
2. Mother generally made most of my decisions for me.
3. If I was right about something, my father generally told me so.
4. If I got into a quarrel my father would try to show me who was right and why.
5. My father seldom asked my opinion on anything.
6. My father thinks I should have as much opportunity as possible within reasonable limits.
7. My father was quite concerned about my doing well in school.
8. I still kiss my father "good night" when I am home.
9. My mother told me that she wished that I had never been born.
10. My mother explained sex matters to me if I asked her about them.
11. My mother gave me encouragement when I needed it most.
12. My father would explain things to me when I was working with him.
13. I felt that my father understood me.
14. My mother almost always kept me dressed better than my young friends.
15. I could "talk back" to my mother if I didn't overdo it.
16. My mother was willing to listen to my side of the story and give it consideration.
17. My father seemed to overdo both "blaming" and "praising."
18. My mother never seemed to notice my "pet" projects.
19. When I asked for something my mother would almost always give it to me.
20. I hardly ever felt that my mother criticized me unjustly.

RELIABILITY AND VALIDITY: Original scales were administered to 100 male and female undergraduate students. The coefficients of internal consistency on the scales were in the .80s or .90s with the exception of father concentration, which was .59. Test-retest reliability coefficients were in the similar range except for father concentration, which was .73. Validity was assessed through scale intercorrelations, the hypothesis being that acceptance and avoidance should be negatively correlated, whereas concentration was not highly correlated with either of the other scales. Validity was also measured through correlation with other scales such as Grigg's Questionnaire (1959) and Utton's Rating Scale (1962). Further validity was established through a comparison of students and prison inmates. For both parents the inmates scored significantly higher on avoidance and lower on acceptance.

BIBLIOGRAPHY:

Brunkan, R. J. "Perceived Parental Attitudes and Parental Identification in Relation to Field of Vocational Choice." *Journal of Counseling Psychology,* 1965, *12,* 39-47.
Brunkan, R. J. "Perceived Parental Attitudes and Parental Identification in Relation to Problems in Vocational Choice." *Journal of Counseling Psychology,* 1966, *13,* 394-402.
Brunkan, R. J., and Crites, J. O. "An Inventory to Measure the Parental Attitude Variables in Roe's Theory of Vocational Choice." *Journal of Counseling Psychology,* 1964, *11,* 3-12.
Grigg, A. E. "Childhood Experience with Parental Attitudes: A Test of Roe's Hypothesis." *Journal of Counseling Psychology,* 1959, *6,* 153-156.
Utton, A. C. "Recalled Parent-Child Relations as Determinants of Vocational Choice." *Journal of Counseling Psychology,* 1962, *9,* 49-53.

FORBES-DYKSTRA HOSTILITY TOWARD AUTHORITY SCALE

AUTHORS: Gordon B. Forbes and Dale Dykstra

AGE: 6 to 12 years

VARIABLE: Attribution of negative traits to authority

TYPE OF MEASURE: Checklist

SOURCE FROM WHICH MEASURE MAY BE OBTAINED: Gordon B. Forbes, Department of Psychology, Millikin University, Decatur, Illinois 62522.

DESCRIPTION OF MEASURE: The Forbes-Dykstra scale consists of faceless line drawings of six authority figures and a standard set of six dichotomous questions about each figure. The authority figures represented are: policeman, judge, mother, father, fireman, and teacher. Each page of the test contains a half-page drawing of one of the authority figures. The questions to be answered "yes" or "no" are the same for each of the figures: "A *(name of authority figure)* likes me, helps me, will hurt me, is my friend, protects me, and is bad." The instrument yields a score that represents the number of negative characteristics the child attributes to the authority figures. The test may be administered individually or administered to small groups using an overhead projector. The format of the instrument is designed to minimize demands on the child's reading or vocabulary skills. With the use of appropriate instructions, the test requires no reading skills from the subject.

RELIABILITY AND VALIDITY: Formal reliability and validity studies are not available. However, females below age 8 attribute very few negative characteristics to authority, and a substantial "floor" effect is found with young females. The instrument appears to detect individual differences among males as young as 6.

BIBLIOGRAPHY:

Forbes, G. B., and Dykstra, D. "Children's Attribution of Negative Traits to Authority Figures as a Function of Family Size and Sex." *Psychological Reports,* 1971, *28,* 363-366.

GAMES INVENTORY

AUTHORS: John E. Bates and P. M. Bentler

AGE: Parents of boys 5 to 12 years

VARIABLE: Masculinity-femininity, gender deviances in boys, age-appropriateness of game choices

TYPE OF MEASURE: "Yes-no" parent questionnaire

SOURCE FROM WHICH MEASURE MAY BE OBTAINED: See Bates and Bentler (1973).

DESCRIPTION OF MEASURE: The Games Inventory is composed of sixty-four names of children's games, which were chosen from a longer list on the basis of correlations with the factors of another gender-deviance measure, the Gender Behavior Inventory for Boys (GBIB) (Bates, Bentler, and Thompson, 1973). The scales of the Games Inventory are: (1) feminine, preschool games (e.g., dress up, play house); (2) masculine, nonathletic games (e.g., kites, play spaceman); (3) athletic games (e.g., basketball, wrestling); and (4) composite (containing all the items of scales 1-3, and scored in the direction of effeminacy).

As examples, the first twenty-five of the sixty-four items of the questionnaire are given below. The parent indicates which of these games his child plays by marking "yes" or "no."

1. Arts and crafts.
2. Ballet.
3. Baseball.
4. Basketball.
5. Blocks.
6. Builds forts and huts.
7. Camping.
8. Card games.
9. Clay modeling.
10. Climb trees.
11. Dancing.
12. Darts.
13. Dodge-ball.
14. Draw and paint.
15. Dress.
16. Dress up.
17. Fishing.
18. Follow the leader.

19. Foot races.   23. Hunting.
20. Football.   24. Indian wrestling.
21. Giant steps ("mother, may I").   25. Jump-rope.
22. Hiking.

RELIABILITY AND VALIDITY: Two types of internal consistency coefficients were obtained with a normal sample of PTA mothers (N = 223) for the scale. Kuder-Richardson formula 20 values are .85, .74, .83, and .72, for scales 1 to 4, respectively. Coefficient *theta* values (Bentler, 1972) are .97, .94, and .93 for scales 1, 2, and 3 respectively. There are several sorts of validity evidence. First, the scale scores of a separate normal PTA sample (N = 66), not used in the original scale construction process, were intercorrelated. The results suggest that scales 1 and 3 are orthogonal, scale 2 has low or moderate relationship with both 1 and 3, and, as would be expected, scale 4 (the composite) relates moderately or highly to all of the other scales. Second, using the same normal cross-validational sample, generally low but significant correlations were obtained between the Games Inventory scales and corresponding GBIB factors, as was predicted. Third, significant age trends (years 5 to 10) were found for all scales in the original normal sample (excluding one 11-year-old, N = 222). Means and standard deviations are reported in Bates and Bentler (1973). Fourth, scales 3 and 4 were found to correlate highly and significantly with independent clinical judgments of degree-of-gender disturbance in a group of seventeen 5- to 12-year-old boys referred because of effeminacy. Fifth, scales 1, 2, 3, and 4 discriminated well between the clinical sample of gender-problem referrals and a matched normal sample (p levels were .005, .044, .004, and .001, respectively) in the predicted directions. It should be noted that while the Games Inventory would be useful for research in deviant gender development and may indeed be useful for diagnostic purposes, not enough evidence has yet been obtained regarding its efficiency in populations of children where the base rate of gender deviance is low. So at this point it should probably be used clinically as a final screening or classification device only with caution. Further validational data are being analyzed (Thompson, Bates, and Bentler, in preparation).

BIBLIOGRAPHY:

Bates, J. E., and Bentler, P. M. "Play Activities of Normal and Effeminate Boys." *Developmental Psychology,* 1973, *9,* 20-27.

Bates, J. E., Bentler, P. M., and Thompson, S. K. "Measurement of Deviant Gender Development in Boys." *Child Development,* 1973, *44,* 591-598.

Bentler, P. M. "A Lower-Bound Method for the Dimension-Free Measurement of Internal Consistency." *Social Science Research,* 1972, *1,* 343-357.

Thompson, S. K., Bates, J. E., and Bentler, P. M. "Gender-Disturbed Boys and Their Families: A Multi-Variable Comparison with Normals and Clinical Controls" (in preparation).

HUNTER'S TEACHER REPORT CARD

AUTHOR: Elizabeth Hunter

AGE: Kindergarten through high school

VARIABLE: Pupils' thoughts and feelings about the teacher

TYPE OF MEASURE: Questionnaire

SOURCE FROM WHICH MEASURE MAY BE OBTAINED: Elizabeth Hunter, Box 803, Hunter College, 695 Park Avenue, New York, New York 10021.

DESCRIPTION OF MEASURE: This is an informal forty-item test, designed to provide feedback to teachers about their own pupils' thoughts and feelings about school and the teacher. The items are suggestions, and it is hoped that teachers will make their own additional items.

As examples, the first fifteen odd-numbered items are given below.

1. My teacher is careful not to hurt the children's feelings.
3. My teacher cares about me.
5. My teacher treats most of the kids fairly.
7. My teacher makes me feel important in this class.
9. My teacher criticizes me.
11. My teacher criticizes lots of kids in the class.
13. The kids in this class pick on each other.
15. We learn from each other in this class.
17. We learn important things in this class.
19. My teacher is nice.
21. My teacher uses ideas that are suggested by pupils.
23. Homework in this class is useful to me.
25. My teacher likes it when we ask questions.
27. Time seems to go by quickly in this class.
29. I deserve the grades I get in this class.

RELIABILITY AND VALIDITY: None reported.

BIBLIOGRAPHY:

Hunter, E. "Report Cards For Teachers." *Childhood Education,* 1972, *48,* 410-411.

IMBER TRUST SCALE FOR CHILDREN AND TEACHERS

AUTHOR: Steve C. Imber

AGE: Grades 4 and 5

VARIABLE: Children and teacher trust

TYPE OF MEASURE: Teachers, rating scale; children, questionnaire rating scale

SOURCE FROM WHICH MEASURE MAY BE OBTAINED: Steve C. Imber, Special Education Department, Rhode Island College, 600 Mt. Pleasant Avenue, Providence, Rhode Island 02908. Cost: $5.00, 5 copies or less; $4.00, 5 to 10 copies; $3.50, 10 or more copies.

DESCRIPTION OF MEASURE: Children's Trust Scale: This research instrument was devised to provide a measure of a child's trust of important individuals around him. The forty-item test presents several situations relating to father, mother, peer, and teacher trust, the outcomes of which are selected from either a "trusting" or "non-trusting" answer. This scale has presently been used with fourth- and fifth-grade children. Teacher's Trust Scale: This is a 5-point rating scale developed to provide a measure of children's trust in addition to and in conjunction with the Imber Children's Trust Scale. There are four components of the teacher's rating of the child's trust: trustworthiness, trust, security, and dependability.

As examples, the first five of the forty items of the Children's Trust Scale are given below.

1. A father promises his son a set of new wheels for Christmas.
   a. He will remember to get the set for him.
   b. He will forget.
2. When teachers give grades (marks) they
   a. are usually fair.
   b. seem to be pretty unfair.
3. A mother looks into her pocketbook and discovers that a dollar is missing. She asks her son i] he has seen it. He says "No."
   a. The mother does not believe him.
   b. The mother believes him.
4. One friend was supposed to meet another after school and didn't show up.
   a. He probably didn't want to come in the first place.
   b. He didn't come because he couldn't.
5. Dad says he'll take Franklin to the movies on Saturday morning. On Saturday
   a. Dad says he can't take him because he has a lot of work to do.
   b. they go to the movies.

RELIABILITY AND VALIDITY: The present scale has been evaluated for reliability; a different version of the Children's Trust Scale yielded a Kuder-Richardson formula 20 reliability coefficient of .83. The Children's and Teacher's Trust Scales appear to have a high degree of face validity. In addition, concurrent validity may be derived through intercorrelations of the Teacher's and Children's Trust Scales, although these scales are not assessing trust in the same manner. These intercorrelations range from .11 (*n.s.*) to .39 (*p* < .01), with an overall correlation of children's and teacher's trust of *r* = .37 (*p* < .01). In addition, there is some indication of construct validity in that teacher trust of the Children's Trust Scale correlated significantly (*p* < .05) with dependent variables of reading and social studies at *p* < .01 for arithmetic, language arts, and science, as predicted. These measures of trust are perceived by the author as having significant potential; however, at the present time, both scales are still relatively crude attempts to measure the concept of trust.

BIBLIOGRAPHY:

Imber, S. C. "Relationship of Trust to Academic Performance." *Journal of Personality and Social Psychology,* 1973, *28,* 145-150.

Imber, S., and Marcia, J. *The Relationship of Trust and Concept Attainment in Fifth Graders.* Unpublished manuscript. State University of New York at Buffalo, 1968.

JUNIOR HIGH SCHOOL STUDENTS' RATING SCALE OF TEACHING EFFECTIVENESS

AUTHORS: L. Grant Somers and Mara L. Southern

AGE: 11 to 14 years

VARIABLE: Teacher behavior

TYPE OF MEASURE: Rating scale

SOURCE FROM WHICH MEASURE MAY BE OBTAINED: Mara L. Southern, Department of Testing and Evaluation, San Jose State University, San Jose, California 95192.

DESCRIPTION OF MEASURE: This is a scale for junior high school students to use to evaluate their teachers. Eight items relating to teacher effectiveness were generated from student-listed "best teacher" traits. Student-generated traits were ranked in frequency of mention, as were teacher-generated traits. The rank order correlation of the two sets of ranked traits was .84, suggesting considerable teacher and student agreement about the important teacher behaviors for effective instruction. The test is scored using a Likert format with a score of 1 assigned to "A" ratings (most positive teacher behavior) and a score of 4 assigned to "D" ratings. Student ratings of ten teachers who taught a total of forty-four classes were obtained with a total of 1,081 student responses made to each of the eight items. Means and standard deviations for the item are not included, as it is suggested that local normative data from a school or school district would best serve as referents.

As examples, the first four items of the eight-item scale are given below.

1. A. This teacher really has a good sense of humor.
   B. This teacher has a pretty good sense of humor.
   C. This teacher has a fair sense of humor.
   D. This teacher does not have a very good sense of humor.
2. A. This teacher almost always understands students of this age and their problems.
   B. This teacher has a pretty good understanding of students this age and their problems.
   C. This teacher sometimes understands students this age and their problems.
   D. This teacher doesn't seem to be able to understand students this age and their problems.
3. A. This teacher always has good control of the class and can be strict when it is necessary.
   B. This teacher usually controls the class and is usually strict when it is necessary.
   C. This teacher is not too good at controlling the class or being strict when it is necessary.
   D. This teacher doesn't control the class and is not strict when he or she should be.
4. A. This teacher is almost always friendly to students.
   B. This teacher is usually friendly to students.
   C. This teacher sometimes has a friendly attitude toward students.
   D. This teacher is not very friendly to students.

The following five items are from Part II of the test.

2. Show me how Nancy (Johnny) would feel *if she wanted to play with you and you couldn't play because it was too late.* Would you feel (examiner names emotions according to sequence). Pick up the face you think and put it on the picture. Why do you think Nancy (Johnny) would feel _____?
3. Show me how Nancy (Johnny) would feel *if you broke her favorite toy.* Would she feel (examiner names emotions according to sequence). Pick up the face you think and put it on the picture. Why do you think Nancy (Johnny) would feel _____?
6. Show me how Nancy (Johnny) would feel *if you left her and went to play with someone else.* Would she feel (examiner names emotions according to sequence). Pick up the face you think and put it on the picture. Why do you think Nancy (Johnny) would feel _____?
10. Show me how Nancy (Johnny) would feel *if you said something bad about her father or mother.* Would she feel (examiner names emotions according to sequence). Pick up the face you think and put it on the picture. Why do you think Nancy (Johnny) would feel _____?
11. Show me how Nancy (Johnny) would feel *if you wouldn't let her play with you.* Would she feel (examiner names emotions according to sequence). Pick up the face you think and put it on the picture. Why do you think Nancy (Johnny) would feel _____?

RELIABILITY AND VALIDITY: The pooled ratings of all teachers in all classes yielded an *alpha* coefficient of .84. Reliability was also determined by randomly splitting student ratings (N = approximately 65 in each random half) for each teacher separately into two groups and performing independent t tests of differences between means for each scale item for each teacher. Of the 64 resulting t-ratios only six were significant beyond the .05 level. Interitem correlations ranged from .55 to .04, all of which were positive. Item three, dealing with maintenance of class control, was consistently less highly related to other items than the remaining seven items were related to one another.

BIBLIOGRAPHY:

Somers, L. G., and Southern, M. L. "A Rating Scale for Evaluation of Teaching Effectiveness for Use with Junior High School Students." *California Journal of Educational Research,* 1974, *25,* 128-133.

Prepared by Mara L. Southern

MICHIGAN GENDER IDENTITY TEST (MIGIT)

AUTHOR: University of Michigan Personality and Language Behavior Research Project

AGE: 18 months and up

VARIABLE: Gender identity

TYPE OF MEASURE: Modified sorting task

SOURCE FROM WHICH MEASURE MAY BE OBTAINED: Alexander Z. Guiora, University of Michigan Personality and Language Behavior Research Project N5714, University Hospital, University of Michigan, Ann Arbor, Michigan 48104.

DESCRIPTION OF MEASURE: The Michigan Gender Identity Test (MIGIT) is a modified sorting procedure permitting a choice of strategies for eliciting either verbal or nonverbal responses. The test consists of two tasks: identification of colored photographs of familiar objects such as dogs and balls (nine pictures) and identification of colored photographs of boys and girls (eight pictures). Each of the two tasks consists of two trials. In the second trial of the boys and girls series, the child is shown a picture of himself/herself as well, taken prior to testing. Attainment of a perfect score requires that the child correctly identify all photographs of dogs and balls and boys and girls, as well as place his/her own picture in the appropriate gender category and identify it as his/her own.

RELIABILITY AND VALIDITY: None reported.

BIBLIOGRAPHY:

Dull, C. Y., Guiora, A. Z., Paluszny, M., Beit-Hallahmi, B., Catford, J. C., and Cooley, R. E. "The Michigan Gender Identity Test (MIGIT)." *Comprehensive Psychiatry,* 1975, *16,* 581-592.
Paluszny, M., Beit-Hallahmi, B., Cooley, R. E., Dull, C. Y., and Guiora, A. Z. "Gender

Identity and Its Measurement in Children." *Comprehensive Psychiatry*, 1973, *14*, 3.

Prepared by Alexander Z. Guiora

MODIFIED "IT" SCALE

AUTHOR: Henry B. Biller

AGE: 4 to 7 years

VARIABLE: Masculinity-femininity of sex role orientation

TYPE OF MEASURE: Test

SOURCE FROM WHICH MEASURE MAY BE OBTAINED: See Biller (1968)

DESCRIPTION OF MEASURE: This is an extensively modified version of Brown's (1956, 1962; Brown and Tolor, 1957) IT Scale used to assess sex-role orientation (0). The IT Scale has been criticized because "IT", the stick figure, actually looks more like a boy than a girl. In the modified instrument, only the face of the IT figure is presented, rather than the whole body. Pilot work revealed that in this way the IT figure was sexually neutral in appearance. Ss are asked to indicate a particular behavior for the "child" from among pictures of the following pairs of items: Indian chief and Indian princess; men's clothes and women's clothes; materials for sewing a handkerchief and for making a model airplane; lipstick and cosmetics, and a razor; tools for fixing broken objects, and washing and ironing apparatus; men's shoes and women's shoes; big boys playing and big girls playing; building tools and cooking utensils; and a man and a woman. When the pictures are of people, the S is asked which person the child would be (in other words, "Here are some big Indians. Which big Indian is the child going to be?") When the pictures are of clothing, the S is asked what clothes the child would wear. (In other words, "Here are some big people's clothes. Which big person's clothes is the child going to wear?") When the pictures pertain to activities, the S is asked which activity the child would perform. (In other words, "Here are some things big people do. Here are some things to bake and cook with, and some things to build with. Which is this child going to do?") A point is given for each masculine choice, and 2 additional points (1 each) are given if the boy, when questioned, gives the child a boy's name and says the child will become a father.

RELIABILITY AND VALIDITY: The modified IT technique yielded a rather skewed distribution. Scores ranged from 0 to 11, with a mean of 8.23 and a standard deviation of 5.50. Split-half reliability computed by the Spearman-Brown formula was .89 ($p <$ .0005). Draw-A-Person and IT scores were correlated .58 ($p <$ .0005). It was expected that the relationships between measures of the same aspect would be higher than relationships among different aspects of masculinity. For instance, the DAP and IT measures should have a higher relationship to one another than to measures of toy and game preference (P) or sex-role adoption (A). The results conformed with such expectations. DAP scores correlated .58 ($df = 185$, $p < .0005$) with IT scores and .79 ($df = 185$, $p < .0005$) with O scores, while correlating only .10 ($df = 185$, $n.s.$) with P scores and .10 ($df = 185$, $n.s.$) with A scores. IT scores correlated .91 ($df = 185$, $p < .0005$) with O scores but only .27 ($df = 185$, $p < .05$) with A scores. Biller (1968) provides additional data on relationships of the modified IT with other variables.

BIBLIOGRAPHY:

Biller, H. B. "A Multiaspect Investigation of Masculine Development in Kindergarten-Age Boys." *Genetic Psychology Monographs,* 1968, *78,* 89-138.

Biller, H. B. "Father Dominance and Sex-Role Development in Kindergarten-Age Boys." *Developmental Psychology,* 1969, *1,* 87-94.

Brown, D. G. "Sex-Role Preference in Young Children." *Psychological Monographs,* 1956, *70* (14) (Whole no. 421).

Brown, D. G. "Sex-Role Preference in Children: Methodological Problems." *Psychological Reports,* 1962, *11,* 477-478.

Brown, D. G., and Tolor, A. "Human Figure Drawings as Indicators of Sexual Identification and Inversion." *Perceptual and Motor Skills,* 1957, *1,* 199-201.

Prepared by Henry B. Biller and Orval G. Johnson

MOTHER-CHILD INTERACTION TEST (MCIT)

AUTHOR: Jay D. Schvaneveldt

AGE: Adolescents and adults

VARIABLE: Perceptions of maternal overprotection of children aged preschool through adolescence

TYPE OF MEASURE: Film test and rating scale

SOURCE FROM WHICH MEASURE MAY BE OBTAINED: Filmed instrument (MCIT) is available from the Educational Media Center at Florida State University, Tallahassee, Florida. There is a nominal rental fee. Item scales are available from Jay D. Schvaneveldt, Department of Family and Child Development, Utah State University, Logan, Utah 84322.

DESCRIPTION OF MEASURE: The MCIT is a detailed battery of items that accompany ten episodes of filmed behavior between parents and children, most of them focusing on mother-child interaction. Subjects view each of the filmed episodes and then respond to an average of ten items per filmed episode in which they rate their perceptions using a 4-point Likert scale. This film test, in conjunction with the rating scales, attempts to overcome some of the serious limitations of traditional paper-and-pencil tests in which subjects only react to an elusive stimulus. The film defines and refines the area of focus and permits greater validity of response, since it approximates real situations.

As examples, the first episode and five of the ten items based on it are given below.

This episode has two subjects. One boy is seven and the other is eight. They are fighting in the backyard of the seven-year-old's home. They slap at each other and wrestle in a half-serious manner. Neither boy appears to hurt the other boy and neither of the boys ever goes to the ground. The mother is seen coming from the porch of the house and comes to where the boys are fighting. She separates them and places a hand on each of their shoulders. She scolds the boys for a period and then directs one boy to go home and gestures for him to leave. As the neighbor boy leaves, the mother turns her attention to her own son and continues to scold him.

1. The mother should have let the boys keep going unless they were inflicting injury upon one another.
2. The mother should not have sent the boy home.
3. The mother should discuss the fighting problem with the neighbor boy's mother.
4. The mother should have directed the boys into some other activity.
5. The mother should have realized that this was a normal activity for boys of this age and have let them continue.

RELIABILITY AND VALIDITY: Test-retest done on fifty-three female subjects who were similar to actual subjects used in the study produced a Spearman-Brown rank-order correlation coefficient of .92. A percentage of specific agreement of the items in two administrations resulted in a 78.54 specific agreement between the two administrations. The MCIT was capable of distinguishing individuals who vary in present state. The filmed episodes coupled with the items were constructed utilizing the following guides: (1) Is the item clear? (2) Is the item sufficiently specific? (3) Is the item significantly related to the concept under investigation? Specialists viewed each episode and ranked the items in regard to these three criteria. It was assumed that mothers and unmarried single coeds would differ in their perceptions of maternal care and control. The data indicated that this was the case.

BIBLIOGRAPHY:

Schvaneveldt, J. D. "Correlates of Perceptions Toward Maternal Overprotection." *Journal of Genetic Psychology,* 1968, *112,* 267, 273.
Schvaneveldt, J. D. "Development of a Film Test for the Measurement of Perceptions Toward Maternal Overprotection." *Journal of Genetic Psychology,* 1968, *112,* 255-266.

PARENT-AFFINITY PERCEPTION SCALE

AUTHORS: Earlene E. Miller and Jay D. Schvaneveldt

AGE: Preschool to junior high

VARIABLE: Perceived parent preference

TYPE OF MEASURE: Questionnaire or structured interview

SOURCE FROM WHICH MEASURE MAY BE OBTAINED: Jay C. Schvaneveldt, Department of Family and Child Development, UMC 29, Utah State University, Logan, Utah 84322.

DESCRIPTION OF MEASURE: The Parent-Affinity Perception Scale consists of thirty statements referring to possible activities where a parent would be involved with the child. They are posed in question form, and the child responds to each item with the word "mother" or "father" depending upon parental preference to perform or engage in each activity. It is designed as a summated-type measure in which each child's responses are summarized and an indication is given as to mother or father preference for that given child. Theoretically, the measure is important in regard to occupational role, sex role, sex typing, and degree of affiliation or affirmation with mothers and fathers as parents.

As examples, the first six of the thirty questions are given below.

1. If you wanted money to spend, whom would you ask, your mother or your father, for the money?
2. If you needed a parent to come to school with you, whom would you ask to go, your mother or father?
3. If you were to take a plane trip, would you rather have your mother or your father go with you?
4. If you were sick and needed to see a doctor, would you want your mother or your father to take you to the doctor?
5. Whom do you think is the happier person, your mother or your father?
6. If you were unhappy, would you rather talk to your mother or your father about what is making you sad?

RELIABILITY AND VALIDITY: A test-retest with an interval of seventeen days indicated a specific percentage of agreement of 92.8. The scale was judged to have face validity, and the item content was of interest to the age and sex of the subject children. The items are clear and understandable and are designed to obtain a discriminative response for parental preference. In addition, an item analysis using the *chi*-square on the upper- and lower-quartile responses indicated that twenty-six of the thirty items discriminated at or beyond the .05 level of significance.

BIBLIOGRAPHY:

Miller, E. E. "Parent-Child Affinity as Perceived by Children." Unpublished master's thesis. Utah State University, Logan, 1972.

Schvaneveldt, J. D., and Miller, E. E. "Parent-Child Affinity as Perceived by Children."
Unpublished research paper. Utah State University, Logan, 1973.

Prepared by Jay D. Schvaneveldt

PARENT DISCIPLINE INVENTORY

AUTHOR: Eric L. Dlugokinski

AGE: 8 to 15 years

VARIABLE: Children's perceptions of maternal induction in peer-conflict situations

TYPE OF MEASURE: Situations inventory

SOURCE FROM WHICH MEASURE MAY BE OBTAINED: Eric L. Dlugokinski, Department of Psychiatry and Behavioral Sciences, University of Oklahoma Health Science Center, P.O. Box 26910, Oklahoma City, Oklahoma 73190. Cost: $1.00 for photocopying and handling.

DESCRIPTION OF MEASURE: The measure consists of six peer-conflict situations in which the child is asked to read and imagine (1) that he is in that situation, and (2) that his mother witnessed or heard about the conflict. He is then asked to check how often his mother might respond to each situation with varied types of reactions (usually, sometimes, rarely, never). There is an average of nine reactions to each situation. After checking the frequency of each reaction he is asked to go back and pick the one thing his mother does most often (1), second most often (2), and third most often (3). The reactions vary from power-assertive responses, to inductive responses, to neutral responses. Final scores for perceived induction and power assertion are obtained by weighting and summing the total ranks for power assertion and induction. A rank of 1 is weighted 3, 2 is weighted 2, and 3 is weighted 1.

The scale is an extension of the scale devised by Hoffman (1970) and was specifically created to assess the degree of perceived induction in peer-conflict situations. Although the scale assesses perceptions of maternal behavior, with slight modifications it could also assess paternal behavior. Induction refers to attempts at communicating to the child the consequences of his action for others and involves using reasoning to develop empathy or perception of the needs of others. The parent in this socialization mode ideally communicates three things: the existence of a rational basis for discipline, independent of power; the value of respect for these rules; and the necessity of self-monitoring. In power assertion, reasoning is replaced by suggestion and exhortation, by demands and threats of punishment. The basic assumptions of this scale are that there is correspondence between reports and experience, and that children are more generous when exposed to a communication that elicits a rational and emphathetic basis for such behaviors. Inductive communication is hypothesized as a socialization practice that can contribute to a value orientation, moral understanding, and behavior sensitive to the rights and feelings of others.

As an example, the first of the six peer-conflict situations of the inventory, together with the maternal reactions, are given below.

Imagine that you and your friend went to the State Fair together. Each of you had the same amount of money to spend. As you were getting ready to leave the fair you had just enough for a hot dog and your bus fare home. You hadn't eaten lunch and you were starved. Your friend pleaded with you to let him use your hot dog money to get home, because he had spent all of his money. Instead, you ate the hot dog and took the bus home yourself. You told your mother exactly what happened. How often do you think she might say or do the following things?
1. Hit or slap you for not giving him your money.
2. Praise you for not spending your money as foolishly as your friend.
3. She wouldn't say or do much of anything because you made it home all right.
4. She wouldn't say much but you could tell she was disappointed in you for leaving your friend helpless like that.
5. Warn you that if you ever did anything like that again she (or your father) would really give you a beating.
6. Tell you how disappointed she was that you thought your stomach was more important than your friend.
7. Say that that will probably teach him to be more careful with his money.
8. She would try to make me imagine all the trouble my friend would have to get home so that I could see all the problems I caused him.

RELIABILITY AND VALIDITY: In a pilot study the test-retest reliability after ten days was .87 for the induction score and .79 for power assertion. Perceived induction correlated positively with four measures of other-centeredness including value statements, mature understanding of kindness, donations to charity, and peer ratings on consideration. Perceived power assertion correlated negatively with perceived induction, but independently it has questionable value as a predictor.

BIBLIOGRAPHY:

Dlugokinski, E. L., and Firestone, I. "Congruence Among Four Methods of Measuring Other-Centeredness." *Child Development,* 1973, *44,* 304-308.

Dlugokinski, E. L., and Firestone, I. "Other-Centeredness and Susceptibility to Charitable Appeals: Effects of Perceived Discipline." *Developmental Psychology,* 1974, *10,* 21-28.

Hoffman, M. L. "Moral Development." In P. H. Mussen (Ed.), *Carmichael's Manual of Child Psychology.* Vol. 12. New York: Wiley, 1970.

PARENT-PEER CROSS-PRESSURES TEST

AUTHOR: Clay V. Brittain

AGE: 13 to 16 years

VARIABLE: Tendencies toward parent vs. peer compliance

TYPE OF MEASURE: Role-conflict test

SOURCE FROM WHICH MEASURE MAY BE OBTAINED: See Brittain (1959). A limited number of copies are available from Clay V. Brittain, Research and Analysis Branch, U.S. Enlisted Evaluation Center, Fort Benjamin Harrison, Indianapolis, Indiana 46249.

DESCRIPTION OF MEASURE: The Cross-Pressures Test consists of twelve items plus an example. Each item briefly describes a situation in which a teenage girl is trying to decide between two alternatives (e.g., which dress to wear, which boy to date). Her parents favor one of the alternatives and her friends favor the other. The subject is asked to indicate which alternative the girl probably selected. The Cross-Pressures Test is designed to assess tendencies toward peer compliance vs. parent compliance. It consists of Forms A and B, which are identical except for the preferences attributed to parents and friends. These are reversed from one form to the other. The two forms are administered a few days apart. In scoring the test, the responses to each item are categorized as peer-compliant (the alternative favored by friends is chosen each time), parent-compliant (the alternative favored by parents is chosen each time), or noncompliant (the same content alternative is chosen, regardless of preferences of parents and friends). The data can be analyzed for situational differences, that is, to what extent tendencies to peer compliance vs. parent compliance differ depending upon the type of choice. The data also can be used to derive indices of peer compliance vs. parent compliance for each individual tested. Thus, the instrument yields information about both situations and individuals.

As examples, the first two of the twelve items on Forms A and B of the test are given below.

Form A

1. For her junior year in high school, Jo is required to take a foreign language. She has her choice of French or Spanish. The French class is taught by Mrs. Alston. The Spanish class is taught by Mr. Martin. Both Mrs. Alston and Mr. Martin are good teachers. However, there are some differences in the way they teach. Mr. Martin seems to know exactly what he wants to do in class and does it. Mrs. Alston is more informal in class. Mr. Martin gives tests more frequently, but Mrs. Alston assigns more homework. Jo isn't sure which one she would like better as a teacher—Mr. Martin or Mrs. Alston. And she doesn't know whether she would prefer French or Spanish. Her friends like Mr. Martin and they think she should take the Spanish course. But her parents think it would be better for her to take the course in French.

On Form B of the test, the paragraph is the same except for the last two sentences which read, "Her friends like Mrs. Alston and they think she should take the French course. But her parents think it would be better for her to take the course in Spanish." The questions and answers are the same.

Form A

2. For the past several weeks Martha has been dating two boys. One of them is Jack and the other is Frank. Jack is good looking and intelligent. He is not especially talkative, but he can hold up his end of the conversation and he is friendly. Frank is in some ways different from Jack. He is not especially good looking, but he is more talkative than Jack and has a good sense of humor. Frank dresses with good taste. Both Frank and Jack have asked Martha to go steady. Many of her girl friends are going steady and Martha would like to go steady. But she isn't sure which she would rather go steady with—Frank or Jack. She has put both of them off about an answer because she can't make up her mind which one she likes better. Martha's mother and father haven't tried to tell her who to date, but Martha can tell that they like Frank. Martha knows that her parents would rather have her go steady with Frank than Jack. But that is not the way Martha's girl friends feel. They like Jack better than Frank. They think that Jack is more desirable as a boyfriend. Her friends would rather see Martha go steady with Jack.

On Form B of the test, the paragraph is the same except for the last six sentences, which read, "Martha's mother and father haven't tried to tell her who to date, but Martha can tell that they like Jack. Martha knows that her parents would rather have her go steady with Jack than Frank. But that is not the way Martha's girl friends feel. They like Frank better than Jack. They think that Frank is more desirable as a boyfriend. Her friends would rather see Martha go steady with Frank." The questions and answers are the same.

RELIABILITY AND VALIDITY: In order to assess reliability, the same form of the CPT was administered twice to fifty-eight teenage girls with an intervening period of two weeks. The stability of response validity from one item to another ranged from a low of 72 percent to a high of 86 percent; that is, better than 80 percent of the subjects chose the same alternative both times. When the alternative forms are administered, response shifts are significantly more frequent than this. It has been found that groups of subjects that are differentiated with respect to responses to the CPT also differ in other ways that indicate construct validity. Evidence of construct validity is presented in the references cited below.

BIBLIOGRAPHY:

Brittain, C. V. "Parents and Peers as Competing Influences in Adolescence." Unpublished doctoral dissertation. University of Chicago, 1959.

Brittain, C. V. "Adolescent Choices and Parent-Peer Cross-Pressures." *American Sociological Review,* 1963, *28,* 385-391.

Brittain, C. V. "Age and Sex of Siblings and Conformity Toward Parents vs. Peers in Adolescence." *Child Development,* 1966, *37,* 709-714.

Brittain, C. V. "An Exploration of the Bases of Peer-Compliance in Adolescence." *Adolescence,* 1967/1968, *2,* 445-458.

Brittain, C. V. "A Comparison of Rural and Urban Adolescents with Respect to Peer vs. Parent Compliance." *Adolescence,* 1969, *4,* 59-68.

PERCEIVED CLOSENESS-TO-THE-MOTHER SCALE

AUTHOR: Barbara Bowens Miller

AGE: Junior high school

VARIABLE: Perceived closeness to the mother

TYPE OF MEASURE: Questionnaire

SOURCE FROM WHICH MEASURE MAY BE OBTAINED: See Anderson (1940).

DESCRIPTION OF MEASURE: The Perceived Closeness-to-the-Mother Scale was developed by selecting eleven items seemingly related to closeness to the mother from the total pool of seventy-seven items on the Anderson Intrafamily Questionnaire (Anderson, 1940). These items are numbers 5, 6, 9, 10, 11, 46, 47, 48, 49, 50, and 51. A subject's score is the sum of his responses to the eleven items; the lower the score, the greater the perceived closeness. The total Anderson Questionnaire may be a useful guidance instrument for professionals interested in perceptions by this age child of his relationship to his family and friends, since other items deal with these relationships.

As examples, two of the eleven items on the scale are given below.

5. I feel that my mother is
   a. very concerned about my health, always afraid I'll be sick.
   b. interested but not anxious about my health.
   c. not very interested or concerned about my health.
6. My mother
   a. helps me with difficult lessons all the time.
   b. helps me with difficult lessons only when I ask her.
   c. never has time to help me with difficult lessons.

RELIABILITY AND VALIDITY: Split-half reliability of Closeness-to-the-Mother Scale corrected by the Spearman-Brown formula was .77. Reliability and validity information on the total questionnaire can be obtained from Anderson (1940).

BIBLIOGRAPHY:

Anderson, J. P. *A Study of the Relationships Between Certain Aspects of Parental Behavior and Attitudes and the Behavior of Junior High School Pupils.* New York: Bureau of Publications, Teachers College, Columbia University, 1940.

Miller, B. B. "Effects of Father Absence and Mother's Evaluation of Father on the Socialization of Adolescent Boys." Unpublished doctoral dissertation. Columbia University, New York, 1961.

PIETY PARENT PERCEPTION QUESTIONNAIRE

AUTHOR: Kenneth R. Piety

AGE: 8 or 9 years to adult

VARIABLE: Patterns of parent perception

TYPE OF MEASURE: True-false questionnaire

SOURCE FROM WHICH MEASURE MAY BE OBTAINED: Kenneth R. Piety, Orange Memorial Hospital, Mental Health Center, 1416 South Orange Avenue, Orlando, Florida 32806.

DESCRIPTION OF MEASURE: This questionnaire discloses patterns of parent perception, revealing the preferred or idealized parent, positive and negative attitudes toward either parent, and degree of closeness and overprotection. The 140 items yield a total inappropriate parent perception score and also a consistency of discrimination score.

As examples, ten selected items from the measure are given below, to be answered "true" or "false."

6. I am more like my father than my mother.
8. Sometimes it seems as if other children have better parents than I do.
15. Sometimes I feel as if I am not loved by either of my parents.
19. My mother often criticizes my father.
27. My mother wants me to become somebody important, but my father does not seem to care much what I do.
30. My parents often disagree about me.
32. Mothers have to suffer more for their children than fathers do.
39. My mother seems to distrust men.
50. My father complains a lot about having to work.
59. It is hard to live up to my mother's plans for me.

RELIABILITY AND VALIDITY: The first form of the test yielded a reliability coefficient of .87 with thirty subjects retested after three months. The questionnaire was subsequently put through an item analysis, and only those items were retained that correlated well with the total score. The test has been validated by picking only those items that would discriminate between experimental groups with established psychosexual conflicts and controls at the .10 level. Validity has also been determined by finding significant relationships between peer ratings, teacher ratings, and this questionnaire scale. The studies that have been done support the hypothesis that there is a relationship between the subject's parent perception score and psychosexual conflicts in role behavior as expressed in social behavior.

BIBLIOGRAPHY:

Piety, K. R. "Perceptual Dissonance and Role Learning." *Journal of Clinical Psychology*, 1966, *22*, 10-14.
Piety, K. R. "Patterns of Parent Perceptions Among Neuropsychiatric Patients and Normal Controls." *Journal of Clinical Psychology*, 1967, *23*, 428-433.

Piety, K. R. "Parent Perception and Social Adjustment Among Elementary and High
    School Students." *Journal of Clinical Psychology,* 1968, *24,* 165-171.

RATING SCALE FOR MASCULINITY
OF SEX-ROLE ADOPTION

AUTHOR: Henry B. Biller

AGE: 4 to 7 years

VARIABLE: Masculinity of sex-role adoption

TYPE OF MEASURE: Rating scale

SOURCE FROM WHICH MEASURE MAY BE OBTAINED: See Biller (1968) or write
Henry B. Biller, Psychology Department, University of Rhode Island, Kingston, Rhode
Island 02881.

DESCRIPTION OF MEASURE: This sixteen-item behavioral rating scale is designed to
be used by teachers in rating kindergarten-age boys on the masculinity of their sex-role
adoption (as distinguished from sex-role orientation or sex-role preference). For the
masculinity of a boy's role adoption to be assessed, it is assumed that his relative assertiveness, aggressiveness, competitiveness, independence, and activity directed toward
physical prowess and mastery of his environment will have to be taken into account.
Furthermore, it is assumed that low masculinity is represented by such behavior as passivity, dependency, and timidity (see Biller, 1968). Nine items are assumed to be characteristics of high masculinity and seven of low masculinity. The teacher rates each
item on a 5-point frequency scale (0 to 4) ranging from "very frequently" to "never."
    As examples, the first five items of the scale are given below.

1. Is active and energetic. (on the move, plays hard)
2. Leads other children. (organizes play activities, assigns tasks to others)
3. Asks for help. (acts helpless, wants someone to do things for him he could do himself)
4. Participates in sports and active games. (plays rough and tumble games where running and balls are involved)
5. Makes own decision. (not swayed by other children when he has decided what he
   wants to play; doesn't ask others what he should do)

RELIABILITY AND VALIDITY: Product-moment correlations between total scores in
ratings by two teachers varied from .75 to .96, with a median of .91 ($p < .0005$).
When only one teacher's rating for each child was considered, split-half reliability computed by the Spearman-Brown formula was .89 ($p < .0005$). Correlations between the
sixteen individual rating-scale items and total A scores ranged from .50 to .78, with a

median correlation of about .60 ($p < .0005$). Biller (1968) provides numerous correlations of this measure with other indices, in general showing rather low correlations.

BIBLIOGRAPHY:

Biller, H. B. "A Multiaspect Investigation of Masculine Development in Kindergarten-Age Boys." *Genetic Psychology Monographs,* 1968, *78,* 89-138.

Biller, H. B. "Father Dominance and Sex-Role Development in Kindergarten-Age Boys." *Developmental Psychology,* 1969, *1,* 87-94.

ROLE KNOWLEDGE TEST

AUTHORS: David R. Heise and Essie P. M. Roberts

AGE: 7 years to adult

VARIABLE: Maturity of role conceptions; sex and social-class biases

TYPE OF MEASURE: Test

SOURCE FROM WHICH MEASURE MAY BE OBTAINED: See Heise and Roberts (1970).

DESCRIPTION OF MEASURE: A child taking the Role Knowledge Test is asked to sort persons according to whether they engage in specific behaviors. The stimuli persons are: baby, brother, son, sister, daughter, high school boy, high school girl, husband, father, wife, mother, sick person, teacher, doctor, and nurse. The behavioral questions are: (1) Who stays inside stores a lot? (2) Who stays at home a lot? (3) Who stays outside a lot? (4) Who goes to school? (5) Who hangs up clothes? (6) Who rips clothes? (7) Who tears up money? (8) Who plays with toys? (9) Who makes grownups do things? (10) Who moves desks around? (11) Who writes on paper? (12) Who cleans tables? (13) Who spends money? (14) Who cares for books? (15) Who fixes clothes? (16) Who earns money? (17) Who builds tables? (18) Who moves children from one place to another? (19) Who fixes food to eat? (20) Who takes toys from one place to another? Scoring keys were obtained from adult responses to the same questions and from psychometric analyses that provided a numerical weight for each item. Separate keys were derived to measure overall maturity, sex bias, and social-class bias in responses.

RELIABILITY AND VALIDITY: The scales for measuring overall maturity, sex, and class biases in role conceptions each consisted of several hundred differentiating items, and scores from these scales had high reliability: .97 for role maturity, .97 for sex bias, and .97 for class bias. The breakdown of the role maturity scale into knowledge scales for separate roles yielded a series of subscales with reliabilities from .19 to .56 with a median value of .38. The correlation between overall role maturity and age was .77. The correlation between sex-bias scores and biological sex was .49. The correlation between class bias and Duncan's prestige index for father's occupation was .62 within the sample of children.

BIBLIOGRAPHY:

Heise, D. R., and Roberts, E. P. M. "The Development of Role Knowledge." *Genetic Psychology Monographs,* 1970, *82,* 83-115.

SEX-ATTITUDE SCALE AND
ROLE-TAKING SEX-ATTITUDE SCALE

AUTHORS: Anthony T. Soares and Louise M. Soares

AGE: High school and older

VARIABLE: Sex attitudes and perceptions of others' sex attitudes

TYPE OF MEASURE: Questionnaire and rating scale

SOURCE FROM WHICH MEASURE MAY BE OBTAINED: Anthony T. Soares and Louise M. Soares, University of Bridgeport, Bridgeport, Connecticut 06602. Cost: $1.25 per specimen set, including postage and handling.

DESCRIPTION OF MEASURE: The Sex-Attitude Scale is designed to tap the sex attitudes of high school students and adults. The items were derived in a pilot project with teenagers from various socioeconomic strata. Form I of the scale consists of forty statements; Form II has thirty-one statements; and Form II (condensed) has twenty statements. The items on Form I are different from those on Form II. The Role-Taking Sex-Attitude Scale consists of three forms: (A) role-playing disadvantaged teenagers' responses, (B) role-playing middle-class teenagers' responses, and (C) role-playing upper-class teenagers' responses. The respondent is asked to take each of the three roles in answering the thirty-one items on each form. The scale can be administered to high school students and adults to obtain role responses relative to the social class of the teenage role. Forms A, B, and C utilize the Form II items of the Sex-Attitude Scale. Both of these scales are scored on a 4-point forced-response format: "yes," "maybe yes," "maybe no," and "no." Subscale scores can be obtained in the following areas: A, Affective ideational, abstract; K, knowledge, cognitive, informational; and I, interrelationship, interactive, boy-girl definitive. Form I contains eighteen A and twenty-two I subscale items. Form II includes sixteen A, six K, and nine I subscale items. Item analysis yields individual responses and comparative responses to discern both similarities and differences in the variables of sex, age, social class, and role-taking insight.

As examples, representative items from the two forms of the scales are given below.

Form I

I item—"Having sex relations with your best girl is O.K."

A item—"It's hard for parents to talk with their children about sex."

Form II

I item—"The more boys that a girl has sex relations with, the more of a woman she shows she is."

K -item—"You can catch syphilis and gonorrhea from germs on a doorknob or toilet seat."

A item—"Are you glad you're what you are—boy or girl?"

RELIABILITY AND VALIDITY: None reported.

BIBLIOGRAPHY:

Soares, A. T., and Soares, L. M. "A Study of Students' Sex Attitudes and Teachers' Perceptions of Students' Sex Attitudes." Paper presented to the meeting of the Eastern Psychological Association, 1969. *Psychology in the Schools,* 1970, 7, 172-174.

Prepared by Louise M. Soares

SEX-ROLE PREFERENCE QUESTIONNAIRE

AUTHOR: Aletha Huston Stein

AGE: Approximately 10 to 15 years

VARIABLE: Preference for masculine and feminine activities

TYPE OF MEASURE: Questionnaire

SOURCE FROM WHICH MEASURE MAY BE OBTAINED: Aletha Stein, College of Human Development, Pennsylvania State University, University Park, Pennsylvania 16802.

DESCRIPTION OF MEASURE: This measure is designed to tap preference for masculine and feminine activities independently. In many earlier measures, masculinity and femininity have been conceived as the opposite ends of one continuum. The assumption underlying the present measure is that there are two continua that may be relatively independent of each other. A second departure from other measures is an attempt to let the subject define what specific activities he or she considers masculine or feminine. Although sex-role definitions are widely shared, individuals may define specific activities in somewhat different ways; preference for jump rope or baseball, for example, may also be affected by many other factors besides sex-appropriateness. For that reason, the items in this measure specify the gender appropriateness of an activity but leave the specific content of the activity open to the child's interpretation, as in the question, "How much do you like boys' books?"

As examples, the first seven of the twenty-two items, to be answered on a 5-point scale from "very interesting" (5) to "not interesting" (1), are given below.

1. How interesting do you think boys' books are?
2. How interesting do you think women's magazines are?
3. How interesting are women's occupations? (jobs you get paid for.)
4. How interesting do you think men's magazines are?
5. How interesting do you think men's jobs are?
6. How interesting do you think girls' books are?
7. How interesting to play with do you think boys' toys are?

RELIABILITY AND VALIDITY: To determine test-retest reliability, fifty-three children were retested after 6 months. The correlations between the two administrations were: boys, masculine scale = .53; girls, masculine scale = .80; boys, feminine scale = .52; girls, feminine scale = .52. In two separate samples, the correlations between the masculine scale and the feminine scale were not significant. Thus, the two scales are independent. The twenty-five items were selected from a pool of forty-two items administered to sixty-four sixth-grade children. All items discriminate significantly between males and females. The median correlations of the items with total scores were: boys, masculine scale = .50; girls, masculine scale = .70; boys, feminine scale = .65; girls, feminine scale = .65. The questionnaire discriminates between males and females (Stein, 1971; and Stein, Pohly, and Mueller, 1971).

BIBLIOGRAPHY:

Stein, A. H. "The Effects of Sex-Role Standards for Achievement and Sex-Role Preference on Three Determinants of Achievement Motivation." *Developmental Psychology,* 1971, *4,* 219-231.

Stein, A. H., Pohly, S. R., and Mueller, E. "The Influence of Masculine, Feminine, and Neutral Tasks on Children's Achievement Behavior, Expectancies of Success, and Attainment Value." *Child Development,* 1971, *42,* 195-207.

STEIN-SOSKIN ADOLESCENT TRUST SCALE (SSATS)

AUTHORS: Kenneth B. Stein and William F. Soskin

AGE: Adolescents

VARIABLE: Interpersonal trust

TYPE OF MEASURE: Likert-type scale

SOURCE FROM WHICH MEASURE MAY BE OBTAINED: Kenneth B. Stein, 517 Moraga Avenue, Piedmont, California 94611.

DESCRIPTION OF MEASURE: Several guidelines were used in constructing the SSATS. First, it should have an obvious rather than a subtle format. Second, the content of the items should represent the significant persons and role agents in the adolescent's world. The instructions are direct and obvious, asking simply, "To what extent do you trust the following people?" Total score is the simple sum of all the item scores.

As examples, selected items from the fifteen-item scale, to be answered on a 5-point scale from "almost never" to "almost always," are given below.

To what degree can you trust the following people?
 3. Trust most white students.
 5. Trust most adults.
 7. Trust most Asian students.
 9. Trust most physicians.
11. Trust most school principals.

RELIABILITY AND VALIDITY: *Alpha* reliability is .81, and test-retest reliability with an eight-month interval is .67. The test is unrelated to age in the high school adolescent range, religious affiliation, parent's education, and type of residential dwelling. It also is not correlated with social desirability response set. Significant positive correlations did occur with smaller family size, residential stability, positive parent-adolescent relations, acceptance of criminal justice system, and democratic principles for social change. High trust is related to internal locus of control. Correlation between SSATS and Rotter Trust Scale (1967) is 15.33. A cluster analysis of SSATS produced three dimensions: trust of authority, trust of peers, and trust of people in the more intimate world. A controlled study found that the more conventional high school students achieved higher trust scores than did relatively disaffected students.

BIBLIOGRAPHY:

Rotter, J. B. "A New Scale for the Measurement of Interpersonal Trust." *Journal of Personality,* 1967, *35,* 651-665.
Stein, K. B., Soskin, W. F., and Korchin, S. J. "Interpersonal Trust and Disaffected High School Youth." *Journal of Youth and Adolescence,* 1974, *3,* 281-292.

STUDENT PERCEPTION OF TEACHER STYLE (SPOTS)

AUTHOR: Bruce Wayne Tuckman

AGE: Grades 6 to 12

VARIABLE: Nondirectiveness in teacher style

TYPE OF MEASURE: Rating scale

SOURCE FROM WHICH MEASURE MAY BE OBTAINED: See Tuckman (1968, 1970, or 1972).

DESCRIPTION OF MEASURE: This student rating scale consists of thirty-two items, each describing a facet of classroom behavior indicative of the directiveness or non-directiveness of teaching style based on the operational definition below. The following behaviors illustrate the concept of directive teaching embodied in this scale: (1) formal planning and structuring of course work; (2) minimization of informal work or small-group work; (3) rigid structuring of such small-group work as is employed; (4) rigid structuring of individual and class activities; (5) emphasis of factual knowledge or knowledge derived from sources of authority (books, school administrators); (6) use of absolute and justifiable punishment; (7) minimization of the opportunity to make and to learn from mistakes; (8) maintenance of formal relationship with students; (9) assumption of total responsibility for grades; and (10) maintenance of formal class-room atmosphere. The scale requires students to rate the intensity or frequency of specific teacher behaviors on 9-point rating scales. Anchor phrases on each of the thirty-two scales are descriptive rather than evaluative. For example, item one asks whether the teacher is interested in "how many facts you know" (directive orientation) or "whether you can think for yourself" (nondirective orientation. The revised SPOTS includes seventeen items taken from the original scale (see Tuckman, 1970).

As examples, four of the seventeen items from the revised scale are given below.

3. The teacher

1	2	3	4	5	6	7	8	9
doesn't like to talk about any subject that isn't part of your course.			talks about your course subject a lot but encourages the discussion of other matters.			likes to talk about different subjects and is interested in your personal opinions.		

4. The students in our class

1	2	3	4	5	6	7	8	9
only speak when the teacher asks them a question.			feel free to ask the teacher questions.			feel free to speak up at almost any time.		

10. When we are working on a group project or in a committee, the teacher

1	2	3	4	5	6	7	8	9
tells us exactly what to do.			suggests ways that the project might be handled.			lets the group members decide how the project should be handled.		

11. The teacher usually

1	2	3	4	5	6	7	8	9
makes all the students do the same thing in class (working, studying).			makes some students work on projects and some students study, depending on how far they are.			lets the students do what they like as long as they complete the number of projects or chapters assigned by the end of the week.		

RELIABILITY AND VALIDITY: The reliability of the SPOTS was established by correlating the mean SPOTS score of each of the thirty-two items for each of the twenty-two teachers with the grand mean SPOTS score for each teacher. The results of the analysis indicated that 78 percent of the item scores were significantly related to the total SPOTS score ($r > .40$). Of this 78 percent, 88 percent of the items correlated above .50, while 64 percent correlated above .60. Interjudge reliability, that is, the extent to which students agreed in their judgment of a teacher, was determined by ranking each student according to the agreement of his SPOTS rating with the mean SPOTS rating for each teacher and correlating these "agreement ratings" with the average SPOTS score for each teacher. It was found that the interjudge reliability was high up to the judge ranked 10 in deviation from the class mean judgment, with an average interjudge reliability of .86.

Validity of the SPOTS is based on a significant correlation of .53 ($df = 21$, $p < .01$) between the average SPOTS ratings for each teacher and the best judgment rating on the Observer Rating Scale (Tuckman, 1970), indicating that given ideal conditions, trained observers can show appreciable agreement with students with regard to the approximate standing of each teacher on the directive-nondirective continuum. A correlation of .31 was obtained between the SPOTS mean for each teacher and the Teacher Style Checklist (Tuckman, 1970) average scores.

BIBLIOGRAPHY:

Tuckman, B. W. *A Study of the Effectiveness of Directive vs. Nondirective Vocational Teachers as a Function of Student Characteristics and Course Format.* Final report, 1968. ERIC document no. ED 028 990.

Tuckman, B. W. "A Technique for the Assessment of Teacher Directiveness." *Journal of Educational Research,* 1970, *63,* 396-400.

Tuckman, B. W. *Conducting Educational Research.* New York: Harcourt Brace Jovanovich, 1972.

TEACHER'S RATINGS OF "MASCULINE" BEHAVIOR

AUTHOR: Donald K. Freedheim

AGE: 7 to 11 years

VARIABLE: Masculinity or boyishness

TYPE OF MEASURE: Likert-type scale

SOURCE FROM WHICH MEASURE MAY BE OBTAINED: Donald K. Freedheim, Department of Psychology, Case Western Reserve University, Cleveland, Ohio 44106.

DESCRIPTION OF MEASURE: The scale consists of sixteen items, eight of which are scored for masculinity. The items define general independence and assertiveness and need not be characterized as masculine as opposed to feminine. Four items may be used to judge adjustment in school, and two items are neutral. Three of the items are scored in reverse.

As examples, the eight items scored for masculinity are given below, with re-verse-scored items marked (R). They are marked on a 5-point scale from "always" to "never."

  1. Stands up for his own rights.
  5. Is active and energetic.
 14. Likes sports and active games.
  7. Leads other children.
 13. Makes own decisions.
  3. Prefers table (quiet) games. (R)
  9. Is timid around others. (R)
 15. Prefers to stay by himself. (R)

RELIABILITY AND VALIDITY: The original study determined the reliability coeffi-cient to be .90. Original validity was determined by cross-validation with teachers' judgments of general "masculine" boys (Freedheim and Borstelman, 1963). Content validity appears high, as rated by the judges' estimate of the items.

BIBLIOGRAPHY:

Biller, H. B. "A Note on Father Absence and Masculine Development in Lower-Class Negro and White Boys." *Child Development,* 1968, *39,* 1003-1006.
Freedheim, D. K., and Borstelman, L. J. "An Investigation of Masculinity and Parental Role Patterns." *American Psychologist,* 1963, *18,* 339.

TEST OF DIFFERENTIAL CONFORMING
TO PEERS AND ADULTS

AUTHOR: Phillida Salmon

AGE: Junior school boys

VARIABLE: Differential conforming to peers and adults as reference groups

TYPE OF MEASURE: Forced-choice questionnaire

SOURCE FROM WHICH MEASURE MAY BE OBTAINED: Phillida Salmon, Child Development, Institute of Education, Malet Street, London WC1, England.

DESCRIPTION OF MEASURE: There are three distinctive features of this test. (1) It consists of a choice situation involving personal subjective preference as against the judgment of objective factors. (2) The technique is designed so that each choice involves either endorsing peer group judgment and simultaneously rejecting adult group judgment or vice versa. Thus indiscriminate conforming is not possible, because the situation involves a single choice between two mutually opposed alternatives, representing peer and adult group norms, respectively. (3) The technique involves a *series* of judgment situations rather than a single one. The purpose of this feature is to enable assessment to be made of *degrees* of conforming to peer or adult pressure.

The items chosen to make up this technique all concern personal preferences, such as preference between different types of holiday, or they concern subjective judgments, such as the judgment of whether lions or tigers are braver. A series of items that are relatively free from a priori bias among boys of this age was established by pilot work. From the results obtained, twenty-eight items were selected, having approximately 50-percent distribution of responses between the two alternatives. For each item, a spurious record of most boys and most grownups is provided, these two judgments being always in opposite directions. Scoring consists of summing, over the twenty-eight items, the number of times the subject endorses peer rather than adult group decisions. This sum represents his peer-vs.-adult conformity score.

The test instructions and five selected items of the twenty-eight questions, with spurious responses indicated, are given below.

We want you to give your own opinion on the questions in this test. There are no right or wrong answers. To show which you choose, you put a cross (x) between the lines next to the thing *you* choose. These questions have been given to a lot of other boys, and also to grownups. You may like to know which was the choice of most boys (B) and most grownups (G.U.).

1. Which do you like best?

Reading about science		Reading about adventure
( )	B.	(x)
(x)	G.U.	( )
( )	You	( )

3. Which car do you think is best?

Rolls Royce		Jaguar
(x)	B.	( )
( )	G.U.	(x)
( )	You	( )

5. Which pop group do you think is best?

The Animals		The Rolling Stones
(x)	B.	( )
( )	G.U.	(x)
( )	You	( )

7. Which do you like doing best?

Swimming		Cycling
( )	B.	(x)
(x)	G.U.	( )
( )	You	( )

9. Which planet would you most like to visit?

Mars		Venus
( )	B.	(x)
(x)	G.U.	( )
( )	You	( )

RELIABILITY AND VALIDITY: The test was administered to sixty London junior school boys, aged 10 and 11. Reliability was not assessed. The study enabled some assessment of the construct validity of the test: (1) a comparison (by the Mann-Whitney U-Test) of the subjects' conforming responses with their valuation (as assessed by repertory grid technique) of peer-vs.-adult approval, showed conformity to peers, as against adult, approval ($Z = 2.10$, $p < .02$, one-tailed test); (2) a comparison (by the Mann-Whitney U-Test) of the subjects' responding in a markedly differential way, both to the conformity test and to the valuation of peer-vs.-adult approval (repertory grid), showed a significant positive relationship between the two types of response ($Z = 2.24$, $p < .05$, one-tailed test). Thus, a marked orientation to either reference group appears to be consistent across both value system and conforming response.

BIBLIOGRAPHY:

Salmon, P. "Differential Conforming as a Developmental Process." *British Journal of Social and Clinical Psychology*, 1969, *8*, 22-31.

THOMPSON'S PUPIL RATING OF TEACHER

AUTHOR: Jack M. Thompson

AGE: Elementary to high school

VARIABLE: Teacher behavior

TYPE OF MEASURE: Rating scale

SOURCE FROM WHICH MEASURE MAY BE OBTAINED: Sonoma County Office of Education, 2555 Mendocino Avenue, Room 111E, Santa Rosa, California 95405.

DESCRIPTION OF MEASURE: The Pupil Rating of Teacher Scale was based upon the Stanford Teacher Competence Appraisal Guide, Secondary Education Project (1962-1963). This revised instrument was similar to the original instrument except for the elimination of items concerned with rating the teacher in areas of professional improvement. In the present instrument, the pupil rates the teacher on nine teaching tasks, utilizing a 5-point scale from "almost never" to "very often," which yields a total average score and an average score/item for group data.

As examples, the first four of the nine items on the scale are given below.

1. We know what the teacher wants us to learn.
2. The class work is just right for us. Not too hard nor too easy.
3. The lessons make sense to us.
4. The materials used to teach the lessons help make the lessons more clear and interesting.

RELIABILITY AND VALIDITY: The original scale was designed for the improvement of instruction and was based upon a model of teaching as a leadership role in a process of inquiry and problem solving. In the present scale, a pilot tryout revealed no language-level problems. Content validity was indicated by agreement between curriculum consultants on inclusion of the items. The validity of the original instrument was demonstrated in the prediction of student-teaching success in two pilot studies, and test-retest reliability was found to be .89. In a study analyzing the relationship between Carl Rogers' helping relationship concept and teacher behavior, the pupil rating of the teacher made a significant contribution to differences between teachers who scored high or low on relationship scores. Those students who rated the teacher highest on teaching tasks perceived them also as being higher on interpersonal relationship variables (Thompson, 1969a, 1969b).

BIBLIOGRAPHY:

Secondary Education Project. *The Stanford Appraisal Guides.* Palo Alto, California: Stanford University, 1962-1963.

Thompson, J. M. "The Effect of Pupil Characteristics Upon Perception of Their Teacher." *Psychology in the Schools,* 1969a, *6,* 206-212.

Thompson, J. M. "The Relationship Between Carl Rogers' Helping Relationship Concept and Teacher Behavior." *California Journal of Educational Research,* 1969b, *20,* 151-162.

TWO SCALES FOR PARENT EVALUATION

AUTHOR: Joseph B. Cooper

AGE: High school and up

VARIABLE: Attitudes of children toward parents

TYPE OF MEASURE: True-false questionnaires

SOURCE FROM WHICH MEASURE MAY BE OBTAINED: Joseph B. Cooper, Department of Psychology, San Jose State University, San Jose, California 95192.

DESCRIPTION OF MEASURE: This is an instrument for assessing attitudes toward parents, one form for father and one form for mother. Originally they were two fifty-item scales used for a study of ideological similarity between college-age subjects and their parents. The scales were later revised and used in a replication study at the high school level. The revised scales consist of twenty-six items each. Subjects respond to the items under one of two sets of directions: true-false or six-position rating. The methods of scoring are as follows. For the true-false responses, each positive statement is credited by 1 point if marked "true," and each negative statement is credited with 1 point if marked "false." The highest possible score is 26; the lowest possible score, 0. For the six-position rating responses, each positive statement is credited the quantity marked; that is, for a negative statement, choice no. 1, meaning "completely false," is credited to the subject's score as 6 points; choice no. 6, meaning "completely true," is credited as 1 point. The lowest possible score is 26; the highest possible score, 156.

As examples, the first five items of the mother form of the scale are given below. After each item the plus or minus indicates directionality; the one-digit number indicates the content category into which the item falls (acceptance, attitude toward sexuality, responsibility, consistency, warmth and outlook on life), and the two-digit number indicates the biserial r for the item, based on true-false responses.

1. She always made me feel free to discuss problems concerning "boy-girl" relationships without feelings of guilt or embarrassment (+, 2, .68).
2. I enjoy being with her because she is warm and affectionate (+, 5, .68).
3. She has made our home cheerful by her presence (+, 5, .73).
4. She has shown little embarrassment or reluctance in talking to me about problems dealing with sex (+, 2, .58).
5. She has taught me many useful and creative things by working with me in a friendly, helpful way (+, 5, .66).

RELIABILITY AND VALIDITY: Test-retest Pearson rs for the true-false scales are .93 for mother scale and .91 for father scale ($N = 84$). Test-retest Pearson rs for the six-position rating scales are .92 for mother and .97 for father ($N = 42$). Kuder-Richardson reliabilities for the true-false scales are .86 for mother and .88 for father ($N = 202$). Odd-even rs for the six-position rating scales are .90 for mother and .94 for father ($N = 160$). All Kuder-Richardson reliabilities and odd-even coefficients are slightly higher for the second administration than for the first. Although the reliability coefficients tend to be slightly higher for the six-position rating responses than for true-false responses, it seems doubtful that (for most purposes) the slight superiority warrants the use of the more involved rating response and scoring procedure.

BIBLIOGRAPHY:

Cooper, J. B. "Two Scales for Parent Evaluation." *Journal of Genetic Psychology,* 1966, *108,* 49-53.
Cooper, J. B., and Blair, M. A. "Parent Evaluation as a Determiner of Ideology." *Journal of Genetic Psychology,* 1959, *94,* 93-100.
Cooper, J. B., and Lewis, J. H. "Parent Evaluation as Related to Social Ideology and Academic Achievement." *Journal of Genetic Psychology,* 1962, *101,* 135-143.
Schultz, J. P., Firettos, A., and Walker, R. "Relationship of Parental Assessment and Anxiety in High School Freshmen." *Psychology in the Schools,* 1969, *6,* 311-312.

Group 3-b

Perceptions
of Peers

DIRECTING THE SCHOOL PLAY

AUTHORS: Nadine M. Lambert and Eli M. Bower

AGE: Grades 3 to 7

VARIABLE: Social relationships

TYPE OF MEASURE: Peer rating

SOURCE FROM WHICH MEASURE MAY BE OBTAINED: Nadine M. Lambert, School of Education, University of California, Berkeley, California 94720.

DESCRIPTION OF MEASURE: Directing the School Play is a peer-rating instrument with greatest applicability in grades 4, 5, and 6, although it has been used with success in grades 3 and 7. It should take no more than 35 to 45 minutes of class time. Section II of the instrument contains descriptions of fourteen hypothetical roles in a play, with instructions directing each pupil to choose a classmate who would be most suitable and natural in each of the roles. In addition, each pupil is to indicate the roles he would prefer or those which he thinks other people would select for him. This section has thirty different quartets of the fourteen roles, and questions seek to discover how a child sees himself in relation to each role. In scoring, each pupil names a classmate for each role in the play. By counting the number of times a pupil is picked for each role, and then counting the number of times each pupil is picked for the *even numbered* (negative) roles, a percentage is obtained that is indicative of the positive or negative perception of each pupil by his classmates.

As examples, two of the fourteen items in Section I and two of the twenty-four in Section II follow.

1. Someone who is the leader when children do something in class or on the playground—someone to whom everyone listens.
2. A smaller younger child who is always falling down and getting hurt.

1. Which of these four parts would you *least* like to play?
   _____ A nice pest—someone who often gets into trouble, but is really nice:
   _____ Someone who is smart and usually knows the answers.
   _____ Somebody who seems always to be late for school and other activities.
   _____ Someone in class who could act the part of the teacher.
2. Which one of these four parts would your classmates pick you to play?
   _____ Someone in class who could act the part of the teacher.
   _____ A person who often gets angry over nothing and gets into lots of fights.
   _____ Someone who is the leader when children do something in class or on the playground—someone to whom everyone listens.
   _____ A nice pest—someone who often gets into trouble, but is really nice.

RELIABILITY AND VALIDITY: The frequency of selections for individual items is associated with the presence (more selections for negative roles) or absence (more selections for positive roles) of learning and behavior problems in school. The percentage of negative selections has also been found to be a good measure of the extent to which the pupil is experiencing difficulties in interpersonal relationships or is perceived by his peers as having learning and behavior problems in the classroom. About half of the items were significantly correlated with clinical criteria derived from psychological, psychiatric, and social-work data on fifth graders. The percentage of negative selections proved to be valid for long-term prediction of high school status.

BIBLIOGRAPHY:

Hartsough, C. S. *Classroom Adaptation of Elementary School Children Varying with Respect to Age, Sex, and Ethnic Status.* Berkeley: University of California, 1973.

Lambert, N. M. *The Prediction of School Adjustment.* U.S. Office of Education, Cooperative Research Project No. 1980. Sacramento: California State Department of Education, 1964.

Lambert, N. M. "Intellectual and Nonintellectual Predictors of High School Status." *Journal of Special Education,* 1972, *6* (3), 247-259.

Lambert, N. M. *Technical Report Supplement: The Development of Instruments for the Nonintellectual Assessment of Effective School Behavior.* Berkeley: University of California, 1974.

Lambert, N. M., and Bower, E. M. *A Process for In-School Screening of Emotionally Handicapped Children.* Atlanta: Educational Testing Service, 1961, 1974.

Lambert, N. M., Hartsough, C. S., and Zimmerman, I. L. "The Comparative Predictive Efficiency of Intellectual and Nonintellectual Components of High School Functioning." *American Journal of Orthopsychiatry,* 1976, *46* (1), 109-122.

Stampp, S. K. "A Longitudinal Study of Peer Ratings and Cognitive Decentering in Elementary School." Unpublished doctoral dissertation, University of California, Berkeley, 1975.

Swain, C. "The Relationship between Classroom Adjustment and Decentering of Thought in Fouth Grade Children." Unpublished doctoral dissertation, University of California, Berkeley, 1975.

Urbansky, C. "The Relationship of School Achievement and Peer Ratings to Behavioral Profiles Determined from Teacher Ratings of Pupil Behavior." Unpublished master's thesis, University of California, Berkeley, 1974.

LEARNING ENVIRONMENT INVENTORY (LEI)

AUTHORS: Herbert J. Walberg and Gary J. Anderson

AGE: 12 years and up, but may be adapted for younger children

VARIABLE: Sociopsychological perceptions of educational groups

TYPE OF MEASURE: Rating scale

SOURCE FROM WHICH MEASURE MAY BE OBTAINED: Gary J. Anderson, Atlantic Institute of Education, 5244 South Street, Halifax, Nova Scotia, Canada. Cost: $5.00 for manual.

DESCRIPTION OF MEASURE: This inventory consists of 105 items measuring fifteen variables: cohesiveness, diversity, formality, speed, environment, friction, goal direction, favoritism, difficulty, apathy, democracy, cliqueness, satisfaction, disorganization, and competitiveness. A typical item is: "Certain students work only with their close friends" (cliqueness). The student responds by indicating the strength of his agreement or disagreement on a 4-point scale. The scales have been adapted for children in the primary and middle grades.

RELIABILITY AND VALIDITY: The internal consistency reliabilities for individual students range from .6 to .8. The predictive validity has been established for American, Australian, Canadian, and Hindi students. About 80 to 90 percent of the variance in cognitive, affective, and behavioral outcomes can be predicted using pretests and the LEI.

BIBLIOGRAPHY:

Anderson, G. J., and Walberg, H. J. "Learning Environments." In Herbert J. Walberg (Ed.), *Evaluating Educational Performance.* Berkeley, California: McCutchan, 1974.
Walberg, H. J. "Educational Process Evaluation." In Michael W. Apple (Ed.), *Educational Evaluation.* Berkeley, California: McCutchan, 1974.

Prepared by Gary J. Anderson

L-J SOCIOMETRIC TECHNIQUE

AUTHORS: Nicholas J. Long and Evelyn Jones

AGE: Kindergarten to adult

VARIABLE: Peer social structure of the classroom

TYPE OF MEASURE: Rating scale

SOURCE FROM WHICH MEASURE MAY BE OBTAINED: See Long and others (1962) and Long (1966).

DESCRIPTION OF MEASURE: The L-J Sociometric Technique was developed to provide classroom teachers with specific information about the peer social structure of the classroom that affects learning and behavioral problems. Each pupil is requested to list the names of three pupils he most prefers and three pupils he least prefers. These scores are weighted, tabulated, and drawn on a target. The sociometric target consists of five concentric bands, each of which represents a specific statistical category. A separate target is drawn for each variable. By comparing the most preferred and least preferred targets, four significant pupil roles are identified: (1) the significantly preferred pupil, (2) the significantly rejected pupil, (3) the significantly ignored pupil, and (4) the significantly split pupil.

RELIABILITY AND VALIDITY: Reliability studies on elementary grades using a test-retest design with a 3-day interval provided coefficients of .82, .87, and .92. Consensus validation by classroom teachers and school psychologists was .88 and .86, respectively.

BIBLIOGRAPHY:

Long, N. J., Cook, A. R., Evans, E. D., Kerr, J., Linke, L. A., Neubauer, B., and Payne, D. C. "Groups in Perspective: A New Sociometric Technique for Classroom Teachers." *Bulletin of the School of Education, Indiana University,* 1962, *38,* 1-105.
Long, N. J. *Direct Help to the Classroom Teacher.* Washington, D.C.: The Washington School of Psychiatry, 1966.

PEER NOMINATION TECHNIQUE

AUTHOR: Richard N. Walker

AGE: Grades 2 to 7

VARIABLE: Seven general behavioral traits: activity, overt aggressiveness, fearfulness, socialness, stability, surgency, and competence

TYPE OF MEASURE: Sociometric

SOURCE FROM WHICH MEASURE MAY BE OBTAINED: See Walker (1967).

DESCRIPTION OF MEASURE: The method derives from "guess-who" devices of Hartshorne and May and of Tuddenham. Children are read a series of sketches descriptive of personality extremes and are asked to nominate the child in their classroom most like each extreme. Nominations are collected on a form that lists names of all children in the class, a copy of which is given to each child. Number of votes is tabulated for each child, scores are ranked, and ranks converted to sten scores. Note that the device can only be used with entire classes, and that scores can only denote status relative to the remainder of the class. (Thus a child's position in a class may show considerable change over time, on any trait, but changes in an entire class cannot be measured.) Besides the seven individual traits, composite scores reflecting self-confidence and self-control can be determined. The method of computing the scores results in every class' having a mean of 5.5 and a standard deviation of 2.0 for boys and girls on each trait.

As examples, the first five of the fourteen peer nomination sketches are given below.

1. This boy is always on the go. He likes to be active and to move around a lot. Outdoors he is always running or playing hard. He has a lot of energy.

2. This boy doesn't move around so much. He walks instead of running. Sometimes he doesn't seem to have much pep.
3. This boy seems to get angry a lot. He always needs to get even when he thinks someone has done something to him.
4. This boy never seems to fight or tease others or say mean things. He just doesn't seem to get angry at people.
5. I think this boy is afraid of some things. He seems to worry about things that might happen, even when they aren't very scary.

RELIABILITY AND VALIDITY: In eight public-school classrooms, two at each grade from third to sixth, votes for half the class were tabulated separately from those of the other half, and the equivalents of split-half correlations were run. Corrected coefficients ranged from .29 to .86 for individual groups by sex and grade for the seven traits, and from .53 to .82 for the total sample. Correlations for the composite factors were close to .80 for every group. The device was administered, then readministered a year later to 239 public school children. Coefficients for the whole group ranged from .42 to .73 over the year's time for the seven traits, and averaged .70 for the composite factors. For 450 subjects, grades 3 to 6, peer ratings correlated from .25 to .57 with teacher ratings on the same seven traits, .50 and .66 on the composite factor scores. For 390 subjects, correlations with corresponding scores on a self-rating temperament questionnaire were all significant but quite low—.12 to .30 for the traits, .25 and .27 for the composite scores.

BIBLIOGRAPHY:

Walker, R. N. "Some Temperament Traits in Children as Viewed by Their Peers, Their Teachers, and Themselves." *Monographs of the Society for Research in Child Development*, 1967, *32* (6).

PEER RATING SCALE (PRS)

AUTHORS: John F. Feldhusen, Kevin P. Hynes, and Frederic W. Widlak

AGE: 6 to 12 years (or grades 1 to 6)

VARIABLE: Socialization

TYPE OF MEASURE: Rating scale

SOURCE FROM WHICH MEASURE MAY BE OBTAINED: John F. Feldhusen, Educational Psychology Section, Purdue University SCC-G, West Lafayette, Indiana 47906.

DESCRIPTION OF MEASURE: The Peer Rating Scale (PRS) assesses the following three aspects of a child's social behavior in the classroom: (1) individual actions that involve leadership, independence, assertiveness, and competitiveness; (2) social interactions that involve cooperation, conformity, authority relations, and control of aggression; and (3) affective relationships evidenced by liking others, social acceptance, being liked, and popularity. Two forms of the PRS are available—a thirty-six-item nonreading form for grades 1 and 2, and a sixty-item reading form for grades 3 through 6. All items are worded positively. A peer rating approach is used, and each child rates three classmates. An individual's score is obtained by averaging ratings of the individual by three of his peers. Preparation time of 30 minutes per class is involved, and administration time is 30 minutes.

As examples, the first five of the twenty items of each of the three sections of the reading form are given below. The child answers "yes," "no," or "sometimes."

1. If this child wants to do something, do the other kids follow?
2. Does this child help other kids on the team?
3. Does this child say nice things about other kids?
4. Does this child speak up and give ideas?
5. Does this child follow the rules when playing games?

1. Is it easy for this child to talk in front of the class?
2. Does this child go along if some kids want to do something else?
3. Do kids like to play with this child at recess?
4. Does this child get really excited when the team is winning?
5. Does this child act nice even when someone is mean?

1. Does this child like to pick kids for a team?
2. Does this child get along with the teacher?
3. Does this child like a lot of other kids?
4. Is this child quick at answering the teacher's questions?
5. Does this child work well with other kids on a team?

RELIABILITY AND VALIDITY: Reliability and validity estimates for both PRS forms are available. For the reading form, internal consistency was .89 for 208 fourth graders, .88 for eighty-six third and fourth graders, and .89 for ninety-three fifth and sixth graders. Interjudge reliability was .45 for 208 fourth graders, .50 for eighty-six third and fourth graders, and .61 for ninety-three fifth and sixth graders. Factor-analytic results for the reading form indicate support for the predicted factor structure of the instrument. For the nonreading form, internal consistency was .65 for 190 first graders and .83 for ninety-three first and second graders, while interjudge reliability was .36 for 190 first graders and .40 for ninety-three first graders. Factor-analytic results show some support of the predicted factor structure.

BIBLIOGRAPHY:

Feldhusen, J., and McDaniel, E. "Social Behavior Assessment of Elementary School Children." Paper presented at the annual meeting of the National Council on Measurement in Education. Chicago, April 1974.

Feldhusen, J., McDaniel, E., Hynes, K., and Widlak, F. *Assessment of Social Behavior of Elementary School Children.* Unpublished manuscript submitted for publication.

Hynes, K. P. "Development of a Peer Rating Scale of Socialization: An Extension of Sociometric Measurement." Unpublished master's thesis. Purdue University, West Lafayette, Indiana, August 1973.

McDaniel, E. D. *Longitudinal Study of Elementary School Effects.* Final Report. Contract EOC-O-725283 U.S.O.E. Purdue University, West Lafayette, Indiana, December 1973.

Widlak, F. W., and Hynes, K. P. "The Development and Empirical Verification of a Peer Rating Scale for Social Behavior of Elementary School Children." Paper presented at the annual meeting of the National Council on Measurement in Education. Chicago, April 1974.

REVISED OBSERVATION OF SOCIALIZATION BEHAVIOR (OSB)

AUTHORS: Jo Lynn Cunningham, Mary P. Andrews, and Robert P. Boger

AGE: 3 to 8 years

VARIABLE: Peer-group interaction

TYPE OF MEASURE: Videotaped observational rating procedure

SOURCE FROM WHICH MEASURE MAY BE OBTAINED: Institute for Family and Child Study, Home Management House Unit No. 2, Michigan State University, East Lansing, Michigan 48824.

DESCRIPTION OF MEASURE: The revised version of the OSB was developed to provide a more precise measure of the interaction component of peer-group interaction. It is a time-sampling rating procedure to be used with videotapes of peer-group interaction in a controlled but unstructured situation. Time-sampling techniques by their very nature break up the total flow of behavior into brief but regular snatches of behavior. The revised OSB attempts to preserve the interaction component by tracing, within each time interval, not only the subject's behavior, but the impact or effect of his behavior on the other peers. In this manner a more complete rating of the communicative act can be secured. The original instrument's scales for verbal and nonverbal communication and peer and group interaction remain with only slight changes. Another procedural change that also improves upon the time-sampling format requires that all behavioral codes refer to the same "bit" of interaction (the first behavior occurring each twenty seconds). With this rating technique a profile of each child's pattern or style of interaction can be derived, in addition to the quantitative and qualitative measures of peer-group interaction. The scoring categories, similar to the categories on the Parent-Child Interaction Rating Procedure (see p. 822), are as follows: response, initiation, object of interaction, impact codes, verbalizations, fantasy, voice tone, social behavior, physical behavior, contact, behavioral tone, and inferred motivation.

RELIABILITY AND VALIDITY: The authors suggest a minimum of 85-percent agreement among observers in using the measure. The behavioral constructs are based on theoretical contributions of social and developmental psychology, and many scales have been adapted from previously validated instruments.

BIBLIOGRAPHY:

Boger, R. P., and Cunningham, J. L. *Observation of Socialization Behavior.* Unpublished manuscript. Head Start Research Center, Michigan State University, East Lansing, 1969.

Cunningham, J. L., and Boger, R. P. *Development of an Observational Rating Schedule for Preschool Children's Peer-Group Behavior.* East Lansing: Institute for Family and Child Research, Michigan State University, 1971. ERIC document no. 056 055.

Prepared by Robert P. Boger

SHEARE'S SURVEY OF STUDENT ATTITUDES TOWARD SPECIAL CLASS MEMBERS

AUTHOR: Joseph B. Sheare

AGE: Grades 7 to 12

VARIABLE: Peer attitudes

TYPE OF MEASURE: Opinionnaire

SOURCE FROM WHICH MEASURE MAY BE OBTAINED: Joseph B. Sheare, Division of Psychological Services, Montgomery County Public Services, Montgomery County Public School, 850 Hungerford Drive, Rockville, Maryland 20850.

DESCRIPTION OF MEASURE: The Sheare Attitude Survey consists of twenty-five declarative statements concerning Special Education class members. It contains twelve positively stated and thirteen negatively stated items. The instrument is a group-administered measure, and items are answered on a 3-point scale. A scored rating from 1 to 3 is given to each response, thereby yielding a score range from 25 to 75.

As examples, five selected items of the twenty-five on the survey are given below. The respondent answers by checking "agree," "disagree," or "undecided."

1. Special Class teenagers should be educated in special schools away from normal teenagers.
9. In my opinion, Special Class Teenagers are the same as regular teenagers except they are not as smart.
15. A Special Class teenager can be as useful to the school as any other teenager.
20. I believe that I would like to see a Special Class teenager on an athletic team if he were able.
24. I believe that having Special Class teenagers in our school will give our school a bad name.

RELIABILITY AND VALIDITY: The reliability of the scale was determined by the test-retest method and the Kuder-Richardson formula. The coefficients are: test-retest (1 month), .91 ($N = 150$); Kuder-Richardson formula 21, .64 ($N = 80$).

BIBLIOGRAPHY:

Sheare, J. B. "Social Acceptance of EMR Adolescents in Integrated Programs." *American Journal of Mental Deficiency,* 1974, *78,* 678-682.

WHO COULD THIS BE GAME

AUTHOR: Nadine M. Lambert

AGE: Kindergarten to grade 3

VARIABLE: Social relationships

TYPE OF MEASURE: Peer nomination

SOURCE FROM WHICH MEASURE MAY BE OBTAINED: Nadine M. Lambert, School of Education, University of California, Berkeley, California 94720.

DESCRIPTION OF MEASURE: The Who Could This Be Game has been developed as a means of analyzing, in a systematic and measurable way, how children are perceived or "seen" by their peers. It is a peer-rating instrument for kindergarten and grades 1, 2, and 3. It must be given individually, and it takes 15 to 20 minutes at the most for each child. The measure is composed of eleven picture cards with a total of twenty scoring items (one or two items on a card). Five of the items are pictures of boys in situations related to problem or negative behavior; five are pictures of boys in situations related to positive or neutral behavior; five are pictures of girls in situations related to problem or negative behavior; and five are pictures of girls in situations related to positive or neutral behavior. The first four items are:

1. Who could this be playing tether ball with another child?
2. Who could this be, being told by the teacher not to do something?
3. Who could this be playing jump rope?
4. Who could this be fighting with this other child?

RELIABILITY AND VALIDITY: Retest reliabilities of from .75 to .82 were found for all grades combined.

BIBLIOGRAPHY:

Hartsough, C. S. *Classroom Adaptation of Elementary School Children Varying with Respect to Age, Sex, and Ethnic Status.* Berkeley: University of California, 1973.

Lambert, N. M. *The Who Could This Be Game Manual.* Berkeley: University of California, n.d.

Lambert, N. M. *The Prediction of School Adjustment.* U.S. Office of Education, Cooperative Research Project No. 1980. Sacramento: California State Department of Education, 1964.

Lambert, N. M. "Intellectual and Nonintellectual Predictors of High School Status." *Journal of Special Education,* 1972, *6* (3), 247-259.

Lambert, N. M. and Bower, E. M. *A Process for In-School Screening of Emotionally Handicapped Children.* Atlanta: Educational Testing Service, 1961, 1974.

Lambert, N. M., Hartsough, C. S., and Zimmerman, I. L. "The Comparative Predictive Efficiency of Intellectual and Nonintellectual Components of High School Functioning." *American Journal of Orthopsychiatry,* 1976, *46* (1), 109-122.

Stampp, S. K. "A Longitudinal Study of Peer Ratings and Cognitive Decentering in Elementary School." Unpublished doctoral dissertation, University of California, Berkeley, 1975.

Group 3-c

Other Environmental Perceptions and Characteristics

ACADEMIC ACHIEVEMENT ACCOUNTABILITY (AAA) SCALE

AUTHOR: Margaret M. Clifford

AGE: Grades 3 to 8

VARIABLE: Locus of control (regarding academic outcomes)

TYPE OF MEASURE: Likert-type scale

SOURCE FROM WHICH MEASURE MAY BE OBTAINED: Margaret M. Clifford, Department of Educational Psychology, University of Iowa, Iowa City, Iowa 52242.

DESCRIPTION OF MEASURE: The AAA consists of eighteen questions pertaining to academic activities. Each question calls for a "yes" or "no" response, and a 5-point scale is provided to assess the strength of the affirmative or negative reply. It can be group-administered in 15 to 20 minutes. It is recommended that the administrator read each question aloud to the students and that the scale be presented by someone other than the students' teacher(s). The score range for this scale is 18 to 90; a high score indicates acceptance of responsibility for academic outcomes. Responses on items 2, 5, 9, 13, 15, and 16 are scored 1 to 5 from left to right; all other items are scored 5 to 1.

The scale, and its method of marking, is given below.

1. Do your marks get worse when you don't work hard?
     YES!   yes   ?   no   NO!
2. Do your marks stay about the same no matter how hard you study?
3. Does studying before a test seem to help you get a higher score?
4. When you make up your mind to work hard, does your school work get better?
5. When you do worse than usual, do you feel it's your fault?
6. Do your marks get better when you do your homework carefully?
7. Do you think studying for tests is a waste of time?
8. If you get a bad mark, do you feel it's your fault?
9. When a teacher gives you a low mark, is it because he doesn't like you?
10. When you really want a better mark than usual, can you get it?
11. Do your lowest grades come when you don't study your assignment?
12. Do your test marks seem to go up when you study?
13. Is a high mark just a matter of "luck" for you?
14. Do you think you deserve the marks you get?
15. Do you usually get low marks even when you study hard?
16. Are tests just a lot of guesswork for you?
17. Do you have much control over the marks you get?
18. When you do poorly in school work, do you feel that you could have done better if you had wanted to?

RELIABILITY AND VALIDITY: This scale has been administered to fourteen different groups totaling more than one thousand students in grades 3 through 8. Indices from school records suggest these samples represent average middle-class students. The lowest Kuder-Richardson formula 20 for these groups was .63, the highest .85, and the median .74. The correlations between Composite Grade Equivalency on Iowa Tests of Basic Skills and AAA are generally in the .30s and significant beyond the .05 or .01 level. Means and standard deviations are relatively stable across grades, averaging approximately 75.0 and 9.0 respectively. Validation with a need-achievement measure and student effort ratings made by teachers are currently being conducted.

BIBLIOGRAPHY:

Clifford, M. M., and Cleary, T. "The Relationship Between Children's Academic Performance and Achievement Accountability." *Child Development,* 1972, *43,* 647-655.

BOWN'S SELF-REPORT INVENTORY
AS ADAPTED BY STEPHENS

AUTHORS: W. Beth Stephens (adapted with the aid of and reproduced by permission of O. H. Bown)

AGE: 18 to 26 years

VARIABLE: Mental health—attitude toward the phenomenal world

TYPE OF MEASURE: Self-report, pencil-and-paper test

SOURCE FROM WHICH MEASURE MAY BE OBTAINED: Beth Stephens, Ritter Hall, Temple University, Philadelphia, Pennsylvania 19122. Cost: Protocol plus instructions for administering and scoring, $0.50 per set; protocol only, $0.25.

DESCRIPTION OF MEASURE: A measure of the way a mentally retarded young adult feels towards self, others, children, authority, work reality, and the future is provided by Stephens' adaptation of Bown's Self-Report Inventory. The forty-eight-item assessment is a self-report, pencil-and-paper test suitable for either individual or group use and requires no special training for administering or scoring. After an item is read to the subject he scores it by placing an X on the correct response. Average duration of the untimed test is 12 minutes. A total mental-health score is obtained by addition of correct responses.

Sample items and the factorial area they represent are given below.

Yes   No   I have done just enough to get by. (work)
Yes   No   This is a pretty good old world and I am glad to be alive. (reality)
Yes   No   My parents trust me and I trust them. (parents)
Yes   No   Thinking back I don't think I ever liked myself very well. (self)

RELIABILITY AND VALIDITY: Test-retest reliability (twenty-one-day interval) of .88

was obtained in a pilot study involving twenty-five randomly selected subjects (CA 18-26; IQ 50-75) from Marbridge Foundation and Austin State School. Construct validity: When total scores for the instrument were included in a factor matrix of scores for the seventy-six predictor variables obtained in the Peck and Stephens study (1968), the measure contributed loadings of .25 or above on two factors. The highest loading, .50, was on a factor termed "openness to stimuli"; a loading of −.27 was on a factor termed "alienation syndrome." Concurrent validity: Significant Pearson product-moment correlations of T-scores for Stephens' adaptation of Bown's Self-Report Inventory total score and T-scores for the eighty criterion variables included in the Peck and Stephens study (1964) of the after-training success of adult male retardates are listed in the Texas Screening Battery (Peck, Stephens, and Fooshee, 1964). A high score on the inventory suggests a happy, well-integrated personality—a retardate who tends to make desirable use of leisure time, who exhibits some skill with finances, who possesses qualities of leadership, dependability, and responsibility, and who is capable of maintaining a positive relationship with a job supervisor and with fellow employees.

BIBLIOGRAPHY:

Peck, J. R., Stephens, W. B., and Fooshee, D. K. *The Texas Screening Battery for Sub-normals.* 1804 Raleigh, Austin, Texas, 1964.
Peck, J. R., and Stephens, W. B. *Success of Young Adult Male Retardates.* CEC Research Monograph. Reston, Virginia: Council for Exceptional Children, 1964.
Stephens, W. B., Peck, J. R., and Veldman, D. J. "Personality and Success Profiles Characteristic of Young Adult Male Retardates." *American Journal of Mental Deficiency,* 1968, *73,* 405-413.

COMFORTABLE INTERPERSONAL DISTANCE SCALE (CID)

AUTHORS: Marshall P. Duke and Stephen Nowicki, Jr.

AGE: 4 years to old age

VARIABLE: Interpersonal distance-personal space

TYPE OF MEASURE: Diagrammatic scale

SOURCE FROM WHICH MEASURE MAY BE OBTAINED: Marshall P. Duke or Stephen Nowicki, Jr., Emory University, Department of Psychology, Atlanta, Georgia 30033.

DESCRIPTION OF MEASURE: The CID is a paper-and-pencil measure corresponding to body-boundary rooms used previously. The figural layout is in the form of a plane with eight radii emanating from a common point, each 80-millimeter radius being associated with a randomly numbered "entrance" to what is presented as an "imaginary round room." Typical instructions ask *S*s to imagine themselves at the center of the "room" and to respond to imaginary persons approaching them along a radius by making a mark on the line indicating where they might feel uncomfortable. Responses are scored as distance (in millimeters) between center and *S*s' marks.

RELIABILITY AND VALIDITY: Several studies of test-retest reliability have resulted in levels varying from .64 to .88 among children, adolescents, and adults. Five studies of construct validity are also supportive. For more information, see Duke and Nowicki (1972) and Duke (1973).

BIBLIOGRAPHY:

Duke, M. "Locus of Control as a Mediating Variable in Interpersonal Distances." Paper presented at the meeting of the American Psychological Association. Montreal, 1973.

Duke, M., Johnson, K., and Nowicki, S. "Differential Effect of Authority Role Cues of Interpersonal Distancing as Mediated by Locus of Control." Unpublished manuscript. Emory University, Atlanta, Georgia, 1972.

Duke, M., and Nowicki, S. "A New Measure and Social Learning Model for Interpersonal Distance." *Journal of Experimental Research in Personality*, 1972, *6*, 119-132.

Duke, M., and Nowicki, S. "Interpersonal Distance: Sibling Structure and Parental Affection Antecedents." *Journal of Genetic Psychology*, 1973, *123*, 35-45.

DOUBLE-ASPECT FACIAL PERCEPTION TASK

AUTHOR: R. John Huber

AGE: 5 years and up

VARIABLE: Human selective attention behavior

TYPE OF MEASURE: Ambiguous stimuli

SOURCE FROM WHICH MEASURE MAY BE OBTAINED: See Huber and Forsyth (1972) and Huber and Davis (1975).

DESCRIPTION OF MEASURE: The stimuli of the measure consist of fourteen pictures, ten of which are used in the testing and four of which are buffer items. The pictures (except for the buffer items) are ambiguous in that they may be seen as either human or nonhuman. See Huber and Forsyth (1972) and Huber and Davis (1975) for detailed information concerning stimulus standardization, administration, and scoring. This double-aspect task has served well as a warmup for other tests, since administration is brief and children find the task fun. The double-aspect task was developed to experimentally test implications of Adler's social interest hypothesis.

RELIABILITY AND VALIDITY: Scores on this measure have been found to be significantly related to degree of adjustment and improvement in therapy. See Huber and Forsyth (1972) and Huber and Davis (1975).

BIBLIOGRAPHY:

Forsyth, G. A., and Huber, R. J. "An Individual Differences Analysis of Double-Aspect Stimulus Perceptions." Paper presented to Psychonomic Society. Boston, Massachusetts, November 1974.
Huber, R. J., and Davis, R. E. "Selective Attention Behavior and Improvement in Therapy as Predicted by Adler's Social Interest Hypothesis." *Journal of Individual Psychology*, 1975, *31,* 79-84.
Huber, R. J., and Forsyth, G. A. "Selective Attention and Social Interest." *Journal of Individual Psychology,* 1972, *28,* 51-59.
Huber, R. J., and Stiggens, R. "Double-Aspect Perception and Social Interest." *Perceptual and Motor Skills,* 1970, *30,* 387-392.

DRAW-A-CLASSROOM TEST

AUTHOR: E. N. Wright

AGE: 4 to 8 years

VARIABLE: Perception of the classroom

TYPE OF MEASURE: System for analysis of children's drawings

SOURCE FROM WHICH MEASURE MAY BE OBTAINED: The ERIC documents are available from ERIC Document Reproductions, Computer Microfilm International Corp., P.O. Box 190, Arlington, Virginia 22210. The detailed manual is available only from the Toronto Board of Education, 155 College Street, Toronto 2B, Ontario, Canada. Cost: $10 for xeroxing and mailing; a set of colored photographs to illustrate the various coding elements, $50 (spaces for inserting these photographs are provided in the manual).

DESCRIPTION OF MEASURE: The Draw-A-Classroom Test was developed to supplement traditional measures in a major study. By asking children to draw their classroom (they are then asked to tell about their drawing, and teachers record their words to assist in coding), the hope was to obtain data reflecting the child's perceptions of school. It proved difficult to develop reliable methods of recording differences among the drawings. In brief, the eventual result was the development of a coding system that was highly reliable, time consuming to employ, and somewhat removed from the clinical approach of the initiators of this idea.

The manual for coders is extremely lengthy and detailed and was evolved in the process of developing interrater reliability. Under Space the coding provides for the presence or absence of frame lines, both circular and straight, partitioning of the drawing, and the inclusion of physical boundaries (both real and implied), walls, ceilings, ground lines, etc. Other variables noted are the amount of space used, whether or not the drawing includes more than the classroom, whether or not the background is shaded, and whether or not there is an established viewpoint. The second section deals with the presence and absence of people: the artist, other children in the classroom, whether or not boys and girls are specified and distinguished, presence or absence of teacher and other adults, and the types of activities and interaction of and among the people in the drawings. The section on Drawing the Person is similar to elements of Goodenough's Scale, although again a presence-absence type of coding is used on each item. The section on Classroom Constants deals with nonhuman elements that each child has an opportunity to deal with: doors, lights, windows, chairs, and tables. Coding again is for presence-absence, as well as organization, relationship among items, use of color, groupings of types of constants, and so forth. The final section is called Objects. It is more general and records the organization, presence, and relationship of objects and their relationship to people: behind/in front of, on/under, perspective, predominance of color, number of colors used, time-by-tense of labels, labeling to indicate use, time by pictorial situation, and classroom atmosphere.

The above summarizes the areas for which reliable coding strategies could be and were developed. The coding procedure is elaborate and very time consuming, and depending on the goals of the project and the available resources, other alternatives should be considered before using this instrument. However, one or more sections could well be used independently as a method of documenting elements of children's drawings.

RELIABILITY AND VALIDITY: Because many of the categories for coding were essentially presence-absence, an attempt was made to develop a rigorous interrater reliability procedure requiring a revision of the items until there would be complete agreement among five independent raters on the majority of a sample of pictures. The following percentages indicate the percentage of 120 drawings on which there was complete agreement among five raters: For Space—on eighteen items, eleven were over 80 percent, four were over 70 percent, and the remaining were over 60 percent. For Persons and Drawing the Person—there were only fifty-six drawings with people, and the percentages based on these fifty-six using only four raters were: Persons (presence and interaction)—nineteen items total, sixteen items over 80 percent, one item over 70 percent, two items over 50 percent. Drawing the Person—twenty items total, twelve over 80 percent, six over 70 percent, two over 60 percent. Classroom Constants—thirteen items total, eight over 80 percent, five over 66 percent. Object Relationship—twelve items total, six over 80 percent, three over 70 percent, three over 60 percent. There is no appropriate evidence on validity for this measure.

BIBLIOGRAPHY:

The "Draw-a-Classroom" Test: An Overview. Toronto, Ontario, Canada: Toronto Board of Education Research Department, 1966. ERIC document no. ED 068 489.

Rogers, R. S. The Effect of Having Previously Attended Junior Kindergarten on "Draw-a-Classroom" Test Scores Obtained in Senior Kindergarten. Toronto, Ontario, Canada: Toronto Board of Education Research Department, 1968. ERIC document no. 067168.

Rogers, R. S. *A Consolidated Report on the "Draw-a-Classroom" Test: A Study of the Drawing Behavior of Children in Toronto Public Schools.* Toronto, Ontario, Canada: Toronto Board of Education Research Department, 1969. ERIC document no. ED 068 580.

Rogers, R. S., and Wright, E. N. "A Study of Children's Drawings of Their Classrooms." *Journal of Educational Research,* 1971, *64,* 370-374.

Scoring Categories and Administration Instructions: Appendix of a Complete Manual for the "Draw-a-Classroom" Test. Toronto, Ontario, Canada: Toronto Board of Education Research Department, 1966.

DRAW-A-PERSON-IN-THE-RAIN PROJECTIVE TECHNIQUE

AUTHORS: Abraham Amchin and Arnold Abrams as described by Hammer (1971) and Jacobs (1974).

AGE: Preschool to adult

VARIABLE: Perceived environmental stress and ego defense mechanisms

TYPE OF MEASURE: Projective drawings

SOURCE FROM WHICH MEASURE MAY BE OBTAINED: J. C. Jacobs, Special Services Division, Plymouth Community Schools, Plymouth, Michigan 48170.

DESCRIPTION OF MEASURE: The subject is simply asked "Please draw a person in the rain." This gives an opportunity to view the subject's perception of the type and degree of environmental stress by viewing the rain drawing in light of the verbalizations offered, and to view the impact of the environmental stress on the subject by viewing and analyzing the differences of the person drawn for this device with that produced for other tests. Usually this test is given following the Draw-a-Person test or the House-Tree-Person Test. Drawings are analyzed by considering the "prevailing mood," by considering the rain drawing in conjunction with the verbalizations offered, and by comparing and contrasting the details of the human figure in the rain drawing with the equivalent details from other drawings. The amount, type, and intensity of the rain is seen as a measure of the subject's perception of environmental stress. The type, size, and number of protections the person has against the rain are seen as the subject's defenses against the stress—his ego defense mechanisms. This is an easy and short procedure, usually taking about 15 minutes, that adds valuable information to a test battery.

RELIABILITY AND VALIDITY: As with all projective techniques, the experience and skill of the examiner are of vital importance. This task should be undertaken only by those already familiar with the interpretation of other projective drawings, such as in the House-Tree-Person Test.

BIBLIOGRAPHY:

Hammer, E. F. *The Clinical Application of Projective Drawings.* Springfield, Illinois: C. C Thomas, 1971.

Jacobs, J. C. *Draw-a-Person-in-the-Rain Projective Technique.* Honolulu, Hawaii: Behavioral Sciences, 1974.

Prepared by Jon C. Jacobs

DULIN-CHESTER INVENTORY OF READING INTERESTS AND MOTIVATIONS TO READING

AUTHORS: Kenneth L. Dulin and Robert D. Chester

AGE: Intermediate and junior high school students

VARIABLE: Reading interests, classroom reward systems, and classroom motivational practices related to reading

TYPE OF MEASURE: Inventory of related rating scales

SOURCE FROM WHICH MEASURE MAY BE OBTAINED: Kenneth L. Dulin, University of Wisconsin-Madison, 456F Teacher Education Building, 225 North Mills Street, Madison, Wisconsin 53706.

DESCRIPTION OF MEASURE: The Dulin-Chester Inventory of Reading Interests and Motivations to Reading has seven subparts. Part One asks students to grade (from a high of A to a low of E) ten reward systems commonly employed in classrooms in terms of how motivating they feel these various reward systems are. Part Two calls for the grading of ten common teacher practices in terms of how encouraging of reading they are. Part Three utilizes the same procedures to evaluate ten frequently used instructional activities, and Part Four evaluates ten enrichment activities. Part Five asks students to rank-order their preferences for ten subject-matter areas about which they might read. Parts Six and Seven each call for the dividing up of 100 points among five different categories in Part Six, literary genre and in Part Seven, kinds of publications (magazines, newspapers, comic books, hardback books, and softback books).

As examples, the ten items of the reward-systems section of the scale are given below, to be rated as follows: A = I feel this would be a *very good* reward for reading. B = I feel this would be a *fairly good* reward for reading. C = I feel this would be only an *average* reward for reading. D = I feel this would be a *fairly poor* reward for reading. E = I feel this would be a *very poor* reward for reading.

1. Getting a grade for how much reading you do.
2. Getting extra credit for how much reading you do.

3. Getting your name on a bulletin board for how much reading you do.
4. Getting stars on a chart for how much reading you do.
5. Getting money for how much reading you do.
6. Getting prizes for how much reading you do.
7. Getting free time in school as a reward for extra reading you've done.
8. Getting a certificate to take home for extra reading you've done.
9. Getting to go to other classes to tell about books you've read.
10. Getting excused from other classwork as a reward for extra reading you've done.

RELIABILITY AND VALIDITY: This instrument has been field-tested at both the fifth- and seventh-grade levels with success. Clear patterns of sex-related, attitude-related, and ability-related preferences have been established.

BIBLIOGRAPHY: None reported.

ELEMENTARY SCHOOL ENVIRONMENT SURVEY (ESES)

AUTHORS: David Sadker and Robert Sinclair

AGE: 9 to 11 years

VARIABLE: School environments (academic and affective)

TYPE OF MEASURE: Questionnaire

SOURCE FROM WHICH MEASURE MAY BE OBTAINED: David Sadker, School of Education, The American University, Washington, D.C. 20016. Cost: $50.00 per school system, one-time charge only.

DESCRIPTION OF MEASURE: ESES measures elementary-school environments as seen and felt by students. Student perceptions of six dimensions are assessed: alienation, humanism, autonomy, morale, opportunism, and academic resources. Each of the six dimensions is measured by seven consecutive items in the forty-two-item true-false questionnaire. Although educators have a variety of tests designed to measure individual differences, there exist only a few techniques available to administrators and researchers that can assess environments and fewer still that can measure elementary environments. ESES can be used to diagnose elementary-school environments, assess programs, evaluate specific school practices, and suggest avenues for the improvement of the elementary-school experience of children.

The following six items illustrate the six different dimensions assessed by the true-false questionnaire.

1. Most of the teachers care about problems that students are having.
8. Most students are not interested in such things as poetry, music, or painting.

15. Students almost always wait to be called on before speaking in class.

22. Many of the students here are unhappy about the school.

29. Students that the principal and teachers know will have it easier in this school.

36. Teachers seldom take their classes to the library so that students can look up information.

RELIABILITY AND VALIDITY: ESES was initially built upon the constructs identified by Pace (1963, 1969) and Pace and Stern (1958) in College and University Environmental Scales. After an administration to over five thousand elementary-school students, ESES was factor analyzed. That factor analysis validated the current six dimensions.

BIBLIOGRAPHY:

Pace, C. R. *College and University Environment Scales: Technical Manual.* Princeton, New Jersey: Educational Testing Service, 1963.

Pace, C. R. "College Environments." In *Encyclopedia of Educational Research.* Toronto, Canada: Macmillan, 1969.

Pace, C. R., and Stern, G. G. "An Approach to the Measurement of Psychological Characteristics of College Environments." *Journal of Educational Psychology,* 1958, *49,* 269-277.

Sadker, D. "Dimensions of the Elementary-School Environment: A Factor-Analytic Study." *Journal of Educational Research,* 1973, *66,* 441-442, 465.

Sadker, D., Sadker, M., and Cooper, J. M. "Elementary School Through Children's Eyes." *Elementary School Journal,* 1973, *73,* 289-296.

Sadker, D., and Sinclair, R. L. *Identifying the Dimensions of Environment Press at the Elementary School Level: A Factor Analysis of Beta Press.* 1972. ERIC document no. ED 066 431.

GRUEN-KORTE-STEPHENS INTERNAL-EXTERNAL (IE) SCALE

AUTHORS: Gerald E. Gruen, John R. Korte, and John F. Baum

AGE: Elementary school-aged children

VARIABLE: Internal vs. external locus-of-control orientations in academic settings

TYPE OF MEASURE: Forced-choice scale

SOURCE FROM WHICH MEASURE MAY BE OBTAINED: Gerald E. Gruen, Department of Psychological Sciences, Purdue University, West Lafayette, Indiana 47907.

DESCRIPTION OF MEASURE: The Gruen-Korte-Stephens Internal-External Scale is a thirty-eight-page booklet with one item on each page. The stem of an item and each alternative to it are illustrated pictorially. The pictures are drawn as stick figures so that they will not have the features of any particular racial or ethnic group. An example of an item is as follows: *The teacher is smiling while the child is reading in front of the class. Imagine you are the child in the picture. Why do you think the teacher would be smiling at you? Would she be smiling because (a) you are trying hard to do your best? or because (b) the teacher likes the story you are reading?* In the first (internal) alternative, the reinforcement (teacher smiling) is contingent on the child's behavior (trying hard), while in the second (external) alternative, the reinforcement is contingent on an event beyond the child's control (teacher likes the story). Cue words were provided below each alternative to aid the subject in remembering the item. Several other features of this scale should be mentioned. The internal alternative appears an equal number of times in the left and right positions, the "heroes" of the pictures are divided equally between males and females, each item that is positively toned is balanced by an item that is negatively toned, and the response mode for this scale is simply to draw an X through the chosen alternative.

RELIABILITY AND VALIDITY: The original scale was administered to 1,100 black, white, and Spanish children of upper-lower to lower-middle socioeconomic status in the public schools of Gary, Indiana. The overall internal consistency of the scale for that sample, as estimated by Kuder-Richardson formula 20, was .76, while that for each grade level was as follows: second, .69; fourth, .70; and sixth, .79. In terms of predictive and concurrent validity, the scale has some encouraging features. In addition to discriminating between age, ethnic, and socioeconomic groups, it proved to be a fairly good predictor of grade-point averages among second graders ($r = .34$). In this regard it was second only to IQ scores ($r = .45$) and had the desirable characteristics of being negligibly correlated with both a measure of IQ and a measure of social desirability. Bottinelli and Weizmann (1973) also have found this measure to be a significant correlate of grade-point average. In addition, the latter investigators reported the only test-retest (two weeks) reliability coefficient available thus far with this measure, a correlation of .83 for a small sample of twenty-three second-grade children. In terms of convergent validity, Stephens and Delys (1973) correlated the Gruen-Korte-Stephens Internal-External Scale with three other measures of locus of control: the Stephens-Delys, Nowicki-Strickland, and Crandall tests. They reported that the intercorrelations among the four tests were generally quite low, and the Gruen-Korte-Stephens Internal-External Scale generally showed the highest intercorrelations with the other tests. Although they did not report the exact correlations among the four tests, they reported that the correlations were seldom higher than the .30s and often lower. The most serious limitation of the scale is the marked skewness of responses. All groups of children chose the internal alternative more often than the external alternative. This was particularly troublesome at the fourth- and sixth-grade levels where the range of scores was quite restricted. At the second-grade level a more acceptable range of scores was found, but responses were still skewed. This suggests that the scale will be most useful with this younger age group. Further work is needed to eliminate the skewness of scores and the nondiscriminating items.

BIBLIOGRAPHY:

Bottinelli, S. B., and Weizmann, F. "Task Independence and Locus-of-Control Orientation in Children." *Journal of Personality Assessment*, 1973, *36*, 375-381.

Gruen, G. E., Korte, J. R., and Baum, J. F. "Group Measure of Locus of Control." *Developmental Psychology,* 1974, *10,* 683-686.

Stephens, M. W., and Delys, P. "A Locus-of-Control Measure for Preschool Children." *Developmental Psychology,* 1973, *9,* 55-65.

LOCUS-OF-CONTROL INTERVIEW (LCI)

AUTHORS: Charlotte Malasky, Milton F. Shore, and Norman Milgram

AGE: 4 to 9 years

VARIABLE: Locus of control in preschool and early school-age children

TYPE OF MEASURE: Semistructured interview

SOURCE FROM WHICH MEASURE MAY BE OBTAINED: Mental Health Study Center, 2340 University Boulevard East, Adelphi, Maryland 20783.

DESCRIPTION OF MEASURE: This Piaget-type exploratory interview was designed for use with young children, particularly those with limited verbal ability. Using the experiences of a preschool child, the interview provides opportunities to explore the child's knowledge and understanding regarding control over himself and the environment. The scale has twenty-five items covering a wide range of activities. Items are scored according to whether an action is taken and how appropriate the response is.

As examples, three of the twenty-five items on the interview, with scoring criteria, are given below.

1. Do you ever think about what you want to be when you grow up? (If "no," ask child to think about it for a moment.) What do you want to be? Do you think you can be a (whatever child names)?
2. Do you think you really will be a (whatever child has named in Question 1)? (If answer is "no," ask): Why do you think you will not be a (whatever the child has named)?
4. Suppose someone gets mad at you. Can you do anything to make him (her) your friend again? (If "yes," ask): What can you do?

Scoring:
1. Yes = 1; No = 0.
2. Yes = 1; No: because not grown up = 1; No: because might change mind = 1; No: because of some obstacle (parents won't let; you have to go to college, etc.) = 0; No: but don't know why = 0.
4. Yes: by self and appropriately (give him something; play with him, etc.) = 3; Yes: by self and inappropriately (scare him, threaten him) = 2; Yes: with outside help (teacher, mother, etc.) = 1; No = 0.

RELIABILITY AND VALIDITY: The scores on the Locus-of-Control Interview were significantly higher for middle-class than for lower-class children and for sixth-grade than for first-grade children. The interaction between social class and grade was not significant. However, a detailed analysis of first and sixth grades separately, while showing no difference between the social classes among first graders (t = 1.49; n.s.), indicated that among sixth graders the middle-class children scored significantly higher than lower-class children (t = 3.19; p < .01). Thus there are developmental and social class differences with greater internal locus of control developing as age increases. But although the scores in children in both social classes rise, there is a greater rise in the middle classes, with a widening discrepancy between the social classes becoming clear in the older children when compared to the younger ones. The authors tested an experimental and a control group of first-grade children, most of whom were black. The experimental group was a Follow-Through program; the controls were in regular first grades. Measures of achievement, nonverbal intelligence, and the LCI were administered. There was a greater difference between the groups as a function of enrichment on locus of control than on either the achievement task or the nonverbal intelligence task.

BIBLIOGRAPHY:

Shore, M. F., Milgram, N. A., and Malasky, C. "The Effectiveness of an Enrichment Program for Disadvantaged Young Children." *American Journal of Orthopsychiatry,* 1971, *41,* 442-449.

Prepared by Milton F. Shore

MODIFIED INTELLECTUAL ACHIEVEMENT RESPONSIBILITY QUESTIONNAIRE (MIARQ)

AUTHORS: Daniel Ringelheim, Irv Bialer, and Hatice Morrissey

AGE: 9 to 15 years

VARIABLE: Locus of control in intellectual academic situations

TYPE OF MEASURE: Forced-choice questionnaire

SOURCE FROM WHICH MEASURE MAY BE OBTAINED: See Ringelheim and others (1970), which is available from Photo Duplicating Service, Library of Congress, or ERIC Document Reproduction Service, National Cash Register Co., Box 2206, Rockville, Maryland 20852.

DESCRIPTION OF MEASURE: The MIARQ is a modified form of the Intellectual Achievement Responsibility Questionnaire (IARQ) (Crandall and others, 1965; Johnson and Bommarito, 1971). Its rationale is identical to the IARQ. However, the MIARQ is designed to be administered to retarded children, and it differs from the IARQ in that (1) there are twenty-four items instead of thirty-four, (2) language levels of items and instructions are simplified, and (3) two introductory examples are given to ensure *S*'s understanding of task requirements. Scoring is identical to that of the IARQ, and the MIARQ yields three separate scores, reflecting the number of positive outcomes for which the child assumes "credit" (I+ score), number of negative event outcomes for which he assumes "blame" (I– score), and total responsibility (Total I score). The higher the score, the more internal the orientation.

As examples, the first five of the twenty-four test items are given below.

1. When you pass a test, is it
    +a. because you studied, or
    b. because it was easy?
2. When you find it hard to understand school work, is it
    a. because the teacher did not explain it enough, or
    –b. because you did not listen carefully?
3. If you can't remember a story, is it
    a. because the story wasn't good, or
    –b. because you just weren't interested?
4. If your parents tell you your school work is good, is it
    +a. because your work is really good, or
    b. because they feel good?
5. When you do better in school, is it
    +a. because you try hard, or
    b. because somebody helped you?

RELIABILITY AND VALIDITY: In the original study (Ringelheim and others, 1970), the sample consisted of 215 "educable" mentally retarded children from public and parochial school special classes and from institutions. They ranged in chronological age from 9 to 15 years, in mental age from 4 to 12 years, and in IQ from 45 to 82. Both boys and girls were represented. Means and standard deviations are presented for ages 9, 11, 13, and 15. A Cronbach *alpha* reliability coefficient of .58 was obtained. Validity was demonstrated by significant correlations with MA, CA, Arithmetic Grade Level, Spelling Grade Level, The Children's Embedded Picture Test, and the Rosenzweig Picture Frustration Test. In a study among twenty-five black and Spanish-surnamed children in an inner-city school, Ward (1973) found test-retest reliabilities of .85 (Total I), .49 (I+), and .73 (I–).

BIBLIOGRAPHY:

Crandall, V. J., Katkovsky, W., and Crandall, V. C. "Children's Beliefs in Their Own Control of Reinforcement in Intellectual-Academic Achievement Situations." *Child Development,* 1965, *36,* 91-109.

Johnson, O. G., and Bommarito, J. W. *Tests and Measurements in Child Development: A Handbook.* San Francisco: Jossey-Bass, 1971.

Ringelheim, D., Bialer, I., and Morrissey, H. *The Relationship Among Various Dichotomous Descriptive Personality Scales and Achievement in the Mentally Retarded: A Study of the Relevant Factors Influencing Academic Achievement at Various Chronological Age Levels.* Final report, U.S. Office of Education, Bureau of

Research, Project no. 6-2685, Grant no. OEG-0-8-062685-1762 (032). February 1970.

Ward, J. G. "Locus of Control, Social Reinforcement, and Task Performance of Black and Spanish-Surnamed Children." Unpublished doctoral dissertation. New York University, New York, 1973.

Prepared by Irv Bialer

NACHAMIE CHILDREN'S MACH SCALE (KIDDIE-MACH)

AUTHOR: Susan Schiffres Nachamie

AGE: 7 to 12 years

VARIABLE: Machiavellian attitudes toward man, world, and interpersonal tactics

TYPE OF MEASURE: Likert-type scale

SOURCE FROM WHICH MEASURE MAY BE OBTAINED: See Nachamie (1969) for scales only; available with administration and scoring from Susan Schiffres Nachamie, 1175 York Avenue, New York, New York 10021.

DESCRIPTION OF MEASURE: The twenty-item Nachamie Children's Mach Scale is based on an item-analysis of fifth- and sixth-grade students' responses to the Christie Adult Mach IV Scale. The construction involved simplification of vocabulary, sentence structure, content, and response categories of Christie's scale. Of the pro-Machiavelli items, five deal with views of human nature, four are concerned with attitudes toward interpersonal tactics, and one with abstract morality. For each pro-Machiavellian item in each category there is a reversal, or anti-Machiavellian item in each category. An example of a pro-Machiavellian item (called an original) is: "Sometimes you have to hurt other people to get what you want." An example of a reversal: "Most people are good and kind." There are five response categories: "Agree very much," "Agree a little," "No answer" (this is not on the response sheet but was included in scoring for respondents who omitted items), "Disagree a little," "Disagree very much." Pro-Machiavelli items are weighted 5, 4, 3, 2, 1 for the above categories. Reversals are weighted 1, 2, 3, 4, 5. Scores obtained on reversals and originals are summed for a total Mach score. The scale may be read aloud to younger respondents (or poor readers) while they follow along.

As examples, the first five of the twenty items of the scale are given below.

1. Never tell anyone why you did something unless it will help you.
2. Most people are good and kind.
3. The best way to get along with people is to tell them things that make them happy.
4. You should do something only when you are sure it is right.
5. It is smartest to believe that all people will be mean if they have a chance.

RELIABILITY AND VALIDITY: The Nachamie Children's Mach Scale and the Christie Adult Mach IV Scale were administered to four sixth-grade classes in a New York City public school. The protocols of ninety-one respondents were scored, analyzed, and compared. There were no sex or racial differences in mean scores on either scale. The correlation of the two scales was .44, equivalent in magnitude and direction to their respective split-half reliabilities. For three out of the four classes tested, split-half reliabilities were in the .50s for both scales, although they were *slightly* higher for the Children's Mach. Response-set, unfamiliarity with paper-and-pencil tests (this was a ghetto school), and the fact that counter-balanced tests tend to decrease reliability may explain low reliabilities. However, the respondents indicated significantly greater ease of comprehension on the Children's Scale ($p < .001$). Validation of the scale was attempted by means of a dice-rolling game in which S could win points in the following ways: by bluffing successfully or telling the truth deceptively when S rolled or by challenging a bluff or believing the truth when S's opponent rolled. Thirty-six dyads, each composed of a high and low scale scorer, matched for sex and race, were tested. Results confirmed the prediction that high scale scorers would win significantly more games than low scale scorers ($p < .002$).

BIBLIOGRAPHY:

Bien, D. "Parental Machiavellianism and Children's Cheating in Japan." *Journal of Cross-Cultural Psychology*, 1974, *5*, 259-270.

Christie, R. "The Machiavellis Among Us." *Psychology Today*, 1970, *4*, 86.

Christie, R., and Geis, G. L. *Studies in Machiavellianism.* New York: Academic Press, 1970.

Nachamie, S. S. "Machiavellianism in Children: Construction and Validation of the Children's Mach Scale." *American Psychologist*, 1966, *21*, 628.

Nachamie, S. S. "Machiavellianism in Children: The Children's Mach Scale and the Bluffing Game." Unpublished doctoral dissertation. Columbia University, New York, 1969.

NOWICKI-STRICKLAND LOCUS-OF-CONTROL SCALE FOR CHILDREN

AUTHORS: Stephen Nowicki, Jr. and Bonnie R. Strickland

AGE: Grade 3 to college

VARIABLE: Generalized expectancies for internal vs. external control of reinforcement

TYPE OF MEASURE: Test

SOURCE FROM WHICH MEASURE MAY BE OBTAINED: See Nowicki and Strickland (1973).

DESCRIPTION OF MEASURE: The Nowicki-Strickland Locus-of-Control Scale for

Children is a forty-item paper-and-pencil test having Yes-No response mode. The test was developed from an item pool of 102 items. The 102 items were given to a group of nine clinical psychology staff members who were asked to answer the items in an external direction. Items were dropped for which there was not complete agreement among the judges, leaving fifty-nine items. Item analysis reduced the test further to the present forty items (N = 152 children ranging from the third through the ninth grade). The authors suggest two short forms, one for grades 3 through 6 and another for grades 7 through 12. These short forms are derived from a subset of items in the complete scale. An adult form of the Nowicki-Strickland Scale is presently being developed (Nowicki and Duke, 1972), as is a preschool version. A variety of samples, ranging from third grade through college, has been used. The main sample consisted of 1,017 children (mostly Caucasian) ranging from the third through twelfth grade in four different communities.

As examples, the first ten of the forty items of the scale are given below.

1. Do you believe that most problems will solve themselves if you just don't fool with them?
2. Do you believe that you can stop yourself from catching a cold?
3. Are some kids just born lucky?
4. Most of the time do you feel that getting good grades means a great deal to you?
5. Are you often blamed for things that just aren't your fault?
6. Do you believe that if somebody studies hard enough he or she can pass any subject?
7. Do you feel that most of the time it doesn't pay to try hard because things never turn out right anyway?
8. Do you feel that if things start out well in the morning that it's going to be a good day no matter what you do?
9. Do you feel that most of the time parents listen to what their children have to say?
10. Do you believe that wishing can make good things happen?

RELIABILITY AND VALIDITY: Estimates of internal consistency via the split-half method corrected by the Spearman-Brown prophecy formula are r = .63 (grades 3 through 5), r = .68 (grades 6 through 8), r = .74 (grades 9 through 11), and r = .81 (grade 12). Approximate sample sizes for the first three groups are three hundred, and for the grade twelve group, eighty-seven. Test-retest reliabilities sampled at three grade levels (Ns not reported) six weeks apart are .63 for the third grade, .66 for the seventh grade, and .71 for the tenth grade. Correlations with the Intellectual Achievement Responsibility Questionnaire (Crandall, Katkovsky, and Crandall, 1965) were computed for 182 third-grade and 171 seventh-grade blacks. Correlations with I- (total of negative events for which S assumes blame) were not significant. Correlations with I+ (total of positive events for which S assumes credit) were significant for both groups: r = .30, and r = .51, respectively. A correlation of .41 with the Bialer-Cromwell Scale (Bialer, 1961) was found in a sample of twenty-nine children 9 through 11 years of age. Internality was found to increase with age, as follows:

Grade	Males Mean	Females Mean
3	18.0	17.4
4	18.4	18.8

Grade	Males Mean	Females Mean
5	18.3	17.0
6	13.7	13.3
7	13.2	13.9
8	14.7	12.3
9	13.8	12.3
10	13.1	13.0
11	12.5	12.0
12	11.4	12.4

Internality was significantly related to achievement test scores for the third-, fifth-through seventh-, tenth- and twelfth-grade males, but not for females.

Significant relationships have been found between internality and higher grade-point averages in a sample of twelfth graders and another of college students. A dissertation study (Roberts, 1971) found significant correlations between internal locus of control and reading achievement for both sexes, and mathematical achievement for males only. Nonsignificant correlations (not reported) with an abbreviated form (odd-numbered items only) of the Children's Social Desirability Scale (Crandall, Crandall, and Katkovsky, 1965) were computed within each grade level. Nowicki and Strickland (1973) report nonsignificant relationships between their scale and intelligence in one sample of twelfth graders and another sample of college students (statistics not reported).

BIBLIOGRAPHY:

Bialer, I. "Conceptualization of Success and Failure in Mentally Retarded and Normal Children." *Journal of Personality*, 1961, *29*, 303-320.

Crandall, V. C., Crandall, V. J., and Katkovsky, W. "A Children's Social Desirability Questionnaire." *Journal of Consulting Psychology*, 1965, *29*, 27-36.

Crandall, V. J., Katkovsky, W., and Crandall, V. C. "Children's Belief in Their Own Control of Reinforcement in Intellectual-Academic Situations." *Child Development*, 1965, *36*, 91-109.

Nowicki, S., Jr., and Duke, M. P. "A Locus-of-Control Scale for Adults: An Alternative to the Rotter." Unpublished paper. Emory University, Atlanta, Georgia, 1972.

Nowicki, S., Jr., and Strickland, B. R. "A Locus-of-Control Scale for Children." *Journal of Consulting and Clinical Psychology*, 1973, *40*, 148-154.

Roberts, A. "The Self-Esteem of Disadvantaged Third and Seventh Graders." Unpublished doctoral dissertation. Emory University, Atlanta, Georgia, 1971.

Rotter, J. B. "Generalized Expectancies for Internal Versus External Control of Reinforcement." *Psychological Monographs*, 1966, *80* (1) (Whole no. 609).

Prepared by Bonnie R. Strickland

PEDERSEN'S PERSONAL SPACE MEASURE (PPSM), CHILDREN'S FORM

AUTHOR: Darhl M. Pedersen

AGE: 5 to 12 years

VARIABLE: Personal space

TYPE OF MEASURE: Test

SOURCE FROM WHICH MEASURE MAY BE OBTAINED: Darhl M. Pederson, Department of Psychology, Brigham Young University, Provo, Utah 84601.

DESCRIPTION OF MEASURE: There are two versions of the PPSM, one for males and one for females. Both consist of twenty-four 8½ X 11 pages placed horizontally. On the left side of each page a standing profile of a person is printed approximately 2 inches from the left and 3 inches from the bottom. A line on which the profile is standing extends 7¼ inches to the right. A movable profile is attached with a paper clip to the upper-right-hand corner of each page. The profiles represent a man (M), a woman (W), a boy (B), or a girl (G). Each of these is presented facing right (R), front (F), or left (L). Ss are instructed that for the first twelve items they are to pretend that "the one that is loose is you, and the one that is not loose might be a man, a lady, a boy your age, or a girl your age." Ss are directed to position the movable profile on the line so that the distance between the profile representing the self and a profile representing another person is as close as possible so that Ss still feel comfortable. Ss are told that their task is the same for the second set of twelve items, except that the self will be the stationary left profile and another person will be the movable right profile. For all items the movable profile is facing left toward the stationary profile. For the first twelve items the left profiles were as follows: M-R, W-R, B-R, G-R, M-F, W-F, B-F, G-F, M-L, W-L, B-L, and G-L. The right profiles were a boy (or a girl) facing left. For the second twelve items the left profiles were in three sets. The first set had a boy (or girl) facing right, the second set had a boy (or girl) facing front, and the third set had a boy (or girl) facing left. The right profiles consisted of three sets of profiles in the order M-L, W-L, B-L, and G-L. Each item is scored by measuring the distance from toe to toe to the nearest centimeters. An overall score is found by summing the item scored.

RELIABILITY AND VALIDITY: None reported.

BIBLIOGRAPHY:

Pederson, D. M. "Developmental Trends in Personal Space." *Journal of Psychology,* 1973, *83,* 3-9.

PROJECTIVE PERSONAL SPACE MEASURE

AUTHORS: Carol J. Guardo and Murray Meisels

AGE: Grade 3 to adult

VARIABLE: Personal space schemata or social schemata

TYPE OF MEASURE: Semistructured projective test

SOURCE FROM WHICH MEASURE MAY BE OBTAINED: Murray Meisels, Department of Psychology, Eastern Michigan University, Ypsilanti, Michigan 48197.

DESCRIPTION OF MEASURE: The test booklet consists of a series of legal-sized pages showing silhouettes, that is, darkened figures in profile, reproduced by offset or multilith processes. The silhouette may be that of a single female, a single male, a group of males, or a group of females. The silhouettes are scaled 1 inch to the foot, and many represent the subjects' age-appropriate peer group, siblings, or adults. The subject is given a cutout manipulable silhouette figure that represents himself and that is also scaled 1 inch to the foot. After the stimulus figure is described in various personal or interpersonal ways (e.g., "a friend," "someone you are afraid of"), the subject is asked to place the manipulable figure on the page "where you would be standing" or in a spatial relation to the printed silhouette. The subject then traces the outline of the manipulable figure. One corner of the cutout figure is notched to allow identification of the face, and the nose-to-nose distance in millimeters between the stimulus figure and the cutout figure is the dependent variable used in data analysis. A test booklet may consist of a varied number of stimulus figures; the test may be administered individually or in groups.

RELIABILITY AND VALIDITY: Guardo (1969) obtained acceptable test-retest reliability (.84) for the measure in a sample of sixth graders and also found that the measure was strongly related to degree of liking for the stimulus figure and degree of acquaintance with the stimulus figure. Meisels and Guardo (1969) obtained essentially the same validational data for degree of liking and acquaintance in samples of third through tenth graders. In addition, they found the differences in figure placements for age and sex to be consistent with knowledge about social development and the formation of sex-role identity (see also Guardo and Meisels, 1971b). Guardo and Meisels (1971a) found closer distance to a parent when the parent was praising the child and greater distance under conditions of reproof. There are several variations on the use of semiprojective measures in the personal space literature (see Duke and Nowicki, 1972, for a recent review), including felt-board techniques (Kuethe, 1962a, 1962b; Levinger and Gunner, 1967), paper-and-pencil measures (Duke and Nowicki, 1972; Tolor, Branningan, and Murphy, 1970), and the use of dolls (Little, 1968). The reliability (Lerner, Karabenick, and Meisels, 1957b) and validity (Weinstein, 1965, 1967; Kuethe, 1962a, 1962b; Haase and Markey, 1973; Tolor, Brannigan, and Murphy, 1970; Little, 1968) data reported for these measures provide support for the use of semiprojective instruments to assess personal space or social schemata.

BIBLIOGRAPHY:

Duke, M. P., and Nowicki, S., Jr. "A New Measure and Social-Learning Model for Interpersonal Distance." *Journal of Experimental Research in Personality,* 1972, *6,* 119-132.

Guardo, C. J. "Personal Space in Children." *Child Development,* 1969, *40,* 143-151.

Guardo, C. J., and Meisels, M. "Child-Parents Spatial Patterns Under Praise and Reproof." *Developmental Psychology,* 1971a, *5,* 365.

Guardo, C. J., and Meisels, M. "Factor Structure of Children's Personal Space Schemata." *Child Development,* 1971b, *42,* 1307-1312.

Hasse, R. F., and Markey, M. J. "A Methodological Note on the Study of Personal Space." *Journal of Consulting and Clinical Psychology,* 1973, *40,* 122-125.

Kuethe, J. L. "Social Schemas." *Journal of Abnormal and Social Psychology,* 1962a, *64,* 31-38.

Kuethe, J. L. "Social Schemas and the Reconstruction of Social Object Displays from Memory." *Journal of Abnormal and Social Psychology,* 1962b, *65,* 71-74.

Lerner, R. M., Karabenick, S. A., and Meisels, M. "Effects of Age and Sex on the Development of Personal Space Schemata Towards Body Build." *Journal of Genetic Psychology,* 1975, *127,* 91-101.

Lerner, R. M., Karabenick, S. A., and Meisels, M. "One-Year Stability of Children's Personal Space Schemata Towards Body Build." *Journal of Genetic Psychology,* 1975, *127,* 151-152.

Levinger, G., and Gunner, J. "The Interpersonal Grid: I. Felt and Tape Technique for Measurement of Social Behavior." *Psychonomic Science,* 1967, *8,* 173-174.

Little, K. "Cultural Variations in Social Schemata." *Journal of Personality and Social Psychology,* 1968, *10,* 1-7.

Meisels, M., and Guardo, C. J. "Development of Personal Space Schemata." *Child Development,* 1969, *40,* 1167-1178.

Tolor, A., Brannigan, G., and Murphy, V. "Psychological Distance, Future Time Perspective, and Internal-External Expectancy." *Journal of Projective Techniques and Personality Assessment,* 1970, *34,* 283-294.

Weinstein, L. "Social Schemata of Emotionally Disturbed Boys." *Journal of Abnormal Psychology,* 1965, *70,* 457-461.

Weinstein, L. "Social Experience and Social Schemata." *Journal of Personality and Social Psychology,* 1967, *6,* 429-434.

Prepared by Murray Meisels and Carol J. Guardo

SCHOOL ENVIRONMENT ASSESSMENT SCALES (SEAS)

AUTHORS: Robert J. Tolsma and Gordon Hopper

AGE: 13 to 18 years

VARIABLE: Perception of the school environment

TYPE OF MEASURE: Questionnaire

SOURCE FROM WHICH MEASURE MAY BE OBTAINED: Robert J. Tolsma, Department of Counseling Psychology, Faculty of Education, University of British Columbia, Vancouver 8, Canada. Cost: $2.00 to cover postage and handling.

DESCRIPTION OF MEASURE: The SEAS is composed of eight subscales entitled Scholarly Affect, Parental Climate, Heterosexual Social Expression, School Spirit, Activity, Authoritarian Press, Creative Self-Expression, and Social Order. The instrument is normed on over three thousand students in rural and urban Iowa schools. It is easily administered in the time limit (usual time 20 minutes) and can be manually or computer scored. Assumptions on which the instrument is based are: (1) Certain psychological aspects of school environments can be measured by assessing student perceptions, (2) consensual perceptions represent the "real" environment, (3) modifying the environment will change perceptions, and (4) the psychological school environment influences student behavior. Each item is selected based on its ability to differentiate among practical size groups (as few as fifty students); thus each item measures group differences as opposed to individual differences. In addition, each item was selected via an analysis-of-covariance model that mitigates the effects of perceptual responses being a function of personality types. The result of the latter procedure yielded items representing behavioral elements in environments that can be directly manipulated.

As examples, eight of the eighty-one items of the SEAS, one item from each subscale, are given below. Items one through forty-nine are answered on a 5-point scale ranging from "almost never" to "almost always or constantly." Items fifty through eighty-one are answered on a 5-point scale ranging from "almost none" to "almost all."

59. *(Scholarly Affect)* _____ of the teachers assign grades fairly.
30. *(Parental Climate)* The teachers _____ express opinions about how a student should dress to come to school.
69. *(Heterosexual Social Expression)* _____ of the boys and girls mix together during class breaks, during noon hours, etc.
75. *(School Spirit)* School spirit is expressed by _____ of the students here.
32. *(Activity)* Students around here can _____ be seen playing checkers, chess, working crossword puzzles, and engaged in other like activities in their spare time.
48. *(Authoritarian Press)* There are _____ comfortable places available where a student can go to just sit and relax.
 3. *(Creative Self-Expression)* Students are _____ encouraged to use the science lab during their free time.
28. *(Social Order)* School property is _____ damaged by students.

RELIABILITY AND VALIDITY: Scale internal consistency reliability estimates are as follows: Scale 1, .76; Scale 2, .69; Scale 3, .59; Scale 4, .82; Scale 5, .59; Scale 6, .54;

Scale 7, .70; and Scale 8, .68. Construct validity is evidenced by the factor analysis; no objective data are available on criterion validity.

BIBLIOGRAPHY:

Menne, J., and Tolsma, R. J. "A Discrimination Index for Items in Instruments Using Group Responses." *Journal of Educational Measurement,* 1971, *8,* 5-7.
Tolsma, R. J. "A Method for the Assessment of High School Environments." Unpublished doctoral dissertation. Iowa State University, Ames, 1971.

SITUATION-AVOIDANCE BEHAVIOR CHECKLIST FOR STUTTERERS

AUTHOR: Eugene B. Cooper

AGE: Unlimited

VARIABLE: Situations avoided by stutterers

TYPE OF MEASURE: Checklist

SOURCE FROM WHICH MEASURE MAY BE OBTAINED: The Speech and Hearing Center, P.O. Box 1965, University, Alabama 35486.

DESCRIPTION OF MEASURE: This is a checklist of fifty situations that the stutterer might try to avoid because of his stuttering behavior. It may be useful to both client and clinicians in terms of identifying problem behaviors related to the stuttering and in terms of assessing behavioral changes. The situations are structured in home, school, and community.
    As examples, the first ten of the fifty situations are given below.

Instructions: Place a checkmark in the box preceding each speech situation that you avoid or would prefer to avoid because of your stuttering.
  1. Using telephone to obtain information.
  2. Ordering in a restaurant.
  3. Making introductions.
  4. Talking to a store clerk.
  5. Meeting someone for the first time.
  6. Talking with my mother.
  7. Saying hello to friends.
  8. Placing a long-distance telephone call.
  9. Talking in a classroom situation.
10. Being interviewed for a job.

RELIABILITY AND VALIDITY: None reported.

BIBLIOGRAPHY: None reported.